CRITICAL DICTIONARY
OF FILM AND
TELEVISION THEORY

CRITICAL DICTIONARY OF FILM AND TELEVISION THEORY

Edited by
Roberta E. Pearson
and
Philip Simpson

London and New York

First published 2001
by Routledge
11 New Fetter Lane, London EC4P 4EE

Simultaneously published in the USA and Canada
by Routledge
29 West 35th Street, New York, NY 10001

Routledge is an imprint of the Taylor & Francis Group

Typeset in Baskerville by Taylor & Francis Books Ltd
Printed and bound in Great Britain by TJ International Ltd,
Padstow, Cornwall

British Library Cataloguing in Publication Data
A catalogue record for this book is available from the British Library

Library of Congress Cataloging in Publication Data
Critical dictionary of film and television theory / edited by Philip Simpson
and Roberta E. Pearson.
p.cm.
Includes bibliographical references and index.
1. Motion pictures–Dictionaries. 2. Television–Dictionaries. 3. Film
criticism–Dictionaries. I. Simpson, Philip. II. Pearson, Roberta E.
PN 1993.45 .C75 2000
791.43'01–dc21

ISBN 0–415–16218–1

Contents

Contributors

Matthew Allen
Curtin University, Australia

Stuart Allan
University of the West of England, UK

Paula Tatla Amad
Chicago University, USA

Karen Backstein
City University of New York–Staten Island, USA

Neil Badmington
Cardiff University, UK

Bruce Bennett
Bolton Institute of Higher Education, UK

Daniel Bernardi
University of Arizona, USA

Sarah Berry
City University of New York, USA

Andy Birtwistle
Canterbury Christ Church University College, UK

David A. Black
Seton Hall University, USA

Gill Branston
Cardiff University, UK

Will Brooker
Cardiff University, UK

Rod Brookes
Cardiff University, UK

Warren Buckland
Liverpool John Moores University, UK

Nick Burton
Canterbury Christ Church University College, UK

Cynthia Carter
Cardiff University, UK

Paula Chakravartty
University of California, San Diego, USA

G. Briankle Chang
University of Massachusetts, USA

Donald Crafton
University of Notre Dame, USA

Hannah Davies
UK

Bella Dicks
Cardiff University, UK

Stephanie Donald
Murdoch University, Australia

Ken Fox
Canterbury Christ Church University College, UK

James Friedman
UCLA Film and Television Archive, USA

Trevor Gigg
Canterbury Christ Church University College, UK

Lee Grieveson
University of Exeter, UK

Alison Griffiths
Baruch College, CUNY, USA

Sarah Gwenllian Jones
Cardiff University, UK

Mike Hammond
University of Southampton, UK

Matthew Hills
Cardiff University, UK

Simon Horrocks
UK

Mark Jancovich
University of Nottingham, UK

Deborah Jermyn
Southhampton Institute, UK

Rakesh Kaushal
Cardiff University, UK

Frank Kessler
Utrecht University, The Netherlands

Petra Kuppers
Manchester Metropolitan University, UK

Antje Lindenmeyer
University of Warwick, UK

Jane Long
University of Western Australia, Australia

Moya Luckett
University of Pittsburgh, USA

Paula J. Massood
Brooklyn College, CUNY, USA

Geoff Mayer
La Trobe University, Australia

Gary McDonogh
Bryn Mawr College, USA

Alan McKee
University of Queensland, Australia

Adrienne L. McLean
University of Texas, Dallas, USA

Peter McLuskie
Light House Media Centre, UK

Máire Messenger Davies
Cardiff University, UK

Edward Miller
College of Staten Island/CUNY, USA

Jen Neuber
Macalester College, USA

Gabriel M. Paletz
University of Southern California, USA

Katy Pantazis
Macalester College, USA

Roberta E. Pearson
Cardiff University, UK

Elayne Rapping
State University of New York, Buffalo, USA

Philip Rayner
Cheltenham and Gloucester College of Higher
Education, UK

Dickon Reed
Canterbury Christ Church University College, UK

Angelo Restivo
Northwestern University, USA

Tico Romao
Cheltenham and Gloucester College of Higher
Education, UK

K. J. Shepherdson
Canterbury Christ Church University College, UK

Philip Simpson
Formerly of Canterbury Christ Church University
College, UK

Clay Steinman
Macalester College, USA

Paul Sutton
Bolton Institute of Higher Education, UK

Allan James Thomas
La Trobe University, Australia

Julia Thomas
Cardiff University, UK

Frank P. Tomasulo
Georgia State University, USA

Berto Trinidad
University of Arizona, USA

William Uricchio
Massachusetts Institute of Technology, USA

Andrew Utterson
Canterbury Christ Church University College, UK

Eva Vieth
Cardiff University, UK

Eva Warth
Utrecht University, The Netherlands

Chris Weedon
Cardiff University, UK

Tony Wilson
Monash University, Australia

Cindy Wong
College of Staten Island, USA

Ben Woodhouse
UK

Nick Yablon
University of Chicago, USA

Introduction

The field of film and television studies has emerged from several related disciplines: literary studies, history, sociology and psychoanalysis among others. During the past three decades the field has adapted paradigms borrowed from these disciplines, as well as evolving others of its own, resulting in a complex and sometimes confusing theoretical apparatus for the study of screen media. Such diversity can bewilder and discourage people who are encountering the field for the first time. Students are assumed to have understood difficult and extensive theoretical concepts in order to progress through their courses, and even more experienced scholars are hard-pressed to keep up with the ever growing knowledge necessary to their academic practice. The *Critical Dictionary of Film and Television Theory* is intended to meet the needs of both these groups by offering an accessible and authoritative introduction to key concepts in the field.

The *Dictionary* is equally intended for use in disciplines that have been affected by the critical and theoretical approaches developed in the past three decades. These disciplines include communication studies, cultural studies, media studies, film studies, art and design, literary studies and American and British studies.

The *Dictionary* gives readers the necessary conceptual framework to understand the language and terminologies of screen studies by offering new students an introductory map of the field, and more experienced students and scholars a reminder of basic concepts. The book is meant to address the concerns of students and teachers in the classroom; its focus, therefore, is on theoretical terms currently in use. For this reason, the film theories preceding the 1960s are not dealt with in detail. The

theoretical paradigms of the *Dictionary*, particularly in relation to television, draw primarily on cultural studies rather than the social sciences. Film and television texts are related to their conditions of production and reception, but greater attention is paid to texts and textual analysis than to factual accounts of television institutions or quantitative studies.

The *Dictionary* takes into account that television texts and practices, in particular, are embedded in national contexts, and contributors from Britain and the United States write with knowledge of their respective media systems. Where possible, reference in the entries is made to programmes that are known on both sides of the Atlantic. Primarily, the *Dictionary* focuses on media systems or cinemas that are British or American, although many of the theoretical concepts explicated in the book can be applied to other areas. For example, the entry on Globalization has direct relevance to the study of the media of the global South.

Using the Dictionary

General

All entries can be accessed through the usual alphabetical listing. Each entry is cross-referenced, indicated by bold type, so that the reader can follow a specific interest through a number of entries. Entries of more than 100 words end with a selected bibliography of some of the key literature in the field.

The *major* entries, of 2,000 or 3,000 words, offer essays about conceptual terms on which the *Dictionary* is based. These concepts have currency in many fields: in the entry Modernism and post-modernism, for example, these theories are discussed in relation to film and television in the last two decades, but the argument made in the entry can be applied to literature and painting. In the same way, the entry on Feminist theory places film and television within the larger political project of feminism and gender stereotyping before examining critical approaches relevant to many academic discourses. In this way, all the major entries provide substantial and authoritative introductions to concepts which students and researchers in cultural studies generally will find accessible. *Minor* entries of 100 to 700 words, such as those on Phenomenology and Binary, fulfil a similar function: terms from philosophy or anthropology are defined in relation to their usage in film and television studies.

Biographical entries of 200 words are included in the alphabetical listing. These give brief details of influential figures in the field, including major publications.

Film and television students

Students of film and television studies, and in the closely allied fields of communications or media studies, can also gain access through the conceptual map, listed at the end of the Introduction, which locates individual entries within an overall scheme. The map groups entries under three main headings: *Contexts*, *Media systems* and *Media studies*. Though there is inevitably a degree of arbitrariness about the headings, they are meant to move from broad social and cultural categories (*Contexts*), through to concepts which can be seen as belonging to categories mostly familiar within the media themselves (*Media systems*), to those categories which have attained particular explanatory force within the study of the media (*Media studies*).

Under these headings, terms are grouped so that readers may relate one term conceptually to another term. The entries on Semiotics, Realism, and Narrative, for example, are all grouped under a heading that indicates their significance in the analysis of the Text under the more general heading of *Media systems*. Though Genre appears under the same general heading, it is offered here as an aspect of production rather than a textual effect. The conceptual map is, therefore, a way of indicating to students of film and television the interrelatedness of key concepts, and, at the same time, to counter the difficulty of dealing with such diverse concepts as, for example, 'vertical integration' and 'queer studies' within the same subject discipline.

Further use

The broad field of film and television studies in the past three decades has drawn on theoretical paradigms from fields as disparate as history, art history, audience research, psychoanalysis and structuralism. It has also been central in the emergence of new fields of study such as gender studies and queer theory. In consequence, researchers and teachers from many disciplines have had to locate their own specialism within the broad field of screen studies, and to make reference to areas of knowledge which have not been their immediate concern. For readers in this situation, the *Dictionary* is intended to offer a brief introduction to most of the theoretical paradigms that have informed film and television studies, and provide substantial bibliographical sources for further research. Cross-referencing in the *Dictionary* emphasizes the cross-disciplinary nature of film and television studies; it also reveals the conflicting and contradictory positions which these studies have traversed in their short history. The entries on Audience, Reading and Reception Theory, and Screen Theory offer instances.

The *Dictionary* is also intended to supplement work done in lectures or seminars in a range of educational contexts by offering teachers and students an accessible and reliable learning resource in a complex field. For example, the central theme of a class or course might be film narrative approached through textual analysis. However, the entries on Genre, Ideology and hegemony, Institution, Studio systems and others, would provide a context with which students might reasonably be expected to familiarize themselves in order to provide a shared background of understanding against which the main theme can be located.

Conceptual map

Group 1: Contexts

art
body, the
children and media
class
culture
gender
history
institution
memory
music and film
national, the
popular, the
race
sport and television
violence

Group 2: Media systems

(i)   Production

African-American cinema
authorship
classical Hollywood and new Hollywood cinema
documentary
genre
pre-Hollywood cinema

(ii)   Marketing and promotion

broadcasting, the United Kingdom
broadcasting, the United States
cable and satellite
globalization
marketing and promotion
public sphere

regulation
studio systems
technological change

(iii)   Texts

acting
narrative
realism
semiotics
space/place

(iv)   Audiences

audience
audience measurement
consumption
cult film and television
fandom
identity
reading and reception theory
sexuality
subject and subjectivity

Group 3: Media studies

base and superstructure
cognitive theory
dialectic and dialectical montage
feminist theory
Frankfurt School
ideology and hegemony
modernism and post-modernism
psychoanalysis
queer theory
stereotype
structuralism and post-structuralism

Acknowledgements

The production of this Dictionary took place over a longer period of time than even its editors expected. Some of the people who were first consulted, Manuel Alvarado, Barry Curtis, Richard Exton, and Tony Pearson among them, may even have forgotten their initial support and advice about the project. Fiona Cairns was the general editor at Routledge who listened sympathetically to the original idea and kept faith, if not always patience, through long periods of slow progress. Production speeded up when Alan Hay, of Canterbury Christ Church University College, made possible the study leave which enabled Philip Simpson to give more time to editing and writing. On the other hand, most of the contributors deserve the thanks of the editors for the speed with which they delivered copy, and for responding with good nature and rapidity to editorial queries which seem maddening to a hard-pressed scholar. A similar recognition should be given to those working for Routledge, including Mina Gera Price, Stephanie Rogers and Rebecca Russell, who dealt with the exceptional complexities of production.

Philip Simpson would like to acknowledge the support and influence of two groups: colleagues in the Radio Film and Television Department at Canterbury Christ Church University College, 1989–99, and those with whom he was fortunate enough to work in the Education Department of the British Film Institute, 1978–89. Neither are to blame for his limitations.

Roberta Pearson would like to acknowledge the many friends and colleagues among the contributors, all of whom produced brilliant entries, most of whom met their deadlines and some of whom stepped in at the last minute to write remaining unassigned entries. Thanks to all – without you the *Dictionary* would never have been published. She would also like to thank several dear friends for their support and encouragement over the long years of her academic career: Karen Backstein, David Black, Maire Messenger Davies, David Paletz and William Uricchio.

Both editors would like to thank Margaret Simpson for providing moral and material comfort when we both knew she had better things to do with her time.

Finally, the editors thank each other for what has been a remarkably enjoyable and stress-free collaboration.

Roberta Pearson
Philip Simpson

A

absence

At the most fundamental level, absence marks all **representation** in so far as an object or world which is not itself present is being 're-presented' through a particular medium. Film theory asserts that the techniques of classical film narration mask this play of absence and presence, thus suturing – or stitching – the spectator into the seamless fabric of the film's diegetic world (see **suture; diegesis**). This view has subsequently been criticized for its inability to account for the multiplicity of spectator positions possible in film viewing.

See also: castration; lack; narrative; psychoanalysis

ANGELO RESTIVO

access

The notion that 'the public' or 'minority groups' should have access to the means of broadcasting to promote their 'voices' or opinions. In Britain, it was originally linked to cable-based community television stations in the 1960s. However, it has subsequently encompassed radio stations reflecting particular ethnic communities, for example, Sunrise FM for the Asian community in Bradford. Most recently, 'access' has become popular on British television through 'video diary' programmes which allow members of the general public to directly address the audience, although some editorial and technical control is kept in the hands of the 'professionals'.

See also: reality effect

PHILIP RAYNER

acting

Acting is perhaps the most discussed and least understood aspect of cinema and television. Since the fictional film gained ascendance in the first decade of the twentieth century, actors have been one of the most visible and important elements of screen narratives. Through the mechanisms of the **star system**, media industries simultaneously create and cater for audiences' engagement with the prominent personalities of film and television. Popular print and broadcast journalism devote considerable space/time to the coverage of these prominent personalities. The publishing industries produce numerous biographies of actors and technical manuals for would-be actors. Academic film and television studies have engaged with this intense popular interest in actors through the analysis of star images, but have for the most part ignored the substance of these stars' performances in films and television programmes. Needless to say, not many bother to write about those actors who have failed to achieve stardom.

The scholarly neglect of acting stems from the subject's resistance to academic analysis. The bias of personal preference militates against the objective distance that scholars prefer to retain *vis-à-vis* their objects of study. Reactions to screen personalities are in some ways complicated, and they are certainly influenced by our reactions to those whom we encounter in everyday life. Our cumulative experiences negatively or positively bias us towards particular actors. We may agree that an actor is a skilled technician but still fail to appreciate his or her artistry or simply not 'like' him or her. A collective historical bias compounds individual bias. Acting is among the most rapidly changing of all cinematic and televisual codes. While contemporary audiences may exhibit impatience with the slower paced editing of the classical Hollywood cinema, the period's performances may induce outright merriment (see **classical Hollywood cinema and new Hollywood cinema**). Scholars are not exempt from such prejudices, and often are all too ready to employ their own aesthetic criteria to evaluate past performance, the practice resulting in, for example, an ahistorical dismissal of much silent film acting as overly stylized, exaggerated or melodramatic. While there are studies of specific actors (e.g., Naremore 1988) or of specific time periods (e.g., Pearson 1992), the problems of personal and historical bias have made the construction of a generalizable theory of acting difficult. This entry will sketch out some of the key issues involved in the study of screen acting and conclude with a brief case study of silent film acting in order to show that a generalizable theory might be neither possible nor desirable.

Let us begin by taking a formalist approach, enumerating the factors one might consider when conducting the analysis of acting in specific film and television texts. The first of these are what might be termed the actor's 'tools', that is, the channels that the individual actor has available to convey meaning to the audience. Richard **Dyer** defines performance, which for the purposes of this entry we will consider interchangeable with acting, thus:

> Performance is what the performer does in addition to the actions/functions she or he performs in the plot and the lines she or he is given to say. Performance is how the action/ function is done, how the lines are said.
>
> The signs of performance are: facial expression; voice; gestures (principally of hands and arms, but also of any limb, e.g., neck, leg); body posture (how someone is sitting or standing); body movement (movement of the whole body,

including how someone stands up or sits down, how they walk, run, etc.).

(Dyer 1979: 151)

Dyer's definition implies that performance entails the creation of a fictional character through actions and dialogue, that is, through the use of the actor's body. At the most basic level, a scholarly analysis of acting might begin with the description of how actors use their bodies, the signs that they deploy. Yet even simple description is quite daunting, considering the complex nature of each of the signs to which Dyer refers. Take the voice, for example, which is itself not one sign but a whole complex of signs – natural, cultural and volitional. An actor's physiology to some extent determines the pitch and resonance of his or her voice. The circumstances of an actor's upbringing, together with his/her theatrical training, will initially determine accent and pronunciation, although skilled actors can vary these factors. The actor must make specific choices about the delivery of dialogue: dynamics, phrasing, intonation and so forth. Film and television scholars have no discipline-specific tools available to analyse the multichanneled communication of the actor's voice, although they might draw upon the knowledge of those competent in vocal technique such as music scholars or voice coaches. Similarly, those interested in body movement might draw upon choreographic notation. In either case, the media studies scholar intent on even a simple description of acting must do a great deal of preparatory and interdisciplinary work, another factor that might account for the subject's relative neglect.

Formal analysis might also examine variations among stage, film and television with regard to the weight each gives to the different signs of performance and the degree of input each permits the actor into the interpretation of his/her **character**. Live theatre foregrounds the voice and body movements relative to facial expression. The need to convey meaning to the entire audience, including those seated furthest from the stage, requires actors to project their voices and exaggerate their gestures and decreases the importance of facial expression, seen clearly only from the first few rows. Relative to film and television, live theatre affords actors the greatest control over the construction of their characters, one reason that many express a preference for this medium. Lengthy rehearsal periods permit actors to explore their characters and to negotiate their interpretations with the director, other cast members and, in some instances, the play's author. The real-life, real-time performance allows an actor to trace the ebb and flow of his/her character's emotions over the course of the play, building to emotional climaxes. Feedback from the live audience can energize or depress the actor, affecting the nature of his/her interpretation in a specific performance.

Screen performances, both cinematic and televisual, give all audience members an 'ideal' view of the actor. This requires a performer to tone down his/her voice and body movements relative to what he/she might do on the stage. The closer scale of film and television in combination with editing allow audiences greater access to the face, enabling actors to rely more upon subtle facial expressions as a way of conveying meaning. Television's smaller screen size foregrounds facial expression even more prominently than does the cinema, since much of the action is filmed in close-up. Relative to their theatrical counterparts, screen actors have less time to work on the interpretation of their characters. Cinema productions have shorter rehearsal periods than theatrical ones, while quickly produced episodic television often has time for no more than a quick run-through to establish the actors' movements relative to one another, the set and the cameras. Since set and location determine shooting order, scenes are usually filmed out of chronological sequence, denying the actor the opportunity to progress through his/her character's actions and emotions as they occur in the plot. In comparison with the stage, the conditions of production and post-production work to minimize the actor's input into the character. Several camera perspectives cover each shot. In the cinema, sequential camera set-ups film the action from long, medium and close shot and varying angles while television productions typically have three or more cameras filming simultaneously, with a director or assistant director who does in-camera editing. During the post-production process, editors make the final decisions about which take will appear in the final cut. Other aspects of the post-production process,

such as sound mixing and the addition of optical effects, influence the audience's understanding of the character but remain completely outside the actor's control. The telling myth of the **Kuleshov effect** testifies to the extent to which cinema and television acting depends upon the interaction of the actor's performance signs with cinematic and televisual codes. In this instance, editing supposedly entirely dictated viewers' different interpretations of precisely the same shot of an actor. The interaction of performance with other codes, as well as the highly collaborative nature of the film and television production process, involving numerous creative personnel, makes determining the actor's specific contribution to the construction of a character exceedingly difficult.

Thus far we have looked at formal textual analysis that aims to describe what the actor does in a performance and the manner in which the conditions of production of different media affect what the actor does. But media studies, concerned with audience reception, also seeks to illuminate conditions of reception (see **reading and reception theory**). How can scholars investigate the meanings that audiences might make of specific actors or specific performances? Here we turn from the textual to the intertextual (see **intertextuality**), since such investigation requires the consideration of groups of films or television programmes starring the same actor as well as texts related to those films or programmes. For the most part, audience response to an actor or a specific performance is conditioned by intertexts. Most proximate among these intertexts are audience knowledge of the actor's persona and of his/her other roles. As Richard Dyer has shown in his pioneering work in both *Stars* (1979) and *Heavenly Bodies* (1986), scholars seeking to understand conditions of reception must examine the interrelationships among the actor, the character he/she portrays in a specific text and the actor's star image, which is composed of myriads of other texts.

An anecdote helps to convey the complexity of such an approach. In summer 1995, Patrick Stewart, long-term member of the Royal Shakespeare Company and Captain Jean-Luc Picard in the long-running US television series *Star Trek: The Next Generation* (1987–1994), played Prospero in the New York Shakespeare Festival's production of *The*

Tempest. In an interview with *SFX* magazine, Stewart recounted the following incident: 'I made the mistake of tugging on the front of my doublet. There was an instantaneous burst of laughter [from the audience]. I was very careful never to do that again' (Craig 1999). Why did Stewart think he had made a mistake and what provoked the burst of laughter? These questions can be answered by speculating about the intertextual frames concerning Patrick Stewart that various spectators might have brought with them to *The Tempest*. Avid *Star Trek* fans, those who participate in **fandom**'s discourse around the programme, would have interpreted the actor's doublet-tugging as a rendition of the 'Picard manoeuvre', the affectionate term fans have given to the actor's habit of pulling down on the front of his uniform tunic. Less devoted fans and more casual viewers, knowledgeable about Stewart's enactment of the Picard role but not part of active fandom, might have recognized the tugging of the doublet as a specifically Picardian gesture. Both these groups laughed at the sudden conjunction between Prospero and Picard engendered by Stewart's gesture. The laughter would have baffled those spectators who had never seen *Star Trek: The Next Generation* and those who thought of Stewart only as a Shakespearean actor (though this is hard to imagine).

This example illustrates the difficulty of analysing conditions of reception: a single gesture, fairly easily described, functioned within complicated interpretive frameworks relating to an actor, his role(s) and his star persona. Difficulties multiply when we consider that *The Tempest* audience would have responded to the interpretation of Prospero based not only on Stewart-specific intertexts, but upon culturally shared and historically specific evaluative frameworks concerning 'good' or 'bad' acting. As noted above, these frameworks change fairly rapidly, but, since approximately the turn of the twentieth century, western culture has valorized acting thought to be 'realistic', that is, acting that replicates the way people are thought to behave in 'real' life and that constructs psychologically credible characters. Since judgements about 'real'-life behaviour vary over time, so do judgements about 'realistic' acting, but the basic principle remains. As we shall see in more detail

below, this principle has structured performance style in the American cinema since the second decade of the twentieth century. It has been most aggressively championed by the proponents of method acting, a system derived from the precepts of the Russian theatre director and actor Konstantin Stanislavsky, which requires actors to get in touch with their sensations and emotions and then channel these into their performances to achieve a psychologically authentic interpretation. Made popular in the United States through the Actor's Studio, founded in 1947, the method became influential in 1950s Hollywood; performers associated with it include Marlon Brando, Rod Steiger, James Dean, Joanne Woodward and Shelley Winters. Although still dominated by the realist principle, the European cinema has been more receptive to anti-realist styles than the American cinema. The silent German cinema imported the acting style of the German Expressionist theatre, which externalized protagonist's extreme psychological states through distorted body postures (see **Expressionism**); Sergei Eisenstein drew on the Soviet experimental theatre, including the acrobatic biomechanics of Vsevolod Meyerhold; and Jean-Luc **Godard** has sought to apply **Brecht**'s principles of the epic theatre in his filmmaking.

The remainder of this entry presents a brief case study of silent film acting in order to illustrate the importance of intertextuality and historical context in the study of performance. In terms of acting, as Peter Kramer (1999) points out, the 'silent period (in particular the 1910s) is perhaps the most thoroughly investigated in film history'. Much of this research does not centre on the analysis of what actors actually did on the screen, but rather deals with topics such as the rise of the star system or the establishment of acting as a profession. But some scholars have asked questions that crucially depend upon the analysis of performance: what were the period's evaluative frameworks for judging good/bad acting? How do acting styles change over time? How do acting styles vary among different national cinemas?

In *Eloquent Gestures*, Roberta Pearson uses the Biograph Studio films directed by D. W. Griffith to examine the transformations in American silent film in a manner that mitigates the problems of personal preference and historical bias through intertextual historicization, that is, through the examination of key period texts such as acting manuals and critical reviews. Pearson argues that the intertextual frames shared by producers and audiences in 1908 were predicated upon theatrical conventions associated with the melodrama but in 1913 were predicated upon knowledge of culturally specific notions about the mimesis of everyday life. The acting style associated with the former frame is dubbed the 'histrionic' while that associated with the latter is known as the 'verisimilar' (see **verisimilitude**). Actors employing the histrionic style drew their gestures from a highly codified lexicon of gestures with specific meanings: for example, the back of the hand to the forehead indicated despair, which they presented in a series of discrete poses. Actors employing the verisimilar code used gestures coded by cultural expectations about how particular characters in particular situations might behave in real life. Concomitant changes in film style helped actors to construct individuated characters whose actions advanced the narrative. In 1908, 10- to 15-minute films consisted of as few as ten to fifteen shots, with the action filmed in long shot, as if within the proscenium arch of the theatre. By 1913, films of the same length contained many more shots and the camera had moved much closer to the action. The closer camera scale permitted actors to employ smaller gestures and rely more on facial expression, while the emergent editing patterns of the classical Hollywood cinema, for example, **point of view shot**, helped actors to convey meaning to spectators. The concepts of the histrionic and verisimilar style permit Pearson to describe and judge acting within the period's own evaluative frameworks, but do not, in and of themselves, explain why the American cinema shifted so rapidly from one style to the other. Such explanation requires broadening the scope of inquiry beyond film texts and directly relevant intertexts to a fuller consideration of the American film industry within its historical context. Pearson argues that the transformation from the histrionic style to the verisimilar one must be understood as part of a more general transformation of the American film industry from a so-called 'cheap' amusement, associated with marginalized groups such as immigrants and the working classes, to a respectable entertainment, patronized by the middle classes. Since the histrionic style was by this time associated with the down-scale melodrama and the verisimilar with the more up-scale Broadway stage, both trade press critics and industry personnel favoured the latter's adoption. Does Pearson's research on the Biograph films provide a generalizable theory of acting? She herself denies that it does. 'This book has not only failed to construct a definitive theory for the study of cinematic performance, but it has proposed an argument the whole thrust of which militates against such a construction, since any particular performance mode must be studied within the context of the specific historical and cultural conditions that gave rise to it' (Pearson 1992: 144).

Ben Brewster and Lea Jacobs also pay attention to cultural and historical context, challenging Pearson's claim that the realism of the verisimilar style became wholly dominant in the American cinema. They argue instead for the continuation of a tradition of 'pictorialism', that is, an appeal to the audience's visual pleasure not integrally tied to narrative development. Part of this tradition of pictorialism was the 'actor's assumption of poses and attitudes' which, Brewster and Jacobs assert, 'was much more important and was important for far longer' than Pearson's account suggests (Brewster and Jacobs 1997: 81). Concerned as they are with this theatrically derived 'pictorialism', Brewster and Jacobs pose questions different from Pearson's. Rather than concerning themselves with simply charting changes in performance style in the silent cinema, their focus on pictorialism causes them to ask: 'How did the actors in the newly forming stock companies in 1907–1908 – actors largely trained in the theatre – adapt pictorial traditions to film? How did their style change in relation to later developments in film technique?' (*ibid.*: 106). They conclude that, while instances of pictorialism can be found in the American cinema through and beyond the 1908 to 1913 period which Pearson discusses, the European cinema's longer-scale shots, longer takes and tendency to stage scenes in depth made it more congenial to the theatrical tradition of striking poses and attitudes.

The above case study of silent film performance illustrates the ways in which film scholars have begun to use an historicized intertextual approach to overcome the problems of personal and historical bias. Yet scholars have barely begun to investigate acting in different time periods, different countries, different genres (comedy, drama, documentary) or different media (cinema versus television).

References

Brewster, B. and Jacobs, L. (1997) *Theatre to Cinema*, Oxford: Oxford University Press.

Craig, J. (1999) 'Rebel with a Cause …', *SFX* (February), p. 27.

Dyer, R. (1979) *Stars*, London: BFI Publishing.

—— (1986) *Heavenly Bodies: Film Stars and Society*, London: Macmillian.

Kramer, P. (1999) 'Biographical Notes', in Peter Kramer and Alan Lovell (eds) *Film Acting as Art and Profession*, London: Routledge.

Naremore, J. (1988) *Acting in the Cinema*, Berkeley: University of California Press.

Pearson, R. E. (1992) *Eloquent Gestures: The Transformation of Performance Style in the Griffith Biograph Films*, Berkeley: University of California Press.

Further reading

Branston, G. (1995) '… Viewer, I Listened to Him … Voices, Masculinity, *In the Line of Fire*', in P. Kirkham and J. Thumim (eds) *Me Jane: Masculinity, Movies and Women*, London: Lawrence and Wishart, pp. 37–50.

Zucker, C. (ed.) (1991) *Making Visible the Invisible: An Anthology of Original Essays on Film Acting*, Metuchen, NJ: Scarecrow Press.

ROBERTA E. PEARSON

actuality

A translation of the French word *actualité*, meaning drawn from life as opposed to fiction. The term actuality has come to refer mainly to early non-fiction filmmaking (pre-1907) in which camera operators filmed scenes of natural beauty, emblems of modernity such as trains and steamships, images of workers or artisans, and a plethora of other scenes that they felt would captivate the imaginations of turn-of-the-century audiences. These simply constructed actualities – a single camera was used, often with no panning device – were the forerunners of **documentary** and are fascinating illustrations of late Victorian culture.

ALISON GRIFFITHS

Adorno, Theodor Wiesengrund

b. 1903; d. 1969

Born in Frankfurt, Germany, Theodor Adorno was a key member of the Frankfurt Institute for Social Research, otherwise known as the **Frankfurt School**, which was associated during its varied history with a pantheon of intellectual figures, including Walter **Benjamin**, Herbert Marcuse, Max **Horkheimer**, and Adorno's assistant, Jürgen **Habermas**. Adorno joined the School in 1938, by which time it had relocated to New York, and in 1947 published with Horkheimer his best-known work, *Dialectic of Enlightenment*.

Adorno's damning of popular music, advertisements and cinema as part of a 'culture industry' which ultimately dominated, deceived and fettered the consciousness of the mass public, was subject to criticism even at the time from his contemporaries such as Benjamin. His view sits uncomfortably with more recent models of **audience** and the popular (see **popular, the**). It can, however, be justified in part by the context in which he wrote: having escaped Germany as it fell under an increasing state control of culture, Adorno found himself in the US during a period of far greater cultural and industrial standardization than today.

See also: Marxist aesthetics

Further reading

Adorno, T. W. (1991) *The Culture Industry*, ed. J. M. Bernstein, London: Routledge.

WILL BROOKER

advertising

Popular, commercial media, film and television depend on advertising (see **popular, the**). Cinema uses advertising primarily to promote films, whereas commercial television depends on advertising to produce programmes and turn a profit. To cover increased costs, cinema has become increasingly advertiser supported, turning to product placement (prominently displaying brand names in films) and tie-ins (with fast-food chains, for example). The presence of advertising changes texts – more noticeably in television, where adverts interrupt shows, than in film. It also plays a part in deciding what films and programmes might be produced as some advertisers will shun programmes that deal with 'controversial' themes and favour tie-ins with films that glamorize their product.

Advertising's relationship with film and television is a long one, shaping the development and forms of both media. American films were quite late in advertising to the general public. Individual films were not advertised until around 1913, with the arrival of the first imported features. Most early advertisements were aimed at exhibitors, not the public, as distributors tried to persuade cinema owners and managers to select their film service. After 1913, film companies started hiring advertising agents and setting up their own promotional divisions, marketing films more individually and towards the public. Advertising has consequently become a central part of reception, helping stimulate demand and shape audiences' understanding of the film.

The advertising potential of the movie theatre was, however, recognized from the start. Filmed advertisements were shown in nickelodeons while the American **serial** films of the teens were often supported by newspapers and publishers, promoting their publications alongside featured tie-ins for make-up and dress patterns. Brand names were also prominently displayed in Cecil B. DeMille's 1920s consumer comedies, advertising records and other necessities for modern life. During the classical period (see **classical Hollywood cinema and new Hollywood cinema**), tie-ins were less pronounced, re-emerging in the 1960s and 1970s to help underwrite the high budgets generally held necessary for a film's success.

Film advertising practices reinforce the similarities between the shop window and the screen noted by such film historians as Jeanne Allen and Charles Eckert. If the screen is the cinema's commodity, then in the case of television it is the audience, since commercial television depends on selling viewers to advertisers. Since the beginning of commercial broadcasts, advertisers have funded programming in two ways: indirectly through spot advertising (single, discrete advertisements) or directly through programme sponsorship. The latter trend was pioneered on American networks and was the norm in the early days of television, with each show featuring one manufacturer's products. In both cases, the programme lures audiences to watch the advertisements. Ratings are assessed to help calculate advertising costs, with advertisers paying the most for time when more people are watching. The programme itself also affects the price as it determines whether viewers fit a specific profile.

Given their importance, it is not surprising that advertisements are the most expensive programmes on television (when cost is calculated by the second). They are designed to have maximum impact in a short period of time (often 30 seconds or less), to catch the viewer's eye and convey their message quickly. Adverts are fleeting by nature – we come across them by chance rather than actively choosing to watch them on television – so every element is specially chosen to promote a specific image of the selected product. This has led critics to examine advertising carefully and critically, positing its lexicon of images as exemplary – a model for film and television analysis. As advertisements build on real-life experiences and fantasies, they also act as a repository of social fantasies at a given moment in time, yielding valuable historical insights.

Advertising can also be regarded as part of what has been called the **flow** of television programming. Instead of regarding television as a set of discrete programmes, it can be seen as a continual process of interrupted and interlocking texts. This approach does not dismiss adverts, but instead sees them as an integral part of the flow, an equally valuable part of the larger television **text**.

References

Allen, J. (1980) 'The Film Viewer as Consumer', *Quarterly Review of Film Studies*, vol. 5, no. 4, pp. 481–99.

Eckert, C. (1978) 'The Carole Lombard in Macy's Window', *Quarterly Review of Film Studies*, vol. 3, no. 1. pp. 1–21.

MOYA LUCKETT

aesthetics

Aesthetics was applied in western culture from the nineteenth century (notably by Immanuel **Kant**) to those critical activities which sought to understand and evaluate the nature and value of **art**, or of beauty more generally, understood as sensuously, not abstractly perceived (see Williams 1983; Eagleton 1992; and see **Williams, Raymond; Eagleton, Terry**). The adjective 'aesthetic' is sometimes used to mean the same as 'formal', though in feminist and black cultural discourses, 'aesthetic' is also used as a noun – a 'feminist aesthetic', for example, signifying a mode of making art which in some way corresponds to the assumed characteristics of the group (see **discourse analysis; feminist theory**).

Emphases on aesthetics have often run the danger of isolating art, or 'beauty', as being composed of ineffable, transcendental, transcultural qualities, accessible only to a contemplative and isolated sensibility: the words 'aesthete' and 'taste' (see Williams 1983; Bourdieu 1986) still evoke these connotations. As such, aesthetics seems at some distance from the *mass* media, but since films and television involve contribution from the other forms, and since film studies sometimes mobilizes art discourses, there does exist a tradition of aesthetic approach to these media.

Feminist, Marxist and black cultural approaches (see **feminist theory; Marxist aesthetics**) have raised questions of **representation**, which link the text to its **culture** in contrast to the supposed 'free-floating' nature of the aesthetic. (In exploring the ideological role of film and television, these incidentally refuse Kant's opposition of 'the useful' and 'the beautiful'.) Such approaches emphasize the historical and relative, rather than

absolute, nature of the aesthetic judgements. For example, the aesthetic splendours of D. W. Griffith's *The Birth of a Nation* (1915) are usually argued to have overpowered white liberals despite the film's racist politics, rather than its racist discourse being *central* to its spectacle, **narrative** and aesthetic power (see Rogin 1985).

In *Distinction*, **Bourdieu** (1986) argues that aesthetic judgements are neither natural nor disinterested but work as the disguised operation of **class** distinction through accumulated cultural capital or competences, which structure audiences' engagements with artistic texts (see also **culture; audience**). He argues for a distinction between a 'bourgeois' and a 'popular' aesthetic (see **popular, the**). The first privileges contemplative distance and knowledgeable pleasure in formal experimentation and innovation, as in 1950s and 1960s '**art cinema**'. The second values a more intense affective experience, and spectator involvement rather than distance, as for popular **genre** cinemas. A post-modern aesthetic (though often argued to be value free) in fact values **pastiche**, irony and **intertextuality** (see also **modernism and post-modernism**).

Despite contemporary theoretical relativism however, films keep appearing which 'everyone' 'just knows' are 'bad'. Their appropriation by **camp**, cult or queer audiences does not solve the persistent problem of aesthetic judgement which they focus (see **cult film and television; queer theory**). For example, can certain aesthetic features valued in narrative, pictorial and even facial appearance/composition be argued as broadly dominant *across* cultures? These have been characterized variously by such terms as 'the Golden Mean'; the 'classical unities' of dramatic structure; a universal sense of symmetry; the 'natural appeal' of baby-like features in a face. Such interests persist in debates on the shaping of a 'good screenplay' or of the importance of 'beauty' to global cinematic stardom and celebrity.

In film and television studies, largely conducted within the political/representational concerns of cultural politics, there is always a distance or delay between the text, with its very specific formal and aesthetic needs and workings, and the broader political processes which link it to its surrounding and penetrating culture (see Gledhill 1995). How can a politics of representation be argued which gives full weight to these formal or aesthetic concerns?

References

Bourdieu, P. (1986) *Distinction: A Social Critique of the Judgement of Taste*, London: Routledge.

Eagleton, T. (1992) *Ideology and Aesthetics*, Oxford: Blackwell.

Gledhill, C. (1995) 'Women Reading Men', in P. Kirkham and J. Thumin (eds) *Me Jane: Masculinity, Movies and Women*, London: Lawrence and Wishart.

Rogin, M. (1985) 'The Sword Became a Flashing Vision: D. W. Griffith's *The Birth of a Nation*', *Representations*, vol. 9, no. 1, pp. 150–95.

Williams, R. (1983) *Keywords*, London: Fontana.

GILL BRANSTON

African-American cinema

The beginning of theoretical and aesthetic issues concerning African-Americans and cinema is concurrent with the earliest American films. In 1895 Thomas Edison projected the first images of American blacks on the screen: a toothless older gentleman laughing for the camera; a watermelon-eating contest between two men; and a woman washing a baby. In so doing, Edison translated African-American **representation** from vaudeville and minstrelsy to screen. These trends continued with the development of film **narrative**, most notably in the form of Harriet Beecher Stowe's *Uncle Tom's Cabin*, the popular novel featuring African-American subject matter which was first adapted for the screen by Edwin S. Porter in 1903, and which by 1928 had been remade at least seventeen times. Also contemporary with the beginnings of American film came protest from African-Americans, who voiced concern about the negative screen images of blacks. While resistance would culminate in the early part of the twentieth century with marches and boycotts surrounding the release of D. W. Griffith's infamous *The Birth of a Nation* (1915), there also emerged a group of African-American entrepreneurs who replied to

these images by making films. This history of early African-American representation suggests that the problem facing African-American cinema was and still is one of definition: how is African-American film to be defined in the context of American filmmaking practices, and how is this cinema to be defined in relation to transnational film of the black **diaspora**?

Major historical studies of African-American film date back to the late 1960s and coincide with an increasing cross-disciplinary interest in black studies, a result of the civil rights movement and new legislation in the United States. The first history of blacks in film was Peter Noble's *The Negro in Films* (1970). Noble's book was soon followed by other historical overviews of African-American involvement in front of and behind the camera: Donald Bogle's *Toms, Coons, Mulattos, Mammies, and Bucks* (1973), Daniel J. Leab's *From Sambo to Superspade* (1976) and Thomas Cripps' *Slow Fade to Black* (1977). These texts provided the first 'images of …' studies, which documented the history of the industry's production of distorted black images and suggested the possible effects of such stereotypes, and they offered histories of African-American involvement in American film (see **stereotype**). In addition, these studies compared Hollywood cinema with films made by independent African-American companies and criticized the latter for their less accomplished production values, despite massive economic disparities.

During the late 1970s, and best indicated by the change in scholarship from Bogle's highly personal interpretive history to Cripps' densely researched social history, African-American film theorists and filmmakers expanded their focus from determining positive and negative stereotypes to an attempt to define cinematic and aesthetic practices that spoke specifically to black social and aesthetic conditions (see **aethetics**). The most important filmmaking to appear at this time was low-budget, independent film produced by a group of students who existed on the periphery of the film industry and who worked under the auspices of the film programme in the Theater Arts Department at the University of California of Los Angeles (UCLA). This group, variously referred to as the LA Rebellion and the LA School of Filmmakers, consisted of African and African-American graduate film students, including Haile Gerima, Zeinabu Irene Davis, Julie Dash and Charles Burnett. In contrast with the few African-American filmmakers working in Hollywood at that time, members of the LA Rebellion expressed political intentions that extended beyond making money and superficially interrogating representation through the reversal of negative stereotypes. They also developed forms that could not be appropriated by Hollywood in the manner that Melvin Van Peebles' *Sweet Sweetback's Baadasssss Song* (1971) had been, its codes adapted and softened by the blaxploitation genre. Rather than replicating Hollywood's emphasis on classical **realism** and linear narrative, members of the LA Rebellion looked to a diverse cross-section of filmmaking influences and styles, including the early African-American filmmaker Oscar Micheaux, the Black Arts Movement, the Black Panthers, Amilcar Cabral, Franz **Fanon**, the 1930s British social documentary (see **Grierson, John**) and the revolutionary **Third Cinema** emerging from Latin American and African countries. Many of the filmmakers adapted filmmaking techniques from Third Cinema and its focus on the effects of colonialism for an American context in order to have their films speak to larger pan-African concerns. In effect, they wanted to free audiences 'from the mental colonisation that Hollywood tries to impose on its audiences, black and white' (Taylor 1985: 167) by changing the way in which African-Americans were represented and by redressing the stereotypes about black people that these representations had produced.

At the same time, film historians and theorists moved away from less rigorous 'images of ...' approaches in an attempt to define the parameters of black cinema, a project that continues today. In *Black Film as Genre* (1979), Thomas Cripps developed his earlier exclusively historical approach in an attempt to define his subject more precisely. For Cripps, black film was a definable genre, which included:

> those motion pictures made for theatre distribution that have a black producer, director, and writer, or black performers; that speak to black audiences or, incidentally, to white audiences possessed of preternatural curiosity, attentiveness, or sensibility toward racial matters; and

that emerge from self-conscious intentions, whether artistic or political, to illuminate the Afro-American experience.

> (Cripps 1979: 3)

Based on this broad description, Cripps allowed for films with **white** participation to be included in the realm of black film, an approach that was becoming increasingly unpopular with African-American social critics and filmmakers who were engaged in replacing negative stereotypes with representations based on an aesthetic that was more positive, more 'authentic' and more exclusively black. Furthermore, the problem with Cripps' definition was that it grouped all black film together as one genre, thereby blurring generic differences among films.

In a move away from Cripps' more sociological and anthropological approach to African-American cinema, in the early 1980s Gladstone Yearwood and others began a discussion of black film aesthetics. This focus placed black film in the context of larger African-American stylistic and thematic ideas, a critical project that mirrored developments in other academic disciplines. Aesthetic approaches to black film sought to understand African-American arts as the products of the political, economic, ideological and formal practices of black life and culture. Significantly, these ideas changed the focus from positive and negative representations to an understanding of how African-American texts signify among audiences (see **text; signifying practice**).

Influential among these early attempts to create a definition of black cinema aesthetics was Clyde Taylor's 'Decolonizing the Image' (1985). Focusing specifically on independent films from the 1960s and 1970s, Taylor distinguished the LA Rebellion school from race films (made between the 1910s and 1940s), Hollywood films and blaxploitation. According to Taylor, the new black cinema, while diverse, was unified in its 'goals of aesthetic individualism, cultural integrity or political relevance'. Further, these films had a defining aesthetic, which could be identified as a 'realness dimension, [a] relation to Afro-American oral tradition, and ... connections with black music' (Taylor 1985: 168). Notably, Taylor's concept of the 'realness dimension', a set of techniques and styles borrowed from documentary filmmaking and Third Cinema, determined many of the future critical approaches to African-American cinema.

African-American cinema – and criticism of African-American cinema – during the mid- to late 1980s was characterized by a variety of interrelated and determining institutional factors, resulting in a dynamic and sometimes explosive intellectual environment. While the early 1980s witnessed attempts to theorize black film, similar projects were underway in literature, led by such theorists as Henry Louis Gates, Jnr. and Houston A. Baker, Jnr. The 1980s also saw the continuing development of African-American Studies departments across the United States. Furthermore, individual film classes and film departments were gaining in academic respectability and stature. As a result, the 1980s marked an increase in the number of African-American filmmakers attending graduate schools at the same time that an increased number of books and dissertations were written and published on African-American cinema. The changes brought about by the introduction of cultural studies reflected the expansion of other curricula concerned with **identity** politics, such as women's studies, gay and lesbian studies, and post-colonial studies (see **canon; queer theory**).

Influenced by a past that was marked by appropriation, distorted images and a theoretical **discourse** devoted to the identification of an authentic black subject, filmmakers like Spike Lee made films targeted primarily at African-American audiences, which dealt specifically with African-American subject matter and emphasized one African-American experience. The focus on 'realness' and authenticity came to a head in the debates surrounding two films, Steven Spielberg's *The Color Purple* (1985) and Spike Lee's *Do the Right Thing* (1989), the former receiving extended criticism from both the white and the black cultural elite, including Lee, because of its 'skewed' representations of African-American men. Also voiced were objections that the film was not made by an African-American filmmaker, an **essentialism** that was still pervasive in mainstream and African-American film studies at the time.

Lee's *Do the Right Thing* brought the issue of who can speak to the foreground of African-American film studies because of the director's claims of authenticity of story and image. In fact, Lee and the film extended the critical evaluations of realism and authenticity as related to African-American image production. In interviews, Lee's claims to truth indicated the two directions in which African-American filmmaking and cultural criticism would progress. First, one that would diverge from Lee's (and others') notions of an authentic or essential black culture in order to acknowledge the diversity of the African-American community; second, one in which the importance of an authentic or real black subject would increase to the extent that both filmmaking style and critique would be proscribed along strictly defined parameters.

One of the major critiques of Lee's discourse of the real was based on its almost theoretically retrogressive belief in the authenticity of the image; that cinema as a representation could capture some unmediated and therefore authentic version of black life. Because of Lee's insistence on the truth-value of his films, especially *Do the Right Thing*, many cultural critics also became concerned that Lee's version of black experience was being mistaken for, or accepted as, the representation of black life as a whole. Critics of this aspect of Lee's filmmaking, a number of them involved in feminist and queer studies or who were more interested in independent filmmaking, argued that Lee's representations of black life were exclusive of women, and gays and lesbians. One of the best examples of this theoretical concern is Wahneema Lubiano's article, 'But Compared to What?', which appeared in a special issue of the *Black American Literature Forum* dedicated to black film, one of many special issues on black film published between 1988 and 1991.

The approach to African-American cinema reflected in the journals indicated an expanded definition of black film and included considerations of filmmakers working outside traditional narrative modes, for instance documentary and experimental film. These discussions of cinema also made reference to a number of African-American and black British artists working in media other than film (for example, video-makers like Marlon Riggs), indicating not only an expansion of the parameters of African-American cinema to include the black diaspora but also a redefinition of film studies as a whole. Importantly, research and writings by Lubiano, bell **hooks**, Michelle Wallace, Tommy

Lott, Ed Guerrero, Jacqueline Bobo and Gloria J. Gibson pointed to the diversity at the foundations of black filmmaking practices. By arguing for the ways in which many black films did not fit into one overarching definition of black cinema, these critics, like Stuart **Hall**, Kobena Mercer and Paul Gilroy in cultural studies, objected to essentialism and posited the idea that, as Tommy Lott states,

> biological criteria are neither necessary nor sufficient for the application of the concept of black cinema. I want to avoid any commitment to an essentialised notion by not giving a definition of black cinema. Rather, the theoretical concern ... is primarily with the complexity of meanings we presently associate with the political aspirations of black people.
>
> (Lott 1991: 223)

In effect, Lott's and other critics' ideas about black cinema rejected biological essentialism for a more complex understanding of the heterogeneity of black film.

At the same time that theorists and filmmakers began to define a more diverse approach to black film, a new group of filmmakers in Hollywood followed Lee. In 1991 Hollywood released more films directed by African-American filmmakers than at any other time in its history. Significantly, such films as John Singleton's *Boyz N the Hood* (1991) and Mario Van Peebles' *New Jack City* (1991) continued the discourses of truth in African-American film and reflected arguments and ideas in popular culture, particularly rap music and its later manifestations as gangsta rap. These male coming-of-age narratives focused on inner-city crime and nihilism, and relied on spectatorial identification with extra-textual references. This resulted in films that identified their urban narratives with actual black culture. This realness quotient defined African-American youth culture through the early 1990s, culminating in the release of Allen Hughes' and Albert Hughes' *Menace II Society* (1993). The Hughes' stated purpose was to make a film that showed 'the hood like it really is'. Like the LA Rebellion filmmakers of an earlier generation, the Hughes adapted contemporary documentary conventions of television journalism and reality programming in order to reference contemporary African-American events, such as

the 1992 Los Angeles riots. The contradiction was that while the films were all highly post-modern (see **modernism and post-modernism**) in their self-conscious approach to form, they maintained a reliance of subject matter, again building on a dichotomy between negative and positive representation.

Soon, film theorists expanded their approaches to African-American cinema beyond proscriptive attempts at definition. Two key histories were published in 1993, Ed Guerrero's *Framing Blackness* and Mark Reid's *Redefining Black Film*. The former text followed a methodological framework that was chronological at the same time as it traced specific themes in Hollywood and independent films made by African-American and other filmmakers. Reid's text offered a critical overview of independent African-American filmmaking and, importantly, focused on films by black women as part of this project. While both books addressed issues of representation, they shifted away from the sociological and essentialized approaches of earlier histories and moved towards a more complex understanding of the meaning and metaphors produced by films and their relationship to particular industrial and political contexts. Similar concerns arose in two anthologies, Manthia Diawara's *Black American Cinema* (1993) and Valerie Smith's *Representing Blackness* (1997), which sought to 'intervene in ongoing debates about black representation in visual media ... [t]o the extent that questions of authenticity and representation have recurred throughout the history of African American film' and to 'expand ... the project of black visual studies' (Smith 1997: 5). As part of this project, articles in both anthologies re-evaluated early race films and filmmakers according to criteria that rejected value judgements about style and form for sustained analyses of aesthetics, politics and industrial context.

In the 1990s and the turn of the new century, African-American film theory and film has struck an uneasy accord with the difficulty of defining itself. What is being produced in film, video and new media is a diverse mix of subject matter and focus, from adaptations of crime novels into **film noir** (e.g., Carl Franklin's *Devil in a Blue Dress*, 1995) to an increase in films with wide-scale distribution by African-American women (e.g., Julie Dash's

Daughters of the Dust, 1991; Cheryl Dunye's *Watermelon Woman*, 1996). This interest in the diverse aspects of African-American cinema can be seen in the number of theoretical texts that deal with more specific parts of African-American culture. For example, recent histories have undertaken more topical studies of early African-American film and filmmakers such as Oscar Micheaux. Furthermore, in the 1990s there was a rising concern with how blackness is performed (see **performance theory**) in various contexts and how it is linked to issues of **gender** and **sexuality**, both in front of and behind the camera. Finally, the definition of black film has been redefined from Cripps' earlier understanding. It is no longer one genre, but many genres, styles and forms, just as African-American experience is understood as no longer an undifferentiated whole.

See also: Bhabha, Homi K.; difference; dominant ideology; multiculturalism; oppositional; race

References

Bogle, D. (1973) *Toms, Coons, Mulattos, Mammies, and Bucks: An Interpretive History of Blacks in American Films*, New York: Continuum.

Cripps, T. (1977) *Slow Fade to Black: The Negro in American Film, 1900–1942*, New York: Oxford University Press.

—— (1979) *Black Film as Genre*, Bloomington: Indiana University Press.

Diawara, M. (ed.) (1993) *Black American Cinema*, New York: Routledge.

Guerrero, E. (1993) *Framing Blackness: The African-American Image in Film*, Philadelphia: Temple University Press.

Leab, D. (1976) *From Sambo to Superspade: The Black Experience in Motion Pictures*, Boston: Houghton Mifflin.

Lott, T. (1991) 'A No-Theory Theory of Contemporary Black Cinema', *Black American Literature Forum*, vol. 25, no. 2, pp. 221–36.

Lubiano, W. (1991) 'But Compared to What?: Reading Realism, Representation, and Essentialism in *School Daze*, *Do the Right Thing*, and the Spike Lee Discourse', *Black American Literature Forum*, vol. 25, no. 2, pp. 253–82.

Noble, P. (1970) *The Negro in Films*, New York: Arno Press.

Reid, M. (1993) *Redefining Black Film*, Berkeley: University of California Press.

Smith, V. (ed.) (1997) *Representing Blackness: Issues in Film and Video*, New Brunswick: Rutgers University Press.

Taylor, C. (1985) 'Decolonizing the Image: New U.S. Black Cinema', in P. Steven (ed.) *Jump Cut: Hollywood, Politics, and Counter-Cinema*, New York: Praeger.

Yearwood, G. (ed.) (1982) *Black Cinema Aesthetics: Issues in Independent Black Filmmaking*, Athens, Ohio: Centre for Afro-American Studies.

Further reading

Cham, M. and Andrade-Watkins, C. (eds) (1988) *Blackframes: Critical Perspectives on Black Independent Cinema*, Cambridge, MA: MIT Press.

Klotman, P. and Gibson, G. (eds) (1993) *Frame by Frame II: A Filmography of the African-American Image, 1978–1994*, Bloomington: University of Minnesota Press.

Screen (1998) vol. 29, no. 4.

Wide Angle (1991) vol. 13, nos 3 and 4.

PAULA J. MASSOOD

agency

'Agency' can be broadly defined as the capacity to make a difference: 'Agency refers not to the intentions people have in doing things but to their capacity of doing those things in the first place (which is why agency implies power: cf. the Oxford English Dictionary definition of an agent as "one who exerts power or produces an effect")' (Giddens 1984: 9). The concept of agency should not be taken to indicate that individuals are free to do whatever they desire: men and women may be able to make a difference, but of course they will never do so in circumstances entirely of their own making.

Discussions of agency have occurred in two major contexts within film and television theory. First, it has been tackled in theories of film **narrative**. Second, agency has featured in discussions over the activities of film and television audiences, where theorists have disputed the degree and type of power that audiences might have (see **audience**).

Where narrative agency is concerned, Bordwell and Thompson define the foremost attribute of classical Hollywood cinema and its narratives as follows: 'that the action will spring primarily from *individual characters as causal agents*' (1993: 82, their italics). Bordwell and Thompson go on to discuss how, even where natural or societal causes may play a part in classical Hollywood narrative (e.g., floods or wars), the personal psychologies of individual characters still carry such narratives. Classical Hollywood narrative depends on sustaining audience identification with narrative heroes (and such figures are typically male), whose aims structure the narrative. Some theorists have described post-1960s Hollywood as the 'new Hollywood', linking the breakdown of the studio system to more disjointed and spectacular forms of 'post-classical' narrative, but Kristin Thompson argues against these assumptions. In *Storytelling in the New Hollywood*, Thompson suggests that Hollywood film narratives from the 1960s onwards have continued to follow the classical pattern:

> motivations are based upon the traits of the characters. Even in *The Poseidon Adventure* [Ronald Neame, 1972], the ship's fatal instability is motivated in an early scene when a greedy company representative is blamed for the vessel not having proper ballast and running too fast.... Characters with sufficient traits to be interesting and to sustain the causal action remain central to Hollywood filmmaking.
>
> (Thompson 1999: 13–14)

Narrative forms other than classical or 'new' Hollywood do not necessarily follow the same approach to narrative agency. Soviet cinema, in the work of such directors as **Eisenstein**, attempted to replace personalized narrative agency (and 'the hero') with an emphasis on collective agency. For example, events of the Russian Revolution are portrayed in *October* (Sergei Eisenstein, 1928) as coming about through the agency of 'the people'. There is no individual protagonist; the people of Russia fulfill this narrative function.

Where audience agency is concerned, debates in film and television theory have tended to swing backwards and forwards between denying and then emphasizing this agency. **Screen theory**, with its reliance on the work of Louis **Althusser**, emphasized the power of the film text to position the spectator. This approach therefore seemed to deny or minimize audience agency; film spectators were placed by texts within a structure of meaning. An emphasis on the power of structures to limit or remove agency represents the other side in the debate over agency. This is the 'structure/agency' problem. Theorists either emphasize agency, and the power that agents have, or they emphasize structures, and render agents seemingly powerless.

David Morley (1992) has traced these two opposed possibilities across the history of film and television theory. *Screen* theory perhaps erred in favour of emphasizing structure over agency (and it was far from alone given the influence of structuralism in the 1970s; see **structuralism and post-structuralism**). The **uses and gratifications** approach to television audiences, on the other hand, stressed individual agency rather than considering social or textual structure. Theoretical approaches to television viewing have since moved through **semiotics**, and this engagement has produced its own version of the 'structure/agency' stand-off. Theorists such as John **Fiske** have emphasized audience activity and agency. David Morley's work, in contrast, has examined the limits to such agency, and the ways in which audience interpretations may be structured by the uneven distribution of social resources. The 'structure/agency' problem has therefore continued to inform various theories of film and television **consumption**.

See also: classical Hollywood cinema and new Hollywood cinema

References

Bordwell, D. and Thompson, K. (1993) *Film Art: An Introduction* (4th edn), New York: McGraw-Hill.
Bordwell, D., Staiger, J. and Thompson, K. (1985) *The Classical Hollywood Cinema*, New York: Columbia University Press.

Giddens, A. (1984) *The Constitution of Society*, Cambridge: Polity Press.

Morley, D. (1992) *Television, Audiences and Cultural Studies*, London: Routledge.

Thompson, K. (1999) *Storytelling in the New Hollywood: Understanding Classical Narrative Technique*, Massachusetts and London: Harvard University Press.

MATTHEW HILLS

agit-prop

Agit-prop is a term derived from the Department of Agitation and Propaganda set up in 1920 in the Soviet Union and is used to describe the desired effects of Soviet filmmaking after the Russian Revolution. After seizing power in 1917, the Bolshevik Party realized the importance of film in manufacturing support for their new government. The term combines complementary functions: the new Soviet films were meant to agitate the public against the former masters of the country, and to provide propaganda for the Bolshevik reorganization of the devastated land. Although original to Soviet-era film, the term has continued to apply to filmmaking with radical ideological purposes.

See also: propaganda

GABRIEL M. PALETZ

Althusser, Louis

b. 1918; d. 1990

Central among recent Marxist philosophers, Althusser's conceptual acuity has been overshadowed by personal tragedy. From his birth near Algiers through his internment in the Second World War to his lengthy tenure at the Ecole Normale Supérieure in Paris, Althusser came to command a prestigious critical position across disciplines, forcing a rethinking of Marxist models, embodied in such works as *For Marx* (first published in 1965). As such, his influence converged with other post-structuralist thinkers such as **Barthes**, **Derrida** and **Lacan**. Yet Althusser's murder of his wife in 1980 revealed a history of mental problems and hid him from the public until his death in a hospital in Paris.

Althusser's restatement of a scientifically theoretical Marxism focuses critical attention on ideology, the subject (see **subject and subjectivity**) and social reproduction. His subtle and complex sense of ideology puts it at the centre of social organization, in both its representations of the world and its limitations on questions about that world (see **ideology and hegemony**). Ideology shapes the existence of the subject, including its social construction of an apparently pre-existing subject. Hence, critical work must look at the operations of this production of the subject and his/her awareness, as well as social representational meanings.

References

Althusser, L. (1969) *For Marx*, New York: Vintage (originally published as *Pour Marx*, 1965, Paris: François Maspero).

GARY McDONOGH

anchorage

Anchorage is a term used in **semiotics** to describe the manner in which an 'open' or **polysemic** text is 'anchored'. Introduced by Roland **Barthes** (1977), it describes the fixing or limiting of a particular set of meanings to a text. Typically associated with printed images, often a newspaper photograph or advertisement, anchorage is usually through the use of a caption or other written text. However, the use of a commentary or voice-over can also have the same purpose for audio and moving image texts. Anchorage acts as a guide for readers and viewers and aims to direct the audience towards the **preferred reading**.

References

Barthes, R. (1977) *Elements of Semiology* (2nd edn; first published 1964), trans. Annette Lavers and Colin Smith, New York: Hill and Wang.

PHILIP RAYNER

arbitrary

A semiotic term that is used to describe a culturally defined relation between signifier and signified or sign and meaning (see **semiotics**). In contrast to **indexical** and iconic signs (see **icon**), which are motivated by causal or similarity relations, arbitrary sign systems – such as language or visual codes – depend on form-content and sign-meaning relations agreed on and handed down within communities. They differ from community to community (e.g., *Liebe, amour,* love; black or white as a sign for mourning) and, though they are in general obligatory for individual community members, are subject to constant cultural renegotiation (e.g., language change, change of dress code).

See also: Saussure, Ferdinand de; semantics

EVA VIETH

archetype

According to the *Merriam-Webster Encyclopaedia of Literature*, an archetype is '[a] primordial image, character, or pattern of circumstances that recurs throughout literature and thought consistently enough to be considered universal'. Film and television traffic in repeated images, characters and patterns of circumstances. The notion of universality, however, has tended not to be favoured by modern film theorists, who, with the exception of the cognitivists, prefer to explore the effects of historically and culturally specific conditions on the processes of image comprehension and interpretation (see **cognitive theory**). Moreover, the term 'archetype' is closely associated with the work, in the area of the 'collective unconscious', of Carl Jung, a major figure in psychology who has, in film studies and elsewhere, been eclipsed to a large extent by **Freud** – the latter being a universalist thinker of a different sort.

None the less, film is replete with patterns, plots, and **narrative** techniques which lend themselves, at least as a first approximation, to description as expressions of archetypes. Looking at films this way can be uselessly broad; allusion to the archetypal murder of Abel by Cain may shed critical light on films in which brother kills brother but not on other cinematic murders. But archetypal analysis can be a useful tool for mapping the experiences and perceptions of both filmmakers and their audiences, particularly with regard to genres which deliberately recycle images, characters and patterns of circumstances. Westerns, for instance, draw on archetypal images (e.g., the Western landscape), characters (e.g., the cowboy) and patterns (e.g., good guys versus bad guys). Applying this schema to each and every Western may not be productive, but the archetype can serve as a point of reference and departure even for films which revise, rethink or even reject it.

See also: genre; Western, the

DAVID A. BLACK

Arnheim, Rudolf

b. 1904

Arnheim studied psychology, philosophy, art history and music history in Berlin, and in 1928 became a film critic. In 1932 he published *Film als Kunst*, later abridged and published in the US, together with several other essays, as *Film as Art* (1957). Arnheim's original book is part of the formative tradition of film theory. It deals mainly with the aesthetic possibilities of silent cinema. His central thesis is that the aesthetic potential of film lies in the limitations of the medium: wherever film is not able to reproduce the conditions of everyday visual perception, the medium can exploit its creative potential. The specific features of film art derive from the absence of sound and colour as well as the lack of three-dimensional depth and spatio-temporal continuity. The coming of sound and colour pushed the medium towards greater perceptual **realism**, resulting in, according to Arnheim, artistic loss. In his essay 'A New Laocoön' (1938), Arnheim condemns sound cinema as an artistically unsatisfactory composite. Escaping Nazism, Arnheim emigrated to the US and became one of the leading theorists of the psychology of art.

References

Arnheim, R. (1957) *Film as Art*, Berkeley: University of California Press.

Further reading

—— (1997) *Film Essays and Criticism*, trans. Brenda Benthian, Madison: University of Wisconsin Press.

FRANK KESSLER

Arnold, Matthew

b. 1822; d. 1888

An English literary critic and poet, actively involved with British politics and education, Arnold is best known for his polemic *Culture and Anarchy* (1869), which can be viewed with hindsight as an early work of cultural studies. Arnold championed 'culture' – embodied by a **canon** of 'high' literary texts – as a means of bettering society, and was scathing towards the contemporary Puritan attitudes which followed merely the letter of the Bible rather than a grander, holistic project of perfection in all spheres. While he viewed his society in terms of strict class divisions – upper-class 'Barbarians', middle-class 'Philistines' and the working 'Populace' – he believed his view of culture could elevate any individual, regardless of social standing. Reading between the lines of *Culture and Anarchy*, though, an anxiety about the politicized working class is almost tangible.

Arnold remains significant within the history of cultural studies because of his elevation of 'culture' – despite his narrow definition of the term, which excluded all 'popular' texts – to a level beyond the trivial and ineffectual.

References

Arnold, M. (1993) *Culture and Anarchy and Other Writings*, ed. Stefan Collini, Cambridge: Cambridge University Press.

WILL BROOKER

art

Throughout western history the nature of art has occupied major thinkers. What we take art to be has far-reaching consequences for that which is not considered art: 'art' as a concept divides and categorizes human production by placing artefacts in a hierarchy. This entry will first chart some of the definitions of art and then consider the relationship between these and the new media forms of film and television in their relevant contexts.

Aesthetics is a branch of philosophy that considers the nature of beauty, value and the criteria by which art is defined. Etymologically, the concept of 'artefact' links all created things in the world to 'art', so 'creation' is one of the core concepts of 'art'. In order to divide created works into categories, criteria for the judging of merit had to be introduced. Western philosophy has taken up the challenge that this involved, and has created a range of different but interlocking systems for the evaluation of human creativity. In relation to the reception of film and television, two aesthetics debates are most pertinent: the problematic of mimesis and the way the arts are situated historically (see **mimetic/mimesis; reading and reception theory**).

From the Greek philosophers onwards one of the core debates regarding human creation was how this activity links to humanity's place in the world. In Plato's *Republic* the concept of *telos* (Greek: end) links human productivity to things beyond the material world, that is, to metaphysics. Humans create by referring mentally to the *telos* of the things to be created. Thus, the production of a table by a carpenter is a mimesis (**representation** or imitation) of the telos or ideal of the 'table'. Drawing a picture of a table is twice removed from the ideal table: it is the imitation of the representation of the table, so art is itself twice removed.

The notion that the abstract and ahistorical 'ideal' of a thing exists outside the direct human conception thus informs the Platonic notion of beauty. The creation of beauty brings with it the moral obligation to continue the human project of making the ideal visible in the world. Aristotle, a pupil of Plato, also dealt with the place of art and his account of tragedy and **catharsis** has been very influential not only on the forms of theatre, but also as a mode of **genre** analysis. The most influential aspects of these aesthetic theories have resided in the view that truth and beauty exist outside the physical world, combined with a moral obligation upon all creators to strive to make this eternal, ahistoric beauty and truth visible in the here and now.

It took until 1790 before a modern philosophical text creating a place for aesthetics as part of a coherent philosophical system was written: **Kant**'s *Critique of Judgement*. The notion that art itself, or our understanding of art, is stable and transcends the historical moment informs this defining text of the Enlightenment, creating a link to the ancients. For Kant, the ability to distinguish true art from the merely pleasing was a function inherent to the human mind. His view of art centres on the notion of disinterest: 'The delight which determines the judgement of taste is independent of all interests' (Kant 1952: 42).

An interesting counter-view to this idea of the universality of aesthetic judgements is put forward by another thinker who has shaped western philosophical thought, although he is not usually associated with the fields of aesthetics: **Hegel**. The point of difference to Kant lies in the historicity of Hegel's account of art. Hegel lays down the framework for an understanding of art as regulated by its mode of production. A historical culture expresses its *Geist*, its essence, spirit or nature, in its art. This historic, situated understanding of art foreshadows contemporary thought on culture. Although the Kantian influence has been much stronger over the history of western aesthetics, Hegel's conception of the relationship between art and society has found its way back into the discussion of art through the ascendance of cultural studies (see **culture**).

In the nineteenth century, philosophers such as Friedrich **Nietzsche** and Arthur Schopenhauer put forward new theses on the function and form of art, which saw artistic activity in a darker light than Kant's belief in the rational but took up Kant's notion of the genius or 'special creator'. The 'will to power' as underlying impetus in the artist opened up an analysis of art's function which was taken up, on the level of the individual, in **Freud**'s work on art and neurosis.

In the late nineteenth century, the always-fragmented study of aesthetics shatters into many different pathways explored under a range of disciplinary headings. Any clear hold on what art is has vanished: art is neither just representation of metaphysical forms, nor self-expression of a

creative genius. All art does not appeal to all people(s), and all art is not produced in the same way. Art now comes in many different forms, among them fine arts, theatre arts, film art. Problems about the status and usefulness of the category 'art' define debates in the twentieth century.

Film (and later television) destabilizes many paradigms of traditional art production: their production encompasses an industrial framework, a large mechanical apparatus and mass production, and questions the possibility of a single 'creator' of its forms. In relation to the historic debates in aesthetics, the main question which film had to answer related to its mimetic quality. What is the relationship between film's potential status as 'art' and its perceived ability to 'reproduce' (mimic) nature? Early film theory attempted to assert art status for the new medium by centring on the problem of naturalism – how well and in what way film represented the **pro-filmic event** (the event before the camera), and how this could be seen as art. For aestheticians trained in a Kantian framework, the camera experiments of the Lumière Brothers would fall outside the criteria for art because they were too close to a 'mere documentation' of reality: they could be 'useful' as documents of the real world. As such, they are not works of art which demand disinterested appreciation. The other kind of early filmmaking, conventionally indexed with Georges Méliès' fantastical film adventures, equally falls foul of the criteria: they are 'mere entertainment', a pleasing of the senses. But film theorists soon started to elaborate on the relationship between reality and filmic photography in order to point to the 'higher' functions of film, thereby redeeming it as an art form.

Two main positions emerged in the battle about the 'role' of film as art: realist and anti-realist ones. Concurrent (and sometimes overlapping) with these debates, there has been a redefinition of the role of all art in culture, rehearsed through the medium of film.

The most influential 'realist' of cinema is André **Bazin**, who wrote in the late 1940s, and his appreciation of cinema is anchored in a film practice which knows sound, colour and a range of well advanced narrative systems. For Bazin, the cinema needs to recreate a new world, based on a realist depiction. Given its unparalleled ability to transport its viewer into a different world than his or her 'real' one, cinema should aim at a new world where we can go and exchange reality for another one.

Siegfried **Kracauer**'s conception of film as art is embedded in a critique of the state of perception in the modern world. This view is combined with a belief in film as an art form that is able to realign modern perception with the world. While the abstractions, speed and technology of modern living alienate us from the world, the technology of cinema can make us see our reality with new eyes. Film 'literally redeems this world from its dormant state, its state of virtual non-existence, by endeavouring to experience it through the camera' (Kracauer 1997). The 'essence' of nature is thus made accessible in film, and it is the obligation of the filmmaker to reveal reality.

Rudolf **Arnheim**'s writing on film from the 1930s onwards encapsulates the formalist, anti-realist stance towards film: he is opposed to a view of cinema as a 'feeble mechanical reproduction of real life'. For film (or any creation) to become art, it has to mould, shape and recreate reality. Arnheim gives many examples of instances where this reshaping can take place: he delineates those aspects of cinema which make it different from 'real' perception. Black-and-white, silent images, the edges of the screen, camera angles, editing, etc. – all of these are aspects of cinema that need to be exploited if film is to become true art. Arnheim points to the montage technique of the Russian school, and shows how film comes into its own with this exploitation of its own possibilities. Arnheim (as well as **Eisenstein**) is one of the first theorists of cinema to analyse the ways in which film makes meaning additional to those associated with the pro-filmic event and the resources of theatre or the fine arts. Arnheim argues that film can have art status when it shows its own essence and difference from the other arts, following the German philosopher Gotthold Lessing who claims that any art must be true to its nature. Film can be true art if it explores its own means.

Finding frameworks for the relationship between reality and film's mimesis of it was thus the first major thrust in film theory's attempt to find its place among the arts. The second effort originated from a group of film critics who assembled around André Bazin's journal *Cahiers du cinéma*. The group proclaimed the existence of individual **authorship** in cinema: great individuals stamped their personal genius on the films made within the production system of the film industry. Film art, just like any other art, has its geniuses, its artists.

All of these theorists of cinema aimed at finding a place for cinema in the canon of western art. A school of thinking which shifted the ground of investigation, though, overtook these efforts. **Structuralism and post-structuralism** removed the question of 'film as art' from the centre stage. The new theory's first interest in film was in its function as a language. The **reality effect** of film was analysed, not the relationship between film and reality. Roland **Barthes** opened up the field, and seminal essays by film theorists such as Colin MacCabe (see **classic realist text**) looked at realism as a product of a specific organization of the film text.

The evaluating framework of traditional aesthetics was no longer seen as the centre of 'film studies'. But the concerns articulated by the early theorists never left film studies: they are concerns that govern film criticism, which was never separate from theory in the writings of Kracauer or Bazin. Writers such as Victor Perkins have continued to produce works in which the relative merit of cinema art works is discussed, sensitive to the special properties of the art form. Historical poetics, as exemplified by the work of **Bordwell** and Thompson, are charting the specific vocabulary of film, without manifestly evaluating different films.

Parallel to the attempts to create an aesthetic of cinema another discipline concerned with art developed over the course of the twentieth century. It is rooted in the historical view of the arts adopted by Hegel, and dovetailed later with the concerns of the structuralist school. In this view of culture and art, all human creation is relational: culture is seen as a network of structures that sustain its existence. What is considered art in any one period depends on the overall value scheme of that culture at that time.

One of the first influential texts that approached the new 'realist' arts of the twentieth century as a situated human endeavour was Walter **Benjamin**'s 1936 essay 'The Work of Art in the Age of

Mechanical Reproduction'. Benjamin celebrates photography and film as new art forms which lack a central attribute of traditional arts: the **aura**. Through their reproducibility, the new forms are not endowed with the traces of a singular human creativity. This makes these new arts more accessible, more democratic: no forbidding 'distance' between maker and spectator comes in the way of joyful consumption. True mass participation and mass imagination are now possible. What is considered 'art' has changed due to technological developments, and other aspects of culture have to change as well to keep up with the pace. Underlying this conception of the relationship between art and society is a developed Marxist model of culture.

Benjamin is well aware of the possibilities of a reactionary appropriation of the new arts. The **Frankfurt School** develops these concerns into one of the most forceful explanations of culture in modernity, but in a much more pessimistic vein. The writing of scholars associated with the School now starts to take into account the latest new arrival on the culture scene: television. Analysing film, radio, magazines and television, Max Horkheimer and Theodor **Adorno** create the designation 'culture industry'. The culture industry's products are characterized by homogeneity – 'all mass culture is identical' (Adorno and Horkheimer 1972: 121) – and predictability – 'As soon as a film begins, it is quite clear how it will end, and who will be rewarded, punished, or forgotten' (*ibid.*: 125). These characterizations stand in direct opposition to what was traditionally considered art: individuality and creativity.

But instead of pointing to the old definitions of art as guarantors of a 'truth' outside the physical world, or a destiny of an art form, members of the Frankfurt School reproduced these categories under a different agenda. Art as the place for creativity is the driving force of human progress. Without art, culture is stable and locked into place. The values of art are therefore not valuable in themselves and ahistorically fixed, but they drive social emancipation.

One of the central tenets of the Frankfurt School is that the culture industry produces products that reproduce the *status quo*. Mass culture is standardized, manipulative fare for a passive mass audience. The Frankfurt School saw the only

beacon of hope in 'authentic culture' – a culture of 'subversive negativity', which is constantly under battle from the forces of commodification. Later scholars questioned this view of the audience as passive and emphasized the productivity of reading. John **Fiske** re-evaluates the cultural work necessary to read popular texts, and tries to show possibilities of resistance to the dominant ideology on a textual level. His optimistic project realigns itself with the notion that good 'art' requires work on the part of the contemplating individual. Feminist scholars such as Ien Ang similarly argue for a revaluation of the 'passive, brainwashed consumer' by showing the complexity of engagements with texts like *Dallas* or other soap operas. These products of the television world are often seen as low, crude and simplistic works which diminish their viewers. Showing the variety of pleasures that can be gained from these programmes counters the condemning view of users of popular culture as inferior 'others'. In the broader field of cultural studies, these questions of resistance, market-place structures, cultural economy and textual engagements are investigated, but within the non-evaluative framework of culture rather than art.

These views of the place of individual voices in a mass cultural field inform debates about modernism and modern art, a wide and vague term applied to a range of art practices in the disciplines of fine arts, time-based art, site-specific art, etc. in the twentieth century (see **modernism and post-modernism**). One of the definitions of modern art sees it as a reflexive practice: the conditions of its own making are foregrounded in it. **Avant-garde** filmmaking and **video art** were in one form or another influenced by the codes and concerns of modern art: rejecting the commercial aspect of their respective media, artists meditated on the possibilities and frontiers of their medium. Their work was soon assimilated into the broader art market, gallery and museum culture. **Art cinema** now exists as a branch of the cinema industry, and **public service broadcasting** is the location for video experiments as well as quality programming. But although film and television art is thus accessible to a wide population and has merged with and used popular cultural forms, the elite aspects of art have not vanished. The cultural theorist Pierre **Bourdieu** introduced the issue of taste within an historical framework: not as Kant's essential judgement, but as an instrument of power that holds social groups in their relative positions. Cultural capital is needed to read and enjoy works of art, and access to it and its use are indicative of social position.

Art might have lost its hold as an absolute value at the same time that film came into its own, but the influences of centuries of debate about the values of creativity are still extensive. It is important to remember that although theorists might have turned away from a consideration of art as an evaluative concept, the world has not. Organizations like the National Endowment for the Arts in the US or the Arts Councils in the UK grant their monies according to their definition of art, and the public and the media react to the outcomes of this public funding in intense media debates. Thus, constant redefinitions and negotiations of 'art practice' continue to structure the creativity of filmmakers, television producers, video artists and audiences.

See also: Marxist aesthetics

References

Adorno, T. W., and Horkheimer, M. (1972) *Dialectic of Enlightenment* (first published 1944), New York: Herder and Herder.

Kant, I. (1952) *Critique of Judgement* (first published 1790), trans. James Creed Meredith, Oxford: Clarendon Press.

Kracauer, S. (1997) *Theory of Film: The Redemption of Physical Reality* (first published 1960), with an introduction by Miriam Bratu Hansen, Princeton: Princeton University Press.

Mast, G. and Cohen, M. (1985) *Film Theory and Criticism. Introductory Readings*, New York, Oxford: Oxford University Press. (Extracts from the works by Arnheim, Bazin, Benjamin and Kracauer are contained in this useful edition, together with other extracts from defining texts of film aesthetics.)

Further reading

Perkins, V. (1972) *Film as Film*, Harmondsworth, Middlesex: Penguin.

Storey, J. (1997) *An Introductory Guide to Cultural Theory and Popular Culture*, NJ, London: Harvester Wheatsheaf.

PETRA KUPPERS

art cinema

Like **film movements**, art cinema is a term whose history is more revealing than its current desuetude suggests. This entry examines some of the resonance which the term held in the past, and raises questions about its current relevance. Its focus is limited to art cinema in Europe and America.

Art cinema in its simplest usage was a way of signalling a type of cinema differing from an assumed norm – that is, the Hollywood studio system. British and American film criticism, at least from the 1940s to the 1960s, easily slipped into the polarities of art versus industry, culture versus entertainment and meaning versus profit: 'art cinema' was shorthand for these divisions. What the term actually meant is more difficult to assess because its uses differed from period to period and nation to nation. (For a detailed and symptomatic history of its use in British film culture in the 1940s, see Ellis 1978.) In most cases, however, the meaning of art cinema was shaped by the way in which writers saw film both in relation to conceptions of **culture** and **art** dominant in their own society and Hollywood cinema.

Steve Neale's (1981) survey of European art cinema shows how the term is a site for a number of discourses, especially those of national cinema, state funding of production and textual practices (see **discourse**). Faced with the economic dominance of American cinema from the 1920s onwards, most European nations at one time or another have been concerned to ensure that films were made whose meanings would have particular relevance in their country of origin. Hollywood's **narrative** strategies and accessible themes, backed by superior marketing and distribution, proposed a universality which was commercially successful, but there have always been aspects of social experience and identity which individual nations sought to assert. In this sense, films as diverse as *Bicycle Thieves* (Vittorio De Sica, 1948) and *Brief Encounter* (David Lean, 1945) were a kind of national cinema which was also art cinema. Before and after American cinematic hegemony, European countries produced films like these which lacked mass popular appeal, but which were consonant with middle-class notions of art as shaped by the classic novel and a broadly humanist ideology (see **ideology and hegemony**). Such films, often called 'quality films', would be modestly successful at home but would have a significant international reputation with critics and minority audiences. Indeed, almost any film subtitled for screening in another country was seen as art cinema in the receiving country. As cultures have become more nervous about designating their own cinemas as 'art cinema', the term 'quality cinema' has assumed some of art cinema's functions.

The mutually reinforcing discourses of national cinema and state subsidy are apparent, for example, in the 1998 British government report, *A Bigger Picture*. The report exemplifies and catalogues the problems that most European film industries have faced since the Second World War: American films are more popular, especially with the young, less formally-educated audience; American films are better distributed; the existence of a sustainable and stable film industry in Britain depends on attracting foreign – including American and European Community – investment. In keeping with the current British government's reluctance to engage with cultural or critical debate, the report relegates issues of art or quality to an appendix. The consumer research reported there neatly summarizes the contradictions of art cinema and national cinema:

> British films are perceived as those which are made in, by and for the UK, with British sensibilities. They are associated with low budgets; good team acting rather than stars; contemporary UK settings; recognisable ordinary people, real life situations (often depressing); a British sense of humour, or with carefully crafted classics and period dramas.

(Department for Culture Sport and Media 1998: 35)

However, the research also reveals that these films are not successful in the British mass cinema market. This is almost exactly the situation described by John Ellis' account of British cinema in the 1940s, and allows us to argue that films like those of Ken Loach and Mike Leigh exactly fulfil the art cinema functions which *Brief Encounter*, for example, fulfilled in the 1940s.

The textual features and aesthetic strategies of art cinemas vary geographically and historically, but derive in part from the need to differentiate themselves from texts produced by Hollywood. But Steve Neale's (1981: 14–15) description of the art cinema text as 'Marked by a stress on visual style ... by a suppression of action in the Hollywood sense, by a consequent stress on character rather than plot, and by an interiorisation of dramatic conflict', and 'marked at a textual level by the inscription features that function as marks of enunciation ... as signifiers of authorial voice and look', is distinctive enough to accommodate the films of the Italian post-war neo-realist movement and the Danish Dogme 95 group (see **film movements**). These features align art cinema with traditional notions of European art, embracing notions of self-expression and **authorship** inflected by the specific national determinations.

Textual distinctiveness is not the only marker of art cinema. As already implied, distribution and exhibition also signal a different mode of existence: audiences for art cinema have often to be reached in different ways or are found in different cinemas from mainstream audiences. A French government decree in 1991 confirmed subsidies to cinemas showing 'œuvres cinématographiques presentant d'incontestables qualités mais n'ayant pas obtenu l'audience qu'elles méritaient' (films of undoubted quality that are not getting the audiences they deserve), highlighting the fact that distribution and exhibition also sustain the existence of art cinema. In other countries this is marked by distribution circuits which emphasize film societies, cinemas independent of American companies, and university and college cinemas.

In defining art cinema 'as Institution', Neale marks it off from **avant-garde**, agitational or otherwise **oppositional** film practices. Art cinema, in his opinion, functions *within* the conception of cinema as a commodity, seeking only to carve out a sector within it which can be inhabited by 'national industries and national film-makers whose existence would otherwise be threatened by the domination of Hollywood'. Neale refers to other possibilities, some centring on the setting up in Britain of Channel 4, which funds feature film production. In the years since his article appeared, Neale's hopes have probably not been fulfilled: New Labour's report, *A Bigger Picture*, has no conception of oppositional cinema, and even, to give an example from the mid-1990s, the anti-authorial rhetoric of Dogme 95 was easily accommodated as another marketable commodity.

In other aspects, tendencies emerging when Neale was writing (in 1981) which he did not mention have been confirmed and serve to complicate the picture. American films given a wide distribution and exhibition often exhibit the textual features of art cinema: certain films by Martin Scorsese, Brian De Palma and Spike Lee fit Neale's description, as do those of independents of a younger generation like Kevin Smith and Whit Stillman. On the other hand, video shops seem to have shelving policies which, on the whole, reinforce the art cinema/mainstream division, though art cinema video suppliers have made such films more accessible to non-metropolitan audiences. Subscription channels, including Channel 4's Film Four, have perhaps widened the range of quality or art cinema films available and might blur some of the sharp divisions between audiences.

In Britain there are more magazines reviewing films, and probably as many newspaper critics, as in the period the 1940s and 1950s, which John Ellis examined in mapping the discourse of art cinema. The narrow critical consensus he noted then may now be less apparent, especially among those reviewers whose education included the study of popular cultural forms. The break-up of the old Hollywood studio system and the emergence of popular 'authors' like Steven Spielberg, Wes Craven and George Lucas, together with the changes in distribution and viewing practices, make it less easy to discern the polarities noted at the beginning of this entry. Art cinema may be dead or it may just be living in different places – fragments in the **mise-en-scène** of *Batman* (Tim Burton, 1989), *Schindler's List* (Steven Spielberg, 1993) or *Wes Craven's New Nightmare* (Wes Craven, 1994), or in the fragmented audiences in the home.

References

Department for Culture Sport and Media (Media Division) (1998) *A Bigger Picture*, London: Department of Culture, Media and Sport.

Ellis, J. (1978) 'The Discourse of Art Cinema', *Screen*, vol. 19, no. 3.

Neale, S. (1981) 'Art Cinema as Institution', *Screen*, vol. 22, no. 1.

PHILIP SIMPSON

audience

The history of audience research can be viewed as a series of oscillations between opposing beliefs in the power of the media to influence audiences on the one hand, and the resistive capabilities of the audience on the other. As a discursive construct, the audience escapes easy definition, as it can mean very different things depending upon who is doing the constructing, the theoretical and methodological assumptions they deploy, and the anticipated outcomes. This difficulty has at times created a paradoxical popular image of media audiences as both dangerously passive and easily stirred into anti-social action by what they view. Given the conceptual and policy centrality of the term, research on audiences has generated a considerable amount of debate on the subject of what audiences do with the media or what the media do with audiences. As a multifaceted concept, then,

> [t]he audience is not merely the site of meanings, beliefs, and attitudes, but also of commodity choices, social relations, experiences, pleasures, behaviours, agencies, bodies, etc. In fact, what we conclude is that the concept of the audience is so unstructured that we would be better off starting from the fact that the concept has been constructed and invoked, in different forms, in different context for different purposes.
> (Grossberg 1989: 19)

In this entry, I trace the genealogy of debates over the audience, paying particular attention to such issues as the impact of gender on reception and ethnographic approaches to the audience and battle over ratings.

Historical overview

The late teens and 1920s saw the proliferation of scholarly studies of media audiences in the US, including the Payne Fund Studies on the impact of motion pictures on young people (1929–32). Statistical in design, these studies measured childhood attendance at the movies and studied the correlation of gender with **genre** preferences, among other variables. Concerns about the deleterious effect of motion pictures on children underpinned much of the research during this period, and the concept of the audience was used to police the activities of so-called vulnerable social groups, such as children, women and immigrants, *and* to highlight cinema's purported immorality. Arguments about the cinema were bound up with contemporary political concerns over immigration, urban vice and changing social mores, and to an extent cinema (and its audience) functioned as a scapegoat for what some viewed as the destructive effects of modernity. The consolidation of the American film industry in the mid-teens coincided with an emerging view of the mass audience that would remain dominant between the two world wars. Many media researchers at the time believed that urbanization and industrialization were creating a society of rootless, alienated individuals who were seen as relatively defenceless against the onslaught of media messages, since their lives were no longer anchored in networks of social relations of pre-industrial times.

The lack of **agency** granted to audiences within this account is symptomatic of the **hypodermic model**, or 'magic bullet' model, of media effects which views media messages as bullets that strike audience members with uniform, immediate and powerful effects. In this model of communication, the passive and atomized audience responds in a predictable, if often irrational, way to the mass media, a response epitomized in Sidney Lumet's 1975 film *Network* and John Carpenter's *They Live* (1988). The audience (and the society) is represented as a monolith that can only ape uncritically what the media tells it to do. This conception of the audience also evokes the model of media effects developed by the **Frankfurt School**, which left little room for audience resistance.

However, by the late 1940s and 1950s the orthodoxy of strong media effects and weak audience was relinquished for a less deterministic model when concern shifted from questions of 'effects' to questions of 'use'. In contrast to the passive audience of the hypodermic needle approach, audiences in the **uses and gratifications** model were active, discerning and selective in their use of the mass media to satisfy a range of psycho-social needs. Two of the earliest uses and gratifications studies were Herta Herzog's 1942 study of women's responses to daytime radio soap operas, and Bernard Berelson's 1945 study of people's reactions to a two-week newspaper strike by New York City newspaper deliverers. Through the use of extensive interviews, which were supplemented by more general questionnaires, uses and gratifications researchers analysed the consumption of media content as audience members subjectively interpreted it. However, by emphasizing function and use over questions of how meaning was derived from media texts, the uses and gratifications approach was criticized for being too individualistic in that different responses to research questions were seen as the result of subtleties in personality and psychology rather than as symptoms of ideology (see **ideology and hegemony**). In contrast, the model of the audience which subsequently developed within cultural studies, while sympathetic to uses and gratifications researchers' emphasis on audience activity, was epistemologically, theoretically and politically quite distinct (Ang 1991).

Cultural studies and ethnographic approaches to the audience

One of the obvious strengths of cultural studies approaches to the audience lies in its integration of empirical methods of audience research with issues of ideology and social **determination**. In contrast to the quantitative (statistical) audience surveys conducted within traditional social science approaches to the media, cultural studies researchers employ a qualitative methodology that situates media consumption within the context of everyday life. Recognizing the folly of isolating media use from other aspects of people's lives, cultural studies researchers relate questions of audience interpretation – what audiences say about their media preferences and habits – to such issues as **gender**, **race** and **class**, seeing television viewing, for example, not as a neutral leisure act but one bound up with identity and social power.

David Morley's influential contribution to audience studies began with his *Nationwide* project conducted at the Centre for Contemporary Cultural Studies in Birmingham, England (Morley 1980). After completing this research, Morley shifted his attention away from differential readings generated by individual programmes to a consideration of the domestic viewing context itself. In his next study, *Family Television: Cultural Power and Domestic Leisure* (1986), Morley examined how family members constructed the meaning of television within their homes, in particular looking at the role of gender in determining viewing patterns, genre preferences and the balance of power in relation to the television set. Morley's research, although limited in extent, revealed that men and women had very clear preferences in terms of genre: men preferred to watch news and documentaries rather than fictional genres such as soap operas and Hollywood **melodrama**. Furthermore, Morley revealed that men and women watched television in different ways; whereas women frequently viewed television while performing other household tasks, men tended to watch television with few interruptions. Morley's findings, therefore, lent weight to the assertions that the reception context was at once a social and cultural phenomenon that could not and *should* not be divorced from wider ideological contexts influencing audiences' perceptions of television.

The emergence of cultural studies in the mid-1970s saw a shift away from the view of the media text as the primary source of meaning, a method associated with structuralist theory (see **structuralism and post-structuralism**). The move was towards a closer scrutiny of the viewer as a member of an interpretive community who could accept the literal meaning of a text, or read a text against the grain, or derive meaning and pleasure in diverse ways, depending on the viewing context.

Morley was not the only researcher investigating the relationship between gender and reception. Dorothy Hobson's 1982 study of female viewers of the British soap opera *Crossroads*, Janice Radway's 1984 research on women's popular romantic fiction, Ien Ang's 1982 investigation of the cross-cultural reception of the US soap opera *Dallas*, and Ann Gray's 1987 study of the uses of video playback technology in the home, related questions of **pleasure**, power and textuality to issues of subjectivity in audience studies (see **subject and subjectivity**). In this research, the audience is seen has having the ability to derive pleasure from television texts in multifarious ways. It is in the work of John **Fiske**, however, that most emphasis was devoted to audience agency.

In *Television Culture* (1987), Fiske argued that audiences mined television texts for meaning in such complex ways that it was futile to perceive of the text, or the viewer for that matter, as a stable entity. In Fiske's words, 'there is no text, there is no audience, there are only processes of viewing' (Fiske 1987). For Fiske, television was best understood as a form of 'structured polysemy' (see **polysemic**), since audiences excavated meaning from texts in heterogeneous and unpredictable ways. Fiske argued that the balance of power in the reading process resided with the reader rather than with the text; there were, then, as many meanings of a given text as there were readers, suggesting that ideological meaning was likewise up for grabs.

While Fiske's argument about the interpretative resistance of audiences was an important point to make in reception theory, many critics felt that he attributed too much power to the audience. Moreover, the sovereign consumer model of the audience implicit in Fiske's argument was, in the minds of some critics, subsumable within the conservative ideology of consumer pluralism which, Morley argued, led to a 'populist neo-liberalist rhetoric which abandon[ed] concern with cultural values, or "quality" television' (Morley 1992). By underestimating the force of textual determinacy, Fiske threatened to divest media institutions of responsibility for the messages they created.

In rejecting monolithic audiences and totalized readings, Fiske made a call for a more ethnographic approach to the study of media audiences, a call repeated by a number of audience researchers who saw the usefulness of ethnographic approaches derived from anthropology for television reception (see **ethnography**). In similar ways to Morley, Fiske argued that 'the study of culture must not be confined to the readings of texts, for the conditions of a text's reception necessarily become part of the meanings and pleasures it offers the viewer' (Fiske 1987). What became known as the 'ethnographic turn' in audience studies was a rallying cry for a method that would remain sensitive to the contingencies of the viewing situation while also taking into consideration the way television was interwoven into the fabric of everyday life. An ethnographic study of reception typically involved some form of participant observation, where researchers conducted interviews with family members in their homes, attempting to discern the rules governing television consumption in general. For example, Marie Gillespie's 1995 study of the role of television 'talk' in the lives of South Asians living in West London investigated television's role among diasporic peoples along a number of different axes, including ethnicity, gender, cultural identity and technology (see **diaspora**). Similarly, James Lull's (1988a) research into television consumption in different global contexts employed research methods that were broadly derived from ethnography. Lull, however, remained sceptical of ethnography's adoption by cultural studies scholars, arguing that 'what is passing as ethnography in cultural studies fails to achieve the fundamental requirements for data collection and reporting typical of most anthropological and sociological research .... Ethnography has become an abused buzz-word in our field' (Lull 1988b).

Notwithstanding Lull's criticisms of ethnography's status within cultural studies, what distinguishes ethnographic methods most from traditional quantitative studies or uses and gratifications research within mass communication is the extent to which they acknowledge the constructed nature of the research process. That is, that the process of gathering knowledge about audiences should take into account the unequal power relations between researcher and respondent. Ethnographic approaches to the study of audiences within cultural studies have therefore paid increasing attention to the specification of ethnographic discourse – who speaks on behalf of whom, for what purpose, and within what institutional context – in order to emphasize the fact that

'research always produces culturally and historically specific forms of knowledge' (Morley 1992). This attention to the politics of doing audience research is quite distinct to the kind of quantitative ratings data generated by organizations such as Nielson Media Research who sell their information to the television industry (see **audience measurement**).

Audience ratings

Some of the earliest methods for quantitative audience research of direct utility to advertising-supported broadcast media included simultaneous telephone interviews and retrospective diaries that recorded participants' recollections of daily media consumption. Both methods were suspect because respondents frequently invented information about their viewing preferences, especially when talking to a researcher on the telephone, either out of embarrassment or in an effort to give the 'right' answer. Furthermore, diaries depended on what audiences *thought* they had watched or listened to in the previous week. Grounded in a behaviourist tradition, these methods constructed television viewing as an isolatable, one-dimensional and knowable act. But if diaries raised problems for researchers in the 1950s, their utility has been further undermined in contemporary living rooms where multichannel cable, remote control channel surfing, video games, pre-recorded videotapes and Web TV, compete with traditional broadcast outlets for audience attention.

With the advent of new technologies such as VCRs, cable and satellite channels and computer games in the 1980s, the ratings industry was under increasing pressure to develop more precise measuring technologies. This situation led to the launch of the 'people meter' in 1987, a box which sat on top of the television and recorded information about which family member was watching which channel at what time. Like the diaries, the people meter required the active co-operation on the part of individual viewers (each family member was given a code), a flaw that led to experimentation with a passive-people meter which recognized the faces of individual family members as soon as they sat in front of the television screen. However, many potential research subjects balk at the idea of their television set doubling up as a surveillance device. This, together with the technical difficulties of accurate results – household pets are occasionally mistaken for family members – has limited the widespread application of this measuring technology.

For the television industry, then, the ever-elusive audience is a commodified audience abstracted in the form of ratings and shares. As a 'currency of negotiation' for the commercial networks and advertising agencies (Ang 1991), this conception of the audience has little in common with 'real' audience members who remain far too undisciplined and unruly. As John Ellis remarks:

> The audience is a profoundly ideological concept, that has very little to do with what viewers are doing or how they are interpellated. Broadcasting institutions are not concerned with 'viewers,' but they are with 'audience.' Viewers are individuals, people who use TV within their domestic and group social contexts. . . . Audiences are bulk conglomerations created by statistical research. They have no voices and are endowed with few broad or educational features. Audiences do not use TV, they watch it and consume it. Broadcasting institutions do not seek viewers, they seek audiences.
>
> (Ellis 1982: 49)

There is, therefore, a fundamental difference between audience *measurement* as carried out by the television industries and television *research* that approaches its object of analysis from an entirely different perceptual and epistemological position (Ang 1991). However, it would be wrong to assume that ethnographic research produces a flawless portrait of audience activity; as Ang argues in *Desperately Seeking the Audience*:

> no representation of the TV audience (empirical or otherwise) gives us direct access to any actual audience; it only evokes 'fictive' pictures of audiences in the sense of fabricated or made up. . . . The social world of actual audiences is therefore a fundamentally fluid, fuzzy, and elusive reality, whose description can never be contained and exhausted by any totalizing, taxonomic definition of 'television audience'.
>
> (Ang 1991: 35)

But this does not mean that attempts to know the audience should be abandoned; on the contrary, Ang is simply emphasizing how overdetermined audience activity actually is, rather than sounding a death knell for empirical research methods (see **determination**). Indeed, in spite of pessimistic proclamations on the impossibility of knowing the audience, empirical research can tell us a great deal about how audiences perceive and use the media.

Within the television industry, though, the complex and multidimensional nature of television viewing will continue to evade industry researchers so long as they rely upon statistics as their primary mode of data. At the same time, as the television set increasingly competes with the **Internet** for audience attention, more areas of Internet content seem to be merging with television's own signifying practices (see **signifying practice**). While electronic technologies redefine audiencehood, they also create new opportunities for audience measurement and targeting – through recording the number of 'hits' registered at a particular Website, for example. However, these data in and of themselves will not explain how people are incorporating the technology into pre-existing work or leisure patterns.

The emergence of the Internet as a popular entertainment and information medium forces us to rethink the concept of the audience. With Internet chatrooms, browsers and portals multiplying by the day, users of electronic technology can choose to be as active or as passive as they like when they surf the Web, seeking out information on local movie listings, participating in an electronic debate that crosses international borders, or choosing to watch television *and* surf the Web at the same time. That the audience will continue to be a volatile, elusive category is a certainty; what is less clear is how notions of audiencehood will play out in the electronic living room of the twenty-first century.

See also: reading and reception theory

References

Ang, I. (1982) *Watching Dallas: Soap Opera and the Melodramatic Imagination*, London: Methuen.
—— (1991) *Desperately Seeking the Audience*, London: Routledge.
Ellis, J. (1982) *Visible Fictions*, London: Routledge.

Fiske, J. (1987) *Television Culture*, London: Routledge.

Gillespie, M. (1995) *Television, Ethnicity and Cultural Change*, London: Routledge.

Gray, A. (1987) 'Behind Closed Doors: Women and Video', in H. Baer and G. Dyer (eds) *Boxed In: Women on and in Television*, London: Routledge, pp. 38–54.

Grossberg, L. (1989) 'The Context of Audiences and the Politics of Difference', *Australian Journal of Communication*, no. 16, pp. 13–36.

Hobson, D. (1982) *Crossroads: Drama of a Soap Opera*, London: Methuen.

Lull, J. (1988a) *World Families Watch Television*, Newbury Park, CA: Sage.

—— (1988b) 'Critical Response: The Audience as Nuisance', *Critical Studies in Mass Communication*, no. 5, pp. 239–43.

Morley, D. (1980) *The 'Nationwide' Audience: Structure and Decoding*, London: BFI Publishing.

—— (1992) *Television, Audiences and Cultural Studies*, London: Routledge. (This book contains a number of Morley's previously published essays and synthesized sections from *Family Television* [1986], and is an excellent resource on the concept of the audience and its application within Morley's research.)

Radway, J. (1987) *Reading the Romance: Women, Patriarchy and Popular Literature*, London: Verso.

Further reading

Jenkins, H. (1992) *Textual Poachers: Television Fans and Participatory Culture*, New York: Routledge.

Jhally, S. and Lewis, J. (1992) *Enlightened Racism: 'The Cosby Show', Audiences, and the Myth of the American Dream*, Boulder: Westview Press.

Moores, S. (1993) *Interpreting Audiences: The Ethnography of Media Consumption*, London: Sage.

Seiter, E., Borchers, H., Kruetzner, G. and Warth E-M. (eds) (1991) *Remote Control: Television Audiences and Cultural Power*, New York: Routledge.

ALISON GRIFFITHS

audience measurement

Audience measurement of television programmes is a quantitative form of audience research. It is almost exclusively concerned with *numbers* of people watching programmes, and, in a strictly limited sense, who these people are. In general terms, it is a form of research with no claim to assess the cultural or social significance of television: it identifies and uses television as a marketable commodity, and is therefore of interest to all those for whom this is television's paramount value. National or regional advertisers and advertising agencies, for example, make use of the data delivered by audience measurement. Their assessment of audience figures influences what they are prepared to pay television companies for the inclusion of **advertising** in programmes, and this, in turn, affects the money available for programme-making. Even **public service broadcasting** organizations are obliged to take into account the number of people watching their programmes in relation to other channels.

Within this narrow conception of television's value, audience measurement is undertaken with a degree of rigour. In the United States and Canada, the best-known company providing 'an estimate of audience size and composition' is Nielsen Media Research, founded in 1923. Nielsen install metering equipment on all the technologies receiving television signals in a sample of over 5,000 households, containing more than 13,000 people, across the US. Nielsen claim that these families are a representative cross-section of the 99 million households with television sets throughout America, accommodating such factors as income group and ethnicity. The meters record what sets are tuned to: almost all programmes and commercials are tracked. 'People meters' on or near the television sets also record who is watching in the households by means of a colour-coded box which each viewer has to remember to switch on and off. Information from these meters is collected electronically each night. Local television audiences in over 200 local markets are measured by diaries in which samples of viewers record their viewing during a measurement week. These are mailed to the company. The samples are cross-checked against each other and other sources, such as the US Census Bureau, to maintain a statistically valid profile of the nation and its viewing habits.

Since the 1970s, advances in technology have enabled Nielsen to 'devote even more resources to the measurement of actual viewing beha-viour.... In addition to providing complete data on set tuning, the Nielsen People Meters measure who is watching TV' (Nielsen Media Research 1999). These more sophisticated measuring tech-niques allow audiences to be conceived in terms of demographic segments rather than sheer numbers. Programmes that deliver 'desirable' demographics, that is, people with the most disposable income (adults aged between 18 and 49) can survive even if their overall ratings are relatively low. In the 1960s, when sheer numbers were the only determinate, the National Broadcasting Company cancelled the television series *Star Trek* because of poor ratings. In the 1980s and 1990s, when 'desirable demo-graphics' count heavily with advertisers, successors of the original series have survived by delivering the right viewers.

In the United Kingdom, the Broadcasters' Audience Research Board Limited (BARB), set up in 1980, is the main source of similar information. It represents the major UK broad-casters, including the BBC, the Independent Television Association and BSkyB. Contractors undertake the actual research. BARB also provide some qualitative research based upon a national panel of 3,000 adults, operating weekly, and 1,000 children operating monthly. Estimates of viewing figures are obtained from samples which are claimed to be representative of households in ITV (Independent Television) and BBC (British Broadcasting Corporation) regions. The samples range in size from 40 to 550 households, depending upon the region. Collectively, these regional samples make up a network sample of 4,484 households representing the viewing behaviour of the 23 million households in the UK. In order to track and check changes in the broadcasting environment or the samples, 40,000 random probability interviews are carried out on a rolling basis throughout the year. As with Nielsen, the numerical data is collected using set and people meters, and downloaded centrally each night.

The power of the numbers collected is now mythical. Just as the dollar bill or the pound coin has economic power out of all proportion to its physical worth, so rating information in television is 'the currency in all transactions between buyers and sellers, which adds up to approximately $44 billion in national and local advertising spending each year' (Nielsen Media Research 1999). More-over, Nielsen claim that 'programmes which have larger audiences are, by definition, the successful ones'. Leaving aside this one-dimensional measure of success, and reservations about whether people always remember to fill in diaries accurately or switch on and off their people meter every time, other researchers have pointed out how vague a term 'watching television' actually is. Research has shown that people switch on television to ignore others, to talk to others, or just to hear voices in the house, as well as to watch the programmes. They watch programmes they don't like because others in the household do, or because others have the power to turn the set off. Men tend to watch programmes with more single-minded attention than women, often because women have domestic responsibilities which they have to undertake alongside viewing. Ratings define the viewer as an isolated abstraction, free from such social pressures and relations, and multiply these indivi-dual figures into an undifferentiated mass. If the complexity of viewing situations and rationales is taken into account, then the crudeness of ratings measurement indicates the limited nature of the Nielsen definition of success. As Stuart **Hall** (1986) has pointed out, these techniques of research tell us more about what producers and advertisers want to hear – and will pay for – than the 'fine-grained interrelationships between, meaning, pleasure, use and choice' in relation to television.

See also: audience

References

Hall, S. (1986) 'Introduction' in David Morley, *Family Television: Cultural Power and Domestic Leisure*, London: Routledge.
Nielsen Media Research (1999). Online. Available: www.nielsenmedia.com

Further reading

Ang, I. (1991) *Desperately Seeking the Audience*, London: Routledge.
BARB (1999). Online, Available: www.barb.co.uk

PHILIP SIMPSON

aura

A term derived from Walter **Benjamin**, aura indicates the halo of distinction that surrounds a work of art. According to Benjamin, an aura arises from an artwork's uniqueness, and its distance – both literal and figurative, in its singular achievement – from a mass public. To Benjamin, the modern age is distinguished by the peeling away of the aura from art objects. The mass (re-)production of many artworks (on postcards, umbrellas, etc.) decreases their uniqueness. Media such as film and television make remote spaces and masterpieces familiar. Movies may surround stars with atmosphere, but of another kind from the aura surrounding works of art before mass industrial culture.

See also: art

GABRIEL M. PALETZ

authorship

This entry traces the history of the idea of authorship in relation to mainstream (as opposed to **avant-garde**) cinema from its introduction by François Truffaut, the critic and filmmaker, through its reworking as part of a structuralist approach to the analysis of film (see **structuralism and post-structuralism**) and the supposed 'death of the author'.

'La politique des auteurs' and auteur theory

'A certain tendency of the French cinema' was the title of the article in the French film magazine, *Cahiers du cinéma*, in July 1954, in which Truffaut proposed what he called 'la politique des auteurs'. The article was a polemical attack on the current state of French cinema written by a young man anxious to start upon his own film career, and oppressed by what he took to be the orthodoxy of his native film industry. This feeling was shared by other writers on the magazine whose enthusiasm, knowledge and ambition led them to argue that what they valued most in cinema, especially in American cinema, was the product of a unified and organizing vision. The vision embodied in the films

was, they argued, that of its author, or auteur, the director. The implication of their critical practice was that some individuals, exemplified by Alfred Hitchcock, could transcend the constraints of the industrial practices of Hollywood and make films which explored recurrent preoccupations in distinctive ways.

As practised by the *Cahiers* critics, under the editorship of André **Bazin**, the *politique des auteurs* may have been a way of creating a context where they could argue for their futures as directors in French cinema. But it also provoked a revision of the way in which cinema was perceived in Europe and America. Andrew **Sarris**, an American film critic and a translator of *Cahiers du cinéma*, translated *le politique des auteurs* as 'auteur theory', thereby giving a rather loose polemical practice a more substantial status. Sarris had his own polemical purposes: he wanted to argue that films produced within an industrial system could have artistic qualities that were conventionally accorded to films from Europe. Throughout the 1960s, most notably in *The American Cinema* (1968), he used the auteur theory much more evaluatively than its originators had proposed. Like them, he was interested in *how* a director could impose himself on a film, but he accorded a greater status to those directors who were capable of such an act of imposition than to those who merely dealt with the material competently. In *The American Cinema* he offered a pantheon of American directors whose work was not only technically competent but revealed a distinguishable personality. Sarris added to *Cahiers*' concern with the mechanics of technical production a claim for an intuitive recognition of the creative tension between the material of the film – the screenplay, the production circumstances, the stars – and the self of the director.

The critical practices of the *Cahiers* critics, and Sarris' more theorized approach, supported the idea of the director as author of the film. But, in arguing that films had an author, both sides were resorting to an aesthetic position which had gained acceptance fairly recently in historical terms. As Michel **Foucault** (1977) has pointed out, in western society, stories, folk-tales, epics and tragedies circulated without reference to their author. Buscombe (1973) identifies the desire to locate *one* author of a text as an aesthetic which rose to prominence in the nineteenth century, and which was later reinforced by copyright restrictions. Sarris' observation in *The American Cinema* that 'the auteur critic is obsessed with the wholeness of art and the artist, and looks at a film as a whole, a director as a whole', places him in a similar position to S. T. Coleridge writing in 1815 of the way Shakespeare's vision unifies all his plays.

Auteur-structuralism

Though Sarris called his approach 'auteur theory', in practice he relied a great deal on setting down his own impressions of films, and on remarks intended to direct the reader's attention to qualities which intuition suggested were apparent in the film text. His practice was scarcely more theorized than that of Truffaut: he did not ground his approach in any explicit theory of how texts were understood, or spell out a methodology. Furthermore, the popularity of Sarris' approach, in the academy and in film culture generally, led to a disregard of the way films are shaped by economic or aesthetic conditions. The influence of the studio (see **studio systems**), for example, or the significance of **genre** for the meaning of a film came to be neglected when so much emphasis was placed on the work of one person.

In the late 1960s two books appeared which developed the notion of authorship in a different direction. In *Visconti*, Geoffrey Nowell-Smith (1967) started from the point that, though there may well be superficial connections between films by the same director (in this case, Italian director Luchino Visconti) at the level of actors, decor or visual style, connections could also be located at a deeper level: 'a structural hard core of basic and often recondite motifs'. The motifs might be stylistic or thematic, but they formed a pattern which underlay one particular work, and which by extension might distinguish one *body* of work from another – that of Visconti from that of other Italian filmmakers of the post-war period, for example. The difference between this approach and that of earlier arguments for film authorship is that the personality or vision of the author is no longer the central concern. This approach was not intended to uncover the personality of the author from his/

her texts and to locate his/her position in a putative hierarchy of talent, but to locate the structures which seem to be shaping the meanings of his/her films. Nowell-Smith talks about the *concept* of authorship as a dimension in understanding cinema, not as a means of reaching the mind or personality of the authors through the text.

Peter **Wollen** theorized and exemplified this approach more fully in the three editions of *Signs and Meaning in the Cinema*, published between 1968 and 1972. Wollen opposed what he regarded as the use of **art cinema** models for the analysis of Hollywood films. Art cinema was rooted in the idea of creativity and films as expression of an individual vision; all films, and especially Hollywood films, were more like a network of different statements, crossing and contradicting one another. By a process of comparison with other films, it was possible to decipher not a coherent message or world view, 'but a structure which underlies the film and shapes it . . . it is this structure which auteur analysis disengages from the film' (Wollen 1972).

Auteur-structuralism recognized the presence of the author's unconscious preoccupations in the text, but constructed these retrospectively from the body of his/her work. There was no claim that the meanings made possible by these structures were the consequence of a creative vision; Wollen attempted to make this distinction clear by distinguishing between Howard Hawks, the director, and 'Hawks' the structure named after him. Wollen sought to acknowledge the necessary presence of the individual on the set, but argued that, in the complex process of industrial production which is filmmaking, his presence was more as an unconscious catalyst than a conscious, creative artist.

Wollen's version of auteur-structuralism is both subtle and polemical. The subtlety lies in the delicate way he appropriates the terms used by Claude **Lévi-Strauss** in his structural analysis of **myth** in oral cultures to locate and describe similar systems of meaning-making in the popular cultural forms of an industrial society. Just as such myths might reconcile the unconscious needs and contradictions of other societies, cinema offered similar satisfactions. Films could be experienced as 'authorless' in the same way as myths which were told and retold to an audience who responded to the telling and the underlying structure, but did not seek for a unifying, artistic vision. The polemical thrust of Wollen's approach is evident in the challenge to the Romantic aesthetics of critics like Coleridge or Sarris who saw themselves as guides to the 'true' meaning of a text. His use of such terms as 'deciphering' and 'decoding' indicates that meanings are being produced in a number of ways by different combinations of elements, and there is no single, essential meaning to be uncovered. The claim is that underlying structures can be objectively revealed, but these may be coded by the text in a number of ways: one coding may draw heavily on the genre of the film, as in the Western, but these elements may also be crossed by another coding associated with the director, John Ford, for example, whose authorial presence is decoded retrospectively (see **Western, the**).

Criticism of auteur-structuralism was swift to follow. Wood (1976), from the position of a traditional critical point of view, found the approach reductive in its implication that structures were the only thing that gave the text its value. Eckert (1973) and Henderson (1973) attacked Wollen and Nowell-Smith for their untheorized appropriation of Lévi-Strauss' structuralism. Henderson castigates what he takes to be a characteristic passage from *Signs and Meaning*:

> The fundamental questions – whether films are like myths, whether modes of myth study are applicable to film study, and whether the auteur theory is compatible with Lévi-Straussian structuralism – are avoided by Wollen, elided by a skilful rhetoric which seems to answer them.
>
> (Henderson [1973] in Caughie 1995: 171)

Failing to establish its theoretical premises in any detail, auteur-structuralists' claims to be more objective than Sarris' impressionism might be challenged on the grounds that the structures which were located in films texts, and the texts themselves, were constructed as objects for attention by the critics themselves. As Henderson (1973, in Caughie 1995) puts it, 'every system of interpretation will produce 'results' which are in full accordance with its methods'.

In the same year, Geoffrey Nowell-Smith (1973) offered a disarming defence of auteur-structuralism that acknowledged the crudeness of its appropriation of the methodology of a structural anthropologist, but laid some claim to having shifted the terrain of the authorship debate to grounds which had produced stimulating results.

'The death of the author'

Roland **Barthes**' assertion that authors must die so that readers can be born was, it seemed, the final flourish and yet another polemic in the authorship debate. Though his essay, 'The Death of the Author', was written in 1968, its first translation into English was published in 1977, and it took its place as another element in a period of intense intellectual debate among film theorists in Europe and the United States. Broadly speaking, the terms of the debate were shaped by a re-emergence of **Marxist aesthetics** mediated by the writing of, among others, Louis **Althusser**, Bertolt **Brecht**, Michel Foucault, Julia **Kristeva**, Jacques **Lacan** and Christian **Metz**. Though their intellectual disciplines and activities were diverse, most addressed the question of the nature and construction of individual **identity**. In this context, the relationship between author, text and reader was inevitably a matter of concern since their analysis of the operation of language provided both a model and a metaphor for understanding the way identities were structured.

As a literary critic, Barthes attacked the assumption that a text was a finished and discrete artefact with a central core of truths which could be excavated by the critic and the reader. He argued that texts were sites for the *production* of meaning. Against the conventional view that the meanings in a text were largely the product of the author, Barthes proposed that meanings in the text were produced at least as much by the activities of the reader. A recurrent image is of the text as a tissue or weave of threads which the reader could pursue into the world of social and cultural relations beyond those related to the circumstances of the author. The text was crossed by a series of codes among which the reader might decipher that of an author, but Barthes' position is that the process of reading is more a *disentanglement* of threads which cover a space. There is no inner core of meanings to be located, only meanings ceaselessly posited for the reader to pursue.

For Barthes, the author does not precede the

text like a parent to a child. The author can only mix afresh the writings which language has already provided for him. Should he wish

> to *express himself*, he ought at least to know that the inner 'thing' he thinks to 'translate' is itself only a ready-formed dictionary, its words only explainable through other words, and so on indefinitely.
>
> (Barthes [1968] in Caughie 1995: 211; italics in original)

The act of writing is not an act of representation or recording so much as a performative act, an act by which something is performed in the here and now in language, in the way that terms like 'thank you' or 'I'm sorry' exist. The text lives only in a recurrent moment of *enunciation*, the term derived from linguistics which Barthes uses to indicate the performative process. Barthes regarded writing as a *practice*, a process of activity and not an attempt to re-create a fictional world corresponding in some way with the real world.

John Caughie's (1981) definitive account of authorship in film theory, *Theories of Authorship*, makes clear how the appropriation of Barthes was much more sophisticated than the opportunistic use made of Lévi-Strauss in the earlier debate. Caughie offers a reminder that the question of the author in the fiction film has always been complicated by the fact that film is a form of enunciation in which any sense of the enunciator is often obscured. If film does not usually have an author or, at least, a narrator in the way in which Dickens' *Oliver Twist* seems to have in those narrative passages which surround the speech of the characters, what *is* its status as an utterance, and how *is* the source of the utterance to be located? How is the relationship of film to the world to be characterized?

Caughie's answer attempts to reconcile Barthes' denial of the author with a recognition that there are continuities and consistencies which can be recognized across texts. Caughie proposes that these features identify an authorial code which is in fact another text constituted from other similar films. The author is thus a figure constructed out of his films; he is, following Barthes, not the originator of film but another text to be seen in relation to the text at which we happen to be looking. The author

is not celebrated as a source of creativity or uncovered as an unconscious structure but is theorized as the enunciator of the film text, the source of the film discourse to be constructed *from* discourse. As Caughie expresses it, 'the fiction of the author' created by the reader from other texts allows a recognition of the distinctive **pleasure** and expectations which affect the viewer's response. In any one John Ford film, for example, we can recognize the marks of the author and these shape our reading of the film.

Caughie, following Nowell-Smith (1967), poses the question of the relationship of the author constructed from the texts, the ideal author, to the historical John Ford, 1894–1978. The theoretical account of authorship summarized in this section is founded on the construction of the subject, that is, the author through the semiotic analysis of texts (see **subject and subjectivity**). But authors-as-subject are not constituted solely by texts: they are social subjects, sexual subjects and historical subjects, and so the identity of the author has to be seen not as an autonomous, discrete identity but as a site where all these discourses of subjectivity intersect (see **discourse analysis**).

Seen in this light, the attempt to provide a theoretically satisfactory answer to the deceptively simple question of who should be regarded as the author of a film has only just begun. After almost a decade in which theorists tacitly ignored the question, a number of writers in the 1990s have returned to it, attempting to take into account the history of the debate outlined here. Timothy Corrigan (1991) asserts the existence of the author as one of the possible layers of meaning that the post-modern array of commerce and culture makes available to audiences: a 'Spielberg production' refers neither to an artist nor a structure, but may indicate a site in the market where an audience can identify a certain style of production which links a film, a book, a T-shirt or an advertising campaign (see **modernism and post-modernism**). Dudley Andrews (1993), perhaps following from Caughie, argues that some readers and viewers *want* to believe in an author, just as some people want to believe in a God, despite assertions of his death. The text exists and the reader exists, and even if the author is only a function of the text, the desire to speculate about the coming into existence of that function, and the peculiar pleasures associated with it, remains.

See also: art

References

Andrews, D. (1993) 'The Unauthorised Author Today', in Jim Collins (ed.) *Film Theory Goes to the Movies*, London: Routledge.

Buscombe, E. (1973) 'Ideas of Authorship', *Screen*, vol. 14, no. 3, pp. 75–85.

Caughie, J. (1995) *Theories of Authorship: A Reader* (5th edn; first published 1981), London: BFI Publishing. (Caughie's book is the definitive publication on the topic. The collection includes most of the key texts for the authorship debates, and each section includes a valuable introduction. The book includes the following articles cited in this entry: R. Barthes, 'The Death of the Author' [1968] and B. Henderson, 'Critique of Cine-structuralism' [1973]. It also has an extensive listing of articles.)

Corrigan, T. (1991) *A Cinema without Walls*, NJ: Rutgers.

Eckert, C. (1973) 'The English Cine-structuralists', *Film Comment*, vol. 9, no. 3, pp. 46–54.

Foucault, M. (1977) *Language, Counter-memory, Practice*, Oxford: Basil Blackwell.

Nowell-Smith, G. (1967) *Visconti*, London: Secker and Warburg.

—— (1973) 'I Was a Starstruck Structuralist', *Screen*, vol. 14, no. 3, pp. 92–9.

Sarris, A. (1968) *The American Cinema: Directors and Directions*, London: E. P. Dutton.

Truffaut, F. (1954) 'Une certain tendence du cinéma français', trans as 'A Certain Tendency of the French Cinema', in Bill Nichols (ed.) (1976) *Movies and Methods*, 2 vols, Berkeley: University of California Press.

Wollen, P. (1976) *Signs and Meaning in the Cinema*, London: Secker and Warburg.

Wood, R. (1976) *Personal Views*, London: Gordon Fraser.

PHILIP SIMPSON

authorship, television

In the 1960s, the filmmakers of the French *nouvelle vague* reconfigured the cinematic landscape by arguing for a *politique des auteurs*. Literally a *policy* rather than a theory proper, it suggested that directors were the authors of their films, putting their visual signature on the work and creating its thematic and narrative consistency, in spite of the interference of studios and producers (see **authorship**). While the idea of the 'author' came under intense scrutiny and outright attack by both semioticians and post-modernists (see **modernism and post-modernism**) – principally by such theorists as Michel **Foucault** – it still resonates strongly in most popular criticism and in the public imagination.

The notion of authorship has only rarely extended to those working in television, and when the term does appear, it usually retains its more traditional, linguistic connotations by focusing on the series creator, often an executive producer and writer. The most well-known creative names in US television history, those considered responsible for a series' look, ideology, story ideas and plotting, include Rod Serling (*Twilight Zone*), Gene Roddenberry (*Star Trek*), Steven Bochco (*Hill Street Blues, LA Law, NYPD Blue*), David E. Kelley (*Picket Fences, Ally McBeal, The Practice*) and Chris Carter (*The X-Files, Millennium*). In Britain, Dennis Potter, almost always solely a writer, similarly has received full credit for the richly complex and reflexive narrative structure of his texts (for example, *The Singing Detective*).

Given the fact that a series can continue to run for many years, however, many possible authors arise at different times of its existence, starting with the producer (who may or may not pen the pilot script), continuing with the writing staff, and eventually extending to the stars. The exact personages involved may alter during a show's lifespan as people drop away and new ones enter the scene: producers wishing (or desired by the networks) to develop a new series pass the baton to a new person. Major actors depart and new ones enter, forcing plot-lines to shift radically.

As commercial, big-budget Hollywood cinema grows more dependent on visual special effects and less reliant on dialogue and plot coherence, print journalists have increasingly begun to pay attention to and analyse the relative power held by the writer in television, as well as the varying trends influencing both. Much of the difference can be attributed to the different industrial structures and needs of the two media – despite their frequently synergistic relationship.

At the present moment, television has an organization reminiscent of the traditional Hollywood studio system (see **studio systems**). While it is rare for today's major film studios to have stars, writers and directors sign up for a five-year contract, this is the norm in television. As in the old Hollywood system, the television producer is the one who determines the course each series will take; puts together the collective operation, including writers, cast and technical staff; and has the final say over each episode. While, in the case of series creators like Bochco, Kelley and Carter, the producer may be both writer and occasional director, the control may also rest in the hands of someone like Aaron Spelling, who presides over many series without actually handling the creative aspect.

The series format additionally constrains the power of authorship: weekly shifts in personnel can mean that individual quirks become subsumed into the need for a regular, overall narrative tone, and speed is always of the essence. Rob Bowman, now a director on *The X-Files*, complained that while working on *Star Trek: The Next Generation*, he was often forced to work quickly and any attempt to develop complicated camera set-ups was discouraged. Because they are involved in every episode, actors often begin to take control, coming up with story ideas and even scripts, suggesting changes in characterization and language, and sometimes directing episodes. Even when the performers have no interest in this, because of their long-term commitment to a series and the fact that their very bodies are the show's material, their physical changes, pregnancies and illnesses demand incorporation into the narrative.

In recent years, as the crossover between film and television has become more frequent, with such names as Steven Spielberg, Barry Levinson, Barbara Kopple, Quentin Tarantino and Tom Hanks signing on as executive producers and directors on series, mini-series and made-for-TV movies, some of the anonymity that shrouded those who work in television has disappeared and authorship has been assigned.

KAREN BACKSTEIN

autonomy, relative

Althusser's challenge to the traditional Marxist formulation of the **base and superstructure** relationship opened up important questions within film and television studies (see **Marxist aesthetics**). In taking issue with what he perceived to be an overly determinist emphasis on the economic base in theorizing how social formations reproduce, Althusser's approach accentuated the 'relative autonomy' (from one another) of the economic, political and ideological levels. Every social formation is a 'structure in dominance' where the economic level – while not always the most dominant – is none the less, by definition, ultimately determinant 'in the last instance'. This line of argument encouraged a radical reconsideration of the significance of **culture** in understanding how social institutions are reaffirmed in ideological terms on an ordinary, lived basis (see **ideology and hegemony**).

Further reading

Althusser, L. (1969) *For Marx* (first published 1965), New York: Vintage.

STUART ALLAN

avant-garde

Deriving from a French term used to describe a company of soldiers sent in advance of the main army to scout and initiate skirmishes, 'avant-garde' was appropriated in the nineteenth century to describe those artistic practitioners ahead of prevailing conventions. As early as 1825, Henri de Saint-Simone used the term to assert approval of Gustave Courbet's provocative position in the artistic field. From that time, an artwork or artist's appraisal as avant-garde has usually implied a positive evaluation, suggesting either an outsider – or even oppositional – stance which the mainstream arts will eventually follow (thus, a *post facto* judgement) or, as in Saint-Simone's use, a taste judgement consistent with the values of progressive cultural elites (a pre-emptive judgement). Thus, the term has been based on the designation of artistic 'progressiveness' and the cultural power of the people making it, since creative activity deemed merely outside conventions by just 'anyone' could be appraised as amateurish, bad or simply irrelevant (see **conventions**).

The term has not been without its difficulties and it has had problems living up to its traditional definitions, at times becoming marketing jargon. On the one hand, the many avant-garde 'isms' associated with modernism (**Constructivism**, Cubism, **Expressionism** and so on; see also **modernism and post-modernism**) turned over so quickly that the avant-garde's leadership position against mainstream arts was overshadowed by its own frenzied struggle to remain ever-fresh. On the other hand, the quick acceptance of the latest radical artistic turn as 'the newest trend', backed by mass circulation publications and fashion designers, all but denied the oppositional or marginal status once a mark of the avant-garde. After the Second World War, the art industry grew increasingly dependent on the new and different, threatening to transform the term avant-garde into a marker of transient orthodoxy and cultural celebrity.

Film has proven to be something of an exception to these trends. The relative stability of a film industry built upon the feature-length dramatic **narrative** and that industry's domination of exhibition, has positioned the avant-garde on the margins, allowing it to retain its oppositional character. Moreover, unlike painting or literature, mainstream and avant-garde film productions have tended to be marked by material differences: the high costs of film production have generally forced avant-garde productions to be relatively short or to rely on less expensive film formats such as 8mm or 16mm. Since the mid-1970s, video offered a way of equalizing conditions of production, with the result that the confusion experienced by mainstream and

avant-garde practice in traditional media has emerged in video as well. For example, many techniques and aesthetic ends associated with video art are quickly appropriated by music video producers, undermining any sense of video art's oppositional status while blurring distinctions between mainstream and avant-garde culture (see **video and art**). Yet in the case of film, the distinctions between the two have remained. Cinema's avant-garde has arguably been of great influence in the evolution of the film medium, a point evident in several developments.

The avant-garde in film has offered a key site of cultural legitimacy to a much-maligned popular mass medium, mapping out cinematic corollaries to most of the twentieth century's modernist movements. This can be seen, for example, in the work of such artists as Fernand Léger, Salvador Dali and Andy Warhol who found in film an extension of their creative interests. And it is apparent in filmmakers' stylistic affiliations with and contributions to such movements as Expressionism, Dadaism and Pop Art. Thanks to this alliance, avant-garde film entered art galleries and museums, and discussions of filmmakers and their work entered art criticism journals. A new legitimacy for the medium particularly in the eyes of cultural elites ensued, encouraging an examination of film's formal characteristics and ultimately opening the door for the serious analysis of more mainstream fare.

In addition, the avant-garde provoked the establishment of an alternative film circuit. From the late 1920s, cinemas and film clubs dedicated to film as art emerged, offering an outlet for alternatives to the dominant Hollywood film, and sometimes providing experiments in cinematic exhibition (for example, New York's Anthology Film Archive). As well, specialized film distribution companies, film journals, and most recently, even television broadcasting companies (such as Arte) all helped to provide an infrastructure for the production, distribution and exhibition of avant-garde work, while providing a discursive framework for its ongoing development (see **discourse analysis**).

Historically, the avant-garde has lurked behind the development of national alternatives to the classical Hollywood cinema. As the examples of

Soviet Constructivism, German Expressionism, and the French poetic realism suggest, local expressive practices could to some extent find broader international markets thanks to discursive positioning within the avant-garde. While it is often true that these movements had already lost their radical edge by the point of their adaptation by feature filmmakers, once exported to new cultural contexts, they seemed to recover it.

Hollywood eventually absorbed and reworked many techniques developed by the international avant-garde, including lighting and editing techniques, compositional strategies and special effects, as evidenced, for example, by Hollywood's appropriation of German Expressionism in **horror** films and **film noir**, or by Stanley Kubrick's use of abstract imaging techniques – associated with Jordan Belson and others – in *2001: A Space Odyssey* (1968). However, although mainstream filmmakers enriched their expressive and stylistic vocabularies, at the same time they subverted the radical potential which had been so central to the avant-garde's deployment of these techniques.

Further reading

Horak, J. C. (1995) *Lovers of Cinema: The First American Avant-garde, 1919–1945*, Madison: University of Wisconsin Press.

WILLIAM URICCHIO

B

Bakhtin, Mikhail

b. 1895; d. 1975

Russian linguist and literary critic. Bakhtin's career and even authorship of writings under other names, such as Volusinov, reflect the complexities of cultural creativity and criticism throughout changing Soviet regimes. Three central themes in Bakhtin's dense and voluminous work have particular value for film and television criticism. The first is his illumination of the complexity of voice and reading in the text, encompassing **heteroglossia** and polyphony as well as **dialogic** reading. Heteroglossia refers to multiple forms of language in its social context – reflecting **class**, **genre**, socially constructed discourses (see **discourse**), and so on – that also permeate the text itself. Polyphony represents a similar vision of voices that coexist within the text, interacting with external forms of language as well as textual structure. Dialogism, an ambiguous term, refers to the construction of meaning among these multiple voices within the text and with referents possibly outside the text. A second important theme from Bakhtin incorporates the Rabelaisian carnivalesque, with its properties of inversion, satire and revolution as text and language turn worlds upside down (see **carnival**). Finally, the idea of the chronotype synthesizes elaboration of time, space and plot, linking his work to both contemporary thought by the French writer Paul **Virilio** and to specific genres.

Further reading

Bakhtin, M. (1968) *Rabelais and his World*, Cambridge: MIT.
—— (1981) *The Dialogic Imagination: Four Essays*, ed. Michael Holquist, Austin: University of Texas Press.
Haynes, D. (1995) *Bakhtin and the Visual Arts*, Cambridge: Cambridge University Press.

GARY McDONOGH

Barthes, Roland

b. 1915; d. 1980

Born in Cherbourg, France, Roland Barthes had by the time of his death in 1980 gained the status of an intellectual celebrity. His reputation extended beyond academic circles, with his books and lectures attracting the 'popular' audience of 1970s Paris in particular. In addition to such works as a semi-fictionalized autobiography, Barthes wrote widely on the topic of language, literature and contemporary cultural practice, and was influenced by linguistic theory and **semiotics**. His *S/Z* was a structuralist analysis of Balzac's novel *Sarrasine* (see **structuralism and post-structuralism**), while *The Pleasure of the Text* interrogated the acts of reading and authorship. Even Barthes' series of articles on aspects of French popular culture, published as *Mythologies* in 1957, drew on semiology for its concept of **myth** as a 'second-order language'.

As 'mythologist', Barthes deciphered his surrounding culture of advertising, recreation and popular journalism to reveal the ideologies at work behind the '**common-sense**' assumptions they projected. While he embraced this culture to an extent, some passages of his work cast him in the role of outsider, condemned to stand apart from the society which he observed.

Further reading

Barthes, R. (1993) *Mythologies* (first published 1957), selected by and trans. Annette Lavers, London: Vintage.
—— (1975) *S/Z* (first published 1970), trans. Richard Miller, London: Cape.

WILL BROOKER

base and superstructure

According to classical Marxist thought, during each historical period, the economic and productive forces and relations of production (the economic base or infrastructure) give rise to the prevailing ideas, laws and ideological mystifications (the superstructure) of that epoch (see **Marxist aesthetics**). From this perspective, a specific economic structure like capitalism produces a specific social structure – the **class** system – and the latter gives rise to epiphenomenal products – laws, books, **art** works, etc. – and particular ways of thinking. Thereafter, through a process of **reification**, ideology (originally defined as 'false consciousness'; see **ideology and hegemony**) functions to perpetuate the economic and social system by making that system appear to be natural and material.

The terms themselves – 'base' and 'superstructure' – suggest a spatial/architectural metaphor in which the latter is 'built on' or 'rests on' the former, just as a house stands on its foundation. In its initial economistic formulation, this relationship was one of economic reductionism and near determinism by which the economy gave rise to the dominant thought of an era or episteme (see **economism; epistemology**). As **Marx** and Engels put it in their *The German Ideology*, 'Life is

not determined by consciousness, but consciousness is determined by life' (1947: 15). Later, in the preface to *A Contribution to the Critique of Political Economy*, Marx rephrased the concept: 'The **mode of production** of material life conditions the general process of social, political, and intellectual life. It is not the consciousness of men that determines their existence, but their social conditions that determine their consciousness' (1974: 425). According to Marx's famous phrase, 'in the last instance', the economic relations *determine* an epoch's ruling ideas, art, literature, legal system, State, politics, educational system, religion, philosophy, morality and so forth, rather than the other way around. So conceived, the superstructure is always derivative of and secondary to the economic base. Furthermore, under capitalism, the economic base is under the control of the bourgeoisie, which owns the material means of production; hence, according to *The German Ideology*, 'the ideas of the ruling class are in every epoch the ruling ideas' (1947: 89). In turn, those ruling-class ideas tend to represent a 'false consciousness', a set of beliefs and mystifications that blind the proletariat to the real and material conditions of their social existence.

Neo-Marxists have reformulated these concepts to allow the superstructure to have more 'relative **autonomy**' from the base; that is, the degree of **determination** may be less strict than the nineteenth-century model mandated and thus individual cultural products or ideas may not be completely dependent on the economic forces of society. Late in life, even Engels clarified this point when in a letter to J. Bloch, dated 21 September 1890, he wrote: 'According to the materialist conception of history, the *ultimately* determining element in history is the production and reproduction of real life. Hence if somebody twists this into saying that the economic element is the *only* determining one, he transforms that proposition into a meaningless, abstract, senseless phrase' (Marx 1974: 294; see also **materialism and idealism; history/histoire**). Part of this may have to do with the effectiveness of the economic base at a particular historical conjuncture. Another factor may be the degree of reciprocity and interaction between base and superstructure, with each having a potential effect on the other. Another explanation that has emerged is that the base essentially sets the *limits* of superstructural thought. The degree of determinism inherent in this model has been the subject of debate and revision since Marx and Engels first proposed it.

For instance, the Italian Marxist Antonio **Gramsci** modified Marx's model by introducing the dialectical concept of hegemony (see **dialectic and dialectical montage; ideology and hegemony**). Lenin and other Marxists tended to emphasize the role of force and coercion as the basis for capital's domination. Gramsci supplemented this narrow, mechanical doctrine with the idea that in order to maintain its hegemonic leadership, especially in transformative moments of potential social upheaval, the ruling class would sometimes use more consensual tactics, even incorporating certain working-class aspirations into the **dominant ideology** or superstructural system. The extension of voting rights during the nineteenth and twentieth centuries, the rise of compulsory public education, and the creation of welfare state health and pension plans, for instance, represented real proletarian aspirations, but these concessions also defused potential rebellion and co-opted nascent class conflict during 'conjunctural' periods of social transformation. In turn, such 'liberal' reforms allowed the bourgeoisie to retain power and privilege and, in the case of public education, to expand its opportunities for indoctrination into the dominant ideology.

Gramsci's ideas can be applied to the modern mass media, which emerged well after his death, in the way that law-and-order movies and television **cop shows (police drama)** – as social texts (see **text**) – present ruling-class ideology under the guise of depicting the working class. Gramsci's progressive notion that the working classes could produce their own cultural institutions led to the dialectical idea of counter-hegemony, a concept that was rigidly denied by the **Frankfurt School** intellectuals.

The members of the Frankfurt School offered a revised model of the base–superstructure theory. Walter **Benjamin**, for example, suggested that changes in technology from the economic base in 'the age of mechanical reproduction' (the era of the printing press and cinema) could produce profound changes in the way art was created, distributed and received. In particular, Benjamin saw the demo-

cratic potential in the medium of film because it could be disseminated to the masses without the aristocratic and fetishistic **aura** that surrounded the high art of the bourgeoisie (see **fetishism**).

Max **Horkheimer** and Theodor **Adorno** expanded and modernized the original, classical notion of base–superstructure by analysing what they called 'the **culture** industry'. This notion contends that 'popular culture' does not come directly from the populace (the working masses) but from monopolistic corporations intent on maximizing profit and distracting the proletariat from their historical mission of revolution (see **popular, the**). The Frankfurt School generally denounced mainstream culture – literature, music and cinema – as a narcotic for the working classes; instead, they praised **avant-garde** and radical modernists (for example, James Joyce and Arnold Schoenberg) who broke from the conventions of middlebrow bourgeois culture (see **modernism and postmodernism**). The assumption was that such changes and contestations in the superstructure could affect and change consciousness, particularly among the influential intellectual class, who would in turn raise consciousness among larger strata of society.

More recently, the neo-Marxist Louis **Althusser** emphasized that in contemporary society, the superstructure can be divided into two groups: the RSAs – the Repressive State Apparatuses (jails, prisons, laws, torture, the military, as well as the government) – which use coercive physical force to control the masses, and the ISAs – the Ideological State Apparatuses (religion, education, parental upbringing, art, philosophy, mass media) – which utilize persuasion and indoctrination to achieve the same end: that is, the acceptance of the social and economic order of capitalism. Althusser believed that the masses were 'always already' interpellated (indoctrinated, hailed) into the dominant superstructural beliefs of a given historical period. The only way out of such interpellation, according to Althusser, was through the 'science' of Marxism.

Although often critiqued by other Marxists for being too pessimistic about the possibility of overcoming the **manipulation** and subjectification (see **subject and subjectivity**) of the RSAs and ISAs of the ruling classes, Althusser did offer hope that the base–superstructure paradigm could be viewed in a less doctrinaire manner. According to Althusser, there are elements of overdetermination and contradiction inherent in the way many factors impinge on the relationship between the economy and its ideology. This suggests that the dominant ideology may contain 'mixed messages' and may not be as monolithic as originally proposed.

Althusser's theoretical schema has also been critiqued as:

1 being excessively theoretical and abstract and therefore not especially practical to the goals of class struggle and revolutionary praxis;

2 separating base and superstructure to such a deterministic degree that the original totality of Marx's conceptualisation of the dialectic is lost, since Marx believed that the economic base involved the production of *both* commodities and social relations; and

3 being too pessimistic about the possibility of individual and collective (class-based) liberation from the thrall of bourgeois interpellation.

In the 1970s, the influential British cinema journal *Screen* applied the Althusserian model to film and television, seeing them as modern ISAs. In particular, *Screen* rejected the role of 'bourgeois **realism**' in Hollywood and mainstream European films as illusory and reactionary (see **Screen theory**). On the one hand, the aesthetic of classic realist films (see **aesthetics; classic realist text**) was thought to be the cinematic equivalent of reification – an unreflective (and unreflexive) view of the world that hid its economic, social, technological and industrial roots. On the other hand, such films generally depicted the *status quo* as natural, normal and God-given. Like the Frankfurt School theoreticians, *Screen* tended to valorize filmmakers (such as Jean-Marie Straub, Nagisa Oshima, Peter **Wollen** and Laura **Mulvey**, and 'structural-materialist' cineastes) who epitomized **avant-garde** values and self-reflexive aesthetics. The idea was that to change the signifier was to change the signified (see **signifying practice**).

Some media critics still accept the classical description of the base–superstructure relationship. Todd Gitlin, for instance, in *Watching Television*, seems to subscribe to a more classical (almost conspiracy theory) view of media: 'Television . . .

shows us only what the nation already presumes, focuses on what the culture already knows – or more precisely, enables us to gaze upon something the anointed seers think we need or want to know' (1986: 3).

Many contemporary media scholars conclude that the realities of the modern mass communications industry require a more post-modernist application of traditional **theory**. For the post-structuralists (see **structuralism and post-structuralism**), film and television have become part of the material world, part of the economy, and, as such, commodity forms or 'cultural capital' (see **cultural capital/cultural reproduction**). In that film and television constitute a reality (or a **reality effect**) for many individual viewers and the mass **audience**, they determine social consciousness and thereby perform the traditional role of the Marxist base. In today's world, the subaltern classes gain most of their knowledge about the world from the mass media, which are therefore especially crucial in relaying information, imagery and ideology throughout contemporary capitalist societies. The dominant classes in those societies thus ensure their class interests and reproduce the system of class inequities through the use of film and television.

Thinkers such as Fredric **Jameson**, Guy Debord and Raymond **Williams** have articulated this modern sublation of base and superstructure. In Jameson's book *Postmodernism*, he states: 'Culture itself is one of those things whose fundamental materiality is now not merely evident but quite inescapable. . . . Culture has become material, a social institution' (1987: xvii, 67). Put another way, in the modern (and post-modern) world, base and superstructure interact more dialectically than they did in Karl Marx's time – in that the mass communications media, especially television, now constitute a sense of reality for most people in a given society and thereby, along with the economic infrastructure, determine social consciousness. Indeed, the modern media industry is part of the economic infrastructure, and its heavily mediated products have become so embedded in daily life that they have achieved the ultimate fate of post-modern culture, **commodification**. In this sense, under the auspices of late capitalism, the media have become part of the material world; superstructure has become base.

References

Althusser, L. (1971) *Lenin and Philosophy*, trans. B. Brewster, New York: Monthly Press.

Benjamin, W. (1969) 'The Work of Art in the Age of Mechanical Reproduction' (first published 1936), in H. Arendt (ed.) *Illuminations*, trans. H. Zohn, New York: Schocken Books.

Boggs, C. (1976) *Gramsci's Marxism*, London: Pluto Press.

Debord, G. (1983) *Society of the Spectacle*, Detroit: Black and Red.

Gitlin, T. (1986) 'Looking Through the Screen', in T. Gitlin *Watching Television*, New York: Pantheon Books.

Horkheimer, M. and Adorno, T. W. (1972) *Dialectic of Enlightenment*, trans. J. Cumming, New York: Herder and Herder.

Jameson, F. (1987) *Postmodernism, or, the Cultural Logic of Late Capitalism*, Durham, NC: Duke University Press.

Marx, K. (1974) 'A Contribution to the Critique of Political Economy', in *On Historical Materialism*, New York: International Publishers.

Marx, K. and Engels, F. (1947) *The German Ideology*, ed. R. Pascal, New York: International Publishers.

Williams, R. (1977) *Marxism and Literature*, Oxford: Oxford University Press.

FRANK P. TOMASULO

Baudrillard, Jean

b. 1929

Born in Reims, France, Jean Baudrillard is usually associated with the more excessive side of postmodern theory. Early writings reveal a drift away from classical Marxism, especially with regard to the category of production, which is deemed inadequate to the analysis of contemporary consumer society. Perhaps the most influential aspect of Baudrillard's work has been his theory of the simulacrum (the copy for which there is no original). From the understanding that advanced capitalist cultures are dominated by images and reproductions, Baudrillard moves to suggest that the real no longer exists: the proliferation of simulacra has created a hyperreality, a 'real without origin or reality' (Baudrillard 1983: 2).

This trajectory culminated in Baudrillard's controversial writings on the Gulf War, in which he claims that the central role played by media and military technologies of reproduction rendered the conflict incomprehensible according to traditional notions of warfare. Thus the Gulf War, for Baudrillard, did not occur. This, for some, was further proof of the author's drift into political irresponsibility.

See also: McLuhan, Marshall; modernism and post-modernism

References

Baudrillard, J. (1983) *Simulations*, New York: Semiotext(e).

—— (1994) *The Gulf War Did Not Take Place*, Sydney: Power Publications.

NEIL BADMINGTON

Bazin, André

b. 1919; d. 1958

An influential French film critic who contributed to many French film journals after the Second World War, Bazin is best known in English-speaking countries for his writing in *Cahiers du cinéma*, which he co-founded in 1951. *Cahiers* was the journal in which François Truffaut, Jean-Luc Godard, Eric Rohmer and others wrote before becoming filmmakers of the French New Wave of the late 1950s and early 1960s.

Though sceptical about the claims of the younger French critics for American auteurs (see **authorship**), Bazin wrote at length about American cinema, and his essays on the Western (see **Western, the**), Orson Welles and William Wyler are still cited with critical respect. Bazin's arguments about cinematic **realism** and deep-focus photography do not sit easily with semiotic or structuralist analyses of these topics, but the seriousness and suggestiveness of his essays on aspects of European and American cinema still make them stimulating reading for film students. Bazin's jargon is free of the complex conceptual writing of current film and television theory.

See also: depth of field; semiotics; structuralism and post-structuralism

Further reading

Bazin, A. (1967/1971) *What is Cinema?* (vol. 1 and 2), Berkeley: University of California Press.
—— (1973) *Jean Renoir*, New York: Dealta Publishing Co.

PHILIP SIMPSON

Benjamin, Walter

b. 1892; d. 1940

A German literary and cultural critic associated with the **Frankfurt School**, Benjamin has greatly influenced film and television theory. His importance derives mostly from his 1936 essay, 'The Work of Art in the Age of Mechanical Reproduction'. Although neglected in his lifetime, Benjamin's ideas have become widely cited.

Benjamin's work displays a fruitful ambivalence towards the power of moving images, a trait which distinguishes him from other Frankfurt School critics. In 'The Work of Art in the Age of Mechanical Reproduction', he argues for film as a radical breakthrough in popular conceptions of **art**. Whereas earlier forms of artworks attained their elite position through an exalted separation from the public, film and television bring images up close to people worldwide, and create a new architecture of spaces and perceptions. The media possess revolutionary capacities, even while Benjamin recognizes their exploitation as business, and as methods for social stultification. Benjamin's writings, dense though not obscure, remain worth reading for their views of the contradictory potential of film and television, and the ambiguous progress of modern life.

See also: flâneur

References

Benjamin, W. (1968) *Illuminations* (first published 1936), New York: Harcourt Brace Jovanovich.
—— (1978) *Reflections*, New York: Harcourt Brace Jovanovich.

GABRIEL M. PALETZ

Berger, John

b. 1926

John Berger studied painting at art college in London, and during his time as a student became increasingly involved with the Communist Party. This political influence informed his Marxist approach to art history and contemporary advertising imagery, which found its best-known expression in the BBC television series *Ways of Seeing* (1972), accompanied by a book of the same name (see **Marxist aesthetics**).

Through a striking combination of visual and textual material, *Ways of Seeing* questions the assumptions of **class** and **gender** behind both traditional oil painting and 1970s publicity stills, revealing the patterns of power, ownership and control which viewers are encouraged to internalize and take for granted. Despite its unequivocal, sometimes polemical tone which allows for little ambiguity in the process of 'reading' the image, the book of the series remains influential, its mode of presenting an argument through photo-essays and brief captions still marking it out from the mainstream of academic texts.

In addition to his art and broadcasting, Berger is also a prolific novelist who won the Booker Prize in 1972. He retired shortly afterwards to complete his fictional trilogy *Into Their Labours*. Berger resides in the French Alps.

References

Berger, J. (1972) *Ways of Seeing*, London: Penguin.

WILL BROOKER

Bhabha, Homi K.

b. 1949

One of the foremost theorists of post-colonial theory, and responsible for renewing interest in Franz **Fanon** in the 1980s, Bhabha's work has significantly changed the analysis of colonial encounters through his attention to desire and fantasy. His articles complicate the understanding of colonial experience as the product of a one-way Eurocentric domination by recognizing that the colonizer envies as much as he fears the colonized (see **Eurocentrism**). This intersubjective tension in the colonial realm has led Bhabha to characterize the colonial situation and also the relationship that exists between metropolitan and post-colonial cultures under the logic of mimicry. Supporting this theory, which incorporates the psychic ambivalence of Lacanian psychoanalysis, is his Derridean-inspired conception of culture as inherently hybrid and radically indeterminate rather than essentially attached to one set of meanings (see **Lacan, Jacques; Derrida, Jacques**). Bhabha's theory of colonial mimicry and cultural **hybridity** has influenced the articulation of race and nation in visual culture produced and theorized by British black cultural studies.

See also: Said, Edward; Spivak, Gayatri

Further reading

Bhabha, H. K. (ed.) (1990) *Nation and Narration*, London: Routledge.
—— (1994) *The Location of Culture*, London: Routledge.

PAULA TATLA AMAD

bias

It is often said that bias, like beauty, is in the eye of the beholder. In discussing the day-to-day activities of reporting, broadcast journalists – and their critics alike – often draw on the metaphor of a mirror to describe how the social world is 'reflected' in news accounts. The pioneering US broadcast reporter Edward R. Murrow once famously stated, for example, that journalism 'must

hold a mirror behind the nation and the world' and that, moreover, 'the mirror must have no curves and must be held with a steady hand' (cited in MacDonald 1979: 310). This language of reflection is similarly employed in critiques of news coverage to pinpoint evidence of 'bias', that is, to question whether a journalist has mirrored reality in an 'objective' manner or, failing that, the extent to which he/she has allowed certain 'distortions' to creep into the reporting process (see **objectivity**).

Not surprisingly, many critical researchers have dismissed the mirror metaphor as too simplistic. Even its advocates, they point out, have to acknowledge the vast number of 'blind-spots' which render certain types of events virtually invisible. The mirror metaphor is also difficult to sustain due to its inability to account for the ideological dynamics embedded in the newsworker's mediation of the social world. This process of mediation involves not only a series of procedures for knowing the world but, equally important, for not knowing that world as well. As Hallin writes of the 'mirroring' qualities of so-called 'objective reporting' of governmental affairs in the US:

A form of journalism which aims to provide the public with a neutral record of events and which, at the same time, relies primarily on government officials to describe and explain those events obviously has the potential to wind up as a mirror not of reality, but of the version of reality government officials would like to present to the public.

(Hallin 1994: 52)

In light of such criticisms, Tuchman's (1978) concept of a 'news net' has been widely regarded as a much more suitable metaphor than that of a reflective mirror. Introduced following her research into newswork practices, the idea of a news net is a more useful way of conceptualizing this imposition of order on the social world. News, in her analysis, is a social resource which, through its very construction, implies a series of particular constraints or limits on the forms of knowledge which can be generated and called 'reality'.

When asked to reflect on how they go about their daily work of producing 'unbiased' news accounts, journalists will often claim that they simply follow their gut feelings, instincts or a hunch about questions of bias. Many insist that they have a 'nose for news', that they can intuitively tell which sources will prove to be significant in constructing an impartial account, and which ones will be too biased to be relevant to the news frame. Underlying the language of news bias, however, is the (usually implicit) assumption that it is possible for journalists to attain complete detachment, impartiality and neutrality in their reporting. Some journalists acknowledge the difficulties (both practical and philosophical) associated with any claim to being fully objective, choosing instead to use a language of 'fairness' and 'balance'.

Allan (1999) has examined these dynamics in relation to what he terms the 'will to facticity'. Once it is recognized that the truly objective news account is an impossibility, he argues, critical attention may turn to the strategies and devices used by journalists to lend to their accounts a factual status. Given that this factual status can never be entirely realized, the notion of a 'will to facticity' pinpoints the necessarily provisional and contingent nature of any such journalistic appeal to non-bias.

See also: documentary; framing; news values

References

Allan, S. (1999) *News Culture*, Buckingham and Philadelphia: Open University Press.

Hallin, D. C. (1994) *We Keep America on Top of the World: Television Journalism and the Public Sphere*, New York: Routledge.

MacDonald, J. F. (1979) *Don't Touch That Dial! Radio Programming in American Life, 1920–1960*, Chicago: Nelson-Hall.

Tuchman, G. (1978) *Making News: A Study in the Construction of Reality*, New York: The Free Press.

STUART ALLAN

binary

The word 'binary' comes from the Latin *binarius*, meaning 'to contain two'. It refers to a quality of descriptive, often structuralist, systems that rely on the opposition of two distinctive features (see **structuralism and post-structuralism**).

Complex items are usually treated as bundles of abstract binary distinctive features; for example, the semantic component analysis describes the meaning components of 'girl' as [+human], [−male], [−adult] (see **semantics**). This example clarifies the problems of binary systems in meaning analysis: there is little reason to assume that the feature [+/− male] is somehow more 'normal', logical or justified than a feature [+/− female]. Other less debatable binary systems include, for example, the basic computer code, on/off structures or biological classification systems. Drawing on the work of structuralists like **Lévi-Strauss**, film theorists have used the concept of binary oppositions in **genre** analysis, seeing the Western, for instance, as built on the contrast between civilization and the wilderness, or the garden and the desert (see **Western, the**). Feminist film theorists have used the concept to analyse the cinematic representation of women: men conventionally are represented as active, woman as passive, men as rational, women as emotional, and so forth.

EVA VIETH

body

Questions about the relationship between body and mind, the body and perception, and the body and identity have been central to western philosophy, and have also informed major inquiries in film and television studies. This entry will delineate ways of thinking about the body in philosophy, drawing on traditions going back to René Descartes and Benedict Spinoza. These lineages will be followed through to the writing of **Foucault**, **Merleau-Ponty**, **Bakhtin** and **Deleuze and Guattari**. The entry selects a range of highly specific applications of body theory to film or television, rather than attempting to draw up tight categories. The boundaries of the body and the ambivalences surrounding its gendered and racial appearance have been of particular interest to cinema and television theory, an issue which is explored in more depth in the **gender**, **race** and **psychoanalysis** entries.

To write about the body is complicated: the body has traditionally been thought as 'other' to the mind, and the cultural and conceptual work of writing. Going back to Plato, the body has been conceptualized as 'mere matter', ready to be worked on and transformed by the active mind. Descartes further developed this ancient conceptualization of the split between mind and body: he viewed the mind as being outside nature, in a completely different realm from (body) matter. This leads to a position where only consciousness is evident to itself, the 'rest' – body, social world – are only experienced through the mind. The traces of this thinking are evident in metaphors of the body as machine: the body is mere matter, animated and dominated by the guiding mind. To curb the body, seen as foreign to intellect and culture, is to achieve a higher level of being.

This view of the relationship between body and mind has been seen as a diminished conception of human agency in the world. Thinkers such as Spinoza theorize consciousness as embodied: the mind/body split is impossible. We only know ourselves through our bodies, there is no other viewpoint from which to cogitate about our condition. Body and matter are therefore as one: every thought has its corresponding movement, since both are anchored in a common ground. Living is becoming – a continuous process.

Both of these traditions of thinking about the body have had an influence on contemporary conceptualizations of it. In relation to gender studies, initial debates focused on the relationship between sex and gender – sex is seen as biological and gender as the cultural interpretation of it. The body is here the raw material, and culture and ideology make it meaningful.

Film theory has taken up a range of different positions *vis-à-vis* the body. Communality has been seen between the advent of film and psychoanalysis, a model that sees the human psyche mapping the body and structuring meaning in relation to sexuality. This depth model, relying on interior mechanisms by which the subject makes sense of its body and thereby becomes social, has had a wide impact on theorizations of film (see **subject and subjectivity**). In particular, **Freud**'s analysis of the importance of vision for gender difference and **Lacan**'s development of

aspects of this theory have had an impact on both semiotic film theory and feminist film theory (see **semiotics; feminist theory**). Hysteria and ambivalences which surround psychically invested body parts such as the womb have been analysed by Julia **Kristeva** in her writing on the 'abject', and have been discussed extensively in film theory in relation to the body-horror genre. The relationship between psychoanalytic theory and race has also been taken up in a range of writings.

The use of the body as meaning-carrier in language, where aspects of body representation link with one or the other **binary** (white/black, male/female), have also had an impact on textual analysis in film and television studies. These models construct social spectators as scanning products for signs which allow value to be attributed, and which therefore structure narrative. White hats for goodies and black hats for baddies in the Western is one such model, relying on the respective value of black and white in western culture at a specific historic juncture (see **Western, the**). In these binary meaning systems, the values of gender can be allocated in opposition to the 'natural' sex of the body shown: Ripley in *Alien* (Ridley Scott, 1979) has a range of stylistic (costume, make-up, posture), narrational and formal (lighting, *mise-en-scène*) attributes which index her as transgressing the realm of the 'female'. Similarly, Sylvester Stallone's position of masculinity can be seen to be threatened and in need of recuperation due to the (culturally indexed as feminizing) display of the naked body in *First Blood* (Ted Kotcheff, 1982). These allocations of value rely on shifting cultural values, on the meanings of privileged signs such as race, class and gender. Historical investigations of the distribution, ambivalences and shifts of these meanings show the moving and unstable nature of the socially-constructed body.

Dichotomous thinking of the body and culture is challenged in the writings of both Judith **Butler** and Luce **Irigaray**. There is no 'neutral' biology, the very act of binary opposition is expression of the work of language. The body is constituted through the political, the body is always articulating and performing its cultural marking. For Butler, gender is **performative**: it needs reiteration, re-inscription, and is therefore open to transformations. This view of the gendered body as a battlefield and place of possible resistance is influenced by Michel Foucault's technology of sex. In *The History of Sexuality* (1978), Foucault theorizes sexuality as the focal point of the productive work of power on the individual body. Foucault's thinking does not challenge the notion of a body as passive 'matter', but he sees any appearance of the body in social relations as already marked: the body is the playing field of power. Power for Foucault is productive: it is the possibility of knowledge. It is the field of forces that constitute themselves into systems, which make relationships between words, values and things possible. Power produces knowledge, and there is no 'real' outside this field of forces. This means that the paradigm of body and soul is reversed: 'The soul is the effect and instrument of a political anatomy; the soul is the prison of the body' (Foucault 1977: 30). The body is bound into a system (the soul) which creates subjectivity, sexuality, depth and relationship: the mechanisms of power and knowledge. Sexuality is not the manifestation of the 'natural' body, but is a power system in which subjects take pleasure in surveying themselves (since sex is seen as the secret heart of the subject, from the Church's fascination with it to psychoanalysis). Sex is a category of classification, structuring all aspects of social life. In Foucault's words:

> Sexuality must not be thought of as a kind of natural given which power tries to hold in check, or as an obscure domain which knowledge tries gradually to uncover. It is the name that can be given to a historical construct: not a furtive reality that is difficult to grasp, but a great surface network in which the stimulation of bodies, the intensification of pleasures, the incitement to discourse, the formation of special knowledges, the strengthening of controls and resistances, are linked to one another, in accordance with a few major strategies of knowledge and power.
>
> (Foucault 1978: 105–6)

Sexuality is inscribed through scrutiny: the confessional of the church, the couch of the psychoanalyst and the endless display of naked bodies, sexual practices and positions, disavowed or open, available on the screen. This intensity of vision, of needing to know, to see, the depth of privacy as a guarantor of pleasure, has influenced film studies.

Linda Williams (1989) uses Foucault's insights into the technology of bodies for her reading of **pornography**. Following film historian Jean-Louis Comolli, Williams aligns pornography and its origins in early cinema with a 'frenzy of the visible' – a need to see all. Cinematic hard-core emerges from a tradition of charting body knowledge through observation and confession. Pleasure is constructed by the technologies at the same moment as they exert pressure on the body to give up its secrets. Williams charts this 'will-to-knowledge/power' back to the stop-motion photography of Eadweard Muybridge, and discusses the history of the fetishization of female bodies (see **fetishism**). Using Foucault's genealogy of sexuality with its ruptures, changes and discontinuities, she sees psychoanalytic models not as 'essentially' true, but as specific developments out of specific alignments of bodies and pleasures. Any crystallization of power is open to resistant forces: for hard-core pornography, the invisibility of the female orgasm destabilizes any attempt to map the human body on a male model.

Another model of the body in society relies on visuality, but here visuality is the source of community, not the (attempted) split into surveyor and spectacle. Bakhtin's notion of the carnivalesque, developed by him in relation to Rabelais' writings, holds a utopian vision of transgression. In the **carnival**, structures are broken, and in a communal display and engagement in the body in all its carnality – lust, excess, vomit and shit – a group affirms its, and their bodies', wholeness. Inversion and hyperbole subvert limits of gender and class. Mary Russo (1994) shows how this model of the body as agent in subversive politics is hard to bring into modernity. Foucault analysed the historical ascendancy of vision and division as part of the power apparatus; the utopian vision of Bakhtin relies on a radical closeness that does not allow for any differentiation into audience and spectacle. In the age of media saturation, and the display of difference framed by the television screen, the distance of vision that can never fully return to the body replaces the nearness of direct physicality. Lacan writes of our culture's obsession with the human figure (an obsession taken over by photography and film from the fine arts); it is anchored to this basic need of mapping bodies and finding the gaze of the other recognizing our own embodied form (see **gaze, the**). Division is at the heart of these theories.

Russo shows how Ulrike Ottinger's **avant-garde** practices use the grotesque, carnivalesque bodies of Bakhtin in an attempt to disrupt the order of western reason. Her film *Freak Orlando* (1981) produces transgressive meanings by the disruption of narrative logic, a surrealist dreamscape of genders, places and connections, questioning any centre through the accumulation of destabilizing images. John **Fiske** (1987) employs the carnivalesque body to show the avenues of resistances possible in popular television shows, but again, the disruption of subject and object positions has to be framed in the power politics of the wider apparatus. Ultimately, the notion of the carnivalesque body can only have limited currency – it is a utopian, nostalgic vision of a folk past.

Foucault offers the possibility of resistances, as well as the hope inherent in seeing any system of organization as historically contingent. But although the body is the surface and articulation of productive power, it remains the merely passive recipient of meaning. Vision is seen as division, producing difference. Other attempts to figure the body try to rethink not only the notion of the body's agency, but also to find other ways of accounting for the interpenetration of subject and world through the senses.

Maurice Merleau-Ponty's phenomenology understands the body and mind not as separate levels of existence, in potential strife with each other. For him, as for Spinoza, the mind is always embodied, and the body is not an object which can be grasped, used or moved by a subject. Instead, the body is always the condition of experience. Embodiment provides a structure for the relation of world and being, it gives form to all knowledge. This form is an organizing spatio-temporal perspective. We have access to the world through our position as perspective: our body is our focus point that organizes inside and outside, psyche and world. Every perception is experienced as world by the subject and, at the same time, is an expression of the subject's being-to-the-world: an expression of its perspectival viewpoint.

In his last, unfinished work, Merleau-Ponty takes even further his understanding of the subject as embedded in the world rather than in opposition to it. He introduces the term 'flesh', a complex notion of the mutual constitution of world and body. The flesh of the world, folding onto itself and felt by the senses, is the precondition of the subject: there is no opposition between inside and outside, merely a different spatial organization. The subject (and her body) is a fold in the flesh of the world. The flesh provides the ground for the differentiation (through perspectival arrangement) which constitutes diverse subjects in the world. Language is the moment of difference (a notion consistent with Ferdinand de **Saussure**'s semiotics): 'language is everything since it is the voice of no one, since it is the very voice of the things, the waves and the forests' (Merleau-Ponty 1968: 153).

The body has been an important aspect of the development of spectatorship studies, and Merleau-Ponty's model of the body, which relies on the notion of perspective and viewpoint, has been received in this field of film theory. Following earlier phenomenological theories of film, such as Jean Mitry's *Esthetique et psychologie du cinéma* (1963), Vivian Sobchack (1992) theorizes a deep affinity between film and the creation of the subject as seen by phenomenology: both rely on 'an expression of experience by experience'. She quotes Mitry who saw cinema as a form 'which must express life with life itself': film is the act of sensing, the condition of life, made visible. When we see a film, we perceive a world, just as we perceive our world. The phenomenological approach is less interested in the specifics of the world seen (this is relegated to the level of secondary meaning) than in the act of perception and sensing itself. Subjects become subjects in the act of sensing: perception is expression (of self).

Sobchack criticizes both the two dominant historical models of film theory, formalist and realist (see **Formalism; realism**), and more recent apparatus theory for failing to take into account the 'system code' of film: the first level of address, that on which all other forms of secondary signification rely. This is the level of shared agreement between film (and its production apparatus) and spectator – the understanding of how to react to the form. For her, this initial agreement of the legibility of film rests on the approximation of film to embodied experience: film gives us the opportunity to experience (and therefore express ourselves through) a different subject: the film itself. Sobchack views film as 'the dialogical and dialectical meeting of two viewing subjects', rather than the static models of subject/object encounters. She also criticizes a passive view of spectators; subjects are 'full with their own embodiment', the film never takes over, it is a meeting of subjects, but not a colonialization of the viewing subject through the film.

French philosophers Deleuze and Guattari offer a radically disjointed, 'rhizomatic', local, anti-systematic theory of the relationship between bodies and world. They take up the Spinozean notion of 'becoming', and view the world as flow and intensities. Identity is a temporary aggregation made of material and psychical things. It is always provisional, only one of a multitude of possibilities. No hierarchy manifests itself, and no metaphysics points beyond the world. Unity is alien to this world: existence is only realized through movement, through becoming. There is no essential distinction between subjects, bodies and world. The 'Body without Organs' is a body that exists in this continuum of intensities, movement and becoming: all 'organs' as self-contained mechanisms are now opened to the flow – this is the tendency towards which all hierarchized, organized bodies move. Similar to Foucault, Deleuze and Guattari see desire as originally productive. In psychoanalytical theory the subject is constructed through lack, but for Deleuze this view of subjectivity is only an effect of a particular alignment of power, a certain configuration of the machine – new alignments can be made.

While the move of eliding body differences in Deleuze and Guattari (as well as Merleau-Ponty) has worried some feminists and other theorists of body politics, the attempted destruction of binaries and metaphysics has captured the imagination of many. For film theorists, Deleuze's and Guattari's model has provided a way of looking at difference without evoking lack. The pleasure of horror films can be seen as the dissolution of a rigid self in a physical experience of flow, not motivated by a lack

which calls for a pre-Oedipal oneness with the mother.

Stephen Shaviro (1993) reads the bodies depicted in David Cronenberg's films as directly expressive: the flesh is in revolt and displays the workings of power, short-circuiting psychoanalytic explanations. As in Sobchack's reading of film, Shaviro sees the Cronenberg films as questioning the unity of the subject. The distance between spectator and what is seen is broken down, the touch of the other implicates the self, and the boundaries are breached. Technologies form machines (aggregations, alignments) with the body on the screen, which interacts directly (viscerally, affectually) with the body of the spectator: we turn in disgust as fly and man (*The Fly*, 1986), video recorder and bellies (*Videodrome*, 1982), merge and live.

Bodies move, produce and receive images and theories. The constant rewriting of configurations of **agency** moves film and television theory. The problems of politics, difference and ethics compel us to keep writing.

References

Deleuze, G. and Guattari, F. (1987) *A Thousand Plateaus: Capitalism and Schizophrenia*, Minneapolis: Minneapolis University Press.

Fiske, J. (1987) *Television Culture*, London, New York: Routledge.

Foucault, M. (1977) *Discipline and Punish: The Birth of the Prison*, London: Allen Lane.

—— (1978) *The History of Sexuality, Volume 1: An Introduction*, London: Allen Lane.

Merleau-Ponty, M. (1968) *The Visible and the Invisible*, Evanston: Northwestern University Press.

Mitry, J. (1997) *The Aesthetics and Psychology of the Cinema* (first published 1963 as *Esthetique et psychologie du cinéma*), Bloomington: Indiana University Press.

Russo, M. (1994) *The Female Grotesque: Risk, Excess and Modernity*, London and New York: Routledge.

Shaviro, S. (1993) *The Cinematic Body*, Minneapolis: Minnesota University Press.

Sobchack, V. (1992) *The Address of the Eye: A Phenomenology of Film Experience*. Princeton, NJ: Princeton University Press.

Williams, L. (1989) *Hard Core: Power, Pleasure, and the*

'*Frenzy of the Visible*', Berkeley: University of California Press.

Further reading

Grosz, E. (1994) *Volatile Bodies: Toward a Corporeal Feminism*, Bloomington and Indianapolis: Indiana University Press.

PETRA KUPPERS

Bordwell, David

b. 1947

David Jay Bordwell, film theorist and historian, has spent most of his professional career teaching at the University of Wisconsin-Madison in the United States. Bordwell is one of the pre-eminent scholars of film, and eventually may be ranked alongside Eisenstein, **Bazin** and Arnheim as one of film theory's most systematic thinkers. In the formative period of his career he wrote passionately of those films and filmmakers whose hermetic styles rewarded the closest scrutiny (see **hermeneutics**). Later he turned his attention to the encompassing institutions of Hollywood, film theorizing (see **theory**) and **historiography**.

With his wife, Kristin Thompson, Bordwell co-authored *Film Art: An Introduction*. Updated regularly since its first publication in 1979, it has given thousands of students their first taste of film form, couched in easily understood writing. One might consider *Narration in the Fiction Film*, published in 1985, to be a sort of graduate sequel to *Film Art*, explicitly extending the formalist principles of poetics into the realm of cinema. In 1994, Thompson and Bordwell published a companion text, *Film History: An Introduction*.

The Classical Hollywood Cinema: Film Style and Mode of Production to 1960 was published in 1985, co-written with Janet Staiger and Thompson. Bordwell's sections gave an account of the historical development of the formal conventions, corporate structures and technologies that constitute American film style. The *Classical Hollywood Cinema* was a watershed in historiography, permanently changing our model of how American film came to be.

Bordwell's cognitive turn in the 1990s was an outgrowth of the formalist interest in the operations of the mind (see **cognitive theory**). Together with Noël Carroll, Bordwell edited the anthology *Post-Theory: Reconstructing Film Studies* (1996). Bordwell offered cognitivism as an alternative to film theory, claiming that it was based not on *a priori* constructs such as **psychoanalysis**, feminism, Marxism and structuralism, but rather on thought, emotion and action.

See also: classical Hollywood cinema and new Hollywood cinema; feminist theory; Marxist aesthetics; structuralism and post-structuralism

References

Bordwell, D. and Carroll, N. (eds) (1996) *Post-Theory: Reconstructing Film Studies*, Madison: University of Wisconsin Press.

Bordwell, D. and Thompson, K. (1985) *Narration in the Fiction Film*, London: Methuen.

—— (1994) *Film History: An Introduction*, New York and London: McGraw-Hill.

—— (1997) *Film Art: An Introduction* (5th edn; first published 1979), New York: McGraw-Hill.

Bordwell, D., Staiger, J. and Thompson, K. (1985) *The Classical Hollywood Cinema: Film Style and Mode of Production to 1960*, New York: Columbia University Press.

DONALD CRAFTON

Bourdieu, Pierre

b. 1930

Bourdieu grew up in rural France and studied in Paris. In the early 1960s he attended the lectures of Claude **Lévi-Strauss**, which confirmed him in his leanings away from philosophy, his original area of study, towards structuralism and sociology (see **structuralism and post-structuralism**). In 1964 he was made Director of Studies at the Parisian Ecole des Hautes Etudes and four years later he founded the Centre of European Sociology, leading research groups and editing the Centre's journal. In 1981 he was appointed Chair of Sociology at the College de France.

Bourdieu's greatest influence on cultural studies is his work *Distinction* (1984), which, drawing on extensive questionnaires, categorizes different contemporary 'tastes' – in leisure interests, foods, holidays, newspapers and so on – according to the respondent's social position. Bourdieu applied to this data his concept of cultural capital, which can best be seen as a kind of currency or points system based on economic and educational status.

Although strictly speaking an exercise in sociology, *Distinction* offers valuable insights into issues of 'audiences', in the widest sense, and the social matrix surrounding their relationships with 'texts'.

See also: audience; culture; text

References

Bourdieu, P. (1984) *Distinction: A Social Critique of the Judgement of Taste*, trans. Richard Nice, London: Routledge and Kegan Paul.

WILL BROOKER

Brecht, Bertolt

b. 1898; d. 1956

Brecht was a German playwright and poet who strongly influenced the development of the worker's theatre and invented the **epic** theatre and a new form of **distancing** effect. Brecht's plays, aimed (sometimes unsuccessfully) at a proletariat audience, strongly expressed his Marxist and pacifist ideas (see **Marx, Karl**). He fled Nazi Germany in 1933 and, after living in several European countries, went to Hollywood. Threatened by the anti-Communist mood of the US Congress, he returned to East Berlin after the war and worked for the Berlin Ensemble. His later work, while still defending Marxist ideology (see **ideology and hegemony**), expresses disappointment with everyday socialism as realized in the German Democratic Republic.

In contrast to the Aristotelian theatre, Brecht developed the epic theatre which was designed to make the spectator rationally contemplate the proceedings on stage. Such plays as *Mother Courage* and *Mahagonny* combine classic and modern forms, songs, panoramas and choruses to present the lifes described not as fate, but as a result of the socio-economic circumstances according to the historical processes defined by Marxism – circumstances that might be different and could be changed. While *The Threepenny Opera* still comes to the conclusion that 'man would like to be good – but the conditions are not like that', Brecht's later works begin to question the responsibility of the individual for social conditions.

The Threepenny Opera was adapted for the screen in 1931, directed by G. W. Pabst and with a scenario by Béla Balázs, although Brecht filed a law suit (which he lost) against the producers for distorting his work. Brecht himself wrote a script for a film, *Whither Germany?* (*Kuhle Wampe*, Slaten Dodow, 1932), which more closely approximated the epic theatre. For the most part, cinema's dependence upon **realism** has militated against Brechtian influences, with the exception of some films made by non-Hollywood directors, for example Jean-Luc **Godard**, who has taken up several principles of the epic theatre.

Further reading

Fuegi, J. (1995) *The Life and Lies of Bertolt Brecht*, London: Flamingo.
Willet, J. and Manheim, R. (eds) (1980) *Brecht, Bertolt: Collected Plays*, London: Eyre Methuen.

EVA VIETH

bricolage

The French term *bricolage* loosely translates as 'tinkering about' or 'do-it-yourself', and was first used as a critical tool by anthropologist Claude **Lévi-Strauss** to describe a process of adjusting pre-existing concepts to fit new situations. His conception of *bricolage* and the *bricoleur* as a jack-of-all-trades has since been applied to film and television to describe an eclectic creative approach to production that mixes potentially disparate styles.

References

Lévi-Strauss, C. (1966) *The Savage Mind*, London: Weidenfeld and Nicholson.

Further reading

Collins, J. (1992) 'Television and Postmodernism', in Robert C. Allen (ed.) *Channels of Discourse Reassembled*, London: Routledge.

BEN WOODHOUSE

broadcasting, the United Kingdom

This entry provides a historical overview of some of the key events and forces that have impacted on the development and course of broadcasting in the United Kingdom. As an integral facet of the social fabric, broadcasting has provided access to events, ideas and experiences ranging widely across cultural and political life (O'Malley 1994: xi). The task here is to identify key moments and processes that have moulded the contours of the British broadcasting system and to locate these in relation to broadcasting's interactions with society. This historical perspective reveals the state's centrality within the development of broadcasting in the UK and helps to explain the shape it has assumed.

The origins of broadcasting

The Italian wireless enthusiast Guglielmo Marconi demonstrated the capabilities of wireless transmission in Britain in 1896, and the magnitude of transmissions advanced incrementally with improvements in technical equipment over the following years. By 1914, broadcasting as it is now understood – the conveyance of sound over large distances – had taken place. The First World War demonstrated the powers of wireless technology, where it was deployed by the military in the guiding of vessels (Briggs 1961: 36). The security issues surrounding wireless led to reluctance on the part of military authorities to relinquish their control in the immediate period following the war. However, by this time many people had built their own receivers, enabling them to tune in to frequencies. Commercial interests lobbied the government for more stations, as set manufacturers were keen to realize the financial possibilities associated with the technology.

In 1920 Marconi began organized radio broadcasting in Britain, with other operators closely watching and expressing interest in involvement. Co-operation, rather than competition, between the different interest groups was envisaged as the most desirable method by which to harness the development of sound broadcasting. The Post Office, as licensing authority, organized a consortium of the leading six wireless set manufacturers, and it was from this arrangement that the BBC emerged in November 1922 with John **Reith** as General Manager.

The British Broadcasting Corporation

The early era of broadcasting was a tentative period with concerns expressed over its feasibility, financing and purpose (Curran and Seaton 1997: 112). The Sykes Committee reported on these issues in 1923 in its capacity as the first inquiry into broadcasting. The Committee concluded that **spectrum scarcity** necessitated broadcasting's status as a national resource. As such, it would not be prudent to use market forces to finance broadcasting and thus **advertising** was rejected. Funding was to come via a licence fee levied on all users and from a proportion from the sale of the wireless sets. These edicts were soon tested when licence fee evasion proved to be high, and with listeners assembling their own sets the company encountered grave difficulties in raising sufficient revenue. Such measures required modification and the Crawford Committee in 1926 considered these issues in its deliberations on the future of broadcasting.

The Committee's recommendations echoed the sentiments of Reith on the need to create a public institution out of broadcasting. Thus, the British Broadcasting Corporation was formed in January 1927 with Reith in control, guided by the notion of public interest. Its unique features of **public service broadcasting** reflected a paternalistic zeal that endowed the BBC with certain obligations, which it could pursue in its capacity as sole broadcaster. The understanding was that broadcasting had a moral duty to improve the **audience** and raise public taste, drawing heavily on the thinking of Matthew **Arnold**. The BBC's role as moral guardian was enunciated through its Royal Charter, a right bestowed by government encapsulating the Corporation's basic duty to inform, educate and entertain. Moreover, a guaranteed source of funding enabled the BBC to develop its programme policy independently from the tastes of the audience it served (Wheeler 1997: 89). A civic role of public enlightenment and social responsibility to shape the character of the public was moulded by the vision and puritanical beliefs of Reith, set alongside the institutional arrangements carved out by the Crawford Committee. Consequently, the BBC provided a unitary national voice to imbue 'Britishness', as outlined by Reith.

Broadcasting had to avert the dangers of creating a culturally illiterate and immoral audience that a market-based system was thought to engender, with its assumed premium on the lowest common denominator programming through the reliance on advertising. Similarly, the possibilities of radio igniting urban disturbance in a period of social unrest were anticipated by the BBC's austere system of **regulation**. The first examination of the BBC's role and worth was illustrated in the General Strike of 1926. With the shutdown of newspapers, the BBC established itself (and radio) as an essential channel of information, and its handling of the dispute fixed a scope of operation which it has largely retained. The degree of coherence between the government and the BBC's conservative obligations, as Reith defined them, oriented the BBC towards a consensual viewpoint that complemented the government's position. While this endorsement of authority avoided the possibility of a take-over and guaranteed its Charter renewal, it confirmed for some that the BBC was merely an extension of government (see Briggs 1961: 360). However, others, like Winston Churchill, felt the BBC had not supported the government enough.

The beginnings of change

During the 1930s, the BBC garnered a national audience but its moral tone was unsuccessful in retaining listeners. The BBC grew as an institution by utilizing improved technical know-how and equipment, steadily employing more personnel and increasing its news output. However, its programming maintained a highbrow edge, predominantly through classical music and talks (Seymour-Ure 1996: 74). Its defined intention of audience improvement was seriously hampered by foreign broadcasters such as Radio Luxembourg and Radio Normandy targeting a dissatisfied British public and providing programmes of an increasingly popular nature. The BBC responded by organizing an Audience Research Department in 1936 to monitor preferences and assess whether these could be accommodated. Changes also occurred in the singular voice the BBC had provided, with regional broadcasting complementing the national service. Reith, becoming increasingly disillusioned with the form the BBC had assumed and the route to which it was being steered, resigned in 1937.

The BBC's role as a national institution was cemented during the Second World War through its ability to provide information, mobilize support and act as a means of social cohesion. It was able to achieve these aims because the war provided the catalyst for the BBC to improve itself in all its areas and foster a sense of empathy with its audience that it had hitherto neglected. The BBC revised its duties and pinpointed public morale rather than public taste, recognizing the urgency of being sensitive to the needs of its audience if it were to play an active part in the war effort. The realization emerged that to raise the spirit of the public the BBC had to speak to people in a language which they understood and on issues that concerned them. Content reflected the realities of the time through the exploration of everyday situations of ordinary folk. BBC writers visited factories and camps to ensure a working-class voice grew from the issues, plots and characters involved in plays and documentaries. Radio also became a ubiquitous element of the domestic sphere with the enduring image of families gathered around their sets while 'Auntie' informed them of the latest events with accuracy and fortitude (Curran and Seaton 1997: 138). While the BBC's interests lay firmly within the same confines as those of the state, it remained autonomous, again resisting state take-over, and thereby enhancing its reputation as an independent purveyor of news. Though the BBC did engage in propaganda, such activity was limited and has since been justified as the occasional lapse or necessary subterfuge in a crucial situation.

The 'craze' of television

As a post-war phenomenon, television has had a profound impact on cultural patterns and has become deeply entrenched within the fabric of everyday life. Its technical origins can be traced to the nineteenth century, although the Scotsman John Logie Baird led the first organized British attempts in the 1920s. The BBC began experimentation into television as an adjunct of radio and offered a small localized service in 1936 which was shut down once the Second World War broke out. The hesitancy with which it was introduced typified Reith's insistence that it was not a serious medium and any interest it held was purely ephemeral.

When the service resumed in 1946, television take-up steadily increased culminating in the Coronation of Queen Elizabeth II in 1953, which was watched on television by an estimated audience of 20 million. This **media event** gripped the nation and played a major role in establishing the medium by potently demonstrating its capabilities. It is perhaps no coincidence that such enthusiasm occurred at the same time as a corresponding fall in radio audiences, which never recovered to the levels commanded during the war. The BBC did not propose a separate philosophy for the operation of television, instead it unilaterally invoked the public service principles that had guided radio (Seymour-Ure 1996: 88). The religious and serious nature of programming mirrored radio output in the 1930s and testified to the influence of a Reithian undercurrent within the ethos of the BBC.

Since its scope and immediacy had been emphasized by its role in the Second World War, broadcasting was the subject of immense scrutiny and review after the war. Although the Beveridge Committee (1948) on television broadcasting reported on the inadequacies of the BBC, it nevertheless dispelled any thoughts of a commercial operator setting up because of the same fears which had moulded the role of radio some 25 years earlier. The Report did additionally recommend that decentralization was essential for the development of television, thereby confirming the need for a regional service. One dissident member of the committee, the Conservative MP Selwyn Lloyd, departed from this line and outlined plans for a commercial network to complement the BBC. His report appealed to the ideas of competition and choice that another operator was thought likely to generate. With Winston Churchill, no ally of the BBC from the time of the General Strike, gaining office in 1953, the Conservative government set about following Lloyd's blueprint. The 1954 Television Act provided the ground rules for which the Independent Television Network (ITV) would work from, and it came into being the following year.

The arrival of commercial television

Importantly, a number of drastic shifts accompanied the new operator, both in terms of reshaping the whole broadcasting system within the UK, but also with the impetus it gave the BBC. Television was to form a whole cultural industry through its growing reach in a period of relative affluence, so the need to satisfy audience tastes was now a compelling consideration. While ITV struggled to establish itself in the immediate period following its inception, it quickly made up this shortfall and expanded significantly in the period 1956 to 1960. The ITV network was composed of a regional system of separate companies with the provision of television within a region the responsibility of a single contractor. In a short period of time ITV gained a commanding foothold within television through the commitment of more entertainment-minded programme-makers than the BBC employed. While there were elements of public service woven into the governing principles of ITV, the main concern was to win a large audience share in order to secure advertising revenue. Some believed this approach would pave the way for lowest common denominator programming (Hood and Tabary-Peterssen 1997: 31). Commercial television did secure this audience share eventually, and its ability to offer higher wages and give openings for creative talent led a steady stream of BBC staff to leave its stuffy, elitist confines for the greater mood of openness which epitomized commercial television.

The Pilkington Committee was established in 1960 to address the issues which ITV had raised and to review the development of television in Britain as a whole, which it accorded a centrality within the nation's culture (Curran and Seaton 1997: 176). Unsurprisingly, the Committee's conception of society and television's importance within it resulted in a barrage of charges against ITV. The Report, published in 1962, asserted that the large profits advertising generated for commercial television had induced a drop in the standards of programming, which a schedule of American imports and popular culture affirmed. Advertising was further castigated for exploiting a vulnerable public susceptible to its purported persuasive and exploitative techniques. Criticism was levelled at the Independent Television Authority (ITA) for its inefficient regulation of the brash new upstart, on the grounds that it did not encourage the network to provide a full and diverse range of content. On this basis the Pilkington Committee recommended the BBC be awarded a second channel, which it subsequently was, in 1963, with the remit of minority interest programming.

The 'golden age' of British television

The support of Pilkington, alongside the watchful eye placed on ITV, led to a period of change in broadcasting, typified by collusion and co-operation rather than competition. Hugh Greene, appointed BBC Director General in 1960, aimed to raise the BBC's audience share and encourage more adventurous programming. Reithian values were relaxed as the BBC expanded its output to cover more sensitive issues and challenge the established values of taste and decency. At the same time, it was recognized that the audience was large enough to accommodate both the BBC and ITV, particularly since they relied on alternative sources of funding. This rendered peaceful coexistence, rather than fierce competition, the order of the day with similar programming schedules on both the BBC and ITV (Wheeler 1997: 92). Increased political news in addition to pioneering

forms of drama, satire and documentary appeared with household names developing among a mass audience. In 1982, Channel 4 became the fourth terrestrial broadcaster as a result of the recommendations of the Annan Committee (1977). Its purpose was to serve minorities who were not effectively catered for at that time, and its status as commercial broadcaster guaranteed it funding via advertising revenue.

New technology, new forms

This period of relative calm was irreconcilably shaken by two developments that worked in tandem to shift the terrain on which British broadcasting had been built. First was the new technology of **cable and satellite**, which brought more operators into broadcasting and broke the 'cosy duopoly' that the BBC and ITV had secured. This was accompanied by governmental willingness to spread technological resources to further its ideological commitment to creating free-market competition in areas where this had not hitherto existed (Seymour-Ure 1996: 68). The doctrine of market provision as the most efficient allocatory mechanism led to the enthusiastic take-up of new technology as the Conservative government led by Margaret Thatcher sought to restructure a broadcasting system which it believed had relied too heavily on an outdated dogma of public service. While new technology nullified the scarcity principle on which public service had been built, its implementation through a market-centred approach changed the character of broadcasting. Within this system the audience became an aggregate of consumers, all of whom had distinct interests that would be served by a profusion of suppliers, each catering to niche markets.

Much of this activity took place in an increasingly hostile environment, with the relationship between government and broadcasters steadily worsening over a series of disputes concerning programme content and the coverage of key political events. Against this backdrop, Prime Minister Margaret Thatcher set up the Peacock Committee (1985) to investigate the financing of the BBC in this new competitive environment (O' Malley 1994: 168). Although the corporate bias of the committee's members may have suggested the likelihood of a recommendation in favour of advertising on BBC channels, the final report, surprisingly, did not advocate such measures. However, the Peacock Report did institute a more commercial system within which both terrestrial broadcasters have had to operate and to which they have been compelled to adapt. With the arrival in 1997 of Channel 5 as the last terrestrial broadcaster, the advertising cake has had to be cut more thinly in order to accommodate the abundance of broadcasters now serving Britain.

The emergence of BSkyB from the merger of Sky and BSB has indicated a new breed of cross-media, **multinational** conglomerates entering the British broadcasting arena, a process likely to accelerate with **convergence**. This has initiated the movement of blockbuster films and major sporting events onto the satellite platform, taking with them viewers. With such a fragmented audience, the BBC has found it increasingly difficult to justify a licence fee given that it has lost audiences who must pay for the extra services they receive from the new suppliers. Hood and Tabary-Peterssen point out that this has the potential to create a two-tier broadcasting system, leaving terrestrial television as the 'poor relation' to the subscription services on the new platforms. Those unable to afford the encrypted channels will not benefit from the range of services offered by the market (Hood and Tabary-Peterssen 1997: 90).

This pattern has continued with the introduction of digital technology into broadcasting, further eroding the scarcity and specialness on which public service broadcasting rested (see **digital communication**). This allows the possibility of hundreds of channels, targeted at defined sections of the audience rather than the general public, so that 'narrowcasting' is a more appropriate term for the provision of television services. The BBC has joined the so-called 'digital revolution' by diversifying into commercial ventures and expanding its base of operation into new fields such as the **Internet**. Similarly, ITV companies have started to offer digital services. This trend has increasingly commodified broadcasting, where a commitment to profit is now seen as the fundamental aim (O'Malley 1994: 178). The question remains as to whether the commercial rationale of these shifts will undermine the cultural foundations that John

Reith so strenuously laid down for broadcasting in the UK.

See also: broadcasting, the United States; Internet; tabloid television

References

Briggs, A. (1961) *The History of Broadcasting in the UK, Volume 1*, London: Oxford University Press.

Curran, J. and Seaton, J. (1997) *Power without Responsibility: The Press and Broadcasting in Britain* (5th edn), London: Routledge.

Hood, S. and Tabary-Peterssen, T. (1997) *On Television* (4th edn), London: Pluto Press.

O'Malley, T. (1994) *Closedown? The BBC and Government Policy, 1979–1992*, London: Pluto Press.

Seymour-Ure, C. (1996) *The British Press and Broadcasting Since 1945* (2nd edn), Oxford: Blackwell Publishers.

Wheeler, M. (1997) *Politics and the Mass Media*, Oxford: Blackwell Publishers.

Further reading

Barnett, S. and Curry, A. (1994) *The Battle for the BBC*, London: Arum Press.

Crisell, A. (1997) *An Introductory History of British Broadcasting*, London: Routledge.

Scannell, P. and Cardiff, D. (1991) *A Social History of British Broadcasting Volume 1*, Oxford: Blackwell.

Sendall, B. (1982) *Independent Television in Britain, Volume 1: Origin and Foundation, 1946–1962*, London: Macmillan.

RAKESH KAUSHAL

broadcasting, the United States

This entry traces the history of broadcasting as a defining enterprise of the twentieth century. The focus on history serves as a way to define the practice of broadcasting and to situate this practice as involving more than just particular industries, programmes and viewers. I begin with a discussion of concepts in order to frame its account of wireless telegraphy, and then turn to radio and television broadcasting in the United States. Further, various genres of broadcasting are included to illustrate key points about the role of broadcasting in the distribution of information and the production of images (see **image; genre**).

Concepts and definitions

Broadcasting is a compound word made from the words 'broad' and 'casting'. It was used an adjective and verb long before its current connection with mechanical media. The word suggested the ability of one speaker to communicate to a large audience simultaneously. This nineteenth-century concept moved into a twentieth-century practice, enabled by moving images. In other words, the broadcasting industry existed as a concept prior to its prototypes and its popularization.

Wireless technology versus broadcasting

Wireless telegraphy, or point-to-point communication, was primarily initiated by Guglielmo Marconi and was used experimentally as early as 1897. In 1899 Marconi 'simulcasted' the results of the America's Cup in Newport, Rhode Island, to an audience in New York City. This was a year after the American victory over the Spanish fleet in Manila Bay; the news of this nautical and military event took one week to reach the American capital. This event also signalled that the American nation was stretched to its largest size – now that geographical conquests had been made realizing manifest destiny, distance was to be shortened through the ether.

Marconi received transmission, not in the form of a human voice, but in the series of dots and dashes that make up Morse code. He received this through the channel of sound waves, without the need for wire. Early radios were set up both to send and to receive these codes; radios have since become just receivers – only broadcasters have transmitters. By 1910, wireless telegraphy was in general use for ship-to-shore communication. This was put into United States law after the sinking of the *Titanic*. This activity was not strictly 'broadcasting' but point-to-point communication. What made broadcasting possible was the invention of the audion tube by Lee De Forest in 1906 – a tube which permitted the modulation of sound. However, Marconi was not interested in following this aspect of radio. He envisaged radio as an alternative to the telephone and telegraph monopolies (because the wireless was not reliant on wires, it had more mobility and was not affected by bad weather).

In 1906 and 1917 there was considerable amateur experimentation with the technology. In *Inventing American Broadcasting*, Susan Douglas (1987) argues that this disparate group was a **subculture** with signifying practices who helped to structure later broadcasting practices – far more so than Marconi and other inventors (see **signifying practice**). These enthusiasts (mostly young, white middle-class men) devised their own wireless sets using umbrellas and other everyday objects, in some instances diverting power taken from railroad and telephone lines. The amateur radio enthusiasts formed organizations and, at first, communicated with one another, trading information and relaying messages. It was only later that they became involved in broadcasting. In some respects, the early radio amateurs can be compared with the 'hackers' or self-taught computer experts who experimented with computer networking and mastered the **Internet**. Considered a nuisance by the military and pushed down to the bottom of the broadcast spectrum by the Act of 1912, the early 'hackers' were experimenting with broadcasting long before companies like the Radio Corporation of America (RCA) and AT&T. They initiated local shows featuring call-ins, live singing and music and the playing of phonograph records.

In 1917 all radio was taken over by the United States Navy to prevent its use by spies, and the development of new equipment was protected from patent infringement suits by government order. Amateurs, who had once been vilified by the military, were recruited by the Navy to operate the radio equipment that was now mandatory on all military boats. President Wilson broadcast to enemy troops, allowing his voice to enter beyond enemy lines.

Radio broadcasting

The broadcasting era (and the end of the era of the amateur broadcaster) begins with the end of the

First World War. The government removed restrictions in 1919, the same year that the Radio Corporation of America (RCA) was formed. The RCA, a government-sanctioned monopoly, consisted of the companies who had the key patents; the National Broadcasting System (NBC) emerged from this conglomeration. RCA/NBC quickly came to control the production of both hardware and software – it built a large percentage of the receivers and owned many of the stations and the programmes.

The broadcast era is usually cited as beginning on 2 November 1920, when an employee of Westinghouse in Pittsburgh broadcast the Harding–Cox presidential election returns and inaugurated a daily schedule of programmes. At this time, broadcasting was run on an experimental, non-commercial, amateur basis. However, the sharp increase in the number of stations throughout the US, and the fact that most were not affiliated to one another, raised the issue of who would pay pay for broadcasting. What was clear, however, was that the government would not fund broadcasting costs or charge the citizenry a rental fee (see **broadcasting, the United Kingdom**).

As Susan Smulyan (1994) argues in her book, *Selling Radio: The Commercialization of American Broadcasting, 1920–1934*, US radio came to be sustained by selling time to sponsors, contributing to the rise of the advertising agencies and the professionalization of the industry. Indeed, later in the Depression and after the Radio Act of 1927 – when many education, labour and independent broadcasters were moved to the lower end of the spectrum, and the network system was moving into place – the advertising agencies took over much of the production of shows in radio's 'golden era'.

While other industries suffered during the Depression, broadcasting emerged as a profitable enterprise. Legislation, first in 1927 and then in 1934, which saw the setting up of the Federal Communications Commission (FCC), helped to institute the particularly American brand of broadcasting. Although the airwaves remained publicly held, the FCC could license out frequencies to stations at its discretion – a policy which had a detrimental effect on educational and public stations. The FCC also mandated that political candidates should be granted equal air time and

there was to be no censorship. Further, although the agency granted licences to private companies, these companies were expected to operate in the public interest. However, the tacit endorsement of commercialization in the American system virtually ensures that certain voices are not heard.

The geography of the US aided in this noncentralized, commercial system: in such a large and diverse country, no single station could cover the entire land mass, whereas a network of similar stations could. In the Soviet Union, for example, where the state operated the radio stations, programmes were transmitted in sixty-two languages over sixty-four stations and there was no need for nationwide broadcasts. Britain and Germany, both smaller in size than the USSR and the United States and more linguistically homogenous, operated nationwide stations owned by the government. Australia had a mixed system of both public and private stations and it centred the stations around the six major cities, where 80 per cent of the population lived (see Smulyan 1994: 671). Canada, which had a restricted number of available frequencies due to its proximity to the US, established a publicly-held radio station that was pioneered by the Canadian National Railroad. This laid the groundwork for a national radio system.

Despite early utopian rhetoric insisting that broadcasting could unite and educate the nation of newly arrived, non-English-speaking immigrants by inviting them to join a common culture (see Covert 1984; Smulyan 1994), broadcasting quickly became a site for popular entertainment with little educational emphasis. Until President Roosevelt's *Fireside Chats* and the encroaching war in Europe, news broadcasts were a slender consideration by most stations. Instead, music programming, early versions of sitcoms (see **situation comedy**) performed by ex-vaudeville stars such as Edgar Bergen, George Burns and Gracie Allen, and **soap opera** became staples of everyday broadcasting. One of the most popular shows, *Amos 'n' Andy*, was a form of vocal blackface – two white performers played stereotyped black men as 'loveable' Harlem cab drivers. Despite protests from black groups, NBC stood by this show and decreed that its entertainment programmes were also education (see NBC 1935).

One of the landmark events in American broadcasting occurred on 30 October 1938, a year after the Hindenburg disaster (when a radio commentator witnessed the explosion of a dirigible airship in New Jersey) and a year before television was presented to a popular audience at the New York World Fair. Orson Welles' Mercury Theatre performed a radio adaptation of Howard Koch's version of Wells' *The War of the Worlds*. This took the form of an imitation of broadcasting itself: live dance music was interrupted by news flashes from the station and reports from the field. The novel was transformed into a news broadcast, and the invasion of the Martians was performed as a simulation of radio broadcasting. Most people at the time were listening to the ventriloquist Edgar Bergen and his dummy in *The Charlie McCarthy Show*. Thus, when they tuned in to Welles' production, they missed the disclaimer at the outset of the programme and mistook the simulated attack as an actual invasion.

News broadcasting became increasingly important during the Second World War – as did propaganda broadcasting. The American-born poet Ezra Pound transmitted for Italian radio in 1941 (after the war he was arrested for treason), and radio was used by the Allies to try to destabilize the Nazi regime. Americans heard live broadcasts and were witness to the word-pictures of the broadcasting commentators. The voices of the American, English, German, Italian and Soviet leaders were broadcast as a way to solidify and reassure the listening public. The war also delayed the public release of television, since wartime production had to focus on weaponry and related items.

Television broadcasting

Although experimentation with television as a technology can be traced back to the beginning of the twentieth century, television broadcasting is a post-war phenomenon, and one which has radically altered everyday life. Until 1952, due to an FCC ban on the issuing of licences, distribution of television stations was uneven and centred in major cities, known as television cities. Programme costs were high and revenues low, even though within specific areas television impacted on radio listening

and decreased visits to the cinema. Thus, producing low-cost programmes was crucial. This meant showing sports events, 'live' music shows with a dancing audience and which had performers lip-synching to taped music, and live variety programmes that focused on sketch comedy and musical acts (like Sid Caesar's *Your Show of Shows*). Vaudeville-type shows also moved to television, starring such performers as Milton Berle and George Burns. *The Ed Sullivan Show*, which became a mainstay of US television broadcasting, cost a mere $5,000 a week to produce, and by 1951 there were twenty-nine evening variety programmes carried on television networks (Bensman 1998).

From television's early days, new forms of broadcasting emerged. These forms included courtroom dramas or re-enactments, children's puppet programmes, variety shows, music/dance shows and crime/detective shows performed live. The showing of silent Westerns with narrators prefigured series like *Gunsmoke* and *The Virginian*. Television broadcasting was becoming diverse in terms of programming, although the defining traits of these genres remained strict. Shows relied on sponsorship of at least one company for production, and a show's name often carried the name of the sponsor – for example, the popular weekly drama programme, *The Goodyear Theatre*.

During the 1950s, when television-set ownership became ubiquitous, radio broadcasting increasingly centred on playing music, with new opportunities to reach different listening audiences. This period saw the rise of the black-oriented radio, with musicians – like B. B. King, for example – receiving their first break as DJs in stations in the South. Although the nation remained very segregated, audiences had access to stations that appealed to many different tastes. Rock 'n' roll, which consisted of white performers adapting African-American musical styles, can be seen as a partial result of post-war musical programming and the opportunity for white musicians to hear black music and disc jockeys (see Cantor 1992).

In the late 1950s, the sitcom became a prevalent **genre**. This programming reflected the growing suburbanization of the US, with young families placed in new housing units (Spigel 1992), and mostly white families watching television broadcasts featuring mostly white, nuclear families where

'*Father Knows Best*'. Around this time, there also emerged some notable drama shows. For example, *The Twilight Zone* and *The Outer Limits* were two **science fiction** series that served to expose the xenophobia and paranoia of the arms race and the Cold War. Little-known shows, shot live from New York, such as the detective show *Johnny Staccato* in 1959 which featured filmmaker John Cassavetes as director/writer, also provided programming of aesthetic diversity. Television-made dramas used popular current styles of **realism** as well as method acting techniques. Some shows later became films, such as *Requiem for a Heavyweight* (Ralph Nelson, 1962); others, such as *Harvest* with James Dean, featured actors who would go on to films.

In the 1960s, major national and global events impacted powerfully upon broadcasting. The assassination of President Kennedy was an historic event, not least because networks transmitted the occurrence over and over to the viewer. President, Kennedy had proven himself an astute and effective user of broadcasting; his use of media and his success in the debates against his opponent, Richard Nixon, perhaps secured him the 1960 election. For the camera, Kennedy knew how to appear energetic, enthusiastic, well prepared and singular. Roosevelt and Kennedy were presidents of the broadcasting era.

In modern western democracy, the role of broadcasting continues to be central to government. In the broadcasting era, the media are not only the primary audience, they also serve to frame the audience's reception of the candidate or policymaker. Leaders strive to adjust this frame.

Another crucial event of the 1960s that serves to highlight the growing impact of television was reportage and footage of the Vietnam War. Although the capacity to transmit and receive in colour pre-dated the 1960s, it was only during the early part of that decade that television was received predominantly in colour. This had relevance to broadcasting: the hues of war were transmitted live to the populace. The war was 'prime timed' (see **prime time**) and this coverage helped to fuel the anti-war movement. Network coverage of the civil rights movement also conferred status on activists; although the news and broadcast organizations were by no means integrated, inclusion of some of the marches and sit-ins in the news allowed more people to become aware of activist and integrationist positions.

Advances in television broadcasting

Many of the technological advancements commercialized and popularized in the 1970s and 1980s were in fact developed far earlier, but for a variety of reasons they were not brought to the market. For example, colour broadcasts began in 1950; a prototype for the VCR was shown as early as 1955; videotape usage began in the mid-1950s; satellite communications were initiated in 1962; and cable transmission was successfully used between New York and Washington in the late 1940s.

More recently, high definition television (HDTV) has been released in the United States, with FCC encouragement. Although this transmission is far clearer, allows for each station frequency to receive up to four images, and is more dynamic than the previous analogue signal, at the time of writing (1998) there are few companies who produce receivers for these signals and the sets remain expensive. Furthermore, consumers seem unaware of the advantages. Because of marketing stress on the Internet, consumers are being told of the coming interface between television and the World Wide Web, which might be the site and source of increased televisual activity (see **information theory**). With the Internet comes an increased focus on narrowcasting, with a more defined audience, interacting with one another, and with the narrowcasting source. This emphasis can perhaps be seen as originating with cable broadcasting. Cable offers many more choices to the viewer, and allows the successful entry of specialized broadcasting entities such as MTV and the Weather Channel.

The industry has enlarged but it remains reliant on popular activity to signal change; this dimension of broadcasting can be seen in its origins with the amateurs whose unruly experimentation established broadcasting procedures. Broadcasting, as a cultural practice, has undergone great structural changes; the introduction of new technology has allowed groups and individuals to reconceptualize the process. Corporations intervene after innovation, and not always in the public interest. Whatever its form and genre, though, broadcasting – as an activity which sends voices and images to many – has served both to re-present and to impact on the sociocultural milieux from which it emerges.

References

Bensman, M. (1998) *Broadcasting in the 1940s*. Online. Available: www.people.memphis.edu/~mbensman/BC40.DAT (14 November 1998).

Cantor, L. (1992) *Wheelin' on Beale: How WDIA-Memphis Became the Nation's First All-Black Radio Station and Created the Sound That Changed America*, New York: Pharos Books.

Covert, C. (1984) 'We May Hear Too Much', in Catherine L. Covert and John D. Stevens (eds) *Mass Media Between the Wars: Perceptions of Cultural Tension, 1918–1941*, Syracuse: Syracuse University Press.

Douglas, S. (1987) *Inventing American Broadcasting, 1899–1922*, Baltimore, MD: Johns Hopkins University Press.

National Broadcasting Company (1935) *Broadcasting to All Homes* (four vols), New York: NBC.

Smulyan, S. (1994) *Selling Radio: The Commercialization of American Broadcasting, 1920–1934*. Washington, DC: Smithsonian.

Spigel, L. (1992) *Make Room for TV: Television and the Family Ideal in Postwar America*, Chicago: University of Chicago Press.

Further reading

Barnouw, E. (1990) *Tube of Plenty*, New York: Oxford University Press.

Koch, H. (1970) *The Panic Broadcast: Portrait of an Event*, Boston: Little Brown and Company.

Marvin, C. (1988) *When Old Technologies Were New: Thinking About Electric Communication in the Late Nineteenth Century*, New York: Oxford University Press.

Streeter, T. (1996) *Selling the Air: A Critique of the Policy of Commercial Broadcasting in the United States*, Chicago: University of Chicago Press.

EDWARD MILLER

Butler, Judith

b. 1956

Judith Butler's work has had an enormous influence on both **feminist theory** and **queer theory**. In *Gender Trouble* (1990), Butler states that there is no female subject because gender is nothing but a performance (see **performance theory**). Masculinity and femininity, as well as homosexuality and heterosexuality, are not fixed identities, but constructs defined in relation to each other. Gay **camp** and lesbian 'butch and femme' role-play are imitative performances, but they are imitations without an original, because there is no stable heterosexual identity. These performances of masculinity and femininity can be truly subversive in unsettling the seeming stability of **gender** binaries (see **binary**).

Butler's work has been useful for analysing films that unsettle gender binaries, either through cross-dressing or through exposing exaggerated masculinity or femininity as a performance. Butler's concept of gender as performance has been linked to Mary Ann Doane's (1990) concept of female identity as masquerade. However, some queer critics contend that Butler underplays the fact that patriarchal masculinity is a masquerade as well.

References

Butler, J. (1990) *Gender Trouble: Feminism and the Subversion of Identity*, London and New York: Routledge.

Doane, M. A. (1990) 'Film and the Masquerade: Theorizing the Female Spectator', in Patricia Erens (ed.) *Issues in Feminist Film Criticism*, Bloomington: Indiana University Press.

Further reading

Butler, J. (1991) 'Imitation and Gender Insubordination', in Diana Fuss (ed.) *Inside/Out*, London/New York: Routledge.

ANTJE LINDENMEYER

C

cable and satellite

Cable and satellite is a term commonly employed to refer to technologies that are used to transmit a range of data and information including television pictures. Cable systems are usually installed below ground. The cables connect the end user – homes or businesses – to a central point that distributes information. Cable television systems normally require some form of decoder to interpret the information and turn it into television images. Satellites are situated above the earth and beam signals which are subsequently picked up by satellite dishes attached to people's homes.

The technological significance of satellite broadcasting is that it is extra-terrestrial; this means it has the potential to evade state boundaries and national control. Information beamed from a satellite can be picked up by anyone within receiving distance of the signals who has the necessary receiving equipment (e.g., a satellite dish), allowing television viewers in the United Kingdom, for example, access to French, German or Scandinavian programming. Satellite television is, then, potentially a truly global technology (see **globalization**).

By contrast, cable technologies operate on a local level. Cable franchises are granted on a regional and local basis by the Independent Television Commission (ITC) in the United Kingdom, and awarded on the basis of competitive tender by the Federal Communications Commission (FCC) in the United States. Cable television has a much longer history in the United States, where geographical diversity and poor quality terrestrial transmission meant that, in many areas, cable distribution of television was the only means of receiving good quality pictures.

Cable operators install and maintain the cable infrastructure in a given area and provide customers with a range of services – including television channels and telecommunications – that can be distributed via their cable network. One of the main services offered by cable operators is access to a wider range of television channels and services, including the content of the main satellite broadcasters and, increasingly, digital and on-line services.

Globalization

The trend towards increasingly international structures of political, social and economic organization represented by, among other things, the relaxation of controls on currency exchange and the liberalization of trade have been both enabled by and reflected in the rise of new media technologies that cross national boundaries, such as cable and satellite television.

While in theory the growth of broadcast outlets should give more access to a diverse range of voices and views, in practice only those organizations with sufficient capital to compete on the international scale which satellite requires have succeeded in reaching a substantial **audience**. Satellite television channels broadcasting across regions mean that cultures as diverse as Indonesia, Japan, Kenya, Sweden and Brazil all have access to variations of the same global media channels and brands, for example, CNN, MTV and the Disney Channel.

Some cultural and political commentators have voiced concern that this trend has led to a homogenization of culture, lifestyle and formal styles and to the erosion of local cultures and tastes. This is of particular concern in relation to children and young people, who are seen as both more vulnerable and more desirable consumers (see **children and media**).

Increasingly, the global reach of big media corporations also has implications for how the media report on and represent particular situations and stories. One of the most articulate critics of this process is Noam Chomsky. Chomsky has written extensively about the relationship between corporate power and the control over the 'public mind' through the media. Given that global media corporations such as Time-Warner and News Corps are themselves representatives of the global power elite, it is hardly surprising that the coverage of issues relating to free trade and the global economy is likely to come from a particular perspective. A perspective which, as Chomsky (1987) argues, serves the interests of the privileged North American and western European elite who are the main beneficiaries of globalization.

Viewer choice

The power of cable and satellite technologies to transmit a greater volume of information has also created many more television channels unhampered by the limits of the broadcast spectrum. The most obvious implication of cable and satellite television, therefore, has been the provision of more choice for the viewer in terms of the amount of television available to him or her, and thus greater power to choose exactly what he/she wants to watch. For example, a sports fan has access to specialized sports channels twenty-four hours a day, seven days a week, and is no longer restricted to watching the highlights of matches once a week on one of the main terrestrial channels when it fits into their schedules.

However, the technological advances in cable and satellite broadcasting that took place throughout the 1980s and 1990s and its accompanying rhetoric of consumer choice cannot be divorced from the political push towards deregulation and privatization which occurred in all areas of public life in the same period (see **deregulation, the United Kingdom; deregulation, the United States**). New technologies, providing the viewer with potentially hundreds of channels and programmes, was hailed by those on the right as the triumph of consumer sovereignty over elitist autocratic institutions, such as the British Broadcasting Corporation (BBC; see **Reith, John**).

The cable and satellite 'revolution' was given its most convincing ideological justification by Rupert Murdoch. Murdoch successfully managed to link technological progress to populist anti-elitism, thus providing a justification for the rolling back of regulation. In his 1989 address to the Edinburgh Television Festival, Murdoch explained how in the age of **spectrum scarcity** (before cable and satellite technologies), 'the people could not be trusted to watch what they wanted to watch so that [television] had to be controlled...by people who knew what was good for us'.

Cable and satellite television has thus been positioned as a more direct form of communication between the viewer and the producer, liberated by the market to respond only to the wants of the audience, unhampered by the heavy hand of a regulating state. However, the claims made concerning the ability of cable and satellite technology to deliver diversity and value to the viewer are problematic. First, unlike universally available terrestrial broadcasting, access to cable and satellite television presents an extra cost to the viewer, either in subscription or in pay-per-view – a cost that not all sections of society can afford. Second, the promise of a diversity of voices and representations enabled by an increase in distribution outlets has so far failed to materialize, largely due to the prohibitively high entry costs of mass media production and distribution, but also because of the free market's tendency to monopoly and merger. This means that while cable and satellite, and now digital technologies, have brought an end to spectrum scarcity, they cannot address the issue of more relevance to the average viewer – that is, content scarcity.

Fragmentation of the audience

Inherent in the move towards a choice-oriented model of television broadcasting is the erosion of the idea of a mass audience. When sports fans can choose sports channels, children can choose children's channels, music fans can choose music channels and so on, who is left watching a mainstream channel based on a consensus of what the population wants to watch in general?

Inevitably, the more channels there are to choose from, the smaller the share of the overall audience each channel will get. This simple equation problematizes the model of a **public service broadcasting** which rests on an idea of the audience as sharing certain common features and interests – national events such as elections or state occasions or defining sporting events such as the FA Cup Final or the Superbowl.

The emergence of specialist television channels enabled by cable and satellite technologies – for example, sport, movie or lifestyle channels – creates specialist markets for particular types of programming and as a consequence assumes a different relationship between broadcaster and viewer. Unlike the days of spectrum scarcity where the choice of **prime-time** viewing might be between two sitcoms, a popular news programme and a soap opera, with specialist cable and satellite programming a music fan can tune in to MTV, a science-fiction fan can watch *Star Trek: Deep Space Nine* and a comedy fan can watch old episodes of his or her favourite sit-com on the Paramount channel.

This audience fragmentation has particular implications for television advertising: general mass-market advertisers will find it increasingly difficult to reach a large, generic audience. However, it has become easier for companies to target a product at specific sections of the audience who are more likely to be watching a specialist channel. This leads to an increased importance placed on market research in the commissioning and production process so that television companies can minimize risk – in terms of investing in programmes that are unlikely to be successful with the target audience – and find out more about their audiences and thus provide more useful information to advertisers.

However, one of the problems with the specialist/individual choice model of broadcasting is that audiences are seldom as regulated as market researchers and advertisers would like them to be. Television audiences frequently have diverse tastes

and make viewing choices based on a number of factors to do with their social situations and daily lives. The fact is that the *same* viewer may enjoy watching a sci-fi channel, CNN and a soap opera such as *Coronation Street*.

A further implication of content scarcity that cable and satellite television has so far produced is the increasing use of re-packaged and re-run programmes. This means that many channels rely on a diet of television nostalgia as an economic way of filling almost infinite hours of broadcast time.

Regulation

The international reach of cable and satellite television also has implications for the way in which television is regulated. Traditionally, nation states have had a high degree of control over television output – either through direct ownership and editorial control or through the licensing of the broadcast spectrum (defined as a national utility). Satellites broadcasting from outside national boundaries become harder to license and control. Although national bodies are still ultimately responsible for regulating any television output received in the country, there has been a move towards *post hoc* regulation.

The other difficulty of regulating a post-cable and satellite television landscape is the large amount of television that is now broadcast which makes it more or less impossible for any one body to monitor the complete television output both nationally and locally. Specialized channels and the development of 'niche' markets have also required a rethinking of regulatory requirements. For example, it would be difficult to apply the same criteria to the Playboy Channel and a channel aimed specifically at children: if someone chooses to watch an adult channel they are expected to take responsibility for what they might see. In this way, judgements about taste and suitability rely increasingly on definitions of audience that also reinforces the increasing importance of **audience** research.

Convergence

Perhaps a greater long-term significance of cable and satellite is the potential for media **convergence**. Convergence is in many ways the offspring of deregulation, allowing companies to operate across media sectors so that a cable television company can also offer telephone services and **Internet** access. Increasingly, with the expanded capability of broadband networks and digital cable services, it will be possible for television to be available on personal computers and for viewers to access the Internet via television. This convergence at the level of services is also being mirrored by the mounting convergence of media ownership through mergers and take-overs between media companies (which also accelerates the trend towards globalization).

The convergence of media technologies is also reflected in greater conjunction in media content, to the extent that television programmes increasingly use formal devices developed on the World Wide Web, or films use **narrative** strategies more reminiscent of computer games. An example of this trend is cross-media events, pioneered by companies like Disney, whereby the release of an animated film is often supported by a computer game, a television cartoon and a themed Website, as well as by merchandising.

See also: broadcasting, the United Kingdom; broadcasting, the United States

References

Chomsky, N. (1987) 'The Manufacture of Consent', *The Chomsky Reader*, London: Serpent's Tail.

HANNAH DAVIES

camera style and lens style

The camera and the lens are the devices for controlling the light and the formation of the image in film and video. Their positioning, movement and operation influence the style and meaning of the images and hence our understanding of the text. The camera angle defines the nature of the shot, and in so doing helps to create the style of the film giving it, as part of the **mise-en-scène**, atmosphere and mood. When there are performers in the scene, positioning of the camera can make the shot appear to be either subjective or objective.

The tendency of frontal wide shots of early cinema, where the narrative would unfold as if on a theatre stage, has, conventionally, been replaced by shots that give the viewer the best possible view of the action (see **classical Hollywood cinema and new Hollywood cinema**). This view may be from the point of view of one of the characters, thereby making it a subjective shot (as the camera is in the position of one of the characters; see **point of view shot**), or it may be a shot from a point of view which gives the audience some narrative information or atmosphere from an objective position. Indeed, in certain cases the shot may be from an 'impossible' position such as the inside of a cupboard (*Blue Velvet*, David Lynch, 1986), the inside of a sound cassette (*Women on the Verge of a Nervous Breakdown*, Pedro Almodovar, 1988) or the back of someone's throat (*Three Crowns of the Sailor*, Raul Ruiz, 1982).

The angle of the camera, whether the shot is subjective or objective, can dictate the feelings of mood and atmosphere. A low angled shot can give the image an imposing or dominating effect; a high angled shot the reverse. When the camera looks down at Roger Thornhill from the top of the United Nations building in New York in *North by Northwest* (Alfred Hitchcock, 1957), the shot gives the impression of the character as being lost and isolated in the space. An 'unnatural' angle that distorts the vertical lines can impart a sense of unease or alienation which can be seen in such films as *The Cabinet of Dr Caligari* (Robert Wiene, 1919), *The Third Man* (Carol Reed, 1949) or *Confidential Report* (aka *Mr Arkadin*, Orson Welles, 1955). **Film noir**, with its formal adventurousness and interest in paranoia and alienation, consistently offered the audience views from low, skewed angles.

The lens controls the photographic element of the image, and in particular **depth of field** and **perspective**. The relationship between the parts of the image that are in focus, and those that are not, is used to draw the audience's attention to significant elements within the shot. This is dependent on depth of field which is controlled by focal length (the magnifying power), the aperture and focusing of the lens. If it is desirable to draw attention away from the background and on to a character in the foreground, one solution is to make sure that the background is out of focus and the foreground is in focus by using a small depth of field. Conversely, deep focus cinematography uses a large **depth of field**, ensuring that most of the image is in focus from foreground to background. This was stylistically fashionable in the 1940s and 1950s, one of the most notable examples being Orson Welles' *Citizen Kane* (1941).

The focal length of a lens also affects perspective, and hence style. A wide-angle (small focal length) lens exaggerates the depth of a scene by altering the perspective relations between the foreground and the background, making the space appear bigger than it is. It will also produce distortion of straight lines at the edges of the frame, making them bulge outwards, or of objects that are very close to the lens. A telephoto lens will reduce depth and produce a flattened image. Stylistically, this compression of the focal planes can give a feeling of claustrophobia.

The film camera can also control the speed of the film, and in terms of style this has an important effect on the image. When the film is speeded up in the camera, it will appear as slow motion when projected, and vice versa. Martin Scorsese has used slight slow motion effect in a number of his films to give a sense of dramatic tension and unease, while fast motion is often used for humorous effect.

Further reading

Bordwell, D. and Thompson, K. (1997) *Film Art: An Introduction* (5th edn), New York: McGraw Hill.

NICK BURTON

camp

According to Susan Sontag's seminal treatment, 'Notes on "Camp" ' (1969 [1964]), camp is a 'certain mode of aestheticism', a specific strategy of reading both popular and high **culture** which is practised mainly by urban groups for whom it serves as a private code, a badge of identity and a form of subversive celebration of their own marginality. Camp readings favour style, artifice, exaggeration, extremity and irony over content, morality and tragedy. Due to its emphasis on the

visual and the extravagant, camp sensibility has been particularly bound up with film (and movie stars such as Bette Davis). While Sontag regards camp as closely associated with modernism (with its roots in nineteenth-century dandyism) and homosexuality, contemporary theorists point to an intrinsic relationship between post-modern culture and camp, a mainstreaming of camp sensibility due to a shared emphasis on signifier over signified, artifice over meaning.

See also: modernism and post-modernism

References

Sontag, S. (1969) 'Notes on "Camp" ' (first published in 1964), in S. Sontag, *Against Interpretation*, New York: Dell.

EVA WARTH

canon

The term 'canon' is used to designate a collection of texts enshrined as aesthetically definitive within a particular **culture** or a particular discipline (see **aesthetics**). Prior to the revolutionary impact of theories of post-structuralism, post-modernism and post-colonialism (see **structuralism and post-structuralism; modernism and post-modernism**), the canon within literary studies comprised those texts considered to be, in Matthew **Arnold**'s phrase, the 'best that has been thought and said'. This canon manifested itself in the similar curriculum content of literary studies courses in Britain, Australia and North America: Shakespeare, Milton, Joyce and so forth. The theoretical, cultural and political upheavals of the 1960s led to a radical questioning of canonical texts as inextricably linked with dominant ideologies (see **ideology and hegemony**). The 'culture wars' in the American academy in the 1980s and 1990s were fought over the contested terrain of the canon, some wishing to defend the so-called great texts and others wishing to replace them, or at least supplement them, with texts produced by hitherto marginalized writers – women, people of colour, gays and lesbians.

In its first few years, film studies too erected a canonical list of great films chosen for their aesthetic qualities and taught in almost all introductory courses – for example, *Citizen Kane* (Orson Welles, 1941), *Battleship Potemkin* (Sergei **Eisenstein**, 1925) and *The Cabinet of Dr Caligari* (Robert Wiene, 1919). The range of films shown in university courses at the beginning of the twenty-first century, however, reflects the more multi-cultural perspective achieved by the 'culture wars', despite the fact that there have been no major canonical debates within the discipline, attesting perhaps to the left-of-centre politics of most film studies instructors. By contrast with film studies, television studies never had a canon of texts deemed to be aesthetically superior. Until the 1980s most television studies was conducted by scholars of a social science bent more interested in political economy and media effects than in textual aesthetics. In the 1980s, cultural studies took up the question of television, but focused on audiences rather than texts, celebrating the supposed resis-tance of viewers to preferred readings encoded by the programmes' producers (see **encoding; pre-ferred reading**). This perspective has resulted in certain genres and even certain programmes receiving vastly more attention than others. For example, much has been written about soap operas in terms of their appeal to women viewers. Similarly, several scholars have written about female fandoms' response to science fiction pro-grammes, particularly *Star Trek* (see **fandom; genre**). These texts might to some extent be deemed canonical, featuring more prominently in university courses than others, although the motivation for their inclusion stems not from aesthetic considerations, but rather from the combination of their relative accessibility and their relation to particular segments of the audience.

Within the realm of media production, however, canonical texts continue to flourish. The British Broadcasting Corporation (BBC) regularly offers viewers costume dramas adapted from literary 'masterpieces'. Many of these are done in con-junction with American broadcasters such as the Arts and Entertainment Channel or the public service station WGBH, which cuts down on production costs and guarantees an overseas market. The American Public Broadcasting Ser-vice has a regularly scheduled programme, *Master-piece Theater*, devoted entirely to supposedly 'classy' British imports usually based on literary sources, although the canonical status of some of these is debatable. American commercial television relies less on literary adaptations, although at least one company, Hallmark Entertainment, specializes in the genre. Hallmark distributes *The Hallmark Hall of Fame* programmes (the one survivor from American television's 'golden age' of weekly, one-off dramatic shows) and specializes in prestigious, high-production values mini-series based on classic literary sources (e.g. *The Odyssey, Gulliver's Travels, Moby Dick* and *A Christmas Carol*). The cinema occasionally also returns to the canonical texts which have featured in its repertoire since the medium's infancy. At the turn of the twenty-first century, for example, film producers returned to the most canonical of all authors, William Shake-speare, producing direct adaptations of his plays, such as *William Shakespeare's Romeo and Juliet* (Baz Luhrmann, 1996) as well as films loosely based on the plays, such as *10 Things I Hate About You* (Gil Junger, 1999) (inspired by *The Taming of the Shrew*).

Further reading

Greenblatt, S. and Gunn, G. (eds) (1992) *Redrawing the Boundaries: The Transformation of English and American Literary Studies*, New York: MLA.

ROBERTA E. PEARSON

carnival

Carnival marks the period of revelry just prior to Lent – a brief time of indulgence and liberty during which all normal rules of social conduct and hierarchy are suspended or overturned. Traceable back to the Roman Saturnalia and continuing through the Middle Ages, carnival remains a vital cultural force throughout the world. Among the most well-known festivities are those in Brazil, where Rio's *escolas de samba* compete yearly, drawing thousands of tourists to the country and bringing money into the local economy; the Caribbean, especially on the islands of Trinidad and Tobago; New Orleans, where marching bands known as krewes toss beads and coins to the crowd during Mardi Gras; and also Venice, Germany, and even the UK with the Notting Hill Carnival.

Through masquerade, satire and mimicry, the poor 'become' the rich, the powerless can safely ridicule religious and other ruling institutions, and even **gender** categories become blurred as men don women's clothes and vice versa. Frequently, gay culture moves into the foreground during carnival, as transvestism becomes a cause for cheering rather than punishment. Carnivalesque imagery glorifies the grotesque, the outsized, and everything associated with the 'lower body', from defecation to genitalia: it includes gigantic **phallus**-like 'clown sticks', statuary of old women giving birth, and depictions of rivers of drink and mountains of food.

Through the writings of Mikhail **Bakhtin**, this real-life celebration became the blueprint for a cultural and literary theory, used to examine texts that shared its liberatory philosophy. Carnivalesque writings and films took a playful and free approach to language, humorously critiqued entrenched powers, and offered a positive and utopian image of the world.

One such work is Brazilian director Carlos Diegues' *Xica da Silva* (1976), a film that relates a fictionalized account of a famous female slave in the late eighteenth century. Xica achieved a modicum of power by seducing a wealthy Portuguese diamond contractor sent to Brazil. Scholars such as Randal Johnson have written of *Xica*'s narrative and lush visual style, locating the carnivalesque in the film's depiction of slaves dressed in aristocratic clothing and wigs, its inversion of power relations in terms of gender and politics, its moments of joyful dance and music, and its brilliant, tropically colourful landscape.

However, *Xica* also reveals the limits of carnival: the power shift it creates lasts only for a brief time, and then relations return to their normal state. In Xica's case, when the Portuguese Crown recalls her lover to Lisbon, her short reign comes to an abrupt halt and she becomes once again a slave and an outcast. In terms of actual carnival, Roberto DaMatta has argued that while this *festa popular* does move those at the boundaries into the centre, and creates a 'special space', it also captures 'the paradox of a people who never organise spontaneously to *protest or demand their rights*, being obviously over-organised, but instead to *have a good time*' (DaMatta 1991: 47). In this way, carnival might actually serve to defuse actual political action.

Similarly, Mary Russo, in her 'Female Grotesques: Carnival and Theory' (1986), suggests that the much-heralded sexual freedom of carnival has not always been positive for women, and that it may have occasioned rape and other forms of physical harassment. Many critics have spoken ambivalently about the way the female body is displayed in Rio's carnival, in which several of the samba school's lead dancers perform in a semi-naked state; in New Orleans' Mardi Gras, there is an additional pressure on women to bare their breasts.

Whether carnival today continues to retain the potential Bakhtin perceived is an interesting question. With its more limited time frame, rigorous organization, and occasionally even physical constriction, carnival maintains a sometimes ambiguous position. As Robert Stam notes: 'Carnival is admittedly the Bakhtinian category most susceptible to co-optation, at times becoming the pretext for a vacuous ludism'. But he also points out that: 'On the positive side, it is ecstatic collectivity, the joyful affirmation of change, a dress rehearsal for utopia' (Stam 1989: 94).

References

Bakhtin, M. (1984) *Rabelais and His World*, trans. Hélène Iswolsky, Bloomington: Indiana University Press.

DaMatta, R. (1991) *Carnivals, Rogues, and Heroes: An Interpretation of the Brazilian Dilemma*, trans. John Drury, South Bend, IN: University of Notre Dame Press.

Johnson, R. (1984) *Cinema Novo × 5: Masters of Contemporary Brazilian Film*, Austin: University of Texas Press.

Russo, M. (1986) 'Female Grotesques: Carnival and Theory', in Teresa de Lauretis (ed.) *Feminist Studies/Critical Studies*, Bloomington: Indiana University Press.

Stam, R. (1989) *Subversive Pleasures: Bakhtin, Cultural*

Criticism, and Film, Baltimore: The Johns Hopkins University Press.

KAREN BACKSTEIN

castration

In Freudian psychoanalysis (see **Freud, Sigmund**), the fear of the loss or the discovery of the lack of a **phallus** was seen as the basic cause for the Oedipus complex (in both sexes, though stronger in males) or 'penis envy' (in females). This position has been thoroughly refuted by modern psychoanalysis: writers such as Deleuze even analyse the Freudian model of 'have and have not' as a reinforcement of capitalism on the level of relationships and psychological development (see **Deleuze, Gilles and Guattari, Félix**). **Lacan**, building on the Freudian model, reinterpreted castration to signify the rupture between the state of nature and its representation, language. Since, for Lacan, the phallus is the main signifier, the fear of castration is an intellectual construct which expresses the anxiety about the rift between the signifier (language) and the signified (everything else). Feminist film theory has linked the male fear of castration to the fetishization of women in the classical Hollywood cinema (see **gaze, the**).

See also: classical Hollywood cinema and new Hollywood cinema; feminist theory; fetishism; signifying practice

EVA VIETH

catharsis

The word catharsis comes from the Greek, meaning 'purification' or 'cleanse'. In *Poetics*, Aristotle describes the effect of the tragedy as arousal of compassion (*eleos*) and fear (*phobos*), and thus the purification of or from such passions. The exact translation and the object of the sentence – spectator or character – is unclear. The interpretations range from education of the audience through providing examples which precipitate psychological 'discharge' and relief of disturbing emotions to 'completion' of the dramatic form in an aesthetically pleasing ending. Though catharsis has lost

relevance in the literary critic's **discourse**, its 'discharge' interpretation plays an important, if somewhat doubtful, part in the discussion about the effects of **violence** in media.

EVA VIETH

censorship

The word 'censorship' has been used to refer to related but different practices: governmental prior restraint on expression; criminal prosecution for obscenity; the actions of various individuals and groups who exert pressure on producers and distributors to alter products or to stop marketing them; the conscious and unconscious evasions and silences practised by producers, writers, directors and others involved in the production of cultural commodities.

In broad terms, two central meanings are often invoked by the use of the word 'censorship' in contemporary debates. First, the control by state institutions of the expression of political or 'immoral' ideas by film and television; and, second, formations of self-regulation operated by cinema and television industries to police the moral, social and ideological content of texts.

With regard to cinema – which is generally defined as 'harmless entertainment' and divorced from the sphere of the political or 'artistic' – censorship concerns have focused on representations of sex, violence and crime. These are central issues also in regard to television, though television has a different relation to the sphere of the political from cinema. Advocates of censorship usually insist that screen representations, because of their visibility and accessibility, affect behaviour more adversely than literary texts. They are seen to have a more profound affect through a process akin to hypnosis, a common trope, visible in early debates about the effects of film texts and more recent debates surrounding 'video nasties' – films on video containing graphic violence (see **video**). The viewer affected badly by screen representation is regarded as peculiarly vulnerable and as potentially dangerous.

This vulnerability and dangerousness has historically been coded in various ways through gender, class, ethnicity and age – and much of the concern about the effects of film and television concentrates on children. Debates about censorship are thus highly charged negotiations over what can be said or shown, heard or seen, marking out the terrain of conflict over discursive practices in a culture that has insistently been linked to concerns about social, political and moral order.

The study of censorship by film and television scholars has tended to regard it as simply a repressive act, involving the blocking and manipulation of parts of some original message or representation. This view has been challenged by Annette Kuhn (1988), whose book on early British film censorship, *Cinema, Censorship and Sexuality, 1909–1925*, utilizes the work of Michel **Foucault** to argue that the power of censorship is not simply repressive but is also productive. 'Regulation' – Kuhn prefers this word to 'censorship' – can be seen not so much as an imposition of rules on a preconstituted entity but as an ongoing and provisional process of constituting objects from and for its own practices.

Kuhn's work in Britain and Richard Maltby's (1983) writing on the self-regulation of American cinema in the 1920s and 1930s, show censorship debates as having determining effects on the shaping of cinema, holding in place certain social conventions – that crime does not pay, or that heterosexual romance will be consummated in marriage – central to the formation of the dominant conventions of cinema, especially classical Hollywood cinema. For Maltby and others, the self-regulatory practices of the industry in the US validated film texts that were seemingly 'innocent' but which could be read in different ways by more 'sophisticated' (or simply older) audiences, for example in such films as *Blonde Venus* (Josef von Sternberg, 1932) and *Casablanca* (Michael Curtiz, 1942). The work of these scholars suggests that we must consider the productive effects of censorship and self-regulation on film and television texts, and more generally on shaping the general conventions of cinema and television.

Censorship must ultimately be seen as a practice of power, a form of surveillance over the ideas, images and representations circulating in particular cultures. The censorship of film and television are but examples from a broader cultural contestation over leisure space and time, stretching back to the 'dime novels', tabloid press and saloons of the nineteenth century and forwards to the **Internet** of the twenty-first century. This is centrally a concern about the leisure practices of seemingly vulnerable or, alternatively, dangerous segments of the population. It should not be forgotten, however, that 'ordinary viewers' can themselves contest representations and in the process take part in the definition of individual and group identity (for example, in the protests of gay men and women over the portrayal of lesbianism in *Basic Instinct* [Paul Verhoven, 1991]). Analysis of precise contestations around censorship will enable us to come to a better understanding of group conflicts, corporate and state power, and the possession and exercise of cultural power.

See also: classical Hollywood cinema and new Hollywood cinema; deregulation, the United Kingdom; deregulation, the United States; entertainment; pornography

References

Kuhn, A. (1988) *Cinema, Censorship and Sexuality, 1909–1925*, London: Routledge.

Maltby, R. (1983) *Harmless Entertainment: Hollywood and the Ideology of Consensus*, Metuchen, NJ: The Scarecrow Press.

LEE GRIEVESON

Certeau, Michel de

b. 1925; d. 1986

Born in Chambéry, France, Michel de Certeau took degrees in Classics and Philosophy and joined the Jesuit order in 1950. The protests and social uprising in France in 1968 nudged his research interests away from religion towards more varied social and intellectual issues, including contemporary politics. These investigations resulted in the books *Culture in the Plural* and *The Practice of Everyday Life*.

De Certeau's influence on cultural studies stems mainly from his theory of 'making do'; that is, the tactical art through which ordinary people avoid, evade and resist the imposed frameworks of a social system, such as the **class** structures described by Pierre **Bourdieu** or the culture of surveillance identified by Michel **Foucault**. For de Certeau, these popular 'tactics' were found in the creative acts of spoken language, in jokes and fables, even through the process of 'walking in the city' (see **flâneur**).

This concept of creative resistance has been taken up by John **Fiske**, Henry Jenkins and others to account for the practices of television fans who make their own meanings within an imposed framework.

References

De Certeau, M. (1998) *Culture in the Plural*, trans, Tom Conley, Minneapolis: University of Minnesota Press.
—— (1998) *The Practice of Everyday Life*, trans. Steven Randall, Berkeley: University of California Press.

WILL BROOKER

channel

A term derived from Shannon and Weaver's (1949) **sender/receiver** model of communications, channel refers to that part of a linear communication process which carries the message. A channel was originally conceived of as being technical in form – the telephone handset, wires and system – but the term now encompasses all types of human communication including the voice, body language and social institutions such as schools or churches. Although mechanistic, the concept is useful in helping break down the encoding/decoding process and identifying how the medium can affect the message and where problems or discrepancies in meaning may occur (see **encoding**).

References

Shannon, C. and Weaver, W. (1949) *The Mathematical Theory of Communication*, Champaign, IL: University of Illinois Press.

PHILIP RAYNER

character

In a similar way to the literary and theatrical traditions on which they draw, television and film are dominated by character-based **narrative** productions; like novels and other antecedent literary forms, films and television shows use the construction of characters both as a means of differentiation of one **text** from another and as a source of continuity among related texts. Television and film, also like literary character-based narratives, have at their disposal a tradition of stock characters on which they can (and do) draw.

Characters in literature may reappear in more than one text (for example, a particular detective in a series of mystery novels). This technique, which capitalizes on reader familiarity and established interest, is taken to extremes in the case of episodic television series, in which the same characters appear for weeks, months or years. In the case of television, this character continuity is part of a larger industry of repetition and serialization. Episodic television benefits from economy of scale, due in part to the reuse of sets, production personnel and actors. The longevity of television characters, while at times a sentimental matter for fans (and a matter of the manufacture of sentiment by producers), contributes to the production and marketing efficiency characteristic of episodic television in general.

Like literature, film is replete with familiar characters, many of whom are essentially instantiations of stock characters whose pre-existing familiarity and popularity provide a degree of automatic marketing. In general, film is much less episodic than television. Nevertheless, there have been important examples of episodic or quasi-episodic film production, such as early serialized fiction films and a variety of many-sequeled films. The appeal of these sequels cannot be explained entirely as a matter of character recognition, but in some cases the marketing of sequels does revolve around character. Moreover, the film and television industries have increasingly tended to merge on criteria of character recognition and even episodic production. The prime example of this merger, in both formal and economic terms, is the *Star Trek* phenomenon. The original television series was followed by a long string of film sequels, and by further television series – which, themselves, have led to feature films. Through all of this, character familiarity and 'brand loyalty' on the part of fans has facilitated the promotion and marketing of the products.

The notion of character also offers some purchase on outlying or ancillary promotional functions in the film and television industries. The **star system**, in essence, involves the creation and popularization of characters (in the guise of being the 'real' versions of the actors behind on-screen characters). The phenomenon of media celebrity in general, as it pertains to sports figures and other non-actors, operates by the creation of semi-fictional characters. Other ostensibly non-fictional characters involved in media production, such as news anchors, reporters and disc jockeys, generate a kind of product differentiation and recognizability which, like the use of overtly fictional characters in narrative texts, can, and frequently does, inspire tremendous loyalty on the part of consumers.

Further reading

Bordwell, D., Staiger J. and Thompson, K. (1985) *The Classical Hollywood Cinema: Film Style and Mode of Production to 1960*, New York: Columbia University Press.

Smith, M. (1995) *Engaging Characters: Fiction, Emotion, and the Cinema*, Oxford: Clarendon Press.

DAVID A. BLACK

chat/talk show

The **genre** of the chat or talk show in its American context has its origins in popular cultural forms such as the tabloid press, women's columns in newspapers and **melodrama** going back to the nineteenth century. The daytime chat/talk show as it is currently configured began in the late 1960s – some suggest that it was the *Phil Donahue Show*, first broadcast in November 1967, which was the template for many others that followed. Early shows were a mix of sensationalism and the liberal, youth-oriented politics of the era (civil rights, women's liberation movement, anti-war move-

ment, etc.). However, over the years they have become increasingly less political in their treatment of social issues and more personal and sensational.

The term 'chat show' or 'talk show' now includes a wide variety of programming: US shows include, for example, *Larry King Live*, the *Oprah Winfrey Show*, *Ricki Lake*, *Jerry Springer*, *David Letterman*, the *Tonight Show*, the *700 Club*, talk radio programmes like *Good Morning America* and local radio shows. Such diverse fare is united by a shared emphasis on informality in conversation rather than in scripted **discourse**. In the British context, television programmes include *Trisha*, *Kilroy*, *This Morning*, *The Big Breakfast*, *TFI Friday* and *Parkinson*. Radio phone-in programmes are a typical feature of BBC's Radio Five Live. Nevertheless, as Shattuc (1997) has argued, when people refer to chat shows, they usually mean 'issue-oriented' daytime television programmes.

According to Shattuc, 'issue-oriented' daytime television chat/talk shows in the United States can be characterized as follows: (i) their content comes from contemporary social issues and problems; (ii) such programmes are organized around audience participation; (iii) the role of an 'expert' is essential in mediating the relationships between guests, audience (both studio and televisual) and the show's host; (iv) such shows assume a largely female audience – their mode of address is therefore structured to best reach this group; and (v) chat/talk shows are produced by non-network companies for broadcast on network-affiliated stations (e.g., *Geraldo*, *Oprah Winfrey Show*, *Phil Donahue Show*). These programmes differ from evening talk shows in that the issues discussed come directly from news and current affairs with an emphasis on exploring human interest questions behind current events. Issues are discussed within a framework of personal experiences primarily taking place in the private sphere.

Audiences for daytime talk shows are actively included in each programme, mostly those in the studio but also those who are watching on television. The audience is also used to provide background reaction to discussions between guests and the show's host. Studio audiences ask questions on behalf of themselves as well as for those watching at home. While there is an appearance of spontaneity to these questions, participants are selected in advance and coached by the host and others working on the programme to ensure that they adhere to the demands of televisual production processes. Audience participation is often subordinate to the questions and responses of more authoritative figures such as the host and expert guests who tend to represent members of the educated middle classes. Daytime talk/chat show audiences are primarily made up of women, because of their scheduling as well as through their 'feminine' mode of address (personal/emotional).

American daytime talk shows are largely independent of the major television networks and relatively inexpensive to produce, but they often result in high profits. Because of their daytime scheduling, they tend to have greater freedom in terms of their content than **prime-time** programmes which are closely regulated by networks. In Britain, increased competition in the television market (with the advent of cable and satellite) has led to a number of incidents where chat/talk shows have been accused of using fake guests to ensure a steady supply of exciting programmes. This has led a number of television critics in the UK to call for tighter regulation of this genre of programming whose content they believe is becoming increasingly sensational.

See also: audience; tabloid television

References

Shattuc, J. M. (1997) *The Talking Cure: TV Talk Shows and Women*, New York: Routledge.

Further reading

Gamson, J. (1998) *Freaks Talk Back: Tabloid Talk Shows and Sexual Nonconformity*, Chicago: University of Chicago Press.
Kurtz, H. (1996) *Hot Air: All Talk, All the Time*, New York: Times Books.

CYNTHIA CARTER

children and media

The topic of children and media crosses extremely diverse fields of academic inquiry. Social concern about protecting the young from cultural representations of anti-social ideas can be traced as far back as Plato, who complained about the bad examples found in poetry (see **representation**). Historically, '**moral panics**' have been raised about the theatre, the novel, cinema, comics and, above all, television – the most popular and pervasive mass medium ever invented, to which nearly all children in the developed world have regular access. Moral panic has resurfaced most recently in concerns about children's access to **pornography** on the **Internet**.

Characterizing all these concerns are: first, a conception of children as especially vulnerable, inexperienced and helpless, and hence in need of protection; and second, a focus on the negative **effects** of media, rather than an interest in their social and cultural benefits for children. Some scholars, as in the case of adult **audience** studies, stress the competence and creativity of even very young children, in their ability to decode media messages. Such scholars look at ways in which film and television can be positive influences in children's lives.

Definitions of childhood

Underlying these debates are changing historical and social attitudes to children and childhood – which, some social theorists argue, should not be seen as synonymous. 'Children' are young human beings – people under the age of 18, according to the United Nations Declaration of the Rights of the Child (1989). 'Childhood', on the other hand, can be seen as a cultural and social construct which varies with time and place, and which, according to Philippe Aries (1962), did not come into being in the West until the seventeenth century. The modern western 'construct' of childhood is not shared in all parts of the world; it functions to separate children from adults, and to institutionalize aspects of their growth, development and care. Thus the 'invention' of childhood is associated with state interventions such as maternity and health care; the removal of children from the workforce; compulsory schooling; and legislation designed to protect children and young people from access to the same rights and freedoms as adults. Such restrictive legislation includes the ban on sales of alcohol and cigarettes to minors – and it also includes the regulation of broadcasting and film and video classification (see **censorship**).

Childhood as a biological state has also been studied by the medical and social welfare professions, which has contributed to spectacular improvements in the rates of children's physical survival in the twentieth century in the developed world. Children's well-being has historically been linked with that of their mothers, and can thus be seen as partly a **gender** issue. Maternal and child health, at least in the West, improved throughout the eighteenth and nineteenth centuries, as a result of which children became more socially valued, and began to become more prominent culturally. Particular media forms aimed specifically at children, such as children's literature, children's toys, and more recently, children's films and television programmes, are now an entrenched part of our culture. The Disney organization, for example, which produces films, cartoons, toys and merchandise aimed at children and their families, is one of the richest corporate empires in the world.

In the twentieth century, developmental psychology has added to the cultural understanding of childhood not only as a period of biological growth and development, but also as a time when the foundations for healthy emotional and cognitive functioning (see **cognitive theory**) are permanently laid down. More recently, psychologists have begun to acknowledge the role of cultural experiences, such as exposure to mass media, as significant in children's development, although still, often, as a source of possible negative influences.

Children's media

All human societies have used stories, songs, nursery rhymes and fables to help socialize their children. Many of these have been intended for adults, but are also meaningful for children – especially traditional folk and fairy tales which, before the widespread use of printing, were passed on orally but are now known primarily through their Disney versions. This has caused some concern among prophets of cultural decline. Studies of children in different societies have shown that once children are old enough to play independently with each other, without adult supervision (from around 4 years old), they develop cultural practices of their own. Games, rituals, songs and rules are passed from one generation of children to the next. Twentieth-century versions of these playground games and songs draw heavily on references to film and television, for example a skipping rhyme collected in the 1950s:

> I like coffee,
> I like tea,
> I like radio
> And TV.

Children's literature

The earliest form of mass media for children was children's books, which became widely popular, at least among middle-class children, in the nineteenth century. These included collections of traditional stories and rhymes and novels written specially for children, such as *The Secret Garden* (Frances Hodgson Burnett, 1911; most recently filmed in 1993 and televised three times for the BBC in 1952, 1960 and 1975). The effect on children of reading books, including adult books and books about violence or sex, has not been studied in the same way as have the effects of film and television. Nowadays, reading is usually seen as wholly beneficial and this probably reflects the greater prestige and cultural capital of print media, compared with film and television (see **cultural capital/cultural reproduction**). Nevertheless, in a world of increasing media convergence, many children's books become television programmes and films, and vice versa, and there is evidence of a relationship between seeing a televised version of a book, and children going on to read the original. One value of televised books, in a society where most television is still not officially archived, is that the existence of print versions helps to guarantee public accessibility of commercial video versions – an important educational consideration, and a further way of circulating cultural capital.

Children's film

Films made especially for children enjoyed a brief flowering in the first half of the twentieth century, before the arrival of television. Special programmes of dramas, serials, newsreels and cartoons were usually seen at Children's Cinema Clubs, held in cinemas at weekends. Children's film, as a way of socializing children into approved values and traditions, has been especially cherished in Eastern Europe. A more liberal form of children's film, in which the child's view may be seen as **oppositional** to the adults', is exemplified by the products of the Children's Film Foundation in the UK, for example the 1947 classic set in Australia, *Bush Christmas* (Ralph Smart). This tradition has also been established in the Middle East, for example the Iranian film *Where Is My Friend's House?* (1989), Latin America, and a number of European countries, for example, the Danish film *Me and Mama Mia* (1989). All of these films are characterized by their focus on the child's perspective, with adult characters being peripheral, if not inimical, to the child protagonist's concerns.

In recent years, children's film in the UK and the US has been largely superseded as a mass entertainment form by children's television drama and 'family films' in which children are featured, but which are aimed primarily at general audiences – for instance, *Home Alone* (Chris Columbus, 1990). However, a recent experiment by the children's department of Carlton UK Television, of making a children's film for screening in **prime time**, could help the **genre** find a new lease of life on television (*Goodnight Mr Tom*, broadcast in December 1998). The main distinction between children's films and family films is usefully made by Bazalgette and Staples (1995) as one of point of view. The children's film is told (and largely shot) from the point of view of the child protagonists (see **point of view shot**). As the authors point out, this means that the family film *Honey, I Shrunk the Kids* (Joe Johnston, 1989) would have to be renamed, 'Mum – Dad Shrunk Us', if it had been made as a children's film.

Children and television

No cultural medium has ever been so widely excoriated, or so extensively and expensively researched for harmful effects on children, as television. Despite this, watching television has been children's most popular leisure time activity in the US and the UK for the last forty years, and continues to be so, despite increasing competition from computers (see **Internet**). Television has been called a plug-in drug; a one-eyed monster; a boob-tube; a creator of couch potatoes; a stimulus to violence, greed and political apathy; a source of alienation, paranoia and anomie; a destroyer of the higher values of civilization such as reading literature and the enjoyment of art, music and theatre; a purveyor of hegemonic imperialism and the main instrument in the plan for world domination by the United States of America. It has been accused of having destroyed childhood altogether.

Positive critics of the medium have emphasized the value of television as a teacher, and as an important form of access to cultural experiences which many impoverished children would not otherwise have. Children themselves continue to vote 'Yes' with the remote control button and to describe television, as in a recent British study (Livingstone and Bovill 1999), as 'my best friend'. The division between children's continuing love of the medium and the continuing adult public **discourse** of disapproval raises questions about children's rights to participate in the debate about their own access to media. This debate goes to the heart of the academic distinction, as mentioned above, between 'childhood' as a cultural variable and 'children', who, regardless of culture, are always younger, smaller and less powerful than adult citizens. They are thus permanently excluded from adult cultural debates, unless – paradoxically – supportive adults make special institutional arrangements to let them join in.

Children's television

One special institutional arrangement for children's participation in the wider culture has been special children's television provision – as in the case of Children's BBC and Children's ITV in the United Kingdom, and the Children's Television Workshop in the United States. With the growth of **cable and satellite**, a number of specialist subscription children's channels, such as Nickelodeon and Fox Kids, have come into being. While the regulatory requirements stipulating times, quotas and, to some extent, content, for special children's programming have been described as paternalistic (see **patri-archy**), despite the fact that most of the people responsible for children's broadcasting have been women, children's television does provide a public forum within which children and their concerns can be represented as central, not peripheral (see also **regulation**).

Children's television in the United Kingdom, the United States and a number of other countries, has provided special original children's drama, such as *Grange Hill* (BBC); *Press Gang* (ITV); *Clarissa Explains it All* (Nickelodeon); special children's news, such as *Newsround* (BBC) and *Real News for Kids* (Fox); magazine programmes such as *Blue Peter* (BBC) and *The Mickey Mouse Club* (Disney Channel), in which children's own discussion of issues is combined with pop music, cartoons and charity appeals; documentaries about children caught up in adult conflicts, for instance *Newsround Specials* on the conflict in Northern Ireland (BBC); children's access programmes, such as *Wise-Up* (Channel 4); phone-ins in which children have interviewed politicians and rock stars, such as *Going Live* (BBC); and 'how-to' programmes, in which children are given ideas for other things to do, such as *Why Don't You Turn Off Your Television and Do Something Less Boring Instead* (BBC).

A long-standing programming tradition, dating from the earliest days of television, is a category of special shows for pre-school children, such as *Sesame Street* (Children's Television Workshop/PBS) in the US, and more recently, *Teletubbies* (Ragdoll Productions/BBC) in the UK, which are designed to aid early language, cognitive and social development. Such programmes are usually produced in conjunction with academic researchers and teachers. Campaigns to preserve and extend children's television as a protected space within broadcasting, have been carried out in both the United States (ACT) and Britain (BACTV/Voice of the Viewer and Listener), and have been successfully translated into legislation – an aspect of children's representation in the **public sphere**.

Children as an audience

Audience studies have become more popular in cultural studies since the ethnographic work of media scholars on television audiences in the 1980s (see **ethnography**). Children as an audience have been studied for much longer than this by social scientists, particularly, as already mentioned, as potential victims of harmful effects. The most frequent area of concern for this research has been the impact of **violence**, and a number of experiments and observational studies were carried out in the 1960s and 1970s to see whether exposure to filmed violence led to children copying aggressive behaviour. Despite some evidence of short-term imitative effects in some children (mainly, though not exclusively, boys), and some evidence of weak statistical correlation between watching television and negative social attitudes, the effects research tradition has never succeeded in convincing cultural studies scholars that media have direct, measurable, harmful 'effects' – or indeed, that such questions are worth researching. The equally unshakeable belief that media *do* have harmful effects – particularly on children – continues, however, to dominate press discussion of child delinquency, as in the case of murders carried out by schoolchildren in the United States and Britain. This continuing press discourse provides evidence of an indirect media 'effect', working diffusely through the press and public sphere. This effect sustains the tradition of 'moral panics' about **technological change** in media, and its impact on children, partly by tapping into genuine parental and pedagogic worries, and partly by fuelling long-standing populist fears both of the new and of the young.

Those who are specifically interested in children in their own right, whether from a behavioural, emotional, cognitive or cultural perspective – or all of these – have come particularly from a tradition of educational research (see Bazalgette and Buckingham 1995). In this tradition, the concern is to establish the cultural contribution of mass media to children's learning and literacy in the broadest sense, including social attitudes and identity formation, as well as their ability to grasp concepts of genre, **narrative** and **metalanguage**. Scholars combining these concerns with a cognitive psychological tradition, on both sides of the Atlantic (Davies 1997) and also in Australia, Israel and Japan, have focused on 'media literacy' – the study of children's understanding of the techniques, 'grammar' and **aesthetics** of film and television, as related to their judgements about content and ideological meanings (see **ideology and hegemony**). This tradition looks at children's cognitive development in terms of their understanding of reality and fantasy, their 'theories of mind' about intentionality and **authorship**, and their ability to distinguish differing degrees of **realism**, credibility and representational **verisimilitude**. These abilities, like many other cognitive processes, appear to improve and diversify with age.

The relationship of children to different forms of media has always been a site of cultural struggle where competing disciplines and ideologies clash. Allied to a desire on the part of many adults to keep their children safe and innocent for as long as possible is an equally powerful tendency in growing children to want to try out taboo experiences and to explore adult 'secrets' through media. This relationship, traditionally negotiated privately, has now become public. The socialization of children through culture is no longer conducted primarily in a local community through stories and practices handed on from parent to child; it is now commodified, conducted through toys, books, films, television shows and computer games produced by commercial organizations. Children have become consumers – valued clients of big corporations (see **commodification**).

The relationship of children to culture is also part of a long-standing struggle about the kinds of messages and images that the whole of society should be allowed to have access to: should a concern for children be allowed to limit the freedom of adults to see and hear whatever they want to, whenever they want to? Traditionally the answer has been – 'yes', up to a point, hence mechanisms such as the 9 p.m. **watershed** in British television, and the film and video classification system. However, new technology such as satellite and cable television and the Internet are making local regulations more difficult to enforce, and access by children to forbidden material harder to police.

One safeguard, as in the past, does seem to be that children, given reasonably supportive environments (including the support of one another – as is the case even with very materially deprived children, such as street children), often seem able to navigate most of their contacts with legitimate forms of adult culture, including representational ones, without permanent harmful effects. It is clearly important for parents, teachers and health workers to identify any harmful effects that come to light in the cases of particular individuals (for instance, fear reactions), and for media producers to be aware of such possible effects. But it is difficult to legislate for each and every one of these cases. It also seems important to help children develop the skills of navigating their culture, by offering them cultural representations which suggest how to do it. The most effective of these representations are likely to be in forms congenial to children – forms which are playful and comprehensible.

The signposting of the path to maturity has been one of the prime functions of storytelling since the beginnings of human society; film and television for children continue this function.

See also: broadcasting, the United Kingdom; broadcasting, the United States; deregulation, the United Kingdom; deregulation, the United States

References

Aries, P. (1962) *Centuries of Childhood*, London: Pimlico.

Bazalgette, C. and Buckingham, D. (eds) *In Front of the Children: Screen Entertainment and Young Audiences*, London: BFI Publishing.

Davies, M. M. (1997) *Fake, Fact and Fantasy: Children's Interpretations of Television Reality*, Mahwah, NJ: Lawrence Erlbaum Associates.

Livingstone, S. and Bovill, M. (1999) *Young People, New Media*, London: London School of Economics and Political Science.

Further reading

Buckingham, D. Davies, H., Jones, K. and Kelley, P. (1999) *Children's Television in Britain*, London: BFI Publishing.

Davies, M. M. (1989) *Television is Good for your Kids*, London: Hilary Shipman.

Home, A. (1993) *Into the Box of Delights: A History of Children's Television in the UK*, London: BBC.

Kline, S. (1993) *Out of the Garden: Toys and Children's Culture in the Age of TV Marketing*, London: Verso.

Opie, I. and Opie, P. (1959) *The Lore and Language of Schoolchildren* (revised 1986), Oxford: Oxford University Press.

Staples, T. (1997) *All Pals Together: The Story of Children's Cinema*, Edinburgh: Edinburgh University Press.

MáIRE MESSENGER DAVIES

cinema of attractions

Published in 1986, during the first decade of the serious scholarly study of the pre-Hollywood cinema, Tom Gunning's important and influential article, 'The Cinema of Attractions: Early Film, its Spectator and the Avant-Garde', pinpointed what the author believed to be the chief and crucial distinction between the early cinema (1894–1907) and the filmmaking styles that succeeded it. Early cinema, according to Gunning, 'was not dominated by the narrative impulse that later asserted its sway over the medium' (1990: 56), and was less 'a way of telling stories' than 'a way of presenting a series of views to an audience' (*ibid.*: 57). Gunning borrowed the term 'cinema of attractions' from Sergei **Eisenstein** to indicate that the early cinema sought an exhibitionist confrontation with the spectator instead of his/her diegetic absorption (see **diegesis**). Unlike the omniscient narrators of realist novels and the classical Hollywood cinema (see **realism; classical Hollywood cinema and new Hollywood cinema**), the early cinema restricted **narrative** to a particular point of view, that of the camera observing the **pro-filmic event** (see **point of view shot**). For this reason, the early cinema evoked a different relationship between the spectator and the screen: rather than being absorbed in a narrative, early film viewers tended to be more interested in the cinema as visual spectacle than as storyteller.

The relative lack of concern for narrative is indicated by the fact that non-fiction films, known then as actualities (see **actuality**), outnumbered fiction films until at least 1904 and perhaps later. Following in the tradition of other contemporary media such as dioramas, postcards and stereopticon views, these films permitted the spectator access to sights and events around the world: famous landmarks, world's fairs, military encounters, royal occasions and the exotic '**Other**'. One of the most popular forms of actuality was the 'phantom ride', a tracking shot taken from the front of a moving train, subway carriage or other form of transport, which reproduced the sensation of travelling through space even as the spectator remained motionless in his/her seat. Even in fiction films, early filmmakers presented their films to the viewer as if they were carnival barkers touting their wares, rather than disguising their presence through cinematic conventions as their successors were to do. This tendency is most apparent in performers playing directly to the camera, as if on stage in a vaudeville theatre or music hall. This rupturing of the diegesis is also seen in the 'trick film', predicated on cinematic special effects – slow motion, reverse motion, stop action substitution. French filmmaker Georges Méliès, whose most famous film is *Trip to the Moon* (1902), specialized in these trick films. Even films which did tell stories were not tremendously concerned about integrating each shot into an unfolding narrative. The Edison Film Company's catalogue copy for *The Great Train Robbery* (Edwin S. Porter, 1903) told exhibitors that the famous medium shot of a bandit shooting directly at the camera could be inserted at either the beginning or the end of the film.

Gunning's formulation of the concept of the cinema of attractions was perhaps the most coherent statement to date of the fundamental credo of those who had begun to specialize in the study of the early cinema. These scholars rejected the hitherto dominant teleological assumption that filmmakers such as Méliès and Porter were important only in so far as their films resembled the established conventions of the classical Hollywood cinema. Conceived of as a cinema of attractions rather than a cinema of narrative integration, the early cinema could now be seen as separate from but equal to its successor. But Gunning also insisted that 'the cinema of attractions does not disappear with the dominance of narrative, but rather goes underground, both into certain **avant-garde** practices and as a component of narrative films, more evident in some genres (e.g., the musical), than in others' (*ibid.*: 57; see **musical, the**). Of course, as Gunning acknowledges, Laura **Mulvey** had already pointed to a tension between narrative and spectacle in the classical Hollywood cinema, in which, she argued, the contemplation of the female form and the visual pleasure it affords (at least to the male spectator) freezes the action. In the late twentieth and early twenty-first centuries, the concept of the cinema of attractions seems yet more relevant with regard to certain genres of the post-classical Hollywood cinema: action-adventure films with the spectacular stunts of their shoot-outs and car chases and science fiction films with the spectacular special effects of their space battles and alien worlds. Indeed, so extreme has this tendency become that many critics complain that characters and storytelling have been lost amid the welter of attractions which the cinema now affords.

References

Gunning, T. (1990) 'The Cinema of Attractions: Early Film, its Spectator and the Avant-Garde', in Thomas Elsaesser (ed.) *Early Cinema: Space, Frame, Narrative*, London: BFI Publishing.

Further reading

Gunning, T. (1990) 'Non-Continuity, Continuity, Discontinuity: A Theory of Genres in Early Films', in Thomas Elsaesser (ed.) *Early Cinema: Space, Frame, Narrative*, London: BFI Publishing.
—— (1996) ' "Now You See It, Now You Don't": The Temporality of the Cinema of Attractions', in Richard Abel (ed.) *Silent Film*, New Brunswick: Rutgers University Press, 1996.
—— (1990) ' "Primitive" Cinema: A Frame-Up? Or, the Trick's on Us', in Thomas Elsaesser (ed.) *Early Cinema: Space, Frame, Narrative*, London: BFI Publishing.

ROBERTA E. PEARSON

cinéma-vérité

Cinéma-vérité is interactionist cinema – 'flies in the soup' – as opposed to observational/direct cinema – 'flies on the wall'. The term is a French translation of Dziga **Vertov**'s title for his newsreels, *Kino-pravda* ('Film-truth'). The filmmaker is, then, an avowed participant in his/her own film. Jean Rouch, and his collaborative work with Edgar Morin, for example *Chronique d'un été* (1961), are representatives of this movement. The camera and the filmmakers are to elicit truth by acting as a catalyst, to provoke people to articulate a truth that is more revealing than the everyday truth.

CINDY WONG

cinematic apparatus

The term 'cinematic apparatus' usually refers to a particular psychoanalytic model of spectatorship based on an analysis of the basic conditions of film reception. The theory was originally formulated by the French film theorist Jean Louis Baudry, but the term itself has been often used to designate the related psychoanalytical theories of Christian **Metz** and Laura **Mulvey**. Although these initial psychoanalytical formulations have been systematically revised over the years, they are none the less credited for initiating theoretical interest in the analysis of spectatorship within film studies.

In broad outline, the theory of the cinematic apparatus consists of an effort to extend the theory of the ideological state apparatus as advanced by Louis **Althusser** to the realm of the cinema. Baudry maintained that the basic conditions of reception rigidly delimit spectatorial response, and he identified three particular determinations which play a significant role in this process: (i) technological determinations arising from the capacity of the projector to represent an illusion of three-dimensional space on screen; (ii) architectural determinations deriving from the arrangement of elements within the space of the film theatre; and (iii) psychological determinations originating from the unconscious mechanisms of the film spectator (see **determination**).

While these three points of determination are analytically distinguished, they were none the less interrelated within Baudry's overall framework. The illusion of three-dimensional space confers an impression of reality on to the fictional world represented on screen. As a result of unconscious drives, this impression of reality in turn induces the film spectator to regress into a childlike state, into what the psychoanalyst Jacques **Lacan** has described as the **imaginary** phase (see **regression**). In such a state, the spectator relives fantasies of plenitude and unity that pleasurably reassure his or her sense of identity. Facilitating this whole process is the whole architectural arrangement of the theatre that hides the projector from view, thereby ensuring that the technical machinery through which the image is noisily produced does not distract attention from the fictional world represented on screen. Other aspects of the theatre, such as its envelopment in darkness during projection and its fixed seating arrangement, are also held to facilitate spectatorial regression. The ultimate ideological function of all these elements working together is to position the spectator into the site of a transcendental subject, a socially constructed position of social identity through which the spectator comes to understand the world and his or her own place in it (see **subject and subjectivity**).

While Baudry's formulation of the cinematic apparatus was widely influential during the 1970s within film theory, its status has since greatly diminished. Three particular problems with his account can be credited with the theory's downfall. First, Baudry's theory appeared to be fundamentally incapable of accounting for the actual diversity of spectatorial response. In his framework, the spectator is stripped of any social or cultural identity and is reduced to a few unconscious mechanisms. Elided from his account, then, is any description of the ways in which **gender**, **race** or **sexuality** may affect film spectatorship. Equally problematic is Baudry's theoretical reliance on only one historical variant of film exhibition. Yet as investigations into film reception demonstrated, the reverse was the case in that throughout the history of the cinema the conditions of exhibition have varied considerably, both historically and culturally. Film theatres have not necessarily been darkened chambers, nor has the projection machinery always been hidden from the view of the spectator. Lastly, Baudry sought the ideological dimension of the cinema at too fundamental a level. By postulating ideological determinations within the very machinery of the cinema, the theory was incapable of

distinguishing politically progressive films from that of the reactionary.

See also: ideology and hegemony; institution; psychoanalysis

Further reading

Baudry, J. L. (1986) 'Ideological Effects of the Basic Cinematographic Apparatus' and 'The Apparatus: Metapsychological Approaches to the Impression of Reality', both essays reprinted in J. L. Baudry, *Narrative, Apparatus, Ideology*, ed. Philip Rosen, New York: Columbia University Press, pp. 286–98, 299–318 (originally published in French, 1970 and 1975 respectively).

TICO ROMAO

Cixous, Hélène

b. 1937

Hélène Cixous was born in Oran, Algeria. Embodying a distinctive brand of feminist philosophy, her broad body of work straddles a number of cultural forms. Whether manifested in her literary criticism and work on **psychoanalysis** and linguistics, her fiction, plays or her expressly theoretical texts, Cixous' ideas are invariably concerned with notions of woman's expression and **identity**. Having established a pioneering centre for Feminine Studies at a Paris university in 1974, Cixous set about redefining feminism from a psychoanalytic perspective. Opposed to the stringently social perspective of traditional Anglo-American feminism, Cixous' work argues for the existence and fostering of an inherently feminine form of writing.

According to this logic, Cixous celebrates a theory of *écriture féminine* ('feminine writing'), a style of poetic writing that is able to reflect and embrace the difference of the **Other**. This type of expression relates, in Cixous' rhetoric, to ideas of authenticity and essential womanhood. When applied to the moving image, this inherently gendered style of writing can be equated to a form of audio-visual expression that is similarly concerned with questioning the types of **narrative** structure founded on patriarchal language (see **gender; patriarchy**).

See also: Derrida, Jacques; feminist theory; Irigaray, Luce; Kristeva, Julia

Further reading

Sellers, S. (ed.) (1994) *The Hélène Cixous Reader*, New York: Routledge.

ANDREW UTTERSON

class

Since the emergence of cinema and television as mass media, their production, texts, distribution and audiences have raised complicated questions about class, **consciousness** and conflict. Sometimes perceived either as vehicles for lower-class sensibilities or as illusions for the disenfranchised, critics and theorists generally have identified both channels of communication with 'popular' as opposed to elite taste (represented by **'art'** films and 'serious' television). The resources necessary to produce and distribute both media, their profits and their ties to further **consumption**, nevertheless have linked them to economic or political elites. Indeed, in addition to their claims to be art, **myth** and information, films and television are also commodities caught up in exchanges that shape class relations. Yet texts, whether depicting heroic workers or bourgeois norms, incorporate many stories and forms of presentations, reaching and appealing to diverse audiences. Hence, media have been appropriated as well by lower classes, **oppositional** readings, revolutionary cinema, independent and grass-roots production, and public access broadcasting. Thus, Jeffery Richards asserts that cinema is 'a common culture which flourished within the pre-existing boundaries of class, gender and region. It transcended those boundaries, without eliminating or lessening their social significance' (1994: 147).

This is not to suggest class dominates **theory** to the same extent that recent criticism has foregrounded **race**, **gender** or ethnic identity (see **ethnicity**). In fact, the editors of *The Hidden Foundation* (James and Berg 1996) note that class

was dropped by the American Society for Cinema Studies in the name of its Task Force on Race and Class in 1989. Yet, class remains embedded in studies of ideology and reception, in intersections of race and gender, and in studies of genres like gangster films or grass-roots **documentary** with strong class referents (see **genre; ideology and hegemony; reading and reception theory**).

All these arguments depend on diverse definitions of class. In a general Marxist paradigm, class refers to both the situation of producers in relation to the means of production – essentially as owner or workers – and the collective consciousness and actions they develop (see **Marxist aesthetics; paradigmatic**). For media as well as Marxist theory, class is linked to struggle as well as concealment of this struggle through ideology. This dual meaning of classes in conflict produces apparently paradoxical situations of film as tools of domination in 'proletarian' regimes or as products consumed by those who disagree with them. Hence, any discussion of class must allow for contradictions – including undeveloped or false consciousness – as well as ambivalent positions. Is the mom-and-pop store owner, the manager or the small businessman closer to the owners or the workers? Do the class positions of children reproduce their parents; or are those of women the same as men in a system based on male placement? Are some categories – whether intellectuals or outlaws – outside the class system in interesting ways? In fact, contradictions are the stuff of movies grappling with class as a **narrative** question, from Charlie Chaplin's films to *Stella Dallas* (King Vidor, 1937) to *Romuald and Juliette* (Coline Serreau, 1989)

Economic positions, however, intersect with other structures and categories of power. In Max **Weber**'s model, class is linked to status, entailing both power and recognition within society, although this again involves negotiating individual trajectories and group solidarity. Another social perspective entails the recognition of consumption as a feature in contemporary class identification, as analysed by Pierre **Bourdieu** (1984). Again, this has dual implications for film both as portrayals of consumption – in, for example, costume dramas – and as a commodity consumed across class lines.

Both perspectives remind us that film and television are complex capitalist enterprises.

Beyond definitions and structures, we must recognize that many interlocking aspects of film and television may be analysed in terms of class. Texts raise fundamental questions of **representation** and form, generally dealt with in terms of ideology. Yet, these must also be linked to production and **agency**. Critics interested in class are also concerned with **audience** – who it is, how the media invent it and how the media are read across classes. Given these many possibilities, this entry will only focus on two primary areas of class identities and conflicts – media and power and media and the disenfranchised.

Media and power

Consider *Titanic* (James Cameron, 1997), a film at once hugely expensive and hugely remunerative globally. Within the straightforward Hollywood plot, upper-class people promote catastrophic situations, while happy steerage passengers dance and sing on their way to America. Love conquers class antagonisms, as a working-class boy meets and redeems a vulnerable upper-class girl (with the help of a newly enriched woman). Yet he dies, along with those below decks, while the rich, cultured girl – and some evil upper-class companions – survive. Despite the happiness of workers, **spectacle** is embodied in the elite. In addition, the romance, to some women who saw the film repeatedly, came through the girl who had love, beauty and then a varied and successful life, not through revolution. As such, *Titanic* conveyed typical messages of unhappy rich and happy poor that justify the romance of the *status quo*. Who leaves the movie wishing they had drowned in steerage?

However, who is the agent here? How is this message produced, who gains and how? Obviously, these actors are not really portraying their own class position – these are parts, in the same way working-class lads like Cary Grant or Fred Astaire came to embody American sophistication. Nor were the director and screenwriter members of the upper class, although they were wealthy as a result. Those who provided finances spent and gained even more; studios are increasingly part of big

business **multinational** conglomerates like Sony, GE or News Corporation. Yet, we should avoid reductionism while noting that overall, the film, while not explicitly propaganda by and for an elite, at the same time generally does not attack them in a forceful way. Hollywood is part of the reproduction of American capitalism in many ways.

This illustrates the complications of ideology, the logical models underpinning explanation and acceptance of 'the way things are'. Many film theories have concentrated on the examination of ideology based on the construction of a subject-position (see **subject and subjectivity**) and the **cinematic apparatus**, whereby Laura **Mulvey**, for example, 'constructed' male spectatorship, rather than bourgeois spectatorship. Moving away from ahistorical psychoanalytic **semiotics**, the intersections of production, text and reception become more complicated. Obviously, for example, Hollywood (Bollywood, Paris, etc.) also sell glamour on and off screen: stars inhabit opulent settings and don fabulous outfits. Yet the extreme rich are often depicted as evil or unhappy as well (as in the long-running Latin American soap opera, *The Rich Also Cry*). But do these works spur revolution? While ideology seems to mask the contradictions of the social system, in a film or television text, contradictions abound that legitimate and reconstitute society.

Hegemony, a concept proposed by the Italian theorist Antonio **Gramsci**, proves useful here (see **ideology and hegemony**). Hegemony refers to the strategic construction of social support for institutions and actions based on the propagation of an ideology that can embrace those in class positions opposed to it. Stories about the evil rich/noble poor and the widespread naturalization of the middle-class viewpoint represent ways of seeing the world, with a concrete political economic foundation. Still, audiences do not watch passively: they use contradictions in texts to construct oppositional readings and to reject messages (and media products).

Perhaps the most difficult concept to deal with in cinema and television criticism (and contemporary Marxist theory) is in fact the growing 'middle class', especially as understood within an American culture that generally avoids discussions of class. Whether it is the white suburban domestic family of 1950s sitcoms or the ambience of ordinariness underpinning movies from the Andy Hardy films (George B. Seitz/Willis Goldbeck/Howard Koch, 1937–1958) to *Ordinary People* (Robert Redford, 1980), American media have reflected and reproduced middling classes in their premises and values. Even the structure of linear narrative, psychological credibility and narrative **closure** in classical Hollywood cinema have been related to issues of bourgeois control and values (see **classical Hollywood cinema and new Hollywood cinema**).

Television studies also talk frequently about constructions of domesticity and the middle-class family in the US from the 1950s family situation comedies (*Donna Reed*, *Father Knows Best*) to the *Cosby Show* and 1990s non-family sit-coms (*Seinfeld*, *Ellen*). Middle-class television families never worry about money, while most live in nice, spacious apartments/ houses with easily resolved dilemmas, whether suburban whites, black families or urbanite gay bachelors. All portray a certain lifestyle as good, moral, valued and 'normal'. Alternatives may be found in soap operas such as *EastEnders* or rare shows with more political messages, including episodes of *Roseanne* and *All in the Family* (see **soap opera**). Audiences may also read these texts critically, against the realities of their own lives and the contradictory messages that texts, sponsors and stars convey.

Class also intersects with race, gender, sexuality, age and ethnicity, involving both hegemonic strategies and oppositional readings/actions. **African-American cinema** in the United States, for example, was regarded for decades as a cinema of the disenfranchised, echoing the roles that blacks were generally forced into in a white-dominated society. Yet, from Oscar Micheaux to contemporary films like *Waiting to Exhale* (Forest Whitaker, 1995), black cinema has dealt with the dilemmas of a black bourgeoisie set apart by education, diction and skin colour. Echoing representations of other ethnic and immigrant traditions, the same family in George Tillman Jnr's film *Soul Food* (1997) juxtaposes criminals and professionals, with expectations divided by gender and generation, yet both inside and outside mainstream conventions. Globally, the intersection of class with race, gender and status pervades *beur* cinema in France and

underlies the divisions revealed and concealed in Brazilian cinema.

Power relations among nations also shape global class relations played out in cinema and television as a commodity. Writing on the popularity of Hollywood among working-class British, for example, V. F. Perkins observes: 'If the clients were an undiscriminating class, their supply came from a whole society that was said to lack class and culture' (1992: 197). While elite Europeans denigrated American class and culture, American influence permeated Europe not only through economic and military power, but also via media disseminating the American dream throughout the world. Here, the message of Hollywood glamour, television's sagas of exaggerated wealth (*Dallas*, *Dynasty*) or the everyday comfort of soap operas and situation comedies took on different class meanings depending on readings in Belfast, Buenos Aires or Bombay. In other national cinematic traditions, class lines have been drawn in different ways, yet while contemporary Iranian cinema provides sharp contrasts in its use of non-actors, children and peasant settings, its products become 'art' films in a global market.

Audience studies elaborate on the complexity of class and reading by grappling with reflective agents as well as mass readership. Again, ideological strategies and contradictions are especially important features of class as process, especially when broadcast television and current film productions cater to fragmented masses, targeting audiences from different backgrounds. Building new inner-city cinemas in African-American neighbourhoods, for example, echoes the marketing of a black middle class on television. Does this respond to real changes in life opportunity or merely reaffirm a segregated consumption that divides American society? Do whites and blacks receive the same messages? Moreover, while black and ethnic audiences define narrowcast groups, they also attend mainstream blockbusters like *Star Wars Episode 1: The Phantom Menace* (1996), with its visions of white domination and stereotyped servants and enemies. Hence, these viewers must balance film and lives through experience as well as through ideological messages.

Working-class media

This section deals with a more explicitly politicized discourse. Mattelart and Seigelaub's *Communication and Class Struggle* (1979), for example, views communications as a battlefield of domination and resistance in capitalist society, adducing **Marx**, Lenin, Gramsci and others as foundation for study. Intellectuals as theorists and critics in the service of class conflict define a position especially important in working-class analysis, demanding historical and cultural analysis of production, text and reading and non-elite voices.

In the early days of cinema, producers and critics worried about how to appeal to mass audiences and, at the same time, what that appeal meant. Critical theorists have researched the implications of the nickelodeon, neighbourhood cinemas and popular film across cultures for insights into the shaping of the twentieth-century working class. Uricchio and Pearson (1993), for example, show how Vitagraph consciously sought to reshape silent cinema into something whose claims of culture were more appealing to middle-class sensibilities. Ross (1997) has explored the complicated traditions of working-class orientation in silent filmmaking that were eclipsed with the consolidation of the studio system in the 1930s. Not only does he include sympathetic depictions by filmmakers such as D. W. Griffith, but he also includes politically motivated filmmaking and distribution like that which created a documentary on the Gastonia Textile Strike. None the less, economic and political shifts forced this practice underground, when McCarthyism made leftist associations of class struggle anathema. Scattered oppositional films still have appeared in the US, including *Salt of the Earth* (Herbert J. Biberman, 1953), *Harlan County USA* (Barbara Koppel, 1976) and *Matewan* (John Sayles, 1987).

Shifts in production do not eliminate later working-class voices. British cultural studies, for example, has reinserted class and opposition into readings (Turner 1990). Sara Dickey (1993) explores broad audience identification with stars (who become politicians) and texts in South Indian films through careful ethnography. In other cases, films may have intertextual meanings – figures like Chaplin, Cantinflas, Sylvester Stallone, Roseanne

Barr or Chow Yun Fat have emerged as working-class heroes. Certain genres also vividly recreate working-class struggles. Gangster films, for example, show the poor striving to be rich and being punished for doing it in the wrong way. Road films have also driven along class lines, from *It Happened One Night* (Frank Capra, 1934) to *Thelma and Louise* (Ridley Scott, 1991). The latter film also raises the question of class in certain women's genres, especially ones which emphasize the long-suffering wife or the fallen woman. Even so, these issues are not located in films *made* by a working class.

The trajectory of film under capitalism should not be taken as the only model for working-class voices. Some cinematic traditions also emerged which took on much more political overtones, viewing cinema as an element on the side of proletarian consciousness in the class struggle. This would be especially identified with Marxist cinema in the Soviet Union and later Marxist regimes, for example, from **Eisenstein** to Andrzej Wajda of Poland, the filmmakers of China after 1949, or modern Cuba. Here, the rhetoric of the filmmakers themselves often refers to a sense of service in and for the popular revolution, which permeates thematic choices, depictions of heroes and villains in class terms, and political messages more or less central to the texts. Yet, scholars have also underscored contradictions as class intersected with other divisions in these societies. Hence Judith Mayne, re-examining the Golden Age of Soviet film from the perspective of feminism, notes that 'in the oppositions of class conflict and nature and culture, women function in similar ways, whether it be to disrupt the category of class as a neat and clear-cut opposition or to problematise the easy fit between nature and culture' (1989: 64).

Independent productions provide another route for working-class expression. Documentaries like Barbara Koppel's *Harlan County USA* explore working-class lives and actions from a sympathetic political standpoint. Yet, class can be manipulated: for example, in *Roger and Me* (1989) director Michael Moore championed workers of Flint, Michigan in opposition to owners, yet he also provided unsympathetic portrayals of people of lower cultural capital. These films must also struggle with canons of objectivity that can straitjacket documentary and news as presentations of a middle-class 'reality' rather than alternatives to it (see **canon**).

Guerrilla cinema, Third World filmmaking (see **Third Cinema**) and Fourth World indigenous filmmaking suggest other relations between people and media. A self-consciously rough style, including the use of hand-held cameras and video, and direct political content converge to make film a tool in the class struggle, although often as a vehicle of reflection as well as action. None the less, the 'authentic' style of *Memories of Underdevelopment* (Tomás Gutiérrez Alea, 1968) can be copied in mainstream television like *NYPD Blue*, blurring form, agency and meanings.

Similarly, community or grass-roots media that facilitate democratizing practices offer another alternative to mainstream media. Here, films and videos are made by groups defined by their position outside power structures, usually, but not exclusively, working class. While the textual strategies of such groups are very often fairly mainstream, the content and message are sometimes related to their own situation and run counter to established discourses. Such works may reach only limited audiences for the purpose of consciousness as well as community building. The idea of television from a working-class base is even more problematic, since it entails not only production but also **access** to distribution. Again, associations with the television of socialist countries often exacerbate problems of control apparent in cinema. Public television and cable television may give more access to non-mainstream producers in the United States and other western countries, but these groups do not control the medium.

Conclusions

As this account suggests, in reviewing issues of film, television and class that have shaped theory in the past (and a proposed agenda for the future), we must be careful to weigh production, text and response. While film and television have reached a global diversity of audiences, as complex and expensive commodities, they remain linked to *control* of economic, political, social and cultural resources. While responses may be critical or oppositional, control of the media is more likely to be associated with upper and middle classes and ideologies of domination, especially in the capitalist system. Marxist traditions of filmmaking as well as criticism, and re-democratization through independents, Third World cinema and grass-roots video offer some alternatives for critics, producers and audiences, but problems of power and influence remain. Class, as an often-overlooked theme, none the less provides critical insights into film and television as producers and reflectors of social change.

See also: feminist theory; globalization; queer theory

References

Bourdieu, P. (1984) *Distinction: A Social Critique of the Judgement of Taste*, trans. Richard Nice, London: Routledge and Kegan Paul.

Dickey, S. (1993) *Cinema and the Urban Poor in South India*, New York: Cambridge University Press,

James, D. and Berg, R. (1996) *The Hidden Foundation: Cinema and the Question of Class*, Minnesota, MN: University of Minnesota Press.

Mattelart, A. and Siegelaub, S. (eds) (1979) *Communication and Class Struggle*, New York: International.

Mayne, J. (1989) *Kino and the Woman Question*, Columbus, OH: Ohio University Press.

Perkins, V. F. (1992) 'The Atlantic Divide', in Richard Dyer and Ginette Vincendeau (eds) *Popular European Cinema*, London: Routledge.

Richards, J. (1994) 'Cinemagoing in Worktown: Regional Film Audience in 1930s Britain', *Historical Journal of Film, Radio and Television*, vol. 14, no. 2.

Ross, S. J. (1997) *Working-class Hollywood: Silent Film and the Shaping of Class in America*, Princeton: Princeton University Press.

Turner, G. (1990) *British Cultural Studies*, Boston: Unwin Hyman.

Uricchio, W. and Pearson, R. E. (1993) *Reframing Culture: The Case of the Vitagraph Quality Films*, Princeton: Princeton University Press.

CINDY WONG AND GARY McDONOGH

classic realist text

The term 'classic realist text' was coined by Colin MacCabe in his article, 'Realism and the Cinema: Notes on Some Brechtian Theses', published in *Screen* in 1974. In the article, MacCabe proposes that **realism** in a film text is less to do with its subject matter and more to do with the **narrative** structure of the film and the way it positions the viewer in relation to the text: 'A classic realist text may be defined as one in which there is a hierarchy amongst the discourses which compose the text and this hierarchy is defined in terms of an empirical notion of truth' (MacCabe 1974: 8).

MacCabe defines the classic realist text as having two essential features:

1　The classic realist text cannot deal with the real as contradictory.
2　In a reciprocal movement, the classic realist text ensures the position of the subject in a relation of dominant specularity.

(MacCabe 1974:12)

MacCabe argues that the film's 'narration of events' is the dominant **discourse**, providing a **metalanguage** which gives the viewer access to the 'truth' not comprehended by the discourse of the characters. Thus, although contradictions may be voiced within the text by the discourses of the characters, the narrational structure ensures that these are all placed by the superior knowledge delivered to the spectator by the narrative: we know more than they can know. Furthermore, the position offered to the spectator is a unified one: not only are contradictions resolved in the text, there are no contradictions produced in the audience. The formal organization of the discourses ensures that what we perceive as the truth or reality of the text is what the film offers. We are not encouraged to consider the film's processes of constructing a 'reality' or our relationship to both the 'reality' of the film and the reality of our experience. The classic realist text offers a singular meaning or set of meanings with regard to reality, and the spectator is not challenged to work out other meanings or question the one proposed.

In arguing that discourses position subjects and can hide both their own construction and the subject's relation to the real, MacCabe is drawing on **Lacan**'s conception of the construction of identity and **Althusser**'s conception of ideology (see **ideology and hegemony; subject and subjectivity**), and therein, perhaps, lies the importance of the article. Like Laura **Mulvey**'s 'Visual Pleasure and Narrative Cinema' (1975), it represents a high point of **Screen theory**, and is a politically-charged attack on the dominant form of cinema: Hollywood. Both MacCabe's and Mulvey's articles depend on the unconscious operations of film on theorized 'spectators': though MacCabe shows some recognition in his reading of *American Graffiti* (George Lucas, 1973) of actual viewers, the 'petrification' of the spectator which he sees as a consequence of the 'reactionary practice of the cinema' ignores the complexity of the meaning-making activities of actual viewers, or assumes that the operations of the unconscious undermine them.

MacCabe acknowledges that some forms of realism may be 'progressive' – when the content goes against the **dominant ideology**, as in the films of Ken Loach, for example – or there may be moments of subversion – as in John Ford's *Young Mr Lincoln* (1939) – when there are lapses which suggest breaks with the construction of reality. But, in the films of Italian neo-realist Roberto Rossellini, he finds *strategies* of subversion:

> Instead of a dominant discourse which is transgressed at certain moments, we can find a systematic refusal of any such dominant discourse.... In *Germany Year Zero* [Rossellini, 1947], for example we can locate a multitude of ways in which the reading subject finds himself without a position from which the film can be regarded.
>
> (MacCabe 1974: 14)

In the main, though, the argument implies the need for a cinema which disturbs the unity of the spectator's position and obliges the audience to contest meanings and to recognize the illusionist nature of mainstream cinema. The Brechtian context of the debate is clear.

From *Screen* volume 16 in 1975 to *Screen* volume 34 in 1994, MacCabe's arguments have been consistently attacked on every ground – as a misrepresentation of **Brecht**, as a total misapprehension of the way Hollywood films produce meanings, and as a denial of individual and group responses to film. MacCabe claimed at the outset, though, that his notes on the classic realist text were no more than 'a set of digressions which take as their starting point some Brechtian theses'. It was a digression which many followed at the time.

References

MacCabe, C. (1974) 'Realism and the Cinema: Notes on Some Brechtian Theses', *Screen*, vol. 15, no. 2.
Mulvey, L. (1975) 'Visual Pleasure and Narrative Cinema', *Screen*, vol. 16, no. 3.

Further reading

MacCabe, C. (1976) 'Days of Hope: A Reply to Colin McArthur', *Screen*, vol. 17, no. 1.
—— (1976) 'Realism and Pleasure', *Screen*, vol. 17, no. 3.
Williams, C. (1994) 'After the Classic, the Classical and Ideology: The Differences of Realism', *Screen*, vol. 35, no. 3.

PHILIP SIMPSON

classical Hollywood cinema and new Hollywood cinema

Hollywood: development of the studio system

In 1887 Harvey Henderson Wilcox registered his 120-acre ranch in an area north-west of Los Angeles and called it 'Hollywood'. By 1903 a village had developed in the area and in 1910 the 5,000 residents voted to become a district of Los Angeles. The search for alternative film sites, other than New York and Chicago, began in 1907 as film companies sent production units to more favourable climates such as Jacksonville, Santa Fe, San Antonio and Cuba. Hollywood, due to a variety of factors, including its climate and topography which allowed year-round production in a wide range of settings including mountains, lakes and beaches, soon became the major production centre. By 1915 there were approximately 15,000 film workers in Hollywood and they produced 60 per cent of American film production.

In 1912 Thomas H. Ince, at his Inceville Studio in California, developed an 'assembly line' system of film production with a division of labour supervised by a production head. This practice was refined and developed by the film studios in California who, by the end of the 1920s, controlled the American film industry through a vertically integrated system of production, distribution and exhibition. Adolph Zukor's Famous Players-Lasky Corporation became the first vertically integrated studio when it purchased a distribution company, Paramount Film Corporation, in 1917. **Vertical integration** was achieved by five studios, the 'majors', over the next eleven years: Metro-Goldywn-Mayer in 1924, the Fox Film Corporation in 1925, Warner Brothers in 1926, and RKO in 1928. The three 'little majors', Columbia, Universal (formed by Carl Laemmle in 1912) and United Artists were also active during this period although they did not purchase theatres. Annette Kuhn estimates that during the 'golden age' of the studio period, from 1930 to 1948, these eight studios controlled 95 per cent of all films exhibited in the United States (Cook 1985: 10).

From 'primitive' to classical

The 'primitive' period of film production in the US extends from the commercial origins of the cinema in 1894 to approximately 1906–8 when, according to Kristin Thompson, there was a decisive shift in the conceptual basis of filmmaking. This change, Thompson argues, was not due to 'either a growing sophistication or a discovery of a natural "grammar" of the medium' but resulted from a major shift in assumptions about the relation of the 'spectator to film and the relation of a film's form to its style' (Bordwell *et al.* 1985: 158). The primitive cinema assumed that a member of the audience was spatially equivalent to his/her counterpart in the theatre. Consequently, the film spectator prior to 1906 was normally placed at a distance from the space of the action and was constituted as looking into this space. In the primitive cinema, for example, the filmmaker provided few cues to direct the spectator's attention and there was little of the redundancy of narrative information which characterizes the classical cinema.

While the primitive viewer experienced a

continuous stretch of time or discrete blocks of time in one-shot scenes, the classical spectator is guided by a range of stylistic techniques which places him/her within, or on the edge of, the **narrative** space. These classical devices are designed to extend that space out towards the plane of the camera as well as shift the spectator's viewpoint periodically into the narrative space. This process is enhanced by increasing the depth of the playing area, greater three-dimensionality of the sets and other stylistic cues, such as lighting and camera composition, to direct spectator attention away from the actual system of narration and towards the story itself (Bordwell *et al*. 1985: 158).

The basis of this change, Thompson argues, came from the adaptation of aesthetic norms found in the nineteenth-century short story, novel and the well-made play. Thompson emphasizes the significance of Edgar Allan Poe's 1842 review of Nathaniel Hawthorne's *Twice Told Tales* and his dictum that a short story, being designed to be read at one sitting, should be characterized by 'the unity of effect or impression' (Bordwell *et al*. 1985: 167). This principle was influential in playwriting manuals later in the century which stressed unity through **motivation** and continuity of action. In 1912 playwriting expert William Archer further advocated that a 'bridge should be provided between one act and another, along which the spectator's mind cannot but travel with eager anticipation' (Bordwell *et al*. 1985: 170). Thompson writes:

> Although conceptions of unity differed somewhat for the short story, novel, and drama, they boiled down to a similar notion. The artwork was to be organised around a single central factor – an intended impression, a theme. No unrelated elements were admissible, and the elements that were present should be motivated. Such ideas were common currency by the time that studios began hiring professional writers from other fields, buying the rights to literary works, and soliciting freelance scenarios from the public.
>
> (Bordwell *et al*. 1985: 170)

Melodrama and the classical Hollywood cinema

In 1922 Hollywood director Frank Borzage pointed out that 'today in the pictures we have the old melodramatic situations fitted out decently with true characterisations'. David **Bordwell** cites Borzage to support his argument that the short story 'struck an average between the fixed character types of the melodrama and the dense complexity of the realist novel, and this average appealed to the classical Hollywood cinema during its formative years' (Bordwell *et al*. 1985: 14). However, theatrical **melodrama** provided Hollywood cinema with more than just 'fixed character types'. Christine Gledhill, for example, concludes that 'twentieth-century popular culture's melodramatic inheritance must be traced through the passage of European melodrama to America, for its transformation there was arguably a determining factor in the emergence of Hollywood aesthetics and its later international power' (Gledhill 1987: 24).

Melodrama, particularly nineteenth-century theatrical melodrama, was influential in the 'emergence of Hollywood **aesthetics**' in many ways, especially its narrative structure. Hollywood absorbed the melodramatic imagination, with its moral Manichaeism, producing a heightened and polarized cinematic mode. The classical Hollywood film is polarized both vertically and horizontally as characters represent moral extremes while undergoing extremes, passing from dramatic heights to depths within a form that is not content merely to record and describe actions. The melodramatic imagination constantly pressures the surface reality to yield its true, ethical, meaning so that by the point of **closure**, **desire** has achieved its full satisfaction:

> No shadow dwells, and the universe bathes in the full, bright lighting of moral Manichaeism. Hence the psychic bravado of virtue, its expressive breakthrough, serves to assure us again and again, that the universe is in fact morally legible, that it possesses an ethical identity and significance. This assurance must be a central function of melodrama in the post-sacred universe: it relocates and rearticulates the most basic moral sentiments and celebrates the sign of the right.
>
> (Brooks 1995: 43)

Peter Brooks, in *The Melodramatic Imagination*, argues that melodrama, including its cinematic manifestation, is a form for a post-sacred era, in which 'polarisation and hyperdramatisation of forces in conflict represent a need to locate and make evident, legible, and operative those large choices of ways of being which we hold to be of overwhelming importance even though we cannot derive them from any transcendental system of belief' (Brooks 1995: viii). The classical Hollywood cinema assumes the existence of a world threatened by the 'suborners of morality' and its fundamental Manichaeism extends to the entire repertoire of dramatic signs, visual and aural. Polarization is not only 'a dramatic principle but the very means by which integral ethical conditions are identified and shaped, made clear and operative' (Brooks 1995: 36). The specific social values and assumptions which constituted these 'integral ethical conditions' were elaborated in the 1930 Production Code which was highly influential in shaping the narrative structure of the Hollywood cinema between 1930 and 1968.

The Production Code and the system of classical Hollywood narration

In 1930 the Motion Picture Production Code proclaimed that no 'picture shall be produced which will lower the moral standards of those who see it. Hence the sympathy of the audience shall never be thrown to the side of crime, wrong-doing, evil or sin'. The Studio Relations Committee, an industry board responsible for implementing the Code, advocated that the studios pass moral judgements on all characters for the benefit of the audience. During the period 1930 to 1934 the most common method of implementing this system of **censorship** involved some form of final retribution, although there were sporadic attempts to provide intermittent denunciation scenes admonishing 'immoral' characters. This practice was referred to as the 'rule of compensating moral values' and in 1934, with the elevation of Joseph Breen as head of the revamped Studio Relations Committee, which became the Production Code Administration, the Code was reinterpreted by Breen in terms of its effect on the overall narrative structure. Breen, through his power of vetting and reworking scripts before they went into production, insisted that the 'voice of morality' be elaborated throughout the entire film and not just appear at the point of resolution (Jacobs 1991: 114–15).

This change reinforced, and tightened, the system of causality in the classical Hollywood film so that the ethical terms articulated by the (moral) ending of a film would now be worked through the film from the beginning. This process eliminated the need, for a time at least, for the 'tacked on' 'moral' endings found in pre-1934 films such as *Baby Face* (Alfred E. Green, 1933) and *Ex-Lady* (Robert Florey, 1933). Concerned with the treatment of illicit sex in Hollywood films, Breen wrote in the 1936 annual report of the Production Code Administration that it is 'not a satisfactory solution, for example, to have the principals simply and suddenly marry in the final scene after leading an alluring life of sin throughout the play' (Jacobs 1991: 114–15). Later, in the 1940s, there were some disruptions to this system of causality in the use of 'dream endings' in such films as *The Woman in the Window* (Fritz Lang, 1944) and *The Strange Affair of Uncle Harry* (Robert Siodmak, 1945). Nevertheless, Breen's dictum about the dissemination of a 'moral voice' throughout the film had a lasting effect on the Hollywood cinema and it contributed to the unification of the narrative process by insisting that the position produced at the point of resolution must appear inevitable and 'natural'. In this way the Production Code 'reinforced patterns of narrative development, of formal unity and closure, typical of the classical Hollywood cinema as a whole. These formal systems unobtrusively circumscribed the representation of female aggressivity, ambition, and illicit sexuality' (Jacobs 1991: 149).

Characteristics of the classical Hollywood film

Jean Renoir in 1926 described the Hollywood films of Charles Chaplin and Ernst Lubitsch as 'cinematic classicism' and in the late 1930s André **Bazin** referred to the Hollywood style as 'classical'. Although the meaning of the term was never exact, the term generally included some notion of the 'invisibility', or transparency, of the narration process. The publication of *The Classical Hollywood Cinema* in 1985, written by David Bordwell, Janet Staiger and Kristin Thompson, brought a precision to the term by taking it back to Aristotle's notion of the unities of dramatic art. Hollywood films are 'classical' in the sense that individual films are bound by rules that set strict limits on innovation. These rules pertain to the composition and aesthetic organization of the film so that it favours unity, balance and order.

The classical Hollywood system, as David Bordwell points out, 'cannot determine every minute detail of the work, but it isolates preferred practices and sets limits upon invention' (Bordwell *et al.* 1985: 4). Standard practices have subsequently coalesced into a system of priorities and constraints thereby establishing rules of acceptable and unacceptable methods. This system permits stylistic changes that are 'functional equivalents', so that a cut-in may replace a track-in, as each device fulfils the same role within the overall paradigm (Bordwell *et al.* 1985: 5). Change is much less likely, however, if it violates the prevailing systems of narrative logic, cinematic time and cinematic space.

By 1917 the essential norms of the classical style were in place. Thereafter, film techniques were developed to intensify such norms as the creation of a 'unified impression'. Editing techniques, for example, were refined because of the need to control potentially disruptive spatio-temporal problems inherent in a medium based on multiple shots and changing locales. This, in turn, encouraged the development of **continuity editing** practices. Match-cutting (see **matching (shots)**), which meant that a cut from one shot to another was linked in various ways, was developed together with the eyeline match so that when a character looks into off-screen space another shot shows the spectator what the character is looking at. Similarly, the **shot/reverse shot** method was favoured as the most 'natural' technique for presenting lengthy dialogue sequences.

Classical techniques are designed to promote narrative clarity so that the spectator knows not only where he/she is in relation to time and space but also in terms of the overall chronology and logic of the plot. Goal-oriented protagonists, character-centred stories and an omniscient narration style, derived from nineteenth-century aesthetic norms, were accompanied by narrative repetition, retardation and redundancy. Classical style also emphasizes the significance of the climax in the overall narrative structure so that all elements, as well as the attention of the spectator, are channelled towards that powerful moment near the end of the drama.

Unity, narrative clarity and a sense of **verisimilitude** are based on a mutually reinforcing system of motivation. Generally, compositional, or causal, motivation is the most significant form of motivation and it normally works simultaneously with intertextual, especially generic, motivation and realistic, or plausible, motivation (see **genre; realism**). Thus, as Bordwell demonstrates, a **flashback** can be motivated compositionally (providing essential story information), realistically (proceeding from a character's memory) and intertextually (occurring in a certain kind of film such as **film noir**), since multiple 'motivation is one of the most characteristic ways that the classical film unifies itself' (Bordwell *et al.* 1985: 19).

This emphasis on continuity and coherence through motivation serves to deflect attention away from the actual process of narration. The narration draws attention to itself only at codified moments, such as the opening or closing moments, and normally avoids what the Russian Formalists describe as 'laying bare' the artificiality of the device (see **Formalism**). While such moments are not totally unknown in the Hollywood cinema, they are normally motivated generically (the elaborate musical number in the musical, for example) or compositionally, such as a montage segment which condenses time. A camera movement that deliberately exposes the system of narration, or even a glance directly into the lens, unmotivated by a reverse shot justifying this intrusion, is unlikely except in comedy where it is generically motivated. Similarly, cross-cutting from one action to another to establish a link between two lines of action or two characters, as in the opening minutes of *Pretty Woman* (Gary Marshall, 1990) when Edward Lewis (Richard Gere) is linked to Vivian Ward (Julia Roberts) via the simple editing techniques of alternating shots, is preferred to parallel editing between two narrative strands that are not temporally and causally linked in some way, as in D. W. Griffith's thematically linked sequences in *Intolerance* (1916).

The 'new Hollywood'

The vertically integrated system developed by the Hollywood studios was threatened in 1938 when the US Department of Justice's Antitrust Division filed suit against the eight studios accusing them of monopolistic practices. The studios avoided prosecution at this time but the case was reopened in 1944 and the Paramount Decree, as the result came to be known, ruled in 1948 that the studios had to separate production from distribution and exhibition and divest themselves of their theatre chains.

This divesture process was not complete until the late 1950s and, in conjunction with other factors, including changing leisure activities, television, rising costs and the growth of independent production, the studios lost most of their power. By the early 1960s the old studio system had largely disappeared. Such terms as the 'new Hollywood' or the 'post-classical' era have been used to signify the changing role of the studios which after 1960 served largely as distributors for 'packaged' productions assembled by independent producers. More recently, the studios have functioned within a system of 'conglomerate vertical integration' involving large corporate structures and the growth of new technologies and markets, including music, publishing, cable and video (Neale and Smith 1998: xvi).

A brief period of relative experimentation in the classical Hollywood cinema occurred in late 1960s and early 1970s as Hollywood selectively assimilated aspects of the European **art cinema**, including morally problematic protagonists, episodic narratives and unresolved or unhappy endings. This cycle, which included such films as *Bonnie and Clyde* (Arthur Penn, 1967), *Easy Rider* (Dennis Hopper, 1969), *Sugarland Express* (Steven Spielberg, 1974) and *Nashville* (Robert Altman, 1975), was short-lived and it was accompanied, and supplanted, by more traditional 'blockbusters' and **'high concept'** films, such as *Airport* (George Seaton, 1970) and 'disaster' films like *Earthquake* (Mark Robson, 1974). A more significant trend emerged with the commercial success of big budget generic films such as *Jaws* (Steven Spielberg) in 1975, *Star Wars* (George Lucas) in 1977 and *Raiders of the Last Ark* (Spielberg) in 1981. The continued success of such films, for example, *Titanic* (James Cameron, 1997), demonstrates the persistence of the classical Hollywood style as the dominant mode of feature filmmaking.

References

Bordwell, D., Staiger, J. and Thompson, K. (1985) *The Classical Hollywood Cinema: Film Style and Mode of Production to 1960*, London: Routledge.

Brooks, P. (1995) *The Melodramatic Imagination: Balzac, Henry James, Melodrama, and the Mode of Excess*, New Haven: Yale University Press.

Cook, P. (1985) *The Cinema Book*, New York: Pantheon Books.

Gledhill, C. (1987) *Home Is Where the Heart Is: Studies in Melodrama and the Woman's Film*, London: BFI Publishing.

Jacobs, L. (1991) *The Wages of Sin: Censorship and the Fallen Woman Film, 1928–1942*, Madison: University of Wisconsin Press.

Neale, S. and Smith, M. (eds) (1998) *Contemporary Hollywood Cinema*, London: Routledge.

Further reading

Belton, J. (1994) *American Cinema/American Culture*, New York: McGraw-Hill.

Bordwell, D. (1985) *Narration in the Fiction Film*, Madison: University of Wisconsin Press.

—— (1997) *On the History of Film Style*, Cambridge: Harvard University Press.

Maltby, R. and Craven, I. (1995) *Hollywood Cinema. An Introduction*, Oxford: Blackwell.

GEOFF MAYER

closure

A defining feature of classical Hollywood cinema is the impulse to ensure that the **text** provides a satisfactory sense of resolution (see **classical Hollywood cinema and new Hollywood cinema**). The audience is not left with unanswered questions, motivation is accounted for, and all the strands of the **plot** are adequately tied up. Closure arguably fulfils an ideological function in this process: its emphasis could be said to distract the audience from the more indeterminate nature of conflicts outside its representation (see **ideology and hegemony**). It can thus be employed as a strategy to promote the **preferred reading** of a text and to inhibit its potential for broader or more ambiguous readings.

DEBORAH JERMYN

code

A combination of rules which, taken together, regulate the association of meaning with a particular **sign** in communication. The sign acquires and sustains its meaning through these codified rules being upheld consensually. Its significance is recognizable, in part, because codes set limits on the plurality of meanings potentially available in a given instance. Just as the Highway Code defines proper conduct for road users, for example, the codes of **news values** enable broadcast journalists to make judgements about what to report (and how) via a conventionalized sense of newsworthiness. Codes are culturally specific, and constantly change over time.

See also: encoding; encoding-decoding model

Further reading

Barthes, R. (1973) *Mythologies*, London: Paladin.

STUART ALLAN

cognitive theory

The study of cognition is the study of the human mind, and how it processes information. This study encompasses intellectual traditions drawn from psychology (in film theory, this includes the therapeutic technique of **psychoanalysis**), from linguistics, and, increasingly, from engineering, through the design of 'artificial intelligence' for computer software. Some of these traditions – particularly psychoanalysis and linguistics (**semiotics**) – have been widely incorporated into the critical study of film, but less so into the study of television. Within modern academic psychology, cognition has tended to be subdivided into discrete

mental processes such as perception, attention, memory, language, imagination. Other kinds of human functioning, such as emotion, social behaviour and pathology (mental illness) have been studied as separate topics. In practice, it is obviously difficult to separate all these properties within any given human being: **memory** may be powerfully affected by emotion, for instance.

The study of cognition has obvious implications for media and cultural studies, which deals with the **representation** of symbolic information and analyses the processes of meaning formation and interpretation. The terms encoding and decoding, to describe the way meaning is formulated in texts and understood by audiences, are also used by cognitive psychologists (see **encoding-decoding model; text**). A strong cognitive theory of the media would argue that the relationship between media and their readers/viewers is heavily mediated by these mental processes, and this view has been especially influential in supporting the idea of the active audience – an audience capable of interpreting, adapting, negotiating with and resisting information, rather than simply passively absorbing it (see **audience**). This view of the audience has ideological implications as well as cognitive ones and challenges the conception of the audience as an undifferentiated 'mass' (see **ideology and hegemony**).

Although there is divergence among cognitive scholars about the exact mechanisms of human information processing, a generally accepted principle is that it is constructive, not simply imitative; people actively modify what they see and hear, as they see and hear it – as in the phenomenon of selective attention. They also reconstruct and rearrange what they remember later. Studies have shown that recalled information will vary according to several factors: the context of reception; the context in which the information is recalled; the subject matter, form and stylistic features of the original information; and people's own predisposing attitudes and experiences, including their experience of different kinds of texts and **narrative** structures.

Cognitive structures

Cognitive theorists have attempted to produce structural models of the way in which people's experiences of both texts and real-life events are mentally organized and stored. These models are metaphorical, drawing on spatial analogies such as files, networks and plans; they have also been characterized as 'scripts' and 'schemas'. Schema theory argues that an individual's memory for people and events is organized according to systematic models based on the individual's social and personal experiences, which are built up over time. Young children, for example, may lack the knowledge schemas which they need to understand adult events. In the case of a wedding, they would need to have relationship (individual/family) and institutional (religion/state) schemas as part of their cognitive repertoire in order to appreciate fully what is going on. Schemas also help to determine how people respond to new information; a child's 'wedding' schema could be used subsequently to try to interpret a funeral, with possibly confusing results.

Similar to schema theory is the concept of cognitive 'scripts' which guide predictions about the outcomes of events and activities, both in the real world and in texts. 'Narrative scripts', or 'story grammar', imply that across cultures there are human expectations (perhaps innate, perhaps learned) that stories will include certain basic structural ingredients such as exposition, complication and resolution (see **structuralism and post-structuralism**). As people develop, they learn to interpret and to predict story outcomes through utilizing these narrative scripts (Kintsch 1977). Narrative script theory has obvious implications for people's ability to read genres such as, for instance, the Western (see **Western, the**) or **horror** film; competent viewers will be guided in their expectations of outcomes by the characteristic conventions and codes of these forms (see **conventions; genre**). Suspense, humour and surprise can be produced by screenwriters and directors thwarting such expectations.

Cognitive film theory

Cognitive film theory has not focused in the same way as cognitive psychology on specific kinds of perceptual, attentional and memory functioning and has confined itself mainly to two broad strands of enquiry. The first focuses primarily on the text

itself and examines to what extent the visual structures of film (not, usually, of television) mirror, or provide analogies to, the structures of the human mind. The second concerns the viewer or audience more directly and asks: what are the cognitive '**effects**' of viewing film and television? With regard to the first approach, theorists such as Christian **Metz** have suggested that it is the 'unconscious' mind, as in dreaming, which is most closely paralleled by the structures of film and the experience of film-viewing. However, spectatorship of cinema has also been compared to the more deliberately conscious state of being an active witness to the performances of others – i.e., a voyeur (see **voyeurism**). These approaches draw on the theory and practice of psychoanalysis.

Psychoanalysis

Psychoanalytic approaches to film apply the theories of Sigmund **Freud** about the structures of the unconscious mind to the structures and imagery of film. Film is seen as an almost literal model of imaginative and unconscious mental processes, including the memory of early experiences such as infantile oral gratification, in which the screen is a version of the breast. Although psychoanalysis has stimulated a great deal of widely respected theoretical writing, more recent critics have expressed intense scepticism of this view of cinema. Psychoanalysis as a model for understanding human thought processes has also not been particularly influential within mainstream cognitive psychology, although it is an important branch of the traditions of clinical and therapeutic psychology.

Cognitive effects

The second approach of cognitive theory concerns cognitive 'effects'. This strand of inquiry includes questions about the cognitive processes that have to be utilized in order to make sense of the conventions and codes employed in film and television. David **Bordwell** (1996) uses the example of the shot/reverse shot (filming one protagonist in a conversation, in three-quarters view, and then shooting the other as if from the first person's point of view; see **point of view shot**) as an example of a technique that could appear to correlate to 'natural' human perceptual activity (although, as Bordwell points out, it does not). This view of cinema technique as a correlate of human perception is described as the 'naturalist' position. Bordwell makes the important point that a cognitive effect such as the understanding of shot/reverse shot does not have to be biologically natural to be seen as culturally universal. Learned effects can be culturally common, too. He points out that, although people do not require special training in order to understand the technique, it is still a piece of artifice which had first to be invented and then 'taught' to audiences.

The question of behavioural, rather than cognitive, effects – such as the imitation of **violence** – is now more frequently applied to television viewing than to film viewing, and has been mainly addressed by social scientists rather than by textual film critics, so it will not be addressed here. Again, though, the distinction between cognition, emotion and behaviour when it comes to evaluating people's responses to media, is somewhat artificial.

Film grammar and linguistics

The analysis of film as a systematic set of codes, conventions and structures which can be learned, modified and represented cognitively, has generated some common ground between cognitive psychology and film and television theory, particularly in linguistics and psycholinguistics. This tradition of studying film and television is indebted to the semiotic teachings of the linguist Ferdinand de **Saussure**. The organization of shots, scenes and narratives into syntagms and paradigms has been empirically tested with audiences, and there is evidence that children can read cartoons along **syntagmatic** and **paradigmatic** lines (Hodge and Tripp 1986). Máire Messenger Davies (1997), in studies with both children and adults, found that the 'foregrounding' effect of close-up shots in television sequences was paralleled by the use of foregrounding in the linguistic structures people used to describe these sequences. Sequences with close-ups in them were more likely to be described using passive sentences (a linguistic foregrounding device) than were sequences which simply showed the same action in mid-shot.

Visual literacy

Audio-visual texts are now the main source of mediated information of any kind for most people in the developed world, replacing the printed word, which for some commentators indicates cultural decline. The 'reading' of film and television requires audiences to derive meanings both linguistically from the spoken word and from pictures. The study of film and television is the study of moving pictures, which are organized, not only spatially as images within a frame (like paintings and photographs), but also temporally and structurally, through narrative and editing. To be 'literate', film and television viewers need to be aware of pictorial conventions such as **perspective**, focus, framing and the symbolic use of colour or objects. They also need to be aware (if rarely consciously) of how camera movement such as zooms and pans, cuts, fades, close-ups, cross-cutting and editing of various kinds, direct interpretation. Film has been described as 'a meeting place of multiple codes' in which not only visual conventions, but also spoken language, music and quite often, written language, are deployed simultaneously. All this provides a great deal of information for the human cognitive system to make sense of, store and utilize.

Teaching through film and television

Although film and television viewing has often been dismissed as cognitively undemanding, educational researchers have tried to establish whether, and how, people learn to 'read' film and television, and whether they can use narrative and wider social schemas to guide their interpretation of stories and to 'resist', or negotiate with, 'dominant' messages. There has been debate about whether this process has commonalities with, or equal value to, print literacy, and this debate is very much part of the wider ideological arguments about cultural value surrounding film and television: is reading Enid Blyton in print intellectually more valuable than watching an adaptation of a Dickens novel on television?

In the early days of both film and television, their educational usefulness was stressed, and both were seen as important new teaching tools. Simultaneously, concerns were raised about their possibly corrupting and destabilizing effects on vulnerable groups, such as the young and the lower classes. This debate is with us still; it is important to point out that, despite high-profile controversies around violence, **commodification** and Hollywood hegemony, film and television continue to be used internationally as educational tools, and this is a significant aspect of their cognitive effects. Cognitive research has been usefully applied to making news bulletins more comprehensible and memorable, through applying structures from memory and script theory to their design (see, for example, Gunter *et al.* 1982); to co-ordinating words and pictures and the pacing of editing to allow time for a narrative point to be absorbed in children's programmes (see Davies 1997); and to science and practical programmes, where the capacity of moving pictures to demonstrate, for instance, biological processes has been shown to be superior to still pictures or to text in enhancing learning. Research on the pre-school educational programme *Sesame Street* found that techniques such as movement, rapid cutting, music and identification with characters were effective in sustaining attention. Learning was enhanced when children watched with adults, and it was also reinforced by later discussion.

The current developments in multi-media computer texts, in which three-dimensional modelling and complex images, sounds and transformations can be simultaneously represented, unlike the two-dimensional linear narratives of film and television, offer new challenges to cognitive theorists. Interaction with these multimedia texts is much more under the control of the user, rather than being primarily controlled by producers and distributors (as with film and television), and this raises important new questions for cognitive scholars.

References

Bordwell, D. (1996) *Post-theory: Reconstructing Film Studies*, Madison: University of Wisconsin Press.
Davies, M. M. (1997) *Fake, Fact and Fantasy: Children's Interpretation of Television Reality*, Mahwah, NJ: Lawrence Erlbaum Associates.

Gunter, B., Berry, C. and Clifford, B. (1982) 'Remembering Broadcast News: The Implications of Experimental Research for Production Technique', *Human Learning*, vol. 1, pp. 13–29.
Hodge, B. and Tripp, D. (1986) *Children and Television*, Cambridge: Polity Press.
Kintsch, W. (1977) 'On Comprehending Stories', in P. Carpenter and M. Just (eds) *Cognitive Processes in Comprehension*, Hillsdale, NJ: Lawrence Erlbaum Associates.

Further reading

Carroll, N. (1988) *Mystifying Movies: Fads and Fallacies in Contemporary Film Theory*, New York: Columbia University Press.
Metz, C. (1974) *Film Language: A Semiotics of the Cinema*, New York: Oxford University Press.
Neumann, S. B. (1991) *Literacy in the Television Age*, Norwood, NJ: Ablex.

MÁIRE MESSENGER DAVIES

commodification

Commodification is the process by which things or material objects, and more recently services and ideas, become commodities to be bought and sold in a market. Commodities are distinguished by the fact that their *exchange value* is more important than their *use value*. In other words, what one is prepared to pay for a commodity is not an objective assessment of its usefulness, but an acceptance of the – largely – social valuation of a commodity's prestige. Value is about judgements made *external* to the objects themselves, thus ensuring that a system of exchange based on these values is always about human social power (Appadurai 1986: 3). A good example can be found in the higher prices normally charged for women's clothes. Many of these clothes are identical in cost of manufacture and utility to men's clothes and yet they cost more because the prevailing system of cultural-economic exchange does not emphasize utility but the possibilities for exchange for profit.

Marx's great insight was the difference between the value of a thing because of its usefulness and the value of a thing as part of an overarching cultural and economic system of exchange. Marx asserted that capitalism succeeds and prospers by separating the producers of goods from those material goods, alienating workers from the results of their labour. Capitalism allows those who own and control the production process to extract surplus value from the labour by selling the goods for more than they cost to produce. Since human consciousness comes into being (for Marx) through the activity of labour, the exploitative nature of the production of goods as commodities (rather than as things in themselves) is fundamentally oppressive (see Lury 1996: 39–41). Through the process of commodity **fetishism**, people become fixed on valuing the objects that are commodities themselves, rather than recognizing the human labour that produces them in the first place.

Marx's theorization of commodification remains significant, but has been developed in ways that reflect a greater understanding of the concomitant cultural and psychological processes in the context of an emergent consumer culture. This intellectual development has refined the blunt hostility of Marxist thought towards commodification, a hostility that presumed consumerism to be capitalist ideological processes designed to lull the subjects of capitalism into passive acceptance of this economic system. Wolfgang Haug (1986), for example, argues that there is an aesthetic element to commodities that is its own use value: that the glamour and beauty of much consumerism does offer consumers 'real' value, as opposed to simply allowing further extraction of surplus value from goods and services (see **aesthetics**). Other theorists, while accepting that commodification operates through generally oppressive regimes of value, allowing (in Veblen's formulation) the maintenance of hierarchy and class status through 'conspicuous consumption' (Veblen 1925), have noted that consumer culture also allows for negotiations and resistance to the dehumanizing operation of the commodity form (Featherstone 1991).

Some of the impetus for this re-examination of commodification has come from the processes at work since 1945, and increasingly since the 1970s, of creating goods and services for exchange in the market place. Under the impact of globally applied policies of economic rationalism, more and more aspects of life that once were provided outside of the market are now being commodified (see **globalization**). This change is particularly apparent in the field of cultural production where the availability for exchange of opera, drama, artworks, sport, public events and so on is much more important than at any previous time. Television, which has almost always been a medium of 'mass market' commodity products, plays a central role in the commodification of culture. In the case of cinema, '**art**' or 'independent' films were once thought to stand opposed to commodified produce and to avoid entry into the exchange systems of consumer culture. Now they take their place firmly with consumerism, their commodification completed in the moment of illusion that allows us to pretend they are 'different' to other filmic commodities, even as we pay our money to see them.

According to Jean **Baudrillard**, capitalist societies are now so highly commodified, so completely consumerist in their economic and cultural organization, that revolutionary changes are at work leading to a decline in the importance of the commodity form and the logic of production, in favour of the central importance of the signifying processes through which commodities acquire their meaning (and thus, from meaning, their value). What is exchanged in the market place is something far less substantial than goods and money (money being the token of exchange for, in the end, other goods and the labour that produces them); rather it is an exchange of meanings and of the *cultural* capital to make and absorb meanings (Lury 1996: 68ff). While some sociologists and anthropologists insist that material culture remains vitally important to understanding commodification (Appadurai 1986: 4–5), commodification, ultimately, implies the irrelevance of the material goods and services to economies of exchange.

References

Appadurai, A. (ed.) (1986) *The Social Life of Things: Commodities in Cultural Perspective*, Cambridge: Cambridge University Press.

Featherstone, M. (1991) *Consumer Culture and Postmodernism*, London: Sage.

Haug, W. (1986) *Critique of Commodity Aesthetics*, Cambridge: Polity Press.

Lury, C. (1996) *Consumer Culture*, Cambridge: Polity Press.

Veblen, T. (1925) *The Theory of the Leisure Class: An Economic Study of Institutions*, London: Allen and Unwin.

MATTHEW ALLEN

common sense

A much broader category than ideology (see **ideology and hegemony**), common sense signifies the uncritical and largely unconscious way of perceiving and understanding the social world as it organizes daily experience. Antonio **Gramsci** (1971) stresses that common sense, despite the extent to which it is 'inherited from the past and uncritically absorbed', may be theorized as a complex and disjointed 'infinity of traces', and as such never simply identical with a class-based ideology. 'Common sensical' beliefs are in a constant state of renewal: 'new ideas', as Gramsci notes, are always entering daily life and encountering the 'sedimentation' left behind by this contradictory, ambiguous, 'chaotic aggregate of disparate conceptions' (1971: 422).

See also: ideological state apparatuses; praxis

References

Gramsci, A. (1971) *Selections From the Prison Notebooks*, New York: International.

STUART ALLAN

condensation

One of four dreamwork codes (see **displacement**), condensation describes the process by which several distinct chains of ideas coalesce in a composite and highly charged idea or image. Because condensation is the basic unconscious mechanism by which overdetermination occurs, it is central to the ideological analysis of **narrative**. The production of any narrative will be marked by unconscious historical contradictions which manifest themselves only through seemingly banal details invested with great emotional charge. The final shot of John Ford's *Young Mr Lincoln* (1939)

condenses the figure of Lincoln with a gothic landscape and a Civil War song, revealing, through analysis, intolerable contradictions at the heart of American mythology.

See also: ideology and hegemony

Further reading

Freud, S. (1965) *The Interpretation of Dreams*, trans. J. Strachey, New York: Avon.

Laplanche, J. and Pontalis, J.-B. (1973) *The Language of Psychoanalysis*, New York: Norton.

ANGELO RESTIVO

connotation

With the complementary term **denotation**, connotation describes a kind of meaning. Connotation refers to the values a word, image or other representation accumulates beyond its formal definition. For example, the word 'rose' explicitly evokes a flower, but it has become associated with, and connotes love, romance, etc. If characters in a film repeatedly travel by car to an ice cream parlour, the car's appearance soon connotes an ice cream scene to the audience. Connotation is a particularly important subject in the works of critic Roland **Barthes**, whose later writings disrupt the denotation-connotation distinction.

See also: semiotics; sign

GABRIEL M. PALETZ

consciousness

The concept of consciousness is much debated in the disciplines of philosophy and psychology. A reductive definition applicable to cultural theory might be 'awareness' – mental processes dealing with images, sensations or memories, with an emphasis on the fact that this refers (i) to both external and internal stimuli, and (ii) this refers not only to rational mental processes. The term has been taken up in a variety of ways by cultural theory.

The work of David **Bordwell** has drawn on cognitive psychology, and the notion of 'schemata' or frameworks in order to explain the rational mental processes involved in the production of meaning from films (see **cognitive theory**). In contrast, phenomenological film theory has tended to emphasize the non-rational elements of consciousness in the experience of watching films (see **phenomenology**). In the Freudian framework which informs much film theory, 'consciousness' itself is less important than that area of the psyche named 'the conscious' – which, of course, gains its importance in contradistinction to 'the **unconscious**' (see **Freud, Sigmund**). In psychoanalytic cultural theory, 'consciousness' is understood to be largely a product of the workings of the 'unconscious' (see **psychoanalysis**). It should be noted that in recent psychoanalytic cultural theory, the term 'consciousness' has been largely replaced by discussions of the formation of 'subjectivity'. Although the terms are not synonymous, they share a common concern with awareness – of how we come to think of who we are, and how we fit into wider society.

The most common use of the term 'consciousness' in cultural theory is in Marxist-derived formulations – particularly 'consciousness raising' and 'false consciousness' (see **Marx, Karl**). In the paradigm of western, or 'critical', Marxism there is a profound emphasis on the fact that consciousness is developed socially, rather than coming from within: as Marx famously writes in *The German Ideology* (1976), 'life is not determined by consciousness, but consciousness by life'. Marx's writing on consciousness in culture is concerned with the way in which 'false consciousness' is instilled. This idea implies that, in a capitalist society, individuals are unable to perceive the 'true' state of affairs – i.e., that modes of production should be the primary concern of analysis of society and culture, and that workers are denied access to the means of production, and alienated from what they produce. The idea of 'false consciousness' means exactly what it says – that individuals do not know what they really should be thinking or feeling.

This leads to particular interpretations of culture. The 'consciousness industry', for example, is Enzensberger's (1970) description of mass culture – a term similar in its implications to the 'culture industry' of the **Frankfurt School**. The suggestion is that mass culture produces false consciousness in consumers, stopping them from understanding how they really think and feel about the society in which they find themselves. This position informs much writing in the 1960s and 1970s, including such work as Judith Williamson's Marxist-informed classic study of advertising, which suggests that consumers are persuaded by adverts to make decisions which are against their (presumably 'real') best interests by the production of a false consciousness (Williamson 1978: 13). This position is now generally understood to be flawed, relying as it does on the impossible idea that it might be possible to have a 'true' consciousness which is not mediated by culture.

In a similar vein, 'consciousness raising' was an important part of such liberatory movements as the women's movement and gay and lesbian liberation, particularly in the 1970s. These social groups aimed to alter the ways in which group members thought about themselves and their place in society. Women's movements and gay liberation identified films as part of a culture which contributed to oppression (Dyer 1990; see **stereotype**). Producing 'affirmation films', which would present more 'positive' representations of women, or homosexuals, contributed to the process of 'consciousness raising' by contributing to different ways of thinking about the individual and his/her place in society.

References

Dyer, R. (1990) *Now You See It: Studies on Lesbian and Gay Film*, London and New York: Routledge.

Enzensberger, H. (1970) *The Consciousness Industry*, New York: Seabury Press.

Marx, K. (1976) *The German Ideology*, Moscow: Progress Publishers.

Williamson, J. (1978) *Decoding Advertisements: Ideology and Meaning in Advertising*, London: Marion Boyars.

ALAN McKEE

Constructivism

Constructivism was a movement associated with such artists as Victor Tatlin and Alexander Rodchenko in Russia around the time of the 1917 revolution. Fundamental to the movement was the concept of relating machinery and engineering to art. As with most modernist and formalist art, the material and the means of production of that art were central (see **Formalism; modernism and post-modernism**). Emerging film artists embraced Constructivism as part of their ideological process: Dziga Vertov, in particular, praised the machine as a radicalizing force, and the camera as being more truthful than the eye. Aleksei Gan, the editor of *Kino-Fot*, the journal of Constructivist cinema, proclaimed that film should be inseparable from its industrial process.

NICK BURTON

consumption

As Raymond **Williams** has pointed out, the word 'consumption' originally had largely negative associations. It meant 'to destroy, to use up, to waste, to exhaust' (Williams 1976: 69). Since the mid-nineteenth century, however, it has begun to acquire another meaning, but one that is still frequently tied to this former sense. During this period, consumption comes to operate as the obverse of production. Production, in this sense, referred to the process through which human labour transformed raw materials into goods, while consumption involved the process through which these goods were bought and sold via the market. In short, contemporary meanings of consumption are the product of an economic system in which there is a division between the producer and the consumer: goods are produced by one group of people with the aim of obtaining profit through their sale to others.

From the first, this meaning carried some negative associations. Production was defined as active and creative so that consumption came to signify that which was passive and uncreative. Moreover, these terms became gendered so that the activity and creativity of production was defined as masculine, and consumption was not only defined as passive and uncreative, but also frivolous, superficial and feminine.

None the less, it would be wrong to suggest that consumption always had entirely negative associations. From the start, debates over consumption were bound up with debates over the best way of allocating goods and services, and hence one finds radically opposed interpretations of consumption, or what became known as consumer culture.

For some, the allocation of goods via the market is essentially democratic and liberating, and this sense can be seen in celebrations of 'consumer choice'. The market is assumed to 'free' individuals and allow them to exercise choice in their setting of priorities. They may, for example, choose to spend more on clothing than on housing, or invest in education rather than entertainment.

However, others have often presented the market as a largely problematic means for the allocation of resources. Such criticisms often include a range of different and sometimes contradictory assumptions about what is wrong with the market. Nor should it be assumed that critiques of the market are necessarily left wing. Conservatives have attacked the market for threatening to displace traditional authority. In many varieties of mass culture theory, including the work of Theodor **Adorno** and the **Frankfurt School**, for example, the objection to the market is that it only respects the standards of commercial success, and threatens to destroy established cultural values.

Certainly, there were those who rightly stressed that the market was not a 'free space' to which all had equal access but that, on the contrary, its structure actually depended on, reproduced and even exacerbated existing inequalities. However, even these criticisms have often been confused with the previous type of criticism as though they were somehow synonymous with one another.

Where these debates concern the politics of the capitalist market as a means of allocating cultural goods, film as a form emerges in the late nineteenth century in relation to specific developments within capitalism. These changes have been referred to as the emergence of a 'consumer culture', which not only involved the development of a new world of consumer goods directed at the middle classes through department stores and the like, but also the emergence of a whole series of popular amusements.

Again, these developments have been seen in different ways. Some critics have viewed them as the vital expression of a popular aesthetic that provided a challenge to bourgeois values (see

aesthetics). For these critics, early cinema is often seen as a potentially radical and disruptive form of **carnival** which was gradually tamed and controlled by the established order (see **cinema of attractions**).

Others, including Stuart Ewen (1976), identify a process by which capital reorganized itself in the early part of the twentieth century. In this process, it is argued, capital managed to not only pacify radical working-class demands, but also solve some internal economic problems, through the extension of consumer culture to the working classes. Henry Ford, for example, is often credited with the insight that mass production not only required a rationalization of production, but also a relatively wealthy working class which would permit the mass consumption necessary for the generation of profit. In other words, by paying his workers a relatively high wage, Ford was able to pacify his workers and provide the basis for the mass consumption necessary for the sale of his cars.

For Ewen and others, capitalism had moved from a period of accumulation, which required a morality of restraint and deferred gratification, to a period in which reproduction became central to the maintenance of capital, a situation that required the stimulation of consumer desires. The twentieth century was a period in which the major problem for capital was the need to find new markets for its goods, a problem which was in part answered by the creation of an affluent working class that could act as the basis for mass consumption.

However, Ewen also suggests that this new consumerism was also used to pacify the work force, and it did so by deflecting working-class demands. Whereas during the late nineteenth century working-class unionization had largely been organized around a demand for control of the production process, the new consumerism allowed capital to offer higher consumer spending in its place. It changed the terms of working-class demands from issues that provided a fundamental challenge to capital to ones that actually serviced the needs of capital itself.

As a result, film was often directly associated with consumer culture and accused of being central to the process that had caused a de-radicalization of working-class culture. However, similar criticisms would also be directed at other media. Television is often directly associated with the stunning prosperity of the United States in the 1950s, and like the consumer culture of the early twentieth century, the prosperity of this period is also identified with a process of de-radicalization and conservatism.

Similarly, the development of video and satellite in the 1980s was also associated with a booming consumer culture that was accused of obliterating historical **memory**, and creating an isolated society in which people retreated from the public spaces of modernity into the privatized consumption of the post-modern world (see **modernism and post-modernism**).

Of course, while these moments are attacked by some, others present them as moments of liberation and choice. The problem is not simply that each historical moment is much more complex than any of these accounts suggest, but also that these accounts frequently rely on inadequate understandings of the activities associated with film and television viewing. In film and television criticism, the activities of viewing are themselves often referred to as forms of consumption, a reference that has a long and confused past. It relies on a fundamental confusion between two moments – that of purchase and that of appropriation (or use) – a confusion that is often central to accounts of consumption in general and consumer society in particular.

This confusion has had particular significance for the analysis of film and television. Mass culture theorists frequently pointed out that the film and television industries differed from, say, the food industries to the extent that while everyone needs to eat to survive, neither film nor television is necessary in order to sustain physical life. Thus, the cultural industries need to not only rationalize and control the process of production but must also rationalize and control the process of consumption in order to ensure regular demand for their goods.

However, mass culture theorists often confuse the act of purchase and the act of appropriation (interpretation). While it might follow that cultural industries need to ensure a regular market for their product and hence to rationalize and control, say, film attendance, it does not logically follow that they must control what audiences do once they have paid for their ticket. Controlling consumption (purchase) in no way necessitates controlling consumption (appropriation).

In other words, consumption has come to refer to two related but distinct stages of a larger process: purchase and appropriation. Remarkably little work has been done on the first of these stages, the stage at which the film or television industries try to ensure a regular audience for their goods. Indeed, this stage is usually simply assumed, and most film and television criticism tends to concentrate on the second stage, the stage at which films and television programmes are appropriated or used. This work falls into two broad approaches – the analysis of spectatorship and interpretation/reception.

The analysis of spectatorship is usually a feature of mass culture theory, **Screen theory** and the use of **cognitive theory** within historical reception studies (see **reading and reception theory**). These approaches see the spectator as an effect of the **text**. For mass culture critics, the spectator existed in a position of 'subjection' (see **subject and subjectivity**). For *Screen* theorists, the spectator was simply a 'position' constructed by the text's **mode of address**. Even those drawing on cognitive theory, only define the spectator as active to the extent that they perform the allotted task of supplying the right materials and so filling textual gaps.

In these approaches, metaphors of consumption are used to define the appropriation of films and television, metaphors which go back to the definition of consumption as the opposite of production. The language of consumption is used to signify passivity and a lack of creativity, but it also frequently draws on metaphors of eating. For mass culture critics, for example, people simply consume 'pre-digested' materials which require no effort on the part of the audience. Many *Screen* theorists drew on a distinction between the closed and the open text in which the first is associated with a spectator who passively 'consumes' the text, and the latter requires a spectator who actively 'writes' the text.

However, such metaphors not only reproduce the notion of film and television audiences as a passive and unthinking mass, they are also highly gendered. They draw on the repeated trope of 'mass culture as woman' in which both mass culture and its audiences are essentially feminized. The ideal consumer is assumed to be 'feminine': passive, childlike and concerned with the superficial world of appearances. As a result, as Barbara Ehrenreich (1983) has pointed out, fears of consumer society are often fears about changing gender roles, and particularly, masculine fears of 'feminization' (see **feminist theory; gender**).

For some critics, though, all film and television viewing involves an active process of interpretation that depends on the pre-existing cultural competences and dispositions of audiences (see **Bourdieu, Pierre**). Audiences not only decode texts (see **encoding-decoding model**) on the basis of the expectations and knowledges with which they encounter a text, but they also respond to it on the basis of their prior predispositions.

These approaches have been far more influential in television criticism than in film criticism, and it is often related to the empirical and/or ethnographic study of audiences (see **empiricism; ethnography**). However, in film studies, there has been a growing interest in the historical reception of films. For these critics, even when one cannot study actual audiences, one can begin to reconstruct the cultural context within which the reception of films took place.

However, film studies still remains more interested in the interpretation of texts than with the cultural politics of film consumption more generally. In contrast, television studies has long been fascinated not only with the different ways in which audiences interpret television texts, but also with the activity of television viewing itself. This has led to research on the ways in which the meanings of television viewing are bound up with the cultural politics of the living room. Despite the fact that film is now consumed through a range of different media – cinema, television, video, satellite, cable – film studies rarely addresses the different meanings that are attached to the activities of consuming of films through these different sites of exhibition and/or retailing.

As many have pointed out, cinema-going is about far more than the viewing of a particular film. Indeed, as Douglas Gomery (1992) has argued, Balaban and Katz became the most successful and imitated exhibitors of their time, 'despite having little access to Hollywood's top films'. Instead of relying on the films, they succeeded by concentrating on other aspects of the cinema-going experience, and so 'differentiated its corporate product through five important factors – location, the theatre building, service, stage shows and air conditioning' (Gomery 1992: 43). Consumption is about far more than either the activities of purchase or interpretation.

References

Ehrenreich, B. (1983) *The Hearts of Men: American Dreams and the Flight from Commitment*, London: Pluto.

Ewen, S. (1976) *Captains of Consciousness: Advertising and the Roots of the Consumer Society*, New York: McGraw-Hill.

Gomery, D. (1992) *Shared Pleasures: A History of Movie Exhibition in America*, Madison: University of Wisconsin Press.

Williams, R. (1976) *Keywords: A Vocabulary of Culture and Society*, London: Fontana.

Further reading

Hollows, J. (1999) *Feminism, Femininity and Popular Culture*, Manchester: Manchester University Press.

Klinger, B. (1994) *Melodrama and Meaning: History Culture and the Films of Douglas Sirk*, Bloomington: Indiana University Press.

Morley, D. (1995) 'Theories of Consumption in Media Studies', in Daniel Miller (ed.) *Acknowledging Consumption: A Review of New Studies*, London: Routledge.

Slater, D. (1997) *Consumer Culture and Modernity*, Oxford: Polity Press.

Uricchio, W. and Pearson, R. E. (1993) *Reframing Culture: The Case of the Vitagraph Quality Films*, Princeton: Princeton University Press.

MARK JANCOVICH

content analysis

This is a method of analysing media output by quantitative research based on breaking down the media's output into different components or categories, whose frequency can then be measured. Meaning is inferred from the number of times a particular feature occurs. For instance, a study could be made of the number of times positive images of particular ethnic minorities appear in advertisements on terrestrial television during peak viewing hours. One of the problems with this type of research is that although it claims to be an objective methodology there are uncertainties about how some categories are defined or interpreted. What, for instance, is meant by a 'positive' image?

Content analysis can be carried out on a small scale, but this can raise problems of reliability and validity of the findings, so it is therefore generally considered more effective when applied to large-scale projects. It is more typically employed on research projects investigating trends, changes or patterns, perhaps over time or across different media – for example, the changes in content of a broadsheet newspaper over a ten-year period. In Britain, content analysis has been used by groups like the **Glasgow University Media Group** (GUMG; 1976, 1980) to investigate bias in the reporting of industrial issues in news and current affairs programmes. The GUMG recorded a series of news bulletins and timed each item, noting the method of presentation and the details of who appeared and for how long. Although the GUMG claimed that its research showed that anti-strike bias existed in the way in which stories were reported, its content analysis does not explain *why* this bias occurred or its effect.

John **Fiske** (1990) notes that content analysis can be a useful check on the more subjective, selective way in which we normally perceive messages: it may be able to provide objective proof to support a subjective belief that women are shown on television in a more limited range of occupations or environments than men. To provide this objective proof, however, a very complex and well designed sample needs to be undertaken and the findings analysed. Content analysis can therefore be very time consuming, especially if it is part of a large-scale research exercise, and it is not always clear that the results justify the work involved and that the 'evidence' cannot be found by other less time-consuming methods.

There are various limitations associated with this type of research. The main criticism is that it implies a **hypodermic model** of the media and only focuses on the output of the media, thus ignoring much of what the reader or viewer might contribute to the creation of the text's meaning. The findings of the GUMG have been criticized on the grounds that they seem to assume audiences do not engage or interpret the news items in any way other than in the way presented by the programmes. Other criticisms of content analysis focus on the difficulty of looking at selected components in isolation and ignoring the more general context within which the texts are produced or the analysis is taking place.

See also: encoding-decoding model; reading and reception theory; stereotype

References

Fiske, J. (1990) *Introduction to Communication Studies*, London: Methuen.

Glasgow University Media Group (1976) *Bad News*, London: Routledge and Kegan Paul.

—— (1980) *More Bad News*, London: Routledge and Kegan Paul.

Further reading

Weber, R. P. (1990) *Basic Content Analysis*, London: Sage.

PHILIP RAYNER

continuity editing

Since the late teens, continuity editing has represented the dominant way mainstream film (and later, television) combined individual shots to create the illusion of coherent space and time. Elements of the system were in place by the early 1900s when such filmmakers as George Albert Smith and James Williamson began to use point of view cutting and matching screen directions across cuts in their early multiple-shot films (see **matching (shots); point of view shot**). Editing variations found in early films suggest that filmmakers experimented before adopting continuity editing. While these choices today might seem odd, they were based on practices used on the stage and in the projection of magic lantern slides.

Editing grants greater flexibility in representing space and time, condenses action, creates more developed characters and varied perspectives on events. It also presents a problem. How can the potentially disruptive break between the 500 or so individual shots in the typical Hollywood film – each one a discrete piece of film – be minimized or erased? Continuity editing presents one solution to this dilemma. Also known as 'invisible editing', it motivates each cut, so that viewers follow content and ignore form (see **motivation**). Developed for the demands of realist narratives, continuity editing creates a coherent **diegesis** marked by continuous space and linear time (see **narrative; realism**).

Filmmakers have to shoot and edit according to a series of rules. These are guided by the principle of repetition and difference. Each shot should repeat an element we have seen before (unless it is establishing something new) to help viewers orient themselves in space. At the same time, it should also show us something different to justify the cut or else it will be noticed. This applies equally to changes in camera position and shot scale. None the less, the system is quite flexible, enabling the wide degree of individual stylization that helps constitute authorial style and the visual variations that mark individual genres (see **authorship; genre**).

To maintain direction across cuts, all cameras must be positioned in accordance with the **180° rule**. This imaginary line, generally referred to as the axis or the 180° line, organizes filmic space and is usually drawn through the centre of the action. If a couple are talking, the line would appear to join them together. It can move with characters and the action. All cameras must be placed on the same side as 'crossing the line' reverses directions across shots. Besides maintaining constant screen direction, the 180° rule ensures some common space (repetition) across shots so that viewers can orient themselves across the cut. The complementary 30° rule mandates a minimum change of 30 degrees in camera placement to produce sufficient difference to help motivate the cut.

As continuity editing requires a balance between repetition and difference, directors generally do not cut from a long shot to a close-up within a scene because the difference is too great and the cut potentially noticeable. Spaces are seamlessly established by cutting from a long shot or establishing shot (which shows the entire scene) to a medium shot (which focuses on characters framed from just below the knees or hips) before cutting into a close-up (face only, or a close image of an object or some part of the body).

Continuity editing usually condenses time to eliminate narratively insignificant actions. In classical Hollywood films (see **classical Hollywood cinema and new Hollywood cinema**), transitions are used if time is manipulated, but contemporary films generally favour straight cuts. Transitions signal larger temporal ellipses: fades to or from black mark large gaps in time; dissolves indicate smaller, but still substantial, temporal ellipses. They also suggest a move into a character's consciousness, as in dream, fantasy or memory sequences.

Besides creating a formally transparent text, these rules generally position viewers as ideal observers. Spectators know more than any character, as the camera generally shows us the best position on the action at any time. This also allows films to trick viewers, as we trust we have the most knowledge but the filmmaker might have led us astray, withholding crucial knowledge till later. Because of its transparency, then, continuity editing encourages viewers to believe they are seeing everything in a direct, unmediated way, hiding the choices that are made and the implications and ideology behind these decisions (see **ideology and hegemony**).

See also: camera style and lens style; perspective

Further reading

Bordwell, D. and Thompson, K. (1997) *Film Art: An Introduction*, New York: McGraw-Hill.

MOYA LUCKETT

conventions

'Conventions' refers to the assumptions shared by the makers and receivers of media texts about what should be included and what should be omitted in a production. Hollywood narratives conventionally have a male protagonist; television newsreaders are conventionally shot front-on in medium close-up. Some conventions are less obvious: viewers now expect a scene in a fiction film to be shown from more than one angle whereas, in reality, a viewer would see it from one position. In addition, conventions may change: technological change made possible the break from scenes shot from one angle; social changes may cause the male protagonist convention to be challenged.

See also: camera style and lens style; narrative; text

PHILIP SIMPSON

convergence

Convergence emerged as a major defining feature of late twentieth-century technology, working towards the concept of the Information Society. Loosely applied, it refers to the innovation in technology which has led to the process of fusion between previously separate forms of storage, transmission and reproduction of information. Such a conjunction within the technological sphere has been witnessed in broadcasting, computing and telecommunications, with information being processed in a common **binary** form. This has occurred largely because the increased capacity afforded by digital technology (see **digital communication**) has enabled separate broadband systems to be closely integrated (Baldwin *et al.* 1996: 3). While computing has long relied on some form of digitalization, telephony signals were formerly transmitted as electronic impulses along wires, while analogue broadcasting signals were relayed through airwaves. Developments in the underlying infrastructure of each sector has enabled these once disparate media to share certain characteristics as delivery systems have adopted common features. This overlapping has been furthered by the common application of identical fibre optic wires.

It is important to emphasize that these shifts are occurring at a varying pace, but there are a number of identifiable changes associated with convergence, the primary effect being that different delivery platforms can now offer fundamentally similar services. For instance, Web television, **Internet** access over mobile phone networks, and on-line newspapers all cross the sectoral divide. These functions were traditionally contained in specific media operating within a particular industrial structure. Sectors are now increasingly reliant on one another, as convergence has propelled discrete markets to merge with, for example, telecommunications operators offering cable television. Importantly, shifts in one context are now being felt in other sectors as they share the same network architecture: increases in television programme costs, for example, will have repercussions for Web television operators. Similarly, progress in set-top box manufacture for high definition television influences all sectors owing to its utilization of the various technologies.

These overlaps indicate a new trend of cross-sectoral alliances with different companies uniting in their quest to capture the largest market share. In this way, technology has ushered in a new pattern of ownership with the potential for one conglomerate to spread from its established base to other markets so that it contains several media channels. The danger is that equipment may become concentrated in a few hands creating vast monopolies spanning the whole media terrain. Thus, convergence in technological forms may permit convergence in ownership patterns which could seriously affect consumer choice (see **consumption**).

For audiences, the benefits are taken to centre around the increase in the number of services available, due to greater processing speed; interactive television is one such service providing opportunities for home shopping and banking. With the opening up of the spectrum, specialist channels have emerged and as these are supported by encryption systems, viewers are able to select their own channel provision accordingly. Another recent development is the mobile package which offers phone provision together with a palm computer as well as a fax. The vision of a grand multimedia apparatus offering total convergence may still be far-fetched, but such technical improvements have been labelled as a potentially empowering tool. Ultimately, though, the use to which audiences put the technology and the demand for information will decide the degree of convergence that will materialize.

While the technology undoubtedly affords positive benefits, the question remains as to the extent to which this will be universally available: convergence could leave some people outside the Information Society. For these reasons, **regulation** also needs to cross boundaries in order to match **technological change**. Regulating media channels according to a separate logic is no longer plausible; regulation may also need to converge if the individual consumer's interests are to be safeguarded.

See also: broadcasting, the United Kingdom; broadcasting, the United States; cable and satellite; commodification; multinational; spectrum scarcity

References

Baldwin, T., Stevens McVoy, D. and Steinfield, C. (1996) *Convergence: Integrating Media, Information and Communication*, Thousand Oaks, CA: Sage.

RAKESH KAUSHAL

cop shows (police drama)

The cop show/police drama has taken diverse approaches in portraying the role of the police and police methods on television. So much so that to identify the cop show as a specific **genre** with its own distinct codes and conventions distinguishable from other television genres is not as simple as it might seem. However, while bearing in mind the shortcomings of genre theory, three main approaches to the police drama are evident, which borrow from one another and other television genres to blend continuously, always adding to the genre's syntax.

Shows like *Columbo* and *Inspector Morse* are good examples of the type of cop show that stems from the literary tradition of detective fiction. In these series, the narrative centres on the act of detection by an iconoclastic hero (Columbo/Morse) whose detached air signals him as being apart from conventional society and accounts for his ability to solve the mystery. The second approach focuses on the police squad and is more akin to the soap opera in the ways that the lives and interrelationships of policemen and women are highlighted. Ensemble cast shows, such as *Z Cars*, *NYPD Blue* and *Blue Heelers* (an Australian series), all have as much in common with serialized soap operas as they have with other police series (see **soap opera**). The third approach is more action-oriented: shows like *The Sweeney* or *Miami Vice* focus on the action and violence of police work expressed in aggressive displays of masculine style and power. Although these are not distinct categories, to consider the wide range of approaches toward portrayals of the police and of the criminals is useful when considering the meanings proposed by television police drama.

More importantly, the cop show deals with what is right and wrong in society: the criminals deviate from what is acceptable behaviour and are punished by our on-screen representatives, the detectives. This is ideologically interesting because of the cop show's relationship with **realism**. The visual style of early British police dramas such as *Dixon of Dock Green* and *Z Cars* is grounded in the realist tradition of British cinema, and the American show *Dragnet* claimed that the narratives were based on actual police cases. 'Names have been changed to protect the innocent', was its only overt admission to fictionalization. In the 1990s, an equivalent can be found in *NYPD Blue*'s unsteady camera style, mimicking the look of fly-on-the-wall documentaries. The strategies employed to suggest the veracity of the image are often at odds with the subject matter itself. Cop shows portray violent crime levels far out of proportion to their actual occurrence in society at large. The police are the viewer's guide through what is essentially a mythic construction of crime and society (see **myth**).

As the genre progressed through the 1980s and 1990s, crime more often started to be addressed as a political problem rather than merely a moral decision on behalf of the criminal. However, this complexity is often negated by the detective's triumphs. Whatever awkward threats to society the criminal represents, defeat by the detective signals narrative **closure** and restoration of normality. This was addressed in *Hill Street Blues* by adopting the serial format of soap operas, often leaving cases unresolved in an attempt to reflect the actual manner in which police business is conducted.

Fictional representations of the police offer a means for society to understand the conflicts and contradictions that involve the upholding of the law and the relationship between the police detective, the criminal and society as a whole. This inevitably raises ideological issues: the conflict between villain and hero can be perceived as conflict between contrasting ideological positions (see **ideology and hegemony**). Marxist critical perspectives might argue that by creating a mythology around the detective and around crime itself, cop shows cannot adequately address the problems which they depict (see **Marxist aesthetics**).

Further reading

Buxton, D. (1990) *From the Avengers to Miami Vice, Form and Ideology in Television Series*, Manchester: Manchester University Press.

Gitlin, T. (1994) *Inside Prime Time* (revised edn), London: Routledge.

Kaminsky, S. M., with Mahan, J. H. (1985) *American Television Genres*, Chicago: Nelson-Hall.

Robards, B. (1985) 'The Police Show', in Brian G. Rose (ed.) *TV Genres: A Handbook and Reference Guide*, Westport, CT: Greenwood Press.

BEN WOODHOUSE

cult film and television

The eclecticism of the term 'cult' is summed up by Jeff Sconce who argues that it 'would include entries from such seemingly disparate subgenres as "bad film", splatterpunk, "mondo" films, sword and sandal epics, Elvis flicks, governmental hygiene films, Japanese monster movies, beach party musicals and just about every other historical manifestation of exploitation cinema from juvenile delinquency documentaries to soft core pornography' (Sconce 1995: 372). In fact, even this list only includes what Sconce calls 'paracinema', a subsection of cult movies more generally.

However, cult movies are not restricted to mainly low-budget, exploitation production, as Sconce's list would seem to suggest. Indeed, in February 1990, British film magazine *Empire* attempted to define the cult movie, but only succeeded in providing another list which included such 'classics' as *The Searchers* (John Ford, 1956), big-budget flops like *One From the Heart* (Francis Ford Coppola, 1982) and art movies like *Last Tango in Paris* (Bernardo Bertolucci, 1972) and *Paris, Texas* (Wim Wenders, 1984).

The introduction of cult television only increases the problem of defining the qualities of a 'cult' object. In fact, the problem itself is probably irresolvable. The 'cult' is not a quality shared by a group of films and television programmes, rather it is a product of the ways in which these texts are read by specific groups. In other words, cult movies are not related to one other on the basis of what they share, but through the ways in which they are classified in opposition to 'mainstream' cinema. However, like the cult itself, the category of the 'mainstream' is not a coherent object, but a product of that opposition.

As a result, it is not simply that different sections of cult **fandom** value different texts and for different reasons, but that even within a single publication there is rarely, if ever, a single and coherent definition of a cult **text**. On the contrary, within fandom there are a number of different, and even contradictory, strategies for identifying and valuing a cult text. Texts are sometimes treated with virtual contempt, as exemplified by the phrase 'so bad it's good'. Here a text is viewed as being so bad that it can be made the object of humorous ridicule. In other cases, a film can be seen as bad, but treated with a kind of patronizing affection. However, not all cult texts are viewed in this way. Some 'bad films' are valued because, in their ineptness, they supposedly make manifest the devices that other texts render transparent. In these films, ineptness is often presented as almost indistinguishable from radical criticism. For example, in the case of one of the classic cult filmmakers, Edward D. Wood, cult movie fandom has presented him in all the above ways: as an object of

ridicule; as provoking a kind of pathos; as ineptly revealing the mechanisms of classic realist texts (see **classic realist text**); and as a perverse individualist who was unable or unwilling to conform to established cultural norms.

All these strategies can be found in the volume *Incredibly Strange Films* (Vale and Juno 1986), which establishes very different relationships to the subjects of its interviews. The director Frank Henelotter, for example, is addressed as a cult fan who shares the same values and tastes as the interviewer. Hershal Gordon Lewis, on the other hand, is presented as a hack who had little sense of what he was doing as a filmmaker, but whose lifestyle and films were almost heroically outrageous. Lewis is therefore presented as undeniably 'cuckoo' and, for this very reason, as a heroic nonconformist. Finally, Larry Cohen is presented as neither a fan nor a freak, but as a serious, if largely unacknowledged, auteur (see **authorship**). Cohen's auteur status is established in two key ways: through the presentation of him as an independent, and even maverick, filmmaker, and through the suggestion that his films display an overtly **oppositional** politics.

These different approaches are, however, largely held together by a preoccupation with the supposed non-conformity and individuality of the cult filmmaker or the cult text. As a result, in the area of cult movies, a disproportionate number of cult texts come from the 'independent' cinema, which is supposed to provide the possibility for greater individual freedom in terms of political opinion and artistic creativity. Unfortunately, rather than individualism, it is precisely the commercial conditions of the independent sector that have encouraged (instead of simply permitted) the more outlandish features of many cult films. It is through their outlandishness that these films promote themselves as *different* from the mainstream. Even in the area of cult television programming, where these notions of independence are not really relevant, and therefore far more difficult to establish, a similar rhetoric can still be identified.

However, while this sense of opposition to, or difference from, the 'mainstream' eventually proves contradictory, it is necessary in order to provide the sense of subcultural authenticity on which cult fandom is based. This sense is reproduced both in the writings of cult fans and in academic accounts, which are often uncritical of the fans' presentations of themselves. In other words, academic accounts not only revolve around very similar oppositions, but are also often eager to identify subcultures as the uncontaminated Other of the dominant culture (see **subculture**). Indeed, as Sarah Thornton has noted in a different context, it is for this reason that 'inconsistent fantasies of the mainstream are rampant in "subcultural studies" ' (Thornton 1995: 93).

None the less, like other subcultural groups, cult fans frequently portray themselves as 'somehow outside the media and culture', as 'grass roots cultures [that] resist and struggle with a colonising mass-mediated corporate world' (Thornton 1995: 116). But despite their oppositional ideology, cult fans are not the products of an authentic self-generation that is later threatened with incorporation by the media and the academy. Instead, the media and the academy have been central to both the formation and maintenance of cult audiences.

Instead of emerging out of some spontaneous sense of affinity, cult movie fandom developed out of the audiences for the art cinema and repertory theatres. It was these institutions which provided the initial spaces for congregation and often acted as the gatekeepers that classified and reclassified films through their advertising and exhibition. And it is these processes of reclassification that are central to the production of the cult movie and cult television.

Despite the common opposition between the 'mainstream, commercial' cinema and **art cinema**, a version of the latter did not emerge through a rejection of commerce, but rather as a result of it. During the late 1940s and early 1950s, when cinema audiences were in decline, many cinemas converted into arts cinemas as a means of staying in business. Nor was it the case that the audiences for these new art cinemas were somehow outside the political economy of culture. On the contrary, they were largely middle class and, even then, largely restricted to specific metropolitan areas. For example, before 1950, 40 per cent of all art cinemas in the United States were located in New York, and Manhattan alone was responsible for 60 per cent of the national revenues of the typical art film. Outside New York City, arts

cinemas were still restricted to college towns like Ann Arbor, Michigan and Madison, Wisconsin.

If this market was a relatively small and exclusive one, it was none the less highly profitable, and in 1952, it was identified as the biggest news in movie exhibition. At this stage, however, the market was mainly for foreign language films, a trend consolidated by the phenomenal success of Roger Vadim's *And God Created Woman* (1956), starring Brigitte Bardot. This movie proved that foreign films could make money, and it also established the practice of selling these films to highly educated Americans on the basis that they dealt with materials which were supposedly taboo in Hollywood in the 1950s.

As the art cinema continued to flourish through the 1950s and 1960s, it was also complemented by the emergence of the repertory film theatre. If the art cinema had managed to legitimate cinema as an art form through its use of foreign films, the college film societies were established to show re-runs of old Hollywood movies. They did more than re-show old films, however, they also recontextualized them. The film societies established a practice of re-examining films which had often been dismissed academically as 'all the same', and discovered gems of film art within that which appeared to be worthless. By 1960, there were 250 college films societies in the US, many of which would become repertory cinemas during the 1960s.

However, these developments were not restricted to issues of exhibition but also to changing academic attitudes. The art cinema, for example, was closely allied to the tastes of mass culture theorists such as Dwight Macdonald who identified with the European art cinema as a means of opposing Hollywood cinema and popular culture more generally. The film societies, on the other hand, were closer to the tastes of the auteur theorists, who offered a re-evaluation of the Hollywood cinema. As a result, the mass culture theorists provided the critique of mainstream, commercial culture which was essential to the production of the cult movie audiences, a critique that distinguished between the conformity of Hollywood cinema and the cinema of independence. Auteurism, in some manifestations, was perhaps even more influential. It introduced the idea that one need not simply value an established high culture, but rather that films of value could be discovered even within the apparently worthless low-budget quickie. Like the cult movie fans after them, auteur theorists overtly championed the apparently 'lowbrow' over the 'highbrow', in order to combat the 'middlebrow' or 'mainstream'. Thus, while they revered films which were made within the Hollywood studio system, they presented them not as a confirmation of that system, but as a critique of it. Furthermore, they tended to prefer what seemed at first sight to be relatively conventional **genre** films, as opposed to the more respectable 'prestige' pictures. This was because these low-budget productions were supposedly less prone to interference from the head office, and therefore provided more freedom for individual directors to express themselves.

In this way, auteur theory established the practice of searching out the overlooked gems from within the apparently worthless low-budget films. However, it was the influence of **structuralism and post-structuralism** that provided the means of celebrating films which were simply downright awful. Some films, it was argued, did not necessarily present a conscious or even unconscious critique of the prevailing ideology, and were thus fully implicated in the supposed conservatism and conformity of mass culture (see **ideology and hegemony**). None the less, these films do not necessarily work as intended. They may try to conform and yet, for some reason, reveal that which other films try to render transparent. In other words, these films let us see the ideology from which they come. Instead of appearing natural, transparent and obvious, the ideology in these films is made manifest and visible, either because it is presented too baldly or because the film fails to smooth over its contradictions. It is through this kind of critical framework that cult fans can appreciate films like *The Phenix City Story* (Phil Karlson, 1955) or *Reefer Madness* (Louis Gasnier, 1936). They are not praised for their inherent artistry, but for either their remarkable lack of artistry or their bald, contradictory, or even hypocritical, ideological positions.

This, however, frequently bleeds into **camp**, a concept that was of particular significance within the New York City art world of the 1960s. Indeed, the films of John Waters and Jim Sharman's *The*

Rocky Horror Picture Show (1975) are positively imbued with the **aesthetics** of camp, and are the most prominent cult movies of the 1970s. They are also examples of another significant stage in the development of the cult movie: the midnight movie. Midnight showings began in New York City during the 1970s, bringing together an eclectic mix: excessively gory art movies like Alexandro Jodorowsky's *El Topo* (1971), horror classics such as George Romero's *Night of the Living Dead* (1968), films in 3-D like Jack Arnold's *The Creature from the Black Lagoon* (1954), and the aforementioned 'camp' movies like *The Rocky Horror Picture Show* and John Waters' *Pink Flamingos* (1972) (both of which were self-consciously designed as cult movies).

More recently, the role of video has changed many of these dynamics. First, video has made previously inaccessible films accessible and has, therefore, threatened their value for cult audiences. However, it has also been associated with a new type of cult movie: the banned video. Initially, the film industry was wary of video, and thought that it might finally destroy cinematic exhibition. As a result, the film companies and distributors refused to release many films on video, and created a space into which others temporarily moved. Although recordings could be taken from terrestrial television, there was still a demand for material on rental, a demand which was met with the release of an eclectic variety of violent and pornographic films, known in Britain as 'video nasties'. In the UK in the 1980s, video nasties became the focus of a moral panic and their censorship created another type of cult movie (see **moral panics**). These banned videos, for example Sam Raimi's *The Evil Dead* (1980) and *I Spit on Your Grave* (Meir Zarchi, 1977), were now rare and inaccessible and the moral panic surrounding them seemed to prove that they were opposed to the supposedly conformist values of mainstream culture. As a result, these films were appropriated by cult movie fandom.

If the discussion has, up to this point, concentrated on the history of cult movie fandom, this is because it predates and prefigures cult television fandom. Indeed, like the cult movie, cult television has largely been the product of changes in the nature of the audience. In the 1980s, for example, the emergence of video, **cable and satellite** threatened the audience for network or terrestrial television programming. This created two different tendencies.

On the one hand, satellite and cable were desperate for material and used reruns as one, relatively cheap, means of filling the hugely increased number of hours in the schedules. As with the college film societies, this development enabled a reappraisal of old television shows and the development of cult fan cultures around them. On the other hand, these developments threatened the audiences for terrestrial or network television. As a result, this forced the American networks to adopt new strategies for securing their audiences. If Hollywood found that, in the late 1940s, it could not simply rely on a regular market and turned to the blockbuster, network television gradually began to focus on the development of 'must see television'. This refers to television programmes that people do not simply watch because they are on, but which audiences will go out of their way to watch and organize their schedules around, for example *ER*, *Seinfeld* and *The X-Files*. These shows are then used as anchors, drawing people to a channel and keeping them there. American networks use these shows to 'own' a particular night, and the results of losing a show can be disastrous, as can be seen by the effect on CBS when the popular comedy series *Seinfeld* came to an end in 1998.

Furthermore, these shows are also often directed at specific sections of the population. Faced with a declining audience base, the networks do not just want to hold on to viewers, they want to hold on to the most profitable viewers, the viewers with the highest spending power for which advertisers will pay the highest prices. These shows are, therefore, usually directed at the most educated and cultured sections of the population, and address their tastes and preferences.

However, it is not just terrestrial television that uses these techniques. In Britain, Rupert Murdoch's company, Sky, built itself, to a large degree, on the basis of its exclusive rights to such cult shows as *The Simpsons* and *Star Trek: The Next Generation*. Indeed, Murdoch has also employed a similar technique in the establishment of a new network, Fox, after which is named one of the most important figures in contemporary cult television, Special Agent Fox Mulder from *The X Files*. What

Fox has recognized is that while most shows fold very quickly, a show designed with cult appeal may not take off immediately, but it may generate a strong enough following to enable it to keep its place in the schedules and slowly build an audience.

It is true that there were cult audiences organized around television programmes before these developments, but these changes have given these cult audiences a new importance for the television companies, and encouraged them to create programmes designed to speak to cult audiences. Indeed, whereas television companies in the past largely ignored cult audiences, they now frequently work with them. Cult television has become almost a market category, as demonstrated by the BBC which directly addresses adverts to cult audiences after shows like *Star Trek*, *The X-Files* and *Buffy the Vampire Slayer*. Further, these adverts invite the audience to visit the BBC's own cult television Webpages.

However, this is a difficult strategy that threatens to alienate cult viewers as much as attract them. After all, cult fandom is based on a sense of exclusivity and opposition to the mainstream, and often reacts against anything that might threaten to blur this sense of distinction. It fears being absorbed or incorporated into the mainstream, but it also fears the dissemination of its specific forms of cultural capital. Once this cultural capital becomes common, it loses its value, and can no longer operate as a way of distinguishing between the authentic subcultural insider and the inauthentic mainstream outsider.

References

Sconce, J. (1995) 'Trashing the Academy: Taste, Excess and an Emerging Politics of Cinematic Style', *Screen*, vol. 36, no. 4.

Thornton, S. (1995) *Club Cultures: Music, Media and Subcultural Capital*, Oxford: Blackwell.

Vale, V. and Juno. A. (eds) (1986) *Incredibly Strange Films*, San Francisco: Research.

Further reading

Gomery, D. (1992) *Shared Pleasures: A History of Movie*

Exhibition in America, Madison: University of Wisconsin Press.

Hoberman, J. and Rosenbaum, J. (1991) *Midnight Movies*, New York: Da Capo.

Jenkins, H. (1992) *Textual Poachers: Television Fans and Participatory Culture*, New York: Routledge.

Lewis, L. A. (ed.) (1992) *The Adoring Audience: Fan Culture and Popular Media*, London: Routledge.

Telotte, J. P. (ed.) (1991) *The Cult Film Experience: Beyond All Reason*, Austin: University of Texas Press.

MARK JANCOVICH

cultural capital/cultural reproduction

Sociologist Pierre **Bourdieu** (1984) uses the concept of 'cultural capital' in his study of distinction. Investigating the social practices of French citizens (see Robbins 1991), Bourdieu discusses how cultural status is created and reproduced within French society. Cultural 'distinction' results both from **consumption** (what clothes are worn, what products are purchased) and how objects are consumed (in line, or not, with the detached aesthetic appreciation of 'legitimate culture'; see **aesthetics**).

The term 'cultural capital' reveals Bourdieu's economistic view of society. This **economism** means that he treats all social relations as if they are economic. He uses the economy as a guiding metaphor, suggesting that in other fields beyond the properly 'economic', people invest in knowledge (reading the right books), in social contacts (networking and knowing the right people), and in culture (having knowledge of appropriate cultural works and how to respond to them). 'Economic capital' is money as we usually understand it; 'social capital' is who we know, and 'cultural capital' is our awareness and knowledge of 'legitimate culture' (high art, classical music, etc.). Just as citizens can possess more or less economic capital, they can also possess differing amounts of social and cultural capital. Bourdieu's key argument is that amounts of these forms of capital are not possessed randomly. In fact, the **class** system is reproduced through the uneven distribution of economic, social and cultural capital. Bourdieu's concept of 'cultural capital' assumes that there is a common, 'official' culture. This carries a legitimacy which all citizens are taught to respect, even if they possess low 'cultural capital'. It is through education that cultural capital can be built up; the better educated one is, the more cultural capital is accrued (Bourdieu and Passeron 1977).

For Bourdieu, different social classes have different levels of forms of capital. The dominant bourgeoisie have both high economic and cultural capital. The dominated bourgeoisie are those, like scholars, intellectuals and bohemians, who have high cultural capital and are well educated, but have lower economic capital. Those possessing the reverse amounts of cultural and economic capital (that is, high economic capital but low cultural capital) can be thought of as *nouveau riche* – they are financially wealthy but somehow 'vulgar', not having had the correct education. Bourdieu maps out other social classes, such as the petit bourgeois (possessing mid-range levels of forms of capital) and the working class (possessing low levels of forms of capital).

Bourdieu's work seems to assume that media use merely reflects the level of cultural capital that is carried by the individual concerned, given his/her position within a social class. For example, Bourdieu analyses how cinema-goers (at the time of his original work) with lower cultural capital were more likely to focus on film as entertainment, displaying a knowledge of film stars. 'Dominated bourgeois' audiences, with higher cultural capital, were more likely to focus on film as **art**, discussing directors' **authorship**. Bourdieu concludes that the level of cultural capital determines whether film is viewed as entertainment or art – the second approach drawing on the skills and knowledges of 'legitimate culture'.

A number of theorists have developed Bourdieu's work in relation to film and television, and popular culture more generally. John Fiske (1992) suggests that cultural capital needs to be analysed alongside 'popular cultural capital' (the knowledge, skills and distinctions of consumers of popular culture). Fiske argues that consumers of popular culture can create new forms of distinction, such as the **fandom** surrounding a television programme. For Fiske, popular cultural capital is often built up by those who feel excluded from cultural capital. School learning is replaced by extra-curricular learning, allowing those who are subordinated in relation to formal education to build self-esteem and self-identity. Fiske views popular cultural capital as compensating for low cultural capital, although not necessarily challenging cultural capital's legitimacy.

While Fiske examines how the mass media can support audience distinctions, Sarah Thornton (1995) has analysed how mass media such as film and television can threaten forms of 'subcultural capital' where fans seek to protect the skills and knowledges of their own 'underground' **subculture**. Both Fiske and Thornton move away from Bourdieu's assumption that distinction, being based on official culture, stems from one set of values shared, albeit unevenly, by all of society.

References

Bourdieu, P. (1984) *Distinction: A Social Critique of the Judgement of Taste*, London: Routledge.

Bourdieu, B. and Passeron, J-C. (1977) *Reproduction in Education, Society and Culture*, London: Sage.

Fiske, J. (1992) 'The Cultural Economy of Fandom', in L. A. Lewis (ed.) *The Adoring Audience*, London: Routledge.

Robbins, D. (1991) *The Work of Pierre Bourdieu*, Milton Keynes: Open University Press.

Thornton, S. (1995) *Club Cultures: Music, Media and Subcultural Capital*, Cambridge: Polity Press.

MATTHEW HILLS

culture

> Culture is one of the two or three most complicated words in the English language.
>
> (Williams 1976: 76)

This entry summarizes the recent history of a word which, as Raymond **Williams** (1976) observed, has 'often provoked hostility or embarrassment'. In the context of film and television studies, 'culture' is difficult to separate from 'cultural theory', which has also shaped our understanding of it. What follows is largely written from a British cultural and educational perspective.

'The best that has been known and thought'

Social and economic changes in nineteenth-century Britain, as elsewhere, created the conditions which drew the attention of thinkers and writers to the condition of people who had moved into cities. Prominent among these was Matthew **Arnold** (1822–1888), critic, poet and inspector of schools. Arnold saw himself as at a distance from those with economic power (the Philistines), those with inherited social power (the Barbarians), and the mass of the people (the Populace). A demonstration by working-class men in Hyde Park, London in 1866 and disturbances in other parts of Britain in the following year, however, gave him the opportunity in *Culture and Anarchy* (first published 1869) to suggest that those with economic or social power should consider, at least in their own interests, their responsibilities with regard to the mass of the people. Arnold understood that moral values would no longer be buttressed by religion and that a shared conception of culture might be the necessary safeguard against 'anarchy' – in part the result of the Philistines' neglect of anything but material values, but more likely one outcome of working-class ignorance, oppression and discontent.

Arnold proposed a definition of culture:

> culture being a pursuit of our total perfection by means of getting to know, on all the matters which most concern us, the best which has been thought and said in the world; and through this knowledge turning a stream of fresh and free thought upon our stock notions and habits, which we now follow staunchly and mechanically.
>
> (Arnold 1963: 6)

Arnold indicated that this studied pursuit of perfection involves 'developing all sides of our humanity, and as a *general* perfection developing all parts of our society' (italics in original). His emphasis is on culture as a process of 'becoming something, rather than in having something, in an inward condition of the mind and spirit'.

Arnold's account of culture now reads like a series of abstractions. This is partly the effect of quoting briefly from a book-length series of essays on culture written in a rhetorical and ironic tone to the British intelligentsia of the late nineteenth century. But it is also because Arnold is attempting to discern the best that can be derived from the secular and religious institutions of his time. Parliamentary politics in Britain was dominated by two parties, whose struggles for power emphasized the competitive ethos of the business classes of Victorian England, and the conservative interests of the traditional land-owners.

Neither side willingly recognized the rights and needs of 'the Populace' – the working class – nor an idea of the state beyond their own class interests. Arnold's idea of culture amounted to a radical attack on the mechanicality of their thinking, and included his conception of the state which challenged individualism and recognized collective obligations to all, irrespective of religious or secular interests, in the context of, for example, state education. Arnold asserts that culture is a *social* idea:

> and the men of culture are the true apostles of equality. The great men of culture are those who have had a passion for diffusing... For carrying from one end of society to the other, the best knowledge, the best ideas of their time... to make it efficient outside the clique of the cultivated and the learned.
>
> (Arnold 1963: 70)

Religion in Britain was dominated by the Anglican church whose relationship with the Establishment ensured that as late as 1871 Oxford and Cambridge masters degrees, professorships and fellowships were not open to 'Dissenters' – that is, non-Anglicans. While opposing such conformity and uniformity, Arnold's idea of culture as 'inward' implies it is a process of change that meets desires beyond the materialistic. About the time he wrote *Culture and Anarchy*, Arnold also wrote 'Dover Beach', a poem which speaks of the retreat of the 'Sea of Faith' and of a world which:

> Hath really neither joy, nor love, nor light,
> Nor certitude, nor peace, nor help for pain.

Culture would enable all to learn live in such a world, and, for Arnold, the means to culture included education, criticism and poetry. In arguing for a new form of national education and in his life's work as an inspector of schools, Arnold

attempted to put into practice the ideas which inform his theoretical writings. Poetry might awaken what Arnold describes in detail as 'the best self' which could discern ends beyond the immediate and the individual.

Raymond Williams (1966) points out the ambiguities that surround Arnold's view of the state, and condemns his misjudgement and fear of working-class extra-parliamentary activity. If we look at the 'touchstone' poetry that Arnold recommends as contributing to the educative process of culture we may see it now more in terms of a 'high culture' curriculum persuasively attempting to transcend personal taste. But Williams also draws attention to Arnold's recognition in his larger argument that culture is about more than the literary ('all sides of our humanity') or the individual.

'The common pursuit of true judgement'

The idea of culture as essentially a critical practice located most effectively in educational institutions owes much to the teaching and writing of F. R. Leavis. Arnold's conception of culture developed in reaction to the changes in British society he witnessed during his own lifetime. Culture offered a process and practice in living which might enable people to deal with the changes. Arnold's urbane rhetorical tone (see **rhetoric**) seemed to be reminding those in power that culture might prevail and that the Populace had to be reached by its civilizing power. In contrast, Leavis' tone now seems harsh and embattled, too conscious of the enemies, on the right and the left, of the kind of culture he espoused. Frank Raymond Leavis taught English at Cambridge University where with other scholars and teachers he produced the quarterly journal *Scrutiny* (1932–1953), whose influence on the study of English was similar to that of *Screen* on film theory and film studies in the 1970s (see **Screen theory**). As Williams suggests (1966: 246), Leavis' cultural position is dramatically suggested by the title of a pamphlet which he wrote in 1930, *Mass Civilisation and Minority Culture*.

Added to the social changes to which Arnold responded positively were the cultural changes of the twentieth century, in particular the development of mass communications and mass literacy.

Located in an English department which seemed not to be responding to these cultural changes, Leavis felt that the organic social relationships, moral values and homogeneous culture which had characterized English society were disappearing. In their place was a shallower understanding of community and a too-ready response to the appeals, emotional and economic, of a materialistic society. Literature, and especially the novel, could remind people of moral values which were under threat, and could define 'life' as it could only be experienced, through individuals:

> A real literary interest is an interest in man, society and civilisation, and its boundaries cannot be drawn.
>
> (Leavis 1962: 200)

The study of literature 'is, or should be, an intimate study of the complexities, potentialities and essential conditions of human nature' (*ibid.*: 184). Leavis was opposed to literary theorizing, preferring to demonstrate specific critical judgements through detailed analysis of passages where he insisted crucial values lay. In his view, a judgement must be:

> a sincere personal judgement but it aspires to be more than personal. Essentially it has the form: 'This is so, is it not?'
>
> (*Scrutiny*, vol. 18, no. iii: 27)

The analysis would be based on the words on the page, but it would express those values, in sexual and social relationships, about the cultivation and understanding of emotions and desires on which society should be based.

On the surface, *Scrutiny*'s antipathy to 'mass' culture was like that of the **Frankfurt School**, but Leavis argued that Marxism placed too great an emphasis on the way society determined cultural production. He was also suspicious of the Marxist position which proposed that a critic's duty was to evaluate literature in relation to class struggle. His deliberate eschewal of **theory** denied him the Frankfurt School's sophisticated theorization of class consciousness (see **Marxist aesthetics**).

Where Arnold implies that culture, through criticism, can respond to and sustain society, Leavis saw culture as a strategy for resistance through criticism: culture opposed to society. *Scrutiny* and Leavis argued that culture depended on a sensitiv-

ity to literary tradition and language of which only a minority was capable. But central to *Scrutiny*'s project was the expansion of that minority by placing English Studies at the centre of humanities education in schools and colleges. Generations of teachers, inside and outside formal education, were trained to read the texts recommended by *Scrutiny* in the way Leavis demonstrated, and to read all other texts evaluatively. Terry **Eagleton** wrote as late as 1983 that the Leavis view of English Studies 'has become a form of spontaneous critical wisdom as deep-seated as our conviction that the earth moves round the sun' (Eagleton: 1989: 31).

The popular arts and popular culture

Eagleton and Williams both acknowledge the effectiveness and appeal of *Scrutiny*'s educational project, but point out that morally responsible behaviour was not exclusive to those who read literature. As Williams observes:

> for good or ill, the majority of people do not yet give reading this importance in their lives; their ideas and feelings are, to a large extent, still moulded by a wider and more complex pattern of social and family life.
>
> (Williams 1966: 297)

Earlier forms of film and television studies were an attempt to set the boundaries of the study of culture wider than English literature by looking more closely at some aspects of working-class life in the middle of the twentieth century. *The Popular Arts* (1964) by Stuart **Hall** and Paddy Whannel exemplifies this moment in British cultural history. The authors challenge the conservative cultural pessimism of Leavis and his colleagues:

> The old culture has gone because the way of life that produced it has gone. The rhythms of work have been permanently altered and the enclosed small-scale communities are vanishing. It may be possible to resist unnecessary increases in scale and to re-establish local initiatives; but if we wish to re-create a genuine popular culture, we must seek out the points of growth within the society that now exists.
>
> (Hall and Whannel 1966: 39)

Hall and Whannel then go on to argue along

familiar lines about making judgemental discriminations in relation to films and television programmes. Close readings of selected texts support the argument that these popular forms demand a different analytical approach from high art, but their moral value is significant:

> The moral statements made by art are made in aesthetic terms...they are embodied in the manner of presentation. To discover the moral meanings in art and entertainment we must first respond to them in their own terms.
>
> (*Ibid.*: 31)

In re-creating a popular culture, Hall and Whannel distinguish between the popular arts and 'mass art'. They contrast the marketing of a mannered style like that of Elvis Presley or Liberace with the performance of Ella Fitzgerald or Miles Davis whose work suggests a complexity of experience and accessible expression: 'helping us to know the feelings we have more intensely and to realise them more subtly'. From a moral rather than political perspective they endorse Theodor **Adorno**'s unsympathetic remark about much popular music: 'the composition hears for the listener'.

As with Leavis, culture here is bound up with critical practice and moral and social responsibility, but Hall and Whannel are more positively responsive to the changes brought about by market forces and the new media. Film, television and music get detailed critical attention, but fashion, magazines and 'teenager' consumption are recognized as part of a 'revolution in cultural taste', and are subject to sensitive comment. Although the comparison between jazz and pop music inevitably favours the former as 'aesthetically and emotionally richer', Hall and Whannel's openness enables them to recognize the Beatles, in 1965, as 'a distinctive break with earlier patterns' if 'essentially child-like, androgynous, pre-pubertal'. Like Arnold and Leavis, their address locates education, inside and outside schools and colleges, as the site where culture is to be re-created, analysed, theorized and understood.

Culture and cultural studies

Raymond Williams' *Culture and Society* has become central to accounts of culture and cultural studies

because it placed on the agenda concerns which continue to inform discussion of the concept. As well as proposing a definition of culture, as his predecessors had done, Williams addressed more directly the *relationship* between culture and society: what were the forces forming or determining culture? How were we to understand artistic intention and individual or group response in the context of mass distribution and **consumption**? How did the possession of power – economic, social and symbolic – affect attitudes to, and the uses of, culture? As with all Williams' books, the tone of voice is interrogative and undogmatic, identifying itself with his formation as Welsh-British working class.

William's initial definition of culture takes up the word's earlier meaning and offers a famous formulation:

> Where culture meant a state or habit of mind, or the body of intellectual and moral activities, it means now, also, a whole way of life.
>
> (Williams 1966: 18)

In *Culture* (1981) this definition is developed using a mode of semiotic analysis (see **semiotics**) that the intervening years had made available:

> Thus there is some practical convergence... between the anthropological and sociological senses of culture as a distinct 'whole way of life' within which, now, a distinctive 'signifying system' is seen not only as essential but as essentially involved in all forms of social activity, and...the more specialised if more common sense of culture as 'artistic and intellectual activities', though these...are now much more broadly defined to include not only the traditional arts and forms of intellectual production but also all the 'signifying practices' – from language through the arts and philosophy to journalism, fashion and advertising – which now constitute this complex and necessarily extended field.
>
> (Williams 1981: 13)

When culture becomes 'a whole way of life' no single discipline can contain the objects of study; furthermore, study is not simply of artefacts or ideas but of 'signifying practices' which entails attention to the processes of production and reception, encoding and decoding (see **encoding-decoding model**). 'Cultural studies' becomes the academic context in which culture is examined; film and television studies can be located within this context with the recognition that they are not discrete and self-contained discourses (see **discourse**). Indeed, as Williams constantly argued, the history of cultural studies in Britain is the struggle to oblige institutions to include those areas of cultural experience which challenged the 'symbolic power' of those controlling academic institutions (see **Bourdieu, Pierre**).

Though the stress in Williams' cultural analyses is on signifying practices which express aspects of human experience and how they relate, the base and superstructure model informs his thinking about the fundamental relationships between culture and society (see **base and superstructure; signifying practice**). In *Marxism and Literature* (1977) and elsewhere, however, he examined in detail the limitations of material determination and resisted theoretical generalizations about cultural formation which could not be grounded in specific analyses of the causes and natures of, for example, changes in signifying practices at specific historical moments. His writing about culture and cultural studies is a continual oscillation between an identification of a cultural phenomenon – a television programme, television itself, a 'key word' – and the anatomizing of the social conjuncture surrounding and structuring it.

The time, in the late 1970s, when Williams' ideas were developing within the British cultural and academic context co-existed with the impact of other theorizations of culture which claimed to be more substantially located in Marxism. Structuralist theories of culture, particularly associated with Louis **Althusser**, and later Michel **Foucault**, gained currency through recent English translations and their circulation in journals like *Screen*. These theories challenged the particular history of individual or social experience as the foundation of cultural practice; the lived experience which a particular reader or viewer brought to any text needed to be understood in relation to his or her antecedent construction as a subject whose identity had been formed with the establishment of **consciousness** (see **Lacan, Jacques; subject and subjectivity**). Subjects were interpellated by

texts or institutions, like culture, which functioned, 'ideologically', on behalf of the state.

'Ideology' added another further dimension to the analysis of culture (see **ideology and hegemony**). Althusser identified culture as an ideological state apparatus, but the distinction, if any, between ideology and culture has since been the subject of continuous debate. However, Althusser's formulation positioned culture once again as having a social function; whereas Arnold argued that culture could reconcile social divisions, Althusserian Marxism proposed that culture as ideology perpetuated social divisions in the interests of those in power – a conclusion which, from a different direction, Eagleton had arrived at in his analysis of Arnoldian culture.

Neither Williams' nor Althusser's account of culture concentrates on popular culture, but the fact that both draw on Marxist social theories led to an examination of the role of culture in the relationship between dominant and subordinate classes. The extension of the idea of culture to include those signifying practices associated with the mass of the people, however, meant that popular culture became the object to be theorized by those with an interest in the social and political function of culture. Film and television occupied a particularly interesting position as media which could be seen as central to the experience of most people and an obvious site for the operation of ideology through culture.

In the late 1970s and early 1980s, the Althusserian and Lacanian modes of explanation provided the platform for Laura **Mulvey**'s attack on the patriarchal nature of mainstream Hollywood cinema. Film, as a popular cultural form was seen to reinforce existing power relations; spectatorship articulated the unconscious male desire to objectify and dominate women. Even those who dissented from psychoanalytic accounts of cinema's ideological apparatus argued that Hollywood narratives, especially those which deployed its version of **realism**, operated to reaffirm an individualistic, white, male supremacist ideology (see **psychoanalysis**). Other ethnic or **gender** groups were effectively marginalized by mainstream cinema and television. John Fiske's analysis of the *Hart to Hart* series in *Television Culture* (1987) stands as an example of this kind of ideological effect (see **ethnicity**).

The development of cultural studies in the 1980s and 1990s further complicated the understanding of culture. The model of culture as a site of hegemonic contestation between dominant and subordinate groups, and the sophistication of encoding and decoding models challenged recently established paradigms and opened up other possibilities. Fiske's own later work, building on that of writers associated with the Birmingham Centre for Contemporary Cultural Studies, indicated ways in which encoded messages from, for example, a multinational company like News Corporation or MTV might be decoded and used by teenage girls to develop their own group culture and identity in a movement of resistance to the dominant encoding. The **binary** polarities of mainstream and marginal cultures were challenged by **queer theory** or a **multiculturalism** which argued that such categorizations ignored the complexities and variety of cultural experience within so-called minorities, and reinforced the cultural domination of groups whose power was, in practice, limited to the need to find new markets, sometimes by attempting to incorporate the culture of groups outside the mainstream. Some accounts of post-modernity present it not as simply a capitulation to consumerism, but as a cultural development which sublated high culture and popular culture, de-centring traditional sources of cultural power (see **modernism and post-modernism**).

The place of film and television has changed both in cultural study and in the culture at large. Changed delivery systems, the fragmentation of audiences and the development of what Jim Collins (1993) calls 'the array' have meant that these cultural phenomena exist in a different way from their first entry into culture. In the academic context, courses ostensibly concerned with national histories or political geographies, for example, now include film and television not as 'accompanying illustrations' but as important ways into understanding a 'whole way of life'.

Culture is indeed a complicated word as Williams warned us. But, so long as we continue to use it to think about the aesthetic, social and political practices of individuals, groups and nations, it should not be otherwise.

References

Arnold, M. (1963) *Culture and Anarchy* (first published 1896), ed. J. Dover Wilson, Cambridge: Cambridge University Press.

Bryson, J. (ed.) (1967) *Matthew Arnold Poetry and Prose*, London: Rupert Hart-Davis.

Collins, J. (1993) 'Genericity in the Nineties: Eclectic Irony and the New Sincerity', in J. Collins *et al.* (eds) *Film Theory Goes to the Movies*, New York: Routledge.

Eagleton, T. (1989) *Literary Theory*, London: Blackwell.

Fiske, J. (1987) *Television Culture*, London: Methuen.

Leavis, F. R. (1962) *The Common Pursuit*, London: Penguin Books.

Hall, S. and Whannell, P. (1966) *The Popular Arts* (2nd edn), London: Hutchinson Educational.

Williams, R. (1966) *Culture and Society, 1780–1950*, London: Penguin Books.

—— (1976) *Keywords*, London: Fontana/Croom Helm.

—— (1977) *Marxism and Literature*, Oxford: Oxford University Press.

—— (1981) *Culture*, London: Fontana.

Further reading

Gomme, A. (1961) 'Criticism and the Reading Public', in B. Ford (ed.) *The Pelican Guide to English Literature: The Modern Age*, London: Penguin Books.

Morley, D. and Chen K-.H. (1996) *Stuart Hall: Critical Dialogues in Cultural Studies*, London Routledge.

Williams, R. (1989) *The Politics of Modernism*, London: Verso.

PHILIP SIMPSON

current affairs

One of the most established broadcast genres, current affairs encompasses news, documentaries, magazine shows, in-depth reporting and other reality-based programmes. Part of British broadcasting's public service mandate since its inception, current affairs programming has helped define the identity of electronic media. Television's properties of 'liveness' has made it more suited to news gathering because, unlike film, it can transmit information immediately. On both sides of the Atlantic, current affairs programming has therefore helped television establish itself as reputable.

Current affairs form one of the dominant genres of early British television (see **genre**). Unlike the largely stage-bound televised plays of the 1930s, current affairs broadcasts were instrumental in establishing an aesthetic form for the new medium. Programmes like the *Picture Page* (1936–1939; 1946–1952), the period's most successful show, broadcast short studio interviews with various guests. Linked by Switchboard Girl, Joan Miller, it drew on television's relationships with telephony, journalism and radio to foreground the intimacy that would become central to the medium. Current affairs also took cameras outside with broadcasts like *The Coronation of King George VI* (1937). This mobile unit also televised other events – for example, sport – and showed viewers some of London's major sights. When BBC television closed down for the Second World War in 1939, current affairs genres had already been established through these fledgling magazine shows and media events. After television reopened in 1946, the number of outside broadcasts soared, supplemented by victory ceremonies commemorating the war's end. However, the genre soon lost ground to light entertainment **quiz shows**, comedies and dramas despite the debut of *Panorama* in 1953, the longest-running current affairs programme on British television, which added investigative journalism to the mix, and the introduction of *BBC Television News* in 1954.

The appearance of *World in Action* on British screens in 1963 heralded further transformations as its hard news stories and examinations of social change associated current affairs with cutting-edge television. The series went on to become the flagship of current affairs shows, winning awards and shaping the genre into the 1990s. These shows also influenced other fictional forms. Several of *The Wednesday Plays* (1964–1970) ventured into similar terrain, taking cameras out of the studio to show viewers new worlds and unfamiliar aspects of society. A documentary-style aesthetic seen in such plays as *Cathy Come Home* (1965) and marked by hand-held camera and jump cuts reinforced this new, gritty 'authenticity'.

Series like *World in Action* and *Man Alive* (1965–1982) made no pretence to **objectivity**, often adopting a radical and critical perspective, reinforced with plenty of evidence. Meanwhile, other forms of current affairs programming favoured comfortable and reassuring formats. Populist news and entertainment magazines like *Tonight* (1957–1965) and *Nationwide* (1969–1984) provided daily commentary on news and current events, softening many of the day's toughest issues. In recent years, these populist incarnations have dominated the genre as programming has extended more towards light news, celebrity trivia, scandal and conflict. Even *Panorama* has turned towards audience-grabbing subjects, most famously in its interview with Diana, Princess of Wales in 1995.

The deregulation of broadcast television and intensified competition from **cable and satellite** have encouraged this shift away from hard news and issues-based investigative journalism on both sides of the Atlantic (see **deregulation, the United Kingdom; deregulation, the United States**). This, in turn, has led to the rise of **tabloid television** with magazine shows centred around scandal, innuendo, crime and celebrity trivia. Tabloid genres like talk shows, nightly magazines and true-life video programmes have become increasingly prominent on US and British television precisely because they are cheap to make and get reasonable ratings.

The **media event**, one of the least frequent but most prestigious and highest rated forms of current affairs, is perhaps more popular today than at any other time in broadcasting history. The most watched programmes on television, for example, Princess Diana's wedding in 1981 and her funeral in 1997, O.J. Simpson's flight in his Bronco in 1994 and his subsequent trial for murder, all extend the genre into its most spectacular incarnation. Whether random and sudden, like deaths and disasters, or pre-arranged like Royal weddings and funerals, media events still maintain their appeal in an increasingly competitive market, cementing television's hold over current affairs.

See also: broadcasting, the United Kingdom; broadcasting, the United States; documentary; live television

Further reading

Barnouw, E. (1990) *Tube of Plenty: The Evolution of American Television*, Oxford: Oxford University Press.

Vahimagi, T. (1996) *An Illustrated Guide to British Television*, Oxford: Oxford University Press.

MOYA LUCKETT

cyberspace

The term 'cyberspace' is usually credited to the science fiction writer William Gibson. Gibson used the term interchangeably with 'the matrix' in his influential science fiction trilogy, *Neuromancer, Count Zero* and *Mona Lisa Overdrive*, to describe the 'consensual hallucination' through which computer users of his near-future are able to visualize the flow of data and information as a virtual landscape. Gibson's protagonists, 'jacking in' to cyberspace, lose their physical selves to this alternate universe in which a company's information banks are simulated as a city-block, anti-piracy software as a wall, and a virus as a battering-ram.

By the mid-1980s, Gibson was regarded as a leading figure in the 'cyberpunk' movement – a science fiction subgenre characterized by its brand-names, counter-cultural protagonists and street-level technology. This central metaphor of his trilogy, which by *Mona Lisa Overdrive* had expanded and developed to engage with cyberspace ghosts, myths, voodoos and even gods, became a staple device of the genre. Although cyberpunk writing delivered a much-needed adrenaline jab to the corpus of science fiction, its potency was diluted by a host of imitators who lacked Gibson's originality and intelligence; as a result, the conventions became stilted and the tropes over-familiar. Gibson's subsequent novels, perhaps paradoxically, have described a future even closer to our own present day, involving technology barely more advanced than currently available, and a scaled-down, less fantastical model of virtual space than that of *Neuromancer*.

Although Gibson's alternative label, 'the matrix', was never taken up outside his fictional world, 'cyberspace' has become a widely-used and often ambiguous term. In the mid- to late 1990s, as **Internet** use became increasingly widespread and accessible, 'cyberspace' was frequently employed to denote the World Wide Web itself, and the term is still commonly used by companies and institutions to describe a service available through the Internet. Thus, an on-line system for ordering books is a 'cyberspace bookshop', and a means of e-mailing a health service is a 'cyberspace hospital'. In fact, services such as these are still primarily text-based, with visual content reduced to decorative logos or illustrations, and communication carried out by typing a request and waiting for the written response – a far cry from Gibson's vertiginous no-place where all information is transformed into the visual.

Another common use of the term is in reference to the on-line 'communities' of multi-user dimensions (MUDs) and their variants. Devotees of MUDs claim that Gibson's cyberspace has already become contemporary fact. Studies such as Rob Shields' edited collection, *Cultures of Internet*, suggest that users do indeed lose track of their physical body when engaged in on-line discussion, sacrificing work, relationships and sleep in their 'normal' lives for the satisfaction of friendships, 'cybersex' and even marriage within the Internet group. As with the examples above, however, MUDs remain an almost entirely text-based form, with all dialogue, actions, gestures and facial expression communicated through written language, retaining strangely old-fashioned qualities despite their reliance on a global computer network.

The ambiguity of 'cyberspace' is compounded by its further use as an analogous term to **virtual reality**, which developed about the same time as the Internet but has not yet been implemented in an accessible, popular form. While most students and office workers have easy access to the Internet, few will encounter virtual reality outside a games arcade. Yet the latter form has far more in common, both in its emphasis on the visual and its accompanying hardware of viewing helmets and eyepieces, with Gibson's original concept.

Finally, the twin concepts of the Internet and virtual reality have been conflated into the 'cyberspace' of recent feature films – perhaps most notably *Johnny Mnemonic* (Robert Longo, 1995), adapted from a Gibson short story, and *The Lawnmower Man* (Brett Leonard, 1992), whose selling-point was a depiction of 'virtual sex'. As an intriguing echo, these films, like most major new releases, were backed by their own Internet sites. Yet screen depiction of cyberspace can be found in unexpected places: Steven Lisberger's *Tron*, which visualized the interior of arcade machines as a glowing virtual landscape remarkably similar to that of *Neuromancer*'s matrix, was released in 1982, when Gibson's novel was still in manuscript.

References

Gibson, W. (1984) *Neuromancer*, New York: Ace Books.

Shields, R. (ed.) (1996) *Cultures of Internet*, London: Sage.

Further reading

Sterling, B. (1988) *Mirrorshades: The Cyberpunk Anthology*, New York: Ace Books.

WILL BROOKER

D

dance and film

From the earliest days of filmmaking, beginning
with the movie camera's utilization as an instrument of movement analysis, dance served as a
favourite screen subject. A set of paradigms for the
combination of these two arts – dance cinematically reconstructed from stage choreography;
dance created by specifically cinematic devices;
and dance situated within a narrative – developed
even before the nickelodeon era had ended.

The silent era

In the early period of cinema, choreography
provided ready-made visual material for the
camera. From vaudeville houses, film captured
both 'high' and 'low' culture. The former included
influential proto-modern dancers such as Loie
Fuller, whose widely imitated performances consisted of a combination of movement, yards of
swirling material that covered the stage, and highly
theatrical lighting. The latter consisted of shapely,
acrobatic 'hoochy-kooch' girls who displayed high
kicks, splits and cartwheels. *Annabella* (Edison,
1897), a hand-tinted film of one of Fuller's
numerous imitators, represents the former style.
In contrast, *French Acrobatic Dance* (Biograph, 1903)
shows dancers performing a range of 'tricks':
backbends and splits, and hopping about on one
leg while gripping the other by the hand to keep it
aloft.

The **narrative** contexts in which these dances
appeared imbued them with sexual implications. In
How Millionaires Sometimes Entertain Aboard their Yachts
(Biograph, 1905), a young girl dances wildly until
she collapses in exhaustion. Similarly, in *Just Before
the Raid* (Biograph, 1904), women in a bar cavort
drunkenly on top of a table. Dance also became
part of a larger anthropological project: cameras
caught 'ethnic' dancers from the Middle East to
Japan, and Edison's cameramen filmed the Native
American snake and eagle dances.

The musical

With the arrival of sound film came the musical,
and studios began producing revues which presented a variety show filled with song and dance
(see **musical, the**). Narrative musicals quickly
followed, and in these films a tension emerged
between the non-narrative musical numbers and
the film's **plot**.

Although choreographers such as George Bal-
anchine showed an interest in cinema, and in
experimenting with the medium (he created a
number of interesting dances for George Marshall's
The Goldwyn Follies in 1938), the first major dance
director of the musical was Busby Berkeley.
Berkeley had an eye for arranging bodies in space,
creating innovative patterns, moving the camera
and cleverly cutting in such a way that movement
flowed seamlessly from shot to shot (see **continuity editing**). The dancers in *42nd Street* (Lloyd
Bacon, 1933), *Gold Diggers of 1933* (Mervyn Le Roy,
1933) and *Footlight Parade* (Lloyd Bacon, 1933)
rarely showed off specific dance techniques.
Instead, the rows and rows of women served more
as bricks in an architectural structure or as parts of
a constantly shifting kaleidoscope.

With his skill and concern for camera style, actor/dancer Fred Astaire changed screen dance considerably in his Hollywood films of the 1930s and 1940s. Although the use of a 'theatrical' context remained, the dance began to emanate more from the narrative, and to serve as an expression of romance and emotion rather than mere spectacle. The camerawork shifted from Berkeley's editing-dependent choreography; instead, an attempt was made to maintain the integrity of the space and follow Astaire's movements unobtrusively. Cutting was kept to a minimum – especially cutaways to audience reaction.

Gene Kelly followed in Astaire's footsteps, eliminating theatrical motivations for choreographic sequences. Musical numbers ranging from 'New York, New York' in *On the Town* (Gene Kelly and Stanley Donen, 1949) to 'I Like Myself' in *It's Always Fair Weather* (Kelly and Donen, 1955) became visualizations of the characters' emotional state. A choreographic shift also took place around this time: in the mid-1940s American theatrical ballet had begun to incorporate jazz and modern dance elements under the influence of such major dancemakers as Agnes de Mille and Jerome Robbins. Kelly took his cue from them, developing lengthy classical pieces that were entire ballets, as in *An American in Paris* (Vincente Minnelli, 1951). Robbins took this further in *West Side Story* (Robert Wise and Jerome Robbins, 1961) through a rare mixture of stylized choreography and naturalistic street settings.

Since the 1980s, the tide has turned back to highly 'edited' dance that fragments both the body and space. Be it Bob Fosse's *All that Jazz* (1979), in which a series of close-ups focus on a shoulder roll, a hip jut or other isolated movement, or the rock-**video** style of *Flashdance* (Adrian Lyne, 1983), the camera is no longer content to follow the dance but plays an active part in its presentation.

Cinedance

The American **avant-garde** began to experiment with combinations of dance and cinematic movement that would create a form of choreography possible only on screen. Maya Deren's *Study in Choreography for the Camera* (1944) is the quintessen-

tial example of the style: leaps that begin in one shot continue into the next, so that the dance floats from one space to an entirely different space in a single jump. Movements broken up into several shots seem to continue longer than any dancer could actually sustain them. In Trisha Brown's *Water Motor* (1978), filmed by Babette Mangolte, the same solo takes place twice. In both cases, the camera maintains its distance, filming the dance in long shot and without cuts; the second version, however, is cinematically slowed down, showing in close detail the flow and change in muscular tension and weight. *Pas de Deux* (1968) by Norman Maclaren uses strobe effects that form multiple images of the dancers' bodies which break apart and rejoin, while Hilary Harris' *Eight Variations on a Dance Theme* (1968) takes a simple and brief piece of choreography and presents it in eight different ways, each version more highly edited than the last.

Further reading

Brooks, V. (1981) *The Art and Craft of Filming Dance as Documentary*, New York: Columbia University Press.

Croce, A. (1977) *The Fred Astaire and Ginger Rogers Book*, New York Vintage Books.

Delameter, J. (1978) *Dance in the Hollywood Film*, Michigan UMI: Research Press.

Film Culture (1965) no. 39 (special issue on Maya Deren).

Mueller, J. (1985) *Astaire Dancing: The Musical Films*, New York: Alfred A. Knopf .

KAREN BACKSTEIN

deconstruction

Deconstruction is a movement in literary and linguistic theory and philosophy, dating from the 1960s and growing out of the work of French philosopher Jacques **Derrida** (see **semiotics**). Although the term 'deconstruction' is sometimes used informally to mean detailed or critical analysis of any kind, deconstruction in the more technical sense involves the systematic questioning, at a fundamental level, of the determinacy of meaning in language and, by extension or by philosophical specialization, in literature, writing and speech (see **determination**). Where other theoretical frameworks, such as structuralism, might operate by establishing units of meaning in texts – even by revealing hidden units of meaning – or by mapping one system of signification onto another, deconstruction forces the issue of indeterminacy of meaning by questioning the underlying metaphysics of meaning: that is, the irreducible meaningfulness of any of the terms in a linguistic or philosophical system, even the ostensibly 'basic' terms.

While its roots and growth in the academic world can be charted fairly accurately, deconstruction cannot really be said to be one theory. Derrida and his earliest followers have had many later followers, and beyond a certain point there is no particular uniformity of thought or practice among them; one branch of the movement may represent a very different approach to literary analysis than another. At times, deconstructionists are united as much as anything else by their critics.

Some critics of Derrida, and explicitly (or otherwise) of the work of at least some of his followers, have expressed concern over what appears to be at once a too easy and an impossibly difficult renunciation of the very idea of meaning in language. Terry **Eagleton** offers a defence of Derrida against such attacks:

> [Derrida] is not seeking, absurdly, to deny the existence of relatively determinate truths, meanings, identities, intentions, historical continuities; he is seeking rather to see such things as the effects of a wider and deeper history – of language, of the unconscious, of social institutions and practices.... [The] widespread opinion that deconstruction denies the existence of anything but discourse, or affirms a realm of pure difference in which all meaning and identity dissolves, is a travesty of Derrida's...work.
>
> (Eagleton 1983: 148)

Other criticism of deconstruction, in particular that of John M. Ellis in *Against Deconstruction* (1989), has pointed to the tendency on the part of at least some deconstructionists to place the movement above the fray of academic discourse and debate. Deconstructionists, Ellis argues, use (or misuse) the notion of indeterminate meaning as a pretext for avoiding a clear, cogent account of the theory itself.

The relevance of deconstruction to film theory takes a path through literary theory and philosophy – disciplines which film theory has drawn on, or stood in the shadow of, depending on one's perspective, for a long time and in many ways. The photographic underpinnings of film raise questions of immanent and determinate meaning at another level from those of written, literary texts. Again, no particular consensus has emerged. Film theorists have drawn on ideas and formulations from deconstruction; it would be extremely unusual for a film theorist to identify him- or herself as a 'deconstructionist', whereas other such labels from literary studies do occur (**genre** theorist, textual analyst, psychoanalytic theorist, etc.).

See also: psychoanalysis; structuralism and poststructuralism

References

Eagleton, T. (1983) *Literary Theory: An Introduction*, Minneapolis: University of Minnesota Press.
Ellis, J. M. (1989) *Against Deconstruction*, Princeton: Princeton University Press.

Further reading

Derrida, J. (1976) *Of Grammatology*, trans. G. C. Spivak, Baltimore: Johns Hopkins University Press.
Culler, J. (1982) *On Deconstruction: Theory and Criticism after Structuralism*, Ithaca, NY: Cornell University Press.

DAVID A. BLACK

Deleuze, Gilles and Guattari, Félix

Deleuze, b. 1925; d. 1995

Guattari, b. 1930; d. 1992

The French writing partnership of the philosopher Gilles Deleuze and practising psychoanalyst and political activist Félix Guattari is best known to the Anglophone world for their two volume *Capitalism and Schizophrenia* (1983; 1987). Although they rarely discuss cinema, their critique of both **psychoanalysis** and Marxism bears directly on the Lacanian/Althusserian paradigm pervasive in English-speaking film theory during the 1970s and early 1980s (see **Althusser, Louis; Lacan, Jacques; Marx, Karl**). However, this critique has entered film theory in a sporadic fashion at best, perhaps due to the formidable conceptual and stylistic difficulty of their writing. Their work has found some currency in post-structuralist media theory, especially with regard to non-linear formats like hypertext or the **Internet** (see **structuralism and post-structuralism**). Of more direct significance for film theory is Deleuze's two volume *Cinema* (Deleuze 1986; 1989).

References

Deleuze, G. (1986; 1989) *Cinema* (vols. 1 and 2), trans. H. Tomlinson and B. Habberjam (vol. 1); trans. H. Tomlinson and R. Galeta (vol. 2), Minneapolis: University of Minnesota Press.

Deleuze, G. and Guattari, F. (1983; 1987) *Capitalism and Schizophrenia* (vols 1 and 2), trans. R. Hurley, M. Seem and H. R. Lane (vol. 1); trans. B. Massumi (vol. 2), Minnesota: University of Minnesota Press.

Further reading

Bogue, R. (1989) *Deleuze and Guattari*, London: Routledge.

ALLAN JAMES THOMAS

denotation

Defining a particular kind of meaning, denotation complements **connotation**. Denotation refers to the circumscribed meanings of a word: 'school' strictly means and denotes an institution of learning, although schools are often associated with other kinds of behaviour. An object in film usually suggests its existence in the world: a sleeping cat on screen *denotes* the actual cat used by the filmmakers, although the image of a cat may also *connote* witchcraft, mystery or domestic plea-

sure. Film, like other forms of art, relies on both denotation and connotation for its effects.

See also: Metz, Christian; polysemic; semiotics; sign

GABRIEL M. PALETZ

depth of field

Depth of field refers to the extent to which all objects in the film frame appear in clear and sharp focus. With a wide-angle lens, everything in both the foreground and the background remains crisp and visible; in a shallow field, only a small portion stands out while the rest stays blurry and undifferentiated. Directors such as Jean Renoir, Roberto Rossellini and Orson Welles often maintained a wide depth of field in their films, carefully arranging décor, performers and movement patterns in such a way as to carry the spectator's eye from the screen's flat surface and give the illusion of three-dimensionality, a style the film critic André **Bazin** lauded for its realist aesthetic (see **aesthetics; realism**).

See also: camera style and lens style

KAREN BACKSTEIN

deregulation, the United Kingdom

Initially coined in the Unites States, deregulation is a term which had limited but powerful currency in discussions of broadcasting policy in the United Kingdom in the late 1980s and early 1990s. Its value now is that the debate about deregulation highlights the differences between the UK and US broadcasting systems (see **broadcasting, the United Kingdom; broadcasting, the United States**). By implication, the debate about deregulation is a debate about ownership and accountability in television, and about public service, as opposed to market-driven, broadcasting.

The UK Conservative government from 1979 to 1997 was committed to the transfer of the ownership of public utilities like electricity, water and transport from public to private bodies. In 1988 it turned its attention to broadcasting, with particular application to television, which, in Britain at that time was largely terrestrial. Since 1955, British television had been regulated by two institutions whose governing bodies are appointed by Parliament: the British Broadcasting Corporation (BBC) and the Independent Broadcasting Authority (IBA). The BBC is funded though an annual licence fee paid by anyone who has a television receiver, and the IBA was responsible for the channels that received income from advertising. Both bodies, though government-appointed, exercised a degree of independence from direct government interference, but, unlike the US Federal Communications Commission, exerted proactive influence over programming in terms of quality or on matters of public concern. The BBC's explicit commitment to educate, entertain and inform was shared implicitly by the IBA.

The Conservative government sought to challenge this 'cosy duopoly' on the grounds that might be summarized as follows:

- it limited the choice of consumers to what the four channels provided;
- it restricted competition in the production of television programmes;
- it fostered inefficient and costly union practices;
- it allowed the BBC too great a distance from the needs and wishes of its audience; and
- the IBA franchise to independent companies brought in too little revenue to government in exchange for their allocation of the limited broadcasting spectrum.

After much public debate the Broadcasting Act of 1990 brought about changes. These were less radical than in other public spheres – initial ideas about making the BBC sell advertising or become a subscription channel, for example, were dropped, but the implications of the changes were significant. Licences for the commercial channels, which are regionally based, were auctioned to the highest bidder, subject to certain quality provisions and specific requirements like news, religious and children's programming. Twenty-five per cent of programmes on all channels, including the BBC, had to be made independently of the five big commercial television companies, and ownership of independent companies was restricted so that

the original regional basis of IBA programming could be retained. The BBC had to set up more effective structures for public access and consultation and the IBA became the Independent Television Commission (ITC) with 'a lighter touch'. This meant that it could not pre-view programmes or intervene in programming policies other than retrospectively – either by fining programme companies or by shortening or revoking licences. Thus the ITC still has to monitor programmes and advertisements and, supported by audience research, seek 'to maintain proper standards' (see **audience**). It also 'supports and encourages high quality and diversity in national and regional services'.

The consequences of these changes are still debated. The auction of licences, it is argued, has led to money being taken away from programme-making to meet the cost of the franchise, a reversal of previous priorities. The BBC has been encouraged to put its energies into selling its programmes and using outside production facilities where these are cheaper, leading to staff and cost-cutting internally. Legislation has been changed to allow fewer companies to own or have influence in other companies. The 'lighter touch' ITC has made some critical reviews of the performance of television companies, and given formal warnings about the screening of violence, sex scenes and bad language. There has been no shortening or revoking of licences.

The biggest changes in the environment of British television have come from other sources. Throughout the 1990s, Rupert Murdoch personally, and his News Corporation institutionally, had attacked British broadcasting, and the BBC in particular, as elitist. With sympathetic support from the Thatcher governments, Murdoch's BSkyB had by the end of the decade become the most successful provider of satellite television to Britain, primarily through the provision of film and sport programming. This has, perhaps, been the most significant form of deregulation in the UK. In 1998, however, the share of the viewing audience for all non-terrestrial channels in the UK, measured individually, was only 12.9 per cent (see **cable and satellite**).

The 'mixed economy' of regulation, through governmental support for broadcasting as a public service, and deregulation, through satellites governed by market forces, still delivers a diversity of programmes which are free at the point of delivery to most UK viewers. The national and cultural homogeneity sustained by arrangement is often commented on, negatively and positively. Current regulation still governs new delivery systems such as digital and cable, though independent companies are entering this market for profit. But the fragmentation of the audience which the extension of these systems will produce may end this homogeneity, and spread revenue from **advertising** more thinly to the detriment of costly and/or minority programming.

Beyond the details and technicalities of recent and current debate on deregulation lies an older one. As Raymond **Williams** (1989) has pointed out, the press and cinema, before television, were seen to be in need of 'regulation' by the moral guardians of church or state. Cinema **censorship** continues to be a mode of regulation where both still have influence, sometimes with the collaboration of business and industry. The most prominent proponents of deregulation have not always been **multinational** media corporations with an interest in constructing the consumer as the representative figure of popular democracy. The argument for deregulation has also sprung from a libertarian conception of the popular, emergent forms which might express and represent the experiences of those without massive economic power – the **Internet** may be only the most recent example.

See also: deregulation, the United States; popular, the

References

BARB. Online. Available: www.barb.co.uk

Williams, R. (1989) *The Politics of Modernism*, London: Verso.

Further reading

Hood, S. and Tabary-Peterssen, T. (1997) *On Television* (4th edn), London: Pluto.

Independent Television Commission (1998) *Factfile*, London: ITC.

Paterson, R. (ed.) (1990) *Organising for Change*, London: BFI Publishing.

PHILIP SIMPSON

deregulation, the United States

Beginning in 1980 with the election of President Reagan, American broadcasting policy has been guided by a philosophy of deregulation. A key component of what came to be known as Reaganomics, this philosophy advocated less government regulation in order to promote free competition and encourage investment in new technology – and eventually to ensure more consumer choices. However, these policies have also ensured increased monopolization in the overlapping industries of **Internet** service providing, telecommunications, broadcasting and cable.

Whereas it may be arguable that this policy has provided more choice to the consumer, it is certainly true that broadcasting in the United States has been further governed by market forces rather than by notions of operating in the public interest. In this new paradigm, it is the consumer and not the citizen whose needs are met. Deregulation has resulted in larger media companies that have been able to develop and move into new markets, creating new alliances between unlikely conglomerates (such as that which exists between Microsoft and the National Broadcasting Company with the cable station and Website MSNBC).

In President Reagan's first administration, the governing body of the communications industry (whose commissioner is appointed by the President), the Federal Communications Commission (FCC), abolished many regulations that applied to radio, simplified licence renewal applications and relaxed regulations for operating television stations. In the guise of decreasing unnecessary bureaucracy and encumbering of dynamic industries, these moves increased the power of already existing broadcasting oligopolies, allowing them to extend their reaches. Another result of these changes was that minority ownership of stations during the Reagan era (1980–1992) actually decreased. In 1984, Congress passed the Cable Communications Policy Act, which allowed cable operators in this rapidly burgeoning industry to set their own rates without any federal government regulation.

The Telecommunications Act of 1996 revealed President Clinton's agenda of accelerating deregulation. Although much of the focus of this Act was an attempt to lend governance to the 'frontier' of the Internet, a key element of the legislation was relaxed ownership and licensing rules in broadcasting. These changes increase the power of major media corporations and decrease the influence that the FCC can have on ensuring that the public interest is met. These changes also forced the FCC to abandon further one of its stated goals: to encourage diversity of ownership in the communication industries.

Previous to the passage of this Act by Congress, broadcast companies were not permitted to own more than twelve television stations. The Act eliminated this restriction, instead allowing one company to own television stations that reach up to 35 per cent of all the nation's homes. This provision enables a major network such as CBS to start a new network. (However, a major network cannot buy another network.) The Telecommunications Act also eased restrictions in radio broadcasting. Before the Act, a network could own only twenty AM and twenty FM stations nationwide. The new Act meant that a network could own up to eight stations within a market that had forty-five stations in the area. In addition – and perhaps most important – the Act encouraged cross-ownership: networks can own television, radio and cable outlets within the same market, encouraging diversified corporations with interests in a variety of communications industries.

One of the key functions of the FCC has been the licensing of stations. As each place on the broadcasting spectrum is not owned by a station but rather is rented, the FCC, acting on the behalf of the people, determines if the station has been operating in the public interest, and can deny or grant licences depending on this key, if ambiguous, factor. In the past, licence renewal was required every five years for television stations and every seven years for radio stations. The Telecommunications Act changed this renewal period to eight years and simplified the licence application, no longer requiring stations to supply additional documentation. Cable television regulation re-

mained outside the purview of the FCC, instead falling under the jurisdiction of local governments, and thereby allowing cable companies to gain control in a variety of markets.

Although the Telecommunications Act was purportedly designed to encourage free competition and eliminate unnecessary governmental interference, it was coupled with the Communications Decency Act, which added three provisions designed to control content on the Internet and in broadcasting and cable (see **censorship**). The Supreme Court overturned the provision on indecent material on the Internet, citing its unconstitutionality, but the two other provisions that affect the television industry remain. First, sexually explicit shows on cable are blocked so that only viewers who subscribe to these channels can view these programmes. Second, all shows are now voluntarily rated by stations and these ratings are read by a 'V-chip', allowing viewers to eliminate the broadcasting of certain 'objectionable' programming. In order to protect children and empower parents, the government has also increased its role in policing what is permissible and proper. As a result, constitutional rights of free speech that protect the print medium do not extend to the broadcasting industry and the ability of the FCC to regulate indecent programming is re-emphasized even as it deregulates.

See also: broadcasting, the United Kingdom; broadcasting, the United States; cable and satellite; deregulation, the United Kingdom

EDWARD MILLER

Derrida, Jacques

b. 1930

French philosopher and literary theorist, Jacques Derrida is best known as the originator of **deconstruction**, a mode of textual analysis whereby the text is 'deconstructed' so that its contradictions, flaws and ambiguities are exposed. Following on from **Nietzsche**, Derrida contends that humanity cannot perceive of any 'reality' outside representation. His work has been hugely influential since the late 1960s, and forms the basis of much post-modernist theory (see **modernism and post-modernism**). In the United States, his theories inspired a 'deconstructionist' movement that is especially active in literary studies and in history.

Derrida's theories have sparked fierce scholarly debate. For some commentators, deconstruction represents a means of breaking with the oppressive truth-claims of modernist discourses (see **discourse**). On the other hand, Derrida's critics – most notably Jürgen **Habermas** – have attacked deconstruction as anti-rationalist, arguing that it undermines the practice of critical reason.

Derrida is Director of Studies at the Ecole des Hautes Etudes en Science Sociales in Paris, and a visiting professor at many universities in Europe and the US.

See also: difference; structuralism and post-structuralism

Further reading

Derrida, J. (1976) *Of Grammatology*, trans. Gayatri Spivak, Baltimore: The John Hopkins University Press.
—— (1978) *Writing and Difference*, trans. Alan Bass, London: Routledge and Kegan Paul.

SARA GWENLLIAN JONES

desire

Desire is generally understood as the identification of a want by the human subject, the fulfilment of which will bring a sense of happiness, satisfaction or completion. The term has been developed extensively by film theorists, literary critics and theorists of **psychoanalysis** in an attempt to explicate the relationship between the (desiring) subject and the (desired) object. But desire, if summed up simply as 'what I want', has given rise to two questions around which there is no simple agreement: what is the mainspring of desire, and how may the 'I' who desires be conceptualized?

In the twentieth century, it is psychoanalytic interpretations of desire and its sources which have been most influential in a western cultural frame. **Freud** and **Lacan** each identified desire as an outcome of the complex psychical processes of traumatic detachment from parent figures. Desire appears as the **unconscious** yearning to make good the sense of loss and **lack** which the establishment of separate subjectivity entails. Lacan identified the **mirror stage** as critical in the passage to autonomous subjectivity, whereby the infant, in viewing its own reflection, experiences for the first time its identity discrete from that of its mother. Simultaneously, the infant experiences a subjectivity fractured between image and the self. Thus begins an unconscious lifetime quest for coherent subjectivity, which manifests itself as desire – for people, commodities and experiences – to fill the gaps. It is a quest which is destined to remain unrealized, since its initial cause can never be reversed.

Criticism of psychoanalytic interpretations of desire has arisen around their inattention to the specific material conditions and histories in which desire has been articulated, experienced and negotiated, as well as their privileging of the individual subject over broader social and cultural context. The production and mediation of desire as a social rather than a psychical construct constitutes the second main interpretative frame among desire theorists. Here, desire has appeared as being dynamically interwoven with relations of power in western society. Theorists argue that the articulation of desire is inextricably bound to prevailing modes of subordination and domination in a society: the avenues through which desire moves are never innocent byways, but are always routes signposted with hierarchical relations of **gender**, **race** and **class**.

Prominent in this field of criticism have been feminist theorists such as Teresa de **Lauretis** (1984) and Catherine Belsey (1994), who have argued that narratives of desire are deeply embedded in and shaped by a patriarchal, imperialist **culture** (see **patriarchy**). Here, desire understood as the will to dominate or to possess the desired object, may express itself as easily in tropes of conquest and colonization of the desired object or **Other** as in culturally 'benign' narratives of sexual love, and may be used to justify the **violence** of the conqueror as readily as the caress of the lover. Further, while romance narratives in text and film may constitute more conventionally understood and acceptable representations of desire, these too are marked by patriarchal and normatively heterosexual relations in which the idealized passivity of the feminine, and the activity and heroism of the masculine, are constantly re-inscribed and given further cultural legitimation.

Theorists have also pointed to the gendered underpinnings of psychoanalytic interpretations of desire, and their implications for film theory. The signification of women as 'lack' within Lacanian models, for example, and their relegation to a passive position within classical literature and filmic narratives as the object of desire rather than occupying the position of the desiring subject, has underpinned a complex debate on the position of the female spectator (see **narrative**). Laura **Mulvey** early on contended that within the logics of dominant filmic/psychoanalytic interpretations in the 1970s, the desiring **gaze** within film and of its audience was established overwhelmingly as male. The **voyeurism** and scopophilia under-pinning the controlling look construct woman as pleasurable **spectacle** whose excessive, threaten-ing (and in psychoanalytic terms, potentially castrating) femininity is contained. In response to such perspectives, the disruption of a gaze and of a desire which take their cues from inside the field of normative power relations, and the development of alternative renderings of desire marked variously by instability, marginality and difference, has preoccupied both theorists and some filmmakers.

See also: feminist theory

References

Belsey, C. (1994) *Desire: Love Stories in Western Culture*, Oxford: Blackwell.

JANE LONG

determination

Whenever anyone employs the term 'determina-tion' within the study of cultural production, or uses any of its cognates such as 'determined', 'caused', 'produced', 'generated', 'effected', etc., one necessarily raises the difficult issue of the nature of social causality. What the concept of determination stakes out, as opposed to these other terms, is the specific manner in which this issue has been thought through within a Marxist framework (see **Marxist aesthetics**). Although one can certainly pursue the question of the nature of social causality in other ways, it is this particular Marxist tradition which has proven to be the most influential within film and television studies.

As a starting point, the concept of determination should be situated in relation to the broader concept of determinism. In its most extreme form, determinism designates the philosophic position that every event has specific historical and social preconditions without which that event could not have occurred. In this view, the identification of the determinations of an event or a particular social phenomenon is equivalent to the discovery of its causes. This extreme formulation of determinism derives from the notions of causality that are found within the natural sciences. But with the recogni-tion that the forms of causality operative in the social sphere do not appear to be comparable to those of the natural realm, this extreme position has consequently been put into question. Instead of treating social determinations as the precise fixing of outcomes, there has been an increasing tendency to understand determinations as the imposition of limits. From this perspective, social determinations do not completely eliminate choice and voluntary action from the social realm, but only set the parameters in which the human agent can operate. It has been through these two opposing formula-tions that the concept of determination has been theoretically developed within the Marxist tradi-tion.

The Marxist concept of determination, however, entails more than just a philosophic reflection on the general nature of social determinism. Also connected with the concept is a particular vision of the basic structure of societies and the interactions occurring within. This vision is encapsulated in the **base and superstructure** model. In the more rigidly deterministic interpretations of the scheme, the economic base of society is perceived to be the sole and ultimate source of social causation with the activities of the superstructure only capable of being passively determined by it (see **econo-mism**). This interpretation was extensively criti-cized, particularly by the Marxist philosopher

Louis **Althusser**. Instead of depriving the super-structure of any real causal effectivity, Althusser claimed that all of the activities that constituted the superstructure should be perceived to be relatively autonomous, having their own independent forms of development, and capable of effecting other aspects of the social formation, including the economic. The image of society that emerges from Althusser's account is one in which the social formation is perceived to be composed of a variety of semi-autonomous instances that causally interact with one another. To describe the interactive nature of these relations, Althusser invokes the Freudian notion of overdetermination, a concept meant to replace the notion of pure unilinear cause and effect relations. On this view, the concept of overdetermination does not just indicate the diversity of factors that one must take into account in the investigation of any particular social phenomenon, but also underscores the fact that social elements can simultaneously determine one another.

Althusser's revision of the base–superstructure model has been significantly influential within film and television studies. Many film theorists have resisted the idea that the form and content of narrative films were somehow directly determined by the economic base of the society in which they were made. Althusser's framework appeared to offer an alternative account in which film production could be seen to be relatively autonomous with respect to the determinations of other social practices. In addition, Althusser's concept of over-determination has been adopted as a means by which to theorize the multiplicity of factors that are involved in the production of any given film or television programme, be they economic, techno-logical or political.

Further reading

Althusser, L. (1969) 'Contradiction and Over-determination', in *For Marx*, trans. B. Brewster, London: Allen Lane.

Williams, R. (1977) *Marxism and Literature*, Oxford: Oxford University Press.

TICO ROMAO

diachronic

Introduced by Ferdinand de **Saussure** at the beginning of the twentieth century, the term 'diachronic' stands in opposition to the term **synchronic**, and refers to the historic-compara-tive style of linguistics as advocated by the grammarians of the nineteenth century. Interested only in historic language development and partly motivated by the search for the Indo-European proto-language, diachronic language analysis was unable to supply a cognitive (see **cognitive theory**) or grammatic model of language and so has been mostly neglected through the decades of the Chomskyan paradigm of generative grammar, which emphasized the grammatical structure of language rather than its historical development. Since the 1960s, a revival of interest in the reasons for language change has seen a return to the study of diachronic language development. The term has been taken up by film scholars to refer to historical analysis as opposed to a synchronic or contempor-ary analysis.

EVA VIETH

dialectic and dialectical montage

The term 'dialectic' has been used to refer to a logical structure where two elements, opposed to each other, create a new and higher meaning through the active work of the reader/spectator. The use of the term is particularly associated with Marxist philosophy, and has influenced Marxist and left-wing theorization of cinema (see **Marxist aesthetics**).

In philosophy, dialectic refers to a principled method of enquiry. In the Socratic technique, truth is sought by the dialogue of two voices, discussing an issue until consensus is achieved. This central theme of the creation of a new unity from two opposing givens also informs G. W. F. **Hegel**'s concept of historical change, a view of history as a step-by-step directional movement. A thesis meets its antithesis and the outcome is a synthesis: a new product that is more than just the sum of the two opposing principles. The synthesis forms the new thesis for the next dialectical step. The dialectic has had its most profound influence on western culture in **Marx** and Engels' re-reading of Hegel's concept. Marxism relies on the principle of opposition and progress for its conception of the historical development towards a socialist, and ultimately communist utopia. The material conditions of existence are the basis for the emergence of the dialectic couple. For this reason, Marx calls his conception of history 'materialist dialectics'. In this conception, the opposing sides are embodied by the powerful (feudal lords, bourgeoisie) against the powerless (slaves, bondsmen or workers). History is conceived as dynamic, moving towards a goal through revolutions as steps in the resolution of conflict.

The **Frankfurt School** questioned Marx's vision of the dialectic as a move forward, with his idealistic vision of mankind as evolving towards greater rationality, and which worked towards a transformation of conflict. The Holocaust disrupts any vision of history as progress. To view catastrophic events such as the Holocaust and Hiroshima as part of a dual structure diminishes their impact on humanity.

In some post-structuralist writing (see **structuralism and post-structuralism**), the dialectic has finally been laid to rest: its conception of progress is not the only part which rings hollow to Jean **Baudrillard**'s concept of history. His vision of a society of simulacra flattens all events and perceptions. No opposition is conceivable: society has lost its taste for the 'real' event of effect and emotion, and all representations/images have the same value. Not only can no antithesis be found, the thesis itself has no power to assert itself.

The dialectic principle had its most profound effect on film theory through the writings and films by Sergei **Eisenstein**. Eisenstein created an **aesthetics** of film by the development of montage as the underlying form of film as **art**.

Soviet film writing approached the aesthetics of film from the basis of montage, with the Soviet filmmaker and teacher Lev Kuleshov pronouncing montage as the founding principle of cinema (see **Kuleshov effect**). In his conception of montage, the shots when joined together formed a composition, similar to artistic activity in the fine arts. Eisenstein took his cue from Kuleshov, but pronounced the dialectic as the important element

of montage. Two opposing images are cut together thereby creating a discord, the aim of which is to stimulate the viewer. The images – in themselves inert and politically neutral – can thus gain a political impetus. The audience can be galvanized, excited and agitated by this **cinema of attractions**. Through dialectical montage, disembodied, abstract concepts can be made tangible, although each shot in a film is a photographic image of what is already there in the world.

The most famous examples of Eisenstein's application of these principles are the montage sequences of the Odessa steps in *The Battleship Potemkin* (1926). The massacre of civilians by the tsarist army in an attempt to quell a revolution is not shot naturalistically; instead, the essence of the experience is brought out through the montage treatment. Montage is used to create meanings beyond the 'tangible'. Eisenstein demonstrated the principles of the dialectical montage in the film in diagrams, showing the progression towards political insight. Soldiers marching down the steps are intercut with a screaming woman – the synthesis is a recognition of oppression. This forms the new thesis, which combined with images of the people fleeing down the steps, leads to the next synthesis: suppression of the forces of the people. A range of different spatial arrangements, shot compositions and length of shots are juxtaposed in this complex sequence. These add to the sense of urgency, the disintegration of the old, and the movement which characterizes the political content of the film, towards its ultimate goal: collective action.

Eisenstein recognized that many effects of the Odessa sequence relied on reactions to the speed of editing or emotional identification, and he tried to distinguish the concept of 'intellectual montage' from the montage of other elements of film. In *October* (1928), he used images which placed metaphors in opposition to each other – for example, the juxtaposition of images of a peacock with a government official. The peacock is extradiegetic, no narrative logic can account for it, yet it acts as a comment on the workings of power. The dividing lines between the various forms of dialectical montage are not very clear: what is the 'unambiguous, simple' meaning of a shot, and at what point does the single shot become a metaphor for something else? Critics of

Eisenstein have also accused his style of cinema of being mechanistic – it relies on manipulation of cerebral and emotional audience responses, allowing no real activity outside the guidance of the director.

In his copious theoretical writings, his view of the affinity of cinema as an artistic practice to Marx's dialectical materialism guides Eisenstein's thinking about the merit of conflict and contrast. Later in his career as a film director, Eisenstein used the principle of contrast to incorporate other elements of film – not just editing – into his conception of dialectical montage. He experimented with colour contrasts and with contrapuntal music.

Eisenstein was fascinated by the dialectical principle of qualitative change (Marx's revolutions), and its application to 'spectator ecstasy' in the cinema. An accumulation of small, quantitative changes suddenly precipitates a major qualitative change in a system. Jacques Aumont (1987) shows how Eisenstein's equation of cinema aesthetics and the history of knowledge threaten to elide the consequences of this qualitative change: how can the audience be galvanized into a transcendence of the **text** into something radically new? What constitutes a 'radically new' perception? These questions define the horizon of a revolutionary cinema.

Eisenstein's foundation of film on principles of contrast has influenced such scholars as Noël Burch (1973) who delineate differences between early and classical cinema based on distinctions of audience involvement (see **classical Hollywood cinema and new Hollywood cinema**). At stake in this casting of film history is not individual films and their political potential realized through the mechanisms of the dialectic, but the disruptive or affirmative character of the whole film medium in its specific historic materialization.

Debates about the relationship between audience identification and alienation in film theory rejuvenated the conception of dialectical principles through the reception of Bertolt **Brecht**, a German dramatist. As playwright, theatre director, scriptwriter and theorist Brecht developed a highly influential 'dialectic of theatre' based on principles for the politicization of audiences. For Brecht, the contrast of two modes of audience address – the dramatic (reliant on character identification and linear development) and the epic (foregoing the dramatic illusion, demonstrative) – can create a theatre which is both pleasurable and political. The audience is actively engaged in creating the synthesis between the two modes, learning how to read the theatre of the social world in the process. Dana Polan (1985) uses Brechtian concepts to argue for a politics of self-reflexive films. He opposes trends that depoliticize and formalize the Brechtian forms of **deconstruction**: cinema needs to embrace fully the political Brecht, a Brecht who is concerned with audience pleasure in identification as much as in formal contrasts. It is only when the spectator initially adopts a position within the constructed world of the theatre (or cinema), that he or she can become sensitive to the political message of the play. The spectator attracted by the fictional world of the play can learn to see the world (of the play, and by extension, the world outside) with other eyes through the mechanisms of distance and negotiation which dialectically interrupt and reconstruct the fictional world presented. The emphasis on an active spectator is the legacy of the political dialectics of cinema or theatre heralded by Eisenstein and Brecht.

Ultimately, though, the core idea of the dialectical principle is redundant in any system which embraces deconstructivist methodologies and sees all meaning as shifting, historical, changing in itself and to its own subject. The moment of forward movement implied by the dialectic is lost when the movement becomes multi-directional and constant. This is the problem posed by Colin MacCabe in 'Realism and the Cinema' (1974). MacCabe attempts to read post-structuralist conceptions of shifting subject positions together with a call for a cinema that is both subversive and progressive (see **classic realist text**). If subversion questions the very ground of subject formation and coherence, how can it be articulated together with a politics of communal, political, forward change? The dialectic principle is founded in a conception of stable oppositions and directions. If these conceptions fail us, we need to look for new ways of engaging in philosophical discourse and to redefine the meaning of politics.

References

Aumont, J. (1987) *Montage Eisenstein*, trans. L. Hildreth, C. Penley and A. Ross, London, Bloomington and Indianapolis: BFI Publishing and Indiana University Press.

Burch, N. (1973) *Theory of Film Practice*, trans. Helen Lane, London: Secker, Martin and Warburg.

MacCabe, C. (1974; reprinted 1993) 'Realism and the Cinema: Notes on Some Brechtian Thesis', in Antony Easthope (ed.) *Contemporary Film Theory*, London and New York: Longman.

Polan, D. (1985) 'A Brechtian Cinema? Towards a Politics of Self-Reflexive Film', in Bill Nichols (ed.) *Movies and Methods* (vol. 2), Berkeley: California University Press.

Further reading

Adorno, T. and Horkheimer, M. (1972) *Dialectic of Enlightenment*, New York: Herder and Herder.

PETRA KUPPERS

dialogic

Dialogic describes the traces of linguistic cross-fertilization that are present in any cultural **text**. According to the Russian Marxist literary critic Mikhail **Bakhtin**, the utterances, ideas or words we find in a text cannot be confined either to the rarefied realm of individual creative consciousness or to the formal, abstract domain of orthodox **semiotics**. Rather, they exist in a concrete social world, and thus in an implicit and open-ended exchange or dialogue between a multiplicity of writers, speakers, readers and audiences (see **audience**). The notion of dialogism allows us to restore the artistic or literary work to this messier sphere of social relations and material forces, where meanings are always plural, interactive and indeterminate. Critics have since appropriated the concept from Bakhtin's studies of literature to evoke the complex and contradictory messages woven into contemporary popular culture.

See also: Marxist aesthetics; popular, the

Further reading

Bakhtin, M. (1981) *The Dialogic Imagination: Four Essays*, trans. C. Emerson and M. Holquist, Austin, TX: University of Texas Press.

Voloshinov, V. and Bakhtin, M. (1986) *Marxism and the Philosophy of Language*, trans. L. Matejka and I. R. Titunik, Cambridge, MA.: Harvard University Press.

NICK YABLON

diaspora

Diasporas are dispersed, multi-generational communities of migrated peoples who have either fled a hostile nation, been exiled or deported, or have left in search of a better life. Often spread over many lands, their members maintain strong community ties and identities across these borders. Being born in the new land does not imply assimilation, but rather the perpetuation of this hybrid identity born from aspects of both the new and home-nation and the condition of exile. Consequently, diasporas challenge concepts of nation and national identity, creating nations without specific homelands, producing nations within and across nations.

See also: globalization; multiculturalism

MOYA LUCKETT

diegesis

A term developed in the study of cinematic discourse, diegesis refers to all things associated with the world of the fiction. In a film's score, for example, all music with a visible or implied source – such as a radio, a stereo, or a band – is diegetic in nature. By contrast, the soundtrack designed to enhance the audience's emotional experience (scary music in a horror film, or the soaring, expressive score that underlies a kiss) is non-diegetic. A voice-over that provides background information, or guides the spectator to a particular point of view, also stands outside the diegesis (see **point of view shot**).

KAREN BACKSTEIN

difference

Difference is a key concept in contemporary cultural theory and politics. Both the impact of post-structuralism and post-modernism on cultural analysis and the growth of new social movements – for example, black liberation, feminism, gay liberation and Third World liberation – have produced radical ideas of difference (see **structuralism and post-structuralism; modernism and post-modernism**). These often envisage a world in which difference might be celebrated as enriching diversity, free from those power relations of hierarchy and exploitation which structure difference in societies governed by **class**, racism and heterosexism.

The work of Jacques **Derrida** has been crucial in the development of recent theories of difference. According to Derrida (1973; 1976), western thought is organized via hierarchical **binary** oppositions. These oppositions are socially produced. Thus, for example, man is privileged over woman, white over black, straight over gay. Against this, Derrida articulates a theory of difference which can lay bare the ways in which hierarchies are established in language. Rereading the structuralist linguistics of Ferdinand de **Saussure**, Derrida theorizes meaning as the temporary effect of a system of differences with no positive terms. Language does not reflect meanings which pre-exist it in the world, it is the site for the production of meaning. This is the case for all signifying practices, including film and television (see **signifying practice**). The chains of signifiers which constitute signification are subject to a continuous process of *différance*, a term which Derrida defines as implying both difference and deferral. Meaning is an effect of difference and is constantly deferred. It can never be finally fixed and there can be no single meaning of a text.

Derrida developed his critique of western thought into a theory of **deconstruction** – a method of reading which aims to expose the implicit assumptions governing particular articulations of meaning. At the level of textual analysis, deconstruction involves the identification of the hierarchical oppositions which govern the meaning of texts. Specific articulations of meaning are always part of the wider body of texts which form the repository of the meanings and values of a particular society. The interrelation between texts is governed by the concepts of the 'trace' and the 'supplement' which point to *différance*, the structuring process of language, and to the existence of other absent possible meanings.

One of the implications of Derrida's theory of difference is that there can be no singular truth, fixed for all times. Truth becomes a social phenomenon and different versions of truth represent different interests. These interests include class, **gender**, **race** and **sexuality**. This challenge to truth has been realized in the theories and practices of the new social movements. These movements have challenged the truth and legitimacy of traditional, hierarchical ideas of difference found, for example, in theories of race and gender which posit essential racial and gender characteristics. There are, for instance, many competing theories of gender difference which often represent patriarchal interests (see **patriarchy**). In particular, feminism has produced both essentialist and non-essentialist theories of difference, influenced by post-structuralism and Freudian and Lacanian psychoanalysis (see Weedon 1999). For example, the French philosopher Luce **Irigaray** has challenged both the construction of woman as intrinsically different or **Other** to the masculine and the psychoanalytic constitution of female difference as **lack** (see Braidotti 1991). New theorizations of difference are also a crucial concern of post-colonial theory where they challenge traditional ideas of race, **culture** and **identity** (see **hybridity**).

See also: feminist theory; queer theory; Spivak, Gayatri

References

Braidotti, R. (1991) *Patterns of Dissonance*, Oxford: Polity Press.

Derrida, J. (1973) *Speech and Phenomena*, trans. D. Allison, Evanston: Northwestern University Press.

—— (1976) *Of Grammatology*, trans. G. Spivak, Baltimore: The John Hopkins University Press.

Weedon, C. (1999) *Feminism, Theory and the Politics of Difference*, Oxford: Blackwell.

CHRIS WEEDON

digital communication

Digital as unifying principle

In technical terms, digital media are those which store, transmit and/or receive data in digital form – that is, in the form of collections of tiny 'on/off' signals (often millions at a time). The term 'digital' is generally understood as the opposite of 'analogue', where analogue media make use of continuously variable forms, such as waves or gradations of light, rather than representing all information in terms of discrete on/off bits. (The term 'bit' has a technical meaning in computer science and digital technology: a single 'bit' is one irreducible unit of memory or information, and is always in either the on state or the off state, represented in **binary** arithmetic, native to computers, as 1 or 0, respectively.)

Digital media represent everything as collections of 'on' or 'off' bits. The surface of a music compact disc is microscopically peopled with patterns of such bits; e-mail is transmitted as a stream of bits, as are World Wide Web documents; digital broadcasts resolve images into bits. Of course, users of digital media see and hear music, texts and images, not bits; it is up to the sending and receiving equipment to handle the encoding and decoding of the binary data (see **encoding-decoding model**). In particular, playback and image-rendering equipment use the digital information to reconstruct sounds and images at a level of resolution high enough, at least ideally, to register as continuous to human perception. This principle – rendering a smooth percept from a set of disconnected units of information – is similar to the phenomenon of looking at a photograph composed of tiny dots from a great enough distance so that the dots coalesce into smooth shapes. Essentially, though at a finer level of resolution, all digital communication works on that principle.

Digital technologies may thus be identified on clear technical grounds. At the same time, many of these technologies do very different things and take very different forms from one another. As much as anything, what connects one digital technology to another – what compact discs share with high definition television (HDTV), or the World Wide Web with cell-phones – is the way in which the term 'digital' has come to symbolize a particular kind of communication, aesthetics and even social order. The term, in fact, is of little relevance to most consumers and viewers of electronic media; none the less, 'digital' has been selected by the electronics and entertainment industries as a signifier of modernity, efficiency and clarity.

To group digital technologies together, then, is to isolate a marketing strategy, operating across media and across borders of consumer functionality, as much as to isolate closely related devices themselves. For many theoretical purposes, too, 'digital' is a meaningless term. For example, a media effects researcher studying the question of addiction to television is unlikely to care whether or not the television signal is digital. The notion of 'digital communication' as a single or unified entity is thus a fiction – though a very compelling one, and one to which many historians and theorists as well as consumers seem to subscribe.

Interoperability and the myth of unified media

The fact that digital media use the same underlying method for storage of many different types of information (text, sound, image, broadcast signal, etc.) makes for interoperability, at least potentially, among the various media. An audio selection may be saved as a computer file, enhanced or manipulated with computer software, sent as e-mail, placed on a publically accessible Website, and so forth. Perfect reproduction of digital information is possible because, unlike the case of analogue representations, digital data are stored entirely as 0s and 1s, in precisely repeatable sequences. This ease of duplication has occasioned concern among corporations involved in the development of digital media, who are eager to maximize profits and restrict competition. The notion of completely replicable units of storage, including entire sound recordings or motion pictures, contravenes the goals of such corporations, even as they market the 'digitalization' of an entire culture.

The interoperability of digital media remains in large part a myth and to some extent a marketing device. It is a myth in that the companies developing the technology tend to introduce competing, proprietary standards for such things as data storage and image-processing software, rather than co-operating on standards. Consumers are therefore often made to choose a particular digital 'world' rather than sharing in a unified world of digital communication. Interoperability's functioning as a marketing device is the other side of the same coin; each company promotes its own system in utopian, world-unifying terms, in spite of the fact that, behind the scenes, universally available, interoperable communications equipment neither exists nor appears to be in the offing.

The realities of planned obsolescence, the fallibility of machines and the unwillingness of ambitious corporations to co-operate with one another all contribute to making the utopian vision rather clearly absurd. None the less, numerous commentators have taken seriously the idea that digital communication differs radically from other forms of electronic and/or mass communication, and that the emergence of digital media promises some kind of fundamental change in human social organization, behaviour and consciousness (see Negroponte 1995).

One of the persistent myths of digitalization – and one which succinctly illustrates the tendency of debate on this issue to focus on relatively unmeaningful details – is the myth of 'service integration' or **convergence**. That is, the promise that, at some point generally described as being just around the corner, the homes of consumers will be provided with telephone, **Internet**, television, radio and various other communication services, all from a single source and all entering the home through a single wire. Both promotional language and ostensibly serious analysis of this promise have focused on the wire – literally, on the replacement of a multiplicity of telephone and cable wires, and possibly outdoor antennas, by a single fibre-optic cable. However, some would argue that the number of wires, be it one or five, running into a home bears no relation to content, nor to habits of media use, nor to issues of interactivity or access to means of production. From this perspective, convergence may be seen as a technologically dazzling but politically digressive and irrelevant detail.

Two books represent opposite ends of the debate over the notion of a digital culture. On the one hand, **Negroponte** (1995) sees digital commu-nication as a determining factor in virtually all of culture and society, and embraces the idea that it sharply divides our age (and the future) from the past. Stoll (1996), on the other hand, makes the point that many non-digital techniques and practices have characteristics and purposes which their ostensible digital replacements do not in fact provide. While sometimes nostalgic rather than cogent in his argumentation, Stoll does system-atically examine and, to a large extent, dismantle the promotional rhetoric and 'hype' surrounding the dissemination of digital technologies.

See also: technological change

References

Negroponte, N. (1995) *Being Digital*, New York: Vintage Books.
Stoll, C. (1996) *Silicon Snake Oil*, London: Pan.

Further reading

Winston, B. (1998) *Media Technology and Society: A History: From the Telegraph to the Internet*, London: Routledge.

DAVID A. BLACK

direct cinema

The direct cinema of the 1960s represented a radical break with classic **documentary** forms of representation established in the 1930s, due to technical and aesthetic innovations it partly shares with **cinéma-vérité**. Both documentary styles rely on the use of lightweight, soundproof 16mm cameras and synchronous sound equipment that allow unhindered access and immersion into the situation being filmed. While *cinéma-vérité* film-makers such as Jean Rouch and Edgar Morin highlight the recording process through interac-tions between camera and characters, direct cinema filmmakers like Robert Drew, Richard Leacock and Frederick Wiseman emphasize non-interventive filmic strategies to achieve the effect of an 'uncontrolled' authenticity. Self-reflexive uses of direct cinema techniques in subsequent decades (for example, *No Lies* by Mitchell Block, 1973, and

Daughter Rite by Michelle Citroen, 1978) have deconstructed this effect as the result of specific representational strategies at the level of **narrative** (crisis structure), shot (long takes, use of zoom lens; see **camera style and lens style**) and montage (chronological editing).

EVA WARTH

discipline

Discipline has effectively two meanings, referring both to highly structured institutions for the production of particular bodies of knowledge and to instances of the insidious exercise of modern power. This is the sense in which the term is used by Michel **Foucault**, whose work mapped out the expanding technologies for the discipline and control of bodies, populations and society. These technologies suffuse such institutions as prisons, hospitals and schools, and often work by setting in place structures of surveillance that are in turn frequently internalized through acts of self-discipline such as confession, itself increasingly popular in the **genre** of television talk shows (see **chat/ talk show**).

LEE GRIEVESON

discourse

This term implies that language is not neutral and universal, but that different social groups use and interpret verbal and non-verbal language in different ways that serve their interests. Thus discourse is the set of conventions (of production and reception) employed by a social group in a particular area of language use. For example, we can distinguish between a dominant discourse of filmmaking (that of Hollywood cinema) and a resistant discourse of filmmaking (that of **avant-garde** cinema), each of which consists of different formal conventions, ideological functions and power relations (see **conventions; ideology and hegemony**). Similarly, we can distinguish between academic and journalistic discourses of film criticism.

See also: discourse analysis; reading and reception theory

BRUCE BENNETT

discourse analysis

Discourse, according to Michel **Foucault** in *The Archaeology of Knowledge* (originally published in French as *L'archeologie du savoir* in 1969), is not to be confused with a **consciousness** embodied in the 'external form of language' (*langage*), nor is it to be reduced to a language (*langue*) complete with a human subject to speak it. Rather, to show why discourse needs to be analysed as a practice with its own forms of sequence and succession, Foucault (1972) introduces the notion of a field of discursive 'events'. Accordingly, a field of discursive events is constitutive of:

> a grouping that is always finite and limited at any moment to the linguistic sequences that have been formulated; they may be innumerable, they may, in sheer size, exceed the capacities of recording, memory, or reading: nevertheless they form a finite grouping.
>
> (*ibid*.: 1972: 27)

Perhaps it is not surprising that questions considered characteristic of language analysis, such as, 'according to what rules has a particular statement been made, and consequently according to what rules could other similar statements be made?', can be, in turn, recast by enquiring, 'how is it that one particular statement appeared rather than another?' (*ibid*.). Foucault is not interested in distinguishing certain (totalized) discursive statements for the ultimate purpose of extracting the hidden 'intentions' of the speaking subject or, alternatively, the 'real meaning' of what was actually said. Instead, to execute a description of a discursive field, a Foucauldian analysis will seek to 'grasp the statement in the exact specificity of its occurrence; determine its conditions of existence, fix at least its limits, establish its correlations with other statements that may be connected with it, and show what other forms of statement it excludes' (*ibid*.: 28). Why, the researcher might ask, could this statement not be other than it was?

How has it come to occupy this space and not another? What is its relation to other statements?

In response to such questions, Foucault proceeds to examine the group of rules immanent in the discursive practice itself. It follows that to 'depresentify' what otherwise would likely have been written off as 'things anterior to discourse', he has to initiate a key move to prioritize for analysis the regular formation of these objects as they emerge within discourse. In this way the definition of these objects can then progress 'without reference to the ground, the *foundation of things*, but by relating them to the body of rules that enable them to form as objects of a discourse and thus constitute the conditions of their historical appearance' (*ibid.*: 48). To grapple with discursive practices, then, is to locate the nexus of regularities that govern their dispersion.

It is at this point that the project Foucault advocates diverges most sharply from linguistic analyses of discourse. While conceding that studies of lexical organization or semantics, for example, have an important role to play for other types of critique, he considers them to be irrelevant to his agenda (see **semiotics**). As he suggests,

> the analysis of lexical contents defines either the elements of meaning at the disposal of speaking subjects in a given period, or the semantic structures that appear on the surface of a discourse that has already been spoken; it does not concern discursive practice as a place in which a tangled plurality – at once superposed and incomplete – of objects is formed and deformed, appears and disappears.
>
> (*ibid.*: 48)

As a result, words or vocabulary (like 'things') are deemed to be unworthy of sustained attention. As Foucault cannot envision returning to a time prior to discourse, nor living beyond the demise of discourse so as to rediscover the forms left behind, he insists that his investigations will remain 'at the level of discourse itself'. Consequently, Foucault writes:

> I would like to show that 'discourses', in the form in which they can be heard or read, are not, as one might expect, a mere intersection of things and words; an obscure web of things, and

a manifest, visible, coloured chain of words; I would like to show that discourse is not a slender surface of contact, or confrontation, between a reality and a language (*langue*), the intrication of a lexicon and an experience; I would like to show with precise examples that in analyzing discourses themselves, one sees the loosening of the embrace, apparently so tight, of words and things, and the emergence of a group of rules proper to discursive practices. These rules define not the dumb existence of a reality, nor the canonical use of a vocabulary, but the ordering of objects.

> (*Ibid.*: 48–9)

Discourses thus cease to be singularly regarded by Foucault as groups of signs (elements referring to representations; see **sign**) but, rather, designate groups of signs organized as practices systematically forming the very objects of which they speak.

Analyses of film or televisual texts, it follows, need to re-conceptualize media institutions as fields on which struggles over *discourses* transpire. In declaring that 'it is in discourse that power and knowledge are joined together', however, Foucault (1980: 100) is at pains to insist that media texts should not be treated as the narrative manifestation of a victory achieved by one discourse (accepted/dominant) over another (excluded/dominated). Rather, in his view, analysis must instead seek to:

> reconstruct, with the things said and those concealed, the enunciations required and those forbidden, [what that discourse] comprises; with the variants and different effects – according to who is speaking, his position of power, the institutional context in which he happens to be situated – that it implies; and with the shifts and reutilizations of identical formulas for contrary objectives that it also includes.
>
> (Foucault 1980: 100)

Hence the need to initiate a key shift in conceptual emphasis so as to engage directly with the discursive practices indicative of cinematic or televisual institutions 'on their own terms'. In so doing, this kind of analytical project may better account for how both the 'saids' and the 'unsaids' are linked to relations of power and resistance.

'Discourse', it follows, 'transmits and produces power; it reinforces it, but also undermines and exposes it, renders it fragile and makes it possible to thwart it' (*ibid.*: 101).

References

Foucault, M. (1972) *The Archaeology of Knowledge*, New York: Pantheon.
—— (1980) *The History of Sexuality, Volume 1*, New York: Vintage.

STUART ALLAN

displacement

One of the four dreamwork codes (with **condensation**, representability and secondary revision), displacement is characterized by the transfer of affect from a repressed idea to a less 'charged' idea with which it is connected by a chain of associations. It is one of the 'primary processes' which govern **unconscious** thought. In **narrative** and **genre** study, the analysis of displacements is central to the symptomatic reading of a text. At its broadest, it can be used to analyse the peculiar features of an entire genre: for example, **melodrama**, which consistently displaces the unconscious fantasies of the characters onto an overloaded **mise-en-scène**.

Further reading

Freud, S. (1965) *The Interpretation of Dreams*, trans. J. Strachey, New York: Avon.
Laplanche, J. and Pontalis, J.-B. (1973) *The Language of Psychoanalysis*, New York: Norton.

ANGELO RESTIVO

distancing

In literary criticism, the term 'distance' describes the level of emotional involvement that the **text** offers the reader. Classic dramatic forms like the Aristotelian theatre tried to draw in the spectator as closely as possible through a code of dramatic **realism**, and even the theatre of enlightenment saw part of its educative function in arousing 'pity and terror' in the audience to reach a cathartic effect (see **catharsis**). For these reasons, events presented on stage had to be perceived as 'natural' and 'familiar' in their emotional impact if not in their everyday occurrence.

By contrast, Russian **Formalism**, in particular Victor Shklovsky (1965), argued that perception, so habitualized, could only lead to the formation of stereotypes, and that the function of literature and drama is defamiliarization (*oistranenie*, Russian 'to make strange'). Shklovsky claimed that:

> Habitualization devours work, clothes, furniture, one's wife, and the fear of war. 'If the whole complex lives of many people go on unconsciously, then such lives are as if they had never been.' And art exists that one may recover the sensation of life; it exists to make one feel things, to make stone *stony.*
>
> (Shklovsky 1965: 12; quotation from Tolstoy's 'Diary')

The Prague School differentiated between 'automization', a use of language that makes the language itself unobtrusive, and 'foregrounding', a use of language that attracts attention to the expression itself. Seen as a whole, Russian Formalism challenged linguistic or stylistic automization rather than political or ideological stereotypes (see **ideology and hegemony; stereotype**).

Though a similar concept, **Brecht**'s plan for the **epic** theatre went much further in employing means in additional to linguistic ones to make the sociopolitical setting of his plays noteworthy and unfamiliar. Brecht made a distinction between dramatic theatre and epic theatre, and the effect each has on the spectator:

> The dramatic theatre's spectator says: Yes, I have felt like that too – Just like me – It's only natural – It'll never change – The sufferings of this man appeal to me, because they are inescapable – That's great art; it all seems the most obvious thing in the world – I weep when they weep, I laugh when they laugh.
>
> The epic theatre's spectator says: I'd never have thought it – That's not the way – That's extraordinary, hardly believable – It's got to stop

– The sufferings of this man appeal to me, because they are unnecessary – That's great art: nothing obvious in it – I laugh when they weep, I weep when they laugh.

(Brecht 1964 in Willett 1964: 71)

To achieve this intellectual distance between spectators and plot, Brecht developed a range of *Verfremdungseffekte*, also called V-effects, estrangement effects or E-effects. He borrowed from classic Greek theatre the employment of masks to change the individual characters into types and the introduction and analysis of the plot via a commentating chorus. His plays tend to be episodic and lead to a usually open, unsatisfying ending which explicitly challenges the audience to 'find their own ending' (for example, *The Good Person of Szechwan*). Since, for Brecht, the spectator's distance from the action and involvement in the subject of a play existed simultaneously, he used effects such as commentaries from the space of the audience or scenes set in front of the stage to 'tear down the fourth wall' between audience and stage. He developed a special style of acting that stressed the distance between actor and character to keep the audience aware of the artificiality of the characters and events they saw. All of these effects were aimed at breaking the illusion which – to Brecht, who embraced **Marxist aesthetics** – kept workers and poor people in misery through an ideology which contructed their condition as inevitable, immutable fate.

Both types of distancing aim at noteworthiness through estrangement, and so are constantly in danger of losing their power by becoming formulaic – as partly happened with Brecht's epic theatre after his death. None the less, both types of distancing remain an important means of exploration in both art and scholarly discourse. Film scholars usually cite the work of Jean-Luc **Godard** as the primary example of cinematic distancing. Peter **Wollen** discusses a particularly apt example, *Vent d'est* (*Wind from the East*, 1970), in his essay 'Godard and Countercinema: *Vente d'est*' (1982).

References

Brecht, B. (1964) *Brecht on Theatre: The Development of an Aesthetic*, ed. and trans. John Willet, London: Eyre Methuen.

Shklovsky, V. (1965; first published 1917) 'Art as Technique', in L. Lennon and Marion Reis (eds and trans.) *Russian Formalist Criticism: Four Essays*, Lincoln: University of Nebraska Press.

Wollen, P. (1982) *Readings and Writings: Semiotic Counter-strategies*, London: Verso.

Further reading

Benjamin, W. (1968) 'What is Epic Theatre?', in *Illuminations*, trans. Harry Zohn, ed. Hannah Arendt, New York: Harcourt Brace and World.

EVA VIETH

documentary

Recording and transmitting 'real-life' events proved one of the first triumphs of film, television and video, respectively. Over time, this relation between medium and 'reality' came to constitute documentary as a **genre**. As Brian Winston observes, since Edward S. Curtis' *In the World of the Head-hunters* (1914), 'despite claims to artistic legitimacy ('creativity') and dramatic structuring ('treatment'), when dealing with the film form we are essentially and most critically in the realm of evidence and witness ("actuality")' (1995: 10).

Through the creation and distribution of multiple interpretations of reality, the practice and criticism of documentary have become deeply intertwined. Moreover, since documentaries often appear marginal to mainstream fictional productions and their analysts, documentary practices have become self-consciously informed about theory and articulations of media and society. Documentarians themselves are often both theorists and critics, whose works manifest their beliefs. This entry explores documentary criticism in relation to production, producers, text, distribution and reception, all of which have reconstituted the genre and its criticism.

We should not assume that theorists/practitioners or their audiences are grappling with a simple, fixed category. The 'public' sees documentary as depicting 'real' events – neither fiction films nor television drama. The documentary form may insist on this difference, while institutions that support documentaries differ from those of fiction film in funding and distribution. Such clear-cut differences, however, belie lengthy theoretical debates about 'truth'. Few documentarians or critics claim that the documentary presents absolute truth; documentary is also a story. Some, however, claim a higher 'truth' or purpose than their fictional counterparts: to them, documentary treats important social issues, forgotten, exotic or famous people, and great historical moments. Yet it may manipulate all these to make other points.

None the less, both documentaries and fictional works use the same technical apparatus; hence, both are constructions. Both present moving images produced under similar technical and cultural constraints. More important, like any cultural production, processes of selection, ingrained frames of reference and formal and **narrative** strategies shape the story, even if 'true'. Again, documentarians have used an awareness of these limits to challenge distinctions between apparent truth and fiction. Works that mix **actuality** footage, interviews, fictional strategies and re-enactments dominate late twentieth-century footage and criticism, raising questions beyond the apparent subject matter of any single work.

Documentaries also have evolved with media technologies. The development of the hand-held camera followed by the video camera altered the genre dramatically. And 'reality' has also changed in relation to the lens. Documentaries often claim to speak for the voiceless. None the less, questions of exploitation remain. Disenfranchised videomakers, meanwhile, who once were subjects, have moved behind the camera as both a response to, and a critique of, documentary power relations.

Finally, divergent audiences and reception complicate the study of documentary. Much of the writing on documentary concentrates on independent documentary films/videos without much regard to distribution. Some subdivide the field in terms of genres (ethnographic, historical) or other extra-textual criteria of use (library or school distribution/educational, industrial, commercial, etc.). However, documentaries often find their widest exposure from television, both commercial and public. On television, they also intersect with other representations of the so-called 'real-life'

materials, including news and the use of actuality footage in American television reality shows.

In this entry, I focus on three major issues in documentary criticism. First, I sketch the history of documentaries and criticism, including the politics of making and distributing documentaries. Second, I investigate the relationship between truth and representation. Finally, I trace questions about the power relationship among documentary, producers, subjects and **audience**.

A brief history of form and criticism

The earliest moving images were indeed 'real', from Auguste and Louis Lumière's train at the station to their record of a baby eating her breakfast. These images were made without altering the 'reality' that was presented; yet they became 'pro-filmic' events (see **pro-filmic event**). These footages are not chunks of reality, but representations, chosen to survive for a century while many other contemporary 'realities' were left unrecorded.

While early cinema was fascinated by its ability to depict and to remember moving images of reality, the camera also could bring back and disseminate images from far away. Colonial French and British filmmakers depicted (and interpreted) the images and peoples of distant, dominated cultures. In the United States, after Edward S. Curtis, Robert Flaherty (1884–1951) made *Nanook of the North* (1922) to show everyday life of the Inuit, whom world movie theatre audiences would never directly encounter. Despite the claims of this and other early documentaries to celebrate 'real' life, all the actions were acted out.

Meanwhile, in the Soviet Union, Dziga **Vertov** created **kino-pravda** – 'film-truth'. He recorded 'life-facts' and organized images into a structural, essential whole. His work showed interesting similarities to other contemporary Soviet filmmakers in both devices like montage and attitudes to progress and technology. In Britain, John **Grierson** (1892–1972) demanded 'the creative treatment of reality' as the essence of documentary as an opposition to studio produced works. With government sponsorship, Grierson made documentaries for social amelioration to educate the masses about everyday people; he also trained generations to follow in Canada and the US. The works were heavily narrated and staged, precluding any direct irruption of the subject voice into their truth. Politics and documentary did not converge only on the left, however. In Germany, Leni Riefenstahl made powerful poetic works like *Triumph of the Will* (1934) as propaganda for Adolph Hitler.

All these works were constructed from selected real-life materials. Yet, the public and documentarians accepted that one might recreate some footage without altering truth. This was partly necessary due to the cumbersome equipment filmmakers used. Filmmakers did not treat what they produced as fiction, either. Indeed, anthropologist Margaret Mead championed documentary 'evidence' about reality in the 1940s and 1950s.

Major changes in filmmaking took place in the 1960s with the introduction of readily portable cameras and synchronized sound recording. While underscoring the artificiality of earlier documentaries, this technology gives the illusion that filmmakers capture 'real life' in action. In the US, this technology facilitated **direct cinema**, which stressed unmediated observation as a goal. Practitioners include the Maysle Brothers (Albert and David), D. A. Pennebaker and Richard Leacock. Films include Leacock's *Primary* (1960), Craig Golbert's *An American Family* (1972) and above all, films by Frederick Wiseman, such as *Titticut Follies* (1967) and *High School* (1968). At the same time, the intimacy and pervasiveness of the documentary eye and the use/reading of these films evoked questions about intrusion into private life: the Loud family responded angrily to their depiction on Public Television's *An American Family*. In France, **cinéma-vérité** developed similar strategies and claims, although filmmakers like Jean Rouch interacted with the subject on film, using the camera to provoke truth.

Changes also took place in documentary distribution and audiences as television became popular. While documentaries had occasionally played in theatres alongside fictional films, their distribution more generally was limited to schools, museums or other specialized settings. Television broadcast documentaries to a large audience, via both commercial and public networks (BBC, PBS, etc.). Commercial and cable networks remain the major channel through which documentary foo-

tage and reality programmes of all kinds, including news, news magazines, star documentaries and MTV shows like *Real Lives*, reach wide audiences. However, as Alan Rosenthal (1988) has argued, some commercial television has certain structures that prescribe roles, given network (and sponsor) control over the content and personnel of documentary productions. US public television has supported controversial films, such as Marlon Rigg's *Tongues Untied* (1989), facing pressure from government and conservative social lobbies. Yet, Ken Burns' *Civil War* (1990) also exemplifies public television documentaries, with high production values and a very safe subject, aimed at a wide audience.

Documentary flourished as both a practice and a theoretical field in the 1980s and 1990s through intersecting forces. Burgeoning film schools used actuality exercises, while such disciplines as anthropology, history and the sciences drew documentaries into the classroom. Industrial films, news programmes and political genres played with the form – and implications of truth – associated with documentary sobriety. A new generation of documentary-makers and critics explored reflections on the claims and form of the genre, epitomized by Nichols, Renov, Winston, Trinh, Michaels and others cited in the following section.

None the less, television documentaries, especially via commercial broadcasting, have been in decline since the mid-1970s because of shrinking ratings. In the late 1990s, news magazines, chat/talk shows and 'reality' shows have replaced more sober television documentaries of the 1960s and 1970s (see **chat/talk show**). Most are cheap and fast to produce; they focus on emotional and sensational subject matters. Though this tendency is still less apparent in Britain than in the US, some critics see similar trends there. In a post-modernist era, where questions of truth and the construction of truth are omnipresent, such representations shamelessly sell truth that conceals fundamental mediations, which independent works are struggling to reveal (see **modernism and post-modernism**). Hence, debates about what documentary is and does have continued to change, entering a new and open context as to what audiences see and interpret.

Truth and representation

Michael Renov, another primary critic of the documentary, designates four fundamental tendencies of the genre: (i) to record, reveal, or preserve; (ii) to persuade or promote; (iii) to analyse or interrogate; and (iv) to express (Renov 1993: 21). Together, these viewpoints and critics underscore dilemmas of truth and **representation**. Claims are made about truth, but this truth also exists in a context beyond its actual relation to events and their place in a world. Documentary makes use of truth for goals that may simply entail recording, but also may go far beyond this representation – persuasion and interrogation do not serve the same ends as recording or expression. Hence, Riefenstahl differs from both Wiseman and a reality-based show like the American television production *Cops*.

Bill Nichols, who has also dominated modern discussion of the documentary, claims that documentary film has a kinship with those non-fictional systems that together make up what we call the **discourse** of sobriety: 'they can and should alter the world itself, they can effect action and entail consequences' (Nichols 1991: 3). However, Nichols asserts that documentary is not a true equal to other discourses of sobriety, like written essays or books, the scientific survey or report. Precisely because of documentary's reliance on the image, on fiction and on narratives, it remains marginal. To understand documentary, Nichols suggests that we look into truth through the relationship between the image (the documentary) and the subject matter in the real world. Nichols (with similarities to Renov) elaborates four modes of documentary representation – expository, observational, interactive and reflexive – which may be illustrated by essential works and practitioners.

The expository mode teaches through direct address, exemplified in Grierson's works (and many lesser educational products). Truth is obviously controlled by the filmmaker with a heavily narrated 'voice of God' and the silence of the subjects.

Observational genres try to observe the subject without interference, seeking 'unmediated' truth. As in direct cinema, filmmakers sought to be 'flies on the wall', presuming that the subject would become accustomed to the camera. Wiseman, however, reinterpreted objectivity by claiming his films are his visions, while asserting that what he saw actually did happen.

Interactive cinema aimed a different consensus model of the truth, exemplified by Jean Rouch. In Rouch's *Chronique d'un été* (*Chronicle of a Summer*, 1961), the audience sees the filmmakers talking about the making of the film, the on-site production of the film, the interviews, the editing and the subjects' reaction to the film. Subjects and audiences must both become participatory; they are, as Winston asserts, 'flies in the soup'.

Practitioners of reflexive documentary question the validity of representation itself. Some of these documentaries argue that representation must encompass the examination of the process of representing reality itself. In *Far from Poland* (1984), Jill Godmilow does not tell the audience about Poland, and the Solidarity movement, so much as about her desire to make the film and how she circumvents her inability to get to Poland. Reflexive documentary also employs techniques used in other documentary modes – re-enactment, intertitles, voice-over and interactive first person address – to highlight representation.

Theorist-filmmaker Trinh T. Minh-Ha has proclaimed that 'there is no such thing as documentary' (quoted in Renov 1993: 90). Her reflexive questioning of documentary practices that promote authentication, like sync-sound and real-time (as in long takes), have both formal and critical implications. In *Reassemblage* (1982), sound is not synchronized nor is the narrative linear, while in *Surname Viet Given Name Nam* (1989), Trinh took pains to use reconstructed interviews which viewers can perceive as staged. Hence, Trinh has argued for the destruction of devices that made audiences complicit in accepting footage as real.

Documentarians choose among these modes, depending on purpose, subject and audience – secondary school films on protozoa tend to be expository rather than questioning observed truth, while politicized explorations of identity often adopt radically reflexive tones. Both the ways in which truth is sought and the visibility of this quest in the documentary respond to extra-textual questions as well. Here, documentaries and criticism are illuminated by the ways in which reality appropriates and interrogates the genre.

Power and presence: rights and voices of the subject

As Nichols points out, unlike narrative films where the maker of the film is separate from the **diegesis**, documentarians are part of the world they portray. Even when the filmmaker is not part of the historical events that are in the film, he/she is a witness and has a relationship with the subject or subject matter. The filmmaker's presence or absence from the film can be interpreted as:

> (their respect or contempt, their humility or arrogance, their disinterestedness or tendentiousness, their pride or prejudice) to the people and problems, situations and events they film.
> (Nichols 1991: 79)

The subjects of documentary also have lives outside the film. Even in documentaries on distant historical subjects, people are connected to the subject by geography, shared national, ethnic, **gender** or **class** background. Subjects in documentary and the filmmakers face consequences beyond the text. While this was not a vocal issue for the Inuit (Flaherty) or Balinese (Mead), since the 1960s it has become a focus of documentary theory and practice.

In *The Things I Cannot Change* (1966), for example, the respected Canadian Film Board sought to talk about the poor through one family, who reviewed the work before it was broadcast. However, the family suffered greatly; neighbours were dismayed that their poverty was exhibited. The filmmaker, despite goals of social reform, was criticized for treating the family as objects, not subjects. This evokes central dilemmas in documentary power – Who is being represented? How? How is the film being received? None of these variables can be controlled with certainty.

Power relations are present from the choice of subjects onward. People of power generally control their images and can challenge unfavourable or inaccurate representations. For most social documentaries, the subjects occupy a lower socioeconomic scale. On the one hand, this resonates with the long-standing goal of documentary to record the forgotten and to effect change. However, some such documentaries also have categorized their subjects as victims. These issues also

underpin individual and group exploration of the expressive documentary. *No Lies* (Mitchell Block, 1973), for example, an important fictional work, directly raises the rights of the documentary subject. The film's two takes about a filmmaker who wants to interview a rape victim shows that the subject is abused not only by the rapist, but also by the filmmaker who intrudes on her life.

Ethnographic film forms a subgenre of documentary that brings the foreign home and captures disappearing worlds (see **ethnography**). Again, a 'scientific' eye may silence the subject; moreover, audiences tend to have little knowledge of the subjects portrayed in the films. Still, David and Susan MacDougall, ethnographical filmmakers and critics, have defended 'participatory cinema' where the filmmaker 'acknowledges his or her entry upon the world of the subjects and yet asks them to imprint directly upon the film aspects of their own culture' (MacDougall 1998: 134). They value the collaborative efforts between the filmmakers and the subjects.

Fourth World indigenous documentary, facilitated by video, promotes alternative works by peoples who proclaim themselves equal to the 'First Nations'. These works are distinguished from ethnographic media primarily through the shared roles of producer, subject and audience. These films/tapes often grapple with retaining and regaining culture and identities. Grass-roots or community video also represents a final appropriation of truth within the witness and purpose of small groups, who affirm their own truth by their limited and highly contextual use of the documentary.

While less significant in the market (or in academic criticism), documentaries made by subjects for themselves show the genre's flexibility amid demands made by claims of truth and power. Eric Michaels (1994), for example, detailed beautifully how the Australian Aborigines appropriated video documentary to cement social and ritual relationships. Moving beyond representation and truth, he called for a processual analysis that encompasses making, transmitting and viewing, and the knowledge which allows texts to come into existence.

Conclusions

Issues of documentary film and television practice

and criticism have evolved for a century. The claim to tell and to find meaning in the truth has set documentarians and their products apart in subject, style, theory, distribution and reading. Yet, critics (including many documentarians) have shown that claims to truth prove neither simple nor self-evident. Moreover, technological advances that have brought greater flexibility, sophistication and distribution to documentaries have exposed artifices and evoked new responses, reforming future films or videos. As documentary products and readings have spilled over into commercial and public television, the video store and the home cinema, theory has re-examined power and representation rather than the formal issues of much film criticism. As such, documentary theory and practice constitute lively fields in their own right as well as an intriguing counterpoint to mainstream film.

References

MacDougall, D. (1998) *Transcultural Cinema*, ed. Lucien Taylor, Princeton: Princeton University Press.

Michaels, E. (1994) *Bad Aboriginal Art*, Minneapolis: University of Minnesota Press.

Nichols, B. (1991) *Representing Reality*, Bloomington: Indiana University Press.

Renov, M. (ed.) (1993) *Theorizing Documentary*, New York: Routledge.

Rosenthal, A. (ed.) (1988) *New Challenges for Documentary*, Berkeley: University of California Press.

Winston, B. (1995) *Claiming the Real*, London: British Film Institute.

CINDY WONG

dominant ideology

'The ideas of the ruling class,' according to **Marx** and Engels, 'are in every epoch the ruling ideas; that is, the class which is the ruling *material* force of society, is at the same time its ruling *intellectual* force' (Marx and Engels 1970: 64–5). These 'ruling ideas', to be understood as the representations of a '**dominant ideology**', are not forced on the

subordinate classes, nor are they to be reduced to 'useful fictions' (see **representation**). Rather, the Marxist position maintains that the capitalist ruling class must work to advance its particular class-specific interests by depicting its ideas, norms and values in universal terms. Thus, these 'ruling ideas' are mobilized as being consistent with the beliefs of ordinary people, as being the only correct, rational opinions available to them (Marx and Engels 1970: 65–6). Media institutions are controlled by members of this ruling class (see **institution**). Each one of these institutions reproduces these 'ruling ideas', to varying degrees, so as to lend justification to the structural inequalities engendered by capitalist society. In this way, the media help to reduce the possibility of radical protests emerging to disrupt the *status quo*.

See also: class; ideology and hegemony; Marxist aesthetics

References

Marx, K. and Engels, F. (1970) *The German Ideology*, New York: International.

STUART ALLAN

drama

'Drama' is a somewhat vague, though useful, term with a wide variety of meanings and applications. The original Greek meaning was simply 'to do', but in modern English usage it generally indicates the performance of a fictional **narrative**. In this sense, drama may be understood to mean the staging and enactment of fictional events for an audience.

Strictly speaking, drama is a mimetic art form consisting of a number of elements including a fictional narrative, characters, staging or setting, acting, effects, costume, dialogue and so forth. However, any kind of performance may be described as dramatic. Martin Esslin points out that 'mime, the circus, street theatre, opera, music hall, cabaret, "happenings", and performance art fall within the boundaries of the dramatic while lacking some of the elements of stricter definitions of the dramatic' (Esslin 1988: 23). To confuse matters further, spectacles such as military parades, concerts, football matches and street carnivals (see **carnival**) are also sometimes described as dramas. The two ingredients that all dramatic forms have are the element of performance and the presence of an audience.

Most commentators agree that drama originated in the religious rituals and ceremonies of ancient Greece. As rituals became increasingly elaborate and **performative**, the distinction between participants and non-participants became one between performers and audience. Eventually, a secular theatre evolved in which there was little or no ritual element. Its primary function was to entertain its audience, and it used professional dramatists, actors and stage crews. Drama continued primarily to be associated with the stage until the advent of accessible screen technologies in the twentieth century. Now, most people see drama on the screen rather than in the theatre.

In critical theory, the dramatic character of film is seldom addressed in its own right and instead generally falls under the auspices of **performance theory**, **authorship**, **genre** theory, or narrative theory. As all fiction film is a form of drama, film theorists have preferred to use more specific terms to describe different genres and filmic elements. An exception is the derivative term **melodrama**, used since the 1970s to describe a type of romantic, sensational and affecting film. Film theory has tended to stress the differences and underplay the similarities between the fiction film and other dramatic forms. Since the 1980s, drama theorists from other disciplines such as theatre studies and anthropology have increasingly challenged this partisanship, arguing that film draws on a variety of performative traditions including theatre, music hall and cabaret, all of which have had some influence on film form and content. In *The Anthropology of Performance*, Victor Turner observes that 'rituals, dramas, and other performative genres are often orchestrations of media, not expressions in a single medium' (1988: 23).

In television studies, on the other hand, television's antecedents in theatre and cinema are more readily acknowledged. The term drama is widely used and again has a variety of meanings. Most large television organizations are responsible for commissioning and/or producing television dramas. One-off dramas, drama series and drama serials are fictional programmes that contain all the dramatic elements of staging and enactment listed above. Television dramas are often further subdivided into generic categories such as costume drama, crime drama, social-realist drama, comedy drama, soap opera and so on.

The term drama is increasingly used in relation to non-fiction television. Docu-dramas and drama documentaries are re-enactments of actual events which blur the boundaries between fact and fiction, documentary and drama. Docu-soaps use real places as settings and 'narrativize' the lives of real people, organizing documentary material so that it takes on dramatic form. Dramatic elements like plot, suspense and resolution are all achieved through careful selection and manipulation of real events.

All documentaries and news programmes seek 'dramatic' events as topics. Used in this sense, drama refers to events of high emotional intensity such as war, famine, crime, political scandal, terrorism and disasters. **News values** and news footage substitute for performance, newsreaders and reporters for performers, while the essential ingredient of audience remains the same.

See also: acting; audience; character; documentary

References

Esslin, M. (1988) *The Field of Drama*, London: Methuen.

Turner, V. (1988) *The Anthropology of Performance*, New York: PAJ Publications.

SARA GWENLLIAN JONES

Dyer, Richard

b. 1945

An academic and critic based in the United Kingdom, Richard Dyer is best known for his writing on the politics of **representation**, works which deconstruct how visual media depict society, particularly in relation to racial and sexual identity. In *Now You See It* (1990), for instance, he traces the history of gay and lesbian cinema, and is one of a number of writers whose work has contributed to the growth in popularity of **queer theory**. *White* (1997) further examines issues of representation, exploring the ways in which racial imagery has permeated contemporary western culture.

A less explicit manifestation of these concerns with representation can be found in Dyer's fascination with the workings of mass entertainment. The Hollywood **star system**, for example, as portrayed in *Stars* (1998), becomes a source of perpetual performance and shifting, constructed personas. In assessing our understanding of popular texts, Dyer reveals the multiple contradictions that have always existed in cinema between screen image and personal identity.

See also: race; sexuality

References

Dyer, R. (1990) *Now You See It: Studies on Lesbian and Gay Film*, London: Routledge.
—— (1997) *White*, London: Routledge.
Dyer, R. and McDonald P. (1998) *Stars* (revised edition), London: BFI Publishing.

ANDREW UTTERSON

E

Eagleton, Terry

b. 1943

The author of a number of important introductions to literary theory, **aesthetics** and ideology, Terry Eagleton has succeeded his teacher and mentor Raymond **Williams** as the leading Marxist literary critic in Britain. He has been largely responsible for acquainting a broad readership with the theories of such European Marxists as Walter **Benjamin**, Louis **Althusser** and Pierre Macherey. Following their example, he advocates a materialist approach to the study of literature, exemplified in his own work on Samuel Richardson and the Brontë sisters (see **materialism and idealism**).

Eagleton's insistence on the historical complexity and political usefulness of such ostensibly normative and traditional categories as 'ideology' and 'aesthetics' has also been influential for cultural criticism in general. His re-reading of these categories has been motivated above all by a desire to steer critics of contemporary culture away from what he perceives as the cultural relativism and political apathy of post-modernism (see **modernism and post-modernism**).

See also: ideology and hegemony; Marx, Karl; Marxist aesthetics

Further reading

Eagleton, T. (1981) *Walter Benjamin, or Towards a Revolutionary Criticism*, London: Verso.

—— (1983) *An Introduction to Literary Theory*, Oxford: Blackwell.
—— (1990) *The Ideology of the Aesthetic*, Oxford: Blackwell.
—— (1996) *The Illusions of Post-Modernism*, Oxford: Blackwell.

NICK YABLON

early television

Most western countries initiated regular television service in the course of the early 1950s, with governments regulating or organizing various commercial, public and state-controlled broadcasting systems. Accordingly, the received history of the medium has tended to reflect distinctly national characteristics. But television's history can be traced back much earlier, underscoring not only the international character of the medium, but also alternate conceptions of how it might be deployed. The early history of television can be divided into three phases: expectations and early technologies (1870s–1920s); mechanical and electronic experimentation (1920s–1930s); and deployment and standard-setting (1930s–1940s).

Although there is considerable debate over when the earliest television transmissions took place, it is clear that as an imagined medium and as a patented technology, the key elements for television were in place well over a decade before the first motion picture images were projected. The televisual, as an imagined medium, was born with the invention of the telephone in 1876. Within one year of the telephone's invention, writers took the idea of directable simultaneity and replaced the grain of the voice with the grain of image. The wedding of telephone and photography and the consequent full-blown descriptions of live 'television' transmissions took many forms. In June 1877, *L'année scientifique et industrielle* included a description of the 'telectroscope' – a device attributed to Alexander Graham Bell which sent live images over a distance. Within two years of the telephone's invention, a now famous cartoon appeared in *Punch* which showed a girl in Ceylon speaking with her parents in London by way of a wide-screen electric camera obscura, attributed to Edison, and a telephone. By 1883 Albert Robida would provide his detailed vision of television as an apparatus capable of entertainment, communication and surveillance. Through these fantasized expressive efforts, an idea of simultaneity already defined and experienced through the telephone quickly took hold in the popular imagination as a quality that could be extended in **image**, effectively establishing a key element in the horizon of expectations that would greet film a decade or so later.

However, television's development was more than imaginary. The patents for what would appear as the first working television systems were filed in 1884. Paul Nipkow's patent for the *elektrisches teleskop*, the so-called 'Nipkow disk', provided the heart of mechanical television systems into the early 1940s. Nipkow's system permitted the instantaneous 'dissection' of images, their transmission as electrical signals and their 'reassembly'. By 1889, Lazare Weiller's phoroscope proved capable of much the same task, except that in place of a spinning disk, Weiller used a revolving drum made of angled mirrors. And, just as projected moving pictures first appeared, Charles Frances Jenkins designed his phantascope – a name that included two devices: one a moving picture system co-designed with Thomas Armat, and the other a television system that promised, but so far as we know, failed, to transmit simple shapes.

By the late 1920s, engineers experimented with the transmission, reception and storage of television signals. Stimulated in part by developments in radio and growing interest from the film industry for possible sound technologies, individuals such as John Logie Baird and Philo Farnsworth and

corporations such as EMI and RCA experimented with a wide array of technologies. John Logie Baird, for example, could claim successful results with colour and three-dimensional television as well as with a disk-based video recording system. Early and perhaps premature efforts to bring television to the public were also initiated, but into the early 1930s the medium was limited by the often idiosyncratic nature of the systems used and the absence of technological standardization. Nevertheless, television remained positioned in the popular imagination, visions of it appearing in films.

In 1935, Germany announced 'the world's first daily, public television broadcasting system', embellishing what was in fact an experimental system with close parallels in the United States, the United Kingdom, the Soviet Union and Argentina. Nevertheless, German broadcasts, centred in Berlin, continued almost unbroken until the end of the Second World War, in contrast to British public television broadcasting which formally began in 1936 and ended with the outbreak of war in 1939.

The 1930s and early 1940s were crucial years for three reasons. First, there was growing convergence over the idea of what, precisely, television was. In Germany, for example, it was conceived variously as radio-like (a domestic appliance, acoustic in emphasis), as film-like (seen in a collective setting, visual), as telephone-like (facilitating point-to-point visual communication) and as a means of telepresence (used for guiding rockets, torpedoes, etc.). But in Germany and most other nations, television as a radio-like appliance providing entertainment and information quickly dominated. Second, there were crucial battles over television's standardization, battles which usually pitted large electronics corporations like RCA, EMI and Telefunken against smaller companies or individual inventors such as Baird, Farnsworth or Fernseh AG. In part, the battle was over technology (what we have inherited as electronic, iconoscope-based television versus alternatives), and in part it was over corporate control of television's infrastructure. Third, the **multinational** character of television's technological development was underscored by licence-sharing agreements among various nations. In 1935, for example, RCA licensed its patents to Hitler's Germany and

Stalin's Soviet Union, and the period gave rise to economic cross-investment as well as technological interdependence.

Early television defined in crucial ways dominant assumptions about the medium's representational capacities, its medial homologues, its place in the public sphere and its technological and economic infrastructure.

See also: broadcasting, the United Kingdom; broadcasting, the United States

Further reading

Abramson, A. (1987) *The History of Television, 1880 to 1941*, London: McFarland.

Shires, G. (1997) *Early Television: A Bibliographic Guide to 1940*, London: Garland.

WILLIAM URICCHIO

Eco, Umberto

b. 1932

A prolific semiologist, cultural critic, essayist, columnist, broadcaster and novelist, Umberto Eco is best known for his analyses of cultural phenomena ranging from Chinese comic strips to Disneyland. In 1968, he set out his theories of **semiotics** in his book, *The Absent Structure*, reprinted in a revised edition as *A Theory of Semiotics* (1976). In 1974 he founded the International Association for Semiotic Studies, and at its first congress described semiotics as 'a scientific attitude, a critical way of looking at the objects of other sciences'. In *The Limits of Interpretation* (1994) he addresses the insights and excesses of Derridean **deconstruction**, stressing the need to consider the roles of both the **text** *and* the reader in the production of meaning.

Eco's interest in semiotics, medievalism and the processes of interpretation was the inspiration for his novels: *The Name of the Rose, Foucault's Pendulum* and *The Island of the Day Before*. Since 1971, Eco has been professor of semiotics at Bologna University, Italy.

See also: Derrida, Jacques; hyperreal; mod-ernism and post-modernism; structuralism and post-structuralism

References

Eco, U. (1976) *A Theory of Semiotics*, Bloomington: Indiana University Press.

—— (1994) *The Limits of Interpretation*, Bloomington and Indianapolis: Indiana University Press.

Further reading

Eco, U. (1983) *The Name of the Rose*, trans. Williams Weaver, London: Secker and Warburg.

—— (1985) *The Island of the Day*, trans. William Weaver, London: Secker and Warburg.

—— (1987) *Travels in Hyperreality*, trans. William Weaver, London: Picador.

—— (1989) *Foucault's Pendulum*, trans. William Weaver, London: Secker and Warburg

SARA GWENLLIAN JONES

economism

A term of opprobrium applied to overvaluing economic **determination**. Both V. I. Lenin and Antonio **Gramsci** used it against those who maintained capitalism would inevitably crash and create preconditions for socialism, even without a revolutionary party. Others applied it to Leninism's promise that socialist economic change would necessarily engender freedom, prosperity and social justice, a promise advocates for capitalism made (if in reverse) after the fall of the Berlin Wall in 1989. These legacies caution those in film and television studies who might think overthrowing the capitalist **mode of production** would itself produce works less racist or heterosexist or individualist.

See also: base and superstructure

CLAY STEINMAN

effects

The entire study of mass communication has assumed that media content has certain effects on audiences, yet researchers often disagree about the nature and extent of assumed effects. It is now widely accepted by media scholars that the media are rarely likely to be the only cause of particular effects, yet their relative contribution has proved to be difficult to assess.

Thinking about media effects has been influenced by various groups and interests, such as mass communication researchers, the government, courts, new technologies, historical change, pressure groups and general public concern over the possible negative influences of media content on audiences (see **audience; audience measurement**). Although the history of media effects research is not linear, it is widely recognized that there have been several phases through which knowledge of media effects has accumulated. The first of these is sometimes referred to as that of the 'all-powerful media', beginning roughly at the turn of the twentieth century and lasting until the late 1930s. During this period, many thought that the media in industrialized countries had a great deal of power to shape people's opinions and behaviour. The press and new media of film and radio became very popular and influential (for both commercial and political purposes) in the space of a few decades.

From the 1930s to the early 1960s, others began to argue that the media were less powerful than originally presumed. This period coincided with the development of mass communication research as a distinct field of academic inquiry. The largely empirical (quantitative; see **empiricism**) focus of early studies sought to measure the effects of media content. The preoccupation with assessing the effectiveness of media messages was related to an increasing interest during this period to the media's ability to persuade, as well as concerns over the possible harmful effects of media content on audiences. Mass communication scholars began to develop communication theories based on mathematical models borrowed from **information theory** to help explain how human and mass communication operates. A central aim was to identify instances of effective and ineffective communication as messages travelled from a 'sender' to a 'receiver'. By the end of this period, a number of studies suggested that although the media have some effects, they operate within a pre-existing structure of social relationships and

cultural contexts which must be taken into account when assessing media effects.

In a third stage of media research, from around 1960 through the 1970s, the notion of a powerful media was 'rediscovered'. Renewed interest in media effects was closely associated with the development of television in the 1950s and growing public concern over its possible influence. Mass communication research increasingly drew on models from psychology to examine people's degree of exposure to media and measure for changes to attitude, opinion and behaviour (in its simplest form, some referred to this as a **hypodermic model** of media effects). The view was that violent media content, in particular, probably had significant negative effects on audiences, especially on children (see **children and media; violence**). During this period, effects researchers became increasingly interested in studying long-term change, coginitions, the influences of social context, prior personal disposition and motivation, as well as climates of opinion, ideologies and media institutions (see **ideology and hegemony; institution**).

A fourth phase of effects research, which developed from late 1970s and continues to the present, saw the emergence of the critical 'social constructivist' model. This approach suggests that media influence is most significant when media producers are able to construct systematic meanings which audiences negotiate within their own personal and collective meaning structures. There has been a concomitant methodological shift away from the extensive use of quantitative methods towards qualitative ones such as textual analysis and audience research. The origins of the new research phase grew out of critical challenges to the empiricist paradigm, epitomized by George Gerbner's (1973) 'cultivation theory'. The media are seen to 'cultivate' certain attitudes and values (see **dominant ideology**) within the context of a particular **culture**. It is argued that heavy television viewers, for example, are more likely to accept the image of reality (that which favours the interests of the economic elite) on television than light viewers. Adherents of this approach conclude that while there are certain measurable media effects, their direction, degree, durability and predictability are uncertain. Instead, effects must be established on a case by case basis, and even then they can only offer limited possibilities of generalization.

See also: censorship

Further reading

Barker, M. and Petley, J. (eds) (1997) *Ill Effects: The Media/Violence Debate*, London and New York: Routledge.

Fowles, J. (1992) *Why Viewers Watch: A Reappraisal of Television's Effects*, Newbury Park and London: Sage.

Gerbner, G. (1973) 'Cultural Indicators: The Third Voice', in G. Gerbner, L. Gross and W. Melody (eds) *Communications Technology and Social Policy*, New York: Wiley.

Schramm, W. and Roberts, D. F. (eds) (1971) *The Process and Effects of Mass Communication*, Urbana and London: University of Illinois Press.

CYNTHIA CARTER

Eisenstein, Sergei M.

b. 1898; d. 1948

Sergei Eisenstein exuded accomplishments: he was a stage designer, stage and film director, theorist, teacher, world traveller, polyglot and inexhaustible storyteller. However, if it had not been for the vicissitudes of his career, he may not have become both a movie director and a theorist. His silent films displayed a vivid creativity, most famously in their use of editing, or montage. When, under Stalin, the new doctrine of **Socialist Realism** became the official Soviet aesthetic, Eisenstein, with other montage directors, suffered a period of retreat and rehabilitation (if not worse).

Eisenstein continually wrote critical articles, but his enforced leave from filmmaking left him more time for critical assessments, often of his previous works. He is best known for his writings on the effects of different kinds, or 'levels', of montage. However, he was also devoted to exploring with his classes details of composition, staging, colour and sound – no fundamental element of film evaded his interest.

See also: agit-prop; dialectic and dialectical montage; Formalism; Marxist aesthetics

Further reading

Eisenstein, S. (1947) *The Film Sense* (first published 1942), New York: Harcourt Brace Jovanovich.
—— (1977) *Film Form* (first published 1949), New York: Harcourt Brace Jovanovich.
Nizhny, V. (1962) *Lessons with Eisenstein*, London: George Allen and Unwin.

GABRIEL M. PALETZ

empiricism

From the rather abstract position of epistemological enquiry, empiricism is an argument that all knowledge, except that which is concerned purely with logical relationships, is substantiated by evidence that comes from the world external to human thought. Like all such philosophical definitions, however, there has been much debate over the precise meaning of such terms as 'evidence' and 'externality', giving rise to many subtly different theories of empiricism. Andrew Morton writes that, 'they all have in common a vague theme, which might be expressed as "it all comes from experience"...the experience of the world around us that we get by using our senses and trying not to let our beliefs influence what we think we perceive' (Morton 1996: 233). At its strongest, such empiricism suggested to John Locke that the human mind at birth was like a blank page, without any pre-existing knowledge. More pragmatically, empiricism demands that, to be truly knowledgeable, one should be sceptical about the formation of one's beliefs and rely on extensive observation of the objective world.

Empiricism is easier to understand if it is located historically. Empiricism and rationalism were competing philosophical visions of knowledge within Europe from the late seventeenth century to the early nineteenth century. Rationalists (such as René Descartes), in direct contrast to empiricism, dismissed perceived or sensed experience as unreliable, and grounded their views in a form of pure reason, emanating from within the conscious thinking subject (see **subject and subjectivity**). Empiricists (particularly in Britain and Ireland) asked the obvious question: how was it possible not to be influenced by the world of experience?

In the late eighteenth century, Kant more or less resolved this dispute for philosophers for a time by arguing that the epistemological categories by which we make sense of the world are 'rational' (that is, not drawn from experience), but that the world of which we seek to make sense is indeed knowable only through experience (see **epistemology**). In other words, knowledge comes from both perception and understanding. Yet a more traditional form of empiricism, with its curious mix of naïveté and scepticism, came to be the dominant *popular* conception of the basis for true beliefs and knowledge, entrenched in a vast array of modern social operations – liberal, socialist and fascistic governance; industrial management practices; political inquiries; legal systems; journalism; medical science; and most of all, the bureaucracies that were characteristic of the nineteenth century.

Variations on the theme empiricism, already the background score of the natural sciences, came to play loudly within the social and human sciences that developed in the nineteenth century. For example, writing history changed from being an essentially literary endeavour to one involving the rigorous, scientific gathering of evidence from archives and other 'reliable' sources and the denial of personal interest by the historian in the topic of their inquiry (see **historiography**). While not completely without challenge, most academic disciplines with the exception of some forms of literary studies, took on an approach that, while not explicitly empiricist, fitted with its key assumption: that knowledge is gleaned from careful analysis of unbiased observation of experience.

Since the 1950s, and latterly by critics working from a (more or less) post-structuralist stance (see **structuralism and post-structuralism**), empiricism has been under serious challenge. The attack is firstly political, arguing that the concepts of impartiality, uninvolved observation, generalization and objectivity central to empiricism's operation are alibis for the entrenched power of the observer, whether in society at large or in a scholarly situation. Secondly, it is claimed, empiricism fails to account adequately for the problem of

whether or not, or in what circumstances, there can be equally valid interpretations of experience leading to conflicting knowledges. What is less clear, however, and particularly so in disciplines involving extensive study of communications, culture and media, is how methods of investigation and research that involve seeking and observing world experiences, rather than inner reflection, can be separated successfully from empiricist assumptions about the knowledge so gained. If this becomes clearer, it might allow an epistemological rearrangement, rather along Kantian lines, between, on the one hand, this limited call to perception and experience and on the other, forms of post-structuralist textualism.

See also: Foucault, Michel; reading and reception theory; text

References

Morton, A. (1996) *Philosophy in Practice: An Introduction to the Main Questions*, Cambridge, MA: Blackwell.

MATTHEW ALLEN

encoding

The term 'encoding' (and its associated term, 'decoding') derives from the code model of meaning that was concurrently developed in **semiotics** and in information theory. In its simplest form, the code model describes communicative processes as a two staged affair that occurs between a sender and a receiver (see **sender/receiver**). In the encoding stage of the process, the sender relays information through a physical medium by pairing a message with a signal on the basis of a socially shared **code**. On receiving the signal, the receiver is able to decode the information by employing the same code by which the information had been originally encoded by the sender. To ensure that the information decoded by the receiver is the same as that encoded by the sender, the encoding and decoding processes must be the precise reverse of each another. Communicative systems such as the Morse code or traffic light signals are the most obvious examples of the code model in operation in its pure form.

Despite the fundamental simplicity of the code model, it is none the less capable of admitting far greater degrees of complexity. The socially shared codes that underlie the encoding and decoding stages need not be simple **binary** pairs, as in the signal/message or signifier/signified dyads, but can also further consist of complex rules of construction. The linguistics of Ferdinand de **Saussure**, for instance, can be profitably seen as a variation on the basic code model through his introduction of such notions of **syntagmatic** and **paradigmatic** relations in his analysis of linguistic systems. Following Saussure's lead, semioticians within both film and television studies, such as Christian **Metz** and Umberto **Eco**, have extended the application of the code model beyond the realm of linguistics in their analyses of cinematic and televisual images. In this respect, Stuart **Hall** has perhaps gone the furthest in the introduction of the concepts of encoding and decoding into media studies by mapping them, respectively, to the moments of the production and reception of media artefacts. Following on from the work of Hall, John **Fiske** and other media studies theorists have deployed the encoding/decoding model to suggest ways in which meanings encoded in a text might be resisted or rearticulated by subordinated groups in society.

The picture that emerges from this perspective of the encoding process is one where the production of film and television texts is treated as being roughly analogous to the production of verbal utterances on the part of a speaker. To communicate, speakers must transform their ideas into the symbolic forms of the language that is used by following the semantic and grammatical rules of sentence construction. Similarly, filmmaking and television production is also characterized as a transformational process in that the initial material intended to be communicated must be transformed into the discursive forms used by the medium in question. The primary difference between these two types of meaning production is that the example of an individual speaker is substituted in the latter case by an **institution** with a specific organizational structure and ownership of technical equipment and property.

This picture of film and television production understood in terms of encoding processes is not without its problems and has been challenged by theorists working within **cognitive theory**. For one thing, it is a matter of intense debate within film and television studies whether the construction of visual images should be analysed on the basis of the code model. Cognitive film theorists, such as David **Bordwell**, have claimed that semioticians have been unsuccessful in identifying the codes that are said to govern the production and comprehension of visual images, at least not to the rigorous extent and detail in which such codes have been identified within linguistics. More damagingly, the assumption that all communication relies exclusively on encoding and decoding processes has itself been questioned. Cognitive film theorists have argued that the comprehension of narrative films relies more on inferential processes than on decoding operations. If this is the case, then the analysis of the production of film and television narratives is less a matter of encoding and more the construction of aural and visual evidence through which spectators are able to infer the communicative intentions of a work.

See also: encoding-decoding model; preferred reading; reading and reception theory

Further reading

Hall, S. (1980) 'Encoding/Decoding', in S. Hall, D. Hobson, A. Lowe and P. Willis (eds) *Culture, Media, Language*, London: Hutchinson.
Sperber, D. and Wilson, D. (1995) *Relevance: Cognition and Communication*, Oxford: Blackwell.

TICO ROMAO

encoding-decoding model

According to Stuart **Hall** (1980: 130), while the encoding and decoding of the televisual news message are differentiated moments (that is, they are not perfectly symmetrical or transparent), they are related to one another by the social relations of the communicative process as a whole. Before this form of **discourse** can have an effect, however, it needs to be appropriated as a personally relevant discourse by the televisual viewer; that is, it has to be meaningfully decoded. For Hall, it is this set of decoded meanings which 'influence, entertain, instruct or persuade, with very complex perceptual, cognitive, emotional, ideological or behavioural consequences' (*ibid.*).

Hall outlines three hypothetical positions (de-rived, in part, from Parkin 1973) from which decodings may be constructed. These ideal-typical reading positions, all of which are available at the moment of decoding, may be distinguished as follows with regard to televisual news:

1 When the viewer of a televisual news account decodes its message in alignment with its encoding, the viewer is occupying the domi-nant-hegemonic position. From this position, Hall argues, the 'authoritative', 'impartial' and 'professional' signification of the news event is being accepted as perfectly obvious or natural. The viewer, operating inside the dominant subjectivity that the news account confers, reproduces the hegemonic definition of the situation in ideological terms (see **ideology and hegemony; subject and subjectivity**).
2 In what Hall characterizes as the negotiated position (see **negotiation**), the viewer under-stands the preferred definition being mobilized by the televisual news account, but does not relate to it as being self-evidently 'obvious' or 'natural'. Although viewers recognize its general legitimacy as a factual report, certain discre-pancies or contradictions within their own personal context are identified. The news account is seen to be encouraging one inter-pretation over and above other possibilities.
3 The final reading position is that which is consistent with an oppositional code. The viewer apprehends the logic of the dominant-hegemonic position in such a manner that the authority of its definition is directly challenged. Hall offers the example of a viewer who follows a debate on the need to limit wages but reads every mention of the 'national interest' as 'class interest' (1980: 138).

It is important to note that these ideal-typical reading positions are being marked for purposes of analytical clarity, and that they are not actual empirical or lived positions. The viewer's engage-ment with an actual televisual newscast is likely to engender a complex range of often contradictory positions as the activity of negotiating meaning is always contingent on the particular social relations of signification in operation (see Gray 1992; Morley 1992).

The encoding-decoding model allows for the issue of textual determination to be addressed as a fluidly heterogeneous process without, at the same time, losing sight of the ways in which it is embedded in relations of power. The status of the televisual news viewer is not reduced to that of a victim who passively acquiesces to the dictates of a 'dominant ideology' being imposed via the **text**, nor is the viewer accorded an ability to identify freely with multiple interpretations of the text. The encoding-decoding model situates this dynamic activity as a negotiated process within certain conditional, but always changing, parameters. As such, it succeeds in highlighting a spectrum of potential positions to be occupied, however fleetingly.

See also: audience; common sense; dominant ideology; encoding

References

Gray, A. (1992) *Video Playtime: The Gendering of a Leisure Technology*, London: Routledge.

Hall, S. (1980) 'Encoding/Decoding', in S. Hall, D. Hobson, A. Lowe, P. Willis (eds) *Culture, Media, Language*, London: Hutchinson, pp. 128–38.

Morley, D. (1992) *Television, Audiences and Cultural Studies*, London: Routledge.

Parkin, F. (1973) *Class Inequality and Political Order*, London: Paladin.

Further reading

Hall, S. (1994) 'Reflections upon the Encoding/Decoding Model: An Interview with Stuart Hall', in J. Cruz and J. Lewis (eds) *Viewing, Reading, Listening: Audiences and Cultural Reception*, Boulder: Westview, pp. 253–74.

STUART ALLAN

enigma

One of five **narrative** codes identified by Roland **Barthes**, enigma – or hermeneutic codes – 'explain' the narrative by controlling when, and how much, information is revealed. An enigma is often a type of disequilibrium where the normal order is overthrown or challenged. This can be by a murder by someone unseen at the beginning of a crime narrative, or it may be the headlines read out at the start of a news bulletin. Usually the enigma is resolved by the narrative's **closure** where the '*status quo*' is restored. **Advertising** is particularly adept at using these codes to gain the audience's attention.

See also: Todorov, Tzvetan

PHILIP RAYNER

entertainment

The notion of entertainment is both a rather debased one and a crucially important one for film and television theorists. 'Entertainment' is often contrasted with 'serious' pursuits; this contrast leads, incorrectly, to the perception that scholars and theorists who study the products of the entertainment industry are engaged in frivolous or lightweight work. The status of film and television as entertainment media has thus slowed film and television theory's ability to gain a foothold in academic institutions.

The majority of film and video productions are created exclusively for entertainment purposes, and every day millions of people spend money and/or time on them. 'Entertainment' makes huge claims on personal and social resources and, whether or not as efficiently and directly as some proponents of theories of media '**effects**' would argue, goes at least some way towards determining and directing the social imagination. Thus, however trivial or ephemeral may be a particular television show or film, the sheer magnitude and sweep of the production and consumption industries makes them suitable candidates for academic study, whether their products are categorized as 'just entertainment' or not.

Academic study of film has also responded to the 'just entertainment' criticism by arguing for the artistic and even philosophical depth of some (though not all) mainstream films, as well as for the artistic potential of film outside of the mainstream once the constraints of the entertainment industry have been lifted. (Unfortunately, the lifting of those constraints is usually accompanied by the lifting of financial support; film is an expensive medium and, however poetic, hardly as easy to produce as poetry.) The most convincing demonstrations of the 'weight' of the medium of film come, not from point-blank assertions of its artistic merit, which often sound reactive and defensive, but from the cumulative effect of the work of theorists and critics who proceed from the assumption that writing about film must be as worthwhile a pursuit as writing about the other arts. Not that all such work is of high quality or lasting interest; but certainly things have reached a point where a denial of the status of film scholars as intellectual peers of scholars in other branches of the humanities indicates a very deeply-entrenched prejudice against film indeed.

Further reading

Modleski, T. (1986) *Studies in Entertainment: Critical Approaches to Mass Culture*, Bloomington: Indiana University Press.

DAVID A. BLACK

enunciation

Narrative theory distinguishes between enunciated (also called *histoire*, or story) – the sequence of events that happen to characters – and enunciation (also called *discours*, or **discourse**) – the manner or mode in which the story is narrated. Enunciation encompasses what would traditionally be called **style** or rhetoric. Christian **Metz** argues that in classical cinema, processes of enunciation are effaced, disguised as elements of the story. This is an ideological operation in so far as it 'dupes' the spectator into believing the story is 'telling itself'. In this view, a politically progressive cinema would reveal the marks of its enunciation, distancing the spectator from a voyeuristic fascination with the image (see **distancing; voyeurism**).

See also: psychoanalysis

ANGELO RESTIVO

epic

The term 'epic' generally refers to very long and expensive films dealing with major historical or religious themes. Often adaptations of important literature or popular novels, epics helped to establish cinema's cultural legitimacy in the teens through early features like *Quo Vadis?* (Enrico Guazzoni, 1913). Epic films often reinforce dominant ideology, support dominant social groups and tend to focus on such major themes as nation, religion and history (see **ideology and hegemony**). Popular before and after the collapse of classical Hollywood, epics are often international co-productions combining extensive location shooting and elaborate sets (see **classical Hollywood cinema and new Hollywood cinema**).

Epic may also refer to Bertolt **Brecht**'s theorizing of theatrical practices, sometimes adopted by **avant-garde** filmmakers, which challenged the dominant form.

MOYA LUCKETT

epistemology

Epistemology is the area of philosophy that deals with knowledge about knowledge: the nature of what we know, how we know we know it, and the reliability, validity and limits of claims to knowledge. In the history of philosophy, epistemological questions have often been debated by rationalists such as Plato, Benedict Spinoza and G. W. Leibniz, who argued that the human mind's reasoning ability is the best source of knowledge; and empiricists like John Locke, George Berkeley and David Hume, who favoured sense experience and its perception as the most reliable method of knowing (see **empiricism**). More recently, constructivists have suggested that human beings project themselves into what they experience, thereby creating knowledge out of their own preconceptions (see **Constructivism**). Social-constructivists believe that knowledge of reality derives from a socially-constructed world view (Berger and Luckmann 1996).

In film and television methodology, most theoreticians have been sceptics, that is, like René Descartes, they doubt whether any knowledge claims about media can stand up under rational or empirical scrutiny. Contemporary thinkers seem to subscribe to the post-structuralist and deconstructionist byword: 'when in doubt, doubt'.

Thus, any 'truth' or 'knowledge' claims would have to be placed in quotation marks, especially when analysing heavily mediated products such as films or television programmes. Although the technological apparatuses of film and video are capable of recording the sights and sounds of the real world (experience), they can also distort those sense impressions through lens choice, editing, lighting, voice-over narration, camera angle and other techniques. Seeing is not always believing.

The seal-hunt sequence in Robert Flaherty's documentary film *Nanook of the North* (1922), for instance, has impressed many with its apparently transparent and realistic view of an Eskimo and his family. Asking the epistemological question, 'How do we know it's real?', raises the spectre of the many liberties Flaherty took with his subject. For instance, the real-life Nanook hunted seals with a rifle, not a harpoon, as shown on screen. Furthermore, rather than wait for hours for a seal to happen along, Flaherty placed a dead seal under the ice and had Nanook pretend to harpoon it, catch it, and struggle with all his strength to haul it out of the Arctic ice. But Flaherty believed that by exaggerating and dramatizing his 'Man against Nature' theme, he was capturing a larger Truth than the mundane reality of Nanook's day-to-day experience. As Mrs Flaherty once said: 'Sometimes you have to lie in order to tell the truth.'

See also: deconstruction; documentary; structuralism and post-structuralism

Further reading

Berger, P. and Luckmann, T. (1966) *The Social Construction of Reality*, Garden City, NY: Doubleday.

Nichols, B. (1991) *Representing Reality: Issues and Concepts in Documentary,* Bloomington: Indiana University Press.

FRANK P. TOMASULO

escapism

The obvious meaning of escapism is 'a seeking of escape, especially from reality', but this has been a term persistently used by some critics to disparage film and television as irresponsible mass cultural/leisure forms – as opposed, for example, to the 'seriousness' of **'art' cinema**. It also implies totally uncritical viewers. The term is often synonymous with '**entertainment**' or **genre** forms, and within them, in a very gendered move, with the musical (see **musical, the**) and **romance** rather than, say, the war film or courtroom drama, which equally provide an entertaining 'escape' for audiences. A key question might be: who is said to escape, into what kind of fictional world, and why?

GILL BRANSTON

essentialism

Esstentialism is one of the enduring philosophical doctrines that responds to the metaphysical inquiry regarding the nature of things. In its most general sense, it states that a thing is what it is and not something else because of its inherent and immutable properties. According to this thesis, the possibility that one can individuate and identify a particular object stems directly from one knowing a set of necessary, intrinsic and invariable characteristics, namely essences, that this object possesses. In western philosophical tradition, essentialism is older than Aristotle; modern essentialists include thinkers such as Edmund Husserl who, using the phenomenological method which he developed, carries on the classical project of uncovering the universal structure underlying reality.

BRIANKLE G. CHANG

ethnicity

Ethnicity, a term which is often used interchangeably with **race** or nationality, is used to designate groups of individuals who supposedly have certain common characteristics. But, sharing with race and nationality an absence of scientifically verifiable markers, ethnicity is an imprecise term. Two related problems hinder precise definition: (i) what are the characteristics deemed to constitute an ethnic affiliation; and (ii) is ethnicity an objective category, assigned by the society, or a subjective category, chosen by the individual, an attribute of birth or a matter of individual agency? Characteristics used to assign individuals to ethnic groups include race, nationality, religion, cultural customs and the person's own sense of group belonging. Although ultimately cultural constructions, race and nationality are attributes of birth and relatively immutable, marked by biological or legal signifiers. An individual may also acquire a religious affiliation and a set of cultural customs at birth, but these are more mutable characteristics than race or nationality; individuals may change their religion and adopt different customs. Indeed, individuals often deliberately change their religion or customs in an attempt to declare a sense of belonging to a group different from that in which they were born, for example, to become British or American rather than Jamaican or Italian. But while these individuals may choose to switch their group affiliations, society may not recognize their choice, still designating them as Jamaican or Italian on the basis of race and nationality, rather than British or American on the basis of religion or customs or declared sense of belonging. In an increasingly globalized and hybridized world, ethnicity becomes an even more complex mixture of subjective choice and external designation, of race, nationality, religion and customs (see **globalization**).

Fortunately, media studies scholars can leave precise definition to the sociologists and use ethnicity as a '**common sense**' conceptual category in the study of production, representation and reception. Not surprisingly, much of the research on the media and ethnicity comes from the United States, perhaps the world's most self-consciously multi-ethnic society, as attested to by the presence of so many 'hyphenated Americans' – African-Americans, Italian-Americans, Asian-Americans and so on. The representation of ethnicity has always been central to the American cinema, whether by omission or commission. The vast majority of American films produced since the beginnings of the cinema reflected the ethnic hierarchies of the American hegemonic order; the default ethnicity was WASP: white, Anglo-Saxon, Protestant (see **ideology and hegemony**).

However, 'WASPness' was represented not as an ethnic affiliation but as the unquestioned norm. To be marked as ethnic was to be different, to be the **Other**, to be outside of and perhaps at odds with the norm. For example, the script of the Warner Bros General Custer biopic, *They Died with Their Boots On* (1941), lists the officers of the seventh Cavalry as 'Cooper...Elliot...Keogh (Irish), Myers (Jewish), Macintosh (half-breed), Commagere (French)' (Kline and MacKenzie 1941: 87). Cooper and Elliot, presumably white Anglo-Saxon Protestants and thus part of the invisible dominant, require no descriptors, but each of the other officers is defined purely in terms of his ethnicity. This held true off-screen as well as on-screen. Hollywood stars, like the characters they portrayed, were represented as overwhelmingly WASP, their non-WASP affiliations whited out, their names and personal histories changed to conform to the dominant. Only rarely, in the days of the classical Hollywood cinema, did a star emerge whose appeal was predicated on ethnicity, for example Rudolph Valentino (see **classical Hollywood cinema and new Hollywood cinema**).

Paradoxically, this reinforcement of hegemony was dictated by an ethnic community, the Jewish studio bosses, who, in their desperation to be 'real' Americans rather than immigrants or outsiders, tried to construct a mono-ethnic Hollywood. But even during the heyday of the studio system, the occasional 'social problem' film addressed ethnicity. For example, in *Gentleman's Agreement* (Elia Kazan, 1947), reporter Gregory Peck, assigned to write a story on anti-Semitism, passes as a Jew in order to experience discrimination directly. But as indicated by their nomenclature, films of this sort conceived of ethnicity as a 'problem', the solution being a melting pot America in which ethnic differences would cease to matter. The social and cultural upheaval of the 1960s gave birth to a new concept of an ideal America however, a multicultural rather than mono-cultural nation. Such a shift in hegemony enabled films to celebrate the country's many ethnic groups and some filmmakers emerged who specialized in representing particular ethnic groups: Francis Ford Coppola and Italian-Americans, Spike Lee and African-Americans, Woody Allen and American Jews.

The space constraints of this entry preclude discussion of research on the role of ethnicity in production and reception, on the representation of ethnicity in television and radio and on the representation of ethnicity in cinemas other than the American. But, living in an increasingly multicultural world, many media studies scholars are concerning themselves with these topics.

See also: African-American cinema; Eurocentrism

References

Kline, W. and MacKenzie, A. (1941) *They Died with Their Boots On*, final script, 17 June 1941, Billy Rose Theatre Collection, New York Public Library for the Performing Arts, Lincoln Center.

Further reading

Bernardi, D. (ed.) (1996) *The Birth of Whiteness: Race and the Emergence of U.S. Cinema*, New Brunswick: Rutgers University Press.

Dyer, R. (1988) 'White', *Screen*, vol. 29, no. 4, pp. 44–64.

Friedman, L. D. (ed.) (1991) *Unspeakable Images: Ethnicity and the American Cinema*, Urbana: University of Illinois Press.

Woll, L. and Miller, R. (eds) (1987) *Ethnic and Racial Images in American Film and Television*, New York: Garland Publishing.

ROBERTA E. PEARSON

ethnography

The term 'ethnography' refers to the practice of collecting and writing up information on human society (often remote native communities) undertaken by a trained anthropologist. An anthropologist typically conducts an ethnographic study by spending at least two years living among an indigenous group during which time cultural practices (see **culture**) are carefully observed and recorded. Through a method of participant observation (immersing oneself in a culture while paying close attention to cultural patterns), the anthropologist-researcher becomes a temporary member of a community, participating either 'overtly or covertly, in people's daily lives for an extended period of time, watching what happened, listening to what is said, asking questions; in fact collecting whatever data are available to throw light on the issues which he or she is concerned' (Hammersely and Atkinson 1983).

Within recent media and cultural studies, ethnography refers to a form of empirical audience research which appropriates some of the methodological precepts of ethnography, such as a reliance on techniques of triangulation (gathering information from a range of sources that can be cross-referenced) with the aim of producing what anthropologist Clifford Geertz (1973) calls a 'thick description' of audience activity (see **empiricism**). According to David Morley, ethnography rests on an ability to 'understand how social actors themselves define and understand their own communication practices, their decisions, their choices, and the consequences of both for their daily lives and their subsequent actions' (Morley 1994). Producing a richly descriptive and interpretive account of how audiences experience television, an ethnographer looks for the rules governing people's uses of the medium, using transcribed interviews with respondents as evidence of deep structures of belief. Even when a researcher is working with a cultural group to which he or she belongs, the experience must be treated as 'anthropologically strange' so as to make explicit assumptions that may have been internalized by the respondents and the researcher.

Although broadly defined ethnographic approaches were first used by a handful of media researchers in the early 1980s – Dorothy Hobson's *Crossroads* (1982) is an early example – the work of David Morley (1994), Marie Gillespie (1995) and James Lull (1988) comes closest to fulfilling the methodological requirements of ethnography (see **audience**). Ethnography's popularity as a research method is both its strength and its weakness, however. On the one hand, ethnography has been hailed as better suited to the vagaries of television viewing and its social and cultural determinants than traditional quantitative methods. On the other hand, some critics fear that ethnography's reliance on description may be inherently unsuited to the critical agenda and commitment to theory of cultural studies. In addition, some anthropologists have objected to the term ethnography being used within cultural studies audience research, arguing that what passes for ethnography within audience research is often a far cry from the kind of systematic observation associated with the extended participant observation practices of anthropologists. Defenders of cultural studies ethnographic research reply that micro-ethnographies produced over relatively brief periods of time can nevertheless provide useful information, especially if the researcher is sensitive to the limitations of the study.

The practice of ethnography has also been invoked in relation to the production and criticism of a specific strand of post-war documentary filmmaking, when the term ethnographic cinema was used to describe the filmmaking activities of such visual anthropologists as Margaret Mead and Jean Rouch. However, non-anthropologists shot some of the most noted ethnographic films – John Marshall's *The Hunters* (1956) and Robert Gardner's *Dead Birds* (1963) are two classic examples. Ethnographic films may be produced within a variety of contexts, ranging from the professional research of an anthropologist in the field to a popular television series, such as *Disappearing World* in the UK. Ethnographic films take as their subject a culture's experiences over a period of time, often focusing on a single individual or family. While some ethnographic films resemble traditional documentaries in form, their concern with representing culture over and above any didactic social message separates them from many other films in the documentary **genre**.

See also: documentary; diaspora

References

Geertz, C. (1973) *The Interpretation of Cultures*, New York: Basic Books.

Gillespie, M. (1995) *Television, Ethnicity and Cultural Change*, London: Routledge.

Hammersley, M. and Atkinson, P. (1983) *Ethnography: Principles in Practice*, London: Routledge.

Lull, J. (1988) *World Families Watch Television*, Newbury Park, Consortium Agreement: Sage.

Morley, D. (1994) *Television Audiences and Cultural Studies*, London: Routledge.

Further reading

Crawford P. and D. Turton (eds) (1992) *Film as Ethnography*, Manchester: Manchester University Press.

ALISON GRIFFITHS

Eurocentrism

Eurocentrism refers to European domination of global space, **history** and **culture**. It exposes and interrogates the ways in which European practices have defined the standards against which all other cultures are judged. European nations have constructed histories to legitimate their conquest of other lands in the name of religion, order, civilization and cultural supremacy. Rather than representing any 'truth', all of these values are profoundly Eurocentric. Subsequent colonizations helped set the stage for Eurocentrism and the global dissemination of European values at the expense of indigenous and native cultures.

European dominance has been naturalized and maintained through history, culture, religion, science and the law – all dominant discourses of power in their own right (see **discourse**). Eurocentrism borrows the '**objectivity**' and 'truth' of science, history, geography and Christianity to legitimize European and western hegemony (see **ideology and hegemony**). Maps testify to the Eurocentric vision of Europe as the centre of the world, casting other nations to the margins and minimizing their land masses. Even the practice of placing the Northern hemisphere at the top of the globe reinforces Eurocentric hierarchies and re-presentational practices which associate power and dominance with the top.

Dominant histories perform a similar function. All culture is traced to Europe, a move which itself demands a certain amnesia, erasing the earlier formation of 'civilization' in such non-European nations as Egypt, Africa, Mesopotamia, Persia and China. This requires some complicated and contradictory thinking. For example, the Egypt of antiquity is represented and reclaimed as white and proto-European while simultaneously it is defined as Middle Eastern in the present.

Eurocentrism values the West more than the East – even within Europe. This helps explain the curious position of the US and Canada in the Eurocentric world view. In many ways, these nations are allied to Eurocentrism, both by virtue of their power, their cultural similarities, and through the histories that place their civilizations as the work of European natives migrating further West. But this also involves a Eurocentric re-visioning of both continents. This perspective privileges white residents of western European descent at the expense of native peoples and non-white, non-European migrants. The predominantly Eurocentric aspects of their culture are seen as representative while non-European elements are either ignored, denigrated or dismissed. A Eurocentric vision of the US emerges that ignores much of its culture, heritage and population, presenting it as a replica of Europe. This also suggests that its culture is 'inferior' despite its economic success.

Eurocentrism refers to the economic and representational practices that reinforce the domination of European culture (see **economism; representation**). Music is judged in relation to the western twelve-tone scale, while **perspective** is privileged in mimetic **art** and photography. This emphasis prevents audiences from understanding other cultures' ways of seeing and hearing the world, and minimizes the values they encode (see **encoding**). Even when non-western cultural productions receive praise and critical validation, it is usually because they can be valued within a Eurocentric perspective. Eurocentrism is even more pronounced in the case of mainstream, popular forms like film and television. On the rare occasions when non-European, non-white characters or events are represented, they are seen through a European perspective. Because of their economic power, these texts dominate the global market.

The formation of canons helped police European domination of art and literature, establishing formal models and parameters for high culture and disseminating these around the globe (see **canon**). Under these conditions, only European (and, to some extent, North American) culture can qualify as 'art'. Simultaneously, all other nations' cultural distinctions are erased and their cultural productions deemed valueless in the face of the canon's international power.

Recently, post-colonial and non-western critics have noted that Eurocentrism has also influenced much theory and, consequently, put forward a western/European agenda. Some forms of post-modernism have been lauded for their emphasis on a multicultural, multi-vocal world, departing from their more singular, Eurocentric predecessors (see **multiculturalism; modernism and post-modernism**).

Eurocentrism also validates other hierarchies found within European nations and across the globe. It privileges masculinity, consigning the East to the less powerful feminine as discussed by Edward **Said**, and presents Christianity as the dominant mode of spiritual belief and the ultimate form of truth.

See also: globalization; national, the

Further reading

Ashcroft, B., Griffiths, G. and Tiffin, H. (eds) (1995) *The Post-Colonial Studies Reader,* London: Routledge.
Said, E. (1978) *Orientalism,* London: Routledge.

MOYA LUCKETT

excess

'Excess' denotes an extravagant, abundant sensation or moment within a **text**, which may be located within the **mise-en-scène**, **narrative** or performance (see **performance theory**). Some genres lend themselves more readily to excess, for example, the musical and **melodrama** (see **genre; musical, the**). Here we can locate excess in the stirring scores, sumptuous decor, moments of high drama and emotional climaxes. These elements of excess can be used to suggest repressed **desire** where it is not more explicitly represented. In terms of performance, excess is to be found in the highly mannered acting style of some stars, suggesting a self-awareness of their performance techniques and status as star (see **acting**).

DEBORAH JERMYN

Expressionism

Originally applied to an anti-naturalistic movement in painting and theatre in the early part of the twentieth century, Expressionism now commonly refers to the distinctive **style** of a number of films produced in Germany *circa* 1919 to 1930. Typically, German Expressionist films use extreme camera angles, high contrast lighting, mobile framing, distorted perspectives and shadowy, nightmarish settings. Examples include Robert Wiene's *The Cabinet of Dr Caligari* (1919) and Fritz Lang's *Metropolis* (1926). **Film noir**'s paranoid mood and style is generally attributed to the influence of German Expressionism.

Further reading

Kracauer, S. (1974) *From Caligari to Hitler: A Psychological History of the German Film,* Princeton: Princeton University Press.

SARA GWENLLIAN JONES

F

fabula

A term originated by the Russian Formalists (see **Formalism**), fabula is one of two basic categories within narratology (the other being **syuzhet**). It describes the actions of the **narrative** as they unfold independent of a speaker's intervention. In the fabula, events would take place in chronological order, just as they would in real life, unaffected by the act of organizing and telling them. Because a literary or cinematic text is always already arranged and given a distinct point of view, the fabula never exists within the work itself, but only as an imaginary construct put together by the spectator.

KAREN BACKSTEIN

faction

'Faction' refers to a mixture of fact and fiction. Faction has caused controversy throughout the history of moving images, with commentators concerned about the effects of fiction masquerading as fact, and about the effects of the dictates of entertainment on factual broadcasting such as **documentary**. Faction is historically associated with the commercial imperatives operating in American television, resulting in a type of dramatized reconstruction which gives priority to 'human interest' aspects, through a thoroughgoing transformation of fact-based material with the aim of maximizing a popular audience. The blurring of borders between fact and fiction has also led scholars to epistemological debates about **realism** and the representation of reality.

See also: epistemology

LEE GRIEVESON

family melodrama

Within the categorical terms of **genre**, 'family melodrama' is a subset of **melodrama**, as the adjective 'family' implies. Melodrama, as a critical category in film and theatre studies, has stretched the boundaries of generic classification enough to be called a 'mode of perception'. Peter Brooks' (1976) concept of the melodramatic imagination attempts to outline and historicize this form as one which makes the world legible through the secularization of the pre-Industrial Revolution religious system 'of mythic explanation and implicit ethics' (Brooks 1976: 18). Most mainstream Hollywood films fall into this category in the sense that the melodramatic involves conflict between the opposing forces of good and evil. These conflicts are made no less powerful by a seeming abandonment to **realism** and acquire their emotional force even in the most elaborate psychological motivations of characters primarily through the 'melodramatic possibilities' of psychology (Brooks 1976: 204). This quality of the combination of realism and melodrama, as Christine Gledhill points out in her introductory essay, 'The Melodramatic Field: An Investigation' (1987: 5–43), has been a crucial dynamic in the emotional and ideological force of Hollywood cinema (see **ideology and hegemony**).

While this all-encompassing definition threatens to include all of Hollywood cinema and a good proportion of **narrative** cinema generally, the family melodrama exemplifies and focuses the dynamics of the melodramatic mode through its recognizable system of human relationships. The family provides archetypal characters who hold considerable social and psychological significance (see **archetype**). A film such as D. W. Griffith's *Way Down East* (1920), for example, turns on the symbolic value of the father, Squire Bartlett (Burr McIntosh), who represents the social prejudices that Anna (Lillian Gish), the central character, struggles to withstand. The family also provides the conduit through which the individual negotiates with outside social forces and at the same time assigns them to a particular social class. In Douglas Sirk's *All That Heaven Allows* (1956), Cary (Jane Wyman) is a well-off widow who is forced to negotiate with her adult children's disapproval of her relationship with her gardener, Ron (Rock Hudson). This treatment of the family as an ideal social unit under threat from, in this case, the transgression of **class** boundaries and its evidence of **desire** in a mature woman, provided the material for an implicit critique of American bourgeois values in the 1950s.

The family melodrama of the 1950s provided the focus for the development of intellectual critique in film studies in the 1970s. Thomas Elsaesser's 'Tales of Sound and Fury: Observations on the Family Melodrama' (in Gledhill 1987) suggested that through the use of widescreen and Technicolor the films of Douglas Sirk provided a means of signifying the psychological state of the characters. This was achieved through the excess of colour and claustrophobic depictions of the suburban home which compensated for the lack of the main characters' ability to express verbally their emotions. More important, it enabled the 'justification for giving critical importance to the **mise-en-scène** over intellectual content or story value' (Gledhill 1987: 52).

The family melodramas of the 1950s in themselves were ideal for critical investigation. They arose at the post-war moment of suburbanization in the United States, the popularization of

Freudian theories of human behaviour (see **Freud, Sigmund**), and the impact of television and Hollywood's response through technological innovations such as widescreen and Technicolor. The potential for the family melodrama as aesthetic subversion outlined by male critics in these films was built on by feminist film critics. Laura **Mulvey** found the family melodrama a form which often explicitly addressed women. For Mulvey, this potential was qualified, however, in the sense that the female point of view produced 'an excess which precludes satisfaction' while the 'irreconcilable social and sexual dilemmas' were ultimately resolved in male-centred family melodramas such as Vincent Minnelli's *Home From the Hill* (1960).

In recent years the emphasis has shifted away from the interpretation of texts for evidence of resistance to, or complicity with, ideological imperatives towards the meanings a text may hold for specific audiences at specific times. Scholars such as Lea Jacobs, Maria LaPlace and Jeanne Allen have undertaken specific studies of the institutional and cultural contexts of melodramas. Studies of television audiences for soap operas, like Ien Ang's (1985) study of audiences for *Dallas*, have used the family melodrama form as the centre of their investigations. Barbara Klinger's (1994) reception study of Sirk melodramas of the 1950s explores their cultural circulation within the contexts of academic discourse, studio practices, the **star system**, popular journalism and gay culture (see **queer theory; reading and reception theory**). Each of these approaches works towards determining the ideological function of texts within specific historical moments. In this regard, the family melodrama continues to hold a central place in the field of film studies.

References

Ang, I. (1985) *Watching Dallas*, London: Methuen.

Brooks, P. (1976) *The Melodramatic Imagination: Balzac, Henry James, Melodrama and the Mode of Excess*, London: Yale University Press.

Gledhill, C. (ed.) (1987) *Home Is Where the Heart Is: Studies in Melodrama and the Woman's Film*, London: BFI Publishing.

Klinger, B. (1994) *Melodrama and Meaning: History,*

Culture and the Films of Douglas Sirk, Bloomington and Indianapolis: Indiana University Press.

MIKE HAMMOND

fandom

Fandom has become a much explored area in both cultural studies and film theory, with work tending to focus on fans of specific television programmes in the first case, and on fans of specific film genres or film stars in the case of the second discipline (see **genre**). In this entry, I initially outline the reasons that have led theorists to focus on fandom; I examine the ways in which academics have reclaimed fandom as an area of study; and I outline two major theoretical approaches which have been taken in relation to film and television fandoms. These approaches are: (i) theories of fandom as an interpretive community (a community built out of shared interpretations of media texts); and (ii) theories of fandom as a form of consumer activity. I suggest a number of limits to each approach, and conclude by addressing possible future directions for the theorization of film and television fandom.

First, then, why the theoretical concern with issues of fandom? The turn to studying fandom has to be located within debates which occurred in film and television theory throughout the 1970s and 1980s. **Screen theory** (work associated with the British journal *Screen*) was heavily criticized for the way in which it conceptualized the responses of film spectators. This body of theory suggested that spectators' responses were implied by film texts themselves. Consequently, there seemed to be no need to examine the readings and responses of flesh-and-blood social spectators in the cinema **audience**. Spectator responses could, it was assumed, be read off from the film in question. Cultural studies scholars such as David Morley opposed this view of 'passive' audience studies, suggesting that it was important to study, from a sociological viewpoint, the actual (or 'empirical'; see **empiricism**) readings made by audiences (see Morley 1992).

However, it was the work of John Fiske which opened the door to fan studies, since Fiske placed a great deal of emphasis not only on studying actual audience readings, but on studying the audience as 'active' in the construction of meaning. As Fiske notes,

> All popular audiences engage in varying degrees of semiotic productivity, producing meanings and pleasures that pertain to their social situation out of the products of the culture industries. But fans often turn this semiotic productivity into some form of textual production that can circulate among – and thus help to define – the fan community.
>
> (Fiske 1992: 30)

For Fiske, audiences could no longer be assumed to be passively positioned by the **culture** industries (producers of media texts). All audiences, by definition, make interpretations and meanings of their own out of popular texts, and indeed it was this capacity for audience remaking that defined popular culture as 'the popular' in Fiske's approach (see Fiske 1989, chapter 5). Fiske turned, therefore, to fans as one highly visible example of his more general thesis of audience activity, arguing that fandom could be distinguished by degree, but not by kind, from the meaning-making activities of audiences more generally (Fiske 1989: 147).

The study of film and television fandom has thus served as part of a wider theoretical shift from textual determinism (the text determines the reader's response) to audience activity (the *socially situated* reader makes meanings from the text, i.e., this is not a merely 'personal' or idiosyncratic process of meaning-making). However, theoretical debate has continued over just how 'active' fans are able to be in their readings of texts. The notion of fandom as a coherent or singular community gathered around a specific text (e.g., '*Star Trek* fans') has also been subjected to criticism.

Work on fandom within cultural studies has therefore reclaimed it as a valuable object of study, to the extent that some academics working in the field have been described as fans of fans (Jameson 1995: 282–3). This description is relevant because it draws attention to the fact that some fan studies have sought to position the fan and the theorist as occupying common ground (see Penley 1997). Fans seem to hold a specific appeal for theorists given that both produce forms of knowledge based around media texts (on fans as especially knowl-edgeable viewers, see Hermes 1995: 15–16). However, this link should not obscure the fact that academics and fans occupy very different social positions and produce differently-valued forms of knowledge (Burt 1998: 15–17). To assume that academics can readily write *as* fans is to miss these significant points.

This leads us into the first theoretical approach: fandom as an 'interpretive community'. The term 'interpretive community' (sometimes written as 'interpretative community') stems from the work of literary theorist Stanley Fish, who famously introduced the notion in his 1980 book *Is There a Text in This Class?* Fish suggested a theoretical approach which could be aligned relatively pain-lessly with the cultural studies move to active audience theory. He argued that there was no such thing as 'the text' as an unchanging structure. Instead, Fish suggested that different groups of readers – drawing on different communal codes and conventions – construct and interpret texts according to their community's reading conven-tions. Fish used this argument to examine different schools of thought within academia, but theorists in cultural studies quickly applied it to the readers of popular texts.

The 'interpretive community' approach was useful to studies of fandom in a number of ways. It helped to explain the fact that fans did not simply make their own independent or idiosyn-cratic readings of texts, but tended to conspicuously agree over what constituted particularly 'good' or 'authentic' episodes of their chosen texts (see Amesley 1989 for a study of *Star Trek* fans as an 'interpretative community' of readers). Henry Jenkins (1992) examined this process of communal debate and agreement as a matter of fan 'initiation' in his seminal study of media fandom, *Textual Poachers*, in which he writes:

> Fandom's institutional structure...does con-strain what can be said about favourite shows and directs attention onto aspects of the original episodes with particular pertinence within fan criticism....An individual's socialization into fandom often requires learning 'the right way' to read as a fan, learning how to employ and

comprehend the community's particular inter-pretive conventions.

> (Jenkins 1992: 89)

This makes clear an aspect of film and television fandom (and fandom more generally) which it is important to keep in mind: fandom occurs and is sustained through social and institutional structures – fan clubs, fan meetings and conventions, fan magazines (see **institution**). It is not *only* an intense personal experience (although other theo-retical approaches place more emphasis on the privatized experiences of fandom, for example Thompson 1995). It is an experience which is located and re-affirmed within social relationships, and this is equally true for film and television fandoms. Camille Bacon-Smith's study of female *Star Trek* fans notes how these fans form into fan 'circles', made up of between ten to thirty fans (Bacon-Smith 1992: 26–31). Each fan 'circle' maintains social links through correspondence and meetings, these being less formal and more frequent than convention attendance (typically occurring at members' homes).

Film critic Mark Kermode has discussed how horror film fans can display interpretive commu-nity through making 'correct' readings within the social space of cinema attendance:

> when special-effects maestro Tom Savini popped up on-screen as 'third bystander from the left'... it was the film-makers' way of winking at the fans in the audience, to which the correct response was a knowing laugh. I remember forming a fleeting bond with a fellow movie-goer at a screening of *The Fly* at the Manchester Oxford Road Odeon in the 1980s when an on-screen doctor preparing to abort Geena Davis' insect foetus turned out to be director David Cronenberg. While everyone else cringed, the two of us chuckled smugly from opposite sides of the auditorium, like ships signalling each other in deep fog.

> (Kermode 1997: 60)

A theoretical focus on fan interpretation fitted into the broadly semiotic models of film and television audiences which were dominant in the 1970s and 1980s, resting particularly well within the cultural studies model of encoding/decoding (see **encoding-decoding model; semiotics**). The emphasis on the communal nature of fandom had the result of drawing attention, at least temporarily, away from conflicts within specific fandoms. It also indicated that fans' communal interpretations were often at odds with the interests of producers, suggesting that fandom could be celebrated, in part, as a form of consumer resistance to producers' patronizing and exploitative views of fans. Work on fandom as an interpretive community has emphasized fans' attention to detail, to (film/television) series **memory** and to continuity. As John Tulloch (1995) notes:

> The [*Doctor Who*] fans' particular competence is their intimate and detailed knowledge of the show; consequently any producer or script editor who needlessly breaches the continuity and coherence of that knowledge is 'insulting their intelligence'.
>
> (Tulloch and Jenkins 1995: 147)

Fans' focus on continuity and textual 'authenticity' typically places them at odds with producers who need to reinvent programme and film formats in order to maintain wider viewer interest (see Brooker [1999] on the Warner Bros *Batman* franchise and fans' definitions of authenticity). Fans can be said to 'resist' this **commodification** of their favoured texts, given that they often act as what we could call 'textual conservationists'. Producers who tinker with established continuity risk generating extremely negative fan responses.

Tulloch's work in particular, given its sociological emphasis, has paid close attention to the issue of fandom not merely as a community but also as a social hierarchy. This is an important point, as otherwise we might be led to believe that fandom is a social space without a pecking order, in which all fans are somehow equal. Where interpretive community approaches tend to emphasize communal agreement and fan resistance to the text-as-commodity, Tulloch indicates that such agreement remains a matter of unevenly distributed (semiotic) power and fan knowledge: some fans have greater power to enforce and reinforce specific readings. These fans tend to be at the apex of their fandom's social hierarchy, and indeed

Tulloch refers to them (fan club presidents, magazine writers and so on) as 'executive fans' (Tulloch and Jenkins 1995: 149; see also MacDonald 1998).

A related approach to film and television fandom is that of fandom as an affective community ('affect' being, broadly speaking, a term for emotion). While interpretive approaches certainly do not ignore the passions which characterize fandom, they tend, to varying degrees, to relegate fan emotion to secondary importance. By contrast, a number of theorists in cultural studies have placed fan emotions and feelings squarely centrestage, for example Larry Grossberg (1992) and Harrington and Bielby (1995), who concentrate on fans of soap opera. Grossberg has noted that:

> The fan's relation to cultural texts operates in the domain of affect or mood...This 'absorption' or investment constructs the places and events which are, or can become, significant to us....These mattering maps are like investment portfolios: there are not only different and changing investments, but different forms, as well as different intensities or degrees of investment.
>
> (Grossberg 1992: 56–7)

Rather than focusing on the semiotic 'decodings' of fandom, such approaches stress that fandom is lived and embodied: it *matters* to people. At the same time, Grossberg makes it clear that he is not merely discussing subjective 'feelings': the affects of fandom are structured and organized. Fandom continues to be theorized as a matter of communal activity, although activity that is focused on the construction of feeling as well as the construction of meaning. Harrington and Bielby (1995) fuse Grossberg's emphasis on fan affect with psychoanalytic approaches to fandom (see **psychoanalysis**), but it is necessary to note that notions of affect and fan 'absorption' are not only relevant to fandoms which are strongly gendered as feminine (such as soap opera fandom). The fact that Grossberg's model of fandom has been most significantly developed in relation to female fans (Harrington and Bielby 1995) and child consumers (Fleming 1996) should provoke theoretical reflection. Why do culturally masculinized fan groups continue to be theorized as interpretive communities while the immersive consumption of toys or soap operas is theorized via work on affect? Fan cultures and issues of **gender** identity remain inseparable in such work. (For a wider discussion of fandom and affect, see Hills 1999a.) Indeed, it is tempting to suggest that academic work occasionally contributes to the very gender constructions that it otherwise so often critiques.

I have already raised the issue of fan activity as a form of resistance to producers' interests and textual commodification. This second major theoretical approach reaches its clearest expression in work which examines how fans actively rewrite their favoured texts. Fans 'appropriate' elements, rewriting characters' relationships in fan fiction. Theorists such as Penley (1997), Bacon-Smith (1992) and Jenkins (1992) have paid considerable attention to fans as consumers who also produce their own texts ('fanzines', derived from 'fan magazines'). Drawing on Michel de **Certeau**'s work, these theorists examine how fans creatively 'poach' from texts. Slash fiction is one example of this textual poaching, in which female fans rewrite source texts such as *Star Trek* or *The Professionals* so that their male lead characters are depicted in homosexual relationships (the term 'slash' comes from the oblique stroke placed between the characters' initials; thus, slash fiction featuring *Star Trek*'s Captain Kirk and Mr Spock is referred to by fans as 'K/S' fiction). Slash fiction, it should be noted, is written by a subsection of fans – a kind of subculture within a subculture – and is vocally contested (if not ridiculed) by other (more mainstream, and usually masculine) sections of fandom.

These approaches tend to celebrate the creative and subversive rewritings which are produced by such fans. Bacon-Smith (1992: 3) opens her study by noting the following temptation: 'the ethnographer wants to jump up and down and scream, "Look what I found! A conceptual space where women can come together and create – to investigate new forms for their art and for their living outside the restrictive boundaries men have placed on women's public behaviour!" ' Such work occasionally tends to celebrate fan 'resistance' without examining the economic and cultural power of the culture industries (for example, the film/television producers' ability to enforce the copyright that they hold over fictional characters).

Fan rewritings may well be tolerated by producers if they do not circulate widely or threaten the 'brand identity' of the narrative franchise concerned. However, as soon as fan rewritings pose a more direct threat to producers' (economic) interests, it is likely that action over copyright will be threatened (see Mikulak 1998).

Despite Jenkins' (1992) work opposing a simplistic celebration of fan activity, later authors have not been as careful in their theorizations of fandom. In a study of how popular films have been revalued by film critics and fan audiences (through the use of such terms as 'cult' and 'camp' film), Greg Taylor (1999) compares his view of film fans ('cultists') to Jenkins' work on television fans:

> Cultism as I have defined it may seem to some analogous to ardent fandom, as recently examined by scholars such as Jenkins (1992)....But fans are not true cultists unless they pose their fandom as a *resistant* activity, one that keeps them one step ahead of those forces which would try to market their resistant tastes back to them. That such activity has grown enormously since the 1950s is one of the key arguments of this study; when Jenkins dissects the resistant tastes and desires of many *Star Trek* fans, he examines a phenomenon certainly tied to popular spectatorship, but also pushed by the growth of marginal, vanguard behaviour into a larger cultural arena.
>
> (Taylor 1999: 161, note 11)

Taylor's approach implies a genuine 'resistance' that film 'cultists' can display but which mere 'fans' may not have access to, being caught up in consumer culture (see **cult film and television**). Apart from implying a valuation of film and a devaluation of television, this separation is highly unstable. How can cultists wholly resist commercialism? Surely they pay to go to the cinema and buy magazines and books related to their cult film tastes? There may be more mileage in Taylor's argument that without the 1950s and 1960s American popularization of film critics' approaches to film (such as the director as auteur; see **authorship**), television fandom would not exist in its current form. Despite Taylor's attempt to promote film above television, he nevertheless identifies the fact that we need to theorize film and television fandom in relation to each other rather than in isolation. This involves considering the history of film and television fandoms, their common languages and their increasing points of overlap.

Theorizing fandom as consumer activity – as semiotic and textual productivity (Fiske 1989; 1992) where fans produce their own texts based on source material – separates fan identities from more everyday 'consumer' identities. Active fans are viewed as more than merely 'consumers' (who are usually still assumed to be passive). However, influential work in film studies (Klinger 1991) has challenged this separation of fan and consumer. Opposing the arguments of Fiske, Barbara Klinger (1991) suggests that fandom can be best theorized not as 'audience activity' and appropriation, but, rather, as follows:

> The process of commodification ... [and] the mini-narratives it produces to background the production of a film *encourage* the spectator to internalise the phenomena of the film by becoming an expert in its behind-the-scenes history. ... In such cases, the individual's manipulation of commodity discourses may not testify to his/her autonomy and ability to react to the system, but to the achieved strategies of these discourses.
>
> (Klinger 1991: 132)

Within Klinger's approach, what looks to Fiske (1989) and Jenkins (1992) like fan 'appropriation' is simply the successful circulation of the film text as a commodity. This is a theoretical debate which will no doubt continue within cultural studies and film studies. Future work on fandom will perhaps need to centrally recognize fans as both active and passive, as both consumers and fans, as both 'anti-commercialist and commodity-completist' (Hills 1999b: 259). Such work will also need to ask whether the term 'fandom' now covers such a multitude of different activities and experiences that a more complex sets of terms and distinctions may be called for in its place (see Kuhn 1999 on enduring fandom; and Hills 1999a on cult fandom).

References

Amesley, C. (1989) 'How to Watch *Star Trek*', *Cultural Studies*, vol. 3, no. 3, pp. 323–39.

Bacon-Smith, C. (1992) *Enterprising Women: Television Fandom and the Creation of Popular Myth*, Philadelphia: University of Pennsylvania Press.

Brooker, W. (1999) 'Batman: One Life, Many Faces', in D. Cartmell and I. Whelehan (eds) *Adaptations: From Text to Screen, Screen to Text*, London: Routledge.

Burt, R. (1998) *Unspeakable Shaxxxspeares*, London: Macmillan.

Fish, S. (1980) *Is There a Text in This Class? The Authority of Interpretive Communities*, London: Harvard University Press.

Fiske, J. (1989) *Understanding Popular Culture*, London: Unwin Hyman.

—— (1992) 'The Cultural Economy of Fandom', in L. A. Lewis (ed.) *The Adoring Audience*, London: Routledge.

Fleming, D. (1996) *Powerplay: Toys as Popular Culture*, Manchester: Manchester University Press.

Grossberg, L. (1992) 'Is There a Fan in the House?: The Affective Sensibility of Fandom', in L. A. Lewis (ed.) *The Adoring Audience*, London: Routledge.

Harrington, C. L. and Bielby, D. (1995) *Soap Fans: Pursuing Pleasure and Making Meaning in Everyday Life*, Philadelphia: Temple University Press.

Hermes, J. (1995) *Reading Women's Magazines*, Cambridge: Polity Press.

Hills, M. (1999a) *The Dialectic of Value: The Sociology and Psychoanalysis of Cult Media*, unpublished Ph.D. thesis, University of Sussex.

—— (1999b) 'Virtual Community and the Virtues of Continuity', *New Media and Society*, vol. 1, no. 2, pp. 251–60.

Jameson, F. (1995) 'On Cultural Studies', in J. Rajchman (ed.) *The Identity in Question*, London: Routledge.

Jenkins, H. (1992) *Textual Poachers: Television Fans and Participatory Cultures*, London: Routledge.

Kermode, M. (1997) 'I Was a Teenage Horror Fan or, "How I Learned to Stop Worrying and Love Linda Blair" ', in M. Barker and J. Petley (eds) (1997) *Ill Effects: The Media / Violence Debate*, London: Routledge.

Klinger, B. (1991) 'Digressions at the Cinema: Commodification and Reception in Mass Culture', in J. Naremore and P. Brantlinger (eds) *Modernity and Mass Culture*, Bloomington and Indiana: Indiana University Press.

Kuhn, A. (1999) ' "That Day *Did* Last Me All My

Life": Cinema Memory and Enduring Fandom',
in M. Stokes and R. Maltby (eds) *Identifying
Hollywood's Audiences: Cultural Identity and the
Movies*, London: Routledge.

MacDonald, A. (1998) 'Uncertain Utopia: Science
Fiction Media Fandom and Computer Mediated
Communication', in C. Harris and A. Alexander
(eds) *Theorizing Fandom: Fans, Subculture and Identity*,
New Jersey: Hampton Press.

Mikulak, B. (1998) 'Fans versus Time Warner:
Who Owns Looney Tunes?', in K. S. Sandler
(ed.) *Reading the Rabbit: Explorations in Warner Bros.
Animation*, New Brunswick, New Jersey and
London: Rutgers University Press.

Morley, D. (1992) *Television, Audiences and Cultural
Studies*, London: Routledge.

Penley, C. (1997) *Nasa/Trek: Popular Science and Sex in
America*, London: Verso.

Taylor, G. (1999) *Artists in the Audience: Cults, Camp,
and American Film Criticism*, Princeton: Princeton
University Press.

Thompson, J. B. (1995) *Media and Modernity*, Cambridge: Polity Press.

Tulloch, J. and Jenkins, H. (1995) *Science Fiction
Audiences: Watching Doctor Who and Star Trek*,
London: Routledge.

MATTHEW HILLS

Fanon, Franz

b. 1925; d. 1961

Born in Martinique, Franz Fanon was educated in
France as a psychiatrist and practised psychiatry in
pre-revolutionary Algeria. He viewed human
suffering and identity in terms of relations of
domination and individual and collective rebellion.
He explored this through social psychology in his
book *Black Skins White Masks* (1967 [1952]), but his
ideas developed in the crucible of Algerian
colonialism and revolutionary activity, which
Fanon chronicled, interpreted and supported in
works such as *The Wretched of the Earth* (1963 [1961],
with a preface by Jean-Paul Sartre). He died in
Washington DC, where he had gone to seek
treatment for leukaemia.

Fanon has been taken as an **icon** by peoples of
colour in the creation and interpretation of film

and representation, and its use in liberation and
revolutionary movements. Recent reflective work,
however, has explored him as a representative
himself of Third World dilemmas in feminism and
gender or relations of power. These dilemmas
made him the subject of an intriguing cinematic
exploration, *Franz Fanon* (1995) by Isaac Julien and
Mark Nash.

References

Fanon, F. (1963) *The Wretched of the Earth*, New York:
Grove (originally published as *Les damnes de la
terre*, 1961, Paris: Maspero).

—— (1967) *Black Skins, White Masks*, New York:
Grove (originally published as *Peaux noires,
masques blancs*, 1952, Paris: Du Seuil).

Further reading

Reed, A. (1996) *The Fact of Blackness: Franz Fanon and
Visual Representation*, London: ICA.

GARY McDONOGH

fantasy

While the term 'fantasy' has multiple connotations
in contemporary screen culture, all of them share a
common root in the work of Sigmund **Freud**.
Freud's notion of an **unconscious** mind whose
impulses are expressed, in disguised form, through
dreams, jokes or slips of the tongue is the basis for
our contemporary understanding of fantasy as a
mode characterized by symbolic meanings, shifted
variants on reality and parallel worlds.

Freudian concepts began to enter popular
discourse in the 1900s and 1910s, at around the
same time as the possibilities of the **cinematic
apparatus** were being explored by its pioneers.
An experimentation with effects and trickery, as in
the work of George Méliès, introduced elements of
the 'fantastic' into a medium which had originally
aimed at faithfully recording 'real' events. This
mode is particularly evident in the cinema of
German **Expressionism**, with its frequent use of
fairy-tale or mystical settings and its employment of
stylized, theatrical set design and lighting to convey

psychological trauma. Siegfried Kracauer, in *From Caligari to Hitler* (1947), reads into these films a disguised expression of dual identity and moral dilemmas – typifying the troubled German mentality of the early part of the twentieth century – which are symbolized through the devices of demons and monstrous mirror-selves.

As German directors fled Nazi control, many of the key traits of Expressionism were exported to the United States where they emerged in subdued, more 'realistic' form. Hollywood, with its obsessive concern for **verisimilitude**, allowed the fantastic to emerge only within the conventions of the musical (see **musical, the**), the comedy, or significantly, in the dream sequence of an otherwise realist film. Few examples of this tendency can be more striking than Alfred Hitchcock's *Spellbound* (1945), which used the designs of Salvador Dali in nightmarish sequences of persecution. True to the popular understanding of Freudian theory, each element of the **mise-en-scène** was interrogated and interpreted within the film to reveal its 'true' meaning.

Though 'fantasy' now denotes a **genre** of itself, whose meaning can also be linked back, as suggested above, to notions of the unconscious and to Expressionism, its dominant traits owe much to the work of British novelists, C. S. Lewis and J. R. R. Tolkien, whose chronicles of Narnia and Middle Earth respectively were first published in the 1950s. Both writers **bricolage** the myths and images of Christianity, Norse legend, Arthurian fable and medieval history into a magical environment, between them setting the framework for an entire generic form. The influence of Tolkien in particular can be seen in the role-playing game *Dungeons and Dragons*, which achieved massive popularity in the 1970s and 1980s. During this period, 'fantasy' became a significant mode in comic books such as Marvel's *Conan*, in arcade games – *Dragon's Lair* and *Gauntlet* – and in television and cinema, from *Krull* (Peter Yates, 1983) and *Clash of the Titans* (Desmond Davis, 1981) to the film adaptation of *Lord of the Rings* (Ralph Bakshi, 1978), the BBC series *The Chronicles of Narnia* and the animated cartoon of *Advanced Dungeons and Dragons*.

A third meaning of the term in contemporary **culture** can be traced to the emphasis, in much of

Freud's theory, on libido and **desire** as a prime impulse of the unconscious mind. Indeed, the 'adult fantasy' film can be seen as an extended dream sequence, a 'what if?' premise leading to a utopian world in which hidden desires are allowed to surface and circulate freely until magically satisfied. The fantastical porn universe, in which beautiful plumbers and secretaries arrive half-naked to work, could even be read as an erotic variant on the skewed world of expressionist fantasy or the parallel realms of 'Tolkienesque' fiction.

These three meanings converge intriguingly in the television series *Xena: Warrior Princess*. While the Amazonian protagonist and her magical, quasi-medieval environment are well within the conventions of *Dungeons and Dragons*-style 'fantasy', the show has found an audience outside the normal demographic of young men, and is enjoyed by lesbian viewers for its erotic subtext (see **queer theory; reading and reception theory**). This notion of reading 'against the grain', with its stress on an alternative meaning disguised and hidden in fantastic elements, is entirely in keeping with Freud's original concept of unconscious desires and the interpretation of dreams.

References

Kracauer, S. (1947) *From Caligari to Hitler: A Psychological History of the German Film*, Princeton: Princeton University Press.

WILL BROOKER

feminist theory

Feminist theory of all kinds begins as a political intervention, a branch of a larger political movement by and on behalf of women, involving organizational and educational attacks on every **institution** and cultural practice founded on the assumptions of sexist and patriarchal ideology (see **ideology and hegemony; patriarchy**). The centrality of feminist theories to academic discourses must be understood as informed by the larger political project that motivates feminism generally: to transform social institutions and forces in ways which empower and gain equality and justice for women (and later, by theoretical extension, to lesbians and gays). But feminist media and film theory holds a special place by virtue of the centrality – recognized early on by feminist activists – of media images, narratives and discourses in relation to the way in which women have been socially and psychologically marginalized in western industrialized societies (see **discourse; image; narrative**).

Since the 1960s, when the second wave of feminism in the United States began, feminists – especially in nations where United States media products are widely available – have had a special interest in the ways in which the mass media have represented girls and women and how the women and girls have been affected by these images. Indeed, it is hardly coincidental that the rise of second wave feminism ran parallel with the enormous expansion of mass media in the post-Second World War industrialized world. In deploying so profuse a barrage of generally stereotypical and demeaning images of femininity (see **stereotype**), the media themselves played a part in arousing the **consciousness** and anger of women, particularly those of the white, educated classes, directed at the way society contrives to keep females in subordinate positions. It was also not surprising that, as academic faculty and students became active in 'consciousness-raising' and activist feminist projects, women began to agitate for programmes which addressed the absence of women theorists and artists, and of feminist perspectives in traditional canonical curricula, and to develop '**oppositional**' theoretical perspectives and analyses to counter and amend traditionally masculinist disciplinary approaches (see **canon**). The importance of media in early feminist political activism understandably led to an academic situation in media study where **theory** assumed a place of importance rivalled only perhaps by feminist literary theory.

Early theoretical approaches

Given the centrality of denigrating media images to the early feminist project, it is not surprising that the earliest approaches to media analyses were of the (now recognizably unsophisticated and under-theorized) **content analysis** variety, which meant that images were evaluated on the basis of their positive or negative connotations. **Gender** stereotypes – the sex kitten, the housewife, the shrew, the spinster, the neurotic, the overly masculine lesbian – long staples of western culture, were endlessly counted and commented on. The absence of images of strong women who were also emotionally and mentally stable, intellectual women who were also sexually attractive and so on, were decried, as demands for the media to amend the situation abounded. This kind of work is still a major focus for feminist writers inside and outside the academy, as the campaigns of liberal women's and lesbian rights organizations illustrate. Moreover, as western media expand and proliferate globally, concern about such images has developed to include negative images and stereotypes of Third World women, women of colour and poor women.

Early academic examples of this kind of work include studies of the treatment of women on television and in newspapers and magazines, on the history of women's portrayals in media and popular culture, and on the traditions of gender representation, its symbols and rituals, from the age of the oil painting to contemporary **advertising**. These have become classics in an enormous body of work in this tradition of feminist media critique of negative images. In more recent years this tradition has expanded to include studies of women of colour and working-class women. bell **hooks**' (1990) work points out how white feminists have failed to address the many ways in which women of colour do not fit classic feminist truisms, and Patricia Turner (1994) has analysed the enormous, if unsung influence, of black popular culture on the larger **white** culture. Many other writers, most prominently Cherrie Moraga and Gloria Anzaldua in their anthology, *This Bridge Called My Back* (1981), have protested the particular, often invisible, ways in which women of colour in many ethnic groups have been victims of media sexism, contrasting this against the very different treatment of white middle-class women. And Lillian Robinson (1978) early on began analysing the similarly demeaning ways in which working-class women have been made invisible, and often doubly oppressed, through media representational norms (see **class**).

Content analysis of this kind remains important for the pressure that it places on media producers, and for the role it plays in educating young and unaware viewers of the underlying ideological assumptions about gender which inform western culture. But it has been criticized for its theoretical and political limitations and weaknesses. Politically, while liberal feminists who do not see corporate society itself as inherently and structurally unfair and oppressive to women (as well as gays, lesbians, people of colour and poor and working-class people), the simple demand that women be given 'equal' opportunity is sufficient. But such demands tend to address the concerns of white, educated women and to ignore or elide the distinctions of **race**, **class** and **ethnicity** which exclude all but the fortunate few from such 'success'.

On the theoretical level, there are even more serious charges to be made about the limits of 'positive image' criticism. It tends, as more recent theorists (Byars 1991) have seen, to 'give precedence to manifest as the bearer of meaning content at the expense of latent content and form'. According to Liesbet Van Zoonen, 'it assumes that frequencies of characteristics are valid indicators of meaning', and 'it produces results whose relation to the actual media experience of producers and audiences is unclear' (Van Zoonen 1994: 73).

Semiotic and psychoanalytic theory

As a result of such critiques, a variety of more theoretically powerful and politically incisive approaches to film and media studies have developed since the 1970s. Many of the earliest borrowed from linguistic and psychoanalytic methodologies in an effort to add depth and complexity to the study of gender images (see **psychoanalysis**). Among the first of these approaches was **semiotics**; this methodology draws on psychoanalytic and linguistic theory to unravel deep structurally embedded layers of meaning in images. It looks closely at the image as it exists on the page. It employs the concept of the **sign**, in which the image is seen to have two components, a signifier – its physical appearance made up of letters and/or images – and a signified – the real-world entity to which it refers. Since signs are only meaningful when understood in relation to other signs,

semiotics analyses the relationship among signs in complex and subtle ways, always assuming that individual cultures develop unique systems of coding, language and imagery which members of that culture internalize from birth. Through the unravelling of the various means by which systems of language and imagery interact, and the ways in which they are coded as meaningful within given cultures, semiotics theorizes the ideological and emotional power such configurations hold over readers. Judith Williamson's (1978) study of advertising imagery is an exemplary work of feminist semiotic analysis. However, in recent years, post-structuralist theory concerned with the **polysemic** nature of texts and with the role of individual viewers in interpreting of them has complicated the analysis of images and undermined the authority of semiotic analysis (see **structuralism and post-structuralism**).

In film theory, which has increasingly followed a different path from media studies, the use of psychoanalytic theory has been a dominant trend among feminists since the 1970s and has greatly influenced the discipline generally. This work is inspired by John **Berger**'s observation, in his book *Ways of Seeing* (1975), about what came to be termed 'the male gaze'. According to Berger: 'men act and women appear. Men look at women. Women watch themselves being looked at'. And this determines not only most relations between men and women but also the relations of women to themselves. For in learning to see herself as observed, rather than as observer, the women in western culture 'turns herself into an object – and most particularly an object of vision: a sight' (1975: 47).

Berger's insight led to a proliferation of feminist psychoanalytic film theory, called also **Screen theory**, because it became the dominant theoretical approach offered in the influential British film journal *Screen*. Laura **Mulvey**'s seminal article in *Screen* in 1975, 'Visual Pleasure and Narrative Cinema', has been called 'the founding document of psychoanalytic feminist film theory'. In the article, Mulvey draws on Freudian and Lacanian psychoanalysis to examine the narcissistic pleasures of identification and the sexual pleasures of looking at others that classic films provide (see **Freud, Sigmund; Lacan, Jacques**). In such theories, pleasure from cinema takes two dominant forms:

scopophilia – the basic human desire to gain sexual pleasure through looking at others, as in **voyeurism** – and narcissistic identification – the need to identify with a 'mirrored' **Other** in order to understand one's own identity. But since the **cinematic apparatus** of film is male-driven and assumes a male viewer as the norm, these drives in women are perverted through the mechanisms and ideologies of classic cinema. Women are placed in the position of being forced to see themselves only as the object of male **desire**, but never as a subject having desires of their own or the agent (see **agency**) in any action portrayed in the narratives of **desire** central to classic film. Female subjectivity, a woman's sense of her own identity, is thus constructed through the cinematic apparatus in a negative way, since the woman is never the subject (see **subject and subjectivity**) but always the object of patriarchal discourse and narrative. Female viewers are forced into a kind of double vision, seeing themselves through the eyes of the **paradigmatic** male viewer as the object of desire and also identifying with the male, since there is no other possibility within the strict confines of the male gaze.

The female pleasure, which would be possible if there were a female central character as active agent in the film, seemed unavailable in the early 1970s, as mainstream film offered few examples of such a protagonist. Further developments in this area by feminists problematized the feminist theorists' position in analysing the absence of women in patriarchal discourse; by pointing it out, feminists are forced to inevitably reproduce and thus reinforce it. Doane (1991) and others offered a limited answer to the dilemma of female pleasure by suggesting that the girl's bond with the mother offers the possibility of homoerotic pleasure in viewing classic cinema representations of women as objects of desire. But the inherently masochistic implications of psychoanalytic theory are not easy to overcome. Nor is the issue of race, since psychoanalytic theory must see women and blacks as essentially 'other', while pathologizing white patriarchal society. The possibilities for escape from its negative imprisonment are hard to find. In recent years, female protagonists as active agents in cinema have become more common (for example, in Ridley Scott's *Thelma and Louise*, 1991). In light of such critiques, more recent feminist psychoanalytic work has to some extent worked to revise and amend the basic assumptions of Freud and Lacan (Flitterman-Lewis 1992). But the limits of psychoanalytic theory, particularly in its failure to theorize an active subject, has made it the object of increasing critique by film theorists and cultural theorists. 'Cognitive' theorists (see **cognitive theory**) have also offered critiques of this approach (Bordwell and Carroll 1997).

Cultural studies: history, institutions and audiences

As Sandy Flitterman-Lewis (1992: 216) has noted, 'psychoanalytic film theory cannot simply be *applied* to television' since the televisual apparatus is distinctly different in many important ways from the cinematic. Television relates to audiences in profoundly different ways, because of its intended functions, its historic development, its small size, the aesthetic quality of its imagery and its placement within the home, rather than the watching of a film in a large-screen, darkened theatre setting, within which viewers are held captive, so to speak. These factors have led those interested in studying television to favour a variety of different approaches, most of which include a concern with the production and reception processes by which texts are produced and audiences are constructed and addressed (see **audience**).

Most academic work has been profoundly influenced by the more leftist theoretical traditions. Marxist feminist scholars have been influenced by the ideas of the **Frankfurt School**, which considered the media industry as a monolithic all-powerful empire of ideology production, with gender, race and class bias as a built-in imperative since the economic hegemony of those who own and control the media demand it. Such work has focused on the economic underpinnings of the media as industry, and on ideological textual analysis of mass media narratives and images. At its most unsophisticated, it has assumed an all-powerful media with viewers, seen as consumers and commodities to be 'purchased' by advertisers, powerless to resist the ideological messages with which they are bombarded. Since women are the primary targets of television producers and sponsors, the role of gender in media texts has been studied with much interest by Marxist feminists. In recent years, many have developed more subtle and complex approaches to media and gender, while remaining focused on the importance of economic forces in the development of texts and the targeting of women viewers.

The most prominent approach to media texts among left-leaning feminist theories has been cultural studies, which maintains a concern with economics and production processes while developing a wide variety of more complex approaches. Originating with the Birmingham School theorists in the late 1960s and early 1970s in the UK, the cultural studies tradition looks not only at how texts are produced and constructed, but also at how audiences receive them. Feminist cultural historians have dug back into the historic past of gender-oriented television and looked at the interactions among historic and social forces of change, the development and the deployment of media technologies in the context of such changes, and the ways in which women were caught up in such changes and targeted by media producers and advertisers as a means to serve political and social needs. Lynn Spigel's *Make Room for TV* (1992) is a groundbreaking study of how television was marketed in the 1950s to a new generation of post-war women poised to enter a world in which women's role in society was increasingly defined in terms of consumerism (see **consumption**).

Feminist cultural theorists have also conducted interesting work on the production process itself, and the complex intertwining of economic and social forces in addressing women audiences. Julie D'Acci's (1994) study on the US television series *Cagney and Lacey* stands as a model of such work in its deft analysis of how progressive and reactionary forces contested for 'control' of the final text. Work such as D'Acci's employs the concepts of encoding to illustrate the complex processes by which gendered messages are produced, and also to illustrate the often **polysemic** and ambiguous meanings such texts may ultimately contain, as a result of complexities in the encoding process (see **encoding**).

Interest in the complexity of the encoding process has been paralleled by an even more robust interest on the part of feminists in the process of decoding, in which audiences, individually and in groups, are analysed in terms of their actual reading practices. This work has been particularly important since it has countered the emphasis on the power of the text and implicitly assumed a passive, non-resistant reader. Feminists have been concerned to counter this emphasis with work which demonstrates that women can resist and oppose dominant hegemonic messages about gender and even participate, in the process of reading texts, in oppositional constructions of meanings of their own.

On one level this work has re-examined gendered texts themselves in an effort to show that popular culture favoured by women is not the demeaning stuff some critics have assumed. They have argued that such generic work often reveals hidden meanings which allow women to feel empowered and respected in ways that male-oriented texts do not. Feminists have analysed texts that are often considered to be the most sexist – soap operas, romance novels, sit-coms – and found them less one-dimensionally oppressive than they might seem. Tania Modleski's *Loving with a Vengeance* (1981) analysed some of these forms and found more value in their representation of women's lives than has generally been granted. She argues that women's forms have been devalued unfairly precisely because they *are* women's forms and speak to women's concerns and values, things a male critical establishment discounts and ignores.

Studies of women readers and viewers of mass culture have furthered the insight into the ways in which texts created by sexist institutions may none the less reveal contradictions, internally, and in the ways in which women themselves receive the texts. Ien Ang (1982), John Fiske (1987) and Janice Radway (1984) offer studies of audiences' 'reading practices' which reveal that women may often 'read against the grain', finding ways to interpret texts to suit their own values and resisting the oppressive dominant message in order to focus on minor subtextual meanings which are more progressive. That texts do not hold a single one-dimensional unambiguous meaning is a position increasingly taken by media scholars. Similarly, readers themselves are increasingly seen as having the power to subvert and reformulate the meaning of even the most oppressively sexist texts. Women who read romances, suggests Radway (1984), find in them moments of liberation from the very different worlds they inhabit within their own sexist marriages. Bobo and Seiter (1991) have done similar work on black female audiences and reached similar conclusions. Finally, feminist media theory has increasingly included studies of gay and lesbian imagery and of the representation of men and boys.

See also: cultural capital/cultural reproduction; pleasure; queer theory; reading and reception theory

References

Ang, I. (1982) *Watching Dallas: Soap Opera and the Melodramatic Imagination*, New York: Methuen.

Berger, J. (1975) *Ways of Seeing*, New York: Penguin.

Bobo, J. and Seiter, E. (1991) 'Black Feminism and Media Criticism: *The Women of Brewster Place*', *Screen*, vol. 32, pp. 286–302.

Bordwell, D. and Carroll, N. (1997) *Post-Theory*, Madison: Wisconsin University Press.

Byars, J. (1991) *All that Heavens Allows: Re-reading Gender in 1950s Melodrama*, Chapel Hill: University of North Carolina Press.

D'Acci, J. (1994) *Defining Women: Television and the Case of Cagney and Lacey*, Chapel Hill: University of North Carolina Press.

Doane, M. A. (1991) *Femmes Fatales: Feminism, Film Theory, Psychoanalysis*, London: Routledge.

Fiske, J. (1987) *Television Culture*, New York: Methuen.

Flitterman-Lewis, S. (1992) 'Psychoanalysis, Film and Television', in Robert Allen (ed.) *Channels of Discourse*, London: Routledge, pp. 203–47.

hooks, b. (1990) *Yearning, Race, Gender and Popular Culture*, Boston: South End Press.

Modleski, T. (1981) *Loving with a Vengeance: Mass-Produced Fantasies for Women*, New York: Methuen.

Moraga, C. and Anzaldua, G. (1981) *This Bridge Called My Back: Writings of Radical Women of Color*, Watertown: Persephone Press.

Mulvey, L. (1975) 'Visual Pleasure and Narrative Cinema', *Screen*, vol. 16, no. 3, pp. 6–18.

Radway, J. (1984) *Reading the Romance: Women, Patriarchy and Popular Culture*, Chapel Hill. University of North Carolina.

Robinson, L. (1978) *Sex, Class and Culture*, New York: Methuen.

Spigel, L. (1992) *Make Room for TV: Television and the Family Ideal in Postwar America*, Chicago: University of Chicago Press.

Turner, P. (1994) *Ceramic Uncles and Celluloid Mammies: Black Images and their Influence on Culture*, Berkeley: University of California.

Williamson, J. (1978) *Decoding Advertisements*, London: Marion Boyars.

Van Zoonen, L. (1994) *Feminist Media Studies*, London: Sage.

Further reading

de Lauretis, T. (1984) *Alice Doesn't: Feminism, Semiotics, Cinema*, Basingstoke: Macmillan.

Taylor, E. (1989) *Prime-Time Families*, Berkeley: University of California Press.

ELAYNE RAPPING

fetishism

In anthropology, the fetish is an object in which a spirit is embodied, and which thus has a magical or spiritual importance. The concept of fetishism in studies of culture is largely taken from two areas of theory which develop this sense of the word: Freudian **psychoanalysis** and Marxist political economy (see **Freud, Sigmund; Marx, Karl**).

In *Capital*, Marx talks of 'commodity fetishism', a concept he uses in an attempt to understand cultural production in capitalist societies. Here, the term implies the way in which the reality of human relations is obfuscated by relations between objects. Human labourers are alienated from their products, which appear detached from the realities of their production. This use of the term applies to the production of all cultural texts in capitalistic societies, and has little descriptive value for making discriminating judgements between such texts.

The concept of fetishism as it is articulated in Freudian psychoanalysis has taken a more central place in the theorizing of film. In the writing of Freud, the concept of the fetish is a straightforward one. Every boy child suffers **castration** anxiety, emerging from the first moment at which he

viewed female genitalia: the threat represented by this person without a penis is that the boy-child's own penis might be cut off. A fetish is then an object from which a man (*sic*) takes sexual pleasure, in order to divert attention away from the threatening female genitalia (Freud 1962). The structure of the fetish is one of disavowal – characterized by the statement, 'I know very well, but all the same . . .'. This is a kind double-think – whereby the man knows very well that the woman has been castrated, but all the same, refuses to acknowledge it.

The writer who is most responsible for introducing this term to the study of films is Laura **Mulvey**, whose article 'Visual Pleasure and the Narrative Cinema' (first published in *Screen* in 1975) proposes that the image of women in film functions as a fetish for male viewers. Mulvey explicitly draws on the terminology of psychoanalysis in order to make this argument. She suggests that the cinema invites two kinds of pleasurable looking – scopophilic and narcissistic, corresponding broadly to the more familiar terms objectification and identification. Mulvey explains scopophilic pleasure – which she insists is a masculine pleasure, and also names 'the gaze' – by suggesting that the image of the woman on the screen 'speaks castration and nothing else' – that is, that its pleasure is the pleasure of the fetish, providing a sexual pleasure which compensates for the fact of the castrated female genitalia (see **gaze, the**). In this logic, all representations of women – except, ironically, those which display the (castrated) female genitalia – are fetishes, inviting scopophilic male pleasure.

It would be rare to find the Freudian analysis of fetishism stated this baldly in film studies. The terminology is often taken up without acknowledgement in the theoretical framework which underlies it, and many writers refer to Mulvey's article merely to cite 'the gaze', without exploring the concepts which sustain her use of the term. While Freud is insistent that it is the penis which is of central concern in fetishism, most recent work in film studies has replaced the Freudian penis with Jacques **Lacan**'s notion of the **phallus**. The concept of fetishism still functions in this post-Freudian economy, where it takes the form of the demand for the maternal 'phallus' rather than the maternal 'penis' (Grosz 1990: 118).

The problems with the concept of fetishism in film studies are those of psychoanalysis more generally: that it is unprovable; that it insists on a level of psychic reality beyond discourse (but which can adequately be explored within discourse); and, despite feminist attempts to rewrite its provenance, provides little in the way of critical tools for understanding women (it is a discourse of masculinity).

References

Freud, S. (1962) 'Fetishism', in *The Standard Edition of the Complete Psychological Works of Sigmund Freud, vol. 21: 'The Future of an Illusion, Civilisation and Discontents and Other Works*, trans. J. Strachey, A. Freud, A. Strachey and A. Tyson, London: The Hogarth Press, pp. 152–7.

Grosz, E. (1990) *Jacques Lacan: A Feminist Introduction*, London and New York: Routledge.

Mulvey, L. (1975) 'Visual Pleasure and the Narrative Cinema', *Screen*, vol. 16, no. 3, pp. 6–18.

ALAN McKEE

film movements

On 13 March 1995, a new film movement came into existence in Copenhagen, Denmark. Its manifesto was a set of rules, a 'Vow of Chastity', which four directors signed. Dogme 95, as the collective called itself, has since become internationally famous and its members were given control of television output on all Danish television channels for the night as 1999 turned into 2000.

Dogme 95 has some of the features of a postmodern phenomenon (see **modernism and post-modernism**): the manifesto is ironically hyperconscious and its presentation is wilfully self-contradictory. In other respects, however, Dogme 95 shows some of the features that have typified earlier film movements. Though the concept of a film movement is currently neglected, it is impossible for any serious history of cinema to ignore the existence of, for example, German **Expressionism**, Italian neo-realism, the French New Wave, British Free Cinema, Young German

Cinema and/or New German Cinema, and their influence on film and television.

Identifying a film movement presents difficulties, but Terry Lovell's (1972) seminal 'sketch' of what the study of a film movement might deliver has as much relevance to an understanding of Dogme 95 as the example she chooses: the *nouvelle vague*, or New Wave, evident in French cinema between 1958 and 1961. Lovell theorizes from a sociological perspective and places the emphasis on those factors outside the text, which determine 'patternings in the forms and themes of the works examined'. The general, and generalizable, point Lovell first makes, however, is that at a specific historical juncture different types of variables combine to effect a certain result – the movement.

Prima facie evidence of a movement's existence may be qualitative and/or quantitative. In the case of the New Wave, the quantitative aspect is that over 100 directors made their first films in France between 1958 and 1961 – a phenomenon labelled at the time by the French newspaper *L'Express* as 'la nouvelle vague'. Qualitatively, many of the films exhibited innovations in **style** and theme that specifically challenged dominant French film styles and practices, challenges made even more explicit in the critical writings of some of the directors. Lovell notes especially that the New Wave films' characters lack a 'social dimension' and a reliance on face-to-face relations, exhibiting the marks of a break with the immediately preceding French cinema. Paradoxically, it is the *presence* of an explicit social dimension that is the marker of difference in the characters, for example, in Italian neo-realist films or those of the New German Cinema, but the significance is the same. The emerging movement challenges the existing cinema. At the same time, New Wave films co-existed with the traditional 'cinema du papa', and exhibited some continuities – a feature equally characteristic of post-war Italian cinema and current Danish cinema.

Lovell lists several determining factors outside the films that shaped their patterns. Summarized, these are:

- *Aesthetic*
- the post-war influx of American films, and the near-obsession with things American;
- the relationship of cinema to the other arts: in

this case, its higher status in France, and the substantial 'cine-literate' audience;
- the New Wave critics in *Cahiers du cinéma* who energetically argued that the post-war tradition of French cinema was degenerate or exhausted.
- *Economic*
- the unpredictable nature of the film industry, in production, distribution and exhibition, outside the heavily capitalized and vertically integrated Hollywood model;
- given that this nature is more or less constant over time, the specific and highly conjunctural crises in the French film industry in this period;
- the political will which led to state intervention in film production and exhibition.

The above list is not exhaustive and only points to the areas of research which need to be further explored in order to obtain a clearer understanding of the causes and processes which determine a film movement. Though the characteristics associated with the New Wave are presented as specific to France, some have wider application: both Geoffrey Nowell-Smith (1985) and Thomas Elsaesser (1976), for example, note that neo-realism and New German Cinema are, in different ways, a response to American cinema. Dogme 95 is also a response to the 'special effects' cinema of the US, and its proponents argue the exhaustion of current forms of Danish cinema and, rather anachronistically, the New Wave.

Lovell's model is, of course, more sophisticated than this summary indicates, though it necessarily lacks empirical detail about the period. Elsaesser's more detailed analysis of the conjuncture, in the late 1960s and early 1970s, out of which Young German Cinema and New German Cinema emerged, has many similarities to Lovell's model and much more detail. But Elsaesser is sceptical about seeing 'a unified group or movement' in German cinema, perhaps because the conditions and the cinematic changes take place over a longer period of time than the New Wave and are dispersed geographically – factors less relevant in Lovell's analysis. Nevertheless, despite its lack of empirical detail, the analysis does move discussion away from simply noting stylistic similarities across a number of films of approximately the same date.

See also: authorship

References

Dogme 95. The full text and 'Vow of Chastity'. Online. Available: www.martweiss.com/english/Film/dogma95.html

Elsaesser, T. (1976) 'The Post-war German Cinema, in Tony Rayns (ed.) *Fassbinder*, London: BFI Publishing.

Lovell, T. (1972) 'Sociology of Aesthetic Structures and Contextualism', in Denis McQuail (ed.) *Sociology of Mass Communications*, London: Penguin.

Nowell-Smith, G. (1985) 'Italian Neo-realism', in Pam Cook (ed.) *The Cinema Book*, London: BFI Publishing.

PHILIP SIMPSON

film noir

Identified by French critics in the 1946, and often described as a movement (see **film movements**) rather than a **genre**, film noir emerged in the United States in the 1940s. Its origins can be traced to numerous sources including pulp novels, 1930s gangster films and the German Expressionist movement (see **Expressionism**). Classic noir films are concerned with the seedy underbelly of America, where crime, corruption and sexual desire intermingle. Recurrent characters include the world-weary detective, the beautiful but deadly *femme fatale* and her male dupes. Visually, its most striking feature is the use of low-key, high contrast lighting, which evokes the immorality of the world explored within the film.

DEBORAH JERMYN

Fiske, John

b. 1939

Fiske is one of the leading writers in the international development of British cultural studies. Assimilating the work of Pierre **Bourdieu**, Antonio **Gramsci**, Michel de **Certeau** and Michel **Foucault**, he has written widely against a reductive anti-mass culture position which refuses to accord **agency** to the consumers of popular culture. He argues that cultural commodities are not simply consumed according to the producer's economic directive but are actively incorporated into the non-regulated meaning-making processes of people's daily lives. People not only consume popular culture but also creatively use it to make sense of social identity and gain resistant pleasure. Consumers are also producers of important cultural capital and meaning in Fiske's terminology. In a similar though more optimistic vein to Stuart **Hall**, Fiske sees popular culture as a site of struggle between dominant incorporation and heterogeneous resistance. Fiske views television programmes and films as semiotic enablers of a diffusion of cultural power from a bottom-up direction (see **semiotics**).

See also: consumption

Further reading

Fiske, J., with Hartley, J. (1978) *Reading Television*, London: Methuen.

—— (1989) *Understanding Popular Culture*, London: Unwin Hyman.

—— (1993) *Power Plays, Power Works*, London: Verso.

PAULA TATLA AMAD

flâneur

The *flâneur*, or 'city-stroller', emerged in nineteenth-century Paris and features heavily in the writings of the French poet Charles Baudelaire and the German cultural critic Walter **Benjamin**. The *flâneur* is the anonymous 'man of the crowd' who wanders through the city observing but not participating in the drama of urban life. In the late twentieth century, cars have made city streets inhospitable to *flânerie*, but there are interesting parallels between *flâneurism*, cinema and television spectatorship, and 'surfing' the **Internet**.

See also: voyeurism

Further reading

Keith T. (ed.) (1994) *The Flâneur*, London and New York: Routledge.

SARA GWENLLIAN JONES

flashback

When watching films or television programmes, we tend to organize the stories being told to us on the basis of the order in which the story information is presented. This articulation of time enables us to organize and construct a chronology by which events are connected. The flashback, as one way in which a director might manipulate time, is a portion of a story that is narrated out of chronological order, switching from story information being told in the present to the narration of an event that occurred before it. While normally associated with the image-track, flashbacks can also occur on a soundtrack.

Further reading

Turim, M. (1989) *Flashbacks in Film: Memory and History*, New York: Routledge.

ANDREW UTTERSON

flow

This term describes a theoretical model suggested by Raymond **Williams**. Williams (1975) argued that network programming was analogous to electricity, a constant flow from shot to shot, scene to scene, programme to programme, advertisement to advertisement. Viewers are carried along the current of television programming towards a potentially continuous and swelling flow of texts and articulations, all in the service of commercial capital. According to the theory, transmission of television texts is centralized while reception of these texts is dispersed yet simultaneous – and takes place in the home. For Williams, this made television a new, far-reaching, and very powerful communication apparatus.

Several scholars have problematized and expanded the notion of flow. John Ellis (1982), for example, argues that television narratives act more through segmentation than continuous flow. Rick Altman (1987), on the other hand, focuses on the ways in which the television soundtrack competes with household flow in an effort to keep the viewer fixated on the **image** and thus the flow of television programming. Nick Browne (1984) further suggests that the serial nature of programming, **advertising** and scheduling ends up linking television flow to the flow of the American work week. Finally, Beverly Houston (1984) synthesizes Williams' notion of flow with **psychoanalysis**, arguing that television spectatorship is analogous to the infant suckling at the mother's breast (making the television set a sort of boob-tube. For Houston, television promises an endless flow that is none the less continually interrupted, thereby creating a **lack** and corresponding **desire** for additional flow/consumption.

Williams' key concept remains central to the theory of television and its relation to contemporary western society. This can be witnessed not only by the work of media scholars, but by the very real flow of current television programming like MTV and the Home Shopping Network. These networks, among many others – terrestrial and cable – are quite adept at keeping viewers attuned to the set, the advertisements and products, and thus the flow of everyday capital.

See also: cable and satellite

References

Altman, R. (1987) 'Television Sound', in Horace Newcomb (ed.) *Television: The Critical View* (4th edn), New York: Oxford University Press.

Browne, N. (1984) 'The Political Economy of the Television Supertext', *Quarterly Review of Film Studies*, vol. 9, no. 3.

Ellis, J. (1982) *Visible Fictions*, London: Routledge and Kegan Paul.

Houston, B. (1984) 'Viewing Television: The Metapsychology of Endless Consumption', *Quarterly Review of Film Studies*, vol. 9, no. 3.

Williams, R. (1975) *Television, Technology and Cultural Form*, New York: Schocken Books.

DANIEL BERNARDI

Fordism

Fordism refers to a logic of production whereby the supply of materials, the subdivision of labour and the assembly process are carefully co-ordinated in order to maximize efficient and standardized output. In the most literal sense of the term, it is associated with Henry Ford and the assembly line production process that he initiated in 1913, which initially cut the time needed to produce a Model T car from 728 minutes to 93 minutes, and eventually enabled his factory to produce a new car every 24 seconds. By reorganizing the production process and controlling the supply of materials and transport, Ford was able to exploit an economy of scale, driving down the prices of his Model Ts from $950 in 1908 to $290 by the mid-1920s, while in the beginning at least, more than doubling the prevailing wage per-hour rate of his employees. In different historical periods Fordism has evoked meanings ranging from the modern (and from a European perspective, often American) assembly line production process generally, to the tyranny of the clock through piece-per-minute production rates (overthrowing artisanal notions of creative involvement), to a socialist vision of production.

Ford's production practices resonated with the post-1913 transformation of the film business in at least three ways. Just as Ford fought a long and hard battle against the automobile trust and their financial backers, the 'independent' studios struggled to break free from the constraints of the film 'trust' (the Motion Picture Patents Company). Just as Ford introduced the minute break-down of jobs and production processes with his introduction of the assembly line, the post-1913 studios developed new logics of production complete with specialized jobs and a carefully co-ordinated and regularized production process aimed at efficient and standardized output (resulting in the classic Hollywood cinema). And just as Ford vertically organized his industry, owning everything from coal mines and glass factories to the transportation infrastructure needed to ship supplies and cars, so, too, did the major film studios attempt to exercise maximum control over their fates, owning or controlling as many aspects of the production, distribution and exhibition process as possible.

The film industry, like Ford, was able to supply the vast market created by growing urbanization and leisure with a standardized and cost-efficient product, in the process both expanding and accumulating power and profits. Some critics complained about the suppression of creativity in a production process that was both fragmented and dominated by a logic of efficiency, while others charged that low prices and easy availability 'flattened' cultural tastes, endangering hierarchies of distinction.

See also: classical Hollywood cinema and new Hollywood cinema; consumption

Further reading

Bordwell, D., Staiger, J. and Thompson, K. (1985) *The Classical Hollywood Cinema: Film Style and Mode of Production Until 1960*, New York: Columbia University Press.

WILLIAM URICCHIO

Formalism

'Formalism' describes an emphasis on form or formal elements in thought and **culture**, and was developed initially as a literary critical method in Russia during the first two decades of the twentieth century. Vladimir **Propp**, Victor **Shklovsky** and others considered such issues as plot structure, tendencies in characterization and **narrative** form and perspective. They wanted to develop a more scientific analysis of a **text**, and were interested in the *process* of **art** rather than the finished text. Shklovsky and his colleagues of the St Petersburg Society for the Study of Poetic Language (OPOYAZ) were interested in making the familiar strange in their criticism (see also **ostranenie**).

The work of the early Russian Formalists helped the development of structural linguistics, structuralism and **semiotics** later in Europe and the United States, through the work of Claude **Lévi-Strauss** and Roland **Barthes** (see also **structuralism and post-structuralism**). In the 1960s film and television theorists applied Formalist theories of literary criticism to film texts.

The term Formalism was more directly applied to film in Russia in the 1920s and here, too, the emphasis was on form over content, a general trait of modernist art (see **modernism and post-modernism**). Shklovsky was one of the first literary critics to apply Formalist theory to the cinema with an analysis of Charlie Chaplin's work. Filmmakers such as **Eisenstein**, Kuleshov (see **Kuleshov effect**) and **Vertov** were considered to be Formalist artists principally because of their work with montage – the dynamic editing system whereby meaning is produced by the juxtaposition of shots, and not always directly related to narrative. Montage systems stress the formal aspects of the medium by highlighting movement and rhythm, and the tonal and graphic qualities on the screen, as well as an intellectual or psychological stimulation which went beyond narrative logic. This was a move away from the 'filmed theatre' which had previously dominated much of early cinema. Kuleshov, Vertov and Eisenstein also wrote about their work, which encouraged theoretical and ideological debate about film and Formalism.

Kuleshov produced a system of movements for his performers that related directly to the montage of the film. There was also a tendency to reject the traditional plot in favour of the plotless film. Vertov's documentary work, for example, has a coherent formal pattern, but little plot, and Eisenstein inhibits psychological identification with character as his actors represent types rather than individuals. The use of non-professional actors who looked the part, rather than interpreting a part, was known as 'typage'. Within the Constructivist ethos, there was a certain mechanistic aspect to the editing of shots. To a greater or lesser extent, the films drew attention to their material and formal construction (see **Constructivism**).

The paradox of a body of work which promoted a revolutionary zeal among the proletariat, while not necessarily meeting the desire for mass entertainment because of its radical and experimental form, disturbed the authorities in Stalin's Soviet Union, and by 1929 the purges of the Formalists had begun. The Soviet authorities criticized the formal experiments and encouraged the filmmakers to make films which would more easily be understood. The term 'Formalism' became an epithet of disdain by the authorities when applied to the filmmakers or any other

artistic experimentation. In 1934 the government instituted the policy known as **Socialist Realism** which decreed that all artistic work should be grounded in '**realism**', and the movement came to an end. Indeed, a charge of Formalism could carry the death sentence (see Christie 1998).

The influence of Formalism was to continue, and the 1960s saw its revival in literary criticism and film theory, and in artistic practice in this area, and many key Russian texts were translated for the first time. The *Tel Quel* group and its publications, which were so influential in development of film theory at this time (and included work by Barthes and Julia **Kristeva**), specifically linked Formalism with **avant-garde** practice. There was also an acknowledgement of the Formalist practices of the Russian filmmakers on emerging avant-garde filmmakers in Europe and the United States.

References

Christie, I. (1998) 'Formalism and Neo-formalism', in J. Hill and P. C. Gibson (eds) *The Oxford Guide to Film Studies*, Oxford: Oxford University Press.

Further reading

Taylor, R. and Christie, I. (eds) (1994) *The Film Factory: Russian and Soviet Cinema in Documents 1896–1939* (2nd edn), London: Routledge.

NICK BURTON

fort/da game

Sigmund **Freud** noticed that his 18-month-old grandson would toss a bobbin over the edge of his cot (*Fort*, 'gone') and then joyfully yank it back by its string (*Da*, 'there'). According to Freud, the child thus overcame the trauma of his mother's periodic absences by reassuring himself that she would return. Indeed, the boy's game allowed him to control her movements: repeatedly controlling the disappearance and return of the toy enabled the infant to gain mastery subconsciously over his mother's comings and goings, thereby ameliorating the separation anxiety of being abandoned. By re-enacting this primary trauma, the boy grew out of his passive infantile fusion with the mother towards more active ego individuation.

Jacques **Lacan** emphasized the role of language and naming objects in the Fort/Da game and the importance of such naming in the infant's development of self-awareness. For Lacan, the Fort/Da game is part of the symbolic order, in that the substitution of concrete objects and words for the absent object of **desire** (the mother) represents an entry into the post-mirror phase world of language and law (*le loi du père*, or the **law of the father**; see also **mirror stage**).

Further reading

Freud, S. (1961) *Beyond the Pleasure Principle*, trans. J. Strachey, London: W. W. Norton.

Lacan, J. (1977) *Ecrits: A Selection*, trans. A. Sheridan, New York: W. W. Norton.

Metz, C. (1982) *The Imaginary Signifier*, trans. B. Brewster, London: Macmillan.

FRANK P. TOMASULO

Foucault, Michel

b. 1926; d. 1984

Growing up and studying in France, Michel Foucault's primary academic interest was psychopathology, a pursuit which resulted in his first published book, and his subsequent doctoral thesis on the history of madness. During the 1970s, Foucault became increasingly politicized, working through the Group for Information about Prisons for penal reform and speaking openly for the gay movement. In the early 1980s he found a new readership among West Coast audiences in the United States, but died mid-decade of Aids-related illnesses.

Foucault's work is concerned with discourses of social power and networks of control, often taking a broad historical perspective to describe changes in the process of regulation. This project is most strikingly expressed in his *History of Sexuality* and in *Discipline and Punish*, which between them offer an account of the way **gender**, deviance, illness and criminality have been channelled and categorized over recent centuries.

The principal metaphor in the latter work is the **panopticon**, which Foucault describes as epitomizing a shift in punishment from the spectacular public torture and shaming of the eighteenth century to the contemporary system of near-invisible surveillance.

References

Foucault, M. (1976) *The History of Sexuality Vol. 1 An Introduction*, trans. R. Hurley, London: Allen Lane 1979.
—— (1984) *The History of Sexuality Vol. 2 The Use of Pleasure*, trans. R. Hurley, New York: Pantheon 1985.
—— (1984) *The History of Sexuality Vol. 3 The Care of the Self*, trans. R. Hurley, New York: Pantheon 1986.

Further reading

Foucault, M. (1984) *Discipline and Punish: The Birth of the Prison*, trans. Alan Sheridan, Harmondsworth: Penguin.

WILL BROOKER

framing

'Framing' often refers to the way in which an image has been composed with regard to what has been chosen to be shown. In a broader sense, however, frames may be conceptualized as 'principles of organization' (Goffman 1974) which work to impose order on the multiple happenings of the social world so as to render them into meaningful events. In the case of broadcast journalism, for example, news frames make the world beyond direct experience look natural; they are 'principles of selection, emphasis, and presentation composed of little tacit theories about what exists, what happens, and what matters' (Gitlin 1980: 6). The subject of often intense **negotiation** between journalists and their editors and their sources, frames help to render 'an infinity of noticeable details' into practicable repertoires. Neither arbitrary nor fixed, frames facilitate the news organization's ordering of the world in conjunction with hierarchical rules of inclusion and exclusion (see **hierarchy of discourses**).

See also: news values

References

Gitlin, T. (1980) *The Whole World is Watching: Mass Media in the Making and Unmaking of the New Left*, Berkeley: University of California Press.
Goffman, E. (1974) *Frame Anaysis*, New York: Harper and Row.

STUART ALLAN

franchise

Franchises are licences issued in the United Kingdom by the government that allow commercial companies to offer broadcasting services, usually local or regional. The Radio Authority administers the allocation of radio franchises, usually for an eight-year period. The Independent Television Commission (ITC) controls the television franchises, which are currently issued for a ten-year period. Although there are programming and quality 'thresholds' to be satisfied, the main criterion for the allocation of a franchise is usually the highest financial bid. However, there have been cases where the highest bidder has been deemed 'too ambitious' and not been awarded the franchise.

See also: broadcasting, the United Kingdom

PHILIP RAYNER

Frankfurt School

Begun as the Institute of Social Research in 1923 in Frankfurt, Germany, then continued into US exile in the 1930s, and later extended in Germany and in the United States, what came to be known as the Frankfurt School consisted of left-wing social critics and philosophers for whom capitalist domination and the potential for its overthrow could be found inscribed in the details of the cultural artefacts, commercial and rarefied, of market society. For film and television theory, the most important figures of the School's first generation are Theodor

Wiesengrund **Adorno**, Walter **Benjamin**, Erich Fromm (for a period of time), Max **Horkheimer**, Leo Löwenthal and Herbert Marcuse. Although their positions were hardly identical (with Benjamin's the most distinctive in its ambivalent relation to modern technologies), as a group they were resolutely antagonistic to what they saw as the **culture** of domination.

Their development of what they called 'critical theory' responded to their historical situation as intellectuals, with radical Marxist sympathies (see **Marx, Karl**), in a world wracked by waves of economic, political and social disaster: first the unanticipated support of the German Social Democrats for the First World War, then the devastation of the war itself and the subsequent years of economic and political crisis, followed by the electoral success and dictatorship of the Nazis in 1933, followed again by war in 1939, and the 1939–1941 alliance of the Soviet Union and the world Communist movement with Germany. Denied by this history was Marxism's promise of a rising proletariat, which was to carry the interests of humankind from the realm of necessity to the realm of freedom. If Marxism's critique depends on its vision of capitalism's overthrow, of what value is that critique once that overthrow no longer can be foreseen?

Yet if the critical theorists' disillusionment with traditional Marxism resonates with our time, their sense of the theoretical possibility for revolutionary change was enabled by their time's experience or historical memory of radical developments in Europe: the Paris Commune of 1871, the St Petersburg workers' councils of 1905 and their short-lived counterparts during the Russian Revolution of 1917 and the 1918–1919 revolutions in Germany and Hungary, as well as the factory councils in Italy. Because they could still see potential for radical transformation, they analysed how objects of commercial culture (Mickey Mouse cartoons, the astrology column of the *Los Angeles Times*, the jitterbug) could at the same time embody the deepest aspirations of their consumers and channel them within the *status quo*, away from possibilities that might allow those aspirations to be fulfilled (see **consumption**).

Present also for them was the emancipatory promise of modernist art (Picasso in painting;

Beckett in theatre; Schönberg in music; surrealist painting and writing; and for Benjamin, the films of Sergei **Eisenstein**), which contained within it deliberate forms not governed by marketing experts or agents of the state. It was in these forms that they saw echoes of a socialist vision of labour not alienated by others' profit or control, as well as of the dialectic of German philosophy (see **dialectic and dialectical montage**). Like Marx, they considered that the dialectic, if linked to a materialist **epistemology**, offered an emancipatory method for understanding the movement of the world.

Their work constitutes one of the twentieth century's major efforts to reconstruct historical materialism as a relevant social theory. This remains true even though they distanced themselves from much of what had come to make Marxism rigid in its analyses and applications. They called their work 'critical theory' in part to stress both its radical and speculative qualities but also to forestall glib denunciations in a period of anti-Communism. The critical theorists opposed tendencies within Marxism to identify itself as a 'science', to claim for itself historical certainty about the ultimate victory of the proletariat, and to see culture as a secondary reflection in the 'superstructure' of the primary economic 'base' (see **base and superstructure**). They were critical of Soviet Communism for its systems of domination, as they were of the modes of global capitalism (see **globalization**).

Aside from Benjamin, who saw emancipatory possibilities in film's editing forms and in a reproducibility that ruptured the aura of sacred culture, they tended to look at film and, later, television in terms of an argument that labelled such media as products of a culture industry. In their later work, they argued that the terms 'mass culture' and 'popular culture' connoted possibilities for production by audience members themselves for each other, a form of intersubjective communication within communities. The culture industry, by contrast, viewed such communities only as fodder for its systems of viewer accumulation and sales. But this was not a theory of film or television in the sense of an ontological account (such as André **Bazin**'s or Maya Deren's or Sergei Eisenstein's; see **ontology**). Rather, it was an analysis of the social

meaning of particular if standardized forms in particular historical situations.

Critical theory would describe most contemporary encounters with culture industry products as governed by a system Marcuse called 'one-dimensional', directing energies along paths carved to the measure of ruling powers, trickling down benefits to others only under pressure. Readings must include this context, or risk reifying their objects (see **reification**). Much quantitatively-oriented empirical work on film and television ignores this, as does research that takes at face value **audience** description of their own responses. At the same time, however, they did not argue that effects could in theory be read off the surface of a work or its conditions of production, certainly not in terms of a **hypodermic model**. Audiences were not objects of simple manipulation. As Adorno maintained in a critique of social-scientific media research: 'It would be naïve to take for granted an identity between the social implications to be discerned in the stimuli and those embodied in the "responses" ' (Adorno 1968: 353). Instead, according to him, analysts of the 'hieroglyphs of social significance' to be found in individual texts should respect both the specificity of the object's forms and its interconnections with others in the world (*ibid.*: 342). They should also insist on self-consciousness about the analytical process, itself a social hieroglyph.

An expert in music, Adorno wrote several detailed studies that suggested how the immanent criticism he argued for might be extended to film and television. Such criticism reads the social within cultural artefacts and, in Adorno's words, 'takes seriously the principle that it is not ideology which is untrue but its pretension to correspond to reality. Immanent criticism...names what the consistency or inconsistency of the work expresses of the structure of the existent....In such antinomies criticism perceives those of society' (Adorno 1981: 32). In its active readings of structural gaps, immanent criticism resembles French post-structuralism and one theoretical wing of British cultural studies (see **structuralism and post-structuralism**). But these stress disconnection and tend to follow or go beyond Louis **Althusser** in his insistence on the 'relative **autonomy**' of cultural forms from economic relations. The Frankfurt School, however, stressed not autonomy but interrelation, which can help us understand how economic, cultural, ideological and political determinations have worked in specific socio-historical moments (such as construction of points of view or the star system in film, or the interruption of programmes by advertisements in commercial television; see **determination; point of view shot**). Understanding this interrelation can also help in theorizing passageways to change. In the cause of this change, Adorno demanded the 'right to go from one *genus* to another, to shed light on an object in itself hermetic by casting a glance at society, to present society with the bill the object does not redeem' (Adorno 1981: 33). The emphasis on relative autonomy has discouraged analysis of this kind – moving from one social realm to another, sketching out the dialectical relations of their forms, illuminating what Fredric **Jameson** has called 'historical tropes' (Jameson 1971: 3–59), even if it does not preclude it in theory.

Although Germanists in the United States have analysed and extended the project of the first generation of Frankfurt thinkers (and of Siegfried **Kracauer**, whose early writings on film influenced Adorno and Horkheimer) in *New German Critique* and *Telos*, and such work thrives in Germany itself, anglophone film and television scholars have tended to dismiss them. In part this has been because the social relations of their time and place mark their writing. They did not treat crucial matters of heterosexism and racism (aside from their studies of fascistic personalities), for example, although these might well be analysed in terms of critical theory. They were unconscious of their own **Eurocentrism**. They did not demonstrate detailed knowledge of film and television textual operations, comparable to their knowledge of literature and music. And although they wrote about **psychoanalysis** and the social bases of contradictory subjectivity, they did not appreciate the complex bonds of **pleasure** and **identity** that stitch together contemporary culture.

However, this dismissal has also tended to include two arguments that may be less persuasive: that the Frankfurt valorization of modernist art betrays their elitism and that their pessimism betrays their political irrelevance. No doubt, as hostile as they tended to be to culture industry products (and as Adorno was, unfortunately, to

African-American jazz), the critical theorists wrote much that could support a view that they were elitists. As I noted above, they did indeed argue for the critical value of a handful of examples of elite art, seeing in them resistance to the culture industry's demands. Yet this does not mean that the theory itself is elitist. They were careful to differentiate their critique of the culture industry from a conservative one rooted in an idealist vision of art's unworldliness. Defenders of what Marcuse in 1937 called the 'affirmative character of culture' might put it otherwise, but for critical theory the conservative insistence that art and culture provide an enclave for the spirit against the mob helps justify existing property relations. 'The truth of a higher world, of a higher good than material existence, conceals the truth that a better material existence can be created in which such happiness is realised' (Marcuse 1968: 121). As for pessimism, aside from Marcuse's optimistic responses of the late 1960s, the first generation critical theorists from the late 1920s could find no movements capable of taking the proletariat's place as the agent of human emancipation. Those who find such agents in post-1968 social movements might reasonably consider the Frankfurt position pessimistic, as might those without confidence or interest in notions of general human emancipation. Indeed, the most prominent of the second generation Frankfurt scholars, Jürgen **Habermas**, grounded a revised emancipatory theory in what he sees as the human desire for intersubjective communication, 'communicative action'. For the others, pessimism was a mood of optimistic refusal, for pessimism requires belief in unrealized potential. Rejection of the Frankfurt School because of their pessimism, because of the desolate images they constructed of everyday life under global capitalism, smacks precisely of the power of positive thinking they sought to eviscerate.

See also: feminist theory; Lukács, Gyorgy; Marxist aesthetics; queer theory; reading and reception theory

References

Adorno, T. W. (1968) 'Scientific Experiences of a European Scholar in America', in D. Fleming and B. Bailyn (eds) *The Intellectual Migration: Europe and America, 1930–1960*, trans. D. Fleming, Cambridge, MA: Belknap/Harvard University.

—— (1981) 'Cultural Criticism and Society', in *Prisms*, trans. S. Weber and S. Weber, Cambridge, MA: MIT.

Jameson, F. (1971) *Marxism and Form: Twentieth-Century Dialectical Theories of Literature*, Princeton: Princeton University Press.

Marcuse, H. (1964) *One-Dimensional Man: Studies in the Ideology of Advanced Industrial Society*, Boston: Beacon.

—— (1968) 'The Affirmative Character of Culture', in *Negations: Essays in Critical Theory*, trans. J. J. Shapiro, Boston: Beacon.

Further reading

Arato, A. and Gebhardt, E. (eds) (1978) *The Essential Frankfurt School Reader*, New York: Urizen.

Bronner, S. E. and Kellner, D. M. (eds) (1989) *Critical Theory and Society: A Reader*, New York: Routledge.

Buck-Morss, S. (1977) *The Origin of Negative Dialectics: Theodor W. Adorno, Walter Benjamin, and the Frankfurt Institute*, Garden City: Macmillan-Free.

Horkheimer, M. and Adorno, T. W. (1972) 'The Culture Industry: Enlightenment as Mass Deception', in *Dialectic of Enlightenment*, trans. John Cumming, New York: Continuum-Seabury.

Jay, M. (1973) *The Dialectical Imagination: A History of the Frankfurt School and the Institute of Social Research, 1923–1950*, Boston: Little, Brown.

CLAY STEINMAN

Freud, Sigmund

b. 1856; d. 1939

An Austrian medical psychologist and founder of **psychoanalysis**, Freud's clinical practice and theories on the human psyche have had a profound influence on western thought. Although often challenged and critiqued, his concepts such as the **subconscious** mind, repression, dream analysis, sublimation, the Oedipus/Electra complex, repetition compulsion, the pleasure principle, infantile sexuality, **castration** anxiety, penis envy and many others have come to define the twentieth-century's view of human motivation and behaviour.

In film and television **theory**, Freud's ideas have been used as methodological paradigms to examine the psychology and motives of fictional characters; the structure and dynamics of classical **narrative** trajectories; **genre** analysis (the subtext of the **horror** film as sexuality); the sources of jokes and humour; the psychology of film **authorship** (the obsessive thematic and cinematic preoccupations of film directors); the **representation** of **gender**; phallic and vaginal iconography; dream and fantasy sequences in films; the conditions of reception of film and television (darkened space, unbidden images, fixed position in the auditorium, heightened susceptibility, the film-as-dream); the process of identification with screen personae, and the source and nature of spectatorial pleasure in the cinema (see **scopophilia**; **voyeurism**).

Further reading

Altman, C. F. (1977) 'Psychoanalysis and Cinema: The Imaginary Discourse', *Quarterly Review of Film Studies*, vol. 2, no. 3, pp. 257–72.

Freud, S. (1975) *The Psychopathology of Everyday Life* (first published 1901), trans. A. Tyson, Harmondsworth: Penguin.

—— (1976) *The Interpretation of Dreams* (first published 1900), trans. J. Strachey, Harmondsworth: Penguin.

Mulvey, L. (1975) 'Visual Pleasure and Narrative Cinema', *Screen*, vol. 16, no. 3, pp. 6–18.

FRANK P. TOMASULO

G

Gadamer, Hans-Georg

b. 1900

Gadamer's **hermeneutics** have been widely influential, from architecture to social theory, as well as in television studies. At the core of his account of texts and their reading or reception are four ideas about how audiences find content intelligible (see **audience; reading and reception theory**). These are:

1 Reception processes are historically located, occurring within a tradition to which reader and **text** belong; this pre-existing 'fusion of horizons' allows audiences some recognition of content as a pre-condition of further interpretation.
2 Such recognition supports readers' informed '**projection**' of meaning, a presumption of textual sense which is checked against **narrative** developments in a conversation-like interaction with content.
3 Reading is therefore pleasurably play-like (see **pleasure**), with audiences continually attending to different aspects of a text, involved and distracted from themselves.
4 Audiences undertake a productive 'hermeneutic circle' of interpretation in which the reader's broad understanding of a text is integrated with the sense attributed to a particular segment (and vice versa), refining the different readings by audience members.

As Jürgen **Habermas** notes, Gadamer's hermeneutics is not substantially political.

See also: cognitive theory

Further reading

Gadamer, H. G. (1979) *Truth and Method*, London: Sheed and Ward.
Warnke, G. (1987) *Gadamer*, Cambridge: Polity Press.

TONY WILSON

gaze, the

The notion of the gaze has been central to feminist film criticism's characterization of the **cinematic apparatus** as patriarchal construct. The first wave of feminist criticism, based on a sociological approach which looked for correspondence between texts and the 'real' world, had examined images of women in imaginative works from high art to mass entertainment with little regard for textual meaning-making. Feminist film criticism, which began to take shape in the mid-1970s, opposed this earlier emphasis on 'content' and focused instead on the question of meaning production through the formal aspects of the **text** such as editing, lighting and so forth. In her seminal article, 'Visual Pleasure and Narrative Cinema', published in 1975, which marked the beginnings of feminist film criticism, Laura **Mulvey** identified the inscription of **patriarchy** in cinema by examining the workings of film as an intricate network of looks. Mulvey singles out three types of looks which constitute the filmic (and, we might add, televisual) organization of the gaze: (i) the camera's look on the profilmic event; (ii) the protagonist's look on other diegetic filmic characters; and (iii) the spectator's look on the screen. By applying pre-Oedipal and Oedipal concepts of Freudian **psychoanalysis** and directly relating the film apparatus to the patriarchal **unconscious**, Mulvey argues that the structuring of the filmic gaze is decidedly male. Thus all three types of looks are organized to construct the spectator as male in accordance with the needs of his unconscious.

The psychic mechanisms instrumental here are **voyeurism** and **fetishism**. Thus the viewing situation in the darkened movie theatre is linked to the voyeuristic scenario of the primal scene with the little boy peeping through a keyhole, a scenario in which looking is related closely to notions of domination and submission, not only in sex scenes but in all screen images in which women are sexualized. Fetishism, on the other hand, answers the male need for alleviating the threat of **castration** posed by women by transforming the female body into that which it lacks, the **phallus** (particularly striking examples of the representation of women as fetish may be found in the von Sternberg films starring Marlene Dietrich). While, in the first mode of looking, the gaze of the camera may be technically neutral, Mulvey argues that the fact that filmmaking is usually restricted to men makes it inherently voyeuristic and male. In the second gaze, the diegetic look of the male characters is mostly organized in fetishistic terms in order to make women objects of the gaze, while the look of the male spectator seems to combine voyeuristic and fetishistic modes of looking.

Despite its impact on feminist film and media studies, Mulvey's conceptualization of the cinematic gaze as inherently gender-specific has raised a host of problems and questions. These have been addressed by feminist critics over the past twenty years, yet crucial issues still remain open. If classical Hollywood cinema constructs its spectator as male despite the actual **gender**, what are the options for female spectators beyond a masochistic identification with the objectified woman on the screen or a transvestite's identification with the male look (Doane 1990)? If voyeurism, with its patterns of domination and subordination, may also be

pleasurable for women, does not the fact that the male look is invested with power (whereas the female gaze is not) prohibit an appropriation of the gaze by women (Kaplan 1983)? How can we account for the pleasure many women experience when watching Hollywood films (Koch 1985)? How are structures of the gaze modified in films addressed to a female audience such as women's films of the 1940s (Doane 1987)? How can we conceptualize a feminist counter-cinema based on a different organization of the gaze (Johnston 1973)?

While these questions have posed a challenge to feminist theory and led to a broadening and diversification of the theoretical spectrum, the notion of a gendered specular regime first applied to cinema by Laura Mulvey, which differentiates between the bearer of the gaze as male and its recipient, the woman defined as the object to be looked at, is still at the core of what constitutes feminist media criticism.

See also: diegesis; feminist theory; Freud, Sigmund; lack

References

Doane, M. A. (1990) 'Film and the Masquerade: Theorizing the Female Spectator', in Patricia Erens (ed.) *Issues in Feminist Film Criticism*, Bloomington: Indiana University Press.

—— (1987) *The Desire to Desire*, Bloomington: Indiana University Press.

—— (1988–89) 'Masquerade Reconsidered: Further Thoughts on the Female Spectator', *Discourse*, vol. 11, no. 1.

Johnston, C. (1973) 'Women's Cinema as Counter-Cinema', in Claire Johnston (ed.) *Notes on Women's Cinema*, London: Society for Education in Film and Television.

Kaplan, E. A. (1983) 'Is the Gaze Male?', in E. Ann Kaplan, *Women and Film. Both Sides of the Camera*, New York: Methuen.

Koch, G. (1985) 'Ex-Changing the Gaze: Re-Visioning Feminist Film Theory', *New German Critique*, 34 (Winter).

Mulvey, L. (1975) 'Visual Pleasure and Narrative Cinema', *Screen*, vol. 16, no. 3.

EVA WARTH

gender

Sex and gender

In film and television theory, gender is not sex. In a common distinction – whose popularization can be traced to feminist writing on culture since the 1970s (see **feminist theory**) – gender can be defined in contradistinction to sex. In this taxonomy, 'sex' refers to the biological and physical differences between men and women; while 'gender' refers to the cultural roles which are built up and linked to those differences. Thus, 'female' and 'male' are sexes, while 'feminine' and 'masculine' are gender roles. The characteristics associated with these roles in western culture include:

- Feminine/masculine
- Passive/active
- Weak/strong
- Emotive/intellectual
- Embodied/abstracted
- Private (home)/public (work)
- **Other**-identified/self-identified
- Process-oriented/goal-oriented
- Secretarial/managerial
- Nurse/doctor

And so on. These **binary** gender roles are always understood to involve hierarchies of value – the emotional and the private must not be allowed to interfere with the rational work of public decision making, the secretarial and nurse roles are merely support for the manager and the doctor and so on.

The distinction between sex and gender is often made in popular **discourse**. However, this is not always the case: at other times, the terms are used interchangeably (so that 'male' and 'female' are referred to as 'genders'). It should be noted, in respect to the different meanings of the term in academic and non-academic cultural sites, that recent theoretical writing has challenged the traditional distinction between sex and gender (see next section).

Like '**race**', the taxonomy of 'sex' provides a way of dividing society into discrete groups of individuals. It provides the basis for the 'identity politics' (see **identity**) commonly known as 'feminism'. The role of 'gender' in this politics has been an ambivalent one.

The need for feminist writing in the 1970s to insist on the distinction between sex and gender can easily be understood. Writers who were championing such political concepts as liberty and equality for women were faced with essentialist arguments which insisted that the behaviours, characteristics and personalities of men and women were determined by nature and could not be changed. Such arguments were used to buttress unequal social institutions – women could not leave the home, join in public life, become politicians, hold powerful positions, and so on, simply because they were biologically incapable of doing so. Women's preference for the private sphere, for abnegating responsibility, for thinking of others before themselves, were all natural.

In the face of such arguments, feminist writing insisted that while sex – the physical distinctions between men and women – might be natural, the behaviours, personalities and characteristics associated with these categories – were not so. Instead, they were cultural and could therefore be changed. (It is worth noting the assumption which is accepted in such a rhetorical move – that if a quality is 'natural' it is therefore both desirable and unchangeable.)

This debate – about whether gender roles are natural or cultural – continues to resonate in popular culture to the present day, with **common sense** understandings of the situation swinging from one side to the other, and a regular roll-call of books by science journalists published each year which claim to 'prove' that gender roles are natural and determined by biology. It should be noted that it is, ultimately, impossible to know to what extent the roles which we name as masculine and feminine are biologically constructed. It is impossible to remove human subjects from culture in order to study them scientifically – this would be not only unethical, but physically impossible.

The work of historians of science such as Anne Fausto Sterling has made clear that, repeatedly throughout history, the claims of the biological sciences to have made 'discoveries' about the 'natural' differences between men and women have later turned out to be based on cultural prejudices. Sterling gives the example of nineteenth-century biological scientists who 'discovered' that women could not study at university as it would dry out their wombs, causing sterility and hysteria. From our contemporary viewpoint, the idea that women are biologically unable to study seems to be obviously untrue – we can now see the cultural assumptions which informed this scientific research. Currently, the most common scientific paradigms which are used to defend arguments that gender differences are really biological differences are sociobiology (argument by metaphor from animals), evolutionary biology (which is hypothesis without replicability) and psychology (a discipline which in fact studies culture and discourse).

Feminist cultural theory strongly argued that gender roles were cultural and changeable and began to examine the ways in which they were sustained and promulgated. In so doing, the analysis of **culture** – including feminist film theory and writing on gender roles in television – became a central part of a feminist project which attempted to show that the gender roles constructed by culture were disabling to women in particular ways.

Gender and film theory: content

Books such as Kate Millett's influential *Sexual Politics* (1971) suggested that the creation of gender roles in culture could be analysed by attention to 'stereotypes' and positive images (see **stereotype**). This terminology suggested that cultural texts supported gender roles by a process simply of repetition of characteristics – women were repeatedly shown to be weak, unable to defend themselves, powerless to take control of their lives and reliant on men. In response was proposed a project of deliberately producing 'positive images'. These representations, it was argued, would provide role models for women. This work sought the abolition of gender roles – although the categories of male and female would remain, the broad binary categories of masculine and feminine which are currently associated with them would be destroyed. Both men and women would be shown as caring, emotional, strong, independent, adventurous, and so on.

Gender and film theory: form

Writers such as Laura **Mulvey** went on to note that more than simply representing male and female characters in different ways, films offered masculine and feminine positions in the way they were structured. In particular, it was noted that women were often presented as 'passive', as 'objects', 'to be looked at'. In contrast, men were 'active', 'subjects' and able to 'look' (see **gaze, the**). This description applied not only to roles in the narrative, but to camera angles, shots, lighting, costuming, editing etc.

Psychoanalysis and gender

Underlying much feminist analysis of the construction of gender roles was a psychoanalytical approach. This provides a curiously ambivalent explanation for the formation of gender roles – partly social/cultural and partly essentialist/biological. Psychoanalytic writing explains the formation of individual subjectivity primarily in relation to sexual difference. In traditional psychoanalytic ways of thinking, there are two kinds of 'psyches' in the world – male and female (later writing attempted to produce psychoanalytic accounts of racial difference, but this is a far less developed process). To the degree that this is understood to be brought about by social/cultural factors – the organization of the western nuclear family, for example – it could be said that psychoanalytic thought is not essentialist. However, in many ways, psychoanalytic cultural relies on biological difference to explain gender – the presence or the absence of a penis (even in Lacanian psychoanalysis, where the physical object of the penis is replaced with the symbolic phallus, the relationship between these two objects remains a close one; see **fetishism; Lacan, Jacques; psychoanalysis**).

Pornography

The idea that the 'feminized' gender role in our culture includes passivity, powerless and the position of being merely an 'object' has also been addressed in writing on **pornography** – and particularly in that tradition represented by Andrea Dworkin. For Dworkin, pornogaphy is the dominant category for understanding gender (an argument which is facilitated by Dworkin's definition of pornography as all cultural texts which show, invite or are violent against women – and her further adoption of interpretive strategies which allow her to show that every representation of women falls into these categories). However, theoretical writing which comes after Dworkin points out that there are other ways to think about pornography than its being about gender – and indeed, other ways to think about gender than its being defined by pornography.

Feminist cultural theory and essentialism

In a way, by challenging gender roles, feminist film theory was inviting its own undoing – at least in the form which it existed – as it challenged 'stereotypes' and championed 'positive images'. For if men and women were represented in identical ways, then the category of 'woman' would begin to degrade – what would then make 'women' different from 'men'?

However, other strands of cultural theory have insisted more strongly on essentialist positions – that the gender roles associated with women in our culture can be traced back to biology and nature. In this approach, rather than trying to change gender roles, the project of feminist cultural theory should be to attempt to revalue them, to celebrate traditionally feminine qualities.

Such an approach can be seen in the work of Luce **Irigaray** and Hélène **Cixous**. The concepts of '*parler femme*' (Irigaray – woman's talking) and '*écriture féminine*' (Cixous – women's writing) suggest that women's cultural expression will be feminine – by which they mean decentred; refusing an over-arching rational point of view; not relying on linear logic; challenging the patriarchal order; excessive, troubling and disturbing, and so on. For these writers, such gendered qualities are not purely cultural but can be linked back to the female body – which allows for decentred and open-ended pleasure, as opposed to the phallic, climax-oriented pleasure associated with men. Thus, 'masculine' forms of cultural production – linear narrative, coherent point of view – cannot produce truly 'feminine' representations.

These arguments are now generally regarded as unconvincing. The idea that particular aesthetic forms are essentially gendered, or have innate tendencies to be either 'radical' or 'conservative', is usually viewed with suspicion, although some such tendencies survive from the 1970s in writing which celebrates **avant-garde** production. It is now more generally accepted that the potential of aesthetic forms to serve particular political ends – to be 'radical', 'subversive' or 'progressive', whatever these terms might be taken to mean – must be judged in terms of the aesthetic and sociopolitical context in which they are used.

Experience

The category of women's 'experience' is also appealed to in order to stabilize gender roles in some 1970s feminist cultural theory. Here, women are more likely to enjoy, understand and relate to the cultural production of other women because they all share a similar outlook, brought about not necessarily by nature, but by common experience. This word, popular in 1970s cultural theory, has now been re-evaluated as it becomes apparent that personal experience is not an unarguable guarantor of truth, it is just as much within discourse as other aspects of culture (see **subject and subjectivity**).

The importance of the sex of the producer of a cultural text can be discussed more usefully within the context of **authorship**: information about the author is, it is accepted in our culture, a suitable intertext to bring to bear on the interpretation of a text. Because our current understandings of **identity** include sex as an important category, knowing that a particular film or television programme is produced, directed or written by a woman can be seen as important – without making any appeal to the ways in which that particular text might contribute to the formation of gender roles.

Masculinity

The attention so far in this entry to feminist writing and the ways in which it has dealt with the construction of (in particular) the 'feminine' gender role should not be taken as implying that it is only women who have gender; nor that the construction of masculinity is in any way less interesting. However, Roland **Barthes**' concept of 'exnomination' can be seen operating in the history of cultural theory around gender. Barthes notes that dominant groups tend to efface themselves from language, rendering themselves the unspoken norm against which everything else is judged. In this way, for several years it appeared that men were simply too obvious and normal to require any explanation. Since the late 1980s, however, this has become increasingly untrue, as an initial trickle of work analysing the construction of masculinity in culture has become something of a flood.

There are occasional early books which analyse 'masculinity in the movies' using the same taxonomy of stereotype/positive image which informs writing on femininity. However, these are largely isolated examples. The later work in the area can be divided into two broad streams.

One stream analyses the production of masculinity in terms very similar to those developed by film studies in order to analyse femininity – analysing the gaze, concepts of stereotypes and so on. In this tradition, pride of place must be given to Richard **Dyer**, who was committed to work in this area long before it gained its current fashionable status. Books providing textual analysis of the construction of masculinity in the cinema now appear at the rate of several a year. It is worth noting Dyer's explicit identification as a gay man, examined and explored in his work, and his attention to the relationship between sexuality and masculinity; this is representative rather than surprising – a certain tangential relation to the simple model of male/female relations produced by early feminist work (including the awareness that men could also be regarded as sexual objects) means that much of the analysis of masculinity is conducted under an explicitly homosexual rubric.

The other stream is a more sociological one, and shades into work produced by the men's movement. In the same way that feminist social movements provided the backdrop for analyses of femininity, the men's movement currently provides an interpretive framework for writing on the ways in which traditional constructions of masculinity 'hurt' men, and the urgent need to intervene in the production of these gender roles in order to protect men (Horrocks 1995). In the analysis of gender roles emerging from the men's movement, these roles must be changed in order to allow men to be more emotional – but there is categorically no desire to retire these gender roles altogether. In this tradition, it is vital that 'masculine' and 'feminine' roles are retained, and that, indeed, they retain much of their current composition (including the need for men to be 'strong' in relation to women). It is only the distribution of the capacity for emotional expression which must be changed.

Challenging sex

Up to this point, this entry has worked with the distinction which was proposed and popularized by feminist cultural theory since the 1970s – that sex (biological) and gender (cultural) can be separated in a functional binary. However, it is important to note that in the 1990s, this taxonomy was challenged – and indeed, in a certain tradition of writing (see **queer theory**), this challenge is now accepted as axiomatic. The most important writer in this regard is Judith **Butler**, who argues that the sex/gender distinction is a misleading one. She notes that the idea that the category of sex – that there are naturally two kinds of people in this world, male and female – is, in itself, a cultural one. In short, the very question, 'are differences between men and women biological and cultural?', makes the assumption that there are two discrete categories of people – named men and women.

Research has pointed out that even at the biological level, it is impossible to make an adequate distinction between male and female. 'Secondary' sexual characteristics, such as the distribution of body hair and body fat are not divided neatly into two groups: for example, a large proportion of women shave, bleach or wax their facial hair to try to fit into these cultural categories. Even in terms of 'primary' sexual characteristics, it is not obvious that easy distinctions can be made. In the biological sciences, definitions of maleness or femaleness sometimes depend on the role taken in reproduction – whether individuals produce sperm or eggs. But by this definition, post-menopausal women would be neither male nor female. If the definition is simply the possession of a penis or a vagina, then the large number of individuals born each year who are intersexed (some estimates suggest 2,000 every year in the United States alone) must be excluded from the definition. Again, these people face surgical intervention to make them either male or female – to make nature fit in with our cultural presupposition that there are only two, discrete and distinct, sexes. Even on a chromosomal level, sex cannot be simply guaranteed: some XY infants are born with 'female' genitalia, and some XX with 'male'.

In short, the work of Butler proposes that the idea that there are two sexes is not a natural one, but is as cultural, and changeable, as the idea that there are two kinds of gender behaviour. Indeed, she goes so far as to propose that, in the absence of a simple 'fact' of biology to sustain this belief, the belief in two sexes is in fact supported by our cultural systems. Or, more simply, that it is the concept of gender which provides the basis on which the concept of biological sex is built – exactly the opposite of what was proposed in 1970s feminist cultural theory.

References

Butler, J. (1990) *Gender Trouble: Feminism and the Subversion of Identity*, New York: Routledge.
Dworkin, A. (1981) *Pornography: Men Possessing Women*, London: The Women's Press.
Horrocks, R. (1995) *Male Myths and Icons*, Basingstoke: Macmillan.
Millett, K. (1971) *Sexual Politics*, London: Hart-Davis.

Further reading

Cowie, E. (1997) *Representing the Woman: Cinema and Psychoanalysis*, Basingstoke: Macmillan.
Erens P. (ed.) (1990) *Issues in Feminist Film Criticism*, Bloomington and Indianapolis: Indiana University Press.
Gledhill, C. (ed.) (1987) *Home is Where the Heart Is: Studies in Melodrama and the Woman's Film*, London: BFI Publishing.
Tasker, Y. (1993) *Spectacular Bodies: Genre, Gender and the Action Cinema*, London and New York: Routledge.

ALAN McKEE

Genette, Gérard

b. 1930

Born in Paris, Gérard Genette is a contemporary of Pierre **Bourdieu** and Jacques **Derrida**, and collaborated with Hélène **Cixous** and Tzvetan **Todorov** in the production of a theoretical journal in 1970. A collection of his articles was first published in 1966. Genette is recognized as a central figure in structuralist theory. Like Aristotle, his concern is to establish a poetics that would locate the institution of literature in society and, like the Russian Formalists, whom he equally acknowledges, Genette attempts to identify the external and internal processes that distinguish literatures (see **Formalism; structuralism and post-structuralism**).

Genette's methodology relies on a close reading of the **text** in order to locate immanent meanings. This is not the close reading of subjective engagement that would produce a new, more detailed interpretation, but a reading that attempts to locate the structures of the texts and what produces those structures. Personal themes or the psychology of the author are less important than, for example, the conventions of the broader culture or the specific **genre** which writer and reader share. Locating these structures places the emphasis on the signifier rather than the signified, and demands an 'anthropological' detachment from the objects or process under analysis (see **signifying practice**).

In relation to film studies, Genette's development of **narrative** analysis has been influential and his extension of notions of intertextuality are also suggestive with regard to television. The logic of his structuralist position argued for the acceptance of **culture** outside canonical 'literatures' as an appropriate object of study: 'Fantomas (a super hero) and Bluebeard may not speak to us as intimately as Swann or Hamlet: they might have as much to teach us'.

References

Genette, G. (1984) *Figures of Literary Discourse, 1966–1972*, trans. Alan Sheridan, New York: Columbia University Press.
Stam, R., Burgoyne, R. and Flitterman-Lewis, S. (1992) *New Vocabularies in Film Semiotics*, London: Routledge.

PHILIP SIMPSON

genre

Genre refers to Hollywood's characteristic production formulas and the recognizably different types of films that these produce – the Western (see **Western, the**), **horror**, comedy and so on. Since the late 1960s, genre criticism has been central to film study, although the favoured genres and the terms of this criticism have shifted over time. Although much writing favours close textual analysis, it might encompass **theory**, criticism, **history**, reception (see **reading and reception theory**) and institutional analysis (see **institution**). Along with **authorship**, genre study helped to shift attention towards the collective meanings produced by a group of films, supplementing individual interpretations of isolated films.

During the 1960s and 1970s, film studies turned to genre criticism to correct some of the assumptions implicit within theories of authorship. Borrowing assumptions from high art, authorship positioned the director as the creative force behind a text and the main source of meaning, repressing the consequences of mass production and collaboration. Films were thus elevated out of the realms of popular culture and transformed into reputable subjects for study. At a popular level, authorship study helped hierarchize films (for example, in Andrew **Sarris**' *The American Cinema* [1968]), supporting the already on-going process of establishing canons of films in accordance with middlebrow tastes (see **canon**). Genre study challenged these ideas and standards of 'taste' acknowledging cinema's mass cultural roots and establishing new criteria for evaluation and new terms of analysis.

Genre reinstated cinema's collaborative, industrial aspects, considering films in relation to the production trends that organized and defined Hollywood production. Historically, studios have divided up production according to genre. Individual budgets and the number of films made in each genre were rationalized to offset costs (sharing sets and costumes over a number of films paid dividends) and to correspond with public tastes. The number of films in each genre varied according to their popularity, although the industry might sacrifice popular genres to save its own reputation during a crisis (as with gangster films in the early 1930s). Generally, though, Hollywood tries to repeat successes, creating variations on popular films that might, over time, stabilize into genres. The appeal of genres also varies with time: while the Western was popular during the 1920s, it lost its appeal for most of the 1930s, making a comeback with John Ford's *Stagecoach* (1939) and finding new audiences and new concerns. This revitalized the genre for the rest of the classical Hollywood period and beyond (see **classical Hollywood cinema and new Hollywood cinema**).

Given that most Hollywood films were (and are) essentially genre productions, it makes sense to analyse them within these terms and to explore the rules guiding the development of these collective variations on Hollywood form. As this line of investigation also depended on the relationships between the films, society and the Hollywood system, it opened up possibilities for social, historical and economic inquiry. However, much of the early work on genre instead concentrated on its conceptual possibilities, particularly in terms of the opportunities and limitations placed on textuality and narrative. While the 'formula filmmaking' characteristic of genre cinema was no longer disparaged, investigation of its characteristics merely replaced analysis of directorial signatures, continuing the predominantly textual approach of authorship criticism.

Early genre studies examined the defining features of specific genres, focusing on iconography (see **icon**), **narrative** and themes. Iconographic studies foregrounded the specificity of the Hollywood form, further extending genre's investment in the characteristics of popular film itself (Buscombe 1970). By focusing on **mise-en-scène**, costume, settings, characteristic images, visual metaphors and even stars (see **star system**), iconographic genre criticism was able to study how popular cinema transformed its concerns into images, and thus explored how the distinctive 'look' of each genre might articulate its own set of social concerns. Like other forms of genre criticism, iconographic analyses foregrounded the importance of **audience** foreknowledge. Supported by promotion from the studios, genres helped audiences to identify films largely on the basis of knowledge gained from prior exposure, establishing a range of audience expectations. This repetition, characteristic of the formulae nature of popular culture, established conventions (visual, narrative, formal) that audiences would quickly identify and understand, establishing a certain textual economy (see **conventions**). Thus audiences might immediately identify a Western through its landscape and setting or a gangster film through its costumes and props, and from these, draw certain inferences about character, themes and narrative.

As Christine Gledhill (1986) notes, these iconographic approaches lent themselves to establishing visual taxonomies for each genre. These tended to repress elements of visual style while narrative itself was generally ignored. Furthermore, the approach only seemed to work for selected genres, like the Western and the gangster film, which had their own distinct look. Consequently, the approach had limited value for some genres, none at all for others (like comedies), and said little about the process of genre as a whole. Elements of this approach persisted, however, as the process of identifying and interpreting specific generic features was extended to narrative, form and style. This led some genre critics (for example, Williams 1984) to outline comprehensive taxonomies and to posit 'ideal' films containing all of a specific genre's characteristic elements and patterns against which all other films in the genre might be measured. As Tom Ryall (1998) suggests, these 'theoretical', *a priori* genre films posit all genres as static and, furthermore, discuss each film in terms of what it *subtracts* from an overall formula. It thus limits any consideration of genre development and denies the social relevance of any individual film or group of texts.

Like auteur studies, genre criticism was strongly influenced by structuralism (see **structuralism and post-structuralism**). Its focus on films as systems seemed equally applicable to a genre or the collective body of a director's work, while its emphasis on the importance of repetition and **difference** offered ways to discuss the variation between films (and even between genres) without falling back on these subtractive 'theoretical' models. Structuralism called for examination of individual systems – be they films, genres or Hollywood cinema as a whole – in terms of their discrete nature and their relationship to one

another. Elements might exist across genres (e.g., romance, the formation of the couple) or be specific to individual genres (the gun-fight in a Western, for example, or the monster in a horror movie), but their significance and meaning varies according to the generic framework and within the genre itself. As Rick Altman (1989) points out, these elements can be arranged into quite different structures, which play an important role in distinguishing genres and establishing the necessary variations across individual films.

Much of this structuralist work also had an ideological dimension (see **ideology and hegemony**). The initial ideological motivations behind genre criticism – the importance of examining film as mass culture and the need to recognize and examine (rather than dismiss) the subtleties of the popular (see **popular, the**) – had been submerged beneath efforts to distinguish genres and examine their textual operations. Influenced by Claude **Lévi-Strauss**, Will Wright's 1975 structuralist analysis of the Western, *Sixguns and Society*, positioned genres as myths (see **myth**). Wright believed that genres represent a society's attempts to communicate with itself about its social organization, problems, customs, history and values. Like any myth, the Western contributed to American culture, as evidenced in the way its iconography and concerns entered the social imagination. Across the genre, films offer various solutions to shared problems, the most popular attracting the largest audiences and therefore offering the most cultural insight into a given historical moment.

Like Wright, Thomas Schatz (1981) highlights genre filmmaking's social importance. Drawing on both structuralism and sociology, he suggests that genres themselves fall into two larger meta-genres – 'rites of order' and 'rites of integration'. Genres of order usually focus on individual male protagonists, who are confronted with solving often violent problems in an unstable public space. The hero has to mediate between antagonistic forces and eliminate the threat, restoring order before he moves on. He is usually not integrated into society, but maintains his individuality – even at the cost of death. Schatz places Westerns, gangster films and detective films within this broader category, and one might also add science fiction, horror and action films. Genres of integration, on the other hand, are broadly feminine, focusing on couples or groups (like the family). They are set in stable, civilized, often private spaces, deal with emotional conflict and are concerned with social integration. Encompassing romance, musicals, screwball comedies and family melodramas (see **family melodrama**), these films explore personal and private desires. Together these genres explore aspects of the relationship between cinema and society, mapping narrative functions onto binary opposed gendered spheres. These films offer models for the resolution of social conflict, posing problems and offering certain solutions, but, as Schatz notes, Hollywood films are better at raising questions than answering them.

Schatz's schematic organization of genres presents certain problems. His invocation of sexual difference fails to account for the more complicated ways protagonists intersect with narrative, theme and setting within many genre films (certainly, for example, male melodramas like *Home From the Hill* [Vincente Minnelli, 1960] have no place in his taxonomy). Meanwhile, his construction of two overriding genres replays other problems in genre classification. His larger categories do, however, suggest ways in which 'feminine' genre films might deal with distinctly different worlds and issues from their 'masculine' counterparts, illuminating the ways in which Hollywood perceived its audiences as gendered subjects.

Other ideological genre criticism was influenced by Jean-Louis Comolli and Jean Narboni's 1969 editorial in *Cahiers du cinéma* (translated in *Screen* in 1971) which proposed a taxonomy of seven categories of film ('a' to 'g') based on their ideological status. Category 'e' was reserved for films that initially appeared to conform to the ideology of the society that produced them, but under closer investigation, revealed cracks and fissures that suggested an internal criticism of that ideology. This category inspired close analysis of many Hollywood films (which, of course, initially appeared as seamless representations of American ideology) for tell-tale ruptures. Once discovered, they evidenced the film's exceptional status as a critique of that society. As genre films had already been associated with social needs and identity, it was hardly surprising that this influenced genre

criticism. Certain genres were heralded for interrogating American ideology, with all its implied conservatism, and for revealing problems and discontinuities in its ways of seeing the world. As a result, critical attention turned towards such genres as **film noir**, **melodrama** and, later, the horror film. While other genres (like the Western) were labelled as dominantly conservative, select individual films, like *Pursued* (Raoul Walsh, 1947) and *The Searchers* (John Ford, 1956), were heralded for their critique of this world view.

While much of this work considered genres or genre films, its approach was quite different from the earlier work that attempted to define genres and place specific films. This had been thwarted by the very difficulty of categorizing films and drawing specific boundaries. Early studies of iconography, for example, relied on the premise that we know a genre when we see it, but as subsequent work proved, recognition was easier than locating a genre's parameters. Initial attempts to define genres faced the tautological problem of selecting the 'essential elements' from films that had already been located within that genre. Certain films were therefore cast as privileged members of a genre and definitions produced based on a limited selection of texts. As time passes, texts and genres change, suggesting that these models need to be historically specific to account for variations over time.

As Schatz (1981) notes, genres have to change because viewers get used to a specific formula. At the same time, the fact that a genre exists at all suggests that audiences like this kind of story so much that they want more variations. Over time, then, the genre has to renew itself, yet still retain some essential similarity. Furthermore, the similarity that defines a film as belonging to one genre rather than another might also change, leading to shifts in emphasis. Indeed, given that genres comment on contemporary social issues and problems, they have to change if they are to retain an audience and remain viable. Some genres, like the Western and the musical have lost their popularity as they no longer have any social relevance for contemporary audiences.

Rather than changing at random, though, Schatz suggests that genres systematically 'evolve'. First of all, they have to be established. Popular films inspire copies, and as the number of pictures based on a specific topic evolves, certain themes are favoured, a 'look' is developed and rules are set up. He calls this the 'experimental stage'. Here, popular films take 'external' or cultural events and adapt them into a movie, and as the process is refined, these events become part of the formula. This gradually becomes distanced from the reality that inspired it, becoming more of a 'formal element', especially as society itself changes. This leads to the 'classic stage', where the genre is at its most recognizable and transparent. Both audiences and producers understand the conventions, which the films follow carefully. After a while, to avoid saturating the audience, the genre becomes more stylized and embellished, becoming less transparent as it enters its period of 'refinement'. This move towards opacity culminates in the 'baroque' or 'self-reflexive' stage, where the genre shows its own awareness of itself, its limitations and its own history and plays with these possibilities. Westerns of the 1950s, like *The Searchers* for instance, play with the idea of the ageing cowboy who can no longer implement the law or act with the authority he once possessed, thus undermining their own original premises. Musicals of the 1950s similarly parody or play with the genre. In *The Band Wagon* (Vincente Minnelli, 1953), for example, Fred Astaire plays an outdated star of musical theatre whose revived career suggests the revision of the genre itself. Meanwhile its stylized musical numbers foreground their own impossibility as stage constructions, rendering them instead mediations on the possibilities of cinema. As Schatz summarizes (1981): 'As a genre's classic conventions are refined and eventually parodied and subverted, its transparency gradually gives way to *opacity*; we no longer look *through* the form (or perhaps "into the mirror") to glimpse an idealised self-image, rather we look *at the form itself* to examine and appreciate its structure and its cultural appeal.' Thus genres emphasize social matters early in their 'evolution', concentrating on form and **aesthetics** later, although both concerns are present throughout.

While Schatz's model of changing genres helps assess genres across time, it does not consider other developments that confuse and obscure definitions. It does not resolve some of the earlier dilemmas, like the problem of cross-genre films (e.g., singing Westerns or their A-film counterparts such as *Seven Brides for Seven Brothers* [Stanley Donen, 1954]) which fulfil the conditions of two separate and unrelated genres – even straddling Schatz's two meta-genres of 'order' and 'integration'. The ease with which genres combine also suggests that this is more of a problem for genre critics than audiences or producers.

The problem of what qualifies a group of films as a genre has never been adequately resolved. According to critics like Tom Ryall (1978), producers, audiences and the film itself all play an equal role in defining genres. Studios take into account audience expectations when producing the film, while during reception its meaning is produced by the audience intersection with the film and coloured by studio-produced promotional materials. While this model draws on genre as a pre-existing concept and framework, it does not define its characteristics nor account for its presence. On the other hand, studio-oriented industrial accounts (e.g., Staiger 1985) discuss how Hollywood rationalized and divided production, yet her work reveals categories like the B-film, prestige productions and current event 'headliners' that do not correspond to any genre within film studies. Critics have also distinguished between genres and cycles, the latter being short-lived variations on a theme or subject (possibly accounting for some of the studio's less well-known genres). This would make film noir a cycle, unlike the Western and comedy which are genres, unless film noir is more a visual style, found across genres. Besides, it is well known that film noir was 'discovered' by French critics several years after the films were produced, raising further questions about how the term should be used. Melodrama is another contested generic category. As Steve Neale (1993) has shown, contemporary academic use of the term does not match that of the film industry's own. In both cases, academics created these 'genres' after the fact, using models from literary criticism, suggesting that they have little relevance to the audience/text/producer triad Ryall proposes. But does this disqualify them from consideration as genres?

These kinds of difficult questions persist, forming the basis of genre theory. Recently, this has been supplemented by work on television genres and national cinema (see **national, the**), extending questions of genre beyond Hollywood film to the likes of British, French and Hong Kong cinema. Debates around genre have been renewed through emphases on different aspects of national culture and how this might be expressed through nationally specific genres such as the heritage film (see **heritage film and television**).

References

Altman, R. (1989) *The American Film Musical*, London: BFI Publishing.

Buscombe, E. (1970) 'The Idea of Genre in the American Cinema', *Screen*, vol. 11, no. 2, pp. 33–45.

Comolli, J.-L. and Narboni, J. (1971) 'Cinema/Ideology/Criticism' (first published 1969), translated in *Screen*, vol. 12, no. 1.

Gledhill, C. (1986) 'Genre', in P. Cook (ed.) *The Cinema Book*, London: BFI Publishing.

Neale, S. (1993) 'Melo Talk: On the Meaning and Use of the Term "Melodrama" in the American Trade Press', *The Velvet Light Trap*, no. 32, pp. 66–89.

Ryall, T. (1978) *Teachers Study Guide, No. 2: The Gangster Film*, London: BFI Education.

—— (1998) 'Genre and Hollywood', in J. Hill and P. Church Gibson (eds) *The Oxford Guide to Film Studies*, Oxford: Oxford University Press.

Sarris, A. (1968) *The American Cinema: Directors and Directions*, London: E. P. Dutton.

Schatz, T. (1981) *Hollywood Genres*, New York: Random House.

Staiger, J. (1985) 'The Producer-Unit System: After 1931', in D. Bordwell, J. Staiger and K. Thompson, *The Classical Hollywood Cinema: Film Style and Mode of Production to 1960*, London: Routledge.

Williams, A. (1984), 'Is Radical Genre Criticism Possible?', *Quarterly Review of Film Studies*, vol. 9, no. 2, pp. 21–5.

Wright, W. (1975) *Sixguns and Society: A Structural Study of the Western*, Berkeley: University of California Press.

Further reading

Collins, J. (1993) 'Genericity in the Nineties', in Jim Collins, Hilary Radner and Ava Preacher Collins (eds) *Film Theory Goes to the Movies*, London: Routledge.

Grant, B. K. (1986) *Film Genre Reader*, Austin: University of Texas Press.

—— (1995) *Film Genre Reader II*, Austin: University of Texas Press.

Neale, S. (1980) *Genre*, London: BFI Publishing.

MOYA LUCKETT

Glasgow University Media Group

From the mid-1970s, critical researchers based at Glasgow University, known collectively as the Glasgow University Media Group (GUMG), have undertaken a series of projects in support of an ongoing argument that the news in Britain (television and print) is biased in favour of powerful, elite points of view (see **bias**). In their groundbreaking study, *Bad News* (1976), which examined the content and language of televisual news reports of industrial relations issues, the GUMG concluded that the news carries out an important ideological role in wider processes of hierarchical economic and cultural reproduction (a conclusion they reaffirmed in later studies). Televisual newscasts present the opinions of the establishment, they argued, in ways that grant legitimacy to needs of capital at the expense of those of labour.

Commentators on the political right have criticized this conclusion for being politically ('left-wing') biased and some critical researchers have suggested that the GUMG assumes that all news is conspiratorially biased in favour of powerful groups in society. Most media commentators agree, however, that the GUMG has been successful in its aim of deconstructing journalistic claims to impartiality and **objectivity**.

See also: dominant ideology; ideology and hegemony

References

Bad News (1976) Glasgow Media Group, London: Routledge and Kegan Paul.

Further reading

Eldridge, J. (ed.) (1993) *Getting the Message: News, Truth and Power*, London: Routledge.

Philo, G. (ed.) (1999) *Message Received: Glasgow Media Group Research 1993–1998*, London: Longmans.

CYNTHIA CARTER

globalization

As we enter a new century, globalization has become a key term in understanding world conditions – economic, political and cultural. It refers to the complex configuration of forces and trends which increasingly transcend national borders in recent decades, creating what is more and more conceived as a 'world culture'. The processes by which such a situation emerges arise from complex developments in the workings of multinational corporate entities whose business dealings, and whose processes of production and **consumption**, increasingly operate on a global scale, eschewing the traditional legal, cultural and political institutions of nation-states.

Malcolm Waters' succinct definition of globalization is as follows: 'A social process in which the constraints of geography on social and cultural arrangements recede and in which people become increasingly aware that they are receding' (Waters 1995: 3). The momentum of such a process, taken to its logical conclusion, implies that at some point a single globalized **culture** and society will emerge to replace the nation-states and tribal entities that now divide and define global populations. Whether such a world culture will in fact arise, and when, is highly debatable. And even more debatable is the nature of such a society, should it actually emerge. Will it be, as cultural imperialists argue, a unified one dominated by an Americanized, western way of life? Or will it, rather, be characterized by great elements of difference, multicentricity and instability?

Whatever the long-term answers to such questions, there is no doubt that globalization is now a major factor in world events as well as local developments, nor is there doubt as to the origins of its development and momentum. While some would argue that the process of globalization originates with the very beginnings of human

history and is inevitable, most theorists see it as a distinctly western European development, at least in origin. Central to this entire process have been two important industrial developments. The rise of Fordist and post-Fordist methods of production by which vast amounts of consumer goods of all kinds are now quickly, efficiently and cheaply manufactured and distributed (see **Fordism**); and the rise and increasing complexity of electronic communication and entertainment media, which have made possible instantaneous global transmission of huge amounts of information and cultural product to virtually every part of the globe, creating the possibility of a truly universal world culture shared by peoples of diverse cultural, technological and economic status. Westernization, or Americanization, are terms often applied to this process, since, up until recently at least, most of the cultural product – films, television programmes, fast-food outlets, theme parks and consumer goods – which makes up the global culture has originated in the United States. Thus, the idea of cultural imperialism arises, in which US culture is seen as colonizing and usurping the indigenous cultures of less wealthy and less powerful nations.

The process has its roots in economic and social developments arising at the end of the Second World War, but its rapid growth and acceleration, and its widespread recognition as a *cultural* process with vast and profound implications begins in the 1980s. Also important is the rise of a world culture characterized by constant processes of migration and leisure travel, as labour power shifts follow the twists and turns of world markets and leisure travel becomes inexpensive and accessible enough for ever larger numbers of people to travel great distances.

All of these factors contribute to a situation that many characterize as post-modern, whereby cultures merge and blend and the homogeneous populations on which national identities were founded give way to a far more diverse and dynamic population in which national identities and cultures are increasingly destabilized and in a process of flux, and in which, increasingly, individual identities and cultures partake of and make reference to global trends (see **modernism and post-modernism**). Whether globalization is indeed a new development which radically transforms world culture and social and intellectual life, as the term 'post-modern' implies, or is rather a trend that has existed, in a much slower, less visible form, since the beginnings of European market capitalism several centuries ago, is highly debatable. But those who argue the latter position see the roots of globalization as inherent in the very beginnings of capitalism, since the need to expand markets has been an ever present function of capitalist logic, bringing with it an inevitable process of colonialism, imperialism and mass production and distribution of goods to global markets.

Classic theories

One of the theoretical debates surrounding globalization revolves around its origins: has it, in some form or another, been in process since the dawn of intentional human history? Has it emerged only with the rise of modernism and capitalism? Or is it a recent, largely cultural, phenomenon associated with post-industrialism and post-modernism? Many theorists have tackled this question, but the earliest and most important, in terms of social and cultural issues, were Emile Durkheim, Max **Weber** and Karl **Marx**. Durkheim (1984) was among the first to recognize and theorize the cultural significance of globalization when he observed the tendency of industrialization to weaken what he called 'the collective consciousness' of individual societies, breaking down allegiances to common rituals and beliefs and beginning the process by which the distinct boundaries separating cultures and societies begin to erode. Weber (1978) furthered the development of the theory by recognizing the tendency of rationalization, inherent in the process of industrialization, to chip away at group commitments to such nationalistic values as patriotism and religious belief. He did not, however, see this trend moving beyond European borders, to less intellectually developed cultures, as later writers would.

The most prescient of early social theorists in this area was undoubtedly Marx (1977) who most thoroughly understood and theorized the tendency of western industrialism to become globalized and imperialistic, and who recognized this trend as having both economic and cultural manifestations. He saw local industries being dislodged by new industries drawing raw materials from distant lands and the commerce and migration resulting from this giving way to new ways of life. Marx wrote that,

> In place of the old wants satisfied by the production of the country we find new wants, requiring... the products of distant lands and climes. In place of the old local and national seclusion and self-sufficiency, we have intercourse in every direction, universal interdependence of nations. The intellectual creations of individual nations become common property. National one-sidedness and narrow-mindedness become... impossible and... there arises a world literature.... National differences and antagonisms between peoples are daily... vanishing, owing to... freedom of commerce, the world-market, uniformity in the mode or production and to the conditions of life corresponding thereto.
>
> (Marx 1977: 224–5)

In these theories lie the core of current understanding of the process of globalization. But it is only a bit later, when the rapid development of mass media made clear the enormous cultural significance of the globalizing tendency, that media theorists took up the issue. For it is only with the modern development of electronic media as a globalized phenomenon that a truly global culture has been made possible. And with the rise of a global culture, theorists of globalization were at last confronted with immense impact of western media images on the consciousness of peoples everywhere. It was Marshall McLuhan (1964) who most famously theorized the concept 'the global village', in which world populations of diverse geographic, ethnic and cultural situations would, ultimately, come to exist, through the technologies of modern media and its global circulation of mediated images and narratives, in a common cultural community. McLuhan's theories, however, were based on radically deterministic assumptions about the primary driving force of technology in shaping society and history (much as Marx's were based on assumptions of economic determinism) and so were somewhat reductive and simplistic in their analyses of how media images and institutions actually develop and circulate. None the less, his insights into the power of mediated images to unify peoples across the globe were seminal to the process of globalization theory. For it has been symbolic, communicative exchange, far more than the more cumbersome and slow processes of economic or political exchange, which has most profoundly transformed the cultures and consciousnesses of people everywhere in ways which have worked to unite us.

McLuhan argued that this reorganization of space through time, what Anthony Giddens (1990) would later term 'time/space distanciation', would transform world cultures and societies. Because electronic media could be virtually instantaneous, he argued, it would make possible the bringing together of widely dispersed locations and events, creating the possibility for the re-emergence of ancient forms of tribalism but on a global scale. Benedict Anderson (1983) elaborated importantly on this aspect of globalization theory with his influential concept of the development of nations as 'imagined communities', replacing the Marxist identity structures based on **class**. Such a shift, argued Anderson, was made possible by the development of mass communication media which brought people together on the basis of cultural rather than economic commonalities.

Dependency and differentiation

In recent years, as the process of globalization has developed, allowing theorists to examine its dynamics and implications in a variety of locales and contexts over a period of time, much controversy has developed (particularly among media theorists) about the impact of the process both on western cultures – from which most texts originate and 'travel' – and on the less wealthy, less powerful cultures which are the recipients of western cultural product. The dominant paradigm, rooted in Marxist social theory, was developed most fully by the theorists of the **Frankfurt School**. They saw the 'culture industries' as a vast, monolithic, all-powerful force which through the power of its images could manipulate audiences (conceived of as an undifferentiated 'mass' of non-resistant, vulnerable minds) into accepting and internalizing messages. This would then produce the 'false consciousness' by which their own class (and now **race**, **gender** and ethnic) identities and interests would give way to beliefs and values which

supported the interests of the moneyed powerful classes who owned the media (see also **ethnicity**). With the advent of globalization, of course, such theories leant themselves easily to theories of 'cultural imperialism' and 'dependency' which saw poorer, less developed cultures and societies being irresistibly swayed toward beliefs and values that favoured the dominant western forces – primarily, of course, the US, which produced and profited from the media texts 'dumped' on them. Such theories are still widely employed by those whose primary focus is macro-economic and political forces and dynamics. This view is most widely connected today with the work of Herbert Schiller (1992). Such theories are implicitly infused with negative implications about the dire 'effects' of media on society and the powerlessness of audiences to resist. This model rests on notions of cultural imperialism and dependency theory, bolstered – at least implicitly – by the equally long-standing models of media reception based on 'hypodermic' and manipulation theories (see **hypodermic model**).

What stands at the centre of dependency theory is a view of culture which is highly economistic in the traditional Marxist sense, in which base and superstructure are seen as wholly separate and hierarchical in structure and the economics of corporate production, in the ideological service of state power, merely reflects and imposes this ideology on other, dependent nations through the conduits of ideological false consciousness which the culture industry generates (see **base and superstructure; economism**). To quote Schiller, 'though the economic measures of domination – control of capital markets and of the infrastructure of international finance – are well understood, the cultural-communications sources of power' are not. But these sources, according to Schiller:

> that influence consciousness are decisive determinants of a community's outlook and the nature and direction of its goals. Thus communication and the flow of messages and imagery *within* and among nations – especially between developed and dominated states – assume a very specific significance. What does it matter if a national movement has struggled for years to achieve liberation if that condition, once gained,

is undercut by values and aspirations derived from the apparently vanquished dominator?

(Schiller 1992: 1)

In recent years, such theories have been challenged by others who perceive the process of textual reception, by individuals and within cultures, as far more complex and dynamic than cultural imperialists assume. Starting with the ideas of reception theorists – in which readers of texts are seen not as wholly passive cultural dupes but as active readers and interpreters of texts, with the ability to 'read against the grain' and 'negotiate' meanings of texts at least to some extent (Radway 1984; Fiske 1987; Ang 1991) – analysts of the effects of globalization have increasingly employed theories of cultural resistance and cross-fertilization to demonstrate that western texts may take on far different meanings when viewed in different geographic and cultural contexts and communities, and by peoples with different assumptions and experiences.

In a well-known study made by Katz and Liebes (1985), different groups of readers – Palestinians living in Israel, Moroccan Jews and matched American groups in Los Angeles – representing different cultural and geographic conditions, made sense of the American prime-time soap opera *Dallas*, which for many years was broadcast and watched with enthusiasm and regularity by a huge audience all over the world, in ways which clearly reflected their own cultural and personal experiences and values (see **soap opera**).

However, works of this kind have themselves been subjected to criticism on the grounds that they give audiences too much control over the construction of the meaning of a text and fail to recognize the power of the text itself – and its economically and politically powerful producers – to incorporate certain cultural and ideological assumptions and values which cannot be fully negotiated and 'read' away. To critics like Armand Mattelart, for example, Katz and Liebes' work seemed to imply that audiences, whose own subjectivities had be formed by different cultural and social conditions and assumptions, could simply transfer those assumptions and ideals to the reading of a text produced in a vastly different cultural situation and confer on it their own

meanings. According to Mattelart, this research 'endorse[s] ... the idea of the absolute freedom of the consumer in the "choice of meaning" ' (Mattelart 1994: 237). Somewhere between these two extremes – the cultural imperialist and the pure reader-reception theory – lies what Sinclair *et al.* (1996) see as a 'middle range' form of analysis in which local and global, cultural and economic, macro and micro forces are seen, in each individual case, to work in unique and complex ways to produce a situation where texts and artefacts originating in the United States, once arriving at a distant point, subtly interact at the level of national, local and tribal institutional and personal sites in ways which alter the texts themselves. In so doing, this creates new cultural contexts in which local viewers experience and interpret the texts. This theorization allows for a way of seeing the process of globalization as having complex and mixed implications, and in which each context and each interpretive community subtly shapes the meaning of texts and its impact on local consciousness.

This formulation allows for the many profoundly important insights of cultural theorists from a wide variety of disciplinary sites who have carefully studied the actual complexities of the processes by which local cultures incorporate and subtly redefine and reshape cultural products as they receive them. As the Indian anthropologist Arjun Appadurai notes:

> The globalization of culture is not the same as its homogenization, but globalization involves the use of a variety of instruments of homogenization (armaments, advertising techniques, language hegemonies, and clothing styles) which are absorbed into local political and cultural economies, only to be repatriated as heterogeneous dialogues of national sovereignty, free enterprise and fundamentalism in which the state plays an increasingly delicate role: too much openness to global flows, and the nation-state is threatened by revolt – the China syndrome; too little, and the state exits the international stage, as Burma, Albania and North Korea in various ways have done. In general, the state has become the arbitrator of this *repatriation of difference* (in the form of goods,

signs, slogans, and styles). But this repatriation or export of the designs and commodities of difference continuously exacerbates the internal politics of majoritarianism and homogenization which is most frequently played out in debates about heritage.

(Appadurai 1990: 16)

Hamid Naficy develops this analysis concretely in a study of the reception of the Walt Disney film *The Little Mermaid* (John Musker, 1989) by his English-speaking Iranian daughter and German-speaking Iranian niece: 'The globalization of American pop culture does not automatically translate into globalization of American control. This globalized culture provides a shared discursive space where transnational audiences...localize it, make their own use of it, domesticate and indigenize it. They may think with American cultural products, but they do not think American' (Naficy 1993: 2). Louise Meintjes (1997) elaborates further, pointing out that 'to regulate and incorporate subordinate groups, the dominant class is forced to reformulate itself constantly so that its core values are not threatened. In reformulating itself it necessarily takes on some features of the subordinate groups that it suppresses'. And Geoffrey Reeves discusses the ' "liberating" role which the music of the dominant music producers may perform when located in the complex class and other mediation of different "national" societies' (Reeves 1993: 338).

Doreen Massey's (1991) work furthers this train of thought, suggesting that once a work or commodity travels abroad, it ceases to be 'American' in its original sense, even as its impact on the culture into which it enters changes slightly the nature of that 'original' culture too. There is no longer a clear sense of 'American culture' as the dependency theorists posed, then. Nor is there any way to clearly distinguish a cultural object – whether a television show, a McDonald's hamburger, Taco Bell enchilada or a brand-name sweater (for example, Benetton) as worn by the multicultural models who advertise it in magazines and billboards everywhere. And by the same token, as the process of globalization continues apace, the United States and other dominant western cultures themselves have been infiltrated and inflected by the cultural products and norms and styles of immigrants, visitors and imported cultural products too, creating a multicultural global scene in which no single environment can any longer be considered culturally 'pure' (see **multiculturalism**).

The implications of this cultural dispersion and diversity seem to support the radical theories cited earlier, in which globalization is seen to inexorably break down the boundaries and indeed the very viability of the nation-state, tending towards the creation of a unified global culture. However, it is far too soon to claim such assumptions have come close to being proven. There are many countervailing forces, economic and political, which mitigate against the easy dissolution of the system of nation-states in the near future, if at all.

References

Anderson, B. (1983) *Imagined Communities*, London: Verso.

Ang, I. (1991) *Desperately Seeking the Audience*, New York: Routledge.

Appadurai, A. (1990) 'Disjuncture and Difference in the Global Cultural Economy', *Public Culture*, vol. 2, no. 2, pp. 1–24.

Durkheim, E. (1984) *The Division of Labor in Society*, New York: Free Press.

Fiske, J. (1987) *Television Culture*, New York: Methuen.

Giddens, A. (1990) *The Consequences of Modernity*, Stanford: Stanford University Press.

Katz, E. and Liebes, T. (1985) 'Mutual Aid in the Decoding of *Dallas*', in Philip Drummond and Richard Patterson (eds) *Television in Transition*, London: BFI Publishing.

Marx, K. (1977) *Selected Writings*, ed. David McLellan, Oxford: Oxford University Press.

Massey, D. (1991) 'A Global Sense of Place', *Marxism Today*, June, pp. 226–43.

Mattelart, A. (1994) *Mapping World Communication*, Minneapolis: University of Minnesota Press.

McLuhan, M. (1964) *Understanding Media*, London: Routledge.

Meintjes, L. (1997) 'Paul Simon's Graceland: South Africa and the Mediation of Musical Meaning', *Ethnomusicology*, vol. 34, no. 1, pp. 37–74.

Naficy, H. (1993) *The Making of Exile Cultures: Iranian*

TV in Los Angeles, Minneapolis: University of Minnesota Press.

Radway, J. (1984) *Reading the Romance*, Chapel Hill: University of North Carolina Press.

Reeves, G. (1993) *Communication and the Third World*, New York: Routledge.

Schiller, H. (1992) *Mass Communication and American Empire*, Boulder: University of Colorado Press.

Sinclair, J., Jacka, E. and Cunningham, S. (1996) *New Patterns in Global Television: Peripheral Vision*, Oxford: Oxford University Press.

Waters, M. (1995) *Globalization*, London and New York: Routledge.

ELAYNE RAPPING

Godard, Jean-Luc

b. 1930

With the release of *A bout de souffle* in 1959, French cinema gave rise to one of its most brilliant talents, director Jean-Luc Godard. Godard's first feature film is a landmark of the *nouvelle vague* (the French New Wave), mixing an appropriation of Hollywood **genre** with a jump-cut editing style and irreverent attitude towards traditional filmmaking techniques. Above all, Godard represents a certain cinephilia – a love of the moving image – a passion fostered during his time as a critic for the influential film journal, *Cahiers du cinéma*. Here, under the auspices of André **Bazin**, Godard helped formulate the 'politique des auteurs' (see **authorship**).

Following a period of popular and critical success, the director's work during the late 1960s reflects a more experimental, modernist agenda. Godard embarked on a series of militant films, both fiction and non-fiction, constructing a series of austere, Marxist-Leninist political critiques. Since 1974, working with his companion and co-director, Anne-Marie Miéville, Godard has continued to work with both film and video. Perhaps the most ambitious of his later projects is *Histoire(s) du cinéma*, a series of documentaries that proclaim both Godard's love for the cinema and the medium's ultimate demise.

See also: Marxist aesthetics; modernism and post-modernism

ANDREW UTTERSON

Gramsci, Antonio

b. 1891; d. 1937

A Marxist activist and theorist, Gramsci's political activities focused on the potential self-rule of Italian workers and peasants, particularly those in the industrial city of Turin. His theoretical work addressed more abstract issues and made a substantial contribution to Marxist theory. His writings on hegemony, coercion and consent, **culture**, and the role of intellectuals in social movements have had a major impact on both contemporary political theory and cultural studies.

One of seven children, Gramsci was born into a lower middle-class family on the island of Sardinia. When Gramsci was about 6 years old, his father was imprisoned for alleged administrative abuses, an event which forced the family into poverty. At the age of eleven, he had to work in order to help support his family.

Gramsci eventually rose to become Secretary General of Italy's Communist Party. Under his leadership, the Party strove to forge a worker–peasant alliance. He organized working-class groups to lecture and inform peasant groups on strategies of incorporation in the revolution. In 1926 the fascist government of Mussolini arrested Gramsci for subversive activities. The prosecutor is reported to have lamented: 'We must stop this brain working for twenty years!' Although prison took a profound toll on Gramsci, it did not stop his brain from working. Indeed, it was in prison that Gramsci produced what has come to be known as the 'Prison Notebooks' – a collection of some thirty-three journals devoted to theory, philosophy and criticism.

In 1937, after eleven years in prison and only two days after receiving a full pardon, Gramsci died of a cerebral haemorrhage. *The Prison Notebooks* were smuggled out of his hospital room by his sister-in-law, Tania Schucht.

See also: ideology and hegemony; Marx, Karl; Marxist aesthetics

Further reading

Hoare, Q. and Nowell-Smith, G. (eds and trans) (1971) *Selections from the Prison Notebooks of Antonio Gramsci*, London: Lawrence and Wishart.

DANIEL BERNARDI

Grierson, John

b. 1898; d. 1972

Scottish **documentary** filmmaker and producer, John Grierson is often credited with having coined the term 'documentary' (although there is some dispute as to whether this is true or not). As founder of the British documentary movement, he is seen as the man behind the nation's 'true' contribution to the art of film. Grierson's interest in media predated his filmmaking career. Financed by a Rockefeller fellowship, he spent 1924–1927 in America studying the media and public opinion. His interests in mass observation shaped the aesthetic and social approach he would later bring to documentary filmmaking.

In 1929, Grierson helped to establish the Film Unit at the Empire Marketing Board, directing *Drifters* (1929) before going on to produce films with such documentarists as Alberto Cavalcanti, Basil Wright, Humphrey Jennings and Harry Watt. He sought 'a creative treatment of actuality', stressing both aesthetic treatment and the film's social impact. After being appointed to the Film Committee of the Imperial Relations Trust, he went to Canada and, in 1939, was appointed head of Canada's National Film Board. He spent the last years of his career working for Scottish television and teaching at Canada's McGill University.

See also: film movements

Further reading

Aiken, I. (1990) *Film and Reform: John Grierson and the Documentary Film Movement*, London: Routledge.
Winston, B. (1995) *Claiming the Real: The Griersonian Documentary and its Legitimations*, London: BFI Publishing.

MOYA LUCKETT

H

Habermas, Jürgen

b. 1929

Described by William Outhwaite (1994) as the 'most important social theorist of the second half of the twentieth century', Jürgen Habermas has reflected on the meaning of modernity in Europe, as a philosopher and a journalist. His contributions to European Marxism have included work on political participation, public opinion, legitimation and communication (see **Marx, Karl**).

His writings demonstrate a commitment to critique modernity, while also producing positive ideals for democratic political behaviour. In his early work, he argues that mass access to mediated debate has had a deleterious effect on the quality of public life. His work has also lent itself, however, to histories of public media, especially film culture, which are not antagonistic to mass entertainment in public spaces. Oskar Negt and Alexander Kluge (1993), major figures in New German Cinema, were influenced by his ideas when they wrote about alternative publics and film. Film theorist Miriam Hansen (1991) also pursued the public nature of film-going in her research of early Hollywood cinema. Habermas is widely used for good reason: he writes accessibly, as an ex-journalist, and passionately, as a true philosopher of the modern age.

See also: modernism and post-modernism

References

Hansen, M. (1991) *Babel and Babylon: Spectatorship in American Silent Film*, Cambridge, MA: Harvard University Press.

Negt, O. and Kluge, A. (1993) *The Public Sphere and Experience*, Minneapolis: Minnesota University Press.

Outhwaite, W. (1994) *Habermas: A Critical Introduction*, Cambridge: Polity Press.

Further reading

Habermas, J. (1987) *The Theory of Communicative Action* (volumes 1 and 2), Cambridge: Polity Press.

—— (1989) *The Structural Transformation of the Public Sphere*, Cambridge: Polity Press.

STEPHANIE DONALD

Hall, Stuart

b. 1932

Stuart Hall grew up in the 1930s in a middle-class Jamaican family. He gained a scholarship to Oxford and left Jamaica in the 1950s to study, going on to teach in secondary schools and colleges in Britain. In 1964 Hall was invited by Richard **Hoggart** to serve as his deputy at the proposed Centre for Contemporary Cultural Studies (CCCS) in Birmingham. Hall became outright head of the CCCS from the late 1960s, following Hoggart's departure for UNESCO, and led the Centre until 1979.

Under Hall's direction, graduate work in Birmingham moved away from literary-based, left-liberal observational studies towards a European Marxism, drawing heavily on sociology and incorporating both feminism and theories of **race**. During this period, the Centre fostered a new intelligentsia in British cultural studies, including Paul Willis, Dick Hebdige, Iain Chambers, Paul Gilroy, Angela McRobbie, Dorothy Hobson and Charlotte Brunsdon. Much of the group's theoretical project emerged in the regular journal *Working Papers in Cultural Studies*, and work was collected in the volumes *Resistance Through Rituals* (1975) and *Policing the Crisis* (1979).

From 1980 until his retirement, Hall was Professor of Sociology at the Open University in the UK. He now holds an honorary position at Goldsmiths' College, University of London.

Further reading

Morley, D. and Chen, K.-H. (eds) (1996) *Stuart Hall: Critical Dialogues in Cultural Studies*, London: Routledge.

WILL BROOKER

Haraway, Donna

b. 1944

Donna Haraway is a feminist biologist and historian of science who analyses the discourses of **race** and **gender** in science and popular culture. Working with and against socialist feminism, feminist philosophy and Foucauldian theory (see **Foucault, Michel**), she is perhaps best known for her development of the concept of the cyborg: a post-modern being that breaches the boundaries between organism and machine, human and animal, male and female, self and other (see **modernism and post-modernism**). Haraway argues against a recourse to 'nature' for a feminist politics addressing the lethal patriarchal use of biological or electronic technologies; instead, she argues for embracing and subverting them, creating 'a cyborg world...in which people are not afraid of their joint kinship with animals and machines, not afraid of permanently partial identities' (Haraway 1991).

Haraway's writing has been used to contest the hegemony of psychoanalytical models of identity within film theory (see **psychoanalysis**), and to provide an analysis of the interrelated discourses of race and gender. Moreover, her theories offer possibilities for a feminist science fiction cinema that does not capitalize on the fear of the **Other**, but celebrates fragmented and marginalized identities.

See also: cyberspace; feminist theory; patriarchy; science fiction

References

Haraway, D. (1991) 'A Cyborg Manifesto', in Donna Haraway, *Simians, Cyborgs and Women*, London: Free Association Books.

Further reading

Haraway, D. (1992) *Primate Visions*, London: Verso.

ANTJE LINDENMEYER

Hegel, Georg Wilhelm Friedrich

b. 1770; d. 1831

A hugely influential philosopher, Hegel unified idealism (see **materialism and idealism**) with a philosophy of history in which *Geist* – a fusion of the human mind with transcendent spirit – is present in a dialectic of thesis, antithesis and synthesis. These describe a process of historical change whereby individuals' relation with society evolves around the initially antagonistic poles of freedom and social cohesion. History controls us in so far as we fail to understand the dialectical form that *Geist* takes. Once understanding is achieved, via the laws of reason, when mind recognizes itself as the ultimate reality, then absolute knowledge brings absolute freedom. Hegel's view of freedom is not, however, based on individuals' empirical desires, but rather in their rational self-realization.

While his style scarcely aids interpretation, difficulties are also inherent in the nature of his ideas themselves. Despite this, his emphasis on the historical roots of conceptual change has been of immense importance. Although substituting material economic forces for *Geist*, **Marx** preserved the notion of an end state – Communism – towards which history was ineluctably moving. Hegel's emphasis on mind also influenced **phenomenology**, as in Jean-Paul Sartre's existentialist work, *Being and Nothingness*.

Further reading

Singer, P. (1983) *Hegel*, Oxford: Oxford University Press.

TREVOR GIGG

heritage film and television

These predominantly British film and television productions are usually set in the past, highlighting moments of national history and glory (such as Elizabethan England or the nineteenth century). They might deal with historically significant people and events or adapt acclaimed literary texts for the screen. In either case, the majority present themselves as part of Britain's literary or cultural heritage.

Heritage film and television is generally linked to literary and cultural tradition and marked as 'prestige' productions. Examples include the films of Ismail Merchant and James Ivory (for example, *A Room with a View*, 1985), costume dramas, adaptations of Shakespeare and serializations of nineteenth-century novels. A heritage production will often use respected actors connected to the theatre (for example, Maggie Smith, the late Sir John Gielgud). Many performers are associated with costume dramas, preserving an undisturbed illusion of the past. Some stars, like Helena Bonham Carter, even bring further links through family ties to the British establishment and minor aristocracy. None the less, these productions are essentially middlebrow and conservative in their form and content.

While heritage dramas have been produced since the silent era, they have recently become more visible. This corresponds to the revived interest in promoting a mythic – mainly English – national identity that developed during the 1980s, affecting the tourist industries as well as cinema and television (see **national, the**). This involved selecting elements from the national past, which were then used to reshape British identity, foregrounding its perpetuation of tradition. Heritage industries were consolidated to market the nation in terms of its historical details: its pastoral landscapes, country houses and gardens, stately homes, churches, ruined castles and other buildings of conventional historical interest. Besides presenting a decorative image rooted in 'antiquity', these endeavours also promoted the specific forms of 'morality' and '**culture**' which these institutions were believed to represent.

Like the heritage industries themselves, heritage film and television advance a specifically bourgeois image of the nation, cloaked in sympathetic nostalgia. As Andrew Higson (1995) has observed in his extended study of the heritage film, these texts market England, not Britain, confining their interest to southern counties and promoting a conservative, middle-class, non-industrial image of the nation. Like the tourist industries, they see heritage as uplifting and 'in the national interest'. Sympathetic towards the **class** structure, they take a romantic approach towards communities and the national character, glossing over contradictions and inequities and repressing social change.

Higson also notes that these productions position the past as an irrecoverable ideal. While it is closed off from the present, the past points to contemporary failings and foregrounds the supremacy of lost values, commodities and ways of life. Heritage film and television often present a fundamentally rural or pastoral nation, projecting an image of a stable, unchanging and 'essential' England sheltered from fast-paced modernity. In contrast, any focus on the city would require some acknowledgement of industrialization, change, dirt, poverty and social inequity. This emphasis on the countryside instead constructs a vision of community, where each individual has his or her place in society, and everyone works together for the common good as opposed to the isolation, atomization and chaos associated with urban and industrial spaces.

This focus on a limited national landscape, coupled with the decorative impulse characteristic of such productions, suggests that these genres create their own sense of 'reality'. As Higson notes, they value authenticity, especially in terms of settings and props where the object's historic **aura** communicates the unchanging values, essential 'truth' and overwhelming superiority of the past. At the same time, this very **mise-en-scène** creates a self-consciously historical **diegesis**, rather than a sense of everyday life set back in time. The emphasis on details, costumes, *mise-en-scène*, and settings slows down pacing, suggesting that the image of the past is more important than the individual acts or desires which inform the **narrative** (see **desire**).

For Higson, heritage films and television constitute a British **genre** or sub-genre. Besides dealing with specifically British (or English) material, they incorporate film and television into British heritage, reclaiming them from Hollywood domination. This makes the heritage film an important element of national cinema, departing from Hollywood conventions in terms of form, content and style. Instead, these genres owe their particular formal attributes – including a certain theatricality – to such elements of the national heritage as literature and portraiture.

See also: memory

References

Higson, A. (1995) *Waving the Flag: Constructing a National Cinema in Britain*, Oxford: Clarendon Press.

MOYA LUCKETT

hermeneutics

The term 'hermeneutic' refers either to a text's establishing an enigma, which it later resolves, or to the reader's own attempted resolution of the puzzle. As the concept is employed by Roland **Barthes** (1974), a film's hermeneutic **code**, for instance, consists of those visual and verbal strategies used to develop a question for the viewer (for instance, the identity of a killer), to which it later provides an answer.

Hans Georg Gadamer's hermeneutics (1979), however, seeks to describe the reader's response to the experience of uncertain meaning found in the text which he/she is viewing. Invariably, but in ways which are empirically complex, this response will be to construct sense-making narratives. Hermeneutics of this kind has functioned as a methodological resource for reception studies of television audiences, supplying such concepts as 'horizon' and 'projection' of understanding (see **reading and reception theory**). In Allen's (1985) writing, for instance, a viewer's 'horizon of expectations' is his or her set of assumptions, drawing on a common knowledge of programme type or **genre**, about likely textual content. According to Radway (1984), again influenced by hermeneutics in establishing how books are consumed, readers make narrative 'projections': they anticipate a story's development, and later scrutinize their predictions for accuracy.

Most importantly, Gadamer's account of the sense-making activities of readers as 'play' is echoed in the widespread understanding of audience responses to television as being ludic. Play-like to and fro scrutiny of content elicits a meaning for a text, while distracting the reader from everyday concerns.

From a methodological perspective, hermeneutic theory urges that in studying audiences, examining their construction of programme meaning is fundamental. It must be distinguished from the erroneous empiricist project of trying to investigate viewers' responses to content whose meaning is taken as already given (see **empiricism**). **Uses and gratifications** theory, for instance, supported inquiry which assumed that audience use of a text had no bearing on how it was understood by them.

Hermeneutic theory, in short, argues that:

1 understanding a text is an interpretative process open to analysis as a 'fusion of horizons', in which the perspectives of those in the programme (indeed of its author; see **authorship**) and those to be found among the audience play against each other to produce new meaning;

2 textual interpretation juxtaposes recognizing a programme's familiarity (allowing understanding to begin with broad awareness of its genre, for instance) alongside the experience of its strangeness, of the cognitive distance between

reader and that which is to be read, a distance (or tension) which must be overcome (released) if understanding is to be attained;

3 understanding employs a 'fore-project', a set of initial assumptions about textual meaning (derived from its familiarity) which the 'facts' of a developing story-line may subsequently require to be revised; the continuing process of checking the fore-project against emerging parts of the programme defines the 'hermeneutic circle' in which a coherent reading of textual content is completed; and

4 understanding is ludic, possessing many features of play, including its fluidity of interaction with a (necessarily open) text, and the pleasurable release which attends its final moments of success.

Hermeneutic theory is to be criticized for overemphasizing the reader's concern to establish textual coherence. The contradictions that it diagnoses are never ideological but merely those of conflict between readers' assumptions and textual content. A hermeneutic account of reading leaves space for gendered (or ethnic and **class**) differences in understanding, but provides little assistance in their interpretation (see also **ethnicity; gender**). The possibility of a reader's critical self-distancing from a text's horizons of understanding the world is scarcely entertained.

See also: phenomenology

References

Allen, R. (1985) *Speaking of Soap Operas*, Chapel Hill: University of North Carolina.
Barthes, R. (1974) *S/Z*, London: Cape.
Gadamer, H. G. (1979) *Truth and Method*, London: Sheed and Ward.
Radway, J. (1984) *Reading the Romance*, Chapel Hill: University of North Carolina.

Further reading

Buckingham, D. (1987), *Public Secrets*, London: BFI Publishing.
Wilson, T. (1995) *Watching Television Hermeneutics:* *Reception and Popular Culture*, Cambridge: Polity Press.

TONY WILSON

heteroglossia

'Heteroglossia' is used by Mikhail **Bakhtin** to suggest the chief quality of the novel. A novel can contain a number of figures from many parts of society whose speech helps define their characters. A novel can also include different kinds of narrators with many possible tones. The several voices united in a novel represent a world of rich interrelationships between kinds of speech and types of people. Bakhtin's term for this verbal and social richness is translated as heteroglossia (literally, 'different tongues'). It applies to film and television as they may also hold a multitude of voices and visual styles.

See also: dialogic

GABRIEL M. PALETZ

hierarchy of discourses

Michel **Foucault** hypothesizes that within every society 'the production of discourse is at once controlled, selected, organised and redistributed according to a certain number of procedures, whose role is to avert its powers and its dangers, to cope with chance events, to evade its ponderous, awesome materiality' (Foucault 1972: 216). He argues that we, as individuals, are all familiar with how these hierarchical relations of prohibition and exclusion work – indeed, by their very *naturalness* or *obviousness*, they frequently pass unnoticed. According to Foucault, 'we know perfectly well that we are not free to say just anything, that we cannot simply speak of anything, when we like or where we like; nor just anyone, finally, may speak of just anything' (*ibid.*). In seeking to correlate this sense of what the individual 'knows perfectly well' to the circulation of discourses across society, the concept of a 'hierarchy of discourses' usefully underscores the thesis that any claim to knowledge or truth is necessarily embedded in unequal relations of power and resistance.

See also: discourse; discourse analysis; ideology and hegemony

References

Foucault, M. (1972) 'The Discourse on Language', Appendix in *The Archaeology of Knowledge*, New York: Pantheon.

STUART ALLAN

high concept

'High concept' is a term that was coined by the American film and television industry to describe productions which are primarily market-driven and distinguished by stars, visual style, advertising concepts and merchandising potential. This production practice grew out of the corporate integration of the entertainment media, the rise of new distribution formats such as home video and cable, and the subsequent emphasis on market research and segmentation. High concept projects are conceived as cross-media marketing campaigns that incorporate a wide range of outlets and ancillary products, such as soundtrack recordings, novelizations, television publicity, music videos and licensed merchandise.

Further reading

Wyatt, J. (1994) *High Concept: Movies and Marketing in Hollywood*, Austin: University of Texas Press.

SARAH BERRY

historiography

Historiography means, literally, 'the writing of history'. The word is derived from the Greek, *historia*, learning by inquiry or by extension narrating what one has learned, and *grapho*, to scratch marks on a tablet and therefore to write or inscribe. A simplistic view holds that historians discover facts which serve as a transparent window on a past that exists independently of the ways in which historians write their histories. But, as most historians now acknowledge, the writing of history is far more problematic than this. Historians must constantly address (sometimes implicitly and sometimes explicitly) several questions that fundamentally structure their writing of history. What subjects are worthy of study? What constitutes reliable evidence? How should this evidence be organized and presented? What interpretations does it justify or exclude? Historians have struggled with these questions since history emerged as a discipline separate from literature and history in the nineteenth century.

One of the founders of the historical discipline, the German scholar Leopold von Ranke, famously declared that the task of the historian was to show history as it actually was ('wie es eigentlich gewesen'). Ranke believed that while the writing of history necessarily involved subjective judgements, historians should have as their ultimate goal the revelation of the essential truth of history, that is, a perfect fit between a written history and the past events it represented. Other historians have rejected the possibility of a perfectly accurate reconstruction of the past, arguing that the fit between written histories and past events must always be contingent and subject to revision. This latter tendency has been encouraged by the advent of post-structuralism and post-modernism, both of which have radically challenged the existence of an objective reality outside the boundaries of linguistic representation and cultural conventions (see **modernism and post-modernism; structuralism and post-structuralism**).

The most radical of current historians would argue that history as past event does not exist except in the form of always already textualized representations, requiring a thorough re-conception of conventional historiographic practices. For example, Alan Munslow argues that 'because today we doubt... empiricist notions of certainty, veracity and a socially and morally independent standpoint, there is no more history in the traditional realist sense, there are only possible narrative representations in, and of, the past, and none can claim to know the past as it actually was' (Munslow 1997: 16). Munslow explicitly rejects the standard to which Ranke wished to hold historians. Richard Evans remains more sympathetic to the Rankean project: 'I will look humbly at the past and say... it really happened, and we really can, if we are very scrupulous and careful and self-critical, find out how it happened and reach some tenable though always less than final conclusions about what it all meant' (Evans 1997: 3). Both Munslow and Evans address debates about the representation of history in an era when critical theory challenges the fundamental processes of representation – language, **narrative**, the **image**.

The problem of narrative

To exemplify the complexities of writing history, we need to consider the question of narrative, that is, how historians tell stories. Prominent historian Simon Schama (1998) has argued that academic historians no longer speak to the general public because, rather than telling stories about individuals and groups of individuals, they organize their materials thematically, in terms of politics or economics or other non-personal historical forces. But narrative is a notoriously slippery word, and Schama implies a rather narrow definition that entails human **agency**. Some historians would argue that writing a history always entails writing a narrative: 'Every work of history has the structure of plot with a beginning, middle, and end. . . . Thus, to argue for a return to narrative, as some traditionalists have done, is to miss the cardinal point that historians have never entirely departed from it' (Appleby *et al.* 1994: 231). A beginning, middle and end are fairly minimal components of narrative; necessary but not sufficient for a definition. Prominent historiographer Hayden White (1978), well known for his speculation on history and narrative forms, adds two other components.

> Theorists of historiography generally agree that all historical narratives contain an irreducible and inexpungeable element of interpretation. . . . The historian must 'interpret' his materials by filling in the gaps in his information on inferential or speculative grounds. A historical narrative is . . . necessarily a mixture of adequately and inadequately explained events, a congeries of established and inferred facts, at once a representation that is an interpretation and an interpretation that passes for an

explanation of the whole process mirrored in the narrative.

> (*ibid.*: 51)

White's explanation and interpretation are again necessary but not sufficient. The kinds of explanations and interpretations that historians make often involve causality; a beginning, middle, end, explanation, interpretation and causality constitute the minimum sufficient components of a definition of narrative. This introduces the question of causality, a problem that philosophers have wrestled with since at least the time of the ancient Greeks. At the most basic level, causality is a temporal connection between events. It may take the form of x produces y produces z. Of course, strictly speaking, this would be a definition of monocausality rather than causality, which might well take the rather more complicated form of a, b, c and x produce d, e, f and y produce g, h, i and z. In fact, E. H. Carr, a leading formulator of historiographic practices, believed, according to Richard Evans, 'that it was the historian's duty to look for a variety of causes of any given event, work out their relationship to one another if there was one, and arrange them in some kind of hierarchy of importance. Causes had to be ordered as well as enumerated' (Evans 1997: 129). But, as Evans points out, the problem of overdetermination often renders difficult the application of Carr's injunction. Events as Evans says, 'may have several sufficient as well as necessary causes, any one of which might have been enough to trigger the event on its own'. Yet Evans concludes that historians usually 'see it as their duty to establish a hierarchy of causes and to explain if relevant the relationship of one cause to another' (*ibid.*: 58).

A brief history of film history

The matter of causation has been key to debates over the writing of film and television history, particularly the tension between the agency of individuals or groups of individuals and that of impersonal historical or textual determinants. Film histories began to be written as early as the 1920s, but it was not until the 1960s that academic film studies became widely accepted in Britain and the United States. Striving to establish themselves as the equal of those in the more traditional disciplines, scholars in these countries sought to position film as **art** by propounding the theory of **authorship**. While the French *Cahiers du cinéma* school championed authorship, it also took up other concerns of its intellectual leader, André **Bazin**, focusing on other issues such as **genre**, **realism** and **film movements**. But British and American 'auteurists' took a rather more simplistic approach, identifying a single controlling mind, usually that of the director, as the primary artist responsible for a film text. Film history became the story of great directors and great films. The authorship approach accounted for historical change in terms of individual agency, but it was a deliberately ahistorical history, predicated on the belief that the aesthetic operates independently of history and ideology. Andrew **Sarris**, whose position as Professor at Columbia University and weekly columnist for *The Village Voice* made him one of the most high profile American proponents of the authorship approach, famously claimed that the measure of a director's greatness lies in his ability to transcend his historical circumstances, particularly the constraints of the producer-dominated studio system. Sarris writes that, 'the auteur theory values the personality of the director precisely because of the barriers to its expression. It is as if a few brave spirits had managed to overcome the gravitational pull of the mass of movies' (Sarris 1968: 31).

The social and cultural upheavals of the 1960s that produced a radical questioning of conventional academic approaches to texts had a profound impact on film studies, producing an emphasis on structuralism, **psychoanalysis** and ideology (see **ideology and hegemony**). Drawing on intellectual developments in France, British scholars associated with the journal *Screen* propounded what became known as **Screen theory**, which postulated a hypothetical spectator whose responses were totally determined by the ideological operations of the text. Here historical causality was attributed to impersonal forces rather than human agency. With some significant exceptions, such as the very influential 'Cinema/Ideology/ Criticism' by Jean-Luc Comolli and Jean Narboni (1976), these perspectives produced a curiously ahistorical film history, centred around the similar underlying structures, or universal psychic drives or dominant ideology that determined film content.

Authorship theory and *Screen* theory isolated producers, texts and spectators from their historical context, but in the 1980s, following on from the pioneering work of Robert Sklar (1994) and Garth Jowett (1976), a new generation of film scholars of a more empirical bent attempted to locate film industries, films and audiences within the fullness of a specific historical moment. Film history became closely aligned to social history, itself a relatively new phenomenon within the traditional historical profession. This perspective, perhaps most influentially set forth in E. P Thompson's *Making of the English Working Class*, published in 1963, shifted many historians' attention from political, intellectual and military history to the history of the everyday lives and culture of non-elites. Film historians influenced by social history looked at the way in which transformations in the **institution** of the cinema related to broader social and cultural transformations: the causality of film history became coterminous with the multiple causalities of history explored by social historians. The conjunction between film history and social history can be seen most clearly in the writings of film scholars about pre-First World War American cinema, which relates the film industry, the films it produced and the audiences it attracted to the social and cultural upheavals attendant on rapid urbanization and massive immigration.

Film and television historiography

This section focuses more closely on the issue of causality by examining the paradigms of historical change employed by various schools of film historians. I draw heavily on Robert C. Allen's and Douglas Gomery's *Film History: Theory and Practice*, which although written in 1985, still remains the best and most accessible discussion of the practice of film history, and by extension television history, and the largely as yet to be written histories of new media.

Individual agency

Aesthetic film histories, those which conceive of cinema primarily as an art form rather than a social phenomenon, attribute causality to individuals or groups of individuals, and examine directors, styles of filmmaking and artistic movements. Given that the directors were almost invariably male, another term for this approach is 'great man' history. In the 1970s most academic film historians abandoned this paradigm; indeed the reaction against it has been so extreme that serious discussions of the agency of individuals (writers, directors, producers) have only begun to re-emerge in the 1990s and usually with regard to television rather than the film industry. A consensus is beginning to emerge in television studies that American producers, those who run the companies which supply programming to the networks and cable channels, have a very direct impact on textual content and programming trends. Gripsrud argues that, 'while the industry's organization and functions may be said to provide a basic tendency toward the *sameness* of texts...the vital *difference* between texts...their *specificity*, can only be fully accounted for with regard to the actual people involved in leading roles in the production process' (Gripsrud 1995: 53). Such producers as Gene Roddenberry and Rick Berman (*Star Trek*), Steven Bochco (*Hill Street Blues*, *NYPD Blue*) and David E. Kelley (*Picket Fences*, *Ally McBeal*) have the status of creator in the US television industry. In Britain, where, by contrast to the United States, much production is in-house and series typically have much shorter runs, the writers (for example, Dennis Potter, Jimmy McGovern, Alan Bleasdale) are seen as the key creative figures.

Technological determinism

Causality is impersonal in this model: technology is conceived of as a force relatively impervious to or completely escaping human agency. Much of the current discussions concerning digital technology (see **digital communication**) and the **Internet** have technological determinism as their implicit model. Many of the advocates of these new phenomena argue that technology will continue to advance at a rapid rate, creating profound changes for the better in culture and society. Others argue that technology is always secondary to the economic motivations and social configurations that determine whether innovations will or will not

be taken up. For example, Brian Winston (1998) has formulated the 'the "law" of the suppression of radical potential' which asserts that powerful financial and political factions can advance or block technological advances depending on whether or not they accord with their interests (see **technological change**). This law helps to explain why the best technology does not always win, as in the case of the United States' adoption of the markedly inferior NTSC format or the case of the VHS format triumphing over the Betamax format.

Economic

Allen and Gomery (1985) distinguish between two economic paradigms: Marxist analysis and industrial analysis. The Marxist approach, often referred to as the political economy paradigm, assumes that ideology, in the form of aspects of the superstructure such as law, religion and communication, legitimizes the power of the ruling class (see **base and superstructure; Marxist aesthetics**). The actions of media industries and the content of the texts they produce must ultimately be understood in terms of upholding the **dominant ideology**. Media studies research on Americanization, **globalization** and cultural imperialism has been strongly inflected by Marxist political economy. Many critics believe that the economic power of American-based **multinational** media organizations leads to the world-wide distribution of film and television texts that exalt American values at the expense of local ones. Allen and Gomery cite Thomas Guback's *The International Film Industry: Western Europe and America Since 1945* as fitting this paradigm, since he characterizes the relationship between the two players as an example of economic imperialism, in which the stronger America exploits the weaker western Europe. The industrial analysis paradigm, unlike the Marxist political economy paradigm, ascribes no ideological motivations to economic actors but, rather, sees them as rationally striving to assure long-term profitability within a capitalist mode of organization. From this perspective, the international distribution of American media products is seen as rational behaviour rather than ideological conspiracy.

Social

The social historian is concerned with the ways in which institutions and structures determine and constrain the actions of individuals. An aesthetic film historian might ask: 'How is Alfred Hitchcock's personal vision reflected in his films?' A social film historian might ask: 'Did differently organized film industries on either side of the Atlantic produce a distinctively "English Hitchcock" and "American Hitchcock"?' Alan and Gomery write that:

> A comprehensive social history of Hollywood would at least include an examination of 1) the organizational structure of the studios 2) the recruitment of personnel 3) the division of labor within each studio 4) the roles played by various participants in the film production process 5) the star system 6) the immediate social context outside the studio (the Hollywood community) and 7) public discourse on Hollywood and the film industry.
>
> (Alan and Gomery 1985: 155)

Since Alan and Gomery in 1985, film historians have addressed many of these issues. One of the best examples of the social history approach is Bordwell, Staiger and Thompson's *Classical Hollywood Cinema* (1985), which relates the day-to-day operation of the studios and the actions of agents fulfilling roles in industrial structures to film style. **Aesthetics** are seen as partially determined by, rather than transcending, industrial organization.

References

Allen, R. C. and Gomery, D. (1985) *Film History: Theory and Practice*, New York: Alfred A. Knopf.

Appleby, J., Hunt, L. and Jacob, M. (1994) *Telling the Truth About History*, New York: W. W. Norton and Company.

Bordwell, D., Staiger, J. and Thompson, K. (1985) *The Classical Hollywood Cinema: Film Style and Mode of Production to 1960*, New York: Columbia University Press.

Comolli, J.-L. and Narboni, J. (1976) 'Cinema/Ideology/Criticism', in Bill Nichols (ed.) *Movies and Methods*, Berkeley: University of California Press.

Evans, R. (1997) *In Defence of History*, London: Granta Books.

Gripsrud, J. (1995) *The Dynasty Years: Hollywood Television and Critical Media Studies*, London and New York: Routledge.

Jowett, G. (1976) *Film: The Democratic Art*, Boston: Little Brown.

Munslow, A. (1997) *Deconstructing History*, London: Routledge.

Sarris, A. (1968) *The American Cinema: Directors and Directions 1929–1968*, New York: E. P. Dutton and Co.

Schama, S. (1998) 'Clio at the Multiplex: What Hollywood and Herodotus Have in Common', *New Yorker*, 19 January, pp. 38–43.

Sklar, R. (1994) *Movie-Made America: A Cultural History of American Movies* (revised and updated 2nd edn; first published 1975), New York: Vintage Books.

White, H. (1978) *Topics of Discourse: Essays in Cultural Criticism*, Baltimore: Johns Hopkins University Press.

Winston, B. (1998) *Media Technology and Society: A History – From the Telegraph to the Internet*, London: Routledge.

ROBERTA E. PEARSON

history

Cinema and television relate in a complex fashion to western culture's dual conception of history as past events and as the representation of those past events. Past events can only be accessed through textual representations, yet most people's **common sense** understanding of history presumes that those past events have an objective, factual reality regardless of their subsequent textualization. The media take part in historical processes as they occur and represent them once they have occurred. The relationship between history and the screen media takes several forms: (i) the history of these media; (ii) the impact these media have on history; (iii) the use of these media as historical evidence; and (iv) the manner in which these media represent history. Point one is addressed in the entry on **historiography**, which considers the approaches media scholars have taken to the history of film and television. This entry briefly discusses points two and three and then undertakes a lengthier consideration of point four, this being the topic to which film and television scholars have to date devoted the most attention.

The impact of the media on history

The print media have always played a role in the historical process, as in, for example, the translation of the Bible into the vulgate as part of the Protestant reformation, or the use of the press by working-class radicals in Britain in the nineteenth century. Since their inception, the image-based media have been viewed by social elites as constituting both a greater threat to social stability and a more powerful tool for social change than ever the print media were. As historians of early cinema have demonstrated, from roughly the first decade of the twentieth century, social elites perceived the new film medium as tied to the period's rapid social transformations such as urbanization, and, in the United States, immigration. In the western democracies, social elites sought to control the medium through regulation of exhibition venues and **censorship** of film texts, as well as to use it for their own ends of 'uplifting' or 'bourgeoisfying' the perceived under-classes. In the 1920s and 1930s, the rulers of autocratic societies, such as Soviet Russia or Nazi Germany, supported film industries that produced **propaganda** films aimed at persuading the populace of the rightness of the new social order, while during the Second World War both Britain and the United States produced propaganda films of their own to boost the morale of civilian populations.

As the first truly mass medium, able to overcome boundaries of nationality and social class, cinema played an important part in the history of the first half of the twentieth century. But the second half of that century would be dominated by a different medium, television, which by about 1960 had replaced cinema as the mass medium in Europe and the United States, becoming more deeply imbricated in historical processes than cinema ever could. As with cinema, social elites have again concerned themselves with the supposed impact of television on the social order, leading media scholars to investigate such topics as the relationship

of television to the democratic process and the potential negative effects of televised depictions of sex or violence. Political scientists have examined the ways in which television has changed the nature of political campaigns in the United States, some arguing that it vitiates democracy by requiring politicians to accumulate vast amounts of money to purchase television time, to emphasize image over issues and to predicate their every move on the perceived reactions of the major television broadcasters. Mass communications specialists have endlessly debated whether television has caused, or at least contributed to, a perceived trend towards increasing violence in the United States.

The precise role that television plays in specific social processes remains subject to debate, but what seems clear is that the medium's characteristics of ubiquity and simultaneity are changing our very notion of history. The combination of advanced, lightweight equipment, satellite technology and the proliferation of television channels means that television can instantly transmit any event in any location, no matter how remote, to vast audiences around the globe. Twenty-four hour news channels such as the Cable News Network predicate their identities on live transmission, whether of presidential speeches or high-profile court cases, while other broadcasters must all rush to the site of the latest significant event, be it earthquake, revolution or sporting event. Television forms instant history, surrounding us with images of ongoing events and fixing the pictures that we will later all remember. As Vivian Sobchack explains:

> Event and its representation, immediacy and it mediation, have moved increasingly toward simultaneity. Early in the century, we thought history was something that happened temporally 'before' and was represented temporally 'after' us and our personal and immediate experience. For an event to 'become' History, an 'appropriate' period of time for reflection upon it seemed necessary. . . . Today, history seems to happen right now – is transmitted, reflected upon, shown play-by-play, taken up as the stuff of multiple stories and significance, given all sorts of 'coverage' in the temporal dimension of the present as we live it.
>
> (Sobchack 1996: 5)

Substantiation of Sobchack's assertion with regard to the period of reflection required for an event to become history requires empirical analysis, but the general point seems to hold true. Audiences today are certainly bombarded with contemporary events that broadcasters frame as having historical import.

The use of the media as historical evidence

The cinema, and television after it, provide a record of the visual texture of bygone ages much thicker than that offered by earlier media such as photography or painting. Historians concerned with what might be termed the **mise-en-scène** of everyday life – fashion, architecture, interior decor and so forth – have yet fully to avail themselves of this evidence source. But the visual media's potential as historical evidence is not limited to this, for films and television programmes, like any other complex text, can be deeply revelatory of what Raymond **Williams** terms a society's structure of feeling, the way of seeing the world that binds the people of an historical period or a geographical area together. The visual media not only shape history but are in turn shaped by history. For example, an historian investigating the relationship between Shakespeare and British national identity in the interwar period would be well advised to view the surviving newsreels documenting such events as the dedication of the Royal Shakespeare Theatre or Stratford's annual celebrations of the Bard's birthday.

Fictional texts can prove every bit as useful as **documentary** ones. An historian concerned with the tumultuous social upheavals of the United States from the 1960s to the 1990s might choose the various incarnations of the television series *Star Trek* as one index. *Star Trek*, now known as 'The Original Series' or 'TOS' to distinguish it from its descendants, first aired in 1966 to a nation that remembered the manufactured euphoria of John F. Kennedy's Camelot but which was also gripped by the Cold War and embroiled in the hopelessness and dissent of the hot war raging on the Asian subcontinent. Captain Kirk's opening voice-over, calling space 'the final frontier' and promising 'to boldly go where no man has gone before' invoked the martial spirit of the Kennedy years, in which the space race had become a means for demonstrating the country's superiority to the Soviet foe. The programme's United Federation of Planets, an intergalactic peacekeeping and exploratory quasi-military organization clearly led by Americans, performed the role that the country's leaders envisioned for the United States as the leader of the so-called Free World. The villains opposing the Federation, the Klingons and the Romulans, strongly resembled America's current enemies, the Soviets and the Chinese. More than thirty years later, however, changes in the fictional Federation paralleled those in the international order: the 1991 feature film *Star Trek VI: The Undiscovered Country* (Nicholas Meyer) centred around the Federations' attempts to achieve détente with the Klingon Empire in a plot that could be argued to have echoed the recent dissolution of the Soviet bloc and the emergence of a new world order dominated by the United States.

In similar fashion, *Star Trek*'s representation of **gender** and **race** responded to the gains made by the feminist and civil rights movements in the decades since the programme's first airing. The Captain of the original Enterprise, James T. Kirk (William Shatner), was an all-American 'man's man' who solved problems with fists and phasers and bedded female aliens across the galaxy. Jean-Luc Picard (Patrick Stewart), the Captain of the Enterprise 1701-D in *Star Trek: The Next Generation*, preferred diplomacy to violence and cerebral activities to sex, his intelligence and sensitivity corresponding to the 1980s and 1990s image of the 'new man'. The next two *Star Treks*, *Deep Space Nine* (1992–1999) and *Voyager* (1995–) featured a black captain and a woman captain respectively. *Star Trek*, as a whole, then, might be taken to reflect the transformations in American culture and society in its three plus decades of production. But this concept of 'reflection' is a fairly facile one, presuming as it does that social and cultural context are the sole determinants of textual meaning. A theory that properly related *Star Trek* to its historical context would account for *Star Trek*'s status as a constructed fiction, considering the economic concerns and organization of the copyright holder, the media giant Paramount/Viacom, more proximate production circumstances such as interaction among creative personnel and budgetary restrictions, textual factors such as **genre** and **narrative** and, finally, **audience** reception, particularly crucial since it was the devotion of TOS' fans that led to a series of feature films and then to three further television series.

The media's representation of history

In an age in which cinema attendance and television viewership far outstrips book sales, professional historians worry about the implications of the media teaching most people their 'history lessons'. Robert Rosenstone sums up historians' concerns thus:

> No matter how serious or honest the filmmakers, and no matter how deeply committed they are to rendering the subject faithfully, the history that finally appears on the screen can never fully satisfy the historian. . . . Inevitably, something happens on the way from page to screen that changes the meaning of the past as it is understood by those of us who work in words. . . . [Cinema] compresses the past to a closed world by telling a single, linear story with, essentially, a single interpretation. Such narrative strategy obviously denies historical alternatives, does away with complexities of motivation or causation, and banishes all subtlety from the world of history.
>
> (Rosenstone 1988: 1173–4)

Rosenstone is not alone in the belief that the visual media usually represent history in a manner somehow inferior to that of the written word. In *Past Imperfect: History According to the Movies*, Mark C. Carnes has compiled essays by several leading historians comparing historical films to the historical record in terms of accuracy and authenticity. Carnes' introduction echoes Rosenstone's criticism: 'Hollywood History sparkles because it is so morally unambiguous, so devoid of tedious complicity, so *perfect*' (Carnes 1995: 9).

Despite their reservations, neither Rosenstone nor Carne would totally condemn the historical film, for both would agree with Robert Toplin that filmmakers have to balance the demands of written history against the cinematic demand to 'fictionalize'. Toplin belives that sometimes this fictionali-

zation can go too far resulting in 'badly distorted images of the past' (Toplin 1996: 2). But traditional academic histories are no more exempt from these kinds of criticism than visual ones, for as historiographer Hayden White has shown written history too must conform to conventions of narrative and genre. Specifically addressing the difference between filmed and written history, White writes:

> No history, visual or verbal, 'mirrors' all or even the greater part of the events or scenes of which it purports to be an account, and this is true even of the most narrowly restricted 'microhistory.' Every written history is a product of processes of condensation, displacement, symbolization, and qualification exactly like those used in the production of a filmed representation. It is only the medium that differs, not the way in which the messages are produced.
>
> (White 1988: 1194)

White's insight that different media represent history in different fashion offers a powerful counter-argument to historians' conviction that filmed history inevitably often seems inadequate by comparison with written history. It also requires film scholars to undertake serious investigation of cinematic forms of historical representation. How do visual strategies of historical representation differ from written ones? We might begin by specifying a precise definition of the history film or television programme. Patterns of production, distribution and audience expectations concerning entertainment that have historically privileged the fictional narrative over the documentary require that the majority of cinematic and televisual representations of history take the form of made-up stories commingled with historical 'facts'. Broadly, these stories fall into two categories: (i) fictional characters in fictional incidents or historical incidents set in an historical time period, e.g., *Gone with the Wind* (Victor Fleming, 1939), *Titanic* (James Cameron, 1997) or *Roots* (ABC, 1977); and (ii) historical characters in historical incidents, including the so-called 'biopics', e.g., *Patton* (Franklin Schaffner, 1970) or *Mosley* (Channel 4, 1998).

In practice, however, the two categories blur, with historical characters appearing in category one texts and fictional characters appearing in category two texts. In fact, the entire notion of the historical film is a rather blurry one; it certainly constitutes nothing as definitive as a genre by virtue of specific textual characteristics that distinguish it from other kinds of films. For example, category one films of fictional characters in fictional incidents set in an historical time period could encompass almost all Westerns (see **Western, the**). But all these texts have in common the fictionalization of history: actors recreate historical characters, art directors recreate period ambience, costume designers recreate period clothing and scriptwriters recreate historical events. It is this last re-creation that critics of the historical film often find most disturbing since they object to the 'distortions' of history which result from scriptwriters inventing scenes having no basis in the historical record. In *Braveheart* (Mel Gibson, 1995), for instance, why is it that William Wallace seduces the Queen of England when the historical record insists they never met? In *Malcolm X* (Spike Lee, 1992), why is the hero's father portrayed as a civil rights martyr when his son's autobiography depicted him as an abusive father and husband? Producers of such texts often respond that these fictionalizations aid in the characterization of the central protagonist, thus serving the needs of an emotional or dramatic truth, rather than of a truth that corresponds strictly with the historical record.

This emotional or dramatic 'truth' conforms to the narrative structure of the classical Hollywood cinema, centred on the actions of characters, rather than to the conventions of written history, which often takes into account impersonal historical forces as well as the actions of individuals (see **classical Hollywood cinema and new Hollywood cinema**). Like the bulk of fiction films produced in Hollywood or in the Hollywood tradition, both cinematic and televisual historical representations tend to focus on the actions of one or two key protagonists, as revealed by the fact that many historical films bear the names of their central characters: for example, *Young Winston* (Richard Attenborough, 1972), *Nixon* (Oliver Stone, 1995), *Michael Collins* (Neil Jordan, 1996). These fairly recent examples coincide with a long-standing tradition: as Custen shows in his book *Bio/Pics* (1992), a great many of the historical films produced during the classical Hollywood period were biographies of individuals. Even films not

bearing the name of an historical figure often construct their stories around the actions of individuals. For example, *Reds* (Warren Beatty, 1981) primarily concerns itself with American journalist John Reed's involvement in the Russian Revolution, while *Glory* (Edward Zwick, 1989) deals with the military exploits of Colonel Robert Shaw of the all-black Fifty-Fourth Massachusetts Volunteer Infantry in the American Civil War. The latter film, using a strategy common to cinematic/televisual historical representations, creates a cast of supporting characters derived not from the historical record but from the screenwriters' imaginations, simplifying history in order more clearly to delineate the narrative arc of the central character. Other films reverse this strategy, the central protagonists being fictional and the supporting characters deriving from the historical record: for example, *Titanic* and *The Birth of a Nation* (D. W. Griffith, 1915). These two films, both **epic** in scope and triumphant at the box office, portray major historical events (the sinking of the *Titanic*, the American Civil War) through stories centred on the romances of fictional characters. As Leger Grindon points out in *Shadows on the Past* (1994), if the history film can be considered to constitute a separate and distinguishable genre, romance is one of its primary components, related to the narrative centrality of the individual. 'The emphasis on characterization in the romance tends to promote personal motives and individual action as the driving force behind history' (Grindon 1994: 15). Some historians may decry this exaltation of the individual over impersonal historical forces, but Simon Schama (1998) suggests that filmmakers are simply fulfilling a need for historical stories that the work of academic historians no longer meets.

If, as Grindon (1994) argues, romance is the central narrative component of the historical fiction, spectacle, or at least visual pleasure, may be the central element of its *mise-en-scène*. Producers may take liberties with the events of the historical record, but ever since the first historical films have laid claim to a visual **realism** manifested in a *mise-en-scène* which conforms to the details of the historical record, often buttressing these claims in publicity that references historical sources. Famous characters must look like their historical progenitors: Napoleon must wear a cocked hat, have a lock of hair falling over his forehead and thrust his hand in his jacket; Lincoln must wear a beard and a stovepipe hat. Sets must manifest correct period detail: the producers of *Titanic* boasted that their set's carpets were manufactured by the very firm that had made the carpets for the original ship. Since western culture still manifests a **bias** towards visual evidence (seeing is believing), the truth claim manifested in the 'correctness' of the *mise-en-scène* can implicitly be extended to narrative events. But as Simon Schama warns: 'It's possible to get all the minutiae right and still get the dramatic core of history wrong' (Schama 1998: 40).

References

Carnes, M. C. (ed.) (1995) *Past Imperfect: History According to the Movies*, New York: Henry Holt and Company.

Custen, G. F. (1992) *Bio/Pics: How Hollywood Constructed Public History*, Rutgers, NJ: Rutgers University Press.

Grindon, L. (1994) *Shadows on the Past: Studies in the Historical Fiction Film*, Philadelphia: Temple University Press.

Rosenstone, R. A. (1988) 'History in Images/ History in Words: Reflections on the Possibility of Really Putting History onto Film', *The American Historical Review*, vol. 93, no. 5, pp. 1173–85.

Schama, S. (1998) 'Clio at the Multiplex: What Hollywood and Herodotus Have in Common', *New Yorker*, 19 January, pp. 38–43.

Sobchack, V. (1996) 'Introduction', in Vivian Sobchack (ed.) *The Persistence of History: Cinema, Television and the Modern Event*, New York: Routledge.

Toplin, R. (1996) *History by Hollywood: The Use and Abuse of the American Past*, Urbana: University of Illinois Press.

White, H. (1988) 'Historiography and Historio-photy', *The American Historical Review*, vol. 93, no. 5, pp. 1193–9

Further reading

Sorlin, P. (1980) *The Film in History: Restaging the Past*, Totowa, NJ: Barnes and Noble Books.

Uricchio, W. and Pearson, R. E. (1993) *Reframing Culture: The Case of the Vitagraph Quality Films*, Princeton: Princeton University Press.

ROBERTA E. PEARSON

history/histoire

Histoire distinguishes the series of events related in a narrative from the *récit*, or the way it is organized and presented to the reader/spectator. The former is always conceived of chronologically, as opposed to the latter, which may jump forwards and backwards in time, or present certain events out of order. Similar to the Russian formalist term **fabula**, this term, a central component of narrative theory, allows the actions within a text to be conceived of as independent from their manifestation in **discourse**. Gérard **Genette**, in his book *Narrative Discourse Revisited*, ultimately found the dichotomy *histoire/récit* unsatisfactory to explain storytelling grammar, unless one also takes into account the very act of narrating or 'telling' the tale.

References

Genette, G. (1983) *Narrative Discourse Revisited*, trans. Jane E. Lewin, New York: Cornell University Press.

KAREN BACKSTEIN

Hoggart, Richard

b. 1918

Richard Hoggart was born to a working-class family in Chapeltown, Leeds. He progressed through scholarships to Leeds University, then taught in adult education while writing his most celebrated work, *The Uses of Literacy*. Following its publication in 1957, Hoggart became professor of English at Birmingham University and in 1964 set up the Centre for Contemporary Cultural Studies (CCCS), aided by Stuart **Hall**.

While Hoggart's influence through the CCCS was immense, and his published work since the 1960s substantial, he is best remembered for *The Uses of Literacy*. The book is both a lyrical reminiscence of his working-class childhood and a scathing attack on the 'candy-floss world' of Americanized consumer culture which he believed was replacing older traditions in British working-class life. While Hoggart's prose style is winning, even beautiful, *The Uses of Literacy* might be found subjective, under-researched and generalized by current standards of cultural studies; it often goes unremarked, for instance, that Hoggart actually invented the extracts from popular crime and romance fiction which serve his polemical argument.

Hoggart's essays are collected in two volumes, *Speaking to Each Other: About Society* and *Speaking to Each Other: About Literature*, both of which were published in 1970. His most recent work is *The Way We Live Now* (1995).

References

Hoggart, R. (1957) *The Uses of Literacy*, Harmondsworth: Penguin.

—— (1970) *Speaking to Each Other: About Society*, London: Chatto and Windus.

—— (1970) *Speaking to Each Other: About Literature*, London: Chatto and Windus.

—— (1995) *The Way We Live Now*, London: Pimlico.

WILL BROOKER

hooks, bell

b. 1952

Born in Kentucky, and christened Gloria Watkins, bell hooks adopted this name to perpetuate those of her mother and grandmother, and the lower case usage to suggest the importance of what is said rather than the speaker. Since 1981 she has published eleven books of critical writing on culture and two autobiographical works, as well as poetry and articles in many journals.

bell hooks writes directly and powerfully about representational forms. Though her writing is clearly informed by theoretical and critical perspectives, her lack of sympathy with the exclusive qualities of much academic writing gives her essays a clarity and accessibility which makes its challenges and provocations unmistakable.

Her main critical objects are the oppressive manifestations of 'white supremacist capitalist **patriarchy**', whether in music, television, films 'or the Clinton administration', though the *sources* of economic and political power in the United States which shape cultures there and elsewhere are her ultimate targets. Her essay, 'Misogyny, Gangsta Rap and *The Piano*', for example, typifies her ability to make connections which place apparently diverse cultural phenomena, and their critical reception, within the same framework for analysis and understanding.

hooks writes from a black feminist perspective shaped by her intellectual and emotional engagement with revolutionary politics and Buddhism. She insists that differences in **class**, **race** and **gender** be acknowledged but not essentialized and seeks a **discourse** of engagement that can transform these differences.

Further reading

For an initial access to bell hooks' writing, online. Available: voices.cla.umn.edu/authors/bell-hooks.html

PHILIP SIMPSON

Horkheimer, Max

b. 1895; d. 1973

Max Horkheimer was born in Stuttgart, Germany. He was a leading figure in the **Frankfurt School**, and is best known in film and television studies for his collaboration with Theodor **Adorno** on their major study of the culture industry in the 1947 *Dialectic of Enlightenment*, a refining of the argument in his 1941 essay 'Art and Mass Culture'. His analysis of conventional social science remains relevant to conventional mass communication research today. He offered a trenchant critique of **empiricism**, arguing that it mystifies the role values play in all investigations, and too often operates as a research tool for the administration of people as objects (see Horkheimer 1972: 188–252).

References

Horkheimer, M. (1972) 'Traditional and Critical Theory', 'Postscript' and 'Art and Mass Culture', in *Critical Theory: Selected Essays*, trans. M. J. O'Connell *et al.*, New York: Continuum-Seabury.

Horkheimer, M. and Adorno, T. W. (1972) 'The Culture Industry: Enlightenment as Mass Deception' (first published 1947), in *Dialectic of Enlightenment*, trans. John Cumming, New York: Continuum-Seabury.

Further reading

Kellner, D. (1989) 'Traditional and Critical Theory' and 'From "Authentic Art" to the Culture Industries', in *Critical Theory, Marxism and Modernity*, Baltimore: Johns Hopkins University.

CLAY STEINMAN

horror

Horror's associations with perverse **desire**, abjection and the **body** have made it central to film studies. A long-established but controversial **genre**, horror has generally been critically maligned. Most classical horrors were B-features, while many of their 1980s high-budget counterparts were dismissed as low brow, appealing to mostly youthful audiences. Rather than blaming horror for individual disturbances, some critics see its excesses as symptomatic of repressed social desires. A knowing genre that plays with how much we can stand to see, horror often draws on prior audience knowledge to create reflexive commentaries about the nature of cinema.

MOYA LUCKETT

humanism

Shaped by the Renaissance, the philosophy of humanism believes in individual potential as the source of general social fulfilment. Humanism proposes that every person should be respected, and without religious motivation. The philosophy trusts in individual rather than mass effort to repair and sustain society. The main features valued by humanism are individual reason, creativity and the capacity to achieve knowledge and harmony with others. Many modernist theories, including those of Karl **Marx**, condemn humanism as impractical and isolating. Yet Marx's theories share the humanist ideal of a society where each individual's worth and abilities are realized.

GABRIEL M. PALETZ

hybridity

Hybridity has become an important theoretical and political concept, particularly in post-colonial theory and theories of **race**. The origins of the term 'hybrid' can be found in botany and biology where, since the eighteenth century, it has been used to denote a cross between two species. In the nineteenth century it was taken up by racial science, which set out to categorize human beings into distinct 'races'. Until the 1860s, the question of whether or not different 'races' were in fact different species was central to theories of race. The polygenists, who argued for separate species, adopted the term 'hybrid' to denote the offspring of sexual relations between people from different racial categories. They advanced various theories about the nature of the 'hybrid', most of which suggested that he/she was unviable. The term 'hybridity' was further used to denote new forms of language – such as Creole and pidgin – which emerged in the contexts of colonialism and slavery.

The term 'hybridity' is also found in the linguistic theory of Mikhail **Bakhtin** where it refers to the dual vocality of language. By this, Bakhtin means the ability of language to signify more than one thing, a feature which gives language its subversive potential. Grammatically, hybrid constructions are the property of a single speaker but contain different speech manners and belief systems: 'It frequently happens that even one and the same word will belong simultaneously to two languages, two belief systems that intersect in a hybrid construction and consequently, the word has two contradictory meanings, two accents' (Bakhtin 1981: 304–5). The subversive potential created by the polyvocality of language is an idea taken up and further developed in recent post-colonial theories of hybridity.

Whereas in the nineteenth century the term 'hybridity' was usually used in the context of racial science to refer to people of mixed race, in the later part of the twentieth century, it was resignified to denote cultural mixing. In this usage, hybridity is most often seen as an effect of the slave trade, colonialism and the ensuing movements of peoples which have created a range of diasporas through-out the world (see **diaspora**). The process of colonialization brought different peoples into close proximity with one another and gave rise to cultural hybridization. Thus, for example, in his groundbreaking work on colonialism, Franz **Fanon** argued that encounters between the colonizer and the colonized transformed both cultures.

In its more recent formulations, hybridity is often used to challenge the very concept of 'racial' categorization. Its function is to deconstruct those **binary** oppositions (see also **difference**) which ground both theories of race and racialized theories of culture. Such oppositions – white/black, advanced/primitive, western/Third World – can then be seen to be cultural rather than natural. Homi K. **Bhabha** (1994), for example, looks both to Fanon and to Bakhtin in his suggestion that hybridity is central to colonial and post-colonial identities. Other post-colonial theorists and critics also stress the hybrid nature of post-colonial diasporic culture and identities (see **Hall** [1990], on Third Cinema, and Gilroy [1993] on the 'Black Atlantic'). Work by feminists of colour also focuses on the importance of hybridity as a challenge to racism, sexism and heterosexism and for understanding new identities and cultural forms in post-colonial societies (see Anzaldúa 1987).

References

Anzaldúa, G. (1987) *Borderlands/La Frontera*, San Francisco: Aunt Lute Books.

Bakhtin, M. (1981) *The Dialogic Imagination: Four Essays*, trans. C. Emerson and M. Holquist, Austin: University of Texas Press.

Bhabha, H. K. (1994) *The Location of Culture*, London and New York: Routledge.

Gilroy, P. (1993) *The Black Atlantic*, London and New York: Routledge.

Hall, S. (1990) 'Cultural Identity and Diaspora', in J. Rutherford (ed.) *Identity, Community, Culture, Difference*, London: Lawrence and Wishart.

Further reading

Young, R (1993) *Colonial Desire. Hybridity in Theory, Culture and Race*, London and New York: Routledge.

CHRIS WEEDON

hyperreal

Like **simulacrum**, the hyperreal is a post-modern concept (see **modernism and post-modernism**). In Baudrillard's relentlessly dystopic vision, the term indicates that the **sign** no longer references the real but has become the dominant symbolic relationship imposed on subjects by the electronic media (see **utopia and dystopia**). **Class** or national conflicts are represented in terms of images exchanged between power groups. Viewers take these images to be a reference to events but their hyperreal function is to mystify and maintain the *status quo* through sustaining the hold of sign systems and their apparent reference to the real. Umberto **Eco**'s more ironical approach suggests that the hyperreal of wax museums is a response to a **desire** for fullness (a Venus de Milo *with arms*) and an abhorrence of emptiness or incompleteness in a spectacle implied by the idea of mere reference. **Fantasy** made real, like Disneyland, is also hyperreal.

PHILIP SIMPSON

hypodermic model

Developed in the 1920s and 1930s, the hypodermic model (or 'magic bullet') theory of media effects views the **audience** as the hapless victims of powerful media messages that strike individuals directly, immediately and with uniform effects. Despite the fact that the hypodermic model was never fully articulated into a formalized set of arguments, it still functions as a shorthand for media critics, a set of naturalized assumptions about the assumed power of the media. It therefore refers more to set of discourses about the mass audience than to a coherent set of theoretical ideas.

See also: discourse

ALISON GRIFFITHS

I

icon

The word 'icon' comes from the Greek *eikon*, meaning 'reproduction' or 'image'. In its broadest sense, 'icon' means anything that bears a perceivable resemblance to an intended object. While medieval iconography concerned itself mostly with the description of mythic harmony expressed through such resemblances, Erwin Panofsky (1939) differentiated between iconography and iconology and so gave the terms their modern meaning. Iconography increasingly denoted descriptive practices of identifying themes, whereas iconology stands for the exploration of the symbolic meaning of figurative forms.

The American semiotician Charles Sanders **Peirce**'s definition of the iconic **sign** as relating to its referent through visual or acoustic imitation (e.g., the stop/go figure on traffic lights, maps, graphs, but also musical sound imitations or sound-imitating poetry) belongs to the field of iconography, whereas the analysis of cultural icons belongs to the field of iconology. The term 'icon' is not widespread in cinema semiotics, which derive more from the French tradition of Ferdinand de **Saussure**, via Christian **Metz**, than from Peirce, although Peter **Wollen** has briefly considered the application of a Peircian **semiotics** to film texts. **Genre** criticism uses the term 'iconography' in a less technical sense than Panofsky, referring to the visual characteristics of specific genres, for example the Western's use of white hats for the good guys and black hats for the bad guys (see **Western, the**).

References

Panofsky, E. (1955) 'Iconography and Iconology: An Introduction to the Study of Renaissance Art' (revised edn), in E. Panofsky, *Meaning in the Visual Arts*, New York: Garden City. ('Iconology and Iconography' first appeared as an Introduction to his book, *Studies in Iconology: Humanistic Themes in the Art of the Renaissance*, New York, 1939).
Wollen, P. (1972) *Signs and Meaning in the Cinema*, Bloomington: Indiana University Press.

EVA VIETH

identity

In her 1998 study of costume drama in British cinema, Pam Cook makes the following point about identity and film:

> with its emphasis on masquerade, [the **genre**] is a prime vehicle for the exploration of *identity*, encouraging cross-dressing not only between characters, but metaphorically between characters and spectators, in the sense that the latter can be seen as trying on a variety of roles in the course of the film.
>
> (Cook 1998: 6)

Here, Cook links elements of 'identity' on screen to processes behind and in front of the screen and to contradictions as well as synthesis. Yet 'identity' also has an immediacy beyond theory, as the 'politics of identity' has become a common designation for strategies of ethnic (see **ethnicity**), **class**, **gender** and other conflicts and their own contradictions. Indeed, critics and producers often tie mass media to the creation or resolution of a 'crisis' in identity, whether national (see **national, thw**), group or individual. None the less, the multiple and seemingly changeable identities of pastiche and travesty constructed in texts and theory also underscore the ambiguities of identity as both a critical and a political term. Its uses may conflate or conceal processes of social formation, relations of self and **Other**, and relations of power within and among groups. Hence, its critical usage must be carefully charted even as the study of identity challenges apparently established categories of race, gender, age, class and nation.

The concept of identity

Identity in social and cultural studies has developed several meanings that influence its readings in film and television (see **reading and reception theory**). Paul Gilroy, while noting its genealogy in psychological and philosophical studies (often oriented to the meaning of the individual), distinguishes three primary current referents. First, identity refers to self or individual constructions of meaning. While this is close to its meaning in earlier theories, it should not be confused with 'identification', which posits psychological or psychoanalytic relations between film and **audience**, as richly explored in work by Laura **Mulvey** and Christian **Metz** (see also **psychoanalysis**). While selves are present in production and formative readings of identity, cultural theories more often deal with *collectivities* or 'others'.

Second, identity may refer to collective categorizations that are meaningful within a larger social framework – hence, 'national identity', 'ethnic identity' or 'gender identity'. Here, there is an implication of sameness as well as an insistence on difference. Nevertheless, identity may reflect categories imposed from outside or the polarization of categories – French identity in relation to Hollywood or African-American identity in relation to 'whiteness' (see **white**). This usage also highlights certain characteristics valued within particular frameworks in which identities must be distinguished, such as landscapes or heroic myths as signifiers of national identity. Finally, this usage ties

critical studies – at least apparently – to politics beyond the text.

Third, identity carries the value of participation and the construction of social labels. As such, theoreticians take the psychological roots of the concept, in the sense of a bounded and integrated personality, and expand them onto a social landscape of complexity and action. The first social usage allows us to interrogate the primary traits of 'African-American', 'queer' or 'working-class' identity. The second usage, meanwhile, poses different investigations, such as, 'does a working-class identity exist in twentieth-century America?', 'How do film and television contribute to the construction of such identity?' or 'What are the conflicts between African-American identity and queer identity?' Thus, the concept 'identity' raises questions of contradictory or contested claims to myths and figures. In both of these latter meanings, however, one must ask who benefits, and how, from constructions or divisions of identity.

Moreover, one must be careful not to reify identities (see **reification**). Many critics have underscored the need to see identity as a process, involving active construction with regard to media as well as change over time. People, moreover, may juggle more than one identity – a vague cultural label is often applied to gender, location or ability in order to avoid reductive categorization, but this remains a dilemma of structure and context. **Hybridity**, or the recognition and fusion of two or more identities – Iranian exile and American citizen, lesbian and black, or the East–West fusion of Hong Kong – also pervades contemporary discussions of identity and how it is explored through media of reflection or reflection on media. These questions arise in films as diverse as *The Crying Game* (Neil Jordan, 1992) where national, gender and racial identities are contested, and *Mississippi Masala* (Mira Nair, 1991) with its Afro-Indian love story.

These bifurcations incorporating internal and external usages as well as differentiated and strategic identities must be kept in mind when identity is applied to film and television. Here, the concept facilitates analysis of **culture** and intention in the production process as well as textual manifestations, whether in the discussion of Hollywood and American identity (inside and outside of the United States), national and transnational television, or 'race' films. At the same time, any analysis must be balanced by the social construction of audience identity. This ranges from the reproduction of dominant **discourse** – the identity of the American 'TV generation' – to alternative ritualizations of identity around classic or cult films (see **cult film and television**), to **oppositional** texts and receptions. All these uses highlight the **text** of film and television as an arena for **negotiation** of identity rather than a simple or transparent representation.

The text itself, obviously, cannot be overlooked. Elements of plot, scene and **myth** are not only features that have been constructed to reinforce identity on screen. These signifying practices are also markers of **difference** for asserting alternative identities (see **signifying practice**). Noël Burch (1979), for example, has argued that the formal elements of Japanese silent cinema embody language and cultural values that reconstitute difference vis-à-vis classical Hollywood cinema (see **classical Hollywood cinema and new Hollywood cinema**). A similar question of aesthetics and identity emerges in Manthia Diawara's (1993) reading of the film *Daughters of the Dust* (1991) by the African-American filmmaker Julie Dash. Diawara contrasts the space and tempo of **narrative** with 'white' forms and identities. It is noteworthy that in all these cases, the formation of identity remains contrastive as well as constituted by concrete elements. Similar textual claims could certainly be made for Iranian cinema by filmmakers like Majid Majidi and Abbas Kourastiami, where prescriptions of Islam favouring child actors, heavily fated plots and inexpensive camerawork have defined a national style – although not necessarily one that redefines transnational culture.

A final caveat must be noted: the spread of studies of identity has been fostered by the emergence of cultural studies since the 1970s, including the concealing usages which Paul Gilroy critiques. Nevertheless, to understand the range of theoretical applications possible, we must incorporate earlier studies that speak to identity without using the term specifically, which are often reassessed by later studies. At the same time, this entry only suggests some of the uses and limits of a term in its critical florescence; other issues, critics and readings deal with these same general points. Here, we focus on the use of 'identity' in the analysis of textual and extra-textual processes, including production and reading. We also delineate possibilities of formation of 'group' identity and the construction of national and transnational identities that use – and shatter – these frameworks.

Looking for group identity

The critical analysis of **African-American cinema** in the United States has always faced the question of African-American identity in American society, informed by thinkers from the formative voices of W. E. B. DuBois and Booker T. Washington through political and intellectual figures such as Franz **Fanon**, Malcolm X, bell **hooks** and Stuart **Hall**. Representation on screen, whether Oscar Micheaux's race films, D. W. Griffith's *The Birth of a Nation* (1915) or Spike Lee's *Malcolm X* (1992), are embedded in history, production and theory as well as reading. J. Ronald Green (1993), for example, suggests historical dilemmas in reviewing the pioneering work of Thomas Cripps, who embedded studies of identity within the dual identity of African-Americans, as posed by DuBois. While Cripps concentrated on assimilation rather than autonomy, Green argued that Micheaux's ambivalent grappling with segregation envisioned a new aesthetic (see **aesthetics**) and a new African-American identity. Yet Cripps (1993), in response, asked where the data on readership and black criticism exist to 'prove' any such identity. While these films use black actors and treat dilemmas of the black population, identity still demands data of interpretation and action.

Other perspectives on identity emerge from a volume on disability and media published by the British Film Institute and the Arts Council of Great Britain (Pointon and Davies 1997). Here, general concerns over the stereotyped representation of the disabled are tempered by recognition that this situation cannot change simply by replacing texts or producers. Those who had learned these stereotypes as disabled could find other identities reinforced. Moreover, the range of people categorized as disabled makes suspect the construction of any synthetic identity that conceals divisions of physical condition, gender, race and politics. Hence, identity provides a central theme of discussion of text and reception because of the political impact of both media and readers, yet theorists and critics need caution in recognizing **dialogic** complexities. In the multiple processes involving the producer, the text, reading and the many constitutive identities of the audience, identity proves a 'messy' business.

In the first case, theory starts from pre-existing constructions of difference: 'black' existed as a category and as agents grappling with identity long before cinema and television. Any oppositional search for black identity was reinforced by segregated theatres as well as movies, production, texts and reading. While *The Birth of a Nation* articulated one aspect of imposed identity construction of blacks by whites, black identity was also shaped by subsequent reactions and protests, engaging political critics as well as specialists in cinema. In the second case, a movement to change the status of the disabled, politically shaped by previous struggles for identity, raises different values of stereotypes, access and incorporation. An individual might not identify as a disabled person at all points in his/her life, much less constitute a collectivity. It is impossible to hold identity as a concept equally applicable in both cases without recognizing complexity, process, context and action.

Yet, any focus on dialogic identity should not underestimate production and text. This proves especially true in reflexive **documentary**, which often represents media about identity. These works can be individualistic, but can also posit broader group questions like those raised by Marlon Riggs' *Tongues Untied* (1989) or Trinh T. Minh-Ha's *Surname Viet, Given Name Nam* (1989). Other documentaries, especially those made by ethnic and/or sexual minorities, with a relatively low budget, question how their group identities have been constructed and imposed on them by the mainstream media. Through their autobiographical works, these filmmakers try to challenge stereotypes by articulating their struggle for self-identity (see **stereotype**).

Distribution creates special settings that define group identities. Screenings of cult films like *The Rocky Horror Picture Show* (Jim Sharman, 1975) entail rehearsals of identity. More 'serious' films like *Amistad* (Steven Spielberg, 1997) or *Shoah* (Claude Lanzmann, 1985) are used to reinforce group identity in other public settings. Similarly, over the history of film and television, generational identities, defined in terms of children, teenagers, adults and senior citizens, have been constituted as identities in both genres and audience. **Fandom**, from Trekkers to teenagers, also facilitates the creation of markers, scenarios and places (conventions) where identity is reaffirmed. The proliferation of cable and audience research has allowed targeted marketing of identities. However, questions of hegemony and **consumption** always remain: who speaks for whom and whose identity is shaped through these actions and experiences?

Group and identity are, therefore, at once independent and interdependent in media, reflecting sometimes problematic axioms of social category as well as genre and audience. This concept can be explored further by examining the meanings of media and identity with regard to one of the primary deconstructive challenges of the twentieth century – national, transnational and hybrid identities (see **deconstruction**).

National identity, globalization and hybridity

Pam Cook's work, noted at the beginning of this entry, focuses on national identity in film as constructed in studios. Here, the recounting of British history was cloaked in glamour and action without an explicitly patriotic agenda. Britishness became an act of imagination, not documentation. Still, Cook warns that elements of nostalgia and home should not be linked only to conservative viewpoints: the left might use this same imagination to claim an alternative form of national unity. Moreover, the construction of identity consistently has faced contradictions within the nation, including those based on the experiences of women or minorities excluded from national efforts.

These constructions of identity emerged from studios and directors rather than specific state projects. Yet they may easily shade over into statecraft within an historical milieu or even the life of a particular director: Frank Capra's Americanness, after all, was part of both *It's a Wonderful Life* (1946) and *Why We Fight* (1942–1945). The first film incorporates classic elements of the good 'little' guy saving the community; the impact of its theatrical release was augmented by generations of holiday screenings on television as well. Capra's work on the *Why We Fight* series served to indoctrinate American soldiers about the values of defeating the Axis. Propaganda and national documentaries raise special concerns: the process of constructing national/Allied identity was not so different from Leni Riefenstahl's *Triumph of the Will* (1934), except for the side one fought on.

This does not imply that such efforts at conscious identity-building as a part of statecraft do not create their own contradictions of identity at the meshing of plans, actions and reading. Luke Gibbons (1996), for example, has shown how the Irish state presumed an identity as a nation, rooted in traditions, which would be reinforced by locally produced programming, especially in television and film. Here, outsiders are viewed as dangerous modernizers in the reconstruction of Irish identity. Yet rural dramas and citizen talks shows, Gibbons has found, as well as some patriotic films, actually subverted this imagined community by questioning Irish myth in its own terms.

Any recognition of interests and boundaries suggests the importance of reading national identity in transnational settings, often epitomized by local opposition to the **globalization** of Hollywood and American television. Kristin Ross (1995), for example, traced the multiple impacts of American imagery, conveyed through media, on a French society that at once rejected and adopted these forms in the aftermath of the Second World War. Neither French nor American society built a simple new transatlantic identity; both engaged in a mutual transaction. Other studies of audience have focused on the widely disseminated American television series *Dallas* in terms of individual and collective readings. Liebes and Katz (1990), for example, found distinctive readings of this series among immigrant Jews in Israel or between Jews and Arabs that confirmed each group's own beliefs and values, their different identities.

Nations themselves are also in flux. Hong Kong and the ambivalence of colonial traditions leading to its 1997 transition to Chinese sovereignty has evoked intriguing critical readings of hybrid identity and concealment in its flourishing film industry. Hong Kong cinema epitomizes the ambiguities and contradictions of cinema that allow spectators to explore their own liminal status and to map out futures. Meanwhile, Hamid Naficy (1993) has looked at identity in terms of those who have moved away to exile rather than the political unit itself. In his careful reading of Iranian television in Los Angeles, Naficy notes the repetition of images of the homeland coupled with visions of new consumption. Here, media are seen as a response to a crisis of identity through a surfeit of presences that allow a new hybridity for exiles also negotiating their ongoing relation to the United States.

A post-modern politics of identity is a major concern of media theory and criticism at the end of the twentieth century (see **modernism and post-modernism**). Myriad studies are produced each year that grapple with issues of identity – gender, race, nation and other possible categories. Yet, Ella Shohat and Robert Stam (1994) warn that the politics of identity may lead to antagonistic self-representation rather than dialogue. Instead, they propose that media might become tools in the pedagogy of mutual and reciprocal relations. Here, the issue of identity in media comes full circle to merge with the politics of identity as a tool for creating the future as well as a reading of past and contemporary texts.

Conclusions

'Identity', as a florescent critical and theoretical concern, proves powerful and liberating in film and television study. Still, critics must be aware of both faddishness and complexity/ambiguity. Identity is constantly caught between production and reading, mediated through text. Moreover, processes off-screen are not necessarily coincident with development of filmic practices or goals. Theorists and critics have recognized that collective constructions of and actions about identity often incorporate social contradictions. These may be concealed by nostalgia, projection or rejection of some 'other', but media may also provide arenas in which contradictions are recognized and grappled with. Hence, the use of this concept also demands careful analysis of who reads movies and television as well as what they do with these readings. Moreover, one must be careful not to reify the term either as a critical discovery or as a political attribute that reinforces polarization: such a powerful analytic tool must be viewed through its consequences as well as its insights.

References

Burch, N. (1979) *To the Distant Observer*, Los Angeles: University of California Press.

Cook, P. (1998) *Fashioning the Nation: Costume and Identity in British Cinema*, London: BFI Publishing.

Cripps, T. (1993) 'Oscar Micheaux: The Story Continues', in Manthia Diawara (ed.) *Black American Cinema*, London: Routledge, pp. 71–9.

Diawara, M. (1993) 'Black American Cinema: The New Realism', in M. Diawara (ed.) *Black American Cinema*, London: Routledge, pp. 3–25.

Gibbons, L. (1996) *Transformations in Irish Culture*, South Bend: Notre Dame.

Gilroy, P. (1996) 'British Cultural Studies and the Pitfalls of Identity', in J. Curran, D. Morley and V. Walkerdine (eds) *Cultural Studies and Communication*, London: Arnold, pp. 35–49.

Green, J. R. (1993) 'Twoness in the Style of Oscar Micheaux', in M. Diawara (ed.) *Black American Cinema*, London: Routledge, pp. 26–49.

Liebes, T. and Curran, J. (1998) *Media, Ritual and Identity*, New York: Routledge.

Liebes, T. and Katz, E. (1990) *The Export of Meaning: Cross-Cultural Readings of 'Dallas'*, New York: Oxford University Press.

Naficy, H. (1993) *The Making of Exile Cultures: Iranian Television in Los Angeles*, Minnesota: University of Minnesota Press.

Pointon, A. and Davies, C. (eds) (1997) *Framed: Interrogating Disability in the Media*, London: BFI Publishing.

Ross, K. (1995) *Fast Cars, Clean Bodies: Decolonization and the Reordering of French Culture*, Cambridge, Mass: MIT Press.

Shohat, E. and Stam, R. (1994) *Unthinking Eurocentrism: Multiculturalism and the Media*, London: Routledge.

CINDY WONG AND GARY McDONOGH

ideological state apparatuses

In Louis **Althusser**'s (1971) conceptual approach to the role of ideology within capitalist society, he first examines what he calls the 'Repressive State Apparatuses', or RSAs. These RSAs, as organizations of physical force centralized within the state itself, include the armed forces, police, courts and prisons – all of which operate through the use, real or implied, of violence. He then proceeds to identify, after Antonio **Gramsci** (1971), the 'Ideological State Apparatuses', ISAs, which operate primarily by *ideology*. Here, the media system, like the educational, familial, religious, trade union and political systems, acts 'massively and predominantly' by ideology to reproduce the structural inequalities of capitalist society. In contending that 'no class can hold state power over a long period without at the same time exercising its hegemony over and in the [ISAs]', Althusser (1971: 146–7) regards the ISAs as both the *stake* of the larger class struggle as well as the *site* where the dominant class encounters the expressed resistance of the exploited or subaltern classes.

See also: dominant ideology; ideology and hegemony

References

Althusser, L. (1971) *Lenin and Philosophy*, London: New Left Books.

Gramsci, A. (1971) *Selections From the Prison Notebooks*, New York: International.

STUART ALLAN

ideology and hegemony

Ideology is one of the most hotly contested concepts in film and televisual theory. Long-standing debates continue to be waged over how to extend its typical dictionary rendering, namely as 'a system of ideas, opinions or viewpoints', so as to theorize the lived materiality of the social relations of meaning production.

In tracing the etymological lineage of 'ideology',

Williams (1983: 153–4) contends that the term 'first appeared in English in 1796, as a direct translation of the new French word *idéologie* which had been proposed in that year by the rationalist philosopher Destutt de Tracy'. According to Tracy's formulation, ideology was to be recognized as 'the philosophy of mind' and, as such, constitutive of a new 'science of ideas' to be distinguished from 'ancient metaphysics'. This scientific conception of ideology would be eventually challenged, in turn, by an explicitly pejorative treatment, one which would enjoy much wider currency in the nineteenth century. Here Williams points to Napoleon Bonaparte's popularization of the term 'ideology' as a means to describe the deliberate falsification of what might otherwise be accepted (in Bonaparte's opinion, at least) as a truthful declaration about the world. To invoke the word 'ideological' to characterize a particular statement was to condemn it to the realm of suspicion, if not outright derision. Not surprisingly, then, to call one's opponent an 'ideologue' was to accuse them of promoting deceitfully abstract ideas, a rhetorical strategy still used today.

The conceptual tensions emergent in these early formulations of how best to define 'ideology' would preoccupy an increasing number of theorists throughout the nineteenth century. Significantly, however, the competing inflections of the term provisionally set down by writers like Tracy, among others, register a profound resonance in the writings of Karl **Marx**. If in Marx's view the approach adopted by Tracy was worthy of close scrutiny, it was none the less deeply misguided in its failure to grasp the structuring influence of economic factors on the ideas of a given period. Indeed, he attacked Tracy as a 'vulgar economist' and, even worse, a 'cold-blooded bourgeois-doctrinaire' (cited in Eagleton 1991: 69). Before turning to Marx's own attempts to shed light on the attendant issues at stake, though, it is important to note that he never actually proffered a formal definition of ideology itself (nor, for that matter, even coined the phrase 'false consciousness'). This observation stands in marked contrast to those claims sometimes made within film and television studies that an analytically coherent or totalized conception of ideology can be attributed to Marxism as a mode of enquiry. Hence the usual

qualifications about distinguishing Marx's own writings from Marxism are particularly pertinent where the concept of 'ideology' is concerned.

Many students and researchers in film and television studies have engaged with Marx's writings on ideology to great advantage. Marx used a variety of expressions and metaphors, often in conjunction with Engels, to describe the combination of **class** forces with ideological processes. Examples drawn from their work include those which appear to signify, first, a form of distortion, such as 'mist', 'camera obscura', 'phantoms', 'inversions on the retina', 'abstractions', 'illusions', 'blocks' or an '*idée fixe*'. A further set of terms suggests some form of reflection, such as 'reflexes', 'echoes' or 'sublimates'. If Marx did not employ the term 'false', he did rely on adjectives such as 'incorrect', 'twisted' and 'dream-like'. Engels, in contrast, wrote: 'Ideology is a process accomplished by the so-called thinker consciously, it is true, but with a false consciousness. The real motive forces impelling him [*sic*] remain unknown to him; otherwise it simply would not be an ideological process. Hence he imagines false or seeming motive forces' (Engels 1959: 408).

An important starting point is a celebrated passage which Marx co-wrote with Engels in *The German Ideology* around 1845:

> The ideas of the ruling class are in every epoch the ruling ideas, i.e. the class which is the ruling *material* force of society, is at the same time its ruling *intellectual* force. The class which has the means of material production at its disposal, has control at the same time over the means of mental production, so that thereby, generally speaking, the ideas of those who lack the means of mental production are subject to it.... In so far, therefore, as they rule as a class and determine the extent and compass of an epoch, it is self-evident that they... among other things... regulate the production and distribution of the ideas of their age: thus their ideas are the ruling ideas of the epoch.
>
> (Marx 1970: 64–5)

Different readings of this and related passages in *The German Ideology* tend to be marked by the relative degree of emphasis each places on the underlying problem of **determination**. For instance, in some readings this text is held up as an example *par excellence* of an economistic reading of ideology, one where references are made to ideology as a negative, restrictive force arising from (and reflective of) a fixed correspondence to the economic realm (see **economism**). For others, a more flexible understanding of ideology as a series of dependent effects (there is no essence of ideology), or as an incoherent 'system of beliefs characteristic of a certain class', is to be reached.

In general, however, of primary interest today is the exposition of ideology as a material practice whereby relations of domination are 'figured out' by the human subject. To this end, attention has tended to focus on the effectivity of dominant ideas so as to discern how the means by which the world is made sense of under capitalism ultimately work to serve ruling interests. As a result, Marx and Engels' declaration that 'the ideas of the ruling class are in every epoch the ruling ideas' (*ibid.*: 64) has sparked considerable debate over the class-specificity of ideology. The broad thesis, as high-lighted in the quotation above, is deceptively straightforward. Ruling ideas become the ideal expression of dominant material relationships, thus individual members of the ruling class, to the degree that they rule as a class, will then *determine* (produce, regulate and distribute) the ideas of their age: 'their ideas are the ruling ideas of the epoch'.

By accentuating the conditions of production of ruling or dominant ideas, Marx and Engels intended to dissolve any idealist dichotomy be-tween the autonomous (see **autonomy, relative**), independent ideas of the ruling class and the ruling class itself (*ibid.*: 65). How, then, to characterize the effectivity of ruling ideas? The representations of the dominant ideology are not forced on the exploited class, nor are they to be reduced to 'useful fictions'. Rather, the ruling class must work to advance its particular interests by depicting its ideas within the terms of *universality*. Ruling interests, like the symbolic processes through which they are spoken, are represented as the common interests of subordinate classes, the only correct, rational ones available (*ibid.*: 65–6). In this way, then, ideological ideas or symbols conceal their dependence on social structures, as well as their relation to determinate forms of politics (as defined by class interests).

This it would appear that Marx and Engels are content to relegate those social practices through which consciousness is organized to a subordinate position *vis-à-vis* the economic realm. Certainly, evidence to support such an assertion appears in Marx's 'Preface' to *A Contribution to the Critique of Political Economy*, a short overview of the Marxist position written almost fifteen years after *The German Ideology*. There Marx writes: 'The mode of production of material life conditions the general process of social, political and intellectual life. It is not the consciousness of men [*sic*] that determines their existence, but their social existence that determines their consciousness' (Marx 1970: 20–1). For Marx, it is during the social production of their existence that individuals *inevitably* enter into *definite relations of production*. Independently of the individual's conscious will, these relations are tied to the material development of the material forces of production. The totality of these relations of production, in turn, 'constitutes the economic structure of society, the real foundation, on which arises a legal and political superstructure and to which correspond definite forms of social con-sciousness' (*ibid.*: 20).

However, a critical question remains unclear: does the mode of production of material life *determine* or simply *condition* the general process of social, political and intellectual life? The point has been contested in terms of the *proper* translation from the German original, to the *real* test of Marx's historical studies. In any case, how this issue is decided for each particular reader will obviously have serious implications for the resultant form of Marxist theorizing.

Should analysis accept a mode of production which *conditions* life processes, for example, then it may accord a degree of relative autonomy to the various superstructural forms from the economic base (see **base and superstructure**). Any model of linear causality where the contradictions of capitalism as an economic system may be resolved and released only with its overthrow, may be also understood to suggest that the same is correct for its dominant social, political and intellectual practices. Evidently, this implicit assumption could also eventually result in the subjection of ideologi-cal analyses to economic analyses. Marxist research would then be reduced to looking to objectively defined class interests, if not class origins, to uncover prefigured ideological relations at work to conceal those contradictions. After all, according to Marx, changes in the economic foundation or base will ultimately lead, 'sooner or later', to the transformation of the *whole immense superstructure* (*ibid.*: 21). The social determination of a *dominated* ideology or, for that matter, the truth and falsity of those ideas to be internalized by subordinate classes through the **dominant ideology**, remains strictly tied to class interests.

Accordingly, analyses need to maintain a distinction between the material transformation of the economic conditions of production, on the one hand, and the 'legal, political, religious, artistic or philosophic – in short, ideological forms in which men [*sic*] become conscious of this conflict and fight it out' (*ibid.*: 21), on the other. **Consciousness**, it follows, is to be explained 'from the contradictions of material life, from the conflict existing between the social forces of production and the relations of production' (*ibid.*). However, should this conflict ever cease to exist, then the bourgeois mode of production itself will be made to collapse (*ibid.*). Therefore, once the transformation of the capitalist social formation has been achieved, the prehistory of human society will be brought to a close (*ibid.*: 21–2). The conceptual constraints of such a teleological presupposition, for some just wishful thinking, were clear: if we are to avoid attributing to ideology a rigidly functional purpose (so that contradictions must at all times be concealed), a new line of enquiry would have to be introduced.

The concept of commodity **fetishism**, outlined by Marx (1984) in the first volume of *Capital*, signals the final movement away from a notion of ideology as a practice located *above* the processes of production. This concept brings to bear a new emphasis on the fetishized forms *immanent to these very processes* (the term ideology appears to have been abandoned). In tracing how it is that the mechanisms of commoditization are deployed throughout the class structure, the entire range of social relations (ruling and non-ruling) are brought to the fore for analysis. An important question then becomes: how is it that the capitalist system itself succeeds in concealing its own social relations? In

advancing beyond explanations linked to conscious efforts to *deceive the masses*, the nature of the commodity itself is problematized by Marx. Specifically, given the transformation of social products into those commodities exchanged on the market, he argues that the actual commodity may be recognized as a *mysterious thing*.

For Marx, the mystical character of the commodity exists 'because in it the social character of men's labour appears to them as an objective character stamped upon the product of that labour; because the relation of the producers to the sum total of their own labour is presented to them as a social relation, existing not between themselves, but between the products of their labour' (*ibid.*: 77). In this way, the qualities of commodities (as products of labour) are rendered both perceptible and imperceptible by the senses. The example of light and the human eye is used by Marx with great effect: 'light from an object is perceived by us not as the subjective excitation of our optic nerve, but as the objective form of something outside the eye itself' (*ibid.*). Hence the appropriateness of Marx's observation that what is in fact a definite social relation between workers assumes, 'in their eyes, the fantastic form of a relation between things' (*ibid.*).

Fetishism is thereby regarded as being inseparable from the production of commodities: producers do not come into social contact with each other until the act of exchange (of their products) is realized (*ibid.*: 77–8). Those characteristics inferred from the products of labour through fetishistic processes are then made to appear *endowed with life* and *natural*. Subsequent to the **reification** of social phenomena, inanimate things are treated as if they had the qualities of the social (material relations between persons) while, concomitantly, definite relations between individuals are formulated as representing characteristics of material objects (social relations between things). Capital is thus made to possess an appearance of productivity which is actually that of the producer, thereby ensuring that the very lived relations of capitalist society work to conceal class antagonisms.

Today, those who are committed to retaining the concept of 'ideology' within a critical context continue to resist this displacement of its features to the realm of commodity fetishism. At the same time, many have argued that the question of class reductionism in ideology must be reconfigured so as to avoid the limitations of a mode of analysis which treats all subjects as class subjects or, in the same vein, holds that each ideological element has a *necessary* class belonging. As a result, the notion of 'hegemony' – derived, in part, from the Greek for 'leader' or 'ruler' enjoying political predominance – has been employed as a means to circumvent economistic readings of ideological imperatives by accentuating their *hegemonic* embodiment in the very process of the subject's discursive constitution. **Laclau** and Mouffe, among other post-Marxists, have highlighted the dangers of reifying a particular approach to theorizing ideological struggle in accordance with an *objective* relation (hence the *necessary* class belonging) between ideological elements. All too often, they insist, this type of conflict is reduced to a 'confrontation between two closed ideological systems completely opposed one to the other, in which victory consists in the total destruction of "bourgeois ideology" ' (Laclau and Mouffe 1982: 94).

Most attempts to define the concept of 'hegemony' attribute its development to **Gramsci**, a radical Italian philosopher who died in 1937 after more than a decade in Mussolini's prisons. Briefly, in his critique of power dynamics in modern societies, Gramsci describes hegemony as a relation of:

'spontaneous' consent given by the great masses of the population to the general direction imposed on social life by the dominant fundamental group; this consent is 'historically' caused by the prestige (and consequent confidence) which the dominant group enjoys because of its position and function in the world of production.

(Gramsci 1971: 12)

It is this implied distinction between consent and its opposite, coercion, which Gramsci recognizes to be crucial. In the case of the coercive force of ruling groups, he underlines the point that it is the 'apparatus of state coercive power which "legally" enforces discipline on those groups who do not "consent" either actively or passively' (*ibid.*). The exercise of this coercive force may involve, for example, the armed forces of the military or the police, courts and prison system to maintain 'law and order'.

This type of coercive control in modern societies is the exception rather than the rule, however, when it comes to organizing public consent. Power, Gramsci argues, is much more commonly exercised over subordinate groups by means of persuasion through 'political and ideological leadership'. It follows that a ruling group is hegemonic only to the degree that it acquires the consent of other groups within its preferred definitions of reality through this type of leadership. In Gramsci's words:

A social group can, and indeed must, already exercise 'leadership' before winning governmental power (this indeed is one of the principal conditions for the winning of such power); it subsequently becomes dominant when it exercises power, but even if it holds it firmly in its grasp, it must continue to 'lead' as well.

(*ibid.*: 57–8)

Subordinate groups are encouraged by the ruling group to negotiate reality within what are ostensibly the limits of '**common sense**' when, in actuality, this 'common sense' is consistent with dominant norms, values and beliefs. Hegemony is to be conceptualized, therefore, as a site of ideological struggle over this 'common sense'.

Gramsci's writings on hegemony have proven to be extraordinarily influential for examining the operation of the media in modern societies. Three particularly significant (and interrelated) aspects of the cultural dynamics of hegemony are the following:

1 *Hegemony is a lived process.* Hegemonic ideas do not circulate freely in the air above people's heads; rather, according to Gramsci, they have a material existence in the cultural practices, activities and rituals of individuals striving to make sense of the world around them. That is, hegemony is a process embodied in what Williams (1977: 110) aptly describes as 'a lived system of meanings and values', that is, as 'a whole body of practices and expectations, over the whole of living: our senses and assignments of energy, our shaping perceptions of ourselves and our world'. It follows that hegemony

constitutes 'a sense of reality for most people in the society' and, as such, is the contradictory terrain on which the 'lived dominance and subordination' of particular groups is struggled over in day-to-day cultural practices.

2 *Hegemony is a matter of 'common sense'*. A much broader category than ideology, common sense signifies the uncritical and largely unconscious way of perceiving and understanding the social world as it organizes habitual daily experience. Gramsci stresses that common sense, despite the extent to which it is 'inherited from the past and uncritically absorbed', may be theorized as a complex and disjointed 'infinity of traces', and as such never simply identical with a class-based ideology. 'Common sensical' beliefs, far from being fixed or immobile, are in a constant state of renewal: 'new ideas', as he notes, are always entering daily life and encountering the 'sedimentation' left behind by this contradictory, ambiguous, 'chaotic aggregate of disparate conceptions' (Gramsci 1971: 422). In critiquing what passes for common sense as 'the residue of absolutely basic and commonly-agreed, consensual wisdoms', Hall (1977: 325) further elaborates on this point: 'You cannot learn, through common sense, *how things are*: you can only discover *where they fit* into the existing scheme of things.'

3 *Hegemony is always contested*. Far from being a totally monolithic system or structure imposed from above, then, lived hegemony is an active process of negotiation; it can never be taken for granted by the ruling group. In Gramsci's words (1971: 348), at stake is 'a cultural battle to transform the popular "mentality" and to diffuse the philosophical innovations which will demonstrate themselves to be "historically true" to the extent that they become concretely – i.e. historically and socially – universal'. Consequently, no one group can maintain its hegemony without adapting to changing conditions, a dynamic which will likely entail making certain strategic compromises with the forces which oppose its ideological authority. Hegemony as a form of dominance is neither invoked nor accepted in a passive manner; as Williams (1977: 112) points out: 'It has continually to be renewed, recreated, defended, and modified [in

relation to] pressures not at all its own'. Hence Gramsci's contention that common sense be theorized as the site on which the hegemonic rules of practical conduct and norms of moral behaviour are reproduced and, crucially, also challenged and resisted.

Significantly, then, this shift to address the cultural dynamics of hegemony displaces a range of different formulations of '**dominant ideology**', most of which hold that media discourse be theorized as 'concealing' or 'masking' the 'true' origins of economic antagonisms, that is, their essential basis in the class struggle. At the same time, this emphasis on the hegemonic imperatives of media discourse allows us to avoid the suggestion that the 'effects' of media discourse on its audience be understood simply as a matter of 'false consciousness'. Instead, this alternative line of enquiry provides important new insights into how media discourses naturalize – to varying degrees – the social divisions and hierarchies of modern society as being *rational*, *reasonable* and *appropriate*, and, in this way, potentially *hegemonic*.

See also: praxis

References

Eagleton, T. (1991) *Ideology*, London: Verso.

Engels, F. (1959). 'Engels to Franz Mehring' (first published 1893), in L. S. Feuer (ed.) *Marx and Engels: Basic Writings on Politics and Philosophy*, New York: Doubleday, pp. 407–10.

Gramsci, A. (1971) *Selections From the Prison Notebooks*, New York: International.

Hall, S. (1977) 'Culture, the Media and the "Ideological Effect" ', in J. Curran, M. Gurevitch and J. Woollacott (eds) *Mass Communication and Society*, London: Edward Arnold, pp. 315–48.

Laclau, E. and Mouffe, C. (1982) 'Recasting Marxism: Hegemony and New Political Movements (Interview)', *Socialist Review* vol. 12, no. 6, pp. 91–113.

Marx, K. (1970) 'Preface' in *A Contribution to the Critique of Political Economy* (first published 1859), Moscow: Progress, pp. 19–23.

—— (1984) *Capital, Volume One* (first published 1867), New York: International.

Marx, K. and Engels, F. (1970) *The German Ideology*

(first published 1845–6), New York: International.

Williams R. (1977) *Marxism and Literature*, Oxford: Oxford University Press.

—— (1983) *Keywords*, London: Flamingo.

STUART ALLAN

image

The image might refer to the visual tracks of a film or television show, a shot or even a single frame. The following might affect their look and meaning: **framing**, **mise-en-scène**, duration and film stock. While images resist conventional semiology, they can be analysed according to Charles Sanders **Peirce**'s structuralist taxonomy. Mainstream films generally privilege **narrative** over specific images but this priority is often inverted in **avant-garde** cinema. Mainstream films sometimes use images that are so arresting they stop the narrative as, for example, with a star's first appearance or a particularly striking special effect.

See also: aesthetics; camera style and lens style

MOYA LUCKETT

imaginary

One of the three 'orders' of psychoanalytic experience (along with the symbolic and the real) proposed by Jacques **Lacan**. The imaginary order comes about through what Lacan calls the '**mirror stage**', when the physically uncoordinated infant achieves an image of bodily coherence by seeing its mirror reflection. This moment is one of fundamental *misrecognition*, since the infant identifies with a coherence it does not yet possess. The imaginary thus indicates a subject decentred in relation to time, in so far as he/she achieves coherence only 'retroactively'. Within the symbolic order, this same retroaction governs the process by which the signifier acquires its meaning or signified, suggesting that the seeming coherence of language is an imaginary effect.

The first wave of psychoanalytic film theory likened the movie screen to a mirror in which the spectator mistook the essentially constructed world of the film for a representation of 'reality'.

See also: enunciation; psychoanalysis; signifying practice; symbolic code

ANGELO RESTIVO

independent cinema

The term 'independent cinema' refers to a cinematic practice that in some way stands as an alternative, or takes an **oppositional** stance, to a dominant, mainstream cinema. The term itself embraces a range of filmmaking practices, both commercial and non-commercial, and extends beyond film production to include systems of distribution and exhibition. As with all forms of filmmaking, independent practice is underpinned and shaped by ideological, technological and economic factors.

At the centre of any understanding of independent cinema is the notion of a dominant cinema. Classical Hollywood cinema has become the model for mainstream cinema in much of the world, and many countries have imitated Hollywood's successful **mode of production** (see **classical Hollywood cinema and new Hollywood cinema**). However, since the early years of the twentieth century there has been a tradition of challenge or opposition to the standardized products and production methods of mainstream cinema. An independent cinema has offered filmmakers the opportunity to tackle subjects and use techniques antithetical to the mainstream, to adopt modes of production at variance with the studio mode, to explore new relationships between the film text and the viewer, and often to pursue filmmaking in a non-commercial context. For this last reason, independent films tend to be funded by private means, state sponsorship (through agencies like the Film Council in Britain and the National Endowment for the Arts in the United States), philanthropic bodies (the Guggenheim Foundation) or by television companies (Channel 4 in Britain and public television in the US).

The term independent cinema has no universal meaning, and is more appropriately considered in relation to specific manifestations of cinematic independence within particular historical and cultural contexts. In Britain an independent cinema grew around the production of experimental, **documentary** and educational films in the 1920s and 1930s. Best known of these are the state sponsored films of the Empire Marketing Board and GPO Film Units, both under the leadership of John **Grierson**. While Grierson was personally satisfied that state sponsorship did not compromise his film units' independence, one must nevertheless question the extent to which any filmmaking practice funded by an external body can be truly independent. Grierson's motivation to work in documentary sprang from his objections to the fiction film, which he described as 'meretricious'. Like many independent films, these were not theatrically distributed; in this case, the films were shown in film clubs, at trades union meetings, to political parties and at schools.

In the US, three broad types of independent film practice developed in the twenty years following the Second World War. Experimental filmmakers like Maya Deren and Stan Brakhage pioneered an American **avant-garde** film practice that placed emphasis on an ideology of film as personal expression. In the early 1960s, taking their lead from the new cinemas of Europe and Japan, feature filmmakers like Shirley Clarke and John Cassavetes pioneered the 'new American cinema', while later in the 1960s the work of Richard Leacock and D. A. Pennebaker in **cinéma-vérité** represented another form of independent film practice.

The reasons why filmmakers choose to work within the independent sector are varied. The militant filmmaking collectives of the 1960s and 1970s (Cinema Action, the Dziga **Vertov** Group) were motivated by political and ideological concerns, which included a rejection of the power structure and organizational model of the Hollywood mode of production. American filmmakers such as Russ Meyer and David Lynch have chosen to work as independents to escape the control and convention of the mainstream, thereby maintaining creative freedom and authorial control at various stages of the production process, yet remain at the margins of commercial cinema. For filmmakers like Jean-Luc **Godard** and Cassavetes independence, among other things, allowed the opportunity to challenge the dominance of the script and work with improvisational techniques of film production – an uneconomic practice in Hollywood terms.

As with sources of finance and modes of production, the distribution and exhibition of independent films varies in its methods. Most independently produced feature films will aim for a limited theatrical release on the **art cinema** circuit, although occasionally a film with strong commercial potential may be picked up for distribution by a studio or one of the major distribution companies. Shorts and documentaries are often distributed and exhibited by collectives, like the film workshops established in the 1960s, or by state subsidized arts organizations.

Further reading

Hillier, J. (ed.) (1999) *American Independent Cinema*, London: BFI Publishing.

Macpherson, D. (ed.) (1980) *Traditions of Independence*, London: BFI Publishing.

ANDREW BIRTWISTLE

indexical

'Indexical', from the Latin *index*, meaning 'indicator'. In the semiotic categorization by Charles Sanders **Peirce**, the class of signs that bear a causal relationship to their referent. In contrast to symbolic signs, which have a purely conventional relation to their referent, and iconic signs (see **icon**), which have a relation of similarity to their referent, indexical signs rely on experience and represent an indication of a further existing object or state; for example, smoke indicates fire, a high pulse indicates fever. Like all other types of signs, indexical signs are context sensitive and ambiguous (a high pulse might indicate excitement).

EVA VIETH

indirect address

Indirect address is a **mode of address** characteristic of realist or classical Hollywood cinema **narrative** wherein camera (and audience) remain unacknowledged by the performers giving the impression that on-screen events have not been staged for the camera/audience, but are being observed secretly (see **classical Hollywood cinema and new Hollywood cinema**). Techniques such as unobtrusive camera movement and **continuity editing** further disguise the signs of construction of a film **text**. A pleasurable illusion of **voyeurism** is reinforced by the darkness of the cinema auditorium.

Laura **Mulvey** suggests that this mode of address is gendered – directed towards a heterosexual masculine spectator, privileging the female body as the object of voyeuristic scrutiny.

See also: feminist theory; gaze, the; gender

BRUCE BENNETT

information theory

Information theory presumes to create abstractions, often mathematical, of the way in which information is processed and circulated; its most common application is in engineering, especially in relation to computing. In essence, information theory makes no comment on the *content* of information and relies on the notion that information is reducible to **binary** data. By holding content constant in this manner, information theory can model information flows in purely probabilistic terms, based on predictability of binary data being received and understood as data. The principal goal of information theory is to seek increased efficiencies by minimizing the time spent in processing information to distinguish it from surrounding non-information.

See also: reading and reception theory

Further reading

Shannon, C. and Weaver, W. (1949) *The Mathematical Theory of Communication*, Champaign, IL: University of Illinois Press.

MATTHEW ALLEN

infotainment/infomercials

'Infotainment' refers to a blurring of the division between 'news' and 'entertainment'. US journalist Neal Gabler regards this development as dangerous because:

> When everything is looked at for its entertainment value, when the news is examined for its entertainment value, when politics is essentially analysed for its entertainment value, when religion is examined for its entertainment value, and when entertainment, frankly, is the pre-eminent value in American life, everything tends to get trivialised. Serious issues that don't conform themselves to entertainment will not get addressed.
>
> (Cited in Kelley 1997: 178)

In the United States, veteran Public Broadcasting System (PBS) journalist, Robert McNeil insists that the news is now much less sober in tone and presentation than it was in his early career. He believes that such changes have had an adverse effect on reporting the news. Although McNeil suggests that some forms of American journalism have always sought to appeal to 'the cheaper end of the carnival side-show', more 'serious' forms of journalism are now following this path (MacNeil, cited in Hickey 1998: 4).

British journalist Simon Hoggart (1995) offers a useful outline of the stages events tend to go through as they are processed into easily digestible stories by news organizations. In the first stage, news is turned into human interest. For example, public issues like gun control are explored 'through the eyes of an innocent victim or, if your agenda is different, someone who saved her own life by keeping a gun at home' (Hoggart 1995: 21). In the second stage, stories that cannot be turned into human interest are 'bit by bit, junked from the schedules'. Finally, if a story has a wider significance this aspect is typically ignored. What particularly troubles Hoggart about the move towards entertainment-led news is that not only is it being turned into the equivalent of fast food, but more important, the 'real, slippery, hard-to-handle news will soon be forgotten' in the process.

Some critics disagree with this assessment, proposing that there is nothing necessarily wrong with the media presenting the news in more entertaining ways. It is argued that infotainment programmes can be useful sources of information on a range of important public issues. Carol Reuss (1999: 231) notes that: 'The infotainment media often appeal to audiences that give little, if any, attention to more serious media. In that respect, those that contain even minimal amounts of information *can* help these people make decisions – they can help make democracy work'. However, Reuss also acknowledges that the infotainment media 'tend to overemphasise entertainment, to oversimplify, trivialise, and titillate', all of which tends to 'confuse their audiences about important issues' (*ibid.*).

In blurring the boundaries of information, entertainment and **advertising**, 1984 is often cited as marking the arrival of the 'infomercial', when the American Federal Communications Commission (FCC) eliminated the regulation limiting the length of television commercials to two minutes. Specifically, an infomercial is a particular type of televisual advertising which is programme-long (in the United States, thirty minutes is the smallest block of airtime a television station will sell without interrupting its programming schedules). Some infomercials take the form of talk shows and include regular hosts and guests who direct all discussion to selling a particular product (see **chat/talk show**). Critics have argued that the product for sale in infomercials is not the merchandise being advertised. Instead, the consumer is being encouraged to associate with a particular lifestyle which is embodied by the acquisition of the material goods which infomercials advertise.

See also: tabloid television

References

Hickey, N. (1998) 'Money Lust: How Pressure for Profit is Perverting Journalism', *Columbia Journalism Review*, (July/August), pp. 1–4.
Hoggart, S. (1995) 'Filleted Fish', *New Statesman and Society*, 24 March, pp. 20–1.
Kelley, J. (1997) 'Prospects for the Future', in E. E. Dennis and R. W. Snyder (eds) *Media and Public Life*, New Brunswick, NJ and London: Transaction Publishers.

Reuss, C. (1999) 'Infotainment Programming', in A. D. Gordon and J. M. Kittross (eds) *Controversies in Media Ethics* (2nd edn), New York: Longman.

Further reading

Franklin, B. (1997) *Newszak and News Media*, London: Arnold.

CYNTHIA CARTER

Innis, Harold Adam

b. 1894; d. 1952

Harold Innis was born in Otterville, Canada. He was a political economist and pioneering communication scholar who, in his early work, developed the 'staple thesis' of economic development arguing against 'continentalism' in *The Fur Trade in Canada* (1930) and *The Cod Fisheries* (1940). During the last ten years of his life, he turned to the study of communication, writing *Empire and Communications* (1950) and *The Bias of Communication* (1951). Innis argued that there are two types of media: those that are 'time biased' and those that are 'space biased'. Time biased media are not easily distributed across space but endure over time (e.g., writing on stone tablets), whereas space biased media are easily distributed over distances but are less durable over time (e.g., print and electronic media). Time biased media are closely linked to traditional, religious societies whereas spaced biased media are characteristic of societies intent on empire building and the expansion of secular power. Globally, there has been a historical shift from time to space biased media. Innis' theories strongly influenced the work of Marshall **McLuhan**.

See also: globalization

Further reading

Kroker, A. (1985) *Technology and the Canadian Mind: Innis/McLuhan/Grant*, New York: St Martins.
Melody, W., Salter, L. and Heyer, P. (eds) (1981) *Culture, Communication and Dependency: The Tradition of H. A. Innis*, Norwood, NJ: Ablex.

CYNTHIA CARTER

institution

When conceptualizing the configuration of social systems, it is convenient for heuristic purposes to separate society into three different levels of organization. At the most fundamental level are the individual social actors without which a society could not be said to exist. Observable at this micro-level is the interpersonal behaviour of individual social agents, arising primarily out of face-to-face interaction. At furthest remove from this level of analysis are the large-scale social structures that are suprapersonal in character and delimit the overall disposition of elements within the totality of the social system itself. Typical examples of such large-scale phenomenon would be the nation-state and **multinational** capitalism. Between these two orders of social organization is situated the institution, a social entity that is an element of the social whole but is itself composed of individual agents and the social practices in which they participate. The analysis of social institutions assumes a large and privileged place within social theory and has taken on increasing significance as a general approach within film and television studies.

Overview of concept

There are two fundamental characteristics connected with the notion of an institution. The first distinguishing feature of an institution is that it is a collective group composed of individual agents. It is this basic sense that is employed when someone describes, for example, the family, the corporation or the judicial system as institutions. One can also speak of an institution as a set of regulative practices. In this respect, one can legitimately describe such things as languages, customs, rituals and conventions (see **conventions**) as kinds of institutions to the extent that they are regularized forms of human activity. What the notion of a regulative practice picks out, then, are the patterned social activities that are normatively sanctioned and associated with the fulfilment of the duties of the social roles of the collective. Hence a family is not merely a group but a hierarchical configuration of social positions that give rise to established patterns of behaviour. What differentiates larger scale social institutions such as the corporation or judicial system from the family is

that the order of complexity has increased through the multiplication of social roles within the group and the increased specification of their attendant duties.

While institutions share these underlying traits, there are none the less distinctions within social theory in terms of the social function they are believed to subserve. Although typologies tend to vary, among the most frequently identified categories are: (i) institutions pertaining to procreation and education, such as the family and the schooling system; (ii) institutions that deal with economic activity, as in corporations and banks; (iii) political institutions that direct and monitor the use of power, such as governments and political parties; and (iv) cultural institutions, such as the art gallery or the museum, which regulate the production and the conservation of cultural artefacts. While it is convenient to distinguish institutions in terms of their social function in this fashion, it is a more difficult matter to keep these social functions entirely distinct. Often the pursuit of a specific goal of an institution, say, the implementation of sex education in schools, will have wider political implications. In addition, social institutions can be perceived to pursue several social functions at once. Cinema and television offer excellent examples. Both the Hollywood film industry and American television have been alternatively analysed as economic enterprises, as political extensions of the dominant social group, or as the producers of popular cultural artefacts. In these multiple guises, it is difficult to ascertain which social function of the Hollywood cinema or of American television should be taken to predominate.

The analysis of institutions in terms of social functions has often been linked to the theoretical position called functionalism. Functionalism advanced the position that societies should be conceived as analogous to organic systems with functionally interdependent components. Just as the human body is composed of different parts, such as the heart or lungs, whose proper functioning ensures the organism's survival, societies too are composed of parts, in this case interrelated institutions that function to ensure the long run stability of the society in question. These institutional pursuits are often conceived in this framework as societal needs. The concept is a difficult one in that societal needs can be taken to refer to, alternatively, the needs of the social system itself (as in the needs of a capitalist society), or to the basic physical and psychological needs of the individuals of the group (as in the need for food and shelter); two senses that are not entirely identical and may even conflict. But even on both these different interpretations of the concept, the fulfilment of societal needs is assumed to be inherently connected with the reproduction of the essential conditions of social existence.

This functionalist account of social institutions is not the only one within social theory. Revised versions of the model have been advanced that place the aims of institutional pursuits elsewhere. Instead of perceiving social institutions as wholly incorporated within the social system and consonant with its general aims, these alternate accounts depict institutions as being semi-autonomous entities. On this view, the objectives of an institution are not necessarily assigned by the social system itself but can be internally developed through a commitment to secure the institution's own long-term continuity. An example from the history of the cinema can illustrate this important point. As a trade organization, the creation of the Motion Picture Producers and Distributors Association (MPPDA) was designed to serve the long-term interests of the American film industry. In particular, its setting up of the Production Code Administration as an internal **censorship** body was motivated by a collective desire on the part of the industry to prevent any potential external interference arising from state or federal intervention. As this example reveals, the institutional objectives of the American film industry were self-serving. The introduction of self-censorship was not intended to further any broader societal goal, as in upholding socially shared standards of decency, but was a strategically motivated move that protected the industry's money-making activities.

Another aspect stressed by the revised functionalist conception of social institutions is the incorporation of social contradictions into the model that were overlooked in the original functionalist account. Societies are not smoothly functioning systems bereft of social discord, nor are social institutions without their own forms of internal conflict. Institutional analysis conducted from this revised framework consequently examines the points of tension where social contradictions may arise. The two most significant areas that have been explored in this respect are inter- and intra-institutional conflict. Inter-institutional conflict refers to the struggles that arise when two or more institutions have opposing aims. Government censorship of certain films released by the film industry is one such example of inter-institutional conflict; the United States Congress' investigations of violence on television are another. Intra-institutional conflict, on the other hand, refers to the contradictions that arise within the institution itself. The Hollywood film industry, for instance, has had its share of labour disputes and its producers and directors have often been at odds with one another. When thinking about social institutions, then, it is important to avoid the danger of conceiving them too monolithically. Institutional analysis is not just the investigation of an optimally functioning machine but also an examination of how institutions conflict and internally unravel.

Institutional analysis and the studio system

The primary manner in which institutional analysis has been applied within media studies has been in the historical investigation of the studio system, particularly that of the classical Hollywood cinema (see **classical Hollywood cinema and new Hollywood cinema; studio systems**). As a distinct methodological approach, the institutional analysis of the studio system constitutes the middle path of film studies. On the one hand, institutional analysis avoids the singular concentration paid to the film **text** itself that sacrifices the wider social picture for a narrow attention to the textual details of a film. On the other hand, the approach is not so encompassing that the analysis of films is swallowed up in the investigation of the broader social currents of history. By examining the immediate social contexts in which films were made, institutional analysis seeks the precise historical link connecting society with text.

It is understandable that as an area of investigation the studio system has been principally studied through an institutional approach. Studio systems clearly exhibit the two fundamental characteristics shared by all institutions. Filmmaking within a studio system is not the solitary endeavour of a lone filmmaker but a collective enterprise with its own organizational structures and divisions of labour that determine the daily chores of the multitude of workers involved in any film production. In addition, studio systems are also typified by their regulative practices that attempt to effect a uniformity of production standards. Standardization as an institutional objective is desirable from the studio system's point of view in that the standardization of production practices is not only cost efficient but also ensures the serial manufacture of 'quality' films. Further motivating the standardization of production practices is the reliance on formulas that have proven previously successful at the box office. While innovation is tolerated, and to a certain extent even promoted, extreme divergence from standard filmmaking practice is generally discouraged.

When examining the regulative practices of studio production, it is useful to break them down into two rough types: product conventions and production conventions. Product conventions dictate the actual form and content of the films to be made. Exemplary in this respect are the canons of classical Hollywood **narrative** (see **canon**): that a classical Hollywood film should have a goal-oriented protagonist; that the story should be conveyed in an intelligible manner; that the temporal and spatial relationships between the shots of a film are to be clearly marked, these are the more obvious dictates of the classical mould. Production conventions, however, refer to the guidelines of how film production itself should be organized. Crucial to the organization of film production within the studio system is the function of the continuity script throughout the preparation, shooting and post-production phases. A detailed continuity script allows film producers to draw up tentative budgets, provides instructions for the actors and technicians as to how scenes are to be performed and filmed during the actual shoot, and, finally, facilitates the reassemblage of the shots during the editing process. While these two different forms of conventions serve different regulative functions within the studio system, it is important to bear in mind their underlying similarity. Conventions are above all shared frames of knowledge that co-ordinate collective behaviour

in the attainment of particular ends. As such, product and production conventions serve the studio system well in the co-ordination of its institutional activities.

Development of institutional analysis within film and television studies

Although historical precedents can be traced far back in the study of the cinema, the historical roots of contemporary institutional analysis are to be found in the auteurism of the late 1960s and early 1970s (see **authorship**). One of the principal criticisms of the auteurist approach was that it elided the collaborative character of film production and presented a false image of the auteur heroically overcoming the institutionally imposed constraints of the film industry. Taking these criticisms into account, certain film theorists sought to contextualize the auteurist approach by marrying it with a more historically sensitive framework. This initial framework was to be **genre** production.

With its repeated use of formulaic narrative structures and reliance on a readily recognizable stock of generic conventions, genre production was the most obvious point at which to situate the auteur within the filmmaking institution. Two works are particularly representative of this approach: Jim Kitses' discussion of the Western in *Horizons West* (1969) and Colin McArthur's analysis of the gangster film in *Underworld USA* (1972). After discussing the conventions associated with each of these respective genres, Kitses and McArthur go on to place the aesthetic strategies of certain auteurs with respect to these institutionalized conventions (see **aesthetics**). In deliberate contrast to previous auteur criticism, Kitses and McArthur maintain that the institutional constraints of genre conventions did not compromise the auteurs' efforts but exerted a positive influence on their films by constraining creative excess and by setting up certain limits in which to work. In a similar fashion, Edward Buscombe attempted to situate a significant portion of Raoul Walsh's *œuvre* within the context of Warner Bros' studio style of the 1940s. In his influential article, 'Walsh and Warner Brothers' (1974), Buscombe claimed that Walsh drew on several elements of the studio's distinctive resources, such as its stars, creative personnel and sets, to integrate his own filmmaking approach with that promoted by the studio. Taken together, what all of these analyses signalled to other film scholars of the time was the necessity of exploring the institutional structure of the filmmaking industry as an area of investigation in its own right.

Despite this newly awakened emphasis on the Hollywood film industry as an institution, auteur critics such as Kitses and McArthur were still far too committed to the auteurist framework to produce any exhaustive analyses of the complex workings of the studio system. Their work inadvertently indicated that a comprehensive understanding of the institutional structure of the American film industry was one of the more underdeveloped areas of film studies. This gap began to be slowly filled during the 1970s and 1980s with the publication of major anthologies and texts devoted entirely to the institutional analysis of the Hollywood studio system. These publications differentiated themselves from other contemporaneous writings in film studies in two important respects. First, this work was produced primarily by film historians who set new standards of historical scholarship in the investigation of film history. Through archival research of internal studio records and an examination of the relevant trade papers of the period, film historians were capable of constructing an intricate picture of the organizational structure and institutional objectives of the Hollywood studio system that eclipsed previous depictions. Representative of such empirical investigation is Thomas Schatz's *The Genius of the System* (1988), which traces the origination and dissolution of the Hollywood studio system in rich, historical detail. In addition to the overall emphasis placed on historical research, these works were further distinguishable from other frameworks in film studies by their thorough discussion of the economic dimension of film production. Film historians contributing to the collection *The American Film Industry* (Balio 1985) conclusively demonstrated how economic issues, particularly that of the institutional drive for profit maximization, permeated almost all aspects of industry structure and policy over the course of its history. This merger of economic analysis with historical explication arguably reached its height in *The Classical Hollywood Cinema* (Bordwell *et al.* 1985). Here, the authors present a compelling case as to how the form and content of classical Hollywood films was largely determined by the institutional context of production in which they were made. In short, institutional analysis has left its indelible stamp on film studies through its complete overhaul of the ways in which the Hollywood cinema is both conceptualized and studied.

It would be a mistake to conclude that the scope of institutional analysis terminates with the investigation of the Hollywood studio system. Other applications of the institutional framework give evidence of the fertility of the approach as a general research strategy. The most obvious manner in which institutional analysis has been extended beyond the realm of the Hollywood cinema has been in the examination of studio systems operating in other national contexts. One pioneering study in this respect has been John Ellis' 'Made in Ealing' (1975), which discusses the internal organization of Ealing studios and the policies it pursued given the particular national context in which it operated. Aside from the study of studio systems in their various national contexts, institutional analysis has also been applied to the growing field of reception studies (see **reading and reception theory**). An early instance of such an application was in the development of the theory of the **cinematic apparatus**. In this psychoanalytical account, the conditions of reception have specific ideological determinations that delimit spectatorial response (see **psychoanalysis**). In contrast to this kind of analysis, and more in keeping with the economic and historical approach that had been previously outlined, is Douglas Gomery's *Shared Pleasures* (1992), which examines the institutional structuring of the conditions of reception from the nickelodeon era to the contemporary period of home **video**. Finally, the institutional framework has been extended to the investigation of the very institutions of film criticism itself. In *Making Meaning* (1989), David **Bordwell** argues that the creation of film criticism is an institutionalized activity, with its own forms of social networks and regulative practices. If so, institutional analysis is not merely an effective framework in the study of the cinema, but can also lead to a genuine sociological understanding of the ways we think about films.

Institutional analysis also furthers our understanding of television, although the institutional approach is rather underdeveloped within television studies as compared to film studies. In the United States, television studies has largely been conducted by social scientists working within the mass communications tradition, who, concerning themselves with the supposed negative effects of television, concentrated on texts and audiences, while cultural studies scholars have reacted against this tradition by celebrating the active audience (see **audience**). Todd Gitlin's pioneering work, *Inside Prime Time* (1985), was one of the first scholarly investigations of the television industry; a comprehensive intra-institutional analysis, including interviews with several leading producers, showing how television programmes get produced (and fail to get produced). Michele Hilmes' *Hollywood and Broadcasting: From Radio to Cable* (1990), an historical inter-institutional analysis, illustrates how the relationship between broadcast institutions and Hollywood has shaped the economics and texts of both industries. Ien Ang's *Desperately Seeking the Audience* (1991) discusses the ways in which the American and European television industries have conceived of and tried to measure their audiences.

References

Ang, I. (1991) *Desperately Seeking the Audience*, London: Routledge.

Balio, T. (ed.) (1985) *The American Film Industry* (revised edn; first published 1976), Madison: University of Wisconsin Press.

Bordwell, D., Staiger, J. and Thompson, K. (1985) *The Classical Hollywood Cinema*, London: Routledge.

Buscombe, E. (1974) 'Walsh and Warner Brothers', in Phil Hardy (ed.) *Raoul Walsh*, Edinburgh: Edinburgh Film Festival, pp. 51–61.

Ellis, J. (1975) 'Made in Ealing', *Screen*, vol. 16, no. 1, pp. 78–127.

Giddens, A. (1977) 'Functionalism: *après la lutte*', in *Studies in Social and Political Theory*, London: Hutchinson, pp. 96–129.

Gitlin, T. (1985) *Inside Prime Time*, New York: Pantheon.

Gomery, D. (1992) *Shared Pleasures*, Madison: University of Wisconsin Press.

Hilmes, M. (1990) *Hollywood and Broadcasting: From Radio to Cable*, Urbana: University of Illinois Press.

Kitses, J. (1969) *Horizons West*, London: Thames and Hudson.

McArthur, C. (1972) *Underworld USA*, London: Secker and Warburg.

Schatz, T. (1988) *The Genius of the System*, New York: Metropolitan Books.

TICO ROMAO

Internet

The Internet refers to the global network of interconnected computers. It is a communications system that allows computers and smaller networks, connected via modems, to speak to one another using mutual languages known as protocols. In its early years, the Internet consisted entirely of plain text files and usage required an extensive knowledge of the multi-user operating system, UNIX. With the development of the World Wide Web in the early 1990s, the Internet became user-friendly and its popularity rocketed. Although 'Web' and 'Net' are often used interchangeably, the Web is actually an interface system that allows users to access and move around the Internet. Web 'browser' programmes use hypertext coding to translate highlighted keywords (hypertext 'links') in the text into unseen commands that communicate with a source computer to bring up the selected files on screen.

Other Web developments have transformed the look and capability of the Internet. Graphical Web browsers such as Netscape Navigator allow images and text to co-exist on screen. Computers equipped with soundcards can download and play sound files, while the development of 'streaming' formats allows sounds to be broadcast and received in a similar way to radio. Movie and animation formats allow moving images, complete with soundtracks, to be accessed via the Internet and played on a computer screen. These developments suggest that Internet technology is rapidly moving towards a convergence with digital television and radio (see **digital communication**).

The Internet consists of a variety of facilities for storing, retrieving and sending information.

Websites are files of linked documents (Web pages) set up and maintained by organizations, institutions, companies or individuals. Together, these constitute the largest databank in the world, allowing users almost instant access to information that once upon a time would have taken months or even years to compile. However, the Internet is largely unregulated and researchers are advised to double-check information posted on Websites which are not hosted by reputable organizations.

Interactive facilities include newsgroups (topic-related discussion groups where visitors can read and 'post' messages), chatrooms (channels which allow users to communicate synchronously) and MUDs (multi-user domains for interactive role-playing games). The most popular and widely used Internet tool is e-mail, which sends and receives electronic messages in a tiny fraction of the time it takes postal mail ('snail mail') to travel.

Scholarly thinking about the Internet roughly divides into two camps: the pessimistic and the cautiously optimistic. Old-school, post-modernist critics like Jean **Baudrillard** and Paul **Virilio** have tended to treat the Internet and other computer media with suspicion, regarding the growing importance of communications and information technologies as symptomatic of the deepening atomization and hyperrealism of late twentieth-century society and culture (see **hyperreal; modernism and post-modernism**). In contrast, Howard **Rheingold** (1993) guardedly argues that some kinds of Internet usage represent attempts to rebuild the sort of community that no longer exists elsewhere in western society. For Rheingold, and other 'optimists', the global and interactive character of the Internet gives it the potential to promote greater social cohesion, access to information and freedom of speech.

Other recurrent topics in the developing field of Internet studies include issues of public access and democratization, regulation and **censorship**, **commodification** and privacy. In particular, the notion of 'virtual identity' has been the object of much research and debate. In virtual environments, Internet users are semi-anonymous and at liberty to construct and alter their on-line identities at will. Determinants such as **gender**, **race**, **class** and age are neither immediately apparent nor fixed in Internet communications. Some feminist critics see the fluidity of virtual identities as a means of moving beyond repressive social categories and related codes of social behaviour. According to Donna **Haraway** (1991), virtual experiences spill over into 'real' life, with liberatory consequences. Overall, most commentators agree that the growth of the Internet has significant political, social and cultural implications that have yet to be fully explored.

See also: cyberspace; Internet and the World Wide Web; technological change; virtual reality

References

Haraway, D. (1991) 'A Cyborg Manifesto', in D. Haraway, *Simians, Cyborgs, and Women*, New York: Routledge.

Rheingold, H. (1993) *The Virtual Community: Homesteading on the Electronic Frontier*, New York: Harper Collins.

Further reading

Porter, D. (ed.) (1997) *Internet Culture*, New York and London: Routledge.

SARA GWENLLIAN JONES

Internet and the World Wide Web

The Internet is a 'network of networks' of computers. A computer network in a school or business, given the necessary hardware and provision of services by a local or regional supplier, can send and receive information in a number of forms to and from computers on other networks around the world. A computer which is part of a network connected in this way is described as being 'on the Internet'.

When one computer on the Internet communicates with another, they exchange digitally formatted information – streams of millions of 0s and 1s. That information is encoded at the sending end and decoded at the receiving end, and may ultimately represent text, images or sounds, or a combination of these elements (see **encoding; encoding-decoding model**). The Internet thus allows for rapid and relatively easy exchange of information and data of various kinds through the single technique of digital representation (see **digital communication**). The popularization of the Internet in the late twentieth century, moreover, opened up the possibility of new methods of sending and receiving moving images and sounds which traditionally would have been the province of television broadcasters and/or cable providers.

The Internet's roots are in the US military: the US Department of Defense funded research into the connectivity of distant computers during the 1960s and beyond. The first network funded in this manner was the ARPANET; as more networks developed, and became interconnected, the growing 'network of networks' became known as the 'Internet' (Hafner and Lyon 1996). Some of the research and many of the early test sites for this type of networking were at universities; accordingly, at least prior to the mid-1990s, most Internet communication was among researchers, scientists, academics and students.

The transmission of digital information on the Internet does not dictate any particular form; that is, given appropriate software and agreed upon standards of encoding and decoding, the data may represent a graphic image, a sound or a block of text, and may be packaged and handled, at the sending and receiving ends, in a variety of ways. Thus an e-mail message behaves very similarly to a sound clip, during the phase of digital transmission along the Internet, though of course the two things take very different forms once they have been processed for human perception.

The Internet thus serves as a kind of common carrier for many different communication services, including e-mail, file transfer, the M-Bone (a real-time video conferencing service), the World Wide Web (see below), telnet (a means of gaining direct access to accounts on distant computers) and so forth. Contrary to the impression often generated by advertisers and by the more utopian commentators on the world of the media, Internet access is not universal. For those outside of universities and businesses, it almost always involves significant expenditures, both on hardware and on connections and services. Still, while it continues to serve a smaller rather than a larger population, the Internet differs from other electronic media in that it does allow for provision of content by members of the general public, and for a degree of interactivity not on offer in any other medium. It may be that Internet saturation of homes will only come about when what Brian Winston (1998) calls 'the suppression of radical potential' has been assured by governmental/corporate interests.

There is no one form of Internet communication, any more than there is one form of communication on the electromagnetic spectrum. However, for various historical and economical reasons, the World Wide Web has emerged as the most high profile and popular of Internet services. The Web, moreover, has attracted significant attention and money from the broadcast industry, in part because it provides an environment for the viewing of video images.

The World Wide Web

Of the many communication services available through the Internet, the one which has achieved the greatest popularity and currency is the World Wide Web; in fact, it is not uncommon for 'Web' and 'Internet' to be used (incorrectly) as synonyms. The popularity of the Web has several causes, and the manner of its popularization has some important implications for the way in which digital technology's reality relates to the expectations surrounding it.

The Web is popular in part because it is a multimedia service. A single Website can include graphics and sound clips as well as text. (How much multimedia functionality actually exists depends largely on the receiving or 'client' software, which has to know what to do with incoming data intended for formatting or delivery as image or sound.) The Web is also popular for its interactive aspects, which allow for retrieval of information from archives, calculation of volatile data (prices, itineraries, etc.), purchasing of goods, playing of games, and other functions.

The underlying characteristic of the Web that probably accounts more than any other for its popularity is its hypertext functionality, which allows for one Web document to include links to other Websites on other computers around the Internet. It is this open-ended navigability among far-flung sites that gave rise to the term 'World Wide Web' by the Web's inventor, Tim Berners-Lee.

The Web has a unique position among Internet services because, introduced almost a decade after the launching of the Internet and more than twenty years after the establishment of the networks on which the Internet was based, it has attracted not only media and consumer attention but the attention of advertisers. Until the mid-1990s, the **advertising** industry had little or no interest in the Internet, which was largely the domain of scholars and researchers. However, as the Web gained in popularity, advertisers began to use it (and e-mail) for advertising purposes.

Comparative history of the Web and American television industries: 'the suppression of radical potential'

The mid- to late 1990s saw the 'discovery' of the Web by advertisers and corporate users, as well as governmental and industrial efforts to enforce limitations on Internet use, and to define the role of the consumer (or 'end-user') as narrowly as possible. These developments in Internet and Web communication in the 1990s provide an instructive case study in the history of technology, and particularly in what Brian Winston calls 'the "law" of the suppression of radical potential' (Winston 1998; see **technological change** for further discussion of Winston's theory).

Prior to the Internet, the traditional model for electronic communication on a mass scale had been government-supported monopoly or near-monopoly, with severely restricted access to the means of production. With its expansion of access to the production or content-provider end of the process, the Internet has the potential to break this mould, and it has started to do so most visibly in the arena of the World Wide Web. Anyone with a Website on a fully Internet-connected machine is on an equal footing, with respect to potential communicative reach, with any and every other Internet user. Unlike television production, where strict distinctions are maintained between mainstream and alternative practices, the Web allows for relatively even-handed provision of content.

Furthermore, and again by contrast with earlier media such as television, the Internet *began* as a comparatively open medium, with content and usage determined by academics and students rather than by advertising executives and their surrogates (network executives). Therefore, the colonizing of the Internet by the advertising industry requires a kind of reversal of history, and provides an unusual glimpse into how governmental and corporate forces go about the processes of suppressing radical potential.

One strategy was revealed in the US Congress' passage of the 1996 Telecommunications Act which, in contravention of the First Amendment to the United States Constitution, included passages placing restrictions on allowable Internet content. (While the Act referred to the Internet, rather than the World Wide Web, it is not unlikely that at least some of those involved in drafting and passing the legislation were unclear about the difference between the two, as they apparently were also about the fact that the Internet is an international medium and not subject to censorship by the US Congress.) Like much rhetoric surrounding commercial television, the Act and its defenders claimed to be concerned with the welfare of children (see **children and media**). As in the case of commercial television, however, that ostensible concern meshed very neatly with the interests of the advertising industry, which is less concerned with children than with keeping in the good graces of conservative consumers. In short, the 1996 Act attempted to do to the Internet what domination throughout history by the advertising industry had already done to US radio and television.

The potential full force of the Internet as a non-traditional medium of electronic communication is also deflected by the practices of large and small companies involved in the provision of on-line services. Internet companies providing space for Websites often disallow the inclusion of interactive programs; and while this often follows from quite understandable security concerns, it has the effect that many individuals' Websites do not, in fact, include all the features of corporate Websites, even though there are no medium-inherent reasons for them not to do so. The Internet and Web thus provide an interesting example of a medium which, already having passed through a relatively open and public phase in its history, is subsequently subjected to reclaiming and staking out by the governmental and corporate forces concerned to mould it into a passive, trivial advertising medium.

See also: cyberspace; Internet; virtual reality

References

Hafner, K. and Lyon, M. (1996) *Where Wizards Stay Up Late: The Origins of the Internet*, New York: Touchstone.
Winston, B. (1998) *Media Technology and Society: A History: From the Telegraph to the Internet*, London: Routledge.

DAVID A. BLACK

intertextuality

In the most basic sense of the term, 'intertextuality' means the relationship of one text to one or more other texts. Just as literary scholars look for earlier versions of the stories of Hamlet or King Lear or note Shakespeare's borrowings from Holinshed's *Chronicles*, film and television scholars may seek the literary or filmic precursors of films and identify the direct citations of other texts. For example, in *Star Trek: First Contact* (Jonathan Frakes, 1996), the obsessed *Starship* captain Jean-Luc Picard seeks revenge on the Borg, a half-biological, half-mechanical alien race that had caused him great harm in the past. One might point to the similarities between the story of *First Contact* and that of Melville's *Moby Dick*, in which a similarly obsessed Captain Ahab seeks revenge on the great white whale responsible for biting off his leg. Indeed, the **text** itself makes this relationship explicit when Picard quotes the Melville novel. Films, of course, quote not only literary sources but film sources as well. For example, in *The Untouchables* (1987), a baby carriage careens down the steps of a railway station during a shoot-out between the good guys and the bad guys. Here director Brian DePalma is quoting the famous Odessa Steps sequence from *Battleship Potemkin* (Sergei **Eisenstein**, 1925) in what film scholars sometimes refer to as an 'homage'.

In 1969, the French structuralist Julia **Kristeva** formulated a more theoretically sophisticated concept of intertexuality that was to have great influence on film and television studies. The simpler formulation of intertextuality referred to above merely related one text to another. Kristeva implied that nothing existed outside of intertextuality: 'Every text takes shape as a mosaic of citations, every text is the absorption and transformation of other texts' (Kristeva 1969: 146). In other words, all texts relate to other texts, which they reference either explicitly or implicitly. The primary object of analysis can be considered the text, while the texts that it references constitute the intertexts or what Umberto **Eco** has called the 'intertextual frame'. This conception of intertextuality makes two key theoretical breaks with past literary and media studies. First, intertextuality forces us to question the nineteenth-century concept of 'the author' (see **authorship**). If all texts reference other texts, then an author is simply the site of intersecting intertextual frames not the creator of a unique and original text. The structuralist conception of intertextuality therefore partially accounts for the decline of the authorship paradigm within film studies (see **structuralism and post-structuralism**). Second, intertextuality forces us to reconceive the relationship between texts and the societies that produce them. Contra a sociologically inclined media studies, texts do not directly 'reflect' the 'real' world, but rather draw on other always already textualized constructions of that world. For example, one would not attempt to judge the representation of **history** in a film such as *The Birth of a Nation* (D. W. Griffith, 1915) against 'real', 'objective' historical events but would rather compare it to other representations of the American Civil War: school textbooks, historical novels, other films and so on.

Scholars see an all-encompassing intertextuality as a key aspect of post-modern popular **culture** (see **modernism and post-modernism; popular, the**). Television studies scholars have written of the extreme intertextual awareness displayed by such cult programmes as *Twin Peaks*, *The Avengers*, *The X-Files* and *Xena: Warrior Princess* (see **cult film and television**). For example, Jim Collins says of *Twin Peaks*: 'The style is aggressively eclectic, utilizing a number of visual, narrative and thematic conventions from Gothic horror, science fiction, and the police procedural as well as soap opera' (Collins 1992: 345). The audience must be in on the game: the programme's 'tonal oscillation and generic amalgamation' encourage viewers 'to activate ever-shifting sets of expectations and coding strategies' (*ibid*.: 347). In the post-modern era, producers and audiences inhabit dense webs of intertexuality within which texts are encoded and decoded (see **encoding; encoding-decoding model**) and texts embrace other texts in a knowing, self-conscious and playful fashion.

References

Collins, J. (1992) 'Television and Postmodernism', in Robert C. Allen (ed.) *Channels of Discourse Reassembled* (2nd edn), London: Routledge.

Kristeva, J. (1969) *Semiotike: Recherches pour une semanalyse*, Paris: Seuil.

Further reading

Culler, J. (1981) *The Pursuit of Signs: Semiotics, Literature, Deconstruction*, Ithaca: Cornell University Press.

Miller, T. (1997) *The Avengers*, London: BFI Publishing, p. 117.

Stam, R., Burgoyne, R. and Flitterman-Lewis, S. (1992) *New Vocabularies in Film Semiotics: Structuralism, Post-Structuralism and Beyond*, London: Routledge.

ROBERTA E. PEARSON

Irigaray, Luce

b. 1930

Luce Irigaray is an important theorist of French feminism, a movement that has been highly influential for feminist film theory (see **feminist theory**). As a philosopher and a psychoanalyst, Irigaray's most influential works – *This Sex Which is Not One* (1985a) and *Speculum of the Other Woman* (1985b) – are concerned mainly with the female body, its connection to language and its representation within the philosophical and psychoanalytic **discourse** (see also **psychoanalysis**). For Irigaray, the female body is linked with touch and contiguity, and she opposes a phallocentric western tradition that has privileged the visible (see **phallus**).

Within feminist film theory, Irigaray's work has been used to criticize a psychoanalytic film theory, drawing on **Freud** and **Lacan**, that centres on the gaze, defining the spectator as masculine and the object of the gaze as feminine (see **gaze, the**). Her writings have been used to analyse feminist film-makers' attempts to create a non-voyeurist feminist aesthetic, especially Sally Potter's *Thriller* (1979) and *Gold Diggers* (1983) and Chantal Akerman's *Jeanne Dielman* (1975).

See also: voyeurism

References

Irigaray, L. (1985a) *This Sex Which is Not One*, Ithaca: Cornell University Press.

—— (1985b) *Speculum of the Other Woman*, Ithaca: Cornell University Press.

ANTJE LINDENMEYER

J

Jakobson, Roman

b. 1896; d. 1982

Semiotician, linguist, literary critic and philosopher, the Russian-born Jakobson was a founder of the Moscow Linguistic Circle before his interests forced him to move to Prague, where he participated in the Prague Linguistic Circle. His concerns dealt not only with the formalities of language but its tensions and creativity, enlivening a Saussurian model with poetic insights and transformative power (see **Saussure, Ferdinand de**). Jakobson fled the Nazis in 1939, and finally arrived in the United States in 1941, where he remained as a professor at Harvard University and then Massachusetts Institute of Technology (MIT) until his death in 1982.

Jakobson's extraordinarily prolific writing on form, **aesthetics**, meaning and communication offer many insights for cinema criticism. He had dabbled in screenwriting in the 1930s and focused on film's metonymic qualities – its play on contiguities (which he cited for Sergei **Eisenstein**, Charlie Chaplin and Buster Keaton) and relations rather than the other pole of linguistic play on which he worked – metaphor and relations of similarity.

See also: semiotics

Further reading

Bradford, R. (1994) *Roman Jakobson: Life, Language, Art*, London: Routledge.
Jakobson, R., with Pomorska, K. (1983) *Dialogues*, Cambridge, MA: MIT Press. (Among discussions of film and more general issues of linguistics, this volume constitutes an accessible introduction.)
Rudy, S. (1990) *Roman Jakobson: A Complete Bibliography of His Works*, The Hague: Mouton.

GARY McDONOGH

Jameson, Fredric

b. 1934

Currently the foremost Marxist literary and cultural critic in the United States, Jameson has consistently worked to make Marxism relevant to the analysis of literature, post-modernity and mass culture. Influenced largely by Gyorgy **Lukács** and Theodor **Adorno**, Jameson's *The Political Unconscious* (1981) sought to approach history as a textually mediated artefact with effects in the real world. His work mediates between the pessimism of a Lukácsian or **Frankfurt School** notion of **reification** and the optimism of a Benjaminian utopia (see **Benjamin, Walter**). Critical of Althusserian Marxism, he has hung on to the notion of totality as the only viable strategy for comprehending the infiltration of capitalism into **culture** in the late twentieth century. Jameson's *Postmodernism, or the Cultural Logic of Late Capitalism* (1991) is one of the most important synthetic analyses of the forms and political possibilities of post-modernism which, in addition to discussions on architecture and video, uncovers the specific relevance of nostalgia to **history** in film.

See also: Althusser, Louis; Marx, Karl; Marxist aesthetics; modernism and post-modernism

References

Jameson, F. (1981) *The Political Unconscious*, London: Methuen.
—— (1991) *Postmodernism, or the Cultural Logic of Late Capitalism*, London: Verso.

Further reading

Jameson, F. (1979) 'Reification and Utopia in Mass Culture', *Social Text*, vol. 1, no. 10, pp. 130–48.
—— (1992) *The Geopolitical Aesthetic: Cinema and Space in the World System*, Bloomington: Indiana University Press.

PAULA TATLA AMAD

Jencks, Charles

b. 1939

Since 1975, the architectural critic Charles Jencks has identified, theorized, and popularized the phenomenon of architectural post-modernism (see **modernism and post-modernism**). He was largely instrumental in bringing about the turn in the 1970s from the elitist purism of International Style modernism to the hybrid pluralism of Robert Venturi and James Stirling, to name his most favoured architects. In the process, he coined the term 'double-coding' to describe the orientation of post-modern architecture, on the one hand towards everyday consumers, local vernacular landscapes, and traditional historicist styles, and on the other towards more esoteric debates concerning the techniques and legacies of modernism. In this respect, post-modernism is more than just another simple expression of anti-modernism.

Although he introduced the vocabulary of **semiotics** into architectural discussions, describing buildings as communicative rather than functional entities, Jencks has not ventured far into theoretical territory. Neither has he been overtly critical of the weaker variants of post-modernism, or of the **multinational** corporate economy which underpins such styles. It is this reluctance which above all distinguishes his position from that of such critics as Fredric **Jameson**.

Further reading

Jencks, C. (1977) *The Language of Post-Modern Architecture*, London: Academy.
—— (1986) *What is Post-Modernism?*, London: Academy.

NICK YABLON

jouissance

Sometimes translated as 'enjoyment', but usually left untranslated to preserve the sexual connotation in the French ('se jouir', which means 'to come'), *jouissance* is the term given by Jacques **Lacan** to the radical, annihilating pleasure of the drives which lie 'beyond the pleasure principle'. With **castration** and entry into the symbolic realm of language, the subject is forever cut off from *jouissance*, and pleasure becomes 'normalized', regulated and channelled into the erotogenic zones.

See also: law of the father; pleasure; psychoanalysis

ANGELO RESTIVO

K

Kant, Immanuel

b. 1724; d. 1804

Although stylistically difficult, Kant is a German philosopher whose contribution to the subject has been of major importance. In taking philosophy to its limits, he sought to explain our knowledge of the world, not as wholly provided by our senses (the central notion of **empiricism**), but through experience as structured by the concepts we bring to it. Accordingly, 'concepts without perceptions are empty; perceptions without concepts are blind'. But this view, far from acting as a precursor to the construction of reality, emanates from regarding concepts as given to us by universal principles of reason. Applied to moral concepts, moral duty consists in testing the universality of principles underlying our actions by applying reason in the form of the Categorical Imperative. **Objectivity** in moral judgements does not, however, extend to **aesthetics**; for 'proofs are of no avail whatever for determining the judgement of taste'. Yet such judgements lay claim to universal validity: the expectation of similar reactions in others. While providing scant resolution of this paradox, Kant's ideas have had significant influence on theories of aesthetics.

See also: epistemology

Further reading

Scruton, R. (1982) *Kant*, Oxford: Oxford University Press.

TREVOR GIGG

kino-pravda

'Kino-pravda' refers to a film series and a concept of filmmaking. Both the series and the concept originated in post-revolutionary Russia and are associated with Dziga **Vertov** (Denis Kaufman). In 1922, Vertov was commissioned to produce 'film newspapers' for the Soviet government. The films followed the official newspaper, *Pravda* ('Truth'), taking the name *Kino-pravda* ('Film-truth', or 'Cine-truth'). Vertov theorized an energetic concept of kino-pravda. He believed that documentaries, transforming the look of unstaged scenes with cinematic devices, could remake our relationships to nature, machines, other classes and nations.

See also: cinéma-vérité; Constructivism; documentary; Formalism

GABRIEL M. PALETZ

Kracauer, Siegfried

b. 1889; d. 1966

A student of George Simmel and a friend of Walter **Benjamin**, Kracauer was a German intellectual who wrote extensively on modern culture, everyday life and the cinema. His writings between 1920 and 1934, when he was forced into exile in the United States, contained incisive critiques of early twentieth century's emerging mass culture which would influence Benjamin and the **Frankfurt School**. One of his most influential essays, 'The Mass Ornament', displays his dialectical fascination with the surface forms of capitalist culture (see

dialectic and dialectical montage). His classic study of cinema, *Theory of Film*, first published in 1960, was concerned with uncovering film's aesthetic specificity which, he argued, stems from the medium's essential connection with photography's ability to record and reveal physical reality. His work has received renewed attention in film and cultural studies for its non-dismissive approach to popular and mass culture and his understanding of cinema as an alternative public sphere.

References

Kracauer, S. (1995) *The Mass Ornament: Weimar Essays*, ed. and trans, and with an introduction by Thomas Y. Levin, Cambridge, MA: Harvard University Press.
—— (1997) *Theory of Film: The Redemption of Physical Reality* (first published 1960), with an introduction by Miriam Bratu Hansen, Princeton: Princeton University Press.

PAULA TATLA AMAD

Kristeva, Julia

b. 1941

Born in Sliven, Bulgaria, Julia Kristeva was taught by Roland **Barthes** in Paris and influenced by Jacques **Lacan**. A psychoanalyst, her concern with the subversive effects of language led to the notion of **intertextuality**, an overlap between voices and texts, that owes much to Mikhail **Bakhtin**, whose writings Kristeva was one of the first to introduce to the West. The fracture of meanings, syntax and grammar that bring language closer to the suppressed elements of the symbolic, such as the **body** and the biological, is, Kristeva argues, of particular significance for women, whose marginality allows them to disrupt the system of language and law. Kristeva's desire to produce a **discourse** that is always in process and confronts the impasse of language can be identified in her own heterogeneous writing, which shatters conventions and undermines traditional ideas of authority and order.

See also: jouissance; law of the father; psychoanalysis; semiotics; symbolic code

Further reading

Kristeva, J. (1980) *Desire in Language: A Semiotic Approach to Literature and Art*, trans. Thomas Gora, Alice Jardine and Leon S. Roudiez, Oxford: Blackwell.
Moi, T. (ed.) (1986) *The Kristeva Reader*, Oxford: Blackwell.

JULIA THOMAS

Kuleshov effect

The 'Kuleshov effect' is the descriptive term given to any montage sequence in which the meaning appears to derive from the relationship of contiguous shots rather than from the 'content' of the individual shots themselves. A Soviet filmmaker and teacher who, like his fellow filmmakers and students Sergei **Eisenstein** and Vsevolod **Pudovkin**, was interested in the **agit-prop** potential of film (and hence in the structural and material basis of its signifying mechanisms), Lev Kuleshov (1899–1970) conducted now famous experiments in Moscow in the teens and 1920s. He interposed an unvarying image of an actor's face with a number of other shots – a bowl of soup, a dead woman in a coffin, a child playing with a toy bear, for example (though Kuleshov and others differed on the precise content of the shots in later characterizations of the experiments) – and found that the expression ascribed to the actor Mozhukin's face changed depending on which shots preceded and followed it.

The result of these experiments led Kuleshov to conclude that the 'content of the shots in itself is not so important as is the joining of two shots of different content and the method of their connection and their alternation'. Or, in the words of his pupil Pudovkin: 'Kuleshov maintained that . . . film-art does not begin when the artists act and various scenes are shot – this is only the preparation of the material. Film-art begins from the moment when the director begins to combine and join together the various pieces of film. By joining them in various combinations, in different orders, he obtains differing results.' Some variation of these two formulations of the power of montage remains the most often cited version of the Kuleshov effect in film theory and history texts. Its explanatory power lies in the way it allows for both the creation of conceptual or abstract meaning through editing, as Eisenstein argued, as well as linear **narrative** sense (Hollywood's **continuity editing** system depends on spectators accepting that shots are linked in time and space and continuous in effect). More idiosyncratic but more precise definitions of the Kuleshov effect are available, however. In the several editions of their book, *Film Art*, David Bordwell and Kristin Thompson (1997) call the Kuleshov effect 'any series of shots that *in the absence of an establishing shot* prompts the spectator to infer a spatial whole on the basis of seeing only portions of the space' (emphasis in the original).

Reports about the actual Kuleshov experiments have always been sketchy and contradictory – was the actor's face neutral, ambiguous or expressionless? How long were the shots? What sort of lighting was used? Stephen Prince and Wayne E. Hensley demonstrate that repeated attempts to replicate the experiments fail to produce the sorts of effects that Kuleshov and Pudovkin claim to have witnessed. While *some* meaning can be produced through editing, a considerable amount of contextualization is required before spectators provide the 'crucial interpretive linkages' that the Kuleshov effect theoretically comprises. We now know that cinematic meaning is never simply 'transmitted' to spectators; rather, they are 'co-constructors' of that meaning and have their own 'cognitive and affective horizons', as Prince and Hensley (1992) write, of 'such factors as race, class, gender, ethnicity, and social and political ideologies of various complexions'. The Kuleshov effect is a myth cloaked in 'empirical garb', in which the terms of science, linguistics and the assembly line are invoked to 'prove' the associational power of montage. In Prince and Hensley's words, the Kuleshov effect might better be understood as part of the 'folklore of the cinema'. At this point, though, it is likely to retain its status as dogma, if only because of the ease with which students grasp its simple, elegant and apparently sensible central point.

See also: Bazin, André; dialectic; kino-pravda; propaganda

References

Bordwell, D. and Thompson, K. (1997) *Film Art: An Introduction* (5th edn), New York: McGraw-Hill.

Prince, S. and Hensley, W. E. (1992), 'The Kuleshov Effect: Recreating the Classic Experiment', *Cinema Journal*, vol. 31, no. 2, pp. 51–75.

Pudovkin, V. (1968) *Film Technique and Film Acting* (first published 1929), ed. and trans. Victor Montagu, London: Vision Press.

Further reading

Levaco, R. (ed.) (1974) *Kuleshov on Film: Writings by Lev Kuleshov*, trans. R. Levaco, Berkeley: University of California Press.

ADRIENNE L. McLEAN

L

Lacan, Jacques

b. 1901; d. 1981

Jacques Lacan was a French psychoanalyst whose re-reading of **Freud** has had a profound impact on media studies, literary studies and the humanities in general. In the 1950s, Lacan began a yearly seminar in which he interpreted the Freudian corpus through the lenses of structuralist anthropology and linguistics (see **structuralism and post-structuralism**). Lacan argued that the **unconscious** was the very effect of the subject's entry into language; that language was radically '**Other**'; and that the subject was constructed by language. Lacan's views generally laid the groundwork for the post-structuralist view of subjectivity. For Lacan, meaning always came at the expense of being, and this fundamental loss effected by language is what constituted the subject as desiring (see **desire**). His innovations in analytic technique led to his expulsion in 1964 from the International Psychoanalytic Association. By then, his seminars had attracted the leading Parisian intellectuals, and his attention turned towards the difficult concept of the real as that which is excluded from symbolization and yet around which the symbolic is structured (see **symbolic code**).

Always dialectical and revelling in paradox, Lacan's writing (collected in *Ecrits*) is notoriously difficult. Transcripts of six of his seminars have been translated into English.

See also: imaginary; psychoanalysis; subject

Further reading

Lacan, J. (various years) *The Seminar of Jacques Lacan*, J.-A. Miller (ed.), New York: Norton. (Books I, II, III, VII, XI, and XX have been translated into English.)

Roudinesco, E. (1997) *Jacques Lacan*, New York: Columbia University Press.

Weber, S. (1991) *Return to Freud: Jacques Lacan's Dislocation of Psychoanalysis*, Cambridge: Cambridge University Press.

Žižek, S. (1991) *Looking Awry: An Introduction to Jacques Lacan through Popular Culture*, Boston: MIT Press.

ANGELO RESTIVO

lack

A theoretical concept that plays across many interrelated registers, lack is connected to:

- the traumatic discovery of sexual difference;
- the lack of being that accrues to both subject and object in the wake of language;
- the essential condition of the human subject as *desiring*;
- the constitutive incompleteness of all signifying systems.

For **Freud**, the child's discovery of the presence/ **absence** of the penis leads to the traumatic realization of **difference**; until then, the child presumed an essential identity among humans. The discovery of sexual difference is the culmination of a series of other, earlier encounters with presence/absence, particularly in relation to weaning and toilet training. But the observed lack of the penis – along with the accompanying fantasies of **castration** – retroactively inserts these earlier encounters into the trajectory of the **phallus**.

Jacques **Lacan** re-situates this entire dynamic in relation to language and the signifier. Lacan argues that being and meaning are fundamentally incompatible; language mortifies being (much in the way that **Hegel** asserts that the word 'murders' the thing). The child's entry into language and into the realm of meaning is thus experienced as a fundamental loss of an (**imaginary**) fullness of being. To illustrate this, Lacan draws on Freud's famous anecdote in *Beyond the Pleasure Principle* centred on his observation of a game played by his infant nephew. The child repeatedly threw away and then retrieved a small bobbin, while simultaneously articulating the words '*fort/da*' ('here/away'; see **fort/da game**). In this example, it is the articulated nature of language as a differential system of sounds that stands in for the presence and absence of an entire series, including the body of the mother, the excremental object and the phallus.

For Lacan, the 'choice' of meaning over being has the quality of a 'forced choice'; it is a 'lose-lose' scenario which thus connects it to castration. Since language as a symbolic system is located outside the subject (and is thus referred to as the '**Other**' with a capital 'O'), and since being (in the form of the **jouissance** of the drives) is located inside the subject, the entry into language is manifested along a 'border' out of which drops the notorious 'object-*a*'. Lacan took pains never to formally define 'object-*a*' in order to allow it to play across many registers. But 'object-*a*' is intimately connected to lack: inaccessible to symbolization, the 'object-*a*' is a kind of illusory residue of the symbolization process which introduces a dislocation between language and world. Language does not 'cover' everything, and out of this impossibility, **desire** is born in the subject, in so far as desire is predicated on something being lacking.

'Object-*a*' is often described as the 'placeholder of desire', lying on the border between the imaginary and the symbolic. It articulates a link between the subject's imaginary identifications before the mirror and the metonymic sliding of language from one signifier to the next, thus in a way 'suspending' the subject in a particular relationship to his/her desire (see **metonymy**).

Needless to say, Lacan's theorization of lack, desire and 'object-*a*' have had far-reaching consequences for all theories of representation, as well as for philosophy generally. Of particular importance to theories of **narrative** – including film theory – is the notion that textual systems in themselves are productive of desire. For not only is the subject constituted by lack, but so too is the symbolic order as the place of the Other. The cultural products that emerge from this field of the Other always bear the stamp of its incompleteness, and construct the spectator or reader so that his/her desire masks this fundamental lack.

See also: law of the father; psychoanalysis; symbolic code

Further reading

Silverman, K. (1983) *The Subject of Semiotics*, New York: Oxford University Press.

Weber, S. (1991) *Return to Freud: Jacques Lacan's Dislocation of Psychoanalysis*, Cambridge: Cambridge University Press.

ANGELO RESTIVO

Laclau, Ernesto

b. 1935

Laclau was born in Buenos Aires, Argentina. His early work represented an important contribution to theories of populism, fascism and ideology, but he is best known for his work, co-authored with Chantal Mouffe, *Hegemony and Socialist Strategy* (1985), a rigorous attempt to formulate a post-Marxist problematic which was not a simple rejection of Marxism (see **Marxist aesthetics**). Drawing on post-structuralist theories (especially those of Jacques **Lacan** and Jacques **Derrida**), Laclau and Mouffe challenged what they saw as the essentialism, reductionism and universalizing nature of classical Marxism, insisting instead on the primacy of articulation and contingency. Within this framework, social and political identities are constructed and partial, rather than being guaranteed by some underlying essence. Hegemony, pushed far beyond **Gramsci**'s account, describes the making of meaningful connections in the absence of guarantees. Because no hegemonic formation can be permanently fixed, there is always the possibility of struggle and rearticulation.

See also: ideology and hegemony; modernism and post-modernism; structuralism and post-structuralism

References

Laclau, E. and Mouffe, C. (1985) *Hegemony and Socialist Strategy: Towards a Radical Democratic Politics*, London and New York: Verso.

Further reading

Laclau, E. (1977) *Politics and Ideology in Marxist Theory: Capitalism, Fascism, Populism*, London: New Left Books.

NEIL BADMINGTON

language/langue

'*Langue*' is French for 'language'. In his 'Cours de linguistique générale', the basis of contemporary **semiotics**, Ferdinand de **Saussure** introduces three levels of language analysis: *langage*, the general human faculty of language acquisition and use; *langue*, the abstract system of a language; and **parole**, the specific verbal behaviour of individuals in speaking and writing a language. Up to the 1960s, the quest for the universals of *langage* and the structure of *langue* took up most of the energies of linguistic analysis. Modern linguistics, specially sociolinguistics and cognitive linguistics, assumes a much more fluent transition between general ability to communicate, the shape of a specific language, the individual use of language and other systems of cognition and perception (see **cognitive theory**). Saussurian semiotics were enthusiastically taken up by film scholars in the late 1960s and the

1970s, most notably in the work of Christian **Metz**.

EVA VIETH

Lauretis, Teresa de

birth date not known

Teresa de Lauretis uses Freudian **psychoanalysis** and **semiotics** to understand the representation of Woman (as distinct from actual women) in film and female spectatorship. In *Alice Doesn't* (1984), she examines how classical cinema and semiotic theories of **narrative** represent Woman as object, as the obstacle/space the hero must overcome, or the reward awaiting him at the end of the journey. Within this Oedipal scenario, the female spectator seems doomed to identify either masochistically with the passive object or sadistically with the active subject. However, placed between the look of the camera and the image on the screen, the female spectator can never easily identify with the subject or the object, but disrupts the narrative system through complex, multiple identifications. In subsequent work, de Lauretis has gone on to develop a theory of a distinctively lesbian sexuality and spectatorship not based on narcissism or identification, but 'a desire that is both at once for the same and for the other' (de Lauretis 1991).

De Lauretis is currently Professor of the History of Consciousness at the University of California, Santa Cruz.

See also: desire; feminist theory; Freud, Sigmund; gaze, the; queer theory

References

de Lauretis, T. (1984) *Alice Doesn't. Feminism, Semiotics, Cinema*, Basingstoke: Macmillan.
—— (1991) 'Film and the Visible', in Bad Object-Choices (eds) *How Do I Look?*, Seattle: Bay Press.

ANTJE LINDENMEYER

law of the father

The 'Law of the Father' is an essential conceptual component of the Oedipal scenario, as it allows a link to be forged between the psychic experience of the individual and the larger social structures of which he/she is a part. The Law of the Father articulates the (presumed universal) prohibition against incest, for which the fantasized punishment (for children of both sexes) is **castration**. There is, however, a lack of symmetry in **Freud**'s version of the Oedipal narrative for boys and for girls around which there is still considerable debate. For some, this marks **psychoanalysis** as tainted by a fundamental phallocentrism, while for others (particularly Jacques **Lacan**) it represents the traumatic, inarticulateable blockage at the core of every symbolic system.

While Freud initially set the Oedipal conflict within the structure of the nuclear family ('the family romance'), he quickly understood that there was a necessary social dimension to the conflict. In *Totem and Taboo*, Freud constructs an originary myth to account for this dimension. (It should be emphasized that Freud is not concerned here with presenting anthropologically verifiable 'facts'; his method is more akin to the philosopher's construction of a hypothetical 'state of nature'.) In a mythical, tribal pre-history, a 'primal father' claimed exclusive sexual rights over the women, thus barring all other men from access to women. The men then formed a pact to murder the primal father and institute the law regulating sexual exchange. The now-dead father served both as memory of the traumatic birth of the law and also as its very guarantor.

Even for Freud, the importance of the father in the Oedipal scenario accrues because of his *symbolic function* rather than because of any 'real' properties he may have. Developing this notion, Jacques Lacan coined the phrase 'Name-of-the-Father' to emphasize that it is the signifier itself that is the bearer of the law. The Name-of-the-Father marks the child's place within the pre-existing social structure, and ultimately it ruptures the **imaginary** unity the child finds in its relationship to the mother's body. In the Lacanian view, language itself is seen as the bearer of the law which is radically **'Other'** (indicated by the capital 'O' to distinguish it from the imaginary 'other(s)' of the **mirror stage**). The subject is thus 'subjected to' language or the signifier as a result of the Oedipal scenario, which can thus be conceived as a kind of patriarchal 'machinery' for the production of subjectivity (see **patriarchy**).

Following from this, one of the central projects of post-1968 film theory was to uncover the ways in which classical cinema was ideologically committed to reproducing the Oedipal scenario in the interest of reinforcing patriarchal law, thus marking cinema as one of culture's main mechanisms of social 'normalization'. Of the many close textual analyses produced in this period, Raymond Bellour's (1979) analyses of Alfred Hitchcock's work is exemplary. Bellour shows how Hitchcock repeatedly stages the fantasy of transgressing the law, only in the end to reaffirm its validity in the production of the normalized, heterosexual couple. In *Psycho* (1960) however, this scenario is radically derailed, thus illustrating what happens to subjectivity when the Law of the Father is foreclosed.

Recent psychoanalytic work has turned its attention to the fact that the symbolic father is necessarily 'haunted' by the trace of his obscene, murdered counterpart, the primal father. This has led to new analyses, for example, of the figure of the homosexual so prevalent in **film noir** (see, for example, Charles Vidor's *Gilda*, 1946). For **queer theory**, the social fantasies surrounding the gay male evoke those surrounding the obscene father, in so far as both are fantasized as immersed in an 'anal enjoyment' which it is the very function of the patriarchal law to repress.

See also: symbolic code

References

Bellour, R. (1979) 'Psychosis, Neurosis, Perversion', *Camera Obscura*, nos 3–4, pp. 104–34.

Further reading

Zizek, S. (1992) *Enjoy Your Symptom!*, New York: Routledge.

ANGELO RESTIVO

Lévi-Strauss, Claude

b. 1908

Doyen of French anthropology, Claude Lévi-Strauss used insights from Ferdinand de **Saussure** and Roman **Jakobson** (with whom he collaborated) to develop structural models in anthropology. Relying on immense reading and profound insight into collected objects and texts rather than extensive fieldwork, he explored the logic underpinning kinship, mythology, **art** and **culture**. His method entails the delineation of fundamental **binary** oppositions and their transformations in relation to myriad variations and apparent anomalies. His seminal works include *Elementary Structures of Kinship*, *The Savage Mind* and his structural analyses of **myth** in both *Structural Anthropology* and the four-volume *Mythologiques*. His exquisitely crafted memoir, *Triste Tropiques*, blends personal history, observation and method.

Scholars in cinema studies have relied on Lévi-Strauss' analysis of binary opposition to explain conflicts in **narrative**. While anthropologists have criticized his lack of engagement with process and people, his synchronic analysis of myth proves illuminating for the study of film texts.

See also: structuralism and post-structuralism

References

Lévi-Strauss, C. (1961) *Tristes Tropiques*, New York: Criterion.
—— (1966) *The Savage Mind*, Chicago: University of Chicago (originally published as *La Pensée sauvage*).
—— (1967) 'The Structural Study of Myth', in *Structural Anthropology*, Garden City, New Jersey: Anchor.
—— (1969) *The Elementary Structures of Kinship*, ed. John Richard von Sturmer and Rodney Needham, trans. James Harle Bell, London: Eyre and Spottiswoode.

Further reading

Leach, E. (1974) *Claude Lévi-Strauss*, New York: Viking.

GARY McDONOGH

live television

Live television is a topic in which the histories of technology, economics and **aesthetics** are deeply intertwined. Furthermore, liveness in television is probably the most significant property of television not shared by film.

The first experiments in television transmission were live; that is, an image appeared on a receiving device simultaneously with its being picked up by the camera. Live broadcasting techniques remained prevalent in commercial television through the mid-1950s, but, gradually, the balance shifted towards the use of film (and later, in some cases, videotape) as the chief production medium. The history of this transition has been thoroughly examined by historian William Boddy in *Fifties Television* (1990). Boddy points out that the reasons behind the transition were by no means aesthetic. In fact, critics of early 1950s television enthused over the higher-end live productions – the so-called 'live anthology dramas' – and expressed considerable disappointment as the US television networks abandoned the form in favour of economically more efficient filmed series. Unlike a weekly drama showcase programme, which required a new script, cast and crew for each broadcast, a filmed series allowed for reuse of casts, crew and sets; in addition, it allows for reruns and distribution to secondary markets, which emerged during the 1950s as the source of the greatest profits in the television industry.

Live television never entirely died out. While it vanished from certain sectors of production, it remained the norm in others, particularly news and sports broadcasts. A few programmes, such as NBC's *Saturday Night Live*, have carried on or taken up the mantle of live production. The ability of television to deliver live images has figured, often accidentally, in a number of the most famous moments in television history (for example, the murder of Lee Harvey Oswald; the 1969 moon landing; the 1986 *Challenger* disaster), and the live broadcast of the coronation of Britain's Elizabeth II in 1953 contributed to the spread of television in that country.

Depending on the circumstances and the content, 'special' live broadcasts sometimes emphasize the event being broadcast and sometimes emphasize the technology itself. In the early 1950s, for example, CBS's weekly news programme *See it Now* often drew attention to the technical feat of live television, including the first live coast-to-coast broadcast in 1951. In 1998, a similar technology-inspired awe could be seen and heard in a Discovery Channel broadcast featuring the first live transmissions from inside a deep-sea diving capsule – specifically, the one at the site of the *Titanic*. The popular American series *ER* broadcast a live episode in 1997, returning for one evening to television's technical roots as a publicity stunt.

'Liveness' also represents a kind of ideal state to which certain types of non-live programming seem to aspire. For example, game shows tend to be produced in clusters (several episodes per day) but broadcast one per day and given a pseudo-live context (with references made to 'yesterday', to the day of the week, etc.). In the case of sports coverage, weather delays are sometimes shown in real time, even if the event has been taped. In spite of the television industry's near abandonment of live television as an aesthetically unique and creative medium, it does seem to place a premium on the emulation, or pretence, of 'liveness'.

See also: broadcasting, the United Kingdom; broadcasting, the United States; chat/talk show

References

Boddy, W. (1990) *Fifties Television: The Industry and its Critics*, Urbana and Chicago: University of Illinois Press.

Further reading

Feuer, J. (1983) 'The Concept of Live Television: Ontology as Ideology', in E. A. Kaplan (ed.) *Regarding Television* (American Film Institute *Monograph* series), Frederick, MD: University Publications of America, pp. 12–22.

DAVID A. BLACK

Lotman, Juri

b. 1922; d. 1993

For Juri Lotman, natural language is a 'primary modelling system' (a system that processes, stores and transmits information), while literature and cinema are 'secondary modelling systems'. Influenced by information theory, Lotman argues that the quantity of information contained in an artistic **text** is dependent on the number of alternative structures that the text can take.

In *Semiotics of Cinema* (1976), Lotman applies this principle to film. First, he identifies conventional (or arbitrary) signs – signs that do not appear automatically in films, but form part of a system of alternatives, including the different types of shot scale, different camera angles, lighting, etc. (see **camera style and lens style**). The filmmaker's selection of the alternatives available is a choice that contains information.

Second, Lotman divides these systems of alternatives into marked and unmarked signs: for example, an eye-level camera is unmarked, in comparison to a low angle, which is marked. The unmarked signs are more predictable than the marked ones, and therefore carry less information. Lotman stresses that each shot and sequence of film consists of multiple signs, some of which are marked, others unmarked. A film can be analysed in terms of the balance it creates between its marked and unmarked signs, and the information they carry.

Rather than presenting a systematic theory of film **semiotics**, Lotman attempts to demonstrate that cinema is a complex modelling system consisting of numerous conventional signs.

References

Lotman, J. (1976), *Semiotics of Cinema* (first published 1973), trans. Mark E. Suino, Ann Arbor: University of Michigan.

WARREN BUCKLAND

Lukács, Gyorgy

b. 1885; d. 1971

Philosopher, literary critic and prominent, albeit

intermittent, figure in the Hungarian Communist Party, Gyorgy Lukács is widely considered to be the founding father of western **Marxism**. Bringing together **Hegel**'s dialectics, **Marx**'s political economy and **Weber**'s sociology, he strove to formulate a systematic and totalizing critique of capitalist modernity.

Although his wide range of interests did not specifically include the nascent mass media, Lukács nevertheless laid the theoretical groundwork for the **Frankfurt School** critique of the 'culture industry'. In particular, he bequeathed to cultural criticism the keyword **reification**, a concept he developed in *History and Class Consciousness* (1971 [1923]) to account for the failure of the working class to grasp itself as subject as well as object, in other words to achieve class consciousness. In his subsequent work, Lukács denounced literary modernism and advocated **realism** – the 'Great Realism' of Balzac and Tolstoy rather than the '**Socialist Realism**' of Zhadanov and Stalin – as the source of a total critique of bourgeois capitalism.

See also: dialectic; Marxist aesthetics

References

Lukács, G. (1971) *History and Class Consciousness: Studies in Marxist Dialectics* (first published 1923), trans. Rodney Livingstone, Cambridge, MA: MIT Press.

Further reading

Lukács, G. (1980) *Essays on Realism*, trans. Rodney Livingstone, ed. David Fernbach, Cambridge, MA: MIT Press.

NICK YABLON

Lyotard, Jean-François

b. 1924; d. 1998

Jean-François Lyotard, became a philosopher of the post-modern, famously through *The Postmodern Condition: A Report on Knowledge* (1984), in which he analysed, in particular, the function of metanarra-

tives as a basis for knowledge (see **metanarrative; modernism and post-modernism**).

Following the failure of his efforts to ground a philosophical system in an economy of the self, **desire** and will that refused to allow truth to be reduced simply to evidence, Lyotard chose, in his words, 'Kant over Freud' (see **Kant, Immanuel; Freud, Sigmund**). He shifted the grounds of his attack on the positivism of scientific rationality to a thoroughgoing critique of the sociolinguistic impossibilities of 'truth'. He described the postmodern as a 'search for new presentations, not in order to enjoy them but in order to impart a stronger sense of the unpresentable'.

His 'linguistic turn', intellectually, was matched by a movement away from narrowly Marxian-left politics. Yet the problem of achieving justice remained crucial for Lyotard. In essence (and in definitive contrast to the modernist restoration undertaken by Jürgen **Habermas**), he argued that no system of open, perfect communicative rationality was possible in face of the *differend*. Put simply, a differend occurs when the achievement of a form of justice requires that the victim of injustice submit to the discourse of those responsible for the injustice. Thus, Lyotard concluded, the quest for perfect communicative community was either too conformist or terrifyingly totalistic, and was itself the cause of injustice and not its solution.

References

Lyotard, J.-F. (1984) *The Postmodern Condition: A Report on Knowledge*, trans. Geoffrey Bennington and Brian Massumi, Manchester: Manchester University Press.

Further reading

Bennington, G. (1988) *Lyotard: Writing the Event*, Manchester: Manchester University Press.
Yeghiayan, E. (1999) *Jean-François Lyotard: A Bibliography*, Irvine: University of California. Online. Available: http://sun3.lib.uci.edu/indiv/scctr/Wellek/lyotard/

MATTHEW ALLEN

M

manipulation

'Manipulation' refers to the process whereby media messages are seen to mould audiences' beliefs. Derived from Marxist theories of the mass media, although not limited to this framework, manipulation describes the way in which audiences' opinions on certain issues are held to be influenced by the content and ideological form of media products. When covering industrial disputes, for example, news and **current affairs** programming frequently manipulate audiences' opinions on key issues through the articulation of what Stuart **Hall** calls a 'preferred meaning', which attempts to close down possibilities for alternative audience interpretations.

See also: Glasgow University Media Group; ideology and hegemony; Marxist aesthetics

References

Morley, D. and Chen, K.-H. (eds) (1996) *Stuart Hall: Critical Dialogues in Cultural Studies*, London: Routledge.

ALISON GRIFFITHS

market place

Commercial forms of popular culture, film and television are dependent on the market place. Variously, this might refer to the **audience**, the exhibition outlet or other competing forms of entertainment. The concept of the market thus involves the intersection between consumers, rival products and venues and is centred around the notion of choice. As all forms of commercial entertainment will only survive if they find an audience and return a profit, the concept of the market place plays an essential role in determining their forms and content.

Popular culture is thus tailored towards its market as producers seek to give the people what they want. In the first half of the twentieth century, most media aimed for a mass market. As competition has intensified within and across media, popular culture has been aimed more at smaller target audiences with specific tastes and needs. In both cases, however, producers need to be familiar with audience tastes and desires if their investment is to pay dividends. One way this is accomplished is through market research, polling the public to identify their preferences or advance screenings of films to assess their reception before their release (see **marketing and promotion**). Currently popular forms, genres and stars receive even more attention as they suggest what audiences want to see (see **genre; star system**). To fulfil the demands of the market, then, producers frequently copy their current successes, fashioning similar stories around stars with proven records, producing spin-off television shows, making sequels for popular films and adapting successes across media. In this way, successful novels beget successful films and television stars appear in big-budget Hollywood features to satiate the desire of the market and return profits.

Conglomeration, especially **multinational** companies, facilitate this multimedia interaction.

Since the 1950s, a series of mergers and take-overs has created large multimedia corporations that control film and television production, publishing and the music industry as well as other unrelated industries. As stars, books and music rights are often held in-house, it is easier and cheaper for film and television production companies to capitalize on their popular successes. As publishers of newspapers and magazines, they also promote their own products and can use contests, ratings, sales and letters to assess audience feedback. While this might permit more effective audience research, it also suggests a short-circuiting of consumers' desires as it might appear that conglomerates do not measure audience tastes so much as impose their own properties on the market. The formation of conglomerates through mergers has also reduced competition, suggesting, perhaps, that consumers no longer have free choice to select the products they like the most.

The market place is also an ideologically informed concept (see **ideology and hegemony**). Indivisible from the idea of commercialized leisure, it is fundamentally capitalist in intent, but as it is predicated on the notion of choice, it also suggests an informed consumer. As such, it is also hailed as an essentially democratic institution, particularly by the producers of popular culture. Borrowing from ideals of free speech, the consumer is positioned as the best judge, selecting and paying for the entertainment that best fits his/her needs. As the consumer is essentially knowledgeable, he/she will select the good ideas and the best products and reject substandard material. The consumer has to be exposed to all kinds of products, however, in order to develop the skills required to distinguish the good from the bad. Good ideas and good products will thus survive and make large profits, the argument runs, whereas poorly made, disreputable material will be rejected.

This idea of a free market suits the producers as it validates the products that return the most money and flatters the consumer. A major threat comes from **censorship**, though, which threatens to limit choice and restrict the market. It also reigns in the industries and suggests that the consumer needs to be protected from the excesses of market-oriented commercial entertainment. Censorship also implies that the biggest-selling product might

be that which appeals to the lowest common denominator, pandering to the worst excesses of the market. It therefore implies a radically different view of choice and of the relations between producers and consumers. The distinction between these two views of market-oriented culture underlines the difference between commercial producers and the public service ethos of uplift that marks non-commercial producers like the early BBC led by John **Reith** (see **public service broadcasting**).

See also: consumption; globalization; popular, the; Reithian

MOYA LUCKETT

marketing and promotion

Film and television promotion refers to several different processes: market research, publicity and **advertising**. While publicity and advertising have a long history in the film industry, marketing is largely a phenomenon of the post-Second World War era, and its impact on film and television has been felt primarily since the 1960s. Market research is conducted before the actual product is created, mainly in the form of focus groups and questionnaires, in order to determine the audience that a particular movie or programme might have. In the case of big-budget films or **high concept** movies, marketing and promotional plans determine most aspects of the production. For example, decisions about a film's title, casting, soundtrack and director will be made as part of an overall marketing strategy, along with plans for advertising, cross-promotion and merchandise licensing. Films and television programmes are often developed specifically because they offer potential 'synergy' between different cross-marketed media products, such as sequel films, television spin-offs, movies or programmes that generate toys or video games. A successful marketing strategy is one that accurately targets an audience and times the movement of the product through different outlets, such as theatrical release, video cassette, airline distribution, cable and broadcast television, syndicated television and international export (Izod 1988: 196).

In both film and television industries, **vertical integration** has created a marketing environment in which films and programmes are developed in order to exploit the ownership of numerous media companies under one corporate umbrella. Deregulation of cross-media ownership and subsequent large-scale mergers have resulted in corporations holding multiple media assets such as film studios, broadcast and cable television systems, music labels, radio stations, book and magazine publishers, computer game and software companies and sports teams. In the United States, the film and television industries have a long history of cross-media promotion, while in many other countries the integration of film and television marketing has been the result of the commercialization of television, the rise of television and film co-production, and the formation of large audio-visual industries which export film and television within a particular 'geolinguistic region' (Sinclair *et al.* 1996: 11). In Europe and elsewhere, 'free market' challenges to national film subsidy and **public service broadcasting**, aided by the rise of **cable and satellite** distribution, have resulted in a far greater emphasis on American-style marketing in the film and television industries. Conglomerate media groups such as Rupert Murdoch's News Corporation, Time-Warner and Bertelsmann AG have supported government deregulation and created **multinational** companies that regularly link products through cross-media promotion.

The studio era of American film production initiated some key elements of contemporary film and television marketing, in particular the **star system** and an emphasis on high production values. In the early studio era, popular stars not only differentiated films from one another, they gave a high market value to any film they appeared in. As the number of films made increased, however, market controls such as block-booking were devised, linking access to movies featuring big stars to the rental of less desirable films without major stars. Until the expansion of regional media industries in the 1980s and 1990s, few national cinemas produced stars that could sell films in foreign markets as successfully as Hollywood, in large part because of the sheer number of American films available to familiarize viewers

with these performers (Finney 1996: 55; see **national, the**). Along with the star system and high-production values, Hollywood studios have long utilized tie-ins with consumer goods to advertise movies and bring in additional revenue. Product placement became common in the 1910s, and press-books were full of cross-promotion ideas linking films to a wide range of products and businesses. The promotional relationship between film and consumer goods initially came to the attention of American film studios as a result of their move into the international market. Exporters noted that demand for American goods overseas increased following the exhibition of Hollywood films, and by 1933, the Warner Bros studio had created a department for merchandising tie-ins and had product placement contracts with General Electric kitchen equipment and General Motors cars. The same year, MGM signed a $500,000 contract with Coca-Cola. Similarly, by 1929 the importance of the female **audience** had made fashion tie-ins a major aspect of film marketing in both the US and UK, as film studios licensed costume designs to garment retailers and distributed large numbers of fashion photographs and publicity copy on costumes to magazines and newspapers (Eckert 1991: 36).

With the end of the studio era in the 1950s, the factory mode of production was replaced by the single-film development package. The number of films produced each year was dramatically reduced and the importance of each film's marketing strategy increased. Without the security of a studio's brand-name or guaranteed exhibition in its theatres, independent producers increasingly sought 'pre-sold' story material such as best-selling novels or successful theatrical productions. Literary agents began to attain the film rights to works by popular authors that were not even written yet, since the authors name alone made the property financable. Producers also looked to star performers to boost the market value of a project, giving talent agencies a much more significant role in film packaging than they had played in the past. Just as Hollywood studios had leveraged star power to differentiate films and stabilize their market value, agents recognized that star value was one of the most bankable aspects of any film package. A forerunner in the trend towards film pre-packaging by talent agents was the Music Corporation of America (MCA), which started as a musical agency and later entered film and television production in the wave of early media mergers that has gradually re-integrated much film and television industry ownership. Other talent agencies like the Creative Artists Agency (CAA), William Morris, and International Creative Management (ICM) now control primary access to both stars and story material, the most important assets in the creation of a high-budget film package.

High concept films have been defined by Justin Wyatt as particularly market-driven projects differentiated according to their target market, visual style, advertising pitch and merchandising potential. This emphasis on market potential grew out of the instability of the post-studio American film industry, the rise of new distribution formats like home video and cable, and subsequent emphasis on designing films based on market research. It also coincided with the increased saturation release of films in many major markets at the same time in conjunction with heavy television advertising (Wyatt 1994: 19). This strategy places the burden of film promotion on advertising rather than reviews, and is intended to reap quick profits before any negative word-of-mouth can circulate. The high concept film is conceived as an entire cross-media marketing campaign that incorporates a wide range of outlets and ancillary products (soundtrack recordings, novelizations, television publicity, music videos, records and merchandise).

High concept cross-marketing also grew out of the new corporate structures produced by the integration of the entertainment media that was marked by the growth of MCA in the 1950s. In 1952, Decca records acquired Universal Pictures, and both companies came under the control of MCA in 1959. One of the first forms of marketing 'synergy' (a term coined in the music industry) was the soundtrack album. Record sales both subsidized film production and generated free film advertising from radio play; a popular film could, in turn, generate huge record sales. By the end of the 1950s Paramount, United Artists, Warner Bros, 20th Century-Fox and Columbia Pictures all owned subsidiary music recording companies (Izod 1988: 157; Smith 1998). The music video format has significantly enhanced the symbiotic relationship between film and music marketing by featuring film clips in videos for soundtrack hits, simultaneously promoting the film, song and performer in a hybrid of radio air-play and movie trailer (see **music and film**).

In the 1980s and 1990s, product licensing became a major source of profits, following the success of toy and ancillary sales for films like *Star Wars* (George Lucas, 1977). Tie-in merchandising usually targets the youth market, and blockbusters like *Jurassic Park* (Steven Spielberg, 1993) and *The Lion King* (Roger Allers and Rob Minkoff, 1994) produced huge sales of licensed products, with *Jurassic Park* producing a billion dollars in sales of 5,000 different products (Magiera 1994: S-8). Product placement also saw a resurgence in the 1990s, with companies like Creative Film Promotions using computer programs to read scripts and co-ordinate each scene with a client's products. During the 1990s most major American consumer goods companies used movie product placement for advertising, and Coke, Pepsi and Anheuser-Busch have special product placement divisions. In 1990, for example, *Total Recall* (Paul Verhoeven) featured 55 references to 28 brand-name products, *Home Alone* (Chris Columbus) made 42 references to 31 brands and *Pretty Woman* (Garry Marshall) made 20 references to 18 brands (Wasko *et al.* 1993: 276).

This phenomenon was certainly nothing new in the context of television. In the 1980s Brazil's TV-Globo began integrating brand-name consumer products into dramatic narratives for advertising revenue, just as American sponsor-produced television had in the 1950s. In TV-Globo's internationally popular telenovellas (soap operas), product placement provides more revenue than the more conventional spot advertising (Barker 1997: 91). In the United States, ongoing television product placement has been compounded by the 1984 repeal of regulations on how long television commercials can be, creating a new generation of integrated 'advertainment' programming such as children's shows designed to sell toys based on programme characters. Numerous television stations purchase such programming in exchange for a share of the licensing profits in an advertising 'barter system' (Mattelart 1991: 128). Similarly, feature films have been generated as part of a larger cross-media marketing campaign for toys (Izod 1988: 186).

The international marketing of television programming was initially marked by an imbalance in distribution whereby the US and UK dominated global television markets and the 'flow' of programming ran primarily from North to South. Herbert Schiller argued that, as a result, television represented 'the channel through which life styles and value systems can be imposed on poor and vulnerable societies' (Schiller 1969: 8–9). But television markets have changed significantly over the last several decades due to the rise of large media industries that dominate the television market in particular 'geolinguistic regions'. For example, Mexico and Brazil export widely in Latin America; Hong Kong and Taiwan in Asia; Egypt in the Middle East; and India in its diasporic populations within Africa and Asia (Sinclair *et al.* 1996: 8). Language difference remains a marketing barrier in some contexts – particularly in the United States – but the successful export of genres like the Latin American telenovella to China, Poland and the former Soviet Union (as well as Italy and France) has made transnational export a goal for many television-producing countries. Programming is thus increasingly designed to be 'repackaged,' as well as dubbed into a variety of languages, in order to conform to local political censorship, genres and time slots. Transnational circulation has, in turn, facilitated the emergence of a cross-cultural star system in both film and television.

See also: deregulation, the United Kingdom; deregulation, the United States; infotainment/ infomercials; market place

References

Barker, C. (1997) *Global Television: An Introduction*, Oxford: Blackwell.

Eckert, C. (1991) 'The Carole Lombard in Macy's Window', in C. Gledhill (ed.) *Stardom: Industry of Desire*, London: Routledge.

Finney, A. (1996) *The State of European Cinema: A New Dose of Reality*, London: Cassell.

Izod, J. (1988) *Hollywood and the Box Office,*

1895–1986, New York: Columbia University Press.

Magiera, M. (1994) 'Promotional Marketer of the Year', *Advertising Age*, 21 March, pp. S-1, S-8.

Mattelart, A. (1991) *Advertising International: The Privatisation of Public Space*, trans. M. Chanan, New York: Routledge.

Schiller, H. (1969) *Mass Communications and the American Empire*, New York: A. M. Kelly.

Sinclair, J., Jacka, E. and Cunningham, S. (eds) (1996) *New Patterns in Global Television: Peripheral Vision*, Oxford: Oxford University Press.

Smith, J. (1998) *The Sounds of Commerce: Popular Film Music from 1960 to 1973*, Princeton: Princeton University Press.

Wasko, J., Phillips, M. and Purdie, C. (1993) 'Hollywood Meets Madison Avenue: The Commercialisation of U.S. Films', *Media, Culture and Society*, no. 15, pp. 271–93.

Wyatt, J. (1994) *High Concept: Movies and Marketing in Hollywood*, Austin: University of Texas Press.

Further reading

Hillier, J. (1993) *The New Hollywood*, London: Studio Vista.

Lewis, J. (ed.) (1998) *The New American Cinema*, Durham and London: Duke Uuniversity Press.

Mattelart, A., Delcourt, X. and Mattelart, M. (1984) *International Image Markets*, London: Comedia.

Wasko, J. (1994) *Hollywood in the Information Age: Beyond the Silver Screen*, Cambridge: Polity Press.

SARAH BERRY

Marx, Karl

b. 1818; d. 1883

One of the most significant social theorists in modern history, Karl Marx was born and educated in Germany, but spent much of his life in England. Active in international socialist politics and a correspondent for the *New York Herald Tribune*, Marx spent most of his life on the study of history, philosophy and economics. Although Marx's prolific writings paid scant attention to **culture**, Marxist theorists in the twentieth century were among the first to examine critically the social context of film and television.

Marxist theorists of culture from the **Frankfurt School** as well as others such as Walter **Benjamin**, Antonio **Gramsci** and Gyorgy **Lukács** considered the relationship between material conditions and human consciousness through **art** and literature. In the 1970s, one prominent school of Marxist cultural theorists concentrated on the reproduction of **dominant ideology** through film. The seminal work of Louis **Althusser** redefined Marxist film criticism through journals like *Cahiers du cinéma* in France and *Screen* in the UK.

Theorists influenced by Marxism have also worked on questions of ownership, consumerism and the commercialization of the media and society, including Raymond **Williams**, Stuart **Hall** and Fredric **Jameson**. One of the most vibrant traditions of Marxist media studies in the context of **globalization** comes from the political economy of mass communication tradition represented by the pioneering work of Armand Mattelart, Dallas Smythe and Herbert Schiller.

See also: class; consumption; ideology and hegemony; Marxist aesthetics; materialism and idealism; mode of production

Further reading

Bottomore, T. (ed.) (1979) *Karl Marx*, Englewood Cliffs, NJ: Prentice Hall.
Mosco, V. (1996) *The Political Economy of Communication*, London: Sage.

PAULA CHAKRAVARTTY

Marxist aesthetics

The term 'aesthetics' has been applied to those critical activities or practices that seek to understand and evaluate the nature and value of **art** and the relationship of art to society. Marxist aesthetics attempt to provide a more rigorous framework for understanding the nature of the arts by placing them in the context of social relationships which are themselves determined by the distribution of economic power.

Though Karl **Marx** wrote little about the arts, the twentieth century has seen a number of Marx's followers explicitly addressing the nature and value of art in society. The 1960s saw a resurgence of interest in Marxist perspectives on art and on the media. The work of the **Frankfurt School**, Walter **Benjamin**, Gyorgy **Lukács**, Lucien Goldmann, Antonio **Gramsci** and Louis **Althusser** received particular attention. These writers shared the belief that Marx's analysis of society was fundamentally correct: material or economic conditions determined all other social practices and social relationships, and an explanation for all social phenomena should be sought in specific historical and social conditions. Art was such a phenomenon, and did not exist in an ineffable realm which transcended material circumstances, but was the result of specific activities by specific people in specific social and economic relationships, and had specific consequences. Marxist aesthetics should, therefore, address these matters.

Marxist aesthetics in the 1970s was much influenced, particularly in film and literary studies, by the work of Althusser, who fundamentally rethought the connection between **base and superstructure** previously accepted by Marxist aestheticians. Althusser asked whether the arts were determined, ultimately, by economic relationships or whether the cultural superstructure might have some degree of autonomy from the base. Despite their relative degree of autonomy, however, might the arts none the less sustain ideologies that obscure the relationships which shape human interaction?

More recently, the work of Marxist scholars like John **Fiske** and Terry **Eagleton** has shifted to a greater concern with how the arts function within the lives of those at the bottom of the economic scale. The Frankfurt School critics argued that the popular arts served as the 'opiate of the people', distracting them from awareness of their real conditions of existence. By contrast, Fiske sees aspects of the popular arts as a site where materially disadvantaged people can show their resistance and rejection of the dominant culture, which he sees as controlled by the economically powerful groups in society. Marxist aestheticians have also concerned themselves in the 1980s and 1990s with post-modernism (see **modernism**

and post-modernism). Fredric **Jameson**, Ann Kaplan and Terry Eagleton discern in post-modernism a reactionary aesthetic based on the denial of **class** relationships, and, in contrast to modernism, a refusal to engage with capitalism's ability to link cultural production to commodities available to consumers.

The recurrent dilemma of Marxist aesthetics seems to be the lingering desire to preserve some element of traditional aesthetic claims that art transcends material values and, at the same time, places them securely in a material, non-transcendent realm of experience open to all. On the one hand, Marxist aesthetic arguments want to locate the arts, and culture generally, as more than leisure activities pursued by those with economic or cultural capital derived from privileged position, often at the expense of those less privileged. On the other hand, they display a reluctance to recognize that the pleasures taken by many less privileged people in cultural forms like film and television are related to the market place, and are not experienced as simply a resistance to social conditions.

See also: Brecht, Bertolt; commodification; Marx, Karl; popular, the

Further reading

Althusser, L. (1977) *For Marx*, trans. B. Brewster, London: NLB.
Williams, R. (1977) *Marxism and Literature*, Oxford: Oxford University Press.

PHILIP SIMPSON

master narrative

As a translation of Jean-François **Lyotard**'s 'grand récit', 'master narrative' introduces connotations of gendered domination into a term which in the original French is comparatively neutral. In this respect, '**metanarrative**', or simply 'grand narrative', are considered by some to convey the sense more accurately.

A master narrative is an overarching **discourse** about, or encompassing, other narratives. One of the key arguments in Lyotard's *The Postmodern Condition* (1984) is that the shift from modernity to

post-modernity involves a breakdown of these totalizing discourses and their associated assumptions of absolute value and universal truth. In place of master narratives, Lyotard champions difference, plurality and small-scale discourses ('petit récits'), each with their own individual and unique set of rules, concepts and methods (see **modernism and post-modernism**).

Lyotard defines discourses of modernity as those which aim to legitimize themselves through 'explicit appeal to some grand narrative, such as the dialectics of Spirit, the hermeneutics of meaning, the emancipation of the rational or working subject, or the creation of wealth' (Lyotard 1984: xxiii). The founding moment of this tendency is the Enlightenment, whose rationalist project is based on absolute concepts of freedom and knowledge. Yet Lyotard's definition also encompasses such varied ideologies as capitalism, Communism and Christianity, and implicitly labels as redundant all large-scale struggles for equality. In so far as campaigns in feminism, black civil rights and the gay movement depend on overarching or universal notions of justice and a long narrative of progress and liberation, they too would appear to stand condemned for their totalizing pretensions.

In a less problematic way, though related still to the project of modernity, we can see master narratives at work in the discourses of science, which aspire to an absolute 'truth' and mastery over the natural world, and in the architecture of the modernist period – Le Corbusier, Frank Lloyd Wright, and the pervasive 'International Style' – with its utopian agenda of social transformation through formal innovation.

Lyotard sees these metanarratives as at best impotent and futile, at worst repressive, totalitarian and 'terrorist' in their imposition of consensus. Grand narratives, he states, have encountered a 'crisis of legitimation' and are no longer credible. Rather than totalizing ideals – the promised lands of absolute truth and freedom – the emphasis is now on the means, on practical skills and strategies. In place of the older grand narrative, Lyotard suggests the 'petit récit' of post-modernity. 'Simplifying to the extreme,' he explains in a much-cited phrase, 'I define postmodern as incredulity toward metanarratives' (Lyotard 1984: xxiv).

Post-modern mini-narratives are characterized

by variety and variation, making no claim to universality. Rather than overarching frameworks and rules, these are discrete 'language games' serving a particular social group or individual. 'Postmodern knowledge,' writes Lyotard, 'is not simply a tool of the authorities; it refines our sensitivity to differences…Its principle is not the expert's homology, but the inventor's paralogy' (Lyotard 1984: xxv). We might well question, however, whether Lyotard's sweeping argument in *The Postmodern Condition*, with its bold subtitle claiming to 'report on knowledge' and internal account of a wide-ranging and progressive cultural shift, does not itself constitute a master narrative.

Recent cultural and screen theorists have taken up the concepts articulated by Lyotard in various ways. John **Fiske** (1991), for instance, echoes Lyotard and Michel de **Certeau** in championing the 'micropolitics' of resistance he sees in television **fandom**, advocating this kind of small-scale negotiation over larger, organized methods of social protest. Other American work on **audience** and popular culture, such as that of Janice Radway and Henry Jenkins, has documented the same process, though not always with Fiske's enthusiasm. More directly, Barbara Creed (1997) refers to the breakdown of patriarchal master narratives in her feminist analysis of the *Alien* films (Ridley Scott/David Fincher/Jean-Pierre Jeunet, 1979–1997), while Peter Brooker and Will Brooker discuss the 'circling mini-narratives' of *Pulp Fiction* (Quentin Tarantino, 1994) as features of a 'progressive' postmodern aesthetic. However, it is perhaps the **Internet**, rather than film and television – with its fragmented content, putative democracy of information, and practice of non-linear reading and writing encouraged by hypertext links and jumps – which most aptly embodies Lyotard's vision of post-modern language games.

References

Brooker, P. and Brooker, W. (eds) (1997) *Postmodern After-Images*, London: Arnold.

Creed, B. (1997) 'From Here to Modernity', reprinted in P. Brooker and W. Brooker (eds) *Postmodern After-Images*, London: Arnold.

Fiske, J. (1991) *Reading the Popular*, London: Routledge.

Lyotard, J.-F. (1984) *The Postmodern Condition: A Report on Knowledge*, trans. Geoff Bennington and Brian Massumi, Manchester: Manchester University Press.

WILL BROOKER

matching (shots)

'Matching' refers to the practice of editing shots so that they appear to be part of the same scene, the same action and the same temporal and spatial reality. Hollywood's **continuity editing** system uses the match on action – a cut which joins together separate shots of the same continuous movement, taken from different camera distances or points of view – to create its 'invisible' style. The continuity system also tends to use 'master shots', to which subsequent shots are visually matched through the placing of characters or actions in smaller spatial sub-units of the original set-up. Since the unified action that the matching shot creates is illusory – it covers up its manipulation of time and space, and the actual labour of filmmaking – the wilful mismatching of shots has at times been seen as **oppositional**.

See also: point of view shot

ADRIENNE L. McLEAN

materialism and idealism

The philosophical distinction between materialism and idealism originates from Karl **Marx**'s early writings and his conception of historical materialism in contrast to classical German Idealism and *philosophical* materialism. Formulated in the *Theses on Feuerbach, Economic and Philosophical Manuscripts* and *The German Ideology*, historical materialism was, for Marx, primarily a method of social history defined by its commitment to concrete research in contrast to abstract philosophical reflection. The centrality of human practice and the denial of the autonomy of ideas from the production and reproduction of social life emphasized the significance of labour in transforming human history. One famous line that lays out the intellectual project of historical materialism in contrast to traditional philosophical inquiry says succinctly, 'the Philosophers have only *interpreted* the world in various ways, the point is to *change* it' (Marx and Engels 1968, 11th Theses).

The philosopher Marx was directly responding to was **Hegel** and his idealist conception of the historical **dialectic**. Marx was intent on turning Hegel 'right side up' in order to conceive of history as the self-realization of human beings (as opposed to God or the spirit), and explain the corresponding dialectical transformation of society from feudalism, to capitalism to (self-realized) Communism. Marx's own writings show a complex understanding of the materiality of ideas:

> The phantoms formed in the human brain are also, necessarily, sublimates of their material life-process, which is empirically verifiable and bound to material premises. Morality, religion, metaphysics, all the rest of ideology and their corresponding forms of consciousness, thus no longer retain the semblance of independence.
>
> (Marx 1978: 154–5)

In contrast to Marx's writings, his collaborator and patron, Friedrich Engels, along with other prominent theorists of the 'Second International', formulated the doctrinal core of dialectical materialism, treating materialism and idealism as mutually exclusive and exhaustive categories. Much of the subsequent debate in western Marxism responds to this reformulation of material reality as epistemologically and ontologically separate from the mind or **consciousness** (see **epistemology; ontology**). At the end of the nineteenth century, 'false consciousness', a term coined by Engels, is contrasted to 'scientific socialism'; the objective of materialism became revealing the true laws of history (**Eagleton** 1991).

Marxist theorists, from Gyorgy **Lukács** in *History and Class Consciousness* to Antonio **Gramsci** in his *Prison Notebooks*, rejected the pejorative reformulation of idealism and ideology criticizing the turn to 'scientific' materialism away from the philosophy of praxis or history. The **Frankfurt School** in the 1930s and 1940s also argued against the crude distinctions invoked by orthodox Marxists, and they attempted instead to develop a materialist approach to a systematic 'critical theory of mass culture'. Their version of 'ideology critique'

sought to explain the lack of revolutionary consciousness through the analysis of the culture industries. They stressed the relative autonomy of 'superstructural' phenomena in a process of 'reciprocal interaction with a socio-economic base' (Kellner 1989).

In the 1950s, the work of E. P. Thompson and Raymond **Williams**, and the early writings of Stuart **Hall**, focused on a materialist analysis of working-class or popular culture 'where consciousness and conditions intersected' (Hall 1980).

By the 1970s, the controversial work of Louis **Althusser** and the structuralist emphasis on the rules of ideology reintroduced the language of 'science' to the study of 'the specific elements of the superstructure'. Althusser rejected the 'socialist humanism' of Marx's early writings. This time, the problem of economic determination was consigned 'to the last instance' and western Marxist cultural studies focused on the 'immanent structures of a particular discourse' (Sparks 1996; see **structuralism and post-structuralism**)

Since the 1970s the question of materialism/ idealism within cultural studies has fractured into many separate discussions. It is difficult to think of an area of critical social theory today that does not at least implicitly touch on the issue. Post-structuralist and post-modern critics have introduced new methods and new subject positions challenging the epistemological tenets of historical materialism (see **modernism and post-modernism**). Within the Marxist, or post-Marxist tradition, the debate in terms of the relationship between consciousness and material conditions has continued in the influential work of Pierre **Bourdieu** and Jürgen **Habermas**.

See also: base and superstructure; class; ideology and hegemony

References

Eagleton, T. (1991) *Ideology*, London: Verso.

Hall, S. (1980) 'Cultural Studies: Two Paradigms', *Media, Culture and Society*, vol. 2, no. 1, pp. 57–72.

Kellner, D. (1989) *Critical Theory, Marxism, and Modernity*, Cambridge: Polity Press.

Marx, K. (1978) 'The German Ideology', in

R. Tucker (ed.) *The Marx-Engels Reader*, New York: W. W. Norton, pp. 147–75.

Marx, K. and Engels, R. (1968) *Selected Works*, London: Lawrence and Wishart.

Sparks, C. (1996) 'Stuart Hall, Cultural Studies and Marxism', in D. Morley and K. H. Chen (eds) *Stuart Hall: Critical Dialogues in Cultural Studies*, London: Routledge, pp. 71–101.

Further reading

Mattelart, A. and Mattelart, M. (1992) *Rethinking Media Theory: Signposts and New Directions*, trans. J. A. Cohen and M. Urquidi, Minneapolis: University of Minnesota Press.

Williams, R. (1980) *Problems in Materialism and Culture*, London: Verso.

PAULA CHAKRAVARTTY

McLuhan, Marshall Herbert

b. 1911; d. 1980

A Canadian, Marshall McLuhan was a media and cultural critic. His most noted works include *The Mechanical Bride* (1951), *The Gutenberg Galaxy* (1962), *Understanding Media* (1964), *The Medium is the Message* (1967, with Q. Fiore) and *Counterblast* (1970). *Understanding Media* propelled McLuhan to international fame with its controversial claim that the development of media technologies has had a far greater social effect on audiences than media content ('the medium is the message'; see **audience**). Distinguishing between 'hot' and 'cool' media, he argued that older 'hot' media extend through space in 'high definition' (they are filled with data), thus encouraging passive audience reception (e.g., photographs, films, newspapers). Newer 'cool' (electronic) media are 'low definition' (they provide little data), requiring audiences to actively complete their messages (e.g., television, radio, telephones). McLuhan optimistically asserted that the rapid spread of electronic media throughout the world would lead to the collapse of spatial and temporal distances between people, turning the planet into a 'global village' of culturally interdependent citizens. McLuhan's

ideas have influenced the work of post-modernist cultural theorists like Jean **Baudrillard**.

See also: globalization; Innis, Harold Adam; modernism and post-modernism; technological change

Further reading

Theall, D. (1971) *The Medium is the Rear View Mirror: Understanding McLuhan*, Montreal and London: McGill-Queen's University Press.

Winston, B. (1998) *Media Technology and Society: A History*, London and New York: Routledge.

CYNTHIA CARTER

media event

A media event is an occurrence which attracts an extraordinary amount of media attention. This attention is generally international in scope, crosses the boundaries between popular news and political event, and usually marks a reference point in the cultural and historical imagination thereafter. For example, the death and the funeral of Diana, Princess of Wales was central to news broadcasts around the world while being, at the same time, the subject of a wide range of media discourse from debates about the constitutional ramifications of her untimely death for the British monarchy to the analysis of Diana as a cultural **icon** within the academy. Other often-cited examples of the media event are the assassination of President Kennedy, the *Challenger* space shuttle disaster, the fall of the Berlin Wall and the O. J. Simpson arrest and trial.

David Dayan and Elihu Katz argue a more specific definition by emphasizing the interruptive quality of these events; the authors state that they 'intervene in the normal flow of broadcasting and our lives' (Dayan and Katz 1992: 5). Emphasizing the ceremonial nature of such events as the wedding of Charles and Diana or the *Apollo* moon landings, Dayan and Katz see media events as films and television programmes which 'claim to be historic, preach reconciliation, celebrate initiative, and are produced and presented with reverence' (*ibid.*: 13). They also stress the importance of the collective experience for these events. The norm of viewing is one in which viewers actively celebrate by watching the event in groups as a special occasion. In this regard, Dayan and Katz attempt to define the media event as a **genre** which includes not only the **text** but also its impact on broadcast scheduling and spectator involvement. Crucial to their overall argument is that the media event can celebrate not only a sense of unity by 'spotlight[ing] some central value or aspect of collective memory' (*ibid.*: ix), but also pluralism where the overarching theme is 'contest' such as the Watergate hearings. By drawing a clear distinction between democratic and totalitarian uses of political ceremony they aim their critique at the types of political ceremony rather than ceremony itself.

While Dayan and Katz outline the specific characteristics of the media event as a genre, other approaches have focused on the way in which they incorporate existing genres as interpretive frames. Here the extensive media coverage presents a multiplicity of 'frames of understanding' by which the events are relayed. A helpful analysis of this phenomenon can be found in the academic film journal *Screen* (Kuhn 1998: 1). In this volume the editors structured a special set of essays on the death of Diana under the headings 'icon', 'story', 'image', 'nation' and 'space'. Each heading outlined the representational traditions which circulated through the media from the first reports of her death through the week prior to the funeral and the funeral itself. The discussion illustrated the characteristics of media events which mobilized and gave voice to a wide range of opinions and responses. For example, Christine Geraghty (in Kuhn 1998) notes the narrative forms which 'built up around her [Diana] in her lifetime...which have been available as people attempt to make sense of her death'. These began with the 'fairy tale romance' but then took on the open-ended structure of soap opera as the media constructed her life within the Royal family and, later, outside of it. Geraghty points out that these forms were drawn on initially by the news media during the week of her death and funeral but were also a central part in the developing story of the mourners' increasing participation in the event as they were interviewed outside the palaces. Geraghty observes that the terms in which a number of

mourners articulated their private feelings were within the values of **soap opera** and that indeed 'talk about private feelings – a staple of soap opera – was valued as the best way of expressing grief', a value which defined the media's coverage of the funeral.

While Dayan and Katz, and Geraghty draw attention to the positive nature of audience appropriation of existing forms, Bill Nichols, in his book *Blurred Boundaries: Questions of Meaning in Contemporary Culture* (1994), laments the way in which the events surrounding the trial of the LA policemen accused of beating Rodney King spilled into 'the Manichean, localised and dramatic channel marked out for it by the mainstream media' (1994: 19). Working from the indexical value of the videotape which shows the police, Nichols argues that the excess of the footage provoked a potential outrage through its presentation as a contest, which ultimately resulted in villainizing the policemen on trial and drew attention away from a critique of the LA police force itself. Here the interpretive frame worked to contain radical response.

Each of these approaches highlights the importance of existing forms in defining the media event and explaining the dynamics of interpretation and social function. Within that, they illustrate the degree of diversity in the debate on how those dynamics operate and to what end.

See also: audience; live television

References

Dayan, D. and Katz, E. (1992) *Media Events: The Live Broadcasting of History*, Cambridge, MA: Harvard University Press.

Kuhn, A. (ed.) (1998) 'Flowers and Tears: The Death of Diana, Princes of Wales', *Screen*, vol. 39, no. 1, pp. 67–85.

Nichols, B. (1994) *Blurred Boundaries: Questions of Meaning in Contemporary Culture*, Bloomington: Indiana University Press.

MIKE HAMMOND

melodrama

Melodrama is a style or **genre** with antecedents as diverse as Greek tragedy and Victorian theatre. Its use has often been pejorative, used to indicate an emotionally manipulative and highly-strung form of drama. After years of neglect in film criticism, it became the focus of great interest among such film theorists as Thomas Elsaesser, Geoffrey Nowell-Smith and Laura **Mulvey** in the 1970s. The surge of attention was made all the more interesting by the diversity of approaches adopted to explore it, encompassing Marxist, psychoanalytic and feminist critiques (see **feminist theory; Marx, Karl; psychoanalysis**).

Marxist criticism has been drawn to the genre for the intriguing position it holds in relation to issues of **class** and capitalism. Significantly, the rise of nineteenth-century melodrama coincided with the rise of capitalism. As the bourgeoisie took on new rights, new demands on the family emerged. The inheritance system meant that the family was instrumental in perpetuating both **patriarchy** and capitalism, and melodrama reveals a preoccupation with these issues. It pivots on an examination of family relationships and domestic tensions, thereby offering a fascinating arena for both male and female roles, since women are frequently key protagonists and men find themselves placed in a sphere where they have traditionally been more peripheral.

Elsaesser (see Gledhill 1987) was among the first to argue that rather than merely reproducing or upholding the values of capitalism and patriarchy, melodrama can be seen to offer a critique of them. Ambivalence and alienation are key motifs of the aesthetic and the pressures of social convention are frequently seen to be the root cause of repression and breakdown. For example, in *All That Heaven Allows* (Douglas Sirk, 1955) a wealthy, middle-aged, middle-class widow is forced to choose between her love for her gardener and her children's demands that she reject him in order to maintain a façade of respectable sobriety, a dilemma which exposes the shallowness of middle-class values and their repression of female **desire**.

A key element of the genre's appropriation as a potentially ideologically subversive form is its use of **mise-en-scène** and **excess**. Nowell-Smith's (see Gledhill 1987) psychoanalytic reading of the genre argues that hysteria or 'the return of the repressed' is not spoken but displaced in melodrama, emerging in its lavish *mise-en-scène* and emotive music. Melodrama opens up problems that it can not accommodate; they can not be contained and strain the formal aesthetic. Exaggerated performance, unlikely plot developments and other moments of anti-realist excess all serve to disrupt the façade of domestic harmony.

Debates surrounding melodrama have been problematized by the difficulty of definition or generic specificity occasioned by the range of forms which fall within its parameters. The categories which have been the focus of most interest within film are the **family melodrama** and the woman's film. The former is characterized by its exploration of an Oedipal trajectory and crisis-stricken masculinity, for example *Rebel without a Cause* (Nicholas Ray, 1955). By comparison, the woman's film, for example, *Stella Dallas* (King Vidor, 1937), was made and marketed with a female audience strongly in mind, and is striking for its use of female subjectivity and fascination with consumerism. This has provided rich territory for feminist theorists, such as Mary Ann Doane, who have explored further subdivisions within the woman's film including the maternal melodrama with its sacrificing mother, and the paranoid or gothic woman's film, in which the heroine is trapped in a menacing home with a sinister love interest who may be persecuting her.

In television studies, critical work on melodrama has focused most strongly on **soap opera**. One can again find a preoccupation with the domestic sphere and the use of female subjectivity. The melodramatic tradition continues in soaps through its use of devices such as stirring music (notably in US **prime-time** soaps), lingering close-ups on faces and significant objects, and narratives marked by coincidences and unexpected events. Christine Geraghty (1991) has argued that the melodramatic aesthetic in soaps is crucial to audience engagement. As psychological motivation is secondary to emotional effect, the use of excess has a space surrounding its significance and it is up to the spectator to bring meaning to this effect.

References

Geraghty, C. (1991) *Women and Soap Opera*, Cambridge: Polity Press.

Gledhill, C. (ed.) (1987) *Home Is Where the Heart Is*, London: BFI Publishing.

DEBORAH JERMYN

memory

'History is not what you thought. *It is what you can remember.*' Despite their parodic intent, the authors of *1066 and All That* (Sellar and Yeatman 1998), the very Memorable History of England, point to a clear distinction between history, often thought to be the province of academics, and memory, often thought to consist of the 'historical intuitions and opinions' of the people (Sellar and Yeatman 1998: 5). Media studies scholars practice **history** and analyse mediated representations of history (see **representation**), yet have paid relatively little attention to issues of memory. This entry seeks to differentiate among various forms of memory, to distinguish history from memory and to consider the relationship of cinema and television to memory.

Memory is often thought of as an individual attribute and individual memory constitutes a form of personal history that is fundamental to **identity**. Persons who suffer neurological damage that incapacitates memory lack the sense of identity that derives from continuity between past and present. Psychological therapy often consists of exploring individual memory to construct a new sense of identity. **Psychoanalysis**, particularly in its traditional Freudian incarnation, seeks to recover the deepest and most repressed memories (see **Freud, Sigmund**). Film studies' engagement with psychoanalysis, however, ignored individual memory, perhaps because of the insistence on universal drives common to all spectators. Of course, individual memory is never entirely isolated or private; rather, individual memories are marked by, and form part of, collective memory. And it is the latter rather than the former that seems particularly pertinent to film and television.

The term 'collective memory' is perhaps the most neutral means of indicating aggregate rather than individual memory, but scholars also refer to public or official memory, cultural memory and popular memory. Some historians speak of individual, group or collective memory as an attribute of individuals or collections of individuals and official or public memory as an attribute of state or civil institutions (see **institution**). Official or public memory originates at the top of social and cultural hierarchies, although it is directed to the people below, often in the interests of maintaining hegemony (see **ideology and hegemony**). Its most prominent texts include museums, monuments and commemorations, whether annual (the United Kingdom's Remembrance Sunday, the United States' Veteran's Day) or one-off (the fiftieth anniversary of VE day, the fiftieth anniversary of Pearl Harbor). In addition, both state and commercial broadcasting systems serve as conveyors of official or public memory, as will be discussed in more detail below. By contrast with official or public memory, the terms 'cultural memory' and 'popular memory' indicate processes that to some degree function apart from public and civic institutions. Liliane Weissberg (1999: 16) suggests that cultural memory, tied as it is to cultural studies, relates to 'low culture', that is to 'popular media and everyday conventions'. The term 'popular memory' points to an even stronger distinction between memory that originates from state and civil institutions and that which emerges from below. Michel **Foucault** wrote:

> People . . . barred from writing, from producing their books themselves, from drawing up their own historical accounts . . . nevertheless do have a way of recording history, or remembering it, of keeping it fresh and using it. This popular history was . . . even more alive, more clearly formulated in the 19th century, where, for instance, there was a whole tradition of struggles which were transmitted orally, or in writing or songs, etc.
>
> (Foucault 1989: 91–2)

Despite addressing popular memory, Foucault employs the term 'popular history', reminding us of the need to differentiate history from memory, something which is not an easy task. Some see memory as an active, continuous link to a past that history merely represents. For example, Pierre

Nora asserts that 'Memory is life, borne by living societies founded in its name.... History... is the reconstruction, always problematic and incomplete, of what is no longer. Memory is a perpetually actual phenomenon, a bond tying us to the eternal present; history is a representation of the past' (Nora 1989: 8). Others distinguish between a formal history predicated on written documents and recorded facts and a quirkier, idiosyncratic popular memory such as that celebrated in *1066 and All That*. Raphael Samuels writes that,

> Popular memory is... the very antithesis of written history. It eschews notions of determination and seizes instead on omens, portents, signs. It measures change genealogically, in terms of generations rather than centuries, epochs or decades. It has no developmental sense of time, but assigns events to the mythicized 'good old days'... or 'once upon a time'. In place of the pedagogues' 'causes' and 'effects' or the scholar's pursuit of origins and climacterics, it deals in broad-brushed contrasts between 'now' and 'then', 'past' and 'present', the new-fangled and the old-fashioned. So far as historical particulars are concerned, it prefers the eccentric to the typical; the sensational to the routine.
>
> (Samuels 1994: 6)

Since most widely circulated media texts are the products of advanced capitalist institutions, they cannot be considered popular in so far as that term might indicate originating with the people (see **popular, the**). But, as the transformations of global capitalism attenuate the traditional structures for the transmission of popular memory such as extended family networks and close-knit stable communities, the media have filled the void, becoming a more active force in the construction of memory. The remainder of this entry discusses the connections between cinema and television and the various forms of memory delineated above – public or official, cultural and popular.

Cinema, television and memory

Although television has replaced the cinema as the mass medium to which all segments of the population attend, films and film stars still play an active part in the cultural memory which Liliane Weissberg (1999: 16) suggests is related to 'popular media and everyday conventions'. Consider, for example, the iconic stars of the classical Hollywood cinema (see **classical Hollywood cinema and new Hollywood cinema**). Just as those who have never read a Conan Doyle story would understand an image of Sherlock Holmes to connote detection and scientific rationality, those who had never seen a Humphrey Bogart or Marilyn Monroe film would understand an image of the former to connote a tough, uncompromising, particularly American brand of masculinity and an image of the latter to connote a playful, innocent sexuality. The culture industry continues to profit from these stars long after their demise, commodifying them in the form of still images – postcards, wall posters and calendars – as well as moving images such as the commercials that reference iconic stars through impersonators or digitalized images or the occasional films that feature star-obsessed characters (such as Woody Allen's *Play It Again Sam* [1972], in which the character played by Allan receives romantic advice from a Humphrey Bogart impersonator). Individual films also feature prominently in cultural memory. For example, the *Star Wars* (George Lucas) phenomenon of 1999 – during which it became almost impossible to avoid the flood of licensed products both in the United States and in Britain, and cinema complexes devoted half their numerous screens to *The Phantom Menace* – derived primarily from the activities of powerful **multinational** companies, but also depended to some extent on the memories of those twenty- and thirty-somethings who had seen the original trilogy in their youth. A better example might be *Gone with the Wind* (Victor Fleming, 1939). The culture industry maintains the film's cultural memory in the form of television showings and commodities such as the Tara plates and Scarlett O'Hara dolls but *Gone with the Wind* seems to have passed into popular memory as well, as attested to by Helen Taylor's book *Scarlett's Women* (1989). Taylor's correspondence with several women respondents shows that the film took on a life of its own within family dynamics, serving as a bond between mothers who remembered the film from their youth and daughters whose mothers initiated them into the film, helping to form their readings of it. Taylor's research shows that a highly commodified form can none the less be claimed by the people for their own use (see **commodification**).

But if, as Nora (1989) and others have argued, memory is a continuous and ongoing process, the continuous, ongoing and ubiquitous medium of television now serves not only as memory repository but as an active force in its construction. This is particularly the case with **public service broadcasting** systems such as the BBC, intended by its founding director, John **Reith**, to be the voice of the nation. The BBC transmits to the nation a series of annual media events that maintain official or public memory by forging links with the past: the Remembrance Sunday ceremonies at the Cenotaph; the Edinburgh Military Tattoo; royal events such as the opening of Parliament, the Trooping of the Colour and the Queen's Christmas message. The BBC, together with ITV, the British commercial television system, also broadcasts one-off media events such as royal marriages and funerals. It was one of the latter, the funeral of Diana, Princess of Wales, that, as does the case of *Gone with the Wind*, illustrates the porousness between different forms of memory. Because of her status as ex-royal and current media celebrity, Diana's death and funeral would have warranted extensive media coverage regardless of the public's reaction to the event. But in this instance popular memory dynamically interacted with the official memory purveyed by state and commercial broadcasters and itself became a part of the **media event**. At the same time as broadcasters endlessly replayed clips of the key events in Diana's life, cameras panned the banks of flowers, stuffed animals, candles and poems that were piled outside the royal palaces, reporters interviewed the pilgrims making their way to these quasi-sacred sites, and news presenters marvelled at the fervency of the public's response. The bottom-up memory of the people, which had enshrined Diana as secular saint, conflicted with the top-down official memory of the Royal Family and its supporters, many of whom had viewed the Princess as a threat to the monarchy's authority.

Media events and the purveyance of memory are not the sole domain of public broadcasting systems. The American commercial networks serve many of the same functions as the BBC, broadcasting annual commemorations such as Veteran's Day ceremonies as well as events presumed to be of import to the nation as a whole. Such broadcasts both remember and actively create new memories. For example, the extensive coverage devoted to John F. Kennedy's assassination and funeral drew on archival footage to memorialize the fallen leader while at the same time shaping the public's memory of the event. Many Americans first learned of the President's demise from television while the most memorable images of the assassination and funeral derive from the television coverage: the Zapruder film of the shots hitting home; the heavily veiled Jackie Kennedy; Kennedy's son saluting his father's coffin; the riderless horse leading the funeral procession. Television recycles these images to mark each significant anniversary of Kennedy's death. In similar fashion, special television programming observes other momentous occurrences such as the thirtieth anniversary of the moon landing or the tenth anniversary of the fall of the Berlin Wall. For those alive at the time of the event, the old footage often recalls the period of one's life in which it was originally viewed, pointing to the complex interactions among media, collective memory and individual memory.

Such complexities reveal that television's memory function is not limited to the creation and enshrinement of official or public memory. The medium maintains cultural memory through forms as diverse as arts programming devoted to the higher end of the cultural spectrum (for example, classical music concerts, Shakespeare plays) and the advertisements for the nostalgic compact discs featuring decade-by-decade compilations of the greatest hits of the post-war period. Sports programming may constitute one of the most conspicuous forms of television's relationship to cultural memory. In the United States and Britain, the sheer amount of time devoted to baseball games and cricket matches attests to the centrality of these sports to their respective nations' identity and cultural memory. The coverage of individual games or matches more specifically invokes the memory of the games, both long and short term. For brevity's sake, let us consider American television's treatment of baseball.

Televised baseball continually invokes the

memory of the game's past. Many regularly scheduled games on the networks and the cable sports channels open by invoking baseball's glorious past, with still photos of famous players, clips of famous plays and tracking shots past old equipment, programmes, baseball cards and newspaper stories. During the 1980s, the initial sequence of NBC's traditional 'Game of the Week' typified this celebratory strategy, linking television, and radio before it, to baseball's history. Through the magic of computer graphics, red, white and blue lines assembled themselves into the Stars and Stripes. The flag then transformed into a facsimile of a baseball ticket. In the frame formed by the ticket, Babe Ruth appeared speaking into a microphone prominently labelled 'NBC'. As the voice-over proclaimed that NBC is 'now in its seventh decade of bringing you baseball's milestones, baseball's memories, baseball's majesty and baseball's magic moments', the visual track displayed well-known plays and players of yore.

Televised baseball also displays a comprehensive short-term memory of the current season and specific games. Baseball, more than any other American sport, is obsessed with record keeping and numbers: official statistics measure every aspect of the game and the players' performances. The televised game both reflects and intensifies this obsession, displaying in graphic form not only the official statistics recognized by the game's arbiters, but more esoteric, computer-generated information. At a pitcher's first appearance, and at a batter's every appearance at the plate, graphics give information about his performance to that point in the season, as well as information about his performance during that specific game. In game telecasts, these graphics combine a picture of the player with numbers and alphabetical abbreviations of baseball terms. Other graphics measure the two teams' performance, again until that point in the season, or during the game, substituting the team's logo for a picture. At the end of each half inning, the graphics summarize the action and scoring up to that point. While most of these graphics display 'official' statistics, some provide information relevant to a particular junction in the game: how many times has player x struck out batting left-handed with men on base and two outs. Occasionally, quotes from players, managers and

umpires, both past and present, appear on the screen. The announcers, among their other functions, serve as keepers of the flame, relating a particular game not only to the current and recent seasons, but to baseball's legendary past. They compare active to past players, tell anecdotes about the game's great and famous and reminisce about their own careers. They also contrast the contemporary game to its previous incarnations, commenting on alterations in rules and playing conditions and not invariably valorizing the present.

Television remembers national history and cultural history. Television also remembers television. The expansion of the television spectrum first through cable and then through digitalization has created a demand for programming to fill the vastly expanded airspace. Industry economics constrain the production of new material and require the endless recycling of popular programmes from the past. In the US, the Nickelodeon Channel was among the first to establish a distinct market niche for these repeat showings, couching its appeal in a canny mixture of nostalgia and post-modern irony (see **modernism and post-modernism**). In Britain, the UK Gold channel engages in a more straightforward celebration of British television history. Television shows no longer in production provide a source of cheap, original programming in the form of clips from a past programme, interspersed with newly filmed footage of cast interviews and a presenter who links the segments together. For example, both the twenty-fifth and thirtieth anniversaries of the long-running television phenomenon *Star Trek* were marked in such fashion. Occasionally even current programmes, faced with budgetary or time constrains, resort to 'clip shows', constructing a **narrative** that serves as an excuse to incorporate scenes from past episodes. The cartoon series *The Simpsons* does this on a fairly regular basis, disarming the viewer through an ironic awareness of the process. Some American programmes now routinely incorporate old material in their prologues, a practice necessitated by the shift from the **series** form of unconnected episodes to the **serial** form of ongoing story lines that took place during the 1980s. Producers aid viewers' memories through a series of clips preceded by the announcement, for example, 'previously on *ER*' or 'previously on *NYPD Blue*'.

The narrative arcs of long-running programmes draw on the memories of both scriptwriters and viewers, who must connect current with past events and fit them all within complex diegetic universes (see **diegesis**). The so-called 'mythology arc' of *The X-Files*, concerning an alien plot to invade the Earth, and the pre-planned five-year story line of *Bablylon 5* are two examples. But the most complex diegetic universe of them all belongs to *Star Trek*, composed as it is of four television series (*Star Trek* [1966–1969], *Star Trek: The Next Generation* [1987–1994], *Star Trek: Deep Space Nine* [1992–1999], *Star Trek: Voyager* [1995–]) and nine feature films. Working within the template laid down by the original series' producer, Gene Roddenberry, scriptwriters strive to create coherency and consistency among these disparate texts, a process resulting in linkages, overlaps and deliberate homages that reference viewers' intertextual memories. The fifth season of *Deep Space Nine* commemorated *Star Trek*'s thirtieth anniversary with an episode called *Trials and Tribbilations*, in which Captain Sisko (Avery Brooks) and several of his crew find themselves on the Enterprise NCC-1701 in the midst of the much loved original series episode *The Trouble with Tribbles*, attempting to foil a plot to assassinate Captain Kirk (William Shatner). The wonders of digital manipulation integrate the casts of the original series and *Deep Space Nine* and the programme concludes with Captain Sisko of the latter talking to Captain Kirk of the former. Over thirty years separate *The Trouble with Tribbles* from *Trials and Tribbilations* and yet both sets of characters inhabit a universe that is recognizably *Star Trek*. And much of the fans' satisfaction derived from the exercise of their *Star Trek* memories: they knew things about the Enterprise NC-1701 that the DS9 characters did not. *Trials and Tribbilations* represents a particularly elaborate knitting together of the *Star Trek* universe, but *Trek* actors regularly make guest appearances on each others' shows. The most important crossover occurred on the big screen in *Star Trek VII: Generations* (David Carson, 1994) when Captain Kirk and Captain Picard (Patrick Stewart) of *The Next Generation* finally met and joined forces to save humanity, the meeting

gaining added poignancy from the fans' intertextual memories of the two captains.

Does the complex diegetic universe of *Star Trek* constitute an example of cultural memory or popular memory? The fact that the universe is produced by one of the richest and most powerful of media conglomerates, Paramount, might identify it as the former. But the fact that the universe would not exist at all if not for the memories of the fans of the original series who consistently clamoured for new texts and then made those texts successful might identify it as the latter.

References

Ben-Amos, D. and Weissberg, L. (1999) *Cultural Memory and the Construction of Identity*, Detroit: Wayne State University Press.

Foucault, M. (1989) 'Film and Popular Memory', in Michel Foucault, *Foucault Live*, New York: Semiotext(e).

Nora, P. (1989) 'Between Memory and History: *Les Lieux de memoire*', *Representations*, 26 (Spring).

Samuel, R. (1994) *Theatres of Memory*, London: Verso.

Sellar, W. C. and Yeatman, R. J. (1998) *1066 and All That*, London: Methuen.

Taylor, H. (1989) *Scarlett's Women: Gone with the Wind and its Female Fans*, New Brunswick, NJ: Rutgers University Press.

Weissberg, L. (1999) 'Introduction', in Dan Ben-Amos and Liliane Weissberg (1999) *Cultural Memory and the Construction of Identity*, Detroit: Wayne State University Press, pp. 7–26.

ROBERTA E. PEARSON

Merleau-Ponty, Maurice

b. 1908; d. 1961

After serving as an army officer in the Second World War, Maurice Merleau-Ponty was appointed Professor of Philosophy at the University of Lyon in 1945. He moved to the Sorbonne in Paris in 1949, and later went on to become the Chair of Philosophy at the College of France from 1952 until his death in 1961.

Philosopher, social critic and a leading

phenomenologist, Merleau-Ponty worked in the field of **phenomenology** in the tradition of Edmund Husserl, but he distinguished himself from transcendental phenomenology through his own theories of existential phenomenology. His major works, *The Structure of Human Behaviour* (1963) and *The Phenomenology of Perception* (1962), refute idealistic suppositions found in classical phenomenology to assert that individual organisms had to be considered in relation to concrete referential structures of perception rather than internal organizations of **consciousness**.

Merleau-Ponty's theory of phenomenology is important to the study of film and television because of the relationship between the viewer, the image on screen and the technology generating the images. One sees the images as a conscious and carnal being, recognizing them by references and perceptions in the world through, and because of, technology. This relationship connects one's own bodily existence to a technological generation of images and sound, creating a perceptual, phenomenological experience.

References

Merleau-Ponty, M. (1962) *The Phenomenology of Perception* (first published 1945), trans. Colin Smith, London: Routledge.
—— (1963) *The Structure of Human Behaviour* (first published 1942), trans. Alden L. Fisherin, Boston: Beacon Press.

BERTO TRINIDAD

metadiscourse

Whereas the term **discourse** can denote the sum or an extract of debates, exchanges and opinions on a certain subject, a metadiscourse analyses the content, structure and function of such a discourse. This does not only include rather technical approaches like linguistic discourse analysis, but also approaches within media, cultural or social studies that theorize about a society or culture based on the different discourses of film, television, print media or public debates. The analytical tools developed within the academic metadiscourse allow a more detailed and objectifiable description of such discourses.

EVA VIETH

metalanguage

Object language talks *within* systems of signification, whereas metalanguage talks *about* systems of signification. For example, the utterance, 'Thou, nature, art my goddess', assigns an object a status, but the utterance, 'In this sentence "nature" is personified', analyses the way language is employed to achieve this assignment. Similarly, metalanguages can talk about how the 'languages' of film, music, traffic signs, etc. achieve signification. Metalanguages are usually developed and defined within the academic **discourse** to facilitate the analysis of, for example, communicative, textual or cultural strategies.

EVA VIETH

metanarrative

The term 'metanarrative' is associated principally with the work of Jean-François **Lyotard**. A metanarrative is a grand, overarching, totalizing story which claims to explain everything about its subject matter. In its desire for universality, a metanarrative subsumes smaller narratives supposedly to unveil the truth of the latter. Examples include: the Enlightenment metanarrative of progress; Marxism's metanarrative of historical or dialectical materialism (see **materialism and idealism**); and feminism's metanarrative of universal **patriarchy** (see **feminist theory**). Postmodernity, for Lyotard, is marked by the feeling that metanarratives are no longer credible. This is not to suggest, contrary to the claims of some critics, that post-modernity is the simple absence of metanarratives (see **modernism and post-modernism**).

NEIL BADMINGTON

metaphor

'If music be the food of love …' is a metaphor: music as food figuratively satisfies the appetite for love – a substitution based on similarity. A metaphor substitutes a word literally referring to one thing with another word or phrase which suggests an affinity between the terms. As you read, your eyes may 'fly' over the lines, metaphorical birds crossing a landscape. A famous example of a film metaphor occurs in Sergei **Eisenstein**'s film *Strike* (1924), in which the editing juxtaposes a massacre of workers with the slaughter of a steer. Metaphor and metonym also figure in **psychoanalysis**.

See also: metonymy

GABRIEL M. PALETZ

metonymy

In contrast to the **metaphor**, the rhetorical figure metonymy signifies an object by naming a subordinated object that has a real, i.e., a spatial, temporal or causal, relation to the intended one: for example, 'reading Lacan' for 'reading books by Lacan'. One of the special metonymic constructions is the synecdoche or *pars pro toto* construction, which names a part of an object/person to stand for the whole or vice versa: for example, 'the hand that rocks the cradle' or 'England lost by six wickets'.

The dichotomy metaphor/metonymy draws attention to the basic difference of two different ways of perception and thought: whereas the metonymy demands no qualitative change and keeps a contingency between signifier and signified, the metaphor renders necessary a change of the semantic plane and so causes a break in reality that can only be bridged by a cognitive process. Roman **Jakobson** found that two different types of damage to the language centre of the brain caused two different afflictions: (i) the inability to maintain **paradigmatic** relations between different language units, which was accompanied by an inability to use or understand metaphors; and (ii) the inability to maintain **syntagmatic** relations between different language units, which resulted in the inability to use or understand metonymies. Christian **Metz** has shown the usefulness of the metaphor/metonymy distinction in the close analysis of film texts.

See also: Lacan, Jacques

EVA VIETH

Metz, Christian

b. 1931

Christian Metz is a French semiotician and structuralist film critic who is interested in the organization of film **narrative**, as well as in linguistic and psychoanalytic theories of spectatorship. One of the most influential writers on cinema in the 1970s and 1980s, Metz examined in his book *Film Language* the ways in which film could be considered a language, the nature of the shot as opposed to the word, and what a grammar of cinematic narrative might be. He developed a classification of sequences and scenes known as *la grande syntagmatique*, based on editing strategies and their role in conveying narrative information. *Language and Cinema* expanded on this theme, separating 'specifically cinematic' codes (such as camerawork and editing) from more generalized codes possible in other arts (such as music, lighting and speech). In *Psychoanalysis and Cinema: The Imaginary Signifier*, Metz used the work of **Freud** and Jacques **Lacan** to focus on the spectator's relationship to the **cinematic apparatus** itself and to individual films. In it, Metz examined the production of meaning and considered issues of linguistics and subjectivity, including **metaphor**, **metonymy**, **condensation** and **displacement**. Challenging the commonly held notion that viewers identified first and foremost with the protagonists on the screen, Metz suggested that the primary identification was with the camera and the act of looking itself.

See also: psychoanalysis; semiotics; structuralism and post-structuralism; voyeurism

References

Metz, C. (1974) *Film Language: A Semiotics of Cinema*

(first published 1968), trans. Michael Taylor, New York: Oxford University Press.

—— (1974) *Language and Cinema* (first published 1971), trans. D. J. Umiker-Sebeok, The Hague: Mouton.

—— (1982) *Psychoanalysis and Cinema: The Imaginary Signifier* (first published 1977), trans. Celia Britton, London: Macmillan.

KAREN BACKSTEIN

mimetic/mimesis

In the loose usage of the term, 'mimesis' is another word for imitation, as derivatives like mimic might suggest. In the context of film and television analysis, however, the concept can be seen as relevant to an understanding of such terms as **realism** and reflection. Mimesis refers to the view that it is the function of art to reproduce appearances, a view which underemphasizes or denies the active nature of production and response.

The Greek philosopher Aristotle's (384–322 BC) *Poetics* is usually cited as the source of this view. Aristotle argued that it was a human instinct to find pleasure in imitation, but he saw imitative possibilities in activities as varied as **epic** tragedy and flute playing. Later aestheticians, particularly in eighteenth-century Britain, narrowed the range of activities but emphasized more strongly the need to look at the given world of appearances for the sources and subject matter of poetry, interpreting the concept of mimesis as a demand for a literal reflection of the world. The critic Samuel Johnson praised Shakespeare because 'his drama is the mirror of life'. Though Johnson's critical practice was more flexible than this observation might suggest, his theoretical position about the arts typified a widespread belief among the intelligentsia of his time that there was a generality about life which artists should strive to reflect through productions which reflected how things appeared.

M. H. Abrams (1976: 14), however, suggests that two developments occurred in the use of mimesis in aesthetic criticism in the eighteenth century that we can see as foreshadowing the similar debate in film. In the first, the emphasis shifted away from the critical evaluation of truth to appearances and began to consider how the audience was affected by the representation. In the second, distinctions were made between the mimetic qualities of different arts forms. Music, architecture and language began to be seen as conventions for what they denoted whereas painting and sculpture were seen as mimetic because, to use twentieth-century terminology, they were iconic – they could represent their objects because they looked like their objects (see **conventions; icon**).

In the late nineteenth century, modernist painters were seen as challenging the mimetic importance of painting head on, and writers from Gustave Flaubert to Virginia Woolf used language which drew attention to the ways in which it constructed, rather than mirrored, reality as experienced (see **modernism and post-modernism**). From 1915 into the 1920s, Russian Formalists (see **Formalism**) such as Viktor Shklovsky, Boris Eichenbaum and Roman **Jakobson** offered a theoretical position diametrically opposed to art as mimesis. They were concerned to identify the distinctive nature of literature and its study. *Difference* from other arts and from the physical world was held to be important. Literature could even 'defamiliarize' the world and the way it is understood. As Bennett (1979) argues, literature could not be a reflection of the world but was a semiotic organization of its signification: 'It does not, as does science, organise the world conceptually, but disorganises the forms through which the world is conceived' (Bennett: 1979: 25).

The iconic potential of film or videotape made its mimetic appeal inevitable. Indeed, mimesis may be the dominant mode in contemporary film and television, and, under the guise of realism, the dominant aesthetic of reviewers. A history of these visual media could be written about the relation between financial investment, new technologies and mimetic effects. David **Bordwell** (1985: 16) offers a theory of narrative as initially mimetic through imitation of the theatre or human perception of the world. However, the non-mimetic potential of film was already apparent in films made by Georges Méliès in the 1890s. Dziga **Vertov** and Sergei **Eisenstein** theorized and practised filmmaking which challenged the mimetic claim to reflect reality by reproducing surface appearances. Their films were used to suggest the forces, which determined appearances, or to reveal the processes by which imitations of life were manufactured. **Avant-garde** film and video sustain this **oppositional** aesthetic.

Television viewers on most evenings, however, consciously or not, seem still to enjoy the pleasures of imitation that attracted Aristotle.

References

Abrams, M. H. (1976) *The Mirror and the Lamp*, London: Oxford University Press.

Bennett, T. (1979) *Formalism and Marxism*, London: Methuen.

Bordwell, D. (1985) *Narration in the Fiction Film*, Madison: University of Wisconsin Press.

PHILIP SIMPSON

mirror stage

The 'mirror stage' is the name given by Jacques **Lacan** to the moment at which the child, somewhere between the ages of 6 months and 18 months, experiencing itself as fragmented and dependent, joyfully identifies with an image of plenitude and independence. Because the infant confuses itself with what it would like to be, this crucial moment in the formation of the ego is one of *méconnaissance* (misrecognition). Although the mirror stage comes to an end, the **imaginary** is not simply replaced by the symbolic; on the contrary, human existence is ceaselessly structured by the inter-related orders of the real, the symbolic and the imaginary.

NEIL BADMINGTON

mise-en-scène

A term taken from French theatre, meaning 'staging an action', the use of *mise-en-scène* in film criticism was popularized in the 1950s by the *Cahiers du cinéma* critics' work on Hollywood. It was adopted in discussions of how the director controlled the framing and content of shots. *Mise-en-scène* can therefore include aspects of setting,

costume, make-up, lighting and the movement of figures within the frame. The *Cahiers* critics argued that, given the restrictions of Hollywood, it was through control of the *mise-en-scène* that a director was able to stamp individual expression on his/her work, enabling the director to become its 'author' (see **authorship**).

DEBORAH JERMYN

mode of address

In examining how a film or televisual **text** 'speaks' to its **audience**, attention turns to the ways in which the implied relationship between addresser and addressee is being constructed. A text's characteristic mode of address – that is, its customary way of talking to its reader – is a complex, discursive accomplishment. Important factors, each of which are typically appropriate to the text's **genre**, include the type of narration (first person or third person, use of pronouns such as 'I' or 'she', etc.), the type and tone of address (direct or indirect, formal or informal, serious or humorous, sincere or ironic, etc.), as well as temporal ('now' or 'then') and spatial ('here' or 'there') indicators. The inscription of an author or speaker in the text or, alternatively, the denial of any such voice so that events appear to narrate themselves, is a richly ideological process (see **ideology and hegemony**).

See also: discourse; history

Further reading

Metz, C. (1982) *The Imaginary Signifier: Psychoanalysis and Cinema*, Bloomington: Indiana University Press.

STUART ALLAN

mode of production

The term 'mode of production' describes the way in which the process of film or television production is organized for any particular film or television programme. Consideration of a film's mode of production requires identification and analysis of the individual production practices that create and shape a film through the stages of pre-production, production and post-production, as well as a consideration of the interrelationship of those practices within the production process as a whole. A mode of production sustains stylistic norms, and critical work on this topic has focused on the way the ideological dimensions of formal norms are created and supported by a particular mode of production.

The term was used by **Marx** in his analysis of the relationship between society and the capitalist mode of production. Drawing on Marxist theory in their study of classical Hollywood cinema, **Bordwell**, Staiger and Thompson (1985: 89) propose that analysis of a film's mode of production must take into account three factors: the labour force, the means of production (the buildings, tools, materials, technology, etc. needed to make a film) and finance. These elements exist in a dynamic relationship, each influencing and influenced by the others.

Much critical work has been concerned with the studio mode of production as the global and economically dominant model of film production (see **studio systems**). The studio mode of production is characterized by a specialized division of labour, whereby the process of making a film is divided into discrete segments, and each worker assigned to repeat a consistent element. When the studio system was established in the early years of the twentieth century, a labour force organized by work functions, with a management structure of hierarchical control, was seen as the most efficient and economical way to arrange work in an organization whose primary goal was the production of profit. The nascent Hollywood studio system adopted and adapted the model of factory production. Thus, strict division of labour in filmmaking is not a natural consequence of the nature of film production but a response to economic demands. In the early years of cinema, films were made by small groups of people in what was essentially a cottage industry. Increased division of labour was a response to the demand for an increased production rate and, as the technology of filmmaking became more complex, an economic need for technical specialization. However, unlike assembly-line manufacture, filmmaking is a collective activity in which co-operation between craft workers is necessary.

In contrast to fiction film, many documentaries, at least in the stages of production (shooting) and editing, do not conform to the studio mode of film practice. **Documentary** filmmakers such as Frederick Wiseman and Nick Broomfield prefer to work with small crews, and perform a range of functions beyond that of direction. Since the establishment of the studio system, there have been modes of film production alternative and **oppositional** to it, reflecting ideological and artistic objections to the system and its output. **Avant-garde** filmmakers Len Lye and Stan Brakhage produced some films single-handedly, both as a response to the economic necessity determined by the non-commercial nature of their work and in order to maintain authorial control over all aspects of the production process. Owning the means of production, although basic, allowed them to produce work that was conceived as improvised personal expression, something that was not possible in the studio mode.

For radical filmmakers in the 1960s, in the United States and Britain, the ideological underpinning of the capitalist studio system and its products was resisted through the establishment of filmmaking collectives. Collective work was seen not just as the democratic ideal for labour practice, but as the politicization of a film's mode of production. Since a mode of production sustains stylistic norms, which have an ideological function, resistance to the studio mode of production was seen as resistance to the capitalist ideology inherent in mainstream film form. Thus, one of the declared aims of the Dziga **Vertov** Group, the film collective formed by Jean-Pierre Gorin and Jean-Luc **Godard**, was not simply to make political films, but to make films politically.

References

Bordwell, D., Staiger, J. and Thompson, K. (1985) *The Classical Hollywood Cinema*, London: Routledge.

Further reading

Wayne, M. (1997) *Theorising Video Practice*, London: Lawrence and Wishart.

ANDREW BIRTWISTLE

modernism and post-modernism

In an age where interactive CD-ROM, domestic **virtual reality** and the relentless spread of the **Internet**'s Web continue to narrow the gap between the individual and new media, thus realizing **Baudrillard**'s (1983) dramatic predictions of a society in which private space has been invaded by 'circuits and networks', there is a certain irony in the fact that much post-modern theory draws on cinema for its examples. Web pages, video – whether amateur, **avant-garde** or commercial – or even television would seem more aptly to embody the contemporary aesthetic than film, which after all celebrated its centenary in 1995 and continues to structure itself around such modernist impulses as **authorship**, **realism** and **genre** (see Denzin 1991).

Despite the status of films like *Blade Runner* (Ridley Scott, 1982) and *Pulp Fiction* (Quentin Tarantino, 1994) as canonical texts within the post-modern theory of the 1980s and 1990s (see **canon**), we should note that the roots of cinema lie in the nineteenth century. Its history remains, in Peter Brooker's (1997) words, 'more analogous to the modern novel than to newer visual media'. In many ways, cinema is the medium *par excellence* of modernism.

Attempting to trap the period of modernism between two neat dates is like catching a cloud; key texts will always escape the boundaries. Cinema poses additional problems because it apparently underwent the same shifts as other forms – from realist to modern to post-modern – at a far more rapid pace, completing in less than 100 years a sequence of changes which took the novel twice as long, and painting several centuries, to achieve. The difficulties in categorization are compounded by the fact that 'modernist' styles can be identified within different national cinemas at various periods, many of which differ significantly from one another. Fredric **Jameson**'s proposal in *Postmodernism, or, the Cultural Logic of Late Capitalism* (1991), that modernist cinema followed two separate histories in turn – one of the silent, one of the sound era – complicates matters while still failing to contain anomalous texts.

In practice, we can argue that the birth of cinema in around 1885 and its coming of age in the 1930s, by which point most of its dominant conventions had been established, locate it squarely in the commonly accepted period of modernism. Moreover, the technology of the apparatus, the inherently experimental nature of all early cinema, the form's urban basis and the process of 'modernization' embodied in the spread of movie theatres to small towns, bind cinema up irrevocably with the core essence and impulses of modernism.

From this point it is possible to identify various key forms of modernist cinema in differing cultural contexts and at different periods, most of which involve some overlap.

Modernism and cinema, 1916–1936

Just as modernism evades neat periodization, so it also resists straightforward definition in terms of its key characteristics. The term serves as an umbrella for styles of art, literature, architecture and music which emerged from very different surroundings and which may have had little in common besides a drive towards experiment and innovation, usually defined against the styles of the previous century. Rather than imply a unified 'modernism', then, we should perhaps talk of disparate modernisms, among which we might list the **aesthetics** of Futurism, Cubism, vorticism, Bauhaus, Dadaism, surrealism and **Expressionism**.

Not all of these styles had a direct influence on filmmaking. There was never, for instance, a recognized 'Dadaist cinema', although Dadaist impulses can be identified in certain films of the avant-garde such as Ferdinand Leger's *Ballet mécanique* (1923–1924). The Dadaism of the 1910s led, rather, into the surrealism of the 1920s, whose ambitious project, a grand **narrative** towards the transformation of human consciousness, finds its visual expression in Luis Buñuel and Salvador Dali's film *Un Chien andalou* (1928). This fragmented collection of scenarios, linked by bizarre transformations, sexual imagery and unpredictable jumps through time and space, displays a typically surrealist interest in Freudian theory of dreams and desires. At the same time, its playful use of Hollywood conventions such as the romantic couple, the explicatory intertitle and **continuity editing** indicates a characteristic tendency towards **pastiche**.

Like Dadaism, Futurism never truly found a home in cinema, but its passion for machines, speed and shock effects inspired key films of the Soviet montage movement such as Dziga **Vertov**'s *Man with the Movie Camera* (1929). Vertov's whirl-wind tour through the modern city, depicting urban life through a 'mechanical eye', makes full use of photographic tricks and surprising juxtaposi-tions to jolt the viewer's expectations and show reality from the new perspectives afforded by technology. Although Futurism had originally embraced Italian fascism, the movement's spirit of revolution through machines seemed to map effectively onto the very different grand narrative of Soviet politics, as can be seen in Sergei **Eisen-stein**'s celebration of farming technology, *The Old and the New* (1929).

Both Soviets and fascists in turn condemned the cinema of German Expressionism, which in the late 1910s took the unusual step of reacting against nineteenth-century tendencies by returning to earlier styles. Robert Wiene's classic of early Expressionism, *The Cabinet of Dr Caligari* (1919), is clearly informed by the **fantasy** and mysticism of folk-tales. Late Expressionism, however, coming enthusiastically to terms with technology, turned its sights to the future and produced Fritz Lang's *Metropolis* (1926), as quintessential a depiction of the modernist city as *Blade Runner* (Ridley Scott) would be of the post-modern. While its view of science, robots and machines remains ambivalent since it could be argued that Lang merely transposes them onto the folk-tale template of magicians and supernatural helpmeets, the film's visual style continues to influence screen culture more than seventy years later. Echoes of its towers and walkways can be found not just in *Blade Runner*, *Batman* (Tim Burton, 1989) and *The Crow* (Alex Proyas, 1994), but in numerous pop videos like Madonna's 'Express Yourself' and Queen's 'Radio Ga-Ga'.

Finally, while classical Hollywood is often regarded as a 'realist' contrast to the experiment of other national cinemas, it too can be seen as inherently modernist. The iconography and themes of the Western (see **Western, the**) and gangster film are bound up with, in the former case, the move from pre-modern agrarian society to the contemporary city, and in the latter with the grit and glory of the urban milieu: its fast cars, new suits, breaking headlines and machine-gun fire. Even a late silent comedy like Charlie Chaplin's *Modern Times* (1936) shows a world of pistons, turbines, screens and advertisements, in its way as vivid a depiction of the near-future workplace as *Metropolis*. On another level, as implied above, cinema was in a sense an agent of modernization in America, bringing the sights and novelties of the city – not just films, but ornate façades, grand foyers and luxurious seating – to small towns. Indeed, Hollywood itself was a town founded on cinema, expanding geographically as the industry thrived and projecting images of American experi-ment and novelty first across the nation, then across the world (see **classical Hollywood cinema and new Hollywood cinema**).

We might note as a postscript that the 'late modernist' cinema of the French New Wave, for instance the work of Jean-Luc **Godard** (and even the collective named after the Soviet director Dziga Vertov with which Godard was later associated), drew not on *The Cabinet of Dr Caligari* or *Un Chien andalou* for their inspiration, but on the popular, mass-market feature films of the American 1930s.

Late modern and early post-modern: the 1960s and 1970s

The case of Jean-Luc Godard illustrates once again the flexibility of boundaries and the extent of overlap between modernism and post-modernism. Fredric Jameson (1992) has called Godard 'surely as post-modern *avant la lettre* as one might have wished in the heyday of *auteurist* high art' – by which he means the cinema of Hitchcock, Renoir and Welles, each with its characteristic, typically modernist, authorial style. Yet Jameson adds that Godard has 'today in full postmodernism become the ultimate survivor of the modern as such'. While Godard's later films are strongly informed by a left-wing 'grand narrative' of social protest and use experimental, avant-garde devices of estrangement to disrupt the viewer's assumptions, they also exhibit a playful, in-jokey pastiche, a fragmentation and stylistic mix-and-match which, as Jameson suggests, can readily be seen as post-modern. 'The true state of affairs', Peter Brooker (1997) concludes from this example, 'is that different modes are possible in the same period'. One might add that different modes are even possible in the same film.

If we allow that Godard's later films demonstrate a post-modern sensibility, we might go on to consider further texts of the same period in a similar light, turning our attention to television. Influenced by Pop Art, fashion and advertising, and catering for an educated, media-aware audience, television shows such as *Batman*, *The Avengers* and *The Man From UNCLE* serve as prime examples of post-modernism in the late 1960s. These shows demonstrate as clearly as any 1980s film the key tendencies of pastiche, fragmentation, **intertextuality**, eclecticism, irony and knowingness. That said, discussion of post-modern screen texts usually takes 1970s cinema as its starting point, with Jameson's case studies of *la mode retro* or nostalgia film.

In his essay, 'Postmodernism and Consumer Society', later reworked in *Postmodernism, or, the Cultural Logic of Late Capitalism*, Jameson cites *American Graffiti* (George Lucas, 1973), *Body Heat* (Lawrence Kasdan, 1981), *Chinatown* (Roman Polanski, 1974), *Raiders of the Lost Ark* (Steven Spielberg, 1981) and *Star Wars* (George Lucas, 1977) as films which in one way or another fondly recall an earlier period through their themes or iconography (see **icon**). He uses these examples to illustrate the concepts of pastiche, or 'neutral' borrowing from other texts, and the lack of historical sense which leads modern cinema to wear the 'masks' of a lost decade.

In the subsequent decade, works of theory – Jean Baudrillard's *Simulations* (1983), Jameson's article on post-modernism in *New Left Review* (1984) and the translation of Jean-François **Lyotard**'s *The Postmodern Condition* (1984) – became elevated, along with a **canon** of film, television and video texts, to the status of post-modern 'classics'. The term became a buzzword reaching far beyond the academy of cultural theory.

Post-modernism in the 1980s

David Cronenberg's *Videodrome* (1982), Susan Seidelman's *Desperately Seeking Susan* (1985), David Lynch's *Blue Velvet* (1986) and Wim Wenders' *Wings of Desire* (1987) have all been held up as key examples of the post-modern aesthetic. However,

none have become quite so ubiquitous in writing on post-modern cinema as Ridley Scott's *Blade Runner* (1982), perhaps for the simple reason that the film illustrates almost every key concept of post-modern theory. Scott's 'retro-fitted' Los Angeles of 2019 provides a concrete visualization of Jameson's concepts of pastiche and schizophrenia, the recycling of signifiers and loss of historical sense. In incorporating high technology and garbage, British punks and Japanese sushi-masters, neon signs for Atari alongside cod-Mayan apartment decor, pop-Egyptian grandeur mixed with Bonsai trees and artificial owls, *Blade Runner* vividly conveys the 'degree zero' of eclecticism described by Lyotard, in which 'one listens to reggae, watches a western, eats McDonalds food for lunch and local cuisine for dinner, wears Paris perfume in Tokyo and "retro" clothes in Hong Kong' (Lyotard 1984).

Accordingly, blade runner Rick Deckard's day begins with a meal of noodles, interrupted by a colleague addressing him in the hybrid 'cityspeak'; his investigation takes him first to Unterwasser street, then to the Urdu snake-maker, Abdul Ben-Hassan; the elevator in his apartment block tells him, 'Thank you. *Danke*', and upstairs he attempts a classical piano piece before venturing out to buy Tsingtao Japanese liquor from a bar playing an American 1940s-style ballad. *Blade Runner* engages with questions of human identity versus machine simulation, and nostalgia for the 'real' in the face of its loss, both of which have become fundamental to post-modern theory (see in particular Jean Baudrillard's 'Simulacra and Simulations' in his *Selected Writings* [1988]).

The road from *Metropolis* picked up another of the 1980s quintessential post-modern icons along the way; Madonna's 'Express Yourself' music video of 1989 was a lavishly eroticized reworking of Fritz Lang's master/slave relationships, with the star in partial male drag. The video epitomizes the qualities of playful sampling which made Madonna a favourite of post-modern critics; as E. Ann Kaplan demonstrates in *Rocking Around the Clock* (1987), the pastiche of *Metropolis* followed an equally wry masquerade by Madonna as Marilyn Monroe.

Post-modern music video, Kaplan suggests, constitutes a genre in itself, and it earned its own television showcase in *Max Headroom*, which began in 1985 following a *Blade Runner*-style pilot titled *Twenty Minutes into the Future*. With perfect logic, the *Max Headroom* video promos were hosted by an eponymous computer graphic, apparently a pure simulation of a charming, tuxedoed presenter, made 'convincing' – that is, imperfect – by apparent malfunctions, twitches and stutters. It is perhaps reassuring that 'Max Headroom' was revealed as an actor in latex and make-up, and fitting that the character went on to advertise hardware for a television and video rental company.

Post-modernism in the 1990s

These examples and others of 1980s post-modern screen culture are covered in detail elsewhere: see, for instance, Barbara Creed, David Harvey, Scott Bukatman and Umberto **Eco** in Brooker and Brooker's *Postmodern After-Images* (1997). As the 1980s themselves become the subject of nostalgia films (Frank Coraci's *The Wedding Singer*, 1998), it seems worthwhile to consider the new forms post-modern film and television have taken in the 1990s, in particular the filters of intertextuality or simply hindsight which now affect our perception of key texts of the previous decade.

First, the process of borrowing and re-borrowing has become increasingly layered and complex as the texts which now constitute 'classic' post-modernism are themselves sampled and recycled, or experienced in a new context. *Blade Runner*, for instance, has since the 1993 release of the director's cut been recast as the 'original' – or, to some fans, the inferior – version of the film, adding a new and unforeseen level to the film's own debates about first generations and simulations.

These increased layers of reference, subtly colouring our perception of the 'original' post-modern texts, have clustered around many of Jameson's examples of the retro mode. Nostalgia operates on a doubled level when a film like *Chinatown* is revisited as *The Two Jakes* (Jack Nicholson, 1990), which recalls not just the 1930s, but also the 1970s of the first movie's release. A whole subgenre of retro films such as *The Rocketeer* (Joe Johnston, 1991), *The Shadow* (Russell Mulcahy, 1994) and *The Phantom* (Simon Wincer, 1996) aim to recreate not so much a period setting

but memories of *Raiders of the Lost Ark*. Nostalgic reworking, as in *Body Heat*, has virtually become a genre in itself: *The Shawshank Redemption* (Frank Darabont, 1994) and *The Hudsucker Proxy* (Joel Coen, 1994) reviving prison drama and screwball comedy respectively, while *The Last Seduction* (John Dahl, 1993), *Romeo Is Bleeding* (Pete Medak, 1992) and *Devil in a Blue Dress* (Carl Franklin, 1995) are discussed as 'neo-noirs' (see **film noir**).

This 'revisiting' can lead to bizarre hybrids. Luc Besson's French-language *Nikita* (1990), remade in Hollywood as *Point of No Return* (John Badham, 1993; UK title, *The Assassin*), bewilderingly switched actors, characters and languages again to become the American television series *La Femme Nikita*. *Wings of Desire* (1987), Wim Wenders' melancholy study of angels in Berlin, was in turn loosely adapted a decade later as *City of Angels* (Brad Siberling, 1997), a Hollywood romance starring Nicolas Cage and Meg Ryan. Not quite tribute and far from parody, this is pastiche without any referent or explanation; selected aspects of the original are simply lifted to the copy and the remainder discarded.

Meanwhile, *Star Wars: A New Hope* has been subject to a series of transformations. Itself a pastiche, it was subsequently pastiched in *Judge Dredd* (Danny Canon, 1995), and so gained the status of an 'original'. Two years later the 'original' *Star Wars* was canonized by many fans as the 'classic' version, in contrast to the perceived gimmicks and unnecessary trickery of Lucasfilm's Special Editions. Science fiction blockbusters such as *Independence Day* (Ronald Emmerich, 1996) and *Lost in Space* (Stephen Hopkins, 1998) consistently attempt through extensive merchandising campaigns to regenerate the buzz of the *Star Wars* 'experience', while Lucasfilm itself currently has the same agenda in its careful leak of information surrounding the new 'prequel' trilogy.

We have surely entered a new phase where the aesthetic identified as 'post-modern' in the 1980s has become so common as to constitute a dominant. The ahistoric eclecticism of *Star Wars* now underlies films from Baz Luhrmann's *William Shakespeare's Romeo and Juliet* (1996) and Ian McKellen's *Richard III* (1995) to *CutThroat Island* (Renny Harlin, 1995) and *Batman and Robin* (Joel Schumacher, 1997). This trend towards the 'naturalization' of the post-modern aesthetic is echoed in television, where in-jokes and cross-references now come ten-a-penny rather than being explicitly signposted. While *Moonlighting* was recognized in the 1980s as an exceptional television show for its pastiche of other forms, late-1990s television relies consistently on wry sideways nods. The stars of *Absolutely Fabulous* appear in *Friends*, Mulder and Scully from *The X-Files* visit *The Simpsons*, *Johnny Bravo* meets *Scooby-Doo*; the tendency towards pastiche is barely remarked on, and certainly not singled out as expressly post-modern as it would have been in the 1980s.

This may seem to fulfil Jameson's pessimistic predictions of empty revisiting, wearing dead masks and touring a historical museum. Perhaps the mausoleum which provided the set for *Reservoir Dogs* (Quentin Tarantino, 1991), or Jack Rabbit Slims, the 1950s-style theme restaurant in *Pulp Fiction* (1994), are part of an 'anything goes' nihilism which some accuse of being inherently amoral and shallow.

In this scenario, *Back to the Future*'s (Robert Zemeckis, 1985) theme park ideal of a safely nostalgic 1950s becomes the dystopic 'utopia' of *The Truman Show* (Peter Weir, 1998) where life is a made-for-TV simulation, and *Blade Runner*'s retro environment is transposed into *Dark City* (Alex Proyas, 1998), where the pastiche of styles is revealed as a malicious experiment imposed by controlling producers. The 'real' world of both films, whether the city initially seems light or dark, is shown to be false, and certainties such as location, memory, history, are stripped of value. The protagonists are stranded in an ahistorical no-place where even human identity is placed in question.

And yet under both these dystopic post-modern texts of the late 1990s, beneath the quotations and layers and simulations, lies a surprisingly traditional trajectory of escape through the salvation of romantic love. If, as Lyotard has argued, the post-modern always contains a germ of modernism, and if periodization always involves an overlap between one form and the next, it is perhaps conceivable that the grand narratives of progress through protest, social renewal and personal enlightenment are retained, even in the most nihilistic depictions of the post-modern condition at the end of the twentieth century.

References

Baudrillard, J. (1983) *Simulations*, New York: Semiotext(e).
—— (1988) 'Simulacra and Simulations', in *Selected Writings*, London: Polity Press.
—— (1992) 'The Ecstasy of Communication' (first published 1983), in C. Jencks, *The Post-modern Reader*, London: Academy Editions.
Brooker, P. and Brooker, W. (1997) *Postmodern After-Images*, London: Arnold.
Denzin, N. (1991) *Images of Postmodern Society*, London: Sage Publications.
Harvey, D. (1989) 'Time and Space in the Postmodern Cinema', in David Harvey, *The Condition of Postmodernity*, London: Basil Blackwell.
Jameson, F. (1984) 'Postmodernism, or, the Cultural Logic of Late Capitalism', in *New Left Review*, no. 146 (July–August).
—— (1991) *Postmodernism, or, the Cultural Logic of Late Capitalism*, London: Verso.
—— (1992) *The Geopolitical Aesthetic*, London: BFI Publishing.
Kaplan, E. A. (1987) *Rocking Around the Clock*, London: Routledge.
Lyotard, J.-F. (1984) *The Postmodern Condition: A Report on Knowledge*, Manchester: Manchester University Press.

Further reading

Benjamin, W. (1983) *Illuminations*, London: Collins/Fontana.
Berman, M. (1983) *All That is Solid Melts into Air*, London: Verso.
Brooker, P. (1992) *Modernism/Postmodernism*, London: Longman.

WILL BROOKER

moral panics

The term 'moral panic' derives from critical work in the sociological study of deviance. However, within film, media and cultural studies, it has often become accepted as simply a descriptive term which refers to a reaction against some perceived threat, usually in the form of an organization campaign to control it.

Moral panics are assumed to be the largely misguided reactions of a repressive dominant culture. These assumptions date back to the origins of the concept. In *Folk Devils and Moral Panics*, Stan Cohen (1980) suggests that 'moral panics' largely invented what they reacted against through the process of 'labelling'. Labelling also introduces another related concept – the folk devil – a *product* of the act of naming or labelling. The folk devil did not refer to a real and existent entity but was rather a **stereotype** composed out of diverse and contradictory materials. In other words, moral panics could produce self-fulfilling prophecies in which certain social groups might identify with and conform to the figure of the folk devil. For example, Cohen suggests that there had been little antagonism between the Mods and the Rockers prior to media reports concerning the supposed clashes between these groups of young people.

However, the causes of moral panics are less clear. If they are not simply responses to a pre-existent threat, then the explanation must be internal rather than external, having more to do with those who experience the sense of moral panic than those who supposedly provoke it. Unfortunately, it is here that work on moral panics is usually most disappointing, and explanations tend to identify two clearly defined causes: ignorance or conspiracy.

It is suggested that moral panics either are simply reactions against that which is strange, or are carefully orchestrated conspiracies in which the folk devil is designed by a social group so as to secure support for measures that will grant them repressive powers. Put another way, the first explanation simply falls back on the assumption that the majority of people harbour some irrational conservatism and/or xenophobia, while the second relies on the action of some coherent, organized and select group with a covert agenda.

Both explanations are implicitly patronizing. They deny any meaningful content to the form of these panics, and allow the critic to position him/herself as the judge who either condemns those associated with these panics for their ignorance or deception, or else seeks to liberate them from their misguided beliefs.

This is not to claim that moral panics are never the product of misunderstandings or even of self-consciously organized campaigns with hidden agendas. Rather, it is to suggest that it is necessary to understand the particular content of specific panics, and the fears on which they are based, instead of dismissing them as irrational.

One area within which this kind of work has been done is the analysis of moral panics over Americanization and Japanization, in which some critics have turned to the notion of '**displacement**'. It is argued that the fears of cultural imperialism, of which concepts of Americanization and Japanization are examples, are not without content, but are rather 'displacements' where one culture projects onto another all those anxieties about itself which it cannot acknowledge to itself (see Morley and Robins 1995).

The analysis of moral panics has a clear concern with media representations. It is through the media that the folk devil is constructed and campaigns against it are organized and legitimated. This work often entails an analysis of news media, but the construction of folk devils is not restricted to the news. Concerns with Japanization, for example, were supposedly disseminated through fictional media, too, and although these texts may be more complex than is sometimes suggested, films like *Rising Sun* (Philip Kaufman, 1993) and *Black Rain* (Ridley Scott, 1989) have been seen as part of this process.

Film and television have themselves been the object of moral panics. The emergence of cinema as a form of popular entertainment provoked moral panics, as did the emergence of television, video and computer games (see **popular, the**). Each new medium is the object of intense concern and calls for **regulation**. However, while the story of these campaigns is often presented as one of incorporation in which the new media is rendered 'safe' and 'unthreatening', such victories are never total.

See also: censorship

References

Cohen, S. (1980) *Folk Devils and Moral Panics*, Oxford: Martin Robertson.

Morley, D. and Robins, K. (1995) *Spaces of Identity: Global Media, Electronic Landscapes and Cultural Boundaries*, London: Routledge.

MARK JANCOVICH

morpheme

A basic term of structural linguistics, 'morphemes' are the smallest meaningful units of a language that cannot be divided into smaller meaningful parts. Linguistic analysis differentiates between two types of morphemes: 'free morphemes' that can function as full words (e.g., *love*), and 'bound morphemes' which cannot stand on their own (e.g., *be* in *be*loved). Morphemes are abstract units defined by their function and can be realized in a language by different allomorphs; for example, the morpheme denoting plural in English is realized as the different allomorphs, cat*s*, hors*es*, or child*ren*.

EVA VIETH

motivation

Motivation links cause and effect, helping the viewer to make sense of a film's story. It also helps determine **realism** by justifying the course of events as they unravel during a film. It binds together the **text** to make it seem plausible, masking the decisions behind **narrative** developments – often through careful foreshadowing. Motivation plays a role in distinguishing mainstream narratives, where events are well motivated, from **art** films, which tend to have poor motivation. Viewers use their knowledge of the world and their experience of watching other films (particularly those from the same **genre**) to judge the strength of motivation.

MOYA LUCKETT

multiculturalism

Multiculturalism refers to the ethnic diversity of many contemporary western cultures. This cultural mix takes many forms – from assimilation to rejection to **diaspora** to **hybridity**. Multicultural analysis considers the relationships between the traditional ethnic cultures of displaced peoples/ immigrants and the dominant culture of their new land. It recognizes the diversity of all cultures and calls for a re-evaluation of **history**, one that considers the consequences of imperialism and conquest.

Multiculturalism foregrounds the way in which cultural differences create hierarchies of power in contemporary society. Mainstream patriarchal culture structurally marginalizes the ethnically different, promoting instead the causes and images of dominant ethnic groups (see **patriarchy**). Multiculturalism interrogates these hierarchies, questioning the terms of dominance used to support one group's claim to power. Instead, it contextualizes the history of ethnic groups and their migrations, analysing the politics and consequences of conquest.

Cornel West (1993) notes that the decolonization of the Third World paralleled First World civil rights movements such as the American Civil Rights Movement of the 1960s. Decolonization prompted disempowered groups to rebel against oppression. Multiculturalism's emphasis on the politics of history helps elucidate why certain groups are silenced, and has consequently empowered people to express anger and call for change. It also questions historical 'truth', showing how ideology is perpetuated through education (see **ideology and hegemony**).

Key contemporary multicultural political debates exist around issues like institutional racism and affirmative action. Leading multicultural critics and theorists such as Gayatri **Spivak** promote greater diversity, fearing the tokenism that leads to the stereotyping which silences other cultures. This can be seen in the marginalization of some cultures – for example, one Asian television show or one Afro-Caribbean politician to cover 'ethnic' interests. As Spivak points out, whether you are **white**, black, Indian or Asian, if people expect you to speak only for that group's interests, they are guilty of homogenizing that culture (see Spivak and Gunew 1993). West (1993) further observes that the media present only the white middle classes as complex individuals.

Spivak stresses that ethnic identities are not pure, but rather are fraught with contradictions. This applies equally to dominant and marginalized or oppressed groups. Indeed, it is the very 'authenticity' of the white man's identity that is used to justify his power. Similarly, once ethnic cultures move overseas, their identities change, as they have to come to terms with new cultural practices and the phenomenon of displacement. Consequently, ethnic identities are not static, but instead depend on contexts and are often multi-layered (as exemplified in diasporas). Multiculturalism calls for a deeper investigation of ethnic identity so the **binary** logic separating white and black – with all its implicit power – might be collapsed.

At the same time, multiculturalism recognizes the need for strategic recognition of non-white ethnicities and their commonalities. In the face of interrogation, ethnic visibility might collapse and, with it, calls for social and political equality. Marginalized groups have had little access to power and have all too often been rendered invisible in popular film and television. Spivak notes two questions endemic within this issue of ethnic identity and culture – that of cultural production and cultural reception. As multicultural critics have observed, production has more power and cultural capital than reception and, correspondingly, it is usually controlled by dominant ethnic groups. This prompts a concentration on white characters and white interests that only reify the *status quo*.

Multiculturalism is thus concerned with white patriarchal culture's attempts to erase cultural difference in order to produce a monocultural society. Many ethnic groups resist such assimilation, attempting instead to preserve oppositional cultural identities. Unfortunately, ethnic and diasporic communities generally do not have the economic means nor the visibility to present themselves as complex and multifaceted – either to other cultures or to themselves. Instead of assimilationist images, positive role models or images of collective, homogeneous community, then, multiculturalism advocates that black and other diasporic cultures interrogate their own diversity. Multiculturalism thus calls for greater self-awareness of the position from which we speak, combined with a greater understanding (and tolerance) of the specificities of **difference**.

See also: African-American cinema; globalization

References

Spivak, G. and Gunew, S. (1993) 'Questions of Multiculturalism', in S. During (ed.) *The Cultural Studies Reader*, London: Routledge.

West, C. (1993) 'The New Cultural Politics of Difference', in S. During (ed.) *The Cultural Studies Reader*, London: Routledge.

Further reading

Harasym, S. (1990) *The Postcolonial Critic: Interviews, Strategies, Dialogues*, London: Routledge.

MOYA LUCKETT

multinational

Multinational corporations, also known as transnationals, are those that have a major base of operation in more than one country. The branch of the corporation that invests in other firms is called the parent company. Media multinationals contribute to an increasing transnational flow of programming and emphasis on production for export rather than national consumption or public service. Multinationals thus lobby against the role of the state in the **regulation** of media and trade.

See also: globalization

Further reading

Mattelart, A. (1979) *Multinational Corporations and the Control of Culture*, Sussex: Harvester Press.

Tomlinson, J. (1991) *Cultural Imperialism: A Critical Introduction*, London: Pinter.

SARAH BERRY

Mulvey, Laura

b. 1941

A feminist film scholar and filmmaker, Laura Mulvey is best known for her essay, 'Visual Pleasure and Narrative Cinema', first published in the British journal *Screen* in 1975, in which she uses Freudian/Lacanian psychoanalytic theories of subject formation to analyse the **pleasure** produced by classical **narrative** cinema (see **Freud, Sigmund; Lacan, Jacques; subject and subjec-**

tivity). Mulvey characterized Hollywood films as splitting the **diegesis** and the spectator's relation to it along lines of **gender** imbalance. The male protagonist (and, through identification with him, the spectator as well) is active, desiring and powerful, while the female is passive, the erotic object of **desire**, a **spectacle** and **image** for the gaze (see **gaze, the**) rather than an active subject.

Subsequently, Mulvey refined and contested many of her original claims, which were meant to be polemical and provocative rather than prescriptive, to '[put] Freud on the political agenda alongside Marx' (Mulvey 1996). Among her films, *Riddles of the Sphinx* (1975), made with Peter **Wollen**, remains the best known for its attempts to create a new kind of visual pleasure through its refusal of classical subject/object relationships.

While Mulvey's first essay will always be a foundational text for feminist film studies, it is unfortunate that it is often the only contact many students have with her rich body of work.

See also: dominant ideology; feminist theory; fetishism; patriarchy; psychoanalysis; queer theory; sexuality; voyeurism

References

Mulvey, L. (1989) *Visual and Other Pleasures*, Bloomington: Indiana University Press.
—— (1996) *Fetishism and Curiosity*, Bloomington: Indiana University Press.

ADRIENNE L. McLEAN

music and film

Music has always been a vital element of the filmic experience, playing an important role in the production, consumption and cultural meaning of cinema. It has become something of an ironic cliché, therefore, that film theory has been largely neglectful of music's significance (and that of sound more generally), concentrating instead on the analysis of cinema's visual construction. To some extent this is a fallacy but it would be fair to argue that much of the substantial literature on film music has often been rendered inaccessible to the general reader through its heavy recourse to musical terminology. Since the 1980s, however, a sustained body of work by authors such as Claudia Gorbman (1987) and Royal S. Brown (1994) has done much to address this lamentable situation, offering theoretical models of film music analysis in language which does not require an intimate understanding of musicology.

Music and silent cinema

For the audience, of course, silent cinema was very rarely silent. From the very first screenings by the Lumière brothers in 1895, films were often accompanied by live music. This could take many forms, ranging from the composition of a score for a specific film, performed in larger venues by a full orchestra, to the completely improvised accompaniment of a solo pianist. In all cases, though, there were practical as well as aesthetic motives behind the inclusion of musical performance in this new form of popular entertainment. Brown suggests that:

> 1) music was needed to cover up the noise from both the audience and the projectors, the latter of which had not yet found their way into soundproofed booths; and 2) music was needed, psychologically, to smooth over natural human fears of darkness and silence.
>
> (Brown 1994: 12)

Most writing on music and silent cinema concentrates on the ways in which the music contributed to the understanding of the **text**. Gorbman (1987), for instance, proposes that film music not only maintained continuity between popular stage melodrama of the late nineteenth century and the new mass entertainment form of the cinema but also compensated for perceived deficiencies in the latter. Cinema's basic visual claims to photographic **realism**, Gorbman notes, were potentially threatened by the lack of sound (particularly speech) to support the image as well as the two-dimensional presentation of the action. Film music, therefore, 'came to replace, or at least compensate for, the lack of, speech. Second, all sound exists in three dimensions; music as sound gave back, or at least compensated for the lack of, the spatial dimension of the reality so uncannily depicted in the new medium' (Gorbman 1987: 37).

Perhaps most significantly, many theories of early film music have focused on the role music played in relation to film **narrative**. Whether following a specific score, cue sheets or improvising, a basic strategy employed by film accompanists was not surprisingly to base their performance on the pace of the action being depicted on screen. This is not to say that the music would follow each and every diegetic movement, a practice principally associated with later cartoons and often referred to as 'mickey-mousing' because of its most famous subject; rather, the accompaniment would attempt to enhance the dramatic impact of a given sequence. A notorious example of this tendency can be found in the music composed and compiled by Joseph Carl Breil to accompany the 1915 premiere of D. W. Griffith's *The Birth of a Nation* (1915). Here, as the Ku Klux Klan ride off to save the film's white heroes from death at the hands of African-American renegades, the Aryan rescue mission is musically supported by a strident score which contains elements of Wagner's 'Ride of the Valkyries'. In this instance, the visceral effect of the image is greatly enhanced by its aural correlate.

Far from merely supporting a film's narrative, however, music can be understood as a commentary on the film image, helping to locate the narrative in a specific historical context and suggest how the audience should interpret the action presented on screen. This is particularly true where film music makes direct reference to existing songs or other musical pieces that a contemporary audience are already likely to know. In the sequence from *The Birth of a Nation* outlined above, for instance, Breil's score also makes deliberate use of the traditional song 'Dixie' which brings with it associations of the American South. As Brown points out:

> the device of incorporating a song such as 'Dixie' or an anthem such as 'The Star Spangled Banner' into the fabric of ongoing music to accompany a film – is one of the strongest trump cards a film composer and/or arranger can play. For even the briefest recognizable snippet of such a piece – can evoke in the listener an entire political mythology.
>
> (Brown 1994: 52)

In the case of *The Birth of a Nation*, the intention of this political mythology is clear: to justify the action of the Klan by positioning them as the defenders of heritage and white honour.

The film score and classical Hollywood cinema

The arrival of the sound film and the development of the studio system as an industrial framework for the production of mainstream American cinema raises different concerns for theorists of film music. One immediate implication is the need to address diegetic as well as non-diegetic music and to understand music's relationship to other elements of the soundtrack such as dialogue and sound effects. The potential to include sound as part of the **diegesis**, for instance, has changed assumptions about the role of non-diegetic music, which is no longer required as a constant soundtrack to the images and, in popular terminology at least, is reduced to the role of 'background music'. Such aesthetic concerns are supported by the negative assessment of mainstream film music by writers from the **Frankfurt School**, most notably Theodor **Adorno** whose criticism of much film music stems principally from its inclusion in the 'culture industry', a factory-like form of artistic production that is best represented in cinema by the Hollywood studio system.

In the context of film production, Adorno and others have raised questions relating to the status of film composers who can be seen as just another cog in the wheel of the industrialized process rather than artists in their own right. Such doubts can be supported by the astonishingly prolific careers of composers like Max Steiner (see Gorbman 1987: 70–98) whose output for specific studios (in Steiner's case principally RKO and Warner Bros) suggested that the pressures of working conditions did little to foster musical creativity. Crucially, however, the opinions of the Frankfurt School theorists were based on analysis of music's role within the text itself. Here, the key problem is presented as film composers' reliance on short repetitive passages of music or 'leitmotifs' which are routinely used as musical shorthand to represent specific characters or situations. While the leitmotif is a convention employed by many respected classical composers such as Wagner, it is suggested that removing these passages from a coherent musical structure renders them simplistic and of little musical value.

As a counter to the position of the Frankfurt School, it has been argued that film music needs to be understood as a different and quite specific cultural phenomenon. Rather than regarding leitmotifs as isolated from their musical context, therefore, it would be better to analyse music as part of a complex audiovisual relationship that does not regard the image and soundtrack as separate entities. This more holistic approach is particularly vital when considering the role of film music and its composers in debates relating to the concept of **authorship**. Indeed, recent theories of film music have signalled the working practice of film composers and the textual function of film music as direct challenges to assumptions about the authorial influence of the director or any other individual.

The relationship between the director Alfred Hitchcock and the composer Bernard Herrmann is a useful illustration of such debates. Although Herrmann's career saw him provide scores for many different directors, his collaboration across a sustained body of work with Hitchcock raises some important questions. First, while Herrmann's contribution to the impact of Hitchcock's films is unquestionable, represented most famously by his 1960 score for *Psycho* and the notorious shower sequence in particular, this can be understood in different ways. In his analysis of *Psycho*'s music, Brown (1994) suggests that Herrmann himself can be considered as the 'author' as parallels can be drawn with the composer's work dating back as far as the 1930s. Conversely, as the sound of Herrmann's music comes to be associated with a particular director, it could be regarded as just one element in an audiovisual nexus that film audiences might recognize as 'Hitchcock', even if it is understood that individual elements are not specifically the work of the director. To complicate matters further, while the sound of Herrman's music might be distinctive, its function within the body of individual films needs to be placed within generic expectations of the film score. Thus, even though the score for *Psycho* is privileged within the film by a lack of diegetic music, Brown concludes that:

The absence of any music coming over a radio, phonograph, or what have you, has the function of heightening the effect of the film-music convention whereby the appearance of non-diegetic music generally 'means' that something out of the ordinary is happening or is about to happen.

(Brown 1994: 165)

Moreover, it should be noted that such debates do not only apply to composers working within the constraints of studio systems, whether in the US or elsewhere. The work of composers such as Ennio Morricone has raised similar questions within the context of **art cinema**.

The introduction of popular music as a significant feature on many soundtracks has different implications for theories of film music and it is here perhaps that the dominant literature of the field is at its weakest. While there have been several studies of popular music's role as a marketing device, sustained treatment of its textual function is harder to find. Yet it is clear that the use of popular music has been a key factor in the development of new cinematic codes. An example of this is the blurring of the diegetic and non-diegetic arenas, which can be illustrated by reference to a sequence from the 1973 Scorsese film *Mean Streets* – when the arrival at a bar of one of the film's main characters, played by Robert De Niro, is accompanied on the soundtrack by a Rolling Stones song, 'Jumping Jack Flash'. Although the audience is encouraged to expect music in the context of this sequence, having already witnessed the presence of a jukebox in the bar, the song is presented at such a volume that it can only be understood as non-diegetic. A little way into the song, however, the music returns to a volume consistent with the diegetic source. Here, then, the use of music clearly signals the process of cinematic construction for the spectator (especially when allied to the use of slow-motion cinematography), challenging assumptions about popular cinema's general aims of not disrupting the relationship between the audience and the cinema screen. In this light, popular music can also be understood as playing a key role in a certain strand of cinematic post-modernism in which the relationship of sound and image is deliberately playful (see **modernism and post-modernism**). A notorious example here is the sequence in *Reservoir Dogs* (Quentin Tarantino, 1991) in which the torture and mutilation of a police officer is accompanied on the soundtrack by the gruesomely ironic lyrics and cheerful tone of Stealers Wheel's 'Stuck in the Middle with You'.

Film music and cultural identity

Music has an important role to play in debates relating to cinema's **representation** of cultural identity. Several studies have concentrated on music's part in the representation of **race** where the use of music can often be understood as a deliberate attempt to influence the audience's perception of a particular social group. Brown (1994), for instance, has suggested that scores for the Hollywood Western regularly employ a particular drum beat to create what he calls aural 'Native Americanicity' (see **Western, the**). A specific example of this tendency is offered by Gorbman (1987) who notes that a recurrent motif is employed in the 1939 John Ford Western *Stagecoach* to herald the appearance on screen of Native Americans as well as the implicit threat this poses to the film's white heroes.

Conversely, it can be argued that film music has often provided an opportunity for marginalized social groups to resist dominant stereotypes and their representation in screen media. In a reception context, for instance, the experience of silent cinema in African-American communities was transformed by the ability to make a film's musical accompaniment appropriate to the audience. Studies of the silent era in Chicago have proposed that the regular employment of jazz to accompany films gave African-American musicians an important role in the interpretation of specific film texts and encouraged audience participation in the spectacle of cinema.

More recently, African-American filmmakers like Spike Lee have used film music as a specific commentary on racial issues. V. E. Johnson's analysis of Lee's *Do the Right Thing* (1989), for example, argues that music has a vital role to play in the way we understand racial relationships within the film, defining the role of certain demographic groups. This is particularly true of the film's portrayal of African-American masculinity through the character of Radio Raheem who symbolizes the notion of resistance to white domination as the confrontational Public Enemy song 'Fight the Power' constantly emanates from his portable sound system. However, Johnson ultimately suggests that the meaning created by music in *Do the Right Thing* (DRT) is often compromised by other internal requirements of the film. She argues:

> that one of DRTs methods for promoting audience sympathy for Raheem and portraying the senselessness of his death is to gradually render Public Enemy's tract familiar via its repetition. Overall, the spatial (noise pollution, because of its unmodulated volume and its encroachment on silent space) and the verbal (politicised lyrics, in comparison with the surrounding environment: that which speaks the unspeakable) content of the song are, finally, rendered relatively nonconfrontational.
>
> (Johnson 1998: 65)

In addition to understanding the role of music in relation to its textual function, film theory has to take into account the different models of film music that operate in specific national contexts, most dramatically in popular Indian cinema (or 'Bollywood' as it has come to be known) where the inclusion of several song and dance numbers in nearly every film is perhaps the defining convention of the form. Addressing this phenomenon, Darius Cooper (1988) has suggested that Indian films regularly employ song and dance sequences for reasons that might not be immediately apparent to the western viewer and require different theoretical paradigms for their explanation.

While much of western cinema is at pains to follow a temporal and spatial continuity within the text in its attempts to construct a rudimentary realism, Indian films habitually break these 'rules' with the introduction of musical sequences. Perhaps most strikingly, such sequences often take place in settings that have no logical justification within the narrative. A good example of this tendency can be found in the 1995 film *Bombay* (Mani Ratnam) when a conversation between the leading protagonists in their urban apartment is suddenly followed by a lavish song and dance number which features the same characters in an unspecified rural location. Although such instances are undoubtedly central to notions of **pleasure** in Indian cinema, Cooper and others prefer to explain the motivation behind this phenomenon by stressing the specific cultural context in which popular Indian film texts operate.

Although song and dance sequences often follow relatively strict conventions, their role is much more subtle than merely providing an entertaining interlude to the epic plots of popular Indian cinema. For one thing, the lyrics regularly ruminate on thematic questions raised by the film, functioning as a sophisticated form of commentary that is not completely external to the diegesis but sufficiently removed to allow a moment of reflection outside of an individual character's subjectivity. This has often provided Indian filmmakers with an opportunity to address issues that might otherwise prove problematic in a country dominated by strict social mores and an industry governed by stringent **censorship**. Treatment of topics such as racial, religious or sexual discrimination, it has been argued, has been less contentious when presented under the guise of 'entertainment'. Song and dance sequences, it should be noted, also provide an arena for a more overt display of sexuality than would be socially acceptable during other parts of the text. Good examples of this tendency can be found in Bimal Roy's 1958 epic *Yahudi*, which features two musical sequences where the display of the female **body** in particular is considerably more explicit that at any other point in the film. Notably, the implication of these sequences is signalled within the text itself as, in each instance, a male onlooker is chided by a female partner for showing too much interest in the spectacle.

See also: musical, the; sound

References

Brown, R. S. (1994) *Overtones and Undertones: Reading Film Music*, Berkeley and Los Angeles: University of California Press.

Cooper, D. (1998) 'The Hindi Film Song and Guru Dutt', *East-West Film Journal*, vol. 2, no. 2, pp. 49–65.

Gorbman, C. (1987) *Unheard Melodies: Narrative Film Music*, Bloomington and Indianapolis: Indiana University Press.

Johnson, V. E. (1997) 'Polyphony and Cultural Expression: Interpreting Musical Traditions in *Do the Right Thing*', in M. A. Reid (ed.) *Spike Lee's Do the Right Thing*, Cambridge: Cambridge University Press.

Further reading

Adorno, T. and Eisler, H. (1994) *Composing for the Films* (first published 1947), London: Athlone Press.

Carbine, M. (1993) ' "The Finest Outside the Loop": Motion Picture Exhibition in Chicago's Black Metropolis, 1905–1928', *Camera Obscura*, 23, pp. 9–41.

Cook, N. (1998) *Analysing Musical Multimedia*, Oxford: Oxford University Press.

Marks, M. M. (1997) *Music and the Silent Film: Contexts and Case Studies, 1895–1924*, New York and Oxford: Oxford University Press.

Skillman, T. (1988) 'Songs in Hindi Films: Nature and Function', in W. Dissanayake (ed.) *Cinema and Cultural Identity: Reflections on Films from Japan, India, and China*, Lanham, MD and London: University Press of America.

Smith, J. (1998) *The Sounds of Commerce: Marketing Popular Film Music*, New York: Columbia University Press.

SIMON HORROCKS

musical, the

A **genre** irrevocably identified with Hollywood, early manifestations of the musical in the 1930s were characterized by simple plots with episodic singing and dancing, evolving later into the 'integrated musical' where performances were motivated and enhanced by the **narrative** (see **plot**). The musical's reputation as frivolous **entertainment** meant early critical neglect, and its many guises were traditionally examined either in terms of rather arbitrary subgenres (e.g., the backstage musical) or through categorization based on studios, their stars and personnel (e.g., MGM producer Arthur Freed). These limitations have since been redressed by attention to the genre's self-reflexivity, its ideological function and its creation of a utopian vision (see **ideology and hegemony**).

See also: classical Hollywood cinema and new Hollywood cinema; music and film

DEBORAH JERMYN

myth

The term 'myth' is variously used to denote particular types and operations of fiction. Its meaning changes according to the discipline and context in which it is used. In anthropology and folklore studies a myth is an allegorical **narrative**, while in Freudian psychoanalytical theory myth refers to a set of archetypes governing the human **unconscious** (see **archetype; Freud, Sigmund; psychoanalysis**). To confuse matters further, in everyday usage the term is applied to any culturally produced belief that is generally understood to be false. In film and television theory, the two main uses of the term are those arising from structural anthropology and **semiotics**.

All cultures produce myths in the form of anonymous, allegorical narratives that explain why the world is as it is, or which explore certain social practices and anxieties. The universality of myth-making and mythology prompted Claude **Lévi-Strauss** to ask whether certain mythic themes, motifs and structures are also transcultural. To test his theory, he analysed myths from a variety of cultures to isolate common elements and relations. He identified certain motifs, such as incest, which are shared by peoples geographically and historically distant from each other. For Lévi-Strauss, any such motif must constitute 'a fragment of a meaningful whole' (1978: 21), suggesting an underlying universal logical structure that all humanity uses to make sense of the world. He identifies this structure as a system of **binary** opposition that, he says, is the organizing principle of all human culture.

Lévi-Strauss' ideas have been widely used in film theory. In his book *Signs and Meaning*, Peter **Wollen** (1972) draws on Lévi-Straussian structuralism,

arguing that the *œuvre* of a given author in film can be analysed in terms of its structural elements and relations in much the same way as Lévi-Strauss analyses myths (see **structuralism and post-structuralism**). Others writers, such as John **Fiske**, have analysed binary oppositions in films as a means of exploring their ideological operations. The application of Lévi-Strauss' analytical methods to films has been criticized on the grounds that such an approach does not take into account the important differences between myths and films. Structuralism does not provide means to address the historical and cultural specificity of films, nor the material conditions and processes which govern their production.

Roland **Barthes** (1993) uses the term myth very differently to identify a particular mode of communication. He bases his theory of myth on Ferdinand de **Saussure**'s account of signification, which he then takes a step further. In Saussurean semiotics, a **sign** is composed of a signifier and a signified. Barthes argues that this is a first-order semiological system (**denotation**). In myth, the first-order sign is appropriated as a signifier in a second-order system (**connotation**). In this way, myth is able to speak about language: it is a **metalanguage**.

In the essays collected in his influential book *Mythologies* (1993), Barthes examines a variety of cultural phenomena that he describes as examples of myth. These include the representation of Romans in Joseph Mankiewicz's film *Julius Caesar* (1953), the cultural significance of plastic, and the iconography of holiness. He proposes a model of myth as 'a type of speech' (Barthes 1993: 109) which functions to 'transform history into nature' (Barthes 1993). Thus, myths are culturally produced concepts that masquerade as nature by disguising their origins in culture. Such myths are culturally specific and usually function to naturalize and uphold power relations.

Barthes variously uses the term myth to mean connotation, **advertising**, propaganda, ideology and **discourse**. Often, he does not adequately distinguish between the diverse cultural processes, operations and concepts that he attempts to identify as examples of myth. A further problem with Barthes' theory of myth is that it supposes the existence of a purely denotative language, a system of communication which operates a value-free relation between the sign and the **referent**. Further, by emphasizing the authority of the text he excludes or ignores questions of polysemy, interpretation and **oppositional** reading.

See also: authorship; ideology and hegemony; polysemic; reading and reception theory

References

Barthes, R. (1993) *Mythologies*, trans. Annette Lavers, London: Vintage.

Lévi-Strauss, C. (1978) *Structural Anthropology, Volume 2*, trans. Monique Layton, Harmondsworth: Penguin.

Wollen, P. (1972) *Signs and Meaning in the Cinema*, London: Secker and Warburg.

Further reading

Lévi-Strauss, C. (1970) *The Raw and the Cooked*, trans. John and Doreen Weightman, London: Jonathan Cape.

SARA GWENLLIAN JONES

N

narrative

The practice of narrative has occupied a central position in the history of film and television production; and the study of narrative has come close to similarly dominating the world of theory. A useful point of entry into the study of narrative is to begin by thinking of it as *story-telling*. The two terms are not synonymous, but they are closely related enough that treating them as near-synonyms is an acceptable first approximation.

Almost everything available to viewers of traditional film and television productions – and considerable amounts of non-traditional, even **avant-garde** production – involves the telling of stories. To start with, every commercial feature film tells one or more stories (stories of love, crime, **horror**, fiction, historical adaptation and so forth). Even **documentary** film, though often very distinct from fiction film in style and subject matter, frequently packages itself in the form of a story of narrative – that is, a filmic representation, using both pictures and words, of a series of events, such as those making up the life-story of a biographical subject.

Television, too, revolves almost entirely around narrative. One striking example is the **soap opera**, which takes the form of a story with no stopping point; this narrative form has been analysed in depth by Robert Allen (1985). Most heavily watched television shows are narrative-based: soap operas, sit-coms, dramas, made-for-television movies and so forth. Less readily apparent, but also true, is the fact that much of what is considered non-fiction television programming (or at least so marketed) also takes narrative form. News, for example, consists to a large degree of stories told to the audience in a very straightforward way – by a presenter staring into the camera supplemented with video clips. Sports events, while not scripted in the way that dramatic or news productions are, also partake of a narrative or story-driven structure; events unfold, drama develops, a resolution emerges. Even commercials, though sometimes given over more to raw assertion and spectacle than to narrative, very often contain miniature stories, involving no more than sketchy, stereotyped characterizations but encapsulating, in some cases, a complete dramatic crisis or life-episode.

As these examples of the saturation of media by narrative suggest, narrative has little to do with what is generally thought of as the distinction between fiction and non-fiction texts. A news broadcast may have a very different style or format from that of a sit-com; but in both cases, the television medium is being used to communicate story-events to the audience. This sharing of ground between fiction and non-fiction has important implications. In particular, it raises the question of how much of our faith in non-fiction – documentary of various types, as well as news – actually comes from the broadcast's style. The study of narrative embraces the study of the shared properties of fiction and non-fiction, and can produce valuable insights into the ways in which non-fiction texts go about convincing us that they do indeed enjoy an elevated truth value.

Narrative: a closer inspection

The concept of 'narrative' stands at the hub of a

cluster of concepts and terms, all of which pertain to the underlying narrative act – the communication of events – and all of which have been analysed and scrutinized by generations of theorists in literature, art history, film studies and other disciplines. Furthermore, while mapping out the basic characteristics of narrative is a relatively simple task at a general level, every component of the process of narrative can be criticized, questioned and subjected to theoretical scrutiny.

A simple account of narrative might run as follows: a narrative is a text, produced by a narrator and addressed or delivered to a narratee in an act of narration. A number of complexities arise even from this simple sketch. Some of these pertain to all narratives, including literary ones. Others are specific to film and/or television.

One issue which has received a great deal of attention from narrative theorists is the relation between the concepts of *narrator* and *author*. It is possible for an author to write a novel, for example, in which one of the fictional characters serves as a narrator (for example, *David Copperfield*, *Moby Dick*). However, many novels do not have identifiable narrators; that is, the story unfolds without the narrator being named.

In the case of film, the narrator/author relationship is, if anything, more complex than it is in the case of literature. Film is a collaborative medium; rarely if ever can we identify one individual who had as much control over the creation of a film (writing, acting, directing, filming, editing, etc.) as an author has over the contents of a novel. The most popular ways of reckoning with this question among film theorists are, first, to concede that there is no equivalent in film to the literary author; and second, to pursue the analogy in respect to a particular contributor to the filmmaking process, generally the director (see **authorship**).

The notion of the narrator of a film is even more elusive. The narrator of a novel may be remote, anonymous and abstract. But we always sense a presence, a mind, behind the narrative; we always feel that the narrator *could* say 'I' at any moment (even if doing so would be strange from the point of view of style). In a film, however, pointing to a consciousness, an 'I' in command of the narrative, is problematic. One area where this has been explored in depth is that of the voice-over narrator.

Like the narrators of novels (who are the stylistic ancestors of voice-overs), voice-over narrators in film may or may not refer to themselves, and may or may not appear in their own stories. They also seem to be in control of the direction and content of the narrative in a way that resembles the control of a literary narrative over the written text. However, voice-over narrators tend to weave in and out of films. During any given film, many of the events depicted take place while the voice-over is silent. In a novel we sense that the text would abruptly stop if the narrator were to stop writing or speaking. In film, the narrative continues, whether the voice-over narrator is speaking or not. Thus the bond between narrator and text has a strength in the case of written narrative that it lacks in the case of film – though creative and even experimental uses of both media can produce results which go beyond this basic understanding.

Whether or not we can identify a narrator in film – even a fictional or anonymous one, or even a voice-over – there is a strong sense that it is being narrated, that the story is being brought to us by some kind of story-telling act or agency. (Film has been compared to dreaming, on the grounds that both represent a kind of narrator-less narrative.) This feeling that film is being narrated has given rise to speculation about the 'inherently narrated' quality of film, the sense in which the technology itself seems to provide a narrative framework, to 'tell' the film, even when no human narrator is present (see Stam *et al.* 1992).

Narrative comprehension

Another key area of concern to narrative theorists in all media is the area of comprehension – that is, the processes by which a narrative text acquires meaning and coherence in the mind of the reader or spectator. This question is closely linked to the question of the comprehension of language in general; indeed, much of the debate over narrative comprehension in film theory has revolved around the relation between narrative and language.

While many theorists have participated in this debate, two of the central ones are Christian **Metz** and David **Bordwell**. Metz wrote several books devoted to exploring the relation between film and language, including the very influential *Psycho-*

analysis and Cinema: The Imaginary Signifier (1982; first published 1977). Bordwell (1985) has taken a different approach, arguing that the comprehension of film – at the level of individual images as well as entire stories or narratives – should not be understood as a form of language comprehension or 'reading' but as proceeding, rather, along lines better described as involving mental processes of 'hypothesis testing'. Such mental activity, according to Bordwell, draws on a mixture of existing knowledge, the data supplied by the film itself, and the mind's ability to search for a meaningful interpretation of those data based on likelihoods and expectations bounded by that knowledge. Language, Bordwell suggests, does not provide a particularly useful framework or metaphor for understanding this kind of psychological process.

Non-narrative

While film and television tend overwhelmingly to involve narrative forms in their productions, there is such a thing as non-narrative imagery. The definition of non-narrative is difficult, however, for several reasons. First, if narrative generally involves the representation of the passage of time, then non-narrative should avoid such representation. In static imagery, such as painting and the decorative arts, this is accomplished in a straightforward manner (for example, wallpaper can tell a story, but need not do so). Literature complicates the case somewhat: even a set of random, unconnected words on a page requires time to read, and the page itself suggests an ordering (even if an ambiguous one) of the words for purposes of reading. This order is reflected in the time required to read, and the sense on the reader's part that the text has a set order.

The element of time is even more difficult to remove from film and television, where the encounter with the text requires the passage of time, almost in the sense that a piece of music occupies a block of time. Thus the sense that a film is telling a story, trying to tell one, or at least behaving, with respect to time, as if it were, can be very compelling.

A second difficulty in defining non-narrative forms in film and television is the role of the viewer, not only in relation to time but also with respect to the perception of meaning in images. If a viewer is predisposed, for instance, to see a story, a drama or

a narrative in the flickering of spots across the screen, then even a film consisting of scratched film leader may well amount to a narrative of sorts for that viewer.

While the search for non-narrative elements in film may be instructive, a more productive approach is to consider *extra*-narrative elements: that is, aspects of film which, while present with or as part of a narrative, have a substance or effect which is not fully accounted for as narrative. In particular, film has an elements of *spectacle*, a visual fullness, which can confer a pleasure of its own on the viewer in ways which go beyond, or lie outside of, the film's narrativity.

Narrative and media history

The difficult search for non-narrative in film and television may suggest that, at some fundamental level, these media must be or 'should' be used in the production of narrative texts. However, while film is certainly a friendly environment for narrative, several theorists and historians have made the point that film did not have to take the course it did, historically. As Christian Metz put it: 'The merging of the cinema and of narrativity was a great fact, which was by no means predestined' (Metz 1974: 93).

If film's technology does not require film to be narrative (and putting aside for the moment the case of seeing narrative in everything), then it becomes important for the historian of narrative film to investigate the question of why the world of film is, in fact, a world of narrative. Important contributions to this line of inquiry have come from historians researching the industrial history of Hollywood, where production of narrative films – films with similar plot elements, recognizable stars, well-established camera and editing practices – was literally a factory activity. Had Hollywood ventured further afield into experimental and/or non-narrative products, production would not have been as efficient or controllable. Marketing narrative films is also an easier task, as they may involve reference to already well-known stories, the inclusion of dramatic moments in trailers and other techniques of dissemination.

References

Allen, R. C. (1985) *Speaking of Soap Operas*, Chapel Hill and London: University of North Carolina Press.

Bordwell, D. (1985) *Narration in the Fiction Film*, Madison, WI: University of Wisconsin Press.

Metz, C. (1974) *Film Language: A Semiotics of the Cinema*, trans. Michael Taylor, New York: Oxford University Press.

—— (1982) *Psychoanalysis and Cinema: The Imaginary Signifier* (first published 1977), trans. Celia Britton, London: Macmillan.

Stam, R. *et al.* (1992) *New Vocabularies in Film Semiotics: Structuralism, Post-Structuralism, and Beyond*, London: Routledge.

Further reading

Branigan, E. (1992) *Narrative Comprehension and Film*, London and New York: Routledge.

DAVID A. BLACK

national, the

With the rise of global media, the concept of 'the national' has become increasingly central to film and television studies. As new technologies allow film, television, the **Internet** and multimedia to cross national borders with increasing speed, concepts of national culture and the idea of the nation itself have demanded closer critical attention. Increased interest in **history** and cultural studies has also led to more studies of national cinemas centred around the relationship between a country's media and its national culture and history, supplementing isolated aesthetic and industrial examinations of cinema or television itself.

Since the late nineteenth century, changes in national boundaries and increased international migrations have sparked interest in the question of national identity. During the early part of the twentieth century, the pseudo-science of eugenics attempted to classify people according to their national origins. Resulting typologies hierarchized ethnic groups, placing fair-skinned Europeans at the top and ranking dark peoples at the bottom end of the scale. These formulas attempted to equate intelligence, manners, behaviour and culture with skin colour and land of origin, using 'nature' and 'science' to elevate some nations above others. Eugenics was one response to the mass migration provoked by industrialization, war and colonization. As some nations (like the United States, the United Kingdom, Germany and France) became richer and more powerful than others, impoverished people travelled across the globe to find work. Others fled in search of freedom from persecution, torture, war and possible death. Eugenics provided 'scientific' justification for limiting migration, ostensibly to preserve domestic peace and national identity.

Although wars have been fought over national boundaries since antiquity, current definitions of 'the national', nationalism and national identity are modern inventions, and can be traced back only as far as the nineteenth century. As Benedict Anderson (1991) has shown, the very concept of the nation is itself predicated on the possibilities of mass communication. For Anderson, the nation can only be an 'imagined community' as its very size, diversity and complexity cannot be experienced first-hand, even in the smallest of countries. Besides, the idea of the nation does not just depend on individuals having some sense about what is transpiring elsewhere in the land, but instead relies on people understanding that this event is happening *now*. The nation thus demands a temporality that connotes a sense of simultaneity.

This sense of community relies on media and arises with the invention of the printing press. Print media from the novel to the daily newspaper helped to establish larger boundaries, enabling people to acquire knowledge about events further afield, thus permitting the creation of a national perspective. As media extended their geographic range and speed, this realm expanded to encompass more global space. The invention of film, radio and television increased media literacy, extending this knowledge and citizenship to more people, while audiovisual moving images offered increasingly vivid recorded experiences of home and the exotic lands beyond.

Print and other recorded media also permitted nations to record their own history beyond oral recollections and collective **memory** for the first time. Besides legitimizing the nation itself, history could be separated from individual minds and experiences, reinventing itself in print as an objective (see **objectivity**), impersonal, collective and truthful account of the past. As education became more widely available, history books helped disseminate citizenship through formal education. Recorded images from film and television have supplemented the book in this task, extending history and the project of citizenship beyond the classroom. National identity is thus formed and reinforced in the present through an intersection with images of the past. While they are often positioned as 'truth', images of the past are generally used to bolster contemporary articulations of national identity, in which the present is usually positioned as superior to the past. At the same time, these older images and texts retain a sense of the traditions, sacrifices and accomplishments that provided the nation with its illustrious present.

This, of course, does not mean that the past is always interpreted in the same way. During the 1960s and the 1990s, for example, Britain has self-consciously tried to modernize its image, with Prime Ministers like Harold Wilson and, most recently, Tony Blair seeking new national identities that break from the past. In both cases, previous national images reified the past and tradition, as Britain still clung to images of former glories and triumphs such as its victories in the Second World War or its more distant cultural and political history. Ironically, in both cases, national history is not effaced but rather re-centred, used not as a consolation for the nation's present diminished status, but rather as an incentive to regain power in a more contemporary fashion. It is thus unsurprising that both periods witnessed increased public and governmental interest in indigenous popular culture.

The concept of the nation has also been at the centre of many of the twentieth-century's major wars and conflicts, including wars in Africa, the Balkans, Northern Ireland, the Middle East and, of course, the two World Wars. The question of a nation's right to possess territory claimed by other countries has been central to these conflicts, often bolstered by individual histories, traditions and religious doctrines. As these wars suggest, the image of a nation does not necessarily depend on its possessing a homeland. In the case of the Jews, for instance, national identity remained strong for centuries despite the absence of a homeland. Even without a nation, they were able to retain a sense of their distinct national ties, despite being dispersed over many and far-flung lands.

During the first half of the twentieth century, literature on nationalism and nations met with unprecedented popular appeal, and its ideas were used to justify the carnage of the First and Second World Wars. Late twentieth-century maps of the world also highlight the increased strength of nationalism, national causes and national identities. As Hobsbawm (1990) notes, following the Second World War, Europe was re-mapped 'according to the principle of nationality...for the first [and] only time'. But, he also notes that nationalism is only one of a set of identifications people might feel, and sometimes it will not be as strong as the kinship they feel with other groups, like family, **race** and **gender**.

Changes in boundaries can redescribe and reinvent the physical properties of the nation, but they may not affect national culture and its idea of 'the national'. Furthermore, this sense of the national is not itself constant, but often changes over very short periods of time. Indeed, as Hobsbawm (1990) notes, national identity itself emerges from transformation and often articulates a specific vision of change. It is particularly desirable for post-war nations to place themselves at the vanguard of change, linking modernity with power, for, in Hobsbawm's words, 'the basic characteristic of the modern nation...is its modernity'.

As Anderson and Hobsbawm suggest, then, the national is not a concrete and unchanging entity, but rather involves images and cultural practices that bind people together. As our major source of mass communication, ideals, collective fantasies, shared knowledge and communal memories, it follows that the media help create the prevailing sense of 'the national' in contemporary culture. Given that the media have mainly been in the hands of powerful western nations which have historically exported their products overseas, it is likely that other smaller and less powerful nations might have problems supporting their own national identities.

Robert Stam and Ella Shohat (1994) argue that it is no coincidence that film was developed at the end of the nineteenth century, during the height of colonialism and western imperialism. They point out that this period also witnessed the invention of **psychoanalysis**, the development of consumerism and widespread interest in eugenics, all of which promoted a specific image of the western individual as a global ideal. Early filmmakers from the Lumière Company and others travelled the globe, bringing back images of 'exotic Third World spectacles' to amaze the inhabitants of European and North American cities. These films advanced the colonial project, reinforcing the supremacy of the 'cultured' First World, turning native cultures into entertainment, spectacles and jokes. Along with photography, film also helped catalogue empires, using the camera's scientific gaze to measure and assess remnants of native life. Entertainment and scientific impulses thus combined to survey native lands, imbuing the camera with western powers and revealing its abilities to police nations.

These films reshaped native lands in tandem with western ideals. The unfamiliar was either disparaged as natives were educated out of 'uncivilized' customs and religions, or rendered exotic, entertaining and marketable overseas (in keeping with the taste for 'Orientalism'). Cameras stayed in western hands, which paid no attention to the ways in which these cultures organized themselves or the ways in which they might like to be represented. Throughout the colonial era, western nations exported their films to their colonies, but often prevented these nations from developing their own cinemas. Native film production was banned in English colonies in Africa, while their French counterparts could only make films under strict government supervision. Either way, it was impossible for indigenous people to create images based on their own national culture and national interests. These nations were often forbidden to make films largely because they had the power to present alternative visions of the nation to the masses which might threaten colonial rule. The economic threat raised by potential competition was usually a secondary consideration

as these were very poor nations, incapable of rivalling the budgets and star appeal of films made in the West.

Indeed, cinema has largely been controlled by western nations for most of its history (with the important exceptions of India and Japan). Most Third World nations have only been able to produce films relatively recently, usually since gaining independence. Many Third World filmmakers choose to work independently, outside the mainstream film industries in their country, as western conglomerates still often own most of them. And most of these filmmakers are interested in film for political and social reasons – including consciousness raising, advancing indigenous national culture and developing their own forms of film language, influenced by native traditions. Consequently, they reject the narrative strategies, form and **aesthetics** of Hollywood and mainstream western cinema, producing films specifically for domestic audiences rather than international markets. Because colonization blocked these populations from spreading knowledge about their own past, many of these films deal with national history, believing that the population needs to understand its own past before there can be real social and political change.

Western nations have also established a long tradition of using cinema to produce and promote national identity. Confronted with the dominance of Hollywood cinema, many European countries have tried to create their own national cinemas to shore up national identity at home and offset the process of Americanization which threatens to engulf not only cinema, but all aspects of national culture. Explicitly 'national' cinemas exist at the most mainstream and experimental ends of the scale, dating back to the moment when the American film industry started dominating world markets during the teens. Many **avant-garde** practices were initiated under this cause. In the early 1920s, for instance, Louis Delluc called for 'specifically French and specifically cinematic' films, motivating the experiments of French Impressionist filmmakers like Abel Gance. More mainstream cinemas advancing explicitly national causes include German **Expressionism**, which incorporated elements of German art, architecture, theatre and literature. Similarly, Soviet montage and British documentaries drew on national traditions and contemporary art and culture to produce nationally distinctive film forms. These films were not simply propaganda for the nation, but were often quite critical of national institutions and policies in order to advance the cause of the community at large and further strengthen the nation itself. These cinemas received international acclaim, were recognized as important movements and inspired Hollywood experimentation (see **film movements**).

Faced with American dominance, even the most affluent western nations have had to take protective measures to preserve national production and domestic film culture. The variety of trade tariffs, import quotas, outright bans and governmental investments reveal the importance of domestic film production, suggesting cinema's key role in national culture. In the United Kingdom, the government has tried to protect the British film industry in a number of ways, establishing quotas and allotting film subsidies (for example, the Eady Levy and, later, lottery grants); Germany has restricted imports (especially in wartime) and helped fund commercial and art cinema; while the Soviet Union nationalized its film industry, banned most imports and even restricted exports to the West. Even in America, national dominance has been preserved through distributors' unwillingness to accept foreign films.

Even though most non-Hollywood films only find audiences and distribution in their own countries, cinema has acquired a reputation as a more international medium than television. Associated with the intimacy of the home, television appears to be the national medium *par excellence*. While many nations face cinema screens filled with Hollywood product and the occasional 'foreign' film, television schedules appear reassuringly home-grown. From its inception, television has focused primarily on the local and the national. The state of early broadcast technologies limited its compass – Britain's first transmissions in 1936, for instance, only reached the London area. BBC Television did not reach other regions until after the service resumed at the end of the war, and even then, some parts of the country would wait for years. Television's first imagined communities, then, were highly localized, making the occasional

long-distance or international transmission a major event and a broadcasting coup. In contrast, the early days of film saw production and exhibition taking place all over the globe.

Television's movement into western homes gathered momentum during the 1950s, a period of intense parochialism, particularly in Cold War America. Viewers retreated from the more public space of cinemas and, through television, found entertainment and distraction within their homes. Television arguably helped foster this inward stance on both sides of the Atlantic, producing national subjects with such programmes as *The Coronation of Queen Elizabeth II* (1953). Despite its international transmission, the unprecedented scale of this event, its revelation of hitherto never seen ceremonies at the heart of national history and mythology, did more than any other broadcast to sell sets and establish television's place in British homes. It also set a precedent for British television, positioning important royal events and displays of British pageantry as major ratings draws. Jet bombers were used to fly the programme to America for transmission later that night, exporting images of British pomp overseas and anchoring certain preconceptions about national identity in foreign minds. This was hardly accidental. This Coronation was designed for television, to promote an image of Britain emerging into opulence and plenty after years of post-war austerity. While far from the truth, the power and scale of the broadcast none the less helped establish new images of Britain around the globe and offered a counter-myth for the people at home.

The emergence of new broadcast technologies, like digital satellite and cable television, have helped extend the medium's physical range across national and continental borders. The idea of television as a national, domestic medium seems to co-exist comfortably with its much-vaunted internationalism. The form this expansion of **cable and satellite** channels has taken to date, however, indicates that these networks might break national boundaries in a different and less utopian fashion. Many stations rely on western programming, often filling schedules with the likes of American sit-coms and dramas. Similarly, American channels such as MTV and CNN are staples of cable systems around the world, their formats sometimes modified to suit local tastes and their programmes fronted by native stars. Given television's importance to national culture, it is hardly surprising that most countries regulate broadcasting to protect it from foreign influence. American laws, for instance, prohibit foreign ownership of television and radio stations, sheltering the people's airways from international influence and corruption. Meanwhile, British regulations limit the amount of overseas programming that can be shown on terrestrial channels. Satellite and cable, however, often escape these regulations, as stations transmit from overseas lands or exist in a space free from current legislation (see **regulation**).

The relationships between cinema and its national origins have been critically discussed since their inception. Critics like Siegfried **Kracauer** have drawn parallels between a nation's cinema and national characteristics, believing that film's status as a popular mass medium enables it to capture national obsessions. As cinema tells stories about national culture, it helps mould and reinforce national identity at home and also shapes the ways in which that culture is understood overseas. These two perspectives may not be entirely in agreement, however, suggesting one flaw in Kracauer's argument. As British heritage films suggest, the national image a country markets overseas might not mirror that land's present domestic situation (see **heritage film and television**).

While films and television shows often reshape history and current concerns, they none the less organize these representations in ways that often reveal master tropes of national identity. Hollywood's emphasis on individualism and happy endings, for example, perpetuates a certain national world view that can be distinguished from Britain's more collective, community-centred productions or the struggles over identity and boundaries that mark most Hong Kong cinema from the 1980s and 1990s. When these national characteristics are most pronounced, they are often used as forms of product differentiation, their 'differences' highlighted and used in marketing the films. As this suggests, in a global market dominated by Hollywood conglomerates, the national is often ultimately dependent on the economic. The images of nations that persist are the ones that sell globally (particularly in the American market), causing most nations to fashion their cinematic (and, increasingly televisual) representations in response to dominant Hollywood paradigms (see **globalization; marketing and promotion**).

See also: Eisenstein, Sergei; Said, Edward; Third Cinema

References

Anderson, B. (1991) *Imagined Communities: Reflections on the Origins and Spread of Nationalism*, London: Verso.

Hobsbawm, E. (1990) *Nations and Nationalism Since 1780: Programme, Myth, Reality*, Cambridge: Cambridge University Press.

Stam R. and Shohat, E. (1994) *Unthinking Eurocentrism: Multiculturalism and the Media*, New York: Routledge.

Further reading

Bhabha, H. (1990) *Nation and Narration*, London: Routledge.

Nowell-Smith, G. (ed.) (1996) *Oxford History of World Cinema*, Oxford: Oxford University Press.

Smith, A. (1979), *Nationalism in the Twentieth Century*, New York: New York University Press.

Thompson, K. (1985) *Exporting Entertainment*, London: BFI Publishing.

MOYA LUCKETT

naturalism and non-naturalism

What is usually meant by the terms 'naturalism' and 'non-naturalism' is apparent in comments, made in 1977, by the well-known British television dramatist Dennis Potter:

> The best non-naturalist drama, in its very structure, disorientates the viewer smack in the middle of the orientation process which television perpetually uses. . . . It shows the frame in the picture when most television is showing the picture in the frame.

(Potter in Creeber 1998: 53)

And, in a later interview, Potter explained: 'I am happy to break the naturalistic mode. I don't want to show life exactly as it is. I hope to show a little of what life is about (*ibid.*). Here Potter was defending the kind of techniques he had begun to use in his work, such as characters directly addressing the camera, behaving like children or lip-synching to songs, in order to subvert the 'naturalistic' conventions of television drama. Implicit in these remarks is a belief that television drama was losing its power to challenge audiences because it had come to rely on the presentation of surface appearances, effacing its methods of production and lulling the audience into a mode of easy identification with characters and their situation. In the same decade, the 1980s, similar assessments were made of film and television productions by Colin MacCabe (see **classic realist text**). In both cases a naturalistic style was seen as limiting the social or political impact of these media.

Paradoxically, about a century earlier it was the radical claims and practices of Naturalism, as a *movement*, that were seen as shocking in the novels of Emile Zola and the plays of August Strindberg and Henrick Ibsen. The features of Zola's novels are conventionally seen as the detailed observation of working-class life, a concern with heredity and an awareness of the impact of social circumstances on the lives of his characters. But Zola, acknowledging the influence of the observational methods and evolutionary hypotheses of Charles Darwin and the physiologist and naturalist Claude Bernard, argued for the novel as a space for experimentally exploring the reaction of characters in individual and social relationships: 'naturalism is not a personal fantasy but . . . the intellectual movement of the century'. The claims he made for scientific method in his writing may now seem spurious, but Zola was anxious to rebut the view that naturalism was no more than photographic **realism**. His novels are an attempt, based on painstaking research, to place the reciprocal relations between individual, groups and society at the centre of his fiction, regardless of political consequences and public taste.

The naturalism acknowledged by Strindberg was of a different, though related order. In the language of his early plays, for example, Strindberg sought to capture the irregularity of speech characteristic of everyday life because his ideas about sexual relationships could not be represented through the 'symmetrical, mathematical construction' of the theatrical dialogue of his time. His scenery was impressionistic, rather than mimetic or spectacular, dispensing with the re-creation of a whole room with furniture and doors in favour of only those chairs and tables central to the action so that 'the imagination is roused and complements what it sees' (see **mimetic/mimesis**). Strindberg also wanted to dispense with footlights and to have actors perform with their backs to the audience, when this seemed appropriate, as part of his desire to break with the artificiality of contemporary theatrical performance. Though Ibsen adopted a different strategy and created detailed rooms, the aim was the same, as Raymond **Williams** notes:

> a real environment had to be reproduced on the stage because within this [Naturalist] perspective . . . an actual environment was in effect one of the actors: one of the true agencies of the action.
> (Williams 1989: 85)

Williams also observes that 'as a movement and as a method [Naturalism] was concerned to show that people are inseparable from their real social and physical environments' (*ibid.*: 113).

Clearly, film and television had the technical ability to reproduce real social and physical environments which might surpass the novel or the stage play. What is suggested by the attacks on naturalism, typified by Potter and others, is that the *methods* of naturalism have been developed at the expense of the *movement*. Methods that had been appropriate to challenge representational orthodoxy became the orthodoxy, and the link with the radical content was broken. The commitment of naturalism to show that actions are shaped by material circumstance and not by idealist notions or out of an unchanging human nature was reversed. Film and television drama used the method to reproduce external reality in telling stereotypical stories of individual success or romance which could vindicate the *status quo*, or suggest that good fortune or individual effort could triumph over disadvantage.

Naturalism will probably continue to be used as the loose description of a style of fictional film or television which ranges from British **soap opera** to the films of Ken Loach via Australian soap opera and American police series, such as *Homicide*. Critics, of any political position, arguing for the social significance of the fictional forms may continue to condemn naturalism as no more than anodyne and superficial reproduction. But as Raymond Williams' account of Naturalism indicates, so long as the lives of the great majority of the people remain wholly disregarded by most arts 'there are social realities that cry out for [Naturalism's] kind of serious, detailed recording and diagnostic attention' (*ibid.*: 115).

See also: verisimilitude

References

Creeber, C. (1998) *Dennis Potter: Between Two Worlds*, London: Macmillan
Williams, R. (1989) *The Politics of Modernism*, London: Verso.

Further reading

Caughie, J. (2000) *Television Drama: Realism, Modernism and British Culture*, Oxford: Oxford University Press.
Strindberg, A. (1968) 'Preface to Miss Julie' (first published 1888), in Richard Ellman and Charles Feidelson (eds) *The Modern Tradition*, trans. Elizabeth Sprigge, New York: Oxford University Press.
Zola, E. (1968) 'The Experimental Novel' (first published 1880), in Richard Ellman and Charles Feidelson (eds) *The Modern Tradition*, trans. Belle M. Sherman, New York: Oxford University Press.

PHILIP SIMPSON

negotiation

This concept has its strongest resonance in **audience** studies. In sharp contrast with attempts to characterize members of a media audience as being passively acquiescent to the dominant message of a given **text**, more sophisticated approaches investigate the ways in which readers make sense of the text through interacting or engaging with its ideological imperatives (see **ideology and hegemony**). In showing how any one text always enables more than one potential reading, researchers can highlight the means by which readers bring to bear their own subjective identities in the process of rendering the text meaningful for themselves. This process is necessarily provisional, contingent and contradictory, regardless of how transparently natural or common sensical the text's claim on reality may appear to be (see **common sense**).

See also: dominant ideology; encoding-decoding model; subject and subjectivity

Further reading

Morley, D. (1992) *Television, Audiences and Cultural Studies*, London: Routledge.

STUART ALLAN

Negroponte, Nicholas

b. 1943

Nicholas Negroponte was a founding member of the Massachusetts Institute of Technology's (MIT) Media Lab. Officially opened in 1985, Media Lab is now, with the support of a large number of blue-chip corporate sponsors, a cutting-edge research and development centre devoted to exploring and promoting the application of digital technologies throughout society.

Negroponte is perhaps best known as the author of *Being Digital* (1995), in which he argues that due to rapid advancements in the flow of information enabled by computer technology, western society is undergoing a change equivalent to the Industrial Revolution. This revolution is the digital revolution. 'Being digital', according to Negroponte, however, is not about technology; rather, it is a way of operating in and understanding the world. This digital world is faster, less hierarchical and more democratic. In essence, Negroponte takes on many of the theorizations of post-modernity, such as time–space compression and the free-flow of information, and gives them an optimistic, technological twist (see **modernism and post-modernism**).

Negroponte has also been an important contributor to *Wired*, the seminal magazine of the new digital frontier, for whom he wrote a regular column between 1993 and 1998. While the breadth of his vision and the emphasis he places on the social use and application of technology avoids unnecessary determinism, it is nevertheless unmistakably North American and utopian (see **utopia and dystopia**). In one of his columns for *Wired*, he confidently predicts that: 'In the future, communities formed by ideas will be as strong as those formed by the forces of physical proximity. Kids will not know the meaning of nationalism'. A position that is contradicted sharply by the actuality of the geo-political struggles of the 1990s throughout the world.

See also: digital communication; Internet; Internet and the World Wide Web

References

Negroponte, N. (1995) *Being Digital*, New York: Knopf.

HANNAH DAVIES

network

A network is any group of radio or television stations that is linked to a central broadcasting source and able to receive and transmit programmes and advertising simultaneously from a centralized source. Nothing prevents a network from being local or regional rather than national, or from being driven by motives other than profit, but the most popular programming has tended to emanate from large commercial national or international networks which, in the United States for example, have acquired control through their ownership of stations and programmes, their ability to attract stars, and hence their ability to attract the appropriate audience group for advertisers. In the mid-1990s large networks began to lose audience share to the new networks made possible by **cable and satellite** broadcasting technologies.

See also: advertising; broadcasting, the United Kingdom; broadcasting, the United States; prime time; public service broadcasting

ADRIENNE L. McLEAN

new film semiotics

The work of Christian **Metz** influenced the formation of 'contemporary' film theory, which consists of two stages – a semiotic stage and a post-structural stage (see **structuralism and post-structuralism**). Film **semiotics** (from the mid-1960s to the mid-1970s), epitomized by Metz's identification of eight basic types of film sequences and by his book *Language and Cinema* (1971), is based on structural linguistics. Post-structural film theory (from the mid-1970s onwards) is based on Althusserian Marxism and Lacanian **psychoanalysis** (see **Althusser, Louis; Lacan, Jacques; Marx, Karl**). Film semiotics was also challenged by 'new film semiotics', an approach to film that combines cognitive science and semiotics. More specifically, new film semiotics is influenced by: (i) Noam Chomsky's transformational generative grammar; (ii) pragmatics; and (iii) by a renewed interest in enunciation.

I will look at all three influences, starting with transformational generative grammar. In his essay, 'Film Semiology as a Cognitive Science' (1995), the new film semiotician Michel Colin charts the relationship between semiotics and cognitive science. He argues that both disciplines address similar issues – language, vision and problem solving. Colin then develops a theory of filmic comprehension (particularly the comprehension based on the combined insights of semiotics and cognitive science). Colin also reformulated Metz's eight basic syntagmatic categories in terms of Chomsky's linguistics. The most remarkable results of this reformulation is that, as with all generative models, the eight actual, manifest **syntagmatic** types are regarded as merely the end result of the generative process. Within the generative framework we can identify and analyse, not only actual syntagms, but also potential syntagms and impossible syntagms. For Colin, the primary aim of Metz's *grande syntagmatique* is not to identify actual syntagmatic types, but to identify a potentially infinite number of possible (and impossible) syntagmatic types.

With regard to the second point, the new film semiotics of Roger Odin is influenced by pragmatics, which posits that the meaning of texts is inherently incomplete and indeterminate, and is completed by the reader's inferential activities guided by contextual information. Pragmatics is concerned with the nature of this knowledge and with outlining the principles that guide readers in their generation of inferences. Odin argues that the film does not signify its own meaning. Instead, reading a filmic image consists of 'applying to [the image] processes that are essentially external to it. This reading does not result from an internal constraint, but from a cultural constraint' (Odin 1995: 213). This framework suggests that there are no inherent differences between, for example, the fiction film and the **documentary** film. Indeed, Odin states that spectators must take up the role of 'documentarizing' subjects in order to comprehend the film on screen as a documentary. Odin offers a useful definition of fiction to explain how, within a pragmatic framework, a documentary film is distinguished by spectators from a fiction film. He argues that, whereas the spectator of a fiction film posits the filmmaker as absent, the documentary spectator must posit the filmmaker as 'real', since the maker of a documentary is assumed to be able to guarantee the truth of what is shown on screen.

Finally, enunciation names the activity that results in speech, in the production of utterances (*énoncés*). The French linguist Emile Benveniste identified two forms of utterance: **discourse** and **story**. Discourse employs words such as personal pronouns within the utterance, indicating particular aspects of its spatio-temporal context (e.g., the speaker and hearer), whereas story is a form of utterance that excludes pronouns. The new film semiotician Francesco Casetti takes to its logical conclusions the analysis of film in terms of personal pronouns (Casetti 1986). Using the categories 'I', 'you' and 'he', he develops a typology of four shot types, which aim to describe the way film orients itself in relation to the spectator. In his final published book, *L'Enonciation impersonnelle ou le site du film* (1991), Metz disputes Casetti's pronoun theory of film, and instead argues that film can only be studied as story. After criticizing Casetti, Metz simply replaced personal pronouns with anaphora – a narrow system of orientation in which one textual element points to another textual element. Moreover, Metz identifies anaphora as a reflexive moment in a film, which results in his identifying filmic enunciation with reflexivity.

The film semioticians mentioned here all share the same project – to combine film semiotics and cognitive science with the aim of understanding the spectator's competence, or the knowledge that spectators deploy to comprehend films.

See also: cognitive theory; semiotics

References

Casetti, F. (1986) *Dentro lo sguardo: Il filme e il sou spettatore*, Milano: Bompiani.

Colin, M. (1995) 'Film Semiology as a Cognitive Science', in Warren Buckland (ed.) *The Film Spectator: From Sign to Mind*, Amsterdam: Amsterdam University Press, pp. 87–110.

Metz, C. (1971) *Language and Cinema*, trans. D. J. Umiker-Sebeok, The Hague: Mouton.

—— (1991) *L'Enonciation impersonnelle ou le site du film*, Paris: Editions Méridiens Klincksieck.

Odin, R. (1995) 'For a Semio-Pragmatics of Film', in Warren Buckland (ed.) *The Film Spectator*, Amsterdam: Amsterdam University Press, pp. 213–26.

WARREN BUCKLAND

news values

One of the most significant aspects of the socialization of journalists is the development of a 'news sense': the acquisition of the news values of journalistic practice in general, and those of the specific genre (print, television, radio) and news organization for which a journalist works. 'News sense' constitutes a notion of what 'reality' supposedly looks like and what is considered important in the world. This 'reality' is then translated into stories for news audiences. This means that once reporters have been 'socialized' within a given newsroom and have learned its specific news values and frames, they soon recognize what should be reported and how. As Ericson *et al.* (1987: 104) argue: 'It [does] not mean that the facts [are] "self-evident" but rather "news-evident" in terms of the criteria learned "day after day and night after night" in the news organization'. In all newsrooms, assumptions around particular groups in society (for example, based on **gender**, **race**, **class**, sexuality and so on) are internalized by reporters, providing them with a ready set of templates to be utilized when writing stories.

One of the most important roles of a journalist is to mediate between events 'happening out there' and news audiences. Journalists select and report on those events according to news values that dictate what is considered newsworthy. As some commentators have argued, news is a cultural product comprised of 'a set of institutional definitions and meanings, which, in the professional shorthand, is commonly referred to as *news values*' (Hall 1984: 149). Together with the bureaucratic organization of the media, news values constitute the conditioning elements of the social production of news. Internalized news values therefore provide a frame for journalists to routinely categorize certain events as 'newsworthy' and, thus, those which are not. These news values are learned by newsworkers in the course of their daily activities of newsgathering and through interaction with other journalists, editors and news sources. The news is not deliberately 'biased' but is instead shaped by the 'steady and unexamined play of attitudes which, via the mediating structure of professionally defined news values, inclines all the media towards the *status quo*' (Hall 1984: 149).

News values dictate that any event must be 'consonant' with the cultural expectations of journalists and readers. Nevertheless, since news workers are always on the look-out for the 'what a story!' happening on which to report, events which seem to challenge cultural expectations will also be regarded as highly desirable to report. It is also fair to suggest that whether or not a particular event becomes news will depend, to some extent, on the range of events occurring and selected for inclusion on any given day. For instance, if a large number of events of a particular type are available for reporting on the same day, a news outlet's requirement for 'balance' will probably dictate that certain items which ordinarily might be included on a 'normal' or, indeed, 'slow' news day could be excluded. Because of this requirement, it may appear that roughly the same number of certain types of events happen daily, and therefore that they are regular, predictable, and 'normal' happenings (in terms of their frequency of occurrence, news type, typical length of report, usual sources, etc.). Despite this, many journalists still tend to regard the news values within which they operate to be 'neutral' and thus that their reporting is objective (see **objectivity**).

See also: bias; framing

References

Ericson, R. V., Patricia, M. B. and Chan, J. B. L. (1987) *Visualizing Deviance: A Study of News Organization*, Toronto: University of Toronto Press.

Hall, S. (1984) 'The World at One with Itself', in S. Cohen and J. Young (eds) *The Manufacture of News: Social Problems, Deviance and the Mass Media*, London: Constable.

Further reading

Allan, S. (1999) *News Culture*, Buckingham: Open University Press.

Carter, C., Branston, G. and Allan, S. (eds) (1998) *News, Gender and Power*, London and New York: Routledge.

Schudson, M. (1995) *The Power of News*, Cambridge, MA: Harvard University Press.

Tuchman, G. (1978) *Making News: A Study in the Construction of Reality*, New York: Free Press.

CYNTHIA CARTER

Nietzsche, Friedrich Wilhelm

b. 1844; d. 1900

The fundamental concern of Nietzsche's work is the collapse of a traditional metaphysical and Christian religious understanding. Nietzsche abhorred Christianity as a false doctrine but also feared that its demise would lead to nihilism unless humanity developed an alternative system of affirmation. In his first book, *The Birth of Tragedy*, published in 1871, he took inspiration from Greek culture and from the German composer Richard Wagner to propose an aesthetic justification for human life. In later works, he stressed the interpretive nature of human knowledge, the illusory character of 'truth' and the need to reconsider value and morality. His profound influence on twentieth-century thought is evident in post-structuralist and post-modernist theory and in the works of Michel **Foucault**, Jacques **Derrida**, Jean-François **Lyotard** and Jürgen **Habermas**.

Nietzsche's reputation suffered as a result of the Nazis' misuse of his theories of the Superman and the Will to Power to justify their eugenics policies.

However, Nazi ideology grotesquely simplifies and distorts Nietzsche's ideas and should not be understood as representative of his philosophical thought.

See also: ideology and hegemony; modernism and post-modernism; structuralism and post-structuralism

Further reading

Nietzsche, F. (1990) *Beyond Good and Evil*, trans. R. J. Hollingdale, Harmondsworth: Penguin.
—— (1993) *The Birth of Tragedy*, trans. Shaun Whiteside, Harmondsworth: Penguin.

SARA GWENLLIAN JONES

O

objectivity

To be an 'objective' reporter – or **documentary**-maker – means being socialized into obeying certain rituals of naming, describing and **framing** realities, even if objectivity is self-reflexively posited as an ideal never to be entirely realized in practice. Attempts to document the means by which broadcast journalists, for example, reproduce a professionalized news culture have sought to examine how social relations shape the norms of objective reportage. In what ways, researchers ask, do these institutional norms centre the predispositions and attitudes of white, middle-class male journalists? In other words, why is it usually the case that these journalists' 'instinctive' judgements about the 'credibility' or 'expertise' of news sources lead to such a small portion of the accessed voices being those of, say, members of ethnic minorities? Similarly, to what extent do male journalists regard their female colleagues as deviating from these norms in their approaches to validating objective truth-claims?

Feminist researchers have sought to intervene in debates about news objectivity. A principal point of contention concerns the gendering of the dominant discourses of 'truth' being mobilized by journalists, that is, the extent to which a **gender** bias is discernible in the objective news reporting. In his exploration of this research, Allan (1999) outlines three distinct modes of enquiry:

- *Neutrality position.* For some feminists seeking to uphold 'objectivity' as a journalistic ideal, the problem is one of male norms being allowed to subjectively distort 'what really took place'. Good reporting, they maintain, is gender-neutral reporting. Advocates of this position call for journalists to observe a rigorous adherence to systematized methods of gathering and processing 'concrete facts' dispassionately so as to ensure that news accounts are strictly 'impartial'. The 'truth' of the 'real world' is to be discovered through these facts; 'gender-biased' journalism can thus be avoided so long as news accounts accurately reflect reality.

- *Balance position.* Other feminists have sought to highlight the gender-specificity of 'objectivity', that is, the essential distinctions between female and male apprehensions of reality. In their view, only women are justified in speaking for women as a social group: personal experience, it follows, stands as the arbiter of 'truth'. Using a language of 'balance', they contend that 'objectivity' is primarily a matter of ensuring that male values are counterpoised by female ones. This is to be achieved by news organizations employing equal numbers of male and female journalists, as well as through changes in newswork practices (such as ensuring that a representative selection of female voices are accessed as news sources).

- *Counter-position.* A further position adopted by some feminists is marked by a resolve to effectively jettison the concept of 'objectivity' altogether due to its perceived complicity in legitimizing patriarchal hegemony (see **ideology and hegemony; patriarchy**). In their view, this concept prefigures a dichotomy between the knower and the known which is untenable: facts cannot be separated out from their ideological, and hence gendered, conditions of production. Moreover, the imposition of this false dichotomy is further masculinized to the extent that it obviates the experiences of women as being outside the realm of what are proclaimed to be universally valid standards of reason, logic and rationality. What counts as 'truth' in a given instance is determined by who has the power to define reality.

It is evident from these differing positions that the relationship between discourses of objectivity and gender relations is politically charged. Feminist efforts committed to deconstructing this relationship have sought to render problematic the often subtle, taken-for-granted strategies through which journalists, knowingly or not, routinely define 'what counts as reality' in alignment with patriarchal renderings of the social world.

Not surprisingly then, the appeal to objectivity becomes a defensive strategy, which assists the journalist in countering charges of sexism (as well as those of racism, among others) being levelled at specific instances of reporting. A journalism genuinely committed to impartiality, its adherents insist, cannot be sexist. So long as the appropriate procedural rules are followed, 'tangible facts' will be separated out from the values expressed through partisan argument and opinion; indeed, it is the task of the 'good' reporter to ensure that this segregation is achieved. Consequently, the journalist's invocation of objectivity may be analysed as a male-centred instance of definitional power to the extent that it ex-nominates (places beyond **common sense**) those truth-claims which do not adhere to masculinist assumptions about the social world.

See also: bias; feminist theory; news values; race

References

Allan, S. (1999) *News Culture*, Buckingham and Philadelphia: Open University Press.

STUART ALLAN

180° rule

The 180° rule is a staging convention characteristic of classical Hollywood cinema which facilitates **continuity editing** through the organization of narrative action along an imaginary '180° line' (or 'axis of action').

As an example, consider a filmed conversation between two people outside a café, a man on the left, a woman on the right; the 180° line runs between the actors. Provided the camera remains on one side of this line, the actors appear on screen in the same places relative to one another and the background – man on the left, woman on the right, and the café behind them – when filmed from any camera position. This means that shots from several positions/cameras can be edited together without spatial or graphic discontinuity which might disrupt the **narrative** flow if the line were crossed.

See also: camera style and lens style; classical Hollywood cinema and new Hollywood cinema

BRUCE BENNETT

ontology

Ontology is the branch of metaphysics concerned with the study and nature of existence and being (literally, 'knowledge of being'). In philosophy, a distinction is made between 'appearance' and 'reality'. This distinction is crucial to the investigation of the truth claims of representational media imagery, especially **documentary** films, **cinéma-vérité** and television news (see **representation**). Because of the **indexical** quality of film and video reproductions of the real world, the **viewer** may mistakenly interpret **photography** and **sound** recordings of reality as real, factual or truthful.

Even the earliest non-fiction films had some degree of preparation, re-enactment, or outright fictional staging. Cinematic techniques – editing, **framing**, camera angle, lens choice, music, voice-over narration, special effects – can also contribute to the **reality effect**, or the equation of a filmed representation with its pro-filmic antecedent (see **pro-filmic event**).

See also: camera style and lens style; music and film

Further reading

Bazin, A. (1967) 'The Ontology of the Photographic Image', in *What Is Cinema?*, trans. H. Gray, Berkeley: University of California Press.

Tomasulo, F. P. (1996) ' "I'll See it when I Believe It": Rodney King and the Prison-House of Video', in V. Sobchack (ed.) *The Persistence of History: Cinema, Television, and the Modern Event*, London: Routledge.

FRANK P. TOMASULO

oppositional

Within film and television culture, the idea of oppositional practices in the production, distribution and exhibition of images gained currency in Britain and the United States in the 1970s. Drawing on Marxist analyses of culture as a site for intellectual struggle, oppositional practices challenged dominant cultural practices which were seen as determined by economic power. Films or programmes were made, for example, without the usual hierarchies of production, and distributed by not-for-profit organizations. Form and content challenged the dominant conventions, especially **realism**. Oppositional practitioners did not merely seek alternatives to the dominant modes but wished to challenge them, and to subvert them where possible.

See also: culture; dominant ideology; independent cinema; Marxist aesthetics

PHILIP SIMPSON

Orientalism

In his highly influential book *Orientalism*, Edward **Said** (1978) traces the history of the **representation** of the East by the West, focusing on the ways in which European, and specially French and British, academics, artists, novelists and colonial officials shaped and reinforced a **discourse** on non-western cultures, particularly Islamic countries and peoples, for use by western peoples. Essential to the production of such a discourse is an 'ontological and epistemological distinction made between "the Orient" and (most of the time) "the Occident" ' (Said 1978: 2).

According to Said, Orientalism constructed an inferior, backward, passive and irrational East by contrast with a superior, modern, active and rational West, in a representation that served to legitimize imperialism and now serves to legitimize post-colonialism. Robert Young has criticized Said for wanting to have it both ways, for arguing, on the one hand, that Orientalism is a misrepresentation, 'that has nothing to do with the Orient', and, on the other hand, that it was a sufficiently accurate representation for 'its knowledge' to be 'put in the service of colonial conquest, occupation, and administration' (Young 1990: 129). Despite Young's and others' criticisms, Orientalism has become a key concept in post-colonial studies and has been used in film and television studies to critique the representations of non-Europeans ranging from Arabs to the indigenous peoples of settler nations.

References

Said, E. (1978) *Orientalism*, New York: Vintage.

Young, R. (1990) *White Mythologies: Writing History and the West*, New York: Routledge.

ROBERTA E. PEARSON

ostranenie

A term coined in 1916 by Victor Shklovsky, *ostranenie* is one of the key concepts of Russian **Formalism**. It translates into English as 'defamiliarization' or, more literally, as 'making strange'. But even though *ostranenie* does refer to the phenomenon of **distancing**, it should not be confused with Bertolt **Brecht**'s 'V-effect'.

According to Shklovsky, our perception of the everyday world becomes automatized, and it is the function of art to 'make strange', or defamiliarize, so that it can be experienced afresh. This basic principle of deautomatization underlies the different functions which *ostranenie* has in Shklovsky's writings. First, it is a differentiating device allowing us to distinguish **art** from the objects of the everyday world. Second, it appears as an artistic device consisting in the creation of unusual perspectives, the use of uncommon expressions and other unaccustomed formal strategies. Shklovsky refers to the example of a Tolstoy short story which is narrated from the point of view of a horse. Third, in the course of time artistic devices themselves become automatized. In such cases, *ostranenie* intervenes as a sort of meta-device, reflecting on the habitualized forms and revealing the way they normally function. This specific phenomenon is also known as 'baring the device'. Finally, for Shklovsky *ostranenie* is also linked to the historical evolution of artistic forms. According to him, all art history is based on a dialectics of automatization and defamiliarization (see **dialectic and dialectical montage**). Art forms that once were original and innovative gradually become habitualized and establish a norm. However, Shklovsky argues that historical evolution is not a linear succession of artistic forms, formal innovation being inspired rather by 'minor' traditions, especially folklore and popular art. Thus *ostranenie* is not really a single concept, but can be seen as one basic principle – the deviation of a form with regard to an established and automatized norm – that Shklovsky uses as a theoretical tool on different levels of analysis.

In film theory, *ostranenie* has been reintroduced by neo-formalist scholars, together with other theoretical concepts of Russian Formalism like **syuzhet** and **fabula**. In the theoretical writings of David **Bordwell** and, more particularly, Kristin Thompson, *ostranenie* plays an important part. As the concept functions on different levels, it fits well into the neo-formalist project which aims at offering an approach to film analysis taking into account the historical context of individual works, while at the same time providing a general framework making explicit neo-formalism's basic theoretical assumptions. Neo-formalist analysis always looks at individual films against a background conceived as a norm. Given its historical prominence, classical Hollywood cinema functions as one of the most pervasive and most important normative backgrounds (see **classical Hollywood cinema and new Hollywood cinema**). However, it must be noted that for neo-formalism, *ostranenie* functions here as a heuristic principle, and not, as with Shklovsky, as a historiographic category (see **historiography**). On a more general level, neo-formalism uses *ostranenie* to define the nature of the artwork. Following rather closely the ideas formulated by Shklovsky, neo-formalism sees the function of art in defamiliarizing the habitual perceptions of the everyday world, while at the same time this assumption allows it to reject a communications model of art. Thus the concept of *ostranenie* enables neo-formalism to postulate a realm for art. Furthermore, it offers an intrinsic criterion, namely the relative complexity of form, to determine which objects are part of it.

Ostranenie is a concept with many different facets. Russian Formalism used it to refer to the functioning of formal aspects in a work of art as well as to patterns of change in art history, and to define the realm of art in opposition to everyday life. Neo-formalism imports it into film theory mainly as an immensely productive heuristic principle, but also in order to find an alternative to theoretical models based on linguistic or communicational concepts.

Further reading

Shklovsky, V. (1965) 'Art as Technique', in *Russian Formalist Criticism: Four Essays*, trans. and ed. L. T. Lemon and M. J. Reis, Lincoln: University of Nebraska Press.

Thompson, K. (1988) *Breaking the Glass Armor*, Princeton, NJ: Princeton University Press.

FRANK KESSLER

Other, the

The concept of the 'Other' has currency in philosophy and **psychoanalysis**, and is predominately used to refer to mechanisms of separation and projection. Othering refers to conceptualizing the unknown (another person, ethnic group,

gender group) as radically different from the self. Since the Other group is created as monolithic and homogeneous, no real contact with individuals can be established. The content of the Other can also be seen as a projection of disavowed or repressed aspects of the self.

The concept has been particularly useful in the analysis of **representation** in **science fiction** films and the media representation of **ethnicity**.

See also: Orientalism; Said, Edward

PETRA KUPPERS

P

panopticon

The panopticon, a prison design, is used by Michel **Foucault** (1977) to represent the operation of power within modern societies. In the panopticon (a central tower surrounded by cells), inmates are potentially always visible to the guard positioned in the centre, while this guard cannot be seen by them. Since inmates cannot be sure when they are being monitored, they behave as if they are constantly being watched.

Foucault's panopticon suggests that modern power operates through hidden surveillance which creates disciplined subjects. His arguments have gathered weight via the rise of **video** surveillance, and have been developed by Michel de **Certeau** (1988).

References

de Certeau, M. (1988) *The Practice of Everyday Life*, Berkeley: University of California Press.
Foucault, M. (1977) *Discipline and Punish: The Birth of the Prison*, London: Allen Lane

MATTHEW HILLS

paradigmatic

The terms 'paradigmatic' and '**syntagmatic**' are employed to describe different relations between sets of elements. Elements that are in a paradigmatic relationship bear a structural resemblance and can replace each other. In language analysis, different nouns can have the function of a subject in a sentence and so are in a paradigmatic relationship, whereas the word order subject–verb–object is defined by syntagmatic rules. The cognitive capacity to understand and employ paradigmatic relationships has been localized in a specific brain area and is closely linked to the ability to understand and employ metaphors.

See also: cognitive theory; metaphor

EVA VIETH

parody

Parody, according to Fredric **Jameson** (1991), is to modernism what **pastiche** is to post-modernism (see **modernism and post-modernism**). Parody relies on the imitation of a recognizable style or idiosyncratic mannerism, and is therefore well-suited to the texts of modernism with their distinctive authorial stamp. Of course, the parodic mode has also found targets in pre-twentieth century literature. James Joyce's *Ulysses*, itself a key modernist text, imitates the styles of Arthurian romance and newspaper headlines among many others, while in previous eras Jane Austen parodied Gothic conventions in *Northanger Abbey*, and Henry Fielding's *Shamela* explicitly mocked Samuel Richardson's novel *Pamela*.

In the post-modern epoch, Jameson argues, parody can no longer operate. Instead of the grand, individual styles of modernism, we are now faced with a vast proliferation of post-modern 'codes', or what Jean-François **Lyotard** calls 'language games'. A fragmented assortment of discourses, each specific to its own social group, has replaced the collective projects typical of modernity. In place of political enlightenment and the struggle for emancipation, we find 'micropolitics' of small-scale resistance; in place of the creative impulse towards experiment and originality which typified the great modernist texts, we find a grab-bag aesthetic of shameless copying and quoting (see **master narrative**).

With this loss of overarching linguistic and artistic norms, parody is stripped of its effect. Post-modernism would no longer recognize *Shamela* as a bawdy deviation from Richardson's 'original', but treat it as a text of no more and no less validity, simply another variation in a pick-and-mix collection of literary styles. Without universally accepted standards, parody is drained of its power to mock or burlesque, and so becomes pastiche. In Jameson's words:

> [Pastiche] is a neutral practice . . . without any of parody's ulterior motives, amputated of the satiric impulse, devoid of laughter . . . the producers of culture have nowhere to turn but to the past: the imitation of dead styles, speech through all the masks and voices stored up in the imaginary museum of a now global culture.
> (Jameson 1991: 17)

This is the aesthetic of Andy Warhol's mass-produced Campbell's soup cans and Roy Lichtenstein's Pop Art Picassos, of Disney's idealized 'Frontierland' and of Madonna's mid-1980s restyling as Marilyn Monroe. As Jameson's tone suggests, he by no means embraces this tendency; rather, he fears that, in addition to the loss of historical sense and originality, pastiche has none of the potential for critique or dissent which was inherent in parody.

In cinema, Jameson writes, pastiche characterizes the nostalgia film; whether this is in such texts as *Chinatown* (Roman Polanski, 1974) and *Raiders of the Lost Ark* (Steven Spielberg, 1981) which explicitly refer back to an earlier historical period and generic mode, or in *Star Wars* (George Lucas, 1977), with its evocation of the 'Saturday morning pictures' serial. The layers of citation have since become more complex as film and television texts gleefully borrow and borrow back from each other in a bewildering spiral of **intertextuality**. *Star Wars* itself is pastiched in *Judge Dredd* (Danny Canon, 1995), *Die Hard with a Vengeance* (John McTiernan, 1995) has Bruce Willis quoting the character he played in *Pulp Fiction* (Quentin Tarantino, 1994), while *Scream* (Wes Craven, 1996) offers a glimpse of a janitor dressed as *A Nightmare on Elm Street*'s (Wes Craven, 1984) Freddy Krueger. On television, *The Simpsons* has featured cartoon versions of *The X-Files*' Mulder and Scully, and an episode of the series *Friends*, set in London, guest-starred actors from the British comedy series *Absolutely Fabulous*.

These cross-references, as Jameson suggests, make no attempt at mockery or critique. We might question, however, whether they are genuinely 'empty' gestures, devoid of any purpose. Surely we can read into *Judge Dredd*'s pastiche an act of homage to George Lucas, just as the performance of a 'tribute' band flatters the original through its imitation. In the cases of *Scream*, *The Simpsons* and *Friends* cited above, the intertextual moment works as a visual gag or in-joke. Furthermore, we might argue not just for the role of homage and humour within this recycling but for the continued existence of a purely satirical mode which can absorb *Airport '77* (Jerry Jameson, 1977), *Top Gun* (Tony Scott, 1986) and *Star Wars* and mutate them into *Airplane* (Jim Abrahams, 1980), *Hot Shots!* (David and Jerry Zucker, 1991) and *Spaceballs* (Mel Brooks, 1987). In this light, to proclaim the death of parody seems premature.

References

Jameson, F. (1991) *Postmodernism: Or, the Cultural Logic of Late Capitalism*, London: Verso.

WILL BROOKER

parole

In Ferdinand de **Saussure**'s theory of language, *parole* – which is to be distinguished from both *langue* and *langage* (see **language/langue**) – names the realm of individual linguistic utterances. *La parole* is made possible, made meaningful, by the underlying structure that is *la langue*. When we use language in everyday contexts, that is to say, the condition of possibility of these statements (*la parole*) is *la langue*. Only by focusing on the latter could linguistics, for Saussure, discern the order in the mass of utterances. For this very reason, he argued, *la langue*, and not *la parole*, is the true object of study.

See also: semiotics

NEIL BADMINGTON

pastiche

Pastiche is generally regarded as a mixing of styles and achieves its effect through intertextual reference (see **intertextuality**), whereby a **text** borrows style, tone or form from another text or texts. In this sense, the concept shares a relationship with **parody**, but without the latter's connotations of ironic mimicry or negative allegiance. Pastiche, in rearticulating the source text in an affectionate or nostalgic manner, has thus elicited criticism as an ineffectual, non-subversive and non-**oppositional** sub-form of parody.

Conceptually part of the post-modern debate, pastiche nevertheless has earlier origins within the context of film and television studies (see **modernism and post-modernism**). One example is the Bugs Bunny cartoon, *What's Opera, Doc?* (Chuck Jones, 1957). In this eight-and-a-half minute animation, a pastiche (and parody) of Wagner's *Ring Cycle* is presented, in which 'high cultural' expectations of operatic **narrative** form and **mise-en-scène** are placed within a cartoon setting, with Bugs Bunny and Elmer Fudd affectionately and absurdly cast as Brünnhilde and Siegfried, respectively. Intertextual borrowing is further enhanced by the accompanying full orchestration provided by the then renowned Warner Bros Orchestra. While specific referential recognition is not essential for the pastiche to work, it does heighten appreciation as we acknowledge the numerous playful references and borrowings.

A more recent example is the animated television series *Beavis and Butt-Head*, which, although satirical in tone, has elements of pastiche within its narrative and stylistic form. Douglas Kellner (1995) provides a useful and entertaining exposition of the series, highlighting its derivatory lineage from source texts as varied as *Wayne's World*

(Penelope Spheeris, 1992) and the television series *The Simpsons* to *Mystery Science Theatre 3000*.

Within post-modernism, pastiche's metamorphosis of earlier texts clearly gives it a substantive role as shown, for example, in television series such as *The Simpsons* and *Third Rock from the Sun*, and in films like *Blade Runner* (Ridley Scott, 1982), *Star Wars* (George Lucas, 1977) and *Raising Arizona* (Joel Coen, 1987). Directed in 1982 by Carl Reiner and starring Steve Martin, *Dead Men Don't Wear Plaid* (1981) provides a pastiche of **film noir**, which overtly integrates original 1940s movie clips to construct, for example, a conversation between Steve Martin and James Cagney. Rather than ridiculing the earlier text, the intent of the new context is to generate humour and an affectionate tone.

A critical view of pastiche as integral to the growth of *la mode rétro* is held by Fredric **Jameson** (1988, 1991). Film and television productions are said to inauthentically replicate rather than reproduce history: a nostalgic referential focus lying in period atmosphere and style. Innovation, Jameson maintains, is thereby usurped by reworking, with 'real' history displaced by multiple pastiches offering a sanitized 'past' to the reader in place of actual experience.

Alternative evaluations of pastiche in film and television are, however, available. Jameson's critique of the age is countered by Jim Collins' (1992) emphasis on the 'knowing' rather than the gullible audience, when faced with pastiche within a post-modern text. Television especially proliferates signs, and identifying the inter-referentiality that such proliferation offers is enjoyed by the relatively sophisticated reader who, for Collins, can differentiate 'constructions' from 'reality'.

An inclination to reject pastiche as facile recycling, albeit without the bite of its near relatives parody and satire, is tempered by recognizing its increasing significance in contemporary productions.

References

Collins J. (1992) 'Television and Contemporary Criticism', in R. C. Allen (ed.) *Channels of Discourse Reassembled*, London Routledge.

Jameson, F. (1988) 'Postmodernism and Consumer

Society', in E. Ann Kaplan (ed.) *Postmodernism and its Discontents*, London: Verso.

—— (1991) *Postmodernism, or the Cultural Logic of Late Capitalism*, London: Verso.

Kellner, D. (1995) *Media Culture*, London: Routledge.

Further reading

Brooker, P. and Brooker, W. (eds) (1997) *Post-modern After-images*, London: Arnold.

Hutcheon, L. (1989) *The Politics of Postmodernism*, London: Routledge.

K. J. SHEPHERDSON

patriarchy

According to the *Oxford English Dictionary*, a patriarch is 'the father or ruler of a family or tribe'. The term 'patriarchy' has been taken up by radical feminists, who have used it to define the oppression of women by men. According to feminists like Kate Millett and Mary Daly, the oppression of women by men is the root and model for all other forms of oppression. Although this concept has been useful as a strategy in order to turn on its head the popular Marxist belief that the oppression of women by men is a mere side effect of an overarching **class** oppression, it can be problematic: it does not allow for historical changes, nor does it allow for cultural differences. Moreover, if patriarchy is an all-encompassing monolithic system, the struggle against it seems doomed from the start (see **Marxist aesthetics**).

For Jacques **Lacan**, a universal patriarchal system is put in place at the moment of entry into language (see **language/langue**): language is shaped by the universal symbolic, which, in turn, is governed by the **law of the father**. As a prerequisite of her entry into language as well as culture, a female subject must accept the fact of her **castration** that marks her as lacking (see **lack**), whereas meaning and fullness are embodied in the **phallus**. Looking at a woman, for a male subject within this system, evokes a fear of castration that is assuaged by fetishistic obsessions that disavow castration and by positioning woman as the

powerless and castrated **Other** to man (see **fetishism**).

This stress on looking and its connection with gendered power relations has made Lacanian **psychoanalysis** attractive for feminist film theory. Laura **Mulvey**, in her influential essay 'Visual Pleasure and Narrative Cinema' (1989), set out to 'fight the unconscious structured like a language while still caught in the language of patriarchy'. Mulvey regards classic Hollywood cinema as a means of gratifying the yearnings of a patriarchal **unconscious**. Cinema provides female stars as objects for fetishistic scopophilia and allows for an illusion of power for the anxious male spectator: he identifies with the male lead who functions as a kind of patriarchal super-ego. Female characters are doubly submitted to the powerful male look: that of the male film star and that of the spectator. They are defined by their 'to-be-looked-at-ness' (Mulvey 1989; see **gaze, the**).

Mulvey has been criticized by some feminist film critics because she does not allow for a female spectator who neither identifies sadistically with the male character nor masochistically with the female character. Some critics have attempted to carve out a more complex position for a female (especially a lesbian) spectator, while others have attempted to show that male spectators masochistically enjoy their disempowerment by a *femme fatale* or a **horror**-movie slasher.

However, feminist film theorists have analysed films not only as products of the patriarchal unconscious, but as products of a patriarchal society that display male-centred codes and conventions. This ties in with a concept of patriarchy not as universal phenomenon but as a 'system of social structures and practices in which men dominate, oppress and exploit women' (Walby 1990) that can vary from culture to culture, and change within time. This leaves room for changes in cinema's images of women. For example, Molly Haskell, in *From Reverence to Rape* (1987), shows how the character of female film stars changes according to the changing needs of society: strong women during the Second World War; passive housewives or doomed *femmes fatales* in the 1950s. This approach avoids constructing a monolithic patriarchy, but it can lead to another constriction: women's roles in film are seen as a mere reflection of changes in society. A deconstructive approach following Judith **Butler**'s contention that **gender** is a performance, and rigid gendered identities can be subverted by ironic performances might, for feminist film theorists, provide a way out of the impasse caused by concepts of psychological or social patriarchy (see **deconstruction**).

See also: feminist theory

Referencs

Haskell, M. (1987) *From Reverence to Rape: The Treatment of Women in the Movies*, Chicago: University of Chicago Press.
Mulvey, L. (1989) 'Visual Pleasure and Narrative Cinema' (first published 1975), in Laura Mulvey, *Visual and Other Pleasures*, Basingstoke and London: Macmillan.
Walby, S. (1990) *Theorising Patriarchy*, Oxford: Blackwell.

ANTJE LINDENMEYER

Peirce, Charles Sanders

b. 1839; d. 1914

As the founder of pragmatism, Charles Peirce's philosophical work was supported and popularized (and somewhat misconstrued) by the philospher William James. To film and television studies, Peirce has contributed one of the most open and subtle **semiotics**, or theory of signs. Peirce believes that although we directly encounter many objects, knowledge of them comes to us by interpreting signs or other impressions of reality. Basic interpretations occur through sense perceptions. Peirce gives the example of a child feeling a stove: heat causes the child to draw back his/her hand, thus becoming a sign of the stove for the infant. Peirce describes three types of signs: **icon**, index or symbol. An icon is related to its object mainly by its similarity or likeness to it; an index by its existential bond – as a weathercock relates to the wind; and a symbol has an arbitrary relationship – an apple symbolizing temptation, for example. The iconic is the most pertinent category for film and

television studies as it includes photographs (**photography**).

See also: indexical; sign; symbolic code

Further reading

Peirce, C. (1982) *Writings of Charles S. Peirce: A Chronological Edition*, Bloomington: Indiana University Press.

GABRIEL M. PALETZ

performance theory

Performance theory is hybrid. Like contemporary film and media theory, it can be related to the proliferation of epistemological paths associated with post-modernism (see **epistemology; modernism and post-modernism**). Approaches employed in the field include Marxist theory, feminism, **phenomenology** and **semiotics** (see **feminist theory; Marxist aesthetics**).

The first problem performance theory encounters is the definition of its fleeting and transitory object, 'performance'; it is past, lost, unrecoverable in the moment that it happens. Each moment of a theatre performance can only be experienced in its presence, and cannot be recreated in the next evening's performance. This insight into the working of performance has had effects in television studies and, consequently, in film studies. An initial focus on the **text** had to be broadened to encompass the whole viewing situation, including **audience**, reception situation and connotations (see **connotation; reading and reception theory**). In his article, 'Invasions Friendly and Unfriendly: The Dramaturgy of Direct Theatre', performance theorist Richard Schechner writes of television news:

> Television news is not made to be kept. . . . It is a multilayered, throwaway flow of images and words combining on-the-spot action with sophisticated editing and framing procedures to create a narrativised and ritualised product.
> (Schechner 1992: 104)

In the article, Schechner explores the making of direct theatre in carnivalesque moments, mediated to a world stage through television (see **carnival**). The moments that he analyses include the fall of the Berlin Wall and the run up to the massacre of pro-democracy demonstrators in Tiananmen Square. By drawing attention to the meanings of rituals, performance theory worries at the same knot which has long occupied media scholars: how can political representation appear in the commodifying stream of television images (see **commodification**)?

Although performance theory centres on the meanings of live performed actions, it shares the insights of semiotic and post-structuralist thinking (see **structuralism and post-structuralism**). Theorists explore the instability of **binary** systems of signification by redeploying Brechtian techniques. Bertolt **Brecht**'s drama theory aimed at the creation of an **epic** theatre, in which identification with the characters was constantly broken by the use of **distancing** effects. Actors addressed the audience directly or shifted between characters, shattering the illusion of a contained realist stage world (see **realism**). The audience had to make sense of the proceedings, not just passively receive an illusion. This obliged the audience to question the 'received wisdom' of their social reality. Film scholars like Peter **Wollen** and Colin MacCabe (see **classic realist text**) have taken up the belief in the political potential of non-realist, alienating cinema.

Performance scholars such as Jill Dolan or Sue Ellen Case have argued that these effects can break through ideological constellations, for instance the binary of **gender**. By showing how each gender position is constructed, the sense of a 'natural' gender position is undermined. These anti-essentialist insights can be linked to Judith **Butler**'s notion of performativity (see **performative**) in gender and Donna **Haraway**'s notion of the cyborg. Film theory writing has taken up these images to explore how hybrid, liminal figures can be seen to disrupt conventional gender representations.

Performance theorist Peggy Phelan uses absence in performances and the function of alienation as her starting point for an investigation of 'visibility politics', merging the concerns of performance and film theory. Drawing on Lacanian frameworks, she shows how performance articulates the impossibility of the subject being seen (see **Lacan, Jacques**). As **psychoanalysis** suggests, the 'I' is forever marking its own loss. Deploying performance paradigms, Phelan re-reads feminist film theory and its attempts to refigure representations of active female subjectivity. She shows how Yvonne Rainer's or Jeannie Livingstone's films can be fruitfully explored through the performative absence of a clear subjectivity:

> Subjectivity can only be 'had', that is to say, experienced and performed (through the performance one has the experience of subjectivity), in the admission and recognition of one's failure to appear to oneself and within the representational field.
>
> (Phelan 1993: 91)

Instead of constructing a female gaze different to the male gaze, the absence of possibility within this system of visibility becomes apparent (see **gaze, the**.

These forms of re-writing from different disciplinary positions can enrich and revivify a theoretical impasse in film and television theory.

References

Phelan, P. (1993) *Unmarked. The Politics of Performance*, London: Routledge.

Schechner, R. (1992) 'Invasions Friendly and Unfriendly: The Dramaturgy of Direct Theatre', in J. G. Reinelt and J. R. Roach (eds) *Critical Theory and Performance*, Ann Arbor: Michigan University Press. (This book includes a wide selection of texts on performance theory by various writers.)

PETRA KUPPERS

performative

While developing the method for analysis of communication later called speech act theory, the philosopher J. L. Austin differentiated communicative expressions into constative speech acts – expressions that describe reality – and performative speech acts –. expressions or, rather, verbal actions that achieve a change of reality by being expressed. The latter are usually bound to the use of performative verbs/formulas such as 'I promise' or 'I now pronounce you husband and wife'. Though speech act theory was influential in the 1960s and 1970s, from the 1980s onwards other theories of communicative actions that – unlike speech act theory – place more importance on the communicative situation have rendered most of Austin's assumptions obsolete. But the notion of performativity has been taken up within cultural studies, most notably in Judith **Butler**'s notion of **gender** as a performed rather than an essentialist attribute.

EVA VIETH

persistence of vision

The term 'persistence of vision' is imprecise in explaining the illusion of movement and the continuity of images in film, but it is often seen as the fundamental optical phenomenon of cinema. In basic terms, it centres on the idea that an image is retained in the eye, or brain, for a short period of time after it is removed from the viewer and then merges into the next image. The phenomenon can be observed when a light is whirled around in the darkness leaving a continuous trace rather than being seen as a moving point.

One of the first studies in this area was by the Frenchman Chevalier d'Arcy who made a series of experiments with a piece of burning coal attached to a revolving wheel, and this was cited in a memoir to the Academie des Sciences in 1765. The study of this optical effect was continued by Peter Mark Roget in 1824, and developed by others including Joseph Plateau and Michael Faraday. Toys such as the phenakistoscope, the praxinoscope and the zoetrope, all used the phenomenon of turning single static images into the illusion of continuous movement, forming an important part of the technological basis of cinema.

The mechanics of film projection means that a series of images are projected on to a screen in rapid succession, alternating with a moment when light from the projector is blocked from the screen by a shutter. If the projection is rapid enough (usually at anything above twelve frames a second) then an illusion of continuity from one image to the

next will occur. This is usually associated with movement. A similar process happens when watching video or television. However, although there will be a continuity from image to image, flicker will be observed unless the rate of images is increased to approximately fifty images per second. To reduce flicker to a minimum, film projectors have shutters which break the light twice while the frame is projected, thus each frame of a film is projected three times on to the screen.

Persistence of vision is a term which has been used very loosely to describe the illusion of movement in film, but in fact it only refers to the fusion of one image into another, and has nothing to do with motion itself. The effect has been more accurately described by psychologists as 'positive afterimages'. As a way of explaining the illusion of motion in cinema, the term has been challenged, particularly by psychologists Susan J. Lederman and Bill Nichols (1981). They dismiss the unscientific claims made by many writers on film, and suggest that the impression of motion is dependent on two distinct perceptual phenomena: *visual flicker* and *apparent motion*.

Visual flicker, or critical flicker fusion, relates more specifically to ideas of persistence of vision, in that if a beam of light is broken more than fifty times a second the viewer cannot detect the interruptions and thus sees the light as continuous. This fusion of the separate images or beams of light is known as critical fusion frequency (CFF). Nichols and Lederman stress the fact that fusion 'creates the impression of a solid, stable world of successive images, *but does not yield the impression of movement*'.

Apparent motion is the term used to describe the visual phenomenon to see movement when there is none. An example of this is to be found in fairground lighting or neon lighting on advertising signs where a fixed line of lights going on and off in succession can give the illusion of a single moving light. This effect was first noted by the psychologist Max Wertheimer in 1912, and became known as the 'phi phenomenon'. David Bordwell and Kristin Thompson in *Film Art* (1995) refer to more recent research which suggests that apparent motion is connected to 'motion analysers' in the human visual system rather than in the process of unconscious thought as previously suggested.

References

Bordwell, D. and Thompson, K. (1995) *Film Art* (5th edn), New York: McGraw Hill.

Nichols, B. and Lederman, S. J. (1981) 'Flicker and Motion in Film', in B. Nichols, *Ideology and Image*, Bloomington: Indiana University Press.

NICK BURTON

perspective

When looking at a scene, closer objects appear to be larger than objects in the distance, even when they are both the same size. Parallel receding lines will appear to converge. This optical law is known as 'perspective', and forms the basis for what might be considered a convincing representation of a three-dimensional space on a two-dimensional surface by giving an illusion of depth. Aerial perspective, the hazing of background planes, can also add to this illusion.

Linear or monocular perspective was theorized during the Renaissance, particularly with the development of lenses and the portable camera obscura. The camera obscura, a darkened room or light-tight box with an aperture to let in light, produces an image of the scene outside on the opposite surface from the aperture. This allowed an opportunity to produce an image automatically, giving a scientifically logical representation of the world, and one which *seemed* highly realistic. In fact, the system was described by some, including Leonardo da Vinci, as a way of recording life by placing a piece of glass between a viewer and a scene and tracing the world in view on the glass.

Perspective can be seen as a system that binds the viewer and the world subtended by the screen together. Monocular perspective fixes the viewer on a single point of vision, as da Vinci proposed by his example of a pyramid of view, with the point at the eye. David **Bordwell** (1985) suggests that, with this system, the distance between objects can be measured, as well as the distance between the scene and the viewer. Perspective places the audience in one particular point of view. With the frame, this gives a kind of rational 'window on the world', a neutral and scientifically logical space where the viewer is invisible.

The central perspective image has depth that relates to the way we see, by offering us a single vanishing point where parallel receding lines appear to converge. Artists were able to use this system to construct images which had a mathematical precision, and this representation of the world became so powerful and seemingly natural that it was taken as the unquestioned way to translate reality within western culture. The invention of **photography** in the nineteenth century offered a mechanical and chemical method of fixing this reproduction of reality on to a two-dimensional surface, without any apparent human interference or interpretation. Cinematic movement of these photographic reproductions of perspective heightened the sense of **realism**.

Heath (1981) and Neale (1985) argue that this powerful impression of reality was, and is, simply an ideal. Actual vision and perception is usually binocular, not monocular, and the viewing processes rely more on scanning than receiving the image as a whole. In addition, it does not work within the essentially curvilinear nature of the sphere of vision. However, the impression of the naturalized 'realistic' world within the frame meant that film was a very suitable medium for naturalism (see **naturalism and non-naturalism**). Through perspective, we can suspend our disbelief very adequately, and Neale (1985) adds that perspective is designed to 'please the scopic drive, the desire to see, to gaze, to look'. Bordwell (1985) considers perspective in broad terms, relating it to the mimetic developments of theatre and literature during the sixteenth and seventeenth centuries and the move towards creating realistic worlds and characters (see **mimetic/mimesis**).

The focal length of a lens can influence perspective relations in a shot (see **camera style and lens style**). A 'normal' lens (50mm for 35mm film) is thought to approximate normal human vision in terms of perspective. But changes in scale relations between the background and foreground with different lenses can influence the meaning of a visual text. Only extreme distortion of normal perspective relations will upset the believability of the image.

Perspective remains one of the key ingredients to entice us into the constructed world on the screen.

See also: depth of field; space/place

References

Bordwell, D. (1985) *Narration in the Fiction Film*, London: Methuen.

Heath, S. (1981) *Questions of Cinema*, London: Macmillan.

Neale, S. (1985) *Cinema and Technology: Image, Sound, Colour*, London: Macmillan.

NICK BURTON

phallus

A complex and politically-charged concept, the phallus is to be distinguished from the penis as bodily organ. For **Freud**, the phallus indicates the symbolic value of the penis: namely, its status as privileged term, one of a series of objects – breast, faeces – that 'fall away' and thus situate the infant within the intersubjective world of exchange. The phallus is to be seen as 'in circulation', not something that the child unproblematically 'has' or does not 'have'. The problem then arises – articulated most forcefully by feminist theorists – as to this privileged status: does it arise from the historical/cultural specificity of **patriarchy**, or is it invariant over time? Freud clearly wants to hold to the latter view.

Jacques **Lacan**, by interpreting **castration** as the loss of the object via symbolization, is able to salvage this universality by making the phallus constitutive of language itself. For Lacan, the phallus is the signifier of signification itself, in so far as language is constituted by both **difference** and **lack**. Recently, **queer theory** has argued that the phallus only 'takes shape' against the background of the repressed formlessness of the anal.

See also: law of the father; psychoanalysis

ANGELO RESTIVO

phenomenology

Phenomenology is the philosophical study of phenomena as they present themselves to human **consciousness** (literally, knowledge of appear-

ances). Although pioneered by J. H. Lambert (as early as 1764), Immanuel **Kant**, George Friedrich **Hegel**, William Hamilton, Eduard von Hartmann, Alexander Pfaender, Charles Sanders **Peirce**, Franz Brentano and others, Edmund Husserl is generally regarded as the founder of modern phenomenology. Later phenomenologists such as Heidegger, Jaspers, Marcel, **Merleau-Ponty** and Sartre became more influential. In **aesthetics**, George Simmel, Roman Ingarden, Michel Dufrenne and Theodor Lipps enlarged the field of phenomenolgy to include literature and art criticism.

Intended to be a presuppositionless founding methodology, phenomenology entails the detailed description of concrete human experiences, especially the non-passive, 'intentional' aspects of consciousness as it confronts being. Because pre-existing attitudes taint our experiences and perceptions, Husserl proposed a preliminary 'reduction' or 'bracketing' step by which the world was held in abeyance, so to speak, in order to focus on the act of consciousness itself. During this step, all ontological claims about existence – our taken-for-granted, **common sense**, everyday experiences and perceptions – are suspended or put into parentheses (see **ontology**). Thereafter, attention needed to be paid 'to the things themselves' (Husserl's watchword), because we encounter consciousness only in its encounter with reality; in short, consciousness must be consciousness of something. Things are the direct objects of consciousness in its purified form, and phenomenology limits one to the data presented in consciousness – to describing rather than explaining – in search of incontrovertible experience.

Phenomenology is therefore neither completely subjective nor entirely objective (see **objectivity**), because we do not arbitrarily, as pure subjects, inject meaning into the *Lebenswelt* (life-world) we experience; neither does reality impose any particular meaning on the act of consciousness or the subject (see **subject and subjectivity**). Furthermore, consciousness is not merely individual or solipsistic; it is also social. Husserl accounted for this in his concept of intersubjectivity and Maurice Merleau-Ponty summarized it thus: 'Truth does not "reside" only in the "inner man," or rather there is no inner man; man is in the world, it is in the world that he knows himself.'

In film and television theory, phenomenology has been used to analyse **authorship**, **representation** and meaning. It has also been used to supplement the aesthetic dimension of a given work and to explain the nature and dynamics of the cinema experience itself, especially the activity or passivity of the viewer. Merleau-Ponty went so far as to call the cinema a 'phenomenological art', in that it utilized the primacy of perception as its chief conveyor of information.

In film **theory**, André **Bazin**, Christian **Metz** and Jean Mitry are associated with phenomenology, although their eclectic viewpoints are far from the pure phenomenology of Husserl.

Further reading

Andrew, D. (1978) 'The Neglected Tradition of Phenomenology in Film Theory', *Wide Angle*, vol. 2, no. 2, pp. 44–9.

Bazin, A. (1976) *What Is Cinema?* (first published 1967), 2 volumes, trans. H. Gray, Berkeley: University of California Press.

Casebier, A. (1992) *Film and Phenomenology: A Realist Theory of Cinematic Representation*, Cambridge: Cambridge University Press.

Husserl, E. (1970) *Logical Investigations* (first published 1900), New York: Humanities Press.

—— (1962) *Ideas: General Introduction to Pure Phenomenology* (first published 1913), New York: Collier Books.

—— (1931) *Cartesian Meditations* (first published 1931), The Hague: M. Nijhoff.

Sobchack, V. (1992) *The Address of the Eye: A Phenomenolgy of Film Experience*, Princeton, NJ: Princeton University Press.

Tomasulo, F. P. (1988) 'The Text-in-the-Spectator: The Role of Phenomenology in an Eclectic Theoretical Methodology', *Journal of Film and Video*, vol. 40, no. 3, pp. 20–32.

FRANK P. TOMASULO

phoneme

'Phoneme' is a linguistic term denoting the smallest abstract sound unit that can be isolated from the stream of sounds of language and that has a potentially distinctive (meaning-differentiating) function. Phonemes can be isolated via the formation of minimal pairs: for example, the minimal pair *cat*/*mat* isolates the phonemes /m/ and /c/ as different phonemes of English. All languages use only a fragment of all possible phonemes; the combination of a fixed set of meaningless phonemes into an unlimited number of meaningful units is one of the universal strategies of human languages. Cinema semioticians, seeking parallels between cinematic meaning-making and verbal language systems, have concluded that there is no filmic equivalent to the phoneme. The shot is the smallest and least divisible of filmic units, yet conveys far more meaning than a linguistic phoneme.

See also: semiotics

EVA VIETH

photography

Photography relates to film and television – particularly film – on a number of historical and theoretical levels. First, cinema has a technological basis in photography: films consist of still photographs shown in rapid succession in such a way that human perception registers continuous movement (see **persistence of vision**). Thus a frame of a motion picture negative is essentially the same as the negative of a still photograph. Film allows for enhancements and variations which take it beyond photography – drawing on film, computer-generation of unphotographable scenes, etc. – and there are elements of film which lie outside of the photographic (**sound**, for example). But film began in photography and continues to have its basis there.

Film also partakes of photography's qualities of **realism**; accordingly, all of the many theoretical and even philosophical debates that have grown up around the photographic image also have a bearing on film. The old adage that 'the camera never lies' has, informally, been carried over to film, while critics of that idea have maintained that in fact the photographic image (moving or still) has to be understood as a creation – not a neutral, perfect replica of reality, but a selective, partial representation of it. This argument succeeds easily in the case of deliberately faked or manipulated images; more radically, it suggests that the camera, like the paintbrush, is a tool of art and of the interpretation of reality, not an instrument of perfect replication.

Television production may or may not involve photography as such. Some programmes are produced on film, while others are produced on videotape or broadcast live. None the less, television shares with film an underlying basis in photo-reproductive technology. Therefore, theorists of television, too, have taken an interest in the issue of photorealism and the status of the medium as an objective recorder and/or interpretive instrument of reality. (Indeed, the phenomenon of **live television**, which bypasses traditional phases of image preservation and the physical editing of preserved material, makes these questions at least as central to television as they are to film.)

Another level of relation between film and photography is that of subject matter: a number of noteworthy and influential films have dealt directly with photographic processes, and in some cases have achieved the status of theoretical essays in their own right. Hitchcock's *Rear Window* (1954), for example, concerns a photographer whose camera lens aids him in his **voyeurism**; the film has been called '[a] brilliant filmic essay on the cinema and on the nature of the cinematic experience' (Stam 1985: 43). Antonioni's *Blow-Up* (1966) involves a photographer who unknowingly captures the body of a murder victim on film. *Blow-Up* explores the relation between photographic and sensory evidence, and has been interpreted by critics as a commentary on the nature of photographic representation. The **avant-garde** film *Nostalgia* [Tarkovsky 1983] consists entirely of shots of photographs, one at a time; each photograph burns before our eyes, while a narrator reads a verbal description of the next one. *Nostalgia* thus engages questions of photography – and cinema – as a medium of truth, **representation**, **memory** and permanence.

References

Stam, R. (1985) *Reflexivity in Film and Literature from Don Quixote to Jean-Luc Godard*, Ann Arbor: University of Michigan Press.

Further reading

Bazin, A. (1967) 'The Ontology of the Photographic Image', in A. Bazin, *What is Cinema?*, volume 1, trans. Hugh Gray, Berkeley and Los Angeles: University of California Press.

DAVID A. BLACK

pleasure

Since the 1960s, the issue of pleasure has been central to media studies, especially as the popular or mass cultural text often produces a kind of 'unreflective' pleasure not traditionally accounted for by **aesthetics**. In the first wave of semiotic- and psychoanalytically-oriented **theory**, the pleasure accorded to the spectator by the classical Hollywood film was suspect because it unthinkingly reproduced dominant (and oppressive) ideological values (see **dominant ideology; psychoanalysis; semiotics**). Thus, in her article 'Visual Pleasure and Narrative Cinema', Laura **Mulvey** (1975) argues that the pleasures of classical Hollywood cinema are available solely to the spectator who assumes a complicity with that cinema's essentially patriarchal **mode of address** (see **patriarchy**). She views the destruction of that erotic pleasure as an important political goal (and by-product) of theoretical analysis. More generally, the **binary** opposition perceived between an aesthetic of pleasure and an aesthetic of **distancing** characterizes a large part of 1970s film theory, leading to a critical position labelled by D. N. Rodowick (1988) as 'political modernism'. However, increasing interest in **oppositional** reading practices (among minorities and subcultural communities), as well as the knowingly ironic viewing positions created by post-modern media products, have led to revaluations of the issue of pleasure in recent film theory (see **modernism and post-modernism**).

Psychoanalysis has been a privileged theoretical discourse in the analysis of pleasure because it sees psychic life as governed by 'the pleasure principle'. In **Freud**'s first model of the psychic economy, the life of the instincts is governed by the pleasure principle, so that the continual internal pressure of the instincts seeks immediate discharge regardless of consequences in the real world. Thus the pleasure principle stands in opposition to the 'reality principle', which seeks to 'bind' the pressure of the instincts so that they can be gratified in socially acceptable ways. In this model, the particularities of **unconscious** processes such as **condensation** and **displacement** can be accounted for by the fundamental disequilibrium produced by these two conflicting ways of handling the energy of the instincts.

However, Freud later encountered the paradoxical clinical fact that seemingly painful symptoms were actually producing unconscious pleasure. Thus, in *Beyond the Pleasure Principle*, Freud revised the early model, so that both the pleasure and reality principles were aligned opposite the death drive. Freud grounds the death drive in the notion that in all complex biological systems, there is an entropic force always pushing towards dissolution of the highly bound energies in the organism.

This suggests that there is another, more radical form of pleasure, which Jacques **Lacan** has termed **jouissance**. Roland **Barthes** mobilizes this Lacanian concept in his analysis of **narrative** fiction: for Barthes, classical narrative produces what he calls the 'text of pleasure', while transgressive modernist narrative produces the 'text of *jouissance*'. Barthes, however, blurs this distinction and shows that through certain kinds of reading practice, the pleasures of the classical text can be radically 'exploded', turning it into a text of *jouissance*.

In the 1990s, Lacanian theorist Slavoj Žižek argued that the post-modern cultural product has a particular affinity for rendering *jouissance*. From the slimy creatures of *Alien* (Ridley Scott, 1979) to the subterranean ants in *Blue Velvet* (David Lynch, 1986), the images in post-modern works often immerse us in the extreme enjoyment of the death drive, while a pulsating, organic Dolby soundtrack seems to blur the boundaries between the inside and the outside of the body. Psychoanalysis links this post-modern fixation on the drives to a more general crisis in the **law of the father** brought about by the organization of capitalism around consumption.

See also: castration

References

Mulvey, L (1975) 'Visual Pleasure and Narrative Cinema', *Screen*, vol. 16, no. 3, pp. 6–18.
Rodowick, D. N. (1988) *The Crisis of Political Modernism*, Urbana: University of Illinois Press.

Further reading

Barthes, R. (1975) *The Pleasure of the Text*, New York: Hill and Wang.
Žižek, S. (1992) *Enjoy Your Symptom!*, New York: Routledge.

ANGELO RESTIVO

plot

The plot in a film or television programme **narrative** can be understood as all the formal and stylistic elements presented in image and sound to make meaning. This is the material actually before the viewer, presented in the order of the film but not necessarily in chronological order. This is unlike the **story**, which can be put together by the audience mentally as a linear set of events – even if they are presented by the plot as, for example, a series of flashbacks (see **flashback**). The plot can also include non-diegetic elements such as music or credits (see **diegesis**).

See also: fabula; syuzhet

NICK BURTON

point of view shot

A point of view shot (POV shot) is one in which the camera is set up to approximate the visual perspective associated with a protagonist or group of protagonists. While this type of play with perspective dates back to early silent cinema, the POV shot is still employed for specific effect in contemporary productions. In one of cinema's joyous anomalies, *Lady in the Lake* (Robert Montgomery, 1946), almost the entire film is structured according to a succession of POV shots.

Further reading

Branigan, E. (1984) *Point of View in the Cinema: A Theory of Narration and Subjectivity in Classical Film*, New York: Mouton.

ANDREW UTTERSON

polysemic

'Polysemic' is a term used to describe the many 'semes', or meanings, that **discourse** always contains. Any **sign** system can be interpreted in different ways, depending on the reader's or viewer's perception. Yet all signs are also 'disciplined' – by the captions in a photograph, or by the way an image corresponds to dominant cultural norms – so as to encourage certain readings. Richard **Dyer**'s characterization of the star image as a 'structured polysemy' incorporates this notion, as does John **Fiske**'s analysis of television to describe the ways programmes are made to mean as much as possible to as many different groups as possible. Polysemy demonstrates the potential for signifying systems to escape their intended meanings, but also that some readings may always be subordinate to others.

See also: audience; code; encoding-decoding model; hierarchy of discourses; semiotics; text

ADRIENNE L. McLEAN

popular, the

As work in cultural studies and social theory has increasingly affected critical practice in film and television, meanings of 'the popular' have become so diverse that its use requires explanation for all but delimited audiences. Cultural elitists have for centuries equated 'popular' with 'debased'. At least as early as the French Revolution, democrats and egalitarians gave the term a more positive meaning, that of being admirable because favoured by the many. In the modern period, with the rise of commodity culture (see **commodification**), 'popular' has been defined in more commercial terms; defenders of the market liken consuming to voting and hence argue that market choice is 'popular' in the sense of being democratic. This line of thought often emanates from executives in the film and television industries, less frequently from the cultural workers within them.

'Popular' has also been used as an adjective preceding '**culture**', although as Raymond Williams (1983) points out, 'Popular culture was not identified by *the people* but by others' (Williams' italics). Williams found an early usage of 'popular culture' in the late eighteenth century, in references to folk culture, 'the culture actually made by the people for themselves'. For some idealist thinkers, this culture articulated the essential character of a people or nation (see **national, the**). Only later was 'popular' extended to the culture consumed by 'the people', but made by elites and their employees. A strain of popular culture studies in the United States has argued that what qualifies profitable commercial culture as 'popular' culture is that so many people like it. According to this argument, enduring forms such as the **melodrama** or the Western (see **Western, the**) can be seen as symptomatic myths of, say, the heterosexual-based nuclear family or masculine individualism and the frontier. Elided in such analyses are matters of marketing, distribution and how profitability is determined, as well as problems of mediation and **representation**, and of power and hegemony (see **ideology and hegemony**), not to mention complexities of audiences, **difference** and reception (see **reading and reception theory**).

It was to exclude such meaning from 'popular culture' and 'mass culture' that the members of the **Frankfurt School** refused their use for anything but what Theodor **Adorno** (1975) described as a 'culture that arises spontaneously from the masses themselves, the contemporary form of popular art'. For them, 'the popular' could be realized only in communities or in a society democratic and egalitarian enough to allow for its expression. In that sense, it functioned as a utopian standard against which contemporary relations could be measured (see **utopia and dystopia**). Accordingly, productions of the capitalist culture industry could never be 'popular' because they were not egalitarian.

Contemporary cultural studies, developed during decades of new social movements since 1968 (and again since 1989), abandons what was a traditional Marxist view of 'popular culture' as the expression of working-class experience and interest (see **Marxist aesthetics**). Instead, cultural studies conceptualizes 'the popular' in neo-Gramscian terms (see **Gramsci, Antonio**) as a field of struggle between multiple subordinated forces and the deployment of state and economic power ('the power-bloc'), a field on which meanings and purposes are contested, or at least can be. Yet despite rejection of the centrality of **class**, this use of 'the popular' remains within a left-wing framework, in which the oppressed continue to be the historical subjects of emancipation. For example, cultural studies tends not to use 'the popular' to describe the Klu Klux Klan, violent sports or neo-fascist discourse, unless it precedes it with an adjective such as 'racist', 'masculinist' or 'right-wing'.

Stuart **Hall** (1981) embeds 'the popular' historically. He locates the term within the centuries-long tradition of struggle of working people and the poor, based on their social position. This 'popular tradition' resisted the processes by which the 'constitution of a whole new social order around capital required a more or less continuous, if intermittent, process of re-education'. For Hall, these ' "transformations" are at the heart of the study of popular culture'. Seeing popular culture as either folk culture or imposed commercial culture misses the point: 'Popular culture is neither, in a "pure" sense, the popular traditions of resistance to these processes; nor is it the forms which are superimposed on and over them. It is the ground on which the transformations are worked'. A similar approach remains useful for studying film and television in contemporary societies marked by advanced oligarchic capitalism. 'There is a continuous and necessarily uneven and unequal struggle, by the dominant culture, constantly to disorganise and reorganise popular culture; to enclose and confine its definitions and forms within a more inclusive range of dominant forms.' This engenders resistance by subordinated groups – at best conscious and strategic, at least the passive resistance of inertia.

While such efforts can be seen as heroic, these struggles are never simply **binary**, for the subjects on both sides of the power divide are themselves fragmented and contradictory, with different relations to power at different moments. Helen Taylor's (1989) study of women's reception of *Gone with the Wind* (Victor Fleming, 1939) shows how a culture industry phenomenon affects its subjects in highly diverse ways. Among them, some speak of the aspirations of the oppressed (here, in terms of **gender**), and some speak of the aspirations of the oppressor (here, in terms of **race**). Even that formulation oversimplifies, however, for within each person, on each topic, there can be a mixture of emancipatory and oppressive responses, as each makes the culture meaningful in diverse terms. For cultural studies, then, 'the popular' includes these processes of making meaning as well as the modes of production and distribution of, in this case, a best-seller and Hollywood super-production, modes in the foreground for traditional left-wing criticism (see **mode of production**).

A more stratified definition focuses on differentiation between what is of the people and what is not of the people, for Hall, between 'what belongs to the central domain of elite or dominant culture, and the culture of the "periphery" '. Yet, as Hall argues, such an opposition founders if it does not take into account that the cultural '*contents* of each category changes' (Hall's italics), in processes of appropriation on both sides of the divide. In order for the categories to be maintained, cultural institutions (college courses, museums, reviews, publicity) work to differentiate between the two, but their dichotomies inevitably shift and slide. Containing this slippage becomes all the more difficult as post-modern consciousness, rejecting traditional cultural hierarchy, increasingly proliferates as **common sense** among the young (see **modernism and post-modernism**).

Of course, arguments about what constitutes 'the popular' also turn on defining 'the people', which seems harder in a time of such fragmentation. Like Hall, John **Fiske** (1990) views 'popular' culture not as the culture of a given empirical group, but as a process that relates to the production of culture within a stratified society. Fiske characterizes 'the people' as a 'relational social force' involving categories and classes that can be occupied by the same person at different times, within a 'general set of forces that oppose the power-bloc'. Each person can move in and out of the realm of 'the people', depending on the category they fill at any given moment (for instance, an executive in her office may be subordinate to her husband at home). Popular culture, then, 'consists of practices which evade, resist, turn or make use of the mechanisms of power and the associated systems that distribute both cultural and material resources' as audiences 'expropriate relevant meanings and pleasures'. Fiske seems to equate 'the popular' with each person's 'own interests' against their subordination, a complex connection, as Taylor's research shows, and one difficult to disentangle from reinforcement of an individualism that esteems whatever a person in a subordinated position happens to enjoy.

While bourgeois culture (for example, most museums and art galleries) treasures disregard for function, Fiske's 'popular' values works that offer 'information for living'. This incorporation into the 'micro-struggles that are part of daily life' not only fills a place in the lives of the audience, but the lives of 'the people' seem to appear in the cultural products themselves. In the television show *21 Jump Street*, one of the actors addresses the audience directly, out of character, and describes what to do in situations of domestic violence like the one dramatized on the show. For Fiske, this illustrates how popular culture crosses over from the **diegesis** of the television show that is scripted and acted into the world of viewers on the other side of the screen, as 'popular realism is raided for its relevance'.

Audiences, in this view, move fluidly between the diegesis of television shows and what happens to them on their side of the screen. Christine Gledhill (1997) observed this in her study of women viewers of soap operas (see **soap opera**). Viewers become involved in the community of the fictional world because they feel its patterns parallel their own lives and experiences. Fiske calls this textual quality 'real-seemingness', which he distinguishes from **realism** because it is relational rather than a textual form. Relevance makes a programme seem real; if it seems real, then there must be some relevance to daily life. This can be true even if at every moment audiences are aware that they are consuming and working on constructed images with purposes other than their own. In this way, 'the people' take what is presented by the power-bloc, and form it into something that is useful against subordination, and therefore make it partly theirs. Popular culture becomes a resource, with benefits that reinforce audience investment in viewing. As Gledhill says: 'Pleasure comes not from the text alone, but from the extension of the text into the thinking, communicating activity and skills of the viewer'.

To sustain its power, commercial culture must seem current and relevant; it must respond to popular struggles, co-opting them perhaps but also offering resources for popular audience response. Engaged as popular culture, commercial culture's products play a part in a social system that circulates ideas, meanings and movements. Cultural creation depends on this interwoven form. Gledhill notes that,

> Multiple pressures towards innovation and renewal mean that popular genres not only engage with social change but also become key sites for the emerging articulation of and contest over change. So the discourses and imagery of new social movements – for example, the women's, gay, or black liberation movements – which circulate into public consciousness through campaign groups, parliamentary and social policy debates, new and popular journalism, and other media representations, provide popular genres with material for new story lines and the pleasures of dramatic enactment.
>
> (Gledhill 1997: 362)

This explains how soap operas have (and have not) changed in response to the women's movement. Advertiser-supported programmes limit the range of changes to those expected to attract and not repel the women they want to bundle for sale to corporations. Not surprisingly, to engage contemporary women, soap opera makers need to allow female characters measures of control not usually allowed in society, or in other popular genres that focus less on women as the primary audience. As Gledhill points out, the soap operas to which women attach importance have become an important part of women's culture because of the large number of women who watch and think and communicate about them. But in an important way these programmes also need to be thought of as women's culture because they are made to appeal to women, drawing on 'female cultural competence', the cultural codes women employ. Soap opera has become an enduring element in some women's lives, and it could be argued that this results from women's power to influence commercial culture to form a **genre** that is specifically their own.

But is it their own? Is this women's genre empowering or does it reinforce subordination? Or both? If both, which matters more for feminism? Gledhill describes women's subject positions, points of empowering intelligibility for soap opera texts (see **subject and subjectivity**). Their pleasure gives these moments of empowerment – or rather, virtual empowerment – greater appeal. Still, do they not also function as psychological compensation for compliance with the social order? In what way and to what extent, then, do women base more of their own identities on their sense of representations of women in their favourite soap than on their own positions in matrices of power? Popular entertainment elicits audience identification (the 'blurring of the lines') for a point of view on the characters and events it represents, and it often represents, as autonomous, positions that social critics would define as subordinated. It thus becomes a potential site for increased subordination to the extent that viewers find these fictional positions real-seeming and identify with them. This seems especially true of the commercials that motivated US soap operas in the first place, commercials which Gledhill ignores even when she talks about the US soaps. Perhaps viewers identify this pleasure with soap opera viewing, binding them even more to the set and its representations. Soap operas undoubtedly contribute to ideas of feminine and masculine identity in society, reinforcing available gender stereotypes entwined with subordination (see **stereotype**). Contemporary soap operas tend to be very different from what we might imagine a feminist soap opera to be, let alone one in which gender subordination and individualism have been overthrown. Yet even soap opera today gives women a socially acknowledged reason to carve out a bit of leisure space and time from inequitably divided work in the home.

Cultural studies tends to resist the view that popular engagement with commercial culture is unlikely to be empowering, seeing this assessment as elitist pessimism. Instead, it insists that the range of possibilities for making meaning is precisely the zone of tension where the popular can be found. What makes commercial film and television popular for these analyses is its necessary passage from the control of its industrial makers to that of its consumers, in all their diversity, as they rework meanings for their own use. In Fiske's words: 'The text's original production (that is, its arrangement of signifiers on the page/screen/airwaves) may well be part of the cultural and economic practices of the power-bloc, but its reading or (re)production occurs in the everyday world.' Yet this world also includes effects and relations whose relevance might be less visible in the moment of reception: acquiescence to war and growing police power, global inequalities, waste, deteriorating and increasingly hazardous physical environments (including the detergents and their packaging hawked on some commercial soap operas), consumption-driven labour and personal debt, thefts of time from friends and loved ones. Also included in this world, but papered over in this culture, are the deleterious effects that political resistance on the part of new social movements has made increasingly visible, such as homophobia, racism and sexism.

With the expansion of the global media environment and the proliferation of receivers of commercial culture, popular culture in the cultural studies sense incorporates ever more parts of more people's lives everyday. Yet evidence for how this has tilted the balance for the subordinated and against the powerful and privileged has been less than overwhelming, while evidence to the contrary, such as growing inequalities of wealth and the increasing commercialization of politics, accumulates all too fast. There are exceptions, and these might one day multiply, radicalizing the valence of what this culture can accomplish. Especially worth considering are efforts by political groups to create popular culture of a different sort, experiences that organize their audiences for change, as have been produced by women's, labour, anti-racist, anti-homophobic, and other groups. This culture is hardly popular in a demographic sense, but it does seek democratic and egalitarian transformation. New and cheaper means of production and distribution allow for a potential explosion of works rooted sufficiently in communities that the term 'popular culture' might well apply, no matter the audience size. Academic cheerleading for the progressive potential of commercial culture validates engrossment in the demographically popular, just as belief in the emancipatory potential of some modernist culture validated attention to those works for earlier generations of socially conscious critics. Still, while commercial culture hypocritically pretends to speak for the people, the lie of modernist culture was not so much the emancipatory claims of its aesthetics as its denial of overlap with relations of property and consequent refusal of the possibility of aesthetic practices in the everyday. Hall and others are right that the designation of 'the popular' is a political act. Traditional elitists and partisans of commercialism, understandably, have no guilty conscience about calling industrial film and television 'popular culture'. For those who envision the popular as a site where people struggle to end subordination, however, the term might more often be held in reserve.

References

Adorno, T. W. (1975) 'Culture Industry Reconsidered', trans. Anson G. Rabinbach, *New German Critique*, vol. 6, pp. 12–19.

Fiske, J. (1990) 'Popular Narrative and Commercial Television', *Camera Obscura: A Journal of Feminism and Film Theory*, vol. 23, pp. 132–47.

Gledhill, C. (1997) 'Genre and Gender: The Case for Soap Opera', in S. Hall (ed.) *Representation: Cultural Representations and Signifying Practices*, London: Sage.

Hall, S. (1981) 'Notes on Deconstructing the Popular', in R. Samuel (ed.) *People's History and Social Theory*, London: Routledge and Kegan Paul.

Taylor, H. (1989) *Scarlett's Women: Gone with the Wind and its Female Fans*, New Brunswick, New Jersey: Rutgers University Press.

Williams, R. (1983) *Keywords: A Vocabulary of Culture and Society*, New York: Oxford.

Further reading

Bourdieu, P. (1984) *Distinction: A Social Critique of the Judgement of Taste*, trans. R. Nice, Cambridge, MA: Harvard University Press.

James, C. L. R. (1993) 'Popular Arts and Modern Society', in A. Grimshaw and K. Hart (eds) *American Civilization*, Oxford: Blackwell.

Löwenthal, L. (1961) *Literature, Popular Culture, and Society*, Palo Alto: Pacific Books.

Marcuse, H. (1968) 'The Affirmative Character of Culture', in *Negations: Essays in Critical Theory*, trans. J. J. Shapiro, Boston: Beacon Press.

McRobbie, A. (1994) *Postmodernism and Popular Culture*, London: Routledge.

Modleski, T. (1983) 'The Rhythms of Reception: Daytime Television and Women's Work', in E. A. Kaplan (ed.) *Regarding Television*, Frederick, MD: American Film Institute-University Publications of America.

Warshow, R. (1970) 'The Gangster as Tragic Hero' and 'Movie Chronicle: The Westerner', in *The Immediate Experience: Movies, Comics, Theatre and Other Aspects of Popular Culture*, New York: Atheneum.

Wright, W. (1975) *Sixguns and Society: A Structural Study of the Western*, Berkeley: University of California Press.

KATIE PANTAZIS AND CLAY STEINMAN

pornography

This entry cannot begin with a simple definition of its subject, for the act of definition has been one of the most contested areas in discussions of pornography. The term itself is not an objective label for a particular group of texts which already have something in common. Rather, different definitions produce different understandings of what pornography actually is. For example, the distinctions between pornography and erotica, **art** and **violence** are being constantly reinvented, and texts are placed and replaced within these categories. Each of these terms carries particular assumptions about the function of texts, and their relationships to wider **culture** and 'society'. However, nobody can finally agree on how to spot a **text** which is, or is not, pornographic.

The dominant approach to understanding pornographic texts in cultural theory has been a feminist one, which insists that the most important aspects of these texts is their construction of **gender** (see **feminist theory**). Since the 1970s, a particular brand of feminist writing has defined pornography as a group of texts which are not only sexually explicit, but which are also degrading to women. The best-known writers in this tradition are Catherine McKinnon and Andrea Dworkin. Using the term 'sexual objectification', these writers argue that pornography causes, creates and indeed *is* a culture in which violence against women is accepted.

The issue of definition becomes central here – for writers in this tradition define pornography as texts which show women in violent and degrading ways. This definition excludes from consideration sexually explicit representations which are not explicitly violent, and which do not feature women (for example, gay male pornography, and sexually explicit representations of men for a female audience). In these arguments the relationship between the consumption of pornography and violence against women is often raised, although it appears that the large amount of scientific research into this popular question has been unable to establish any such link (Longford 1972). In a way, though, this is a red herring – for McKinnon, pornography does not simply promote (physical) violence against women, it *is* (cultural) violence against women.

This position on the function and effects of pornography has been challenged on several counts, including that:

1 the definition is self-fulfilling. If pornography is defined as images of violence against women, then study of these texts will find violence against women.
2 Much of this writing assumes that the desire to see sexually explicit imagery is an essentially masculine attribute – it does not allow for the possibility that women might have any such sexual desire.

In the 1990s, other ways of discussing pornography emerged, challenging the focus on gender and power relations as the only paradigm for approaching these texts. For example, studies of gay male pornography have suggested the ways in which this has helped to form communities. These new approaches are linked by their examination of 'pornography' not as a series of texts with unique and identifiable characteristics, but as a discursive category, which changes and serves different purposes over time. Thus, the concerns of feminist writers about pornography need not be understood as the function of a particular group of texts: rather, pornography might exhibit particular structures of looking which are also apparent in other cultural sites (such as advertisements, for example).

The changing nature of pornography, meanwhile, suggests that rigid definitions do not well serve discussions of this area: the emergence of the male stripping act the Chippendales, the continuing growth of pornographic magazines for women, and the immense popularity of the sexually explicit Black Lace range of novels for women suggest that definitions which insist on pornography's necessary tendency to degrade women are ill-founded.

See also: censorship

References

Longford Committee Investigating Pornography (1972) *Pornography: The Longford Report*, London: Coronet Books.

Further reading

Dworkin, A. (1981) *Pornography: Men Possessing Women*, London: The Women's Press.
Waugh, T. (1996) *Hard to Imagine: Gay Male Eroticism in Photography and Film From Their Beginnings to Stonewall*, New York: Columbia University Press.
Williams, L (1989) *Hard Core: Power, Pleasure and the 'Frenzy of the Visible'*, Berkeley and Los Angeles: University of California Press.

ALAN McKEE

praxis

The concept of 'praxis' broadly refers to a 'unity between spontaneity and conscious direction'. Analogous to the relationship between **theory** and practice, a radical praxis engenders a direct correspondence between concepts and ideas with actual, lived experiences of oppression. Antonio

Gramsci's (1971) use of the phrase 'philosophy of praxis', ostensibly as a code word for Marxism intended to elude the attention of his prison censors, places a crucial emphasis on praxis as the basis for making moral and political judgements. Such judgements, to have validity, must always be concretized in relation to reality – as opposed to referring only to objective, 'extra-human' laws of history. Debates about how best to elaborate on Gramsci's approach to praxis have been extended across film and television studies, particularly with regard to various efforts to develop a critical pedagogy.

See also: common sense; ideology and hegemony; Marxist aesthetics

References

Gramsci, A. (1971) *Selections From the Prison Notebooks*, New York: International.

Further reading

Femia, J. V. (1987) *Gramsci's Political Thought*, Oxford: Clarendon Press.

STUART ALLAN

preferred reading

Though producers of texts can never be sure that the **audience** will share an intended meaning, texts can be produced in such a way that **oppositional** or alternative readings are discouraged. Through the way the **text** is structured, the reader or spectator is encouraged to adopt a preferred reading, rather than to negotiate a wider range of potential meanings. However it is more evident in some texts than others: an 'open' text allows for ambiguity, whereas a 'closed' text will have a strongly prescribed preferred meaning. Furthermore, reception theory suggests that no text can carry inherent meaning in itself.

See also: reading and reception theory

DEBORAH JERMYN

pre-Hollywood cinema

Film scholars have over the past few years constructed a rough chronology in which the first two decades or so of cinema history – approximately from 1894, the year of the first commercially successful moving pictures, until approximately 1917, the year when 'modern' cinematic conventions became fairly standardized – is called the 'pre-Hollywood cinema', the term attesting to the world-wide hegemony that the American film industry achieved after the First World War. Scholars further break this period down into two subsidiary periods: (i) the early or 'primitive' cinema, from approximately 1893 to 1907, in which films looked very much different from today and may be fairly inaccessible to a modern audience unaccustomed to the period's cinematic conventions; and (ii) the 'transitional cinema', from approximately 1907 to 1917, in which dominant conventions emerged though did not yet become standardized.

Until the 1970s film historians almost entirely ignored this period, writing only of the few 'authors' such as Edwin S. Porter, D. W. Griffith and Charles Chaplin who were seen as the relatively primitive precursors of the great directors to follow. But in 1978, FIAF (the International Federation of Film Archives) brought together a group of film scholars and archivists in Brighton in the United Kingdom (home of the Brighton School of English filmmakers) to survey the surviving fiction films from the years 1900 to 1906. The Brighton conference provoked further interest in the early cinema and established a credo for subsequent investigations: these films were separate but equal, worthy of study in their own right, not simply as detours or signposts on the road to the classical Hollywood cinema (see **classical Hollywood cinema and new Hollywood cinema**). In the first post-Brighton years, the early cinema movement concentrated primarily on textual analysis, cataloguing the techniques and style of the pre-1907 cinema. But, as historians moved forward in time to the transitional cinema, they broadened their concerns to include production, reception and the larger cultural/social context of the period. This brief overview of the pre-Hollywood cinema begins by looking at the industries, it then proceeds to texts and concludes with a section on audiences.

Industry

Various nations lay claim to the invention of moving pictures, but the cinema, like so many other technological innovations, has no precise originating moment and owes its birth to no particular country and no particular person. In the last decade of the nineteenth century, inventors/ entrepreneurs in several countries presented their publics with the 'first' moving pictures: Thomas Edison in the United States; the Lumière brothers in France; Max Skladanowsky in Germany and William Friese Greene in the United Kingdom. None of these men can be called the primary originator of the film medium, however, since only a favourable conjunction of technical circumstances made such an 'invention' possible at this particular moment: improvements in photographic development; the invention of celluloid, the first medium both durable and flexible enough to loop through a projector, and the application of precision engineering and instruments to projector design. But pride of place must be given to the Lumière brothers who are frequently, although perhaps inaccurately, credited with projecting the first moving pictures to a paying audience.

Owners of a photographic equipment factory, August and Louis Lumière experimented in their spare time with designing a camera that they dubbed the 'cinematograph'. In December of 1895, they executed their most famous and influential demonstration of their new invention, projecting ten films to a paying audience at the Grand Café in Paris. The cinematograph's technical specifications initially gave it several advantages over its competitors in terms of production and exhibition. Its relative lightness made it able to function as a camera, a projector and a film developer, and its lack of dependence on electric current (it was hand-cranked and illuminated by limelight) made it extremely portable and adaptable.

The Lumière travelling cameramen used the adaptable cinematograph to shoot, develop and project films, this practice pointing to a key distinction between the early period and the studio system in which the industry attained the specialization and division of labour characteristic of large-scale capitalist enterprises. Initially, production, distribution and exhibition all remained the exclusive provenance of the film manufacturers while American studios such as Edison and Biograph usually supplied a projector, films and even a projectionist to the vaudeville houses that then constituted one of the primary exhibition sites. As opposed to the strict division of labour and assembly-line practices that characterized the Hollywood studios, production during this period was non-hierarchical and collaborative. One of the most important of early film 'directors', Edwin S. Porter, who had worked as a hired projectionist and then as an independent exhibitor, joined the Edison Company in 1900, first in the capacity of mechanic and then as head of production. Despite his nominal position, Porter actually controlled only the technical aspects of filming and editing while other Edison employees with theatrical experience took charge of directing the actors and of the **mise-en-scène**. Early in the transitional period, studios, following the practice of the theatrical industry, hired directors who were initially simply in charge of the actors but whose responsibilities quickly broadened to include supervising other emerging specialists such as scriptwriters, property men and wardrobe mistresses. Soon, the bigger American studios employed several directors, giving each his own cast and crew and requiring him to turn out one fifteen-minute reel a week. This required the creation of yet another job category, the producer, who oversaw the whole process, co-ordinating among the individual units.

During the early cinema period, exhibition was integrated into pre-existing venues of what might be termed 'popular culture' and 'refined culture', the establishment of specifically filmic exhibition venues not coming until 1905 in the United States and a little later in most other countries. In the United States, films were shown in the popular vaudeville houses, which by the turn of the century catered for what could loosely be called a middle-class audience, or at least to people willing to pay 25 cents for an afternoon's or evening's entertainment. Travelling showmen, who lectured on educational topics, toured with their own projectors and showed films in local churches and opera houses, charging their audiences, at least in large metropolitan areas, the same $2 that it cost to see a Broadway show. Cheaper and more popular venues included tent shows, set up at fairs and carnivals, as well as temporary shows at rented storefronts, the forerunners of the famous nickelodeons. Early film audiences in the United States, therefore, tended to be quite heterogeneous, dominated by no one class. Early exhibition in Britain, as indeed in most European countries, followed much the same pattern, with primary exhibition venues being fair grounds, music halls and disused shops. Travelling showmen played a crucial role in establishing the popularity of the new medium, making films an important attraction at fairgrounds. Given that fairs and music halls attracted primarily working-class patrons, early film audiences in Britain, as well as on the Continent, had a more homogeneous class base than in the United States.

The practice of selling rather than renting films worked fairly well for the travelling showmen who perforce changed their audiences from show to show, but militated against the establishment of permanent exhibition sites, dependent on attracting repeat customers from the same neighbourhood through frequent programme changes. Having to purchase a large number of films made the latter practice prohibitively expensive. The new 'film exchanges' which began to appear in the United States *circa* 1903, solved this problem by buying the films from the manufacturers and renting them to exhibitors, making permanent exhibition venues feasible and increasing the medium's popularity. Improvements in projectors also facilitated the rise of the nickelodeons, so called because of their initial admission price of a nickel, since exhibitors no longer had to rely on the production companies to supply operators. By 1906, nickelodeons were, in the popular phrase of the period, springing up like mushrooms in every city in the United States. Cinema-specific venues appeared slightly later in European countries than in the United States, but by the early teens on both sides of the Atlantic smaller sites such as the nickelodeon began to give way to larger, more comfortable theatres, the precursors of the lavish picture palaces that dominated exhibition during the cinema's 'golden age' of the 1920s, 1930s and 1940s.

At the beginning of the First World War, the film industry's production and distribution practices look relatively familiar from a twenty-first century vantage point, but there was one vital difference. Prior to the First World War, it was European not American firms that dominated global markets, with France the strongest exporter and Italy occupying a favourable market position as well. A figure of around 60 to 70 per cent of all the films imported into the United States and other European countries were of French origin. Pathé, the strongest of the French studios, forced into aggressive expansion by the relatively small domestic demand, established offices in major cities around the world, supplemented them with travelling salesman who sold both films and equipment, and, as a result, dominated the market in countries that could support only one film company. American manufacturers initially concentrated primarily on the domestic market, but had begun an international expansion that resulted in their being well-placed to step into the number one position in 1914 when European film industries reeled from the effects of the First World War. In 1907 Vitagraph became the first of the major American firms to establish overseas distribution offices, but in 1909 other American producers established agencies in London, which remained the European centre for American distribution until 1916. The devastation the war left in its wake permitted American firms to build on their pre-existing international distribution and the US industry quickly established the dominant global position that it still enjoys today.

Texts

The key distinction between early cinema and the subsequent transitional and classical cinemas is that the early filmmakers tended to preserve the spatial and temporal unity of what film scholars call the **pro-filmic event**, that is, the action which takes place in front of the camera. Until roughly 1907, filmmakers concerned themselves primarily with the individual shot, preserving the spatial aspects of the pro-filmic event rather than using cinematic intervention to create temporal relations or story causality. They set the camera far enough from the action to show the entire length of the human body as well as the spaces above the head and below the feet, kept it stationary except for occasional reframings to follow the action, particularly in exterior shots, and fairly infrequently intervened through such devices as editing, lighting or camera angles. This long-shot style is often referred to as a tableau shot or a proscenium arch shot, the latter appellation stemming from the supposed resemblance to the perspective an audience member would have from the centre front row of a theatre. Concerning themselves primarily with the individual shots, early filmmakers tended not to be overly interested in connections between shots, that is, editing, and hence did not elaborate conventions for linking one shot to the next, for constructing a continuous linear **narrative** and for keeping the viewer oriented in time and space. Until 1902–1903, the majority of films consisted of one shot and were what we would today call documentaries, known then, after the French usage, as actualities (see **actuality**). By 1903–1907, the multi-shot, fiction film gradually began to dominate, with simple narratives structuring the temporal and causal relations between shots. However, some of these films' editing patterns look rather strange from the perspective of the dominant conventions that were to emerge later. To a modern eye one of the strangest of editing devices is overlapping action, which results from filmmakers' desire both to preserve the pro-filmic space and to emphasize the important action by essentially showing it twice. Georges Méliès' *A Trip to the Moon*, perhaps the most famous film of 1902, covers the landing of a space capsule on Earth's satellite in two shots. In the first shot, taken from 'space', the capsule hits a grinning and then grimacing man in the moon in the eye. In the second shot, taken from the 'moon's surface', the capsule once again lands. These two shots, which seem to show the same event twice, first from 'space' and then from the 'moon's surface', can disconcert a modern viewer, who may conclude that Méliès mistakenly failed to trim the few frames from the head of the second shot that would have made the sequence accord with the cinematic representation of a continuous, linear time expected by today's audiences.

By contrast to the one to two minute time of the early films, the average film of the transitional period reached a standard length of a 1,000-foot reel and ran about fifteen minutes in length. The increased use of editing patterns that resemble and presage the conventions of the classical Hollywood cinema together with the abandonment of the tableau shot for three-quarter shot framing most obviously distinguish these films from those of the early period. The decreased distance between action and camera contributed to the increased emphasis on individualized characters and facial expression, as did editing, used both to emphasize moments of psychological intensity and to externalize characters' thoughts and emotions. Crucial in the transition to the classical cinema was the emergence of psychologically credible characters, created through performance style, editing and dialogue intertitles, whose motivations and actions seemed realistic and helped to link together a film's disparate shots and scenes. In this period also, conventions for linking the different spaces of one scene together and orienting the viewer spatially became established practice, as filmmakers no longer insisted on preserving the integrity of the pro-filmic event, but rather created an artificial cinematic space through editing.

The emerging conventions of the transitional period created internally coherent narratives and decreased reliance on intertextual references that facilitated viewer understanding. The early cinema must be seen in the context of the rich popular culture of the age, drawing heavily during its infant years on the narrative and visual conventions of the other forms of entertainment with which audiences would have been familiar. Vaudeville, with its variety format of unrelated acts and lack of concern for developed stories, constituted a very important source material and, in general, the earliest filmmakers relied on such media as the **melodrama** and pantomime (emphasizing visual effects rather than dialogue), magic lanterns, comics, political cartoons, newspapers and illustrated song slides. Many of the early multi-shot films depend on audiences' pre-existing knowledge of the subject matter rather than on cinematic conventions for the requisite narrative links between shots. For example, *L'Epopée Napoléonienne* (Pathé, 1903–1904) presents Napoleon's life through a series of tableaux, drawing on well-known historical incidents (the coronation, the burning of Moscow) and anecdotes (Napoleon standing guard for the sleeping sentry) but with no attempt at causal linear connection or narrative development among its fifteen shots. Filmmakers of the transitional period continued to use well-known sources for inspiration, but used cinematic conventions to create spatial and narrative links between shots.

Audiences

Since the great bulk of research on the pre-Hollywood cinema has focused on the United States, this last section deals only with that country, although many aspects of the American experience of the introduction of the new cinematic medium were paralleled in European countries. In the early cinema period the dominance of the non-fiction film, redolent of the didacticism beloved of the Victorians and Edwardians, exhibition in 'respectable' venues (vaudeville and opera houses, churches and lecture halls) and a mixed class audience kept the new medium from posing a threat to the cultural *status quo*. But the triumph of the story film *circa* 1905 and the concomitant rise of the nickelodeons resulted in a sustained assault against the film industry by state officials and private reform groups. The industry's critics asserted that the dark, dirty and unsafe nickelodeons showed unsuitable fare, were often located in tenement districts and were patronized by the most unstable elements of American society: workers, immigrants, women and children who were all too vulnerable to the physical and moral hazards posed by the picture shows. Although we have no truly accurate information on the subject, most impressionistic reports seem to agree that, in urban areas at least, audiences were predominantly working class, many were immigrants, and sometimes a majority were women and children. While the film industry asserted that it provided an inexpensive distraction to those who had neither the time nor the money for other entertainments, reformers feared that 'immoral' films – those which dealt with crime, adultery, suicide and other unacceptable topics – would unduly influence these most susceptible of viewers and worse yet, that the promiscuous mingling of races, ethnicities, genders and ages

would give rise to sexual transgressions. State officials and private reform groups devised a variety of strategies for containing the threat posed by the rapidly growing new medium. The regulation of film content, mandating what could and could not be shown on the screen, seemed a fairly simple solution and in many localities reformers called for official municipal **censorship**. Far more effective and long lasting than externally imposed censorship was the industry's own self-monitoring, begun in 1909 with the founding of the National Board of Censorship, which in 1913 became the National Board of Review. State and local authorities also devised various ways of regulating the exhibition sites. The so-called 'blue laws', which prohibited certain activities on the Christian Sabbath, were invoked to shut the nickelodeons on Sundays, often the wage-earners' sole day off and hence the best day at the box office. Authorities also struck at box-office profits through state and local statutes forbidding the admission of unaccompanied children, and thus depriving exhibitors of a major source of income. Zoning laws were used to prohibit the operation of nickelodeons within close proximity to schools or churches. In counter-attacking, the industry attempted to form alliances with influential state officials, educators and clergymen by offering evidence (or at least making assertions) that the new medium provided information and clean, amusing entertainment for those otherwise bereft of either education or diversion. The more powerful members of the industry did not resist, and indeed often encouraged, the incorporation of health and safety requirements into local ordinances dictating the construction of new exhibition venues and the upgrading of old ones. By 1913, the year in which New York City passed a major ordinance regulating the construction of new exhibition venues, the battle for respectability had been largely won and cinema was well on its way to becoming the mass medium of the first half of the twentieth century. But debates over the regulation of film content through self-censorship and/or government censorship continue to this day.

Further reading

Abel, R. (ed.) (1996) *Silent Film*, New Brunswick: Rutgers University Press.

—— (1998) *The Cine Goes to Town: French Cinema 1896–1914*, Berkeley: University of California Press.

Bowser, E. (1990) *The Transformation of Cinema, 1907–1915*, New York: Charles Scribner's Sons.

Chanan, M. (1980) *The Dream that Kicks: The Prehistory and Early Years of Cinema in Britain*, London: Routledge and Kegan Paul.

Elsaesser, T. (ed.) (1990) *Early Cinema: Space, Frame, Narrative*, London: BFI Publishing.

Gunning, T. (1991) *D. W. Griffith and the Origins of American Narrative Film: The Early Years at Biograph*, Chicago: University of Illinois Press.

Musser, C. (1990) *The Emergence of Cinema: The American Screen to 1907*, New York: Charles Scribner's Sons.

Pearson, R. E. (1992) *Eloquent Gestures: The Transformation of Performance Style in the Griffith Biograph Films*, Berkeley: University of California Press.

Stokes, M. and Maltby, R. (eds) (1999) *American Movie Audiences: From the Turn of the Century to the Early Sound Era*, London: BFI Publishing.

Thompson, K. (1985) *Exporting Entertainment: America in the World Film Market, 1907–34*, London: BFI Publishing.

Uricchio, W. and Pearson, R. E. (1993) *Reframing Culture: The Case of the Vitagraph Quality Films*, Princeton: Princeton University Press.

ROBERTA E. PEARSON

prime time

In the United States, prime time refers to the portion of the television schedule, between 8.00 p.m. and 11.00 p.m. with an extra hour on Sunday (Gitlin 1994), and between 7.00 p.m. and 10.00 p.m. in Britain (Fiske 1987), when the largest and/or relatively affluent audiences are most likely to be watching. On commercial television, it is during this period that **advertising** costs are highest since television companies compete for high ratings by providing programmes which are most likely to attract the biggest audiences or those with large disposable incomes.

Marketing surveys (based on age, income, **gender**, education, etc.) are undertaken on a continual basis by companies such as the Statistical Research Incorporated and its Systems for Measuring And Reporting Television (SMART) system and Neilsen Media Research's 'Neilsen Ratings' in the US. In Britain, audience data is collected by enterprises such as RSMB Television Research through its Broadcasters' Audience Research Board (BARB) Television Audience Measurement. All of these organizations claim to provide advertisers with a clear picture of shifting demographics of different television programming timeslots. This information is particularly important in terms of reaching large groups of consumers during the peak prime-time viewing period when advertisers are seeking to reach specific audiences for their products. The publicly-owned British Broadcasting Corporation (BBC) is also interested in obtaining information about audiences in order to verify the popularity of its programming and therefore defend its operations based on a universal broadcasting licence fee.

From the early 1970s until the mid-1990s, the American Federal Communications Commission (FCC) regulated media ownership and programming via its 'fin-syn' rules (financial interest and syndication), its aim to restrict the major television networks from producing more than 20 per cent of their own prime-time programming. Fin-syn rules sought to encourage diversity in media ownership and output. In 1993, a US District Court ruled that since ownership and content diversity had been achieved, fin-syn rules were no longer needed to safeguard against the formation of network monopolies.

In Canada, the state regulator, the Canadian Radio and Television Commission (CRTC) has been mandated since the 1970s to ensure that there is a minimum percentage of 'Canadian content' in prime time by regulating the amount of non-Canadian (especially US) content on Canadian television (both commercial and public stations). Media commentators note that Canadian content regulations, particularly severe during prime time, have been an important factor in the development of indigenous Canadian media and audiences for Canadian television programming.

In Britain, the government's Family Viewing Policy is used to regulate content on both public service and commercial television, stipulating that in early prime time (until 9.00 p.m.), programming must be suitable for 'family viewing' (that is, minimal swearing, sex and violence). After the 'nine o'clock watershed' (see Paterson 1980) it is assumed that children will either be in bed or that their television viewing will be directly controlled by their parents.

See also: audience; broadcasting, the United Kingdom; broadcasting, the United States; children and media; deregulation, the United Kingdom; deregulation, the United States

References

Fiske, J. (1987) *Television Culture*, London: Routledge.

Gitlin, T. (1994) *Inside Prime Time*, London: Routledge.

Paterson, R. (1980) 'Planning the Family: The Art of the Television Schedule', *Screen Education*, vol. 35, pp. 79–85.

Further reading

Ang, I. (1991) *Desperately Seeking the Audience*, London and New York: Routledge.

Kottak, C. P. (1990) *Prime-Time Society: An Anthropological Analysis of Television and Culture*, Belmont, CA: Wadsworth.

CYNTHIA CARTER

proairetic code

One of five codes deployed by Roland **Barthes** in analysing the way a realist literary text disguises its artifice and is made to seem a 'natural' form. Interplaying with the hermeneutic, cultural, symbolic and semic codes, it is part of a process that draws in the reader. The proairetic (action) code organizes the sequence of events or actions forwarding the **narrative**. A woman reads a letter, a man searches a room: these actions are recognizably like events in the real world but are literary devices. The proairetic code is particularly effective in Hollywood cinema.

See also: hermeneutics; realism; symbolic code

PHILIP SIMPSON

pro-filmic event

Literally everything 'before the film', the pro-filmic event consists of whatever is placed before the camera to be filmed. The pro-filmic therefore includes the **mise-en-scène** generally – actors and their movement and performance styles, lighting, sets and props, costume and make-up. It always functions in concert with the limits placed, by **framing** and editing, on the spectator's access to the events that the camera records. Because the pro-filmic event is constructed of time and space as well as the objects that inhabit them, and because the *mise-en-scène*, framing, camerawork and editing are chosen, and therefore imply a point of view, the pro-filmic event must be considered to be narrational – constructing the story world for specific effects.

See also: cinema of attractions

ADRIENNE L. McLEAN

projection

In its technical sense, projection is the diffusion and magnification of successive film frames onto a screen. Pre-cinematic devices, such as the zoetrope, offered individual viewers the illusion of movement; however, it is only with projection, as a means of amplifying this illusion, that the cinema can be said properly to exist.

In **psychoanalysis**, projection operates as a defence against excessive, therefore unpleasurable, internal stimuli. It involves the projection onto others, in almost cinematic fashion, of unconscious images (qualities, feelings or wishes) that a subject refuses to recognize in him or herself.

See also: Freud, Sigmund; image; Lacan, Jacques; persistence of vision

PAUL SUTTON

propaganda

Propaganda, at its simplest, means the dissemination of information. It is the promotion of ideas or concepts with the intent to influence a specific **audience**. The term has been applied to a diverse range of activity in film and media practice to include the institutionalized efforts of government 'information agencies', the attempt to manage or shape the reporting of news events or the techniques of **advertising**. All of these examples share a common objective or purpose: to persuade their targeted audience to endorse and/or act on the intended message. The pejorative nature of the term lies in its emphasis on persuasion with intent to benefit the sender of the message with little or no regard for accuracy or **objectivity**. There are three broad ranges of propaganda: white, grey and black. These ideologically-loaded terms provide not only a means of categorization but reflect the moralistic discourse which surrounds the term. Each of these categories is determined by the reliability, or identifiability, of the source of the information. 'White' is where the source of the information is known and the information generally accurate, such as the majority of the reportage during the Gulf War. 'Grey' propaganda's source is not clearly known and the information is unreliable. Jowett and O'Donnell (1986) give the example of the Voice of America's denial of CIA involvement in the Bay of Pigs invasion in Cuba as grey propaganda. An information source that presents a false identity to impart deceptive and inaccurate information is a form of 'black' propaganda. An example of black propaganda is the effort by the Germans during the Second World War to undermine morale in Britain by setting up a radio station purporting to be British and reporting inaccurate war news (Jowett and O'Donnell 1986: 17–18).

Propaganda has been a central part of the history of cinema since the earliest days. The sinking of the Maine and the Spanish-American War in February 1898 provided film companies such as Biograph and Edison with the opportunity to attract audiences with patriotic and inflammatory representations of the events in Havana (for a full account, see Musser 1991: 127–31). During the First World War both sides attempted to bolster popular support for their cause at home and abroad. The British official war film, *The Battle of the Somme* (1916), served the dual purpose of presenting images of the troops at the front for the people at home *and* presenting the case to neutral countries such as the United States. Its celebrated 'actual battle scene', in which men are seen to fall among the barbed wire, is generally accepted as having been faked. Nevertheless, the image was potent enough to be presented as 'informative' at special screenings in the United States.

The two modes, the theatrical and the realistic, which film propaganda has incorporated historically are suggested in Dziga **Vertov**'s statement of his desire 'to substitute the document for *mise-en-scène*'. The Soviet cinema of the 1920s, and particularly Vertov, sought to report the life of the new socialist nation through a rejection of the invented film play and a reinvigorated approach to the newsreel which accentuated the real-life experience of its audience. His method called for a use of montage with 'judgement-speed-attack' in order to bring about the 'exposure of the very heart of your film-objects' (for a full account of Vertov's ideas, see Leyda 1983).

Conversely, the techniques of the Hollywood industry, at least from the 1920s, has presented illusionistic narratives which concern themselves primarily with goal-oriented protagonists within a world which generally allows the achievement of those goals. With notable exceptions such as **film noir**, the Hollywood film industry, with its star system and focus on the spectacle of a Utopian world, has been seen as effective propaganda for American cultural imperialism of the twentieth century (see **utopia and dystopia**).

The pretence to objectivity is a quality shared by both the theatrical and the realistic approaches to propaganda. Bill Nichols (1991) discusses the problem of objectivity in film and media forms by recognizing three definitions. The first is a view distinct from the perspective of characters or social actors, the second is one free of personal bias and the third allows the audience freedom to determine their own views. He points out that the formal structure of the frame of the camera compromises the possibility of the first quality in that there is always an implicit viewpoint when an object is framed or lit a certain way. The second is not possible in that even apparently unbiased representation speaks from the limitations of the values and discourses of its historical and social moment (see **bias**). The result is often that 'objectivity masks the viewpoint of institutional authority'. Finally, he suggests that rhetoric is at work even in the definition of objectivity which emphasizes freedom of choice, pointing out the debatable status of the concept of the 'free subject' (Nichols 1991: 196–8). In this regard, there is a danger that the definition of propaganda slips into the realms of ideology where all meaning is produced in order to benefit or perpetuate existing power structures (see **ideology and hegemony**). It may be best understood, then, as a form of persuasive rhetoric which loses its effectiveness at the moment it is identified as 'propaganda'.

References

Jowett, G. and O'Donnell, V. (1986) *Propaganda and Persuasion*, London: Sage Publications.

Leyda, J. (1983) *Kino: A History of the Russian and Soviet Film* (revised edn), Princeton: Princeton University Press, pp. 176–9.

Musser, C. (1991) *Before the Nickelodeon: Edwin S. Porter and the Edison Manufacturing Company*, Berkeley and Los Angeles: University of California Press, pp. 127–31.

Nichols, B. (1991) *Representing Reality: Issues and Concepts in Documentary*, Bloomington: Indiana University Press, pp. 196–8.

Further reading

Pronay, N. and Spring, D. W. (eds) (1982) *Propaganda, Politics and Film, 1918–1945*, London: Macmillan.

MIKE HAMMOND

Propp, Vladimir Iakovlievitch

b. 1895; d. 1970

Vladimir Propp was a Russian folklorist and student of literature. In his book *The Morphology of the Folktale*, first published in 1928, Propp constituted the **genre** of the folk narrative by reference to recurrent character roles and narrative units or functions which are similar throughout the world. Groups of characters then participate in the narrative units to form a story. This highly synchronic and formal analysis none the less allowed for classification of recurrent figures in folktales in an international index. Film scholars have used Propp's morphological analysis to understand the **narrative** structure of cinema.

Yet these tales, so dissected, lost their context and nuance, the point which Claude **Lévi-Strauss** attacked in the 1960s. Propp had, in fact, explored the historical formation and use of such tales in his second major volume, *The Historical Roots of Fairy Tales*, which he had begun as the final chapter of *Morphology*, and which was published in the USSR in an incomplete edition in 1946. It only became available much later in other European languages. Here he linked the formal system of his earlier work to the origins of the folktale in historical ritual and ethnographic interpretation (see **ethnography**).

References

Propp, V. (1975) *The Morphology of the Folktale*, Austin: University of Texas Press.

GARY McDONOGH

psychoanalysis

Although the publication of the founding texts of psychoanalysis was coincident with the birth of the cinema, **Freud** did not interest himself in 'the invention without a future'. By the 1920s, however, psychoanalytic ideas had diffused throughout the European intelligentsia and surrealists like Salvador Dali began to explore the affinities of film and dreams.

The first major theoretical deployment of psychoanalysis in media studies came from the **Frankfurt School**. Dissatisfied with current Marxist theories of **culture** and subjectivity (see **Marxist aesthetics**), the Frankfurt School thinkers saw psychoanalysis as a possible way to forge a connection between the individual and the social-historical. In the analysis of fascism, for example, the Frankfurt School insisted on the importance of 'reading' cultural phenomena – from opera and philosophical tradition to radio broadcasting and public spectacles – as contributing to the production of a 'mass psychology' which invested the fascist regimes with consent. With a few notable exceptions, the Frankfurt School produced little detailed work on the cinema; and their preference for high modernist over mass culture – as well as their narrowly conceived notion of ideology – were impasses to a fully developed psychoanalysis of culture.

In the 1960s, the Marxist philosopher Louis **Althusser** achieved a fundamental reconceptualization of the notion of ideology, one which opened new avenues for the psychoanalytic study of culture (see **ideology and hegemony**). Drawing directly on the work of psychoanalyst Jacques **Lacan**, Althusser defined ideology as the 'imaginary misrecognition of the subject's relation to [his] real conditions of existence'. Ideology was no longer seen as a circumscribed set of political doctrines, but as rather the result of a complex interaction between the social subject and the myriad institutional discourses (in Lacanian terms, the 'Symbolic Order' or '**Other**') that gave this subject the ('**imaginary**') illusion of his/her seamless connection to the social world. By arguing that ideology operated via a fundamental and unconscious psychic process, that of misrecognition, Althusser was able to resolve several fundamental paradoxes in former theories of ideology: for example, why individuals would act in contradiction to their own **class** interests and, related to this, how capitalist ideology manages to reproduce itself. Althusser called the institutional structures that disseminated and 'policed' ideological discourses 'ideological state apparatuses', ranging from the patriarchal family, to the school, to the institutions of the state (see **ideological state apparatuses; patriarchy**). Curiously, cinema and television were not discussed at great length. However, the notion that the cinema in particular was a potent ideological state apparatus was crucial to the radicalization of film theory in the 1960s, a radicalization which deployed Lacanian psychoanalytic theory to an even greater extent than Althusser had.

The main organs for psychoanalytic film theory were the French journal *Cahiers du cinéma*, and, later, the British journal *Screen*. In 1968, the editors of *Cahiers* published a collectively authored analysis of John Ford's *Young Mr Lincoln* (1939) which showed the power of a psychoanalytically informed ideological analysis of a film. The analysis begins with the assumption that any re-telling of such a central national story – especially in a period of deep economic crisis – would inevitably be overdetermined by a range of conflicting historical imperatives, and that the points of overdetermination would manifest themselves within the narrative economy of the film itself. Thus, much as the psychoanalyst looks for the seemingly banal detail that is strangely charged with affect, the editors of *Cahiers* looked for unexpected condensations and displacements which were seen as symptoms of larger historical contradictions at work in the film (see **condensation; displacement**). For the editors of *Cahiers*, the analysis of *Young Mr Lincoln* was to mark an editorial shift towards criticism as a form of political action.

Theory of the apparatus

Cahiers' analysis of *Young Mr Lincoln* inspired a number of close analyses of other classical Hollywood films which applied psychoanalytic theory to the films' narrative economies in order to produce critiques of the ideological operations of the texts. As early as 1970, however, psychoanalytic film theory moved in yet another direction, as theorists like Jean-Louis Baudry asserted a profound affinity between the cinema and the psyche. Baudry based his argument on a view of cinema not simply as a popular cultural form but as an interlocking set of technological developments, institutions, social practices, discourses and 'texts' – in short, as an 'apparatus', as Michel **Foucault** had developed the term in relation to the origins of modernity. In claiming that the cinematic apparatus in a sense 'reduplicated' the psychic apparatus, Baudry was making a claim not about a particular narrative situated within a particular historical period, but about an essential condition of the cinema itself. Although not fully appreciated at the time, the move towards the apparatus thus introduced a fundamental schism within psychoanalytic film theory, one whose effects are still felt today.

Baudry argued that there was a central ideological effect that was intrinsic to the **cinematic apparatus** itself – namely, what he called 'idealism', by which he meant the installation of the viewing subject as a unified, self-possessed being seamlessly attuned to a surrounding world over which he exerted power. The cinematic apparatus was thus the culmination of a long line of developments in both philosophy and visual practices, developments which included, among other things, the invention of **perspective** painting in the Renaissance and Descartes' formulation of a gulf between thinking subject and material object. Both of these latter developments were seen by Baudry as fundamentally ideological in so far as they provided the western, male subject with an *illusion* of mastery, both of himself as a unified being and of the world around him, as his prerogative. Baudry's invocation of philosophy was especially important, for it ultimately led to the conclusion that *representation itself* is inherently ideological. Thus Baudry repeatedly cited Plato's cave as the archetypal scene of the cinema.

This, of course, is an argument by analogy; and as Baudry extended his argument into the properly psychoanalytic, the analogies multiplied, leaving him open to criticisms which will be taken up here in due course. To summarize, Baudry argued that the conditions of movie spectatorship – darkened room, 'immobility', 'receptivity' to a chain of images – resembled those of dreaming, and that just as dreaming allows one to regressively experience one's primal, repressed desires, so too does the cinematic apparatus. Thus, psychoanalysis allows us to see that the cinema's 'reality effect' is itself the ideological illusion of a culture which, since Plato's cave, has longed to bring under control the very unruliness of perception. If this telescopic view of western philosophy smacks of intellectual hubris (as many have claimed), a more properly psychoanalytic criticism would be this: if dreams are indeed the 'royal road to the unconscious', it is nevertheless the case that the dream is only the beginning of a process which is the *work* of psychoanalysis. Even if the analogy between film and dream were granted, then the analysis of condensations and displacements – precisely the

analysis performed by *Cahiers* on *Young Mr Lincoln* – would be the necessary next step.

In 1975, Christian **Metz** attempted, in *Psychoanalysis and Cinema: The Imaginary Signifier*, to produce a fully psychoanalytic account of the cinema as a signifying system. Metz built on Baudry's basic arguments regarding the relation of cinema to psyche, but he complicated it considerably by mobilizing a full range of psychoanalytic concepts. Principal among them was the concept of identification. Colloquially, we all understand the ways in which we identify with various characters in a fiction, but from the psychoanalytic point of view, these are always *secondary* identifications. Before such identifications are possible, the human subject must have had to identify narcissistically with him/herself. As elaborated in an early work of Lacan, this primary identification occurs when the infant sees itself reflected in the mirror: the awkward and uncoordinated infant misrecognizes itself as a unified, coherent being (see **mirror stage**). What Lacan calls the '**imaginary** order' involves precisely this 'nostalgia for unity' in a subject constitutively split. The cinema screen, like the mirror, presents us with virtual objects in a virtual world; but unlike the mirror, it excludes from us our own image. Our unthinking fascination with the cinematic image is grounded on this fundamental evocation of the imaginary.

To present Metz's further arguments in their complexity is beyond the scope of this entry. Briefly, however, Metz links the (logically primary) imaginary appeal of the cinema to other aspects of the psychic economy, aspects connected to the subject's entry into language (or the Symbolic Order). For Lacan, the self-contained unity effected by the imaginary order is broken by several crucial, traumatic events, all of which require the child to accept the reality of **difference**: events which include the discovery of sexual difference (via the fantasy of the primal scene, the witnessing of the parental sexual act), and the accession to language (whose locus is radically *outside* the subject). The child of either sex is faced with the traumatic realization that he/she doesn't have 'it', and out of this **lack**, **desire** is born. For Metz, the cinema is marked by the same fundamental paradox of **absence**/presence that the human discovers on entry into the Symbolic. From this basic idea, Metz derives his conclusions that the cinema positions its spectators as voyeurs, its connoisseurs as fetishists; and, at its most fundamental level, stages always a 'missed encounter' between the presence that marks the shooting and the absence that marks the viewing (see **fetishism; voyeurism**).

Feminist theory and psychoanalysis

As well as Metz's book, 1975 also saw the appearance of two works whose effect on feminist film theory was galvanic: one was a polemical essay (Laura **Mulvey**, 'Visual Pleasure and Narrative Cinema'), the other, a film (Chantal Akerman, *Jeanne Dielman, 23 Quai du Commerce, 1080 Bruxelles*). Perhaps most remarkable was the way in which Akerman's film seemed a perfect example of the kind of reflexive, anti-pleasure aesthetic that Mulvey argued for in her essay. Mulvey (see Rosen 1986) argued for a politicized use of psychoanalysis, one which realized that the psychoanalytic insights into sexual difference might provide a **discourse** that could unmask the mechanisms underlying patriarchal social and psychic structures. (At the same time, it should be noted that some feminist theory in this period also saw the discourses of psychoanalysis themselves to be 'phallocentric' and thus in need of critique.)

Mulvey argued that classical narrative cinema, especially Hollywood cinema, constructed its sequences in such a way that the male character always controlled the field of vision shown to the spectator. That is to say, the man controlled both the film's 'local', perceptual points of view and also its global, narrative point of view. Within this viewing or scopic regime, the woman was not authorized to actively look, but was rather the (fetishized) object of the look of the man. She was the 'spectacle' for which the narrative's causal chains were interrupted. Classical cinema thus reproduced formally the sexual power relationships of the patriarchal culture. Mulvey further argued that the woman's fetishized status was signalled by the way in which she was often presented not in full-figure, but rather, through editing, as fragmented. The editing thus symptomatized the very fear that underlies the fetish, that is, **castration**, so that the classical cinema provided a way for the male spectator to displace his castration anxiety onto the woman. Mulvey concluded with a call to resist the pleasures of classical cinema in favour of a cinema which refused to make technique 'invisible' but rather foregrounded the materiality of its production.

For feminist analysis of ideology, the question Mulvey's argument raised was this: if it is true that women spectators have taken, and continue to take, pleasure in viewing the spectacularized display of, for example, Rita Hayworth in *Gilda* (Charles Vidor, 1946), then how are we to account for this? Mulvey's argument seems to answer that such pleasures were evidence of 'false consciousness'; but accepting that answer would return us to a view of ideology which Althusser's work had superseded. It was precisely this conundrum that Mary Ann Doane attempted to resolve – from within the psychoanalytic paradigm – in her 1982 essay 'Film and the Masquerade' (see Mast *et al.* 1992). While accepting Mulvey's basic view that popular film forms consigned woman to being the object of the look, Doane argued that the woman's spectacularized performance was precisely that – a performance. Indeed, femininity itself could be seen as a performance, which allowed for the possibility that the woman was actively controlling what the man looked at, and by extension what the camera recorded.

Following Mulvey, feminist film theorists produced an enormous body of work, especially focused on the analysis of Hollywood cinema and its genres. But Doane's essay on the masquerade is a pertinent place to conclude this section for two reasons. First, it was probably the earliest articulation of the notion of **gender** performativity in film studies (see **performative**). Second, and more important, while Doane worked solidly within the psychoanalytic model, it is not difficult to see how the questions raised by the essay might very well lead to the repudiation of that model, in favour of reading and reception studies, cultural studies or new historicist studies of the film-going audience (see **reading and reception theory**).

Revisionism

What all the criticisms had in common was the view that psychoanalytic film theory was totalizing – that, aside from sexual difference, it assumed a homogeneous spectator, ignoring the specificities of real (historical) spectators, the particularities of their racial, class or subcultural positions. There were those who thought, however, that psychoanalysis – as a theory of subjectivity and its relation to the social – was still the most powerful explanatory model around, whatever the weaknesses in its film-theoretical guise. Thus, among those who did not abandon psychoanalysis outright, the 1980s were a time for regrounding psychoanalytic film theory on suppler conceptual schema. Ultimately, and perhaps ironically, this led to the abandonment of the theory of the apparatus and a return to the analysis of narrative.

In 'Primary Identification and the Historical Subject', Thomas Elsaesser (see Rosen 1986) attempted to introduce historical and cultural specificity into the analysis of spectator positioning. To do this, he looked not at the classical Hollywood system of enunciation, but rather at an alternative embodied in the films of the New German Cinema director Rainer Werner Fassbinder. Cleverly calling Baudry's philosophical history a 'negative teleology', Elsaesser argued that while there was merit in Metz's arguments about the mirroring effects of cinema, only the analysis of non-hegemonic systems of filmic enunciation could ground those effects within a historical context. Since Fassbinder's films were pre-eminently about seeing and being seen, they presented an ideal corpus for such an analysis. Ultimately, Elsaesser demonstrated that the scopic regimes of Fassbinder's films reflected the traumatized subjectivity in post-war Germany, allegorizing at one and the same time fascism's insistence on the total visibility of everyday life and the post-war repression of this traumatic history.

Yet another fertile avenue pursued, beginning in the 1980s, was that of **fantasy**; a concept which, though crucially important to psychoanalysis, was never mobilized by the psychoanalytic film theory of the 1970s. In psychic life, fantasy is that which provides the 'set' for the staging of scenarios of desire. Because fantasy can range from the highly individual to the social – the various mythologies of nationhood being common examples of social fantasy – the concept allows for great fluidity in the spectatorial positions taken in relation to the filmic text, while at the same time according the

film the power to organize or orchestrate meanings within the social dimension of fantasy. Such approaches to psychoanalytic textual analysis are relatively new, and have found most fertile ground in analyses of televisual **advertising**, **pornography** and other textual systems clearly connected to structures of fantasy.

From desire to drive

In 1989, Joan Copjec published 'The Orthopsychic Subject' in the journal *October*, in which she argued brilliantly that earlier psychoanalytic film theory was based on incomplete or misunderstood readings of Lacan, and that only by incorporating the difficult Lacanian concepts of the real and the drives could a properly psychoanalytic theory of the subject be constructed. In adopting the model of the mirror, film theory ended up assuming a model of total visibility, whereas psychoanalysis insists that something always, constitutively, remains hidden from view. This is evident, for example, in film theory's use of the very problematic concept of the gaze (see **gaze, the**). Film theory situated the gaze on the side of the viewing subject, at the point where the lines of perspective meet; Lacan, in contrast, situated the gaze on the 'other side' of the field of visuality, within 'another scene' which produced the sense that something hidden lay behind our view of the world, subtending it, making it indeed visible. As Copjec (1995) argues, film theory was actually deploying the concept of gaze set forth by Michel Foucault in his discussion of the **panopticon** as the quintessentially modern apparatus of visuality. The subject produced by this apparatus is, as Copjec puts it, 'inculpable' – not guilty.

In so far as this 'not guilty' subject is the product of post-modernity, some have argued for a renewed psychoanalysis of the subject, now oriented towards the drive rather than towards desire. Desire is predicated on a distance from the ferocity of the drives, a distance guaranteed by the Law (see **law of the father**). This Law has become radically ironized in the post-modern, in such a way that the post-modern subject is thrown into his/her own private enjoyment (**jouissance**), with no recourse to a larger, public sphere being possible. Finally, because the drive and its *jouisssance* are located on the side of what Lacan calls the real, it should be expected that signs of the real would emerge forcefully in post-modern art, and the work of Slovenian theorist Slavoj Zizek (1991) has been of crucial importance in developing this line of analysis. Previously, film theory had focused exclusively on the imaginary and the symbolic, reasoning that since the real was that which was constitutively foreclosed from language, it was impossible to talk about. However, the experience of the uncanny is a quintessential experience of the real. As Zizek has noted, the visual field in the post-modern work of art is often marked by the uncanny stain or point of unreadability. Such stains are greeted with both fascination and anxiety; they mark the point at which the (formerly hidden) gaze erupts into visuality, consequently dissolving the depth effect which the gaze is supposed to guarantee.

See also: feminist theory; modernism and post-modernism; phallus; subject and subjectivity; symbolic code

References

Copjec, J. (1995) 'The Orthopsychic Subject', in *Read My Desire*, Boston: MIT Press.

Mast, G., Cohen, M., Braudy, L. *et al.* (1992) *Film Theory and Criticism* (4th edn), New York: Oxford University Press. (This volume contains the essays mentioned in this entry by the *Cahiers* editors, Baudry, Metz (excerpted), Mulvey and Doane.)

Metz, C. (1982) *Psychoanalysis and Cinema: The Imaginary Signifier* (first published 1975), London: Macmillan.

Mulvey, L. (1975) 'Visual Pleasure and Narrative Cinema', *Screen*, vol. 16, no. 3.

Rosen, P. (ed.) (1986) *Narrative, Apparatus, Ideology*, New York: Columbia University Press. (An invaluable anthology which contains the essays mentioned in this entry by the *Cahiers* editors, Baudry, Metz (selections), Mulvey and Elsaesser.)

Zizek, S. (1991) *Looking Awry: An Introduction to Jacques Lacan through Popular Culture*, Boston: MIT Press.

Further reading

Mayne, J. (1993) *Cinema and Spectatorship*, New York: Routledge.

Penley, C. (1989) *The Future of an Illusion*, Minneapolis: University of Minnesota Press.

Restivo, A. (1997) 'Lacan According to Zizek', *Quarterly Review of Film and Video*, vol. 16, no. 2, pp. 193–206.

Silverman, K. (1983) *The Subject of Semiotics*, New York: Oxford University Press.

Weber, S. (1991) *Return to Freud: Jacques Lacan's Dislocation of Psychoanalysis*, Cambridge: Cambridge University Press. (The finest introduction to Lacan for the advanced student.)

Zizek, S. (1989) *The Sublime Object of Ideology*, New York: Verso. (Ground-breaking reconceptualization of Lacan, which covers all the issues raised in this entry, and a great deal more.)

ANGELO RESTIVO

public service broadcasting

Since the early days of broadcasting, the idea of public service has played a key part in shaping broadcast policy, and it continues to inform debates about the role and effects of television and radio today. This is particularly the case in Europe, where broadcasting policy grew out of a tradition of social welfare provision and state involvement in the lives of its citizens. This is in opposition to the United States where broadcasting quickly fell under the heading of business and commerce and was not troubled by the public service ethos until the 1960s when it was subject to the same social currents that had given rise to the civil rights movement.

Public service broadcasting (PSB) can be characterized by listing its dominant principles. First, it is a system dedicated to the public good rather than private gain. Second, PSB carries with it the democratic urge towards universal access where broadcast services are not restricted to particular social, economic or geographical communities but are made available to the population as a whole. Third, PSB resists the 'common denominator' principle and seeks to provide a range of programmes that may not necessarily appear in more commercial broadcasting schedules. Finally, PSB institutions and personnel are accountable to the public rather than private investors or particular political interests.

However, these principles can only be taken as a rough guide. It is more profitable to think of PSB in terms of its historical evolution and to investigate the various ways in which it has been defined, interpreted and expressed by broadcasting institutions and by those responsible for setting out broadcasting policy. A key voice in the formulation of PSB policy in the United Kingdom has been John **Reith**, the first Director General of the British Broadcasting Corporation (BBC) between 1927 and 1938. Reith believed broadcasting should take a lead role in shaping and 'improving' the tastes of its audience and to this end weighted the BBC radio schedule with plays, classical music, poetry and so forth; essentially reflecting the values and cultural preferences of the British middle classes rather than those of the ordinary listener. However, while residues of a **Reithian** philosophy remain, it would be difficult to find wide and unqualified support for his broadcasting model today. Indeed, by the 1960s and 1970 it was becoming increasingly apparent that the ambitions of PSB were out of step with broader cultural trends and that the notion of a 'common good' underpinned by shared cultural standards was erroneous.

PSB, then, is a problematic concept, and has become increasingly malleable and open to interpretation rather than fixed to any single, universal definition or broadcasting model. It has been at its most coherent and forceful when compared against commercial systems, in particular American broadcasting models. However, even commercial models can, if they deliver the right kind of programmes (that is, **current affairs** as opposed to **quiz shows**, information programmes rather than **entertainment**, etc.), claim to provide a public service. Indeed, this was the case in Britain in the 1970s when many observers believed that the BBC's commercial rival, ITV, was overtaking the Corporation in its commitment to, and provision of, a public service.

It should be noted that PSB has perhaps been as much a product of the technical limitations of broadcasting as it has been predetermined by national and cultural idiosyncrasies. For most of its history broadcasting has suffered **spectrum scarcity** which has limited the number of channels available for public reception. As such, broadcasting has largely been treated as a scarce national resource held by the state in the interest of the public rather than entrusted to private companies for individual gain. With the emergence of **cable and satellite**, and thus the end of channel scarcity, many observers have claimed that a public service-dominated broadcasting model is becoming increasingly untenable.

See also: broadcasting, the United Kingdom; broadcasting, the United States; deregulation, the United Kingdom; deregulation, the United States; public sphere

Further reading

MacCabe, C. and Stewart, O. (eds) (1986) *The BBC and Public Service Broadcasting*, Manchester: Manchester University Press.
McDonnell, J. (ed.) (1991) *Public Service Broadcasting: A Reader*, London: Routledge.
Williams, R. (1974) *Television: Technology and Cultural Form*, London: Fontana.

PETER McLUSKIE

public sphere

The term 'public sphere' has developed to delineate the distinction, in modern societies, between the realm of private, domestic affairs and experiences in which personal life is ostensibly regulated by the desires and resources of individuals and families, and that of the broader arena in which institutional matters of commerce and state are negotiated. The origin of the concept dates from the emergence of the modern industrial order which created a social system whereby home and workplace were severed, geographically, instrumentally and culturally. Before that, home and work, based largely in an agrarian setting, were physically, socially and psychologically joined, as men, women and children worked side by side in common, life-supporting enterprises. However, the arrival of industrialism meant that men left home to pursue work and state affairs, children were sent to school – which served as training grounds for industrial life – and women remained at home to care for the physical and emotional needs of family members.

The most important development in public sphere theory, and its relation to contemporary mass media, has been the work of Jürgen **Habermas** (1984; 1987; 1989) who has analysed the rise of the public/private division. Habermas traced the rise of the split to the relations between the capitalist economic order and the state in the seventeenth and eighteenth centuries. For Habermas, material reproduction was the function of the official capitalist economy and of the modern administrative state, both of which are 'system-integrated'. But the economy is part of the private domain, while the state is public. And symbolic reproduction, for Habermas, involving socialization, nurture, cultural transmission, occurs in the realm of 'life-world': the private family and public sphere (Livingstone and Lunt 1994; Calhoun 1996). This public sphere, an arena in which private citizens, acting in a capacity separate from both private life and the workings of government and the market place, come together to discuss and deliberate on matters of state, creating an arena in which public opinion can be negotiated among autonomous free individuals that can then affect matters of state. To quote Habermas:

> By the public sphere we mean first of all a realm of our social life in which something approaching public opinion can be formed. Access is guaranteed to all citizens. A portion of the public sphere comes into being in every conversation in which private individuals assemble to form a public body. They then behave neither like business or professional people transacting private affairs, nor like members of a constitutional order subject to the legal constraints of a state bureaucracy. Citizens behave as a public body when they confer in an unrestricted manner...about matters of general interest....We speak of the political public sphere in contrast for example to the literary one, when public discussion deals with objects connected to the activity of the state.

> Although state is so to speak the executor, it is not a part of it...Only when the exercise of political control is effectively subordinated to the demand that information is accessible to the public does the political public sphere win an institutionalized influence over the government through the instrument of law-making bodies.
>
> (Habermas 1984: 49)

The very essence of democracy, for Habermas, lay in the ability of private citizens to freely deliberate and affect elected officials through the power of public opinion; economics and state power had to be kept out of such arrangements. Habermas' somewhat Utopian model for this body of deliberation was the coffee house in which men of affairs gathered in the eighteenth century. But, as Habermas understood, the complexities of modern life, and particularly the rise of the electronic mass media, has complicated the viability and the nature of such a model. He noted that, 'in a large public body this kind of communication requires specific means of transmitting information and influencing those who receive it.... Today newspapers and magazines, radio and TV are the media of the public sphere' (Habermas 1984: 49). But therein lay a serious problem for Habermas, since the mass media in capitalist democracies have been at least in part corporate and profit-making enterprises. Thus, the original model, whereby influence travelled from socially-integrated to system-integrated realms, has now been reversed, so that the private realm and the public sphere are increasingly colonized by corporate and state power, undermining both the private life and the democratic role of the public sphere.

Habermas' belief in the past existence of an functioning bourgeois public sphere which has gradually eroded because of the rise of mass media, has in recent years been questioned by such media theorists as Geoff Eley (1993) and James Curran (1991). To the extent that the original public sphere model for Habermas' theory did exist in earlier centuries, it was, as theorists and feminists (see Fraser 1991; Ryan 1993) have pointed out, already compromised by political problems. These meeting places were restricted by **race**, **class** and **gender** to a very narrow range of the general population, a matter which has given rise to much criticism and debate about the Habermasian model as a democratic ideal. The issue of gender has complicated current analyses and debates on the public sphere because, more than even race and class discrimination, Habermas' public sphere theory works to virtually eliminate women, whose labour has traditionally been relegated to the domestic arena, from consideration. Indeed, the gendered nature of the division of labour created by the private/public split gave rise in the 1960s to the phrase 'the personal is political'. This referred to the growing awareness of the political implications of the modern development in which women were essentially isolated in the home, cut off from the institutions and activities through which common social and political affairs were managed, and deprived of access to public power and, in Simone de Beauvoir's words, of the right to 'take responsibility for the world'. Issues of public sphere theory, as they relate to media issues as well as all other areas of modern life, have been of particular importance to feminists concerned with gender theory and politics.

But perhaps the most important issue in recent years arising from debate about the existence and viability of a democratic public sphere within which citizens might deliberate so as to affect state negotiations – one to which questions of race and class, and especially gender, are central – concerns the role of the mass media in western democracies. In the 1990s and beyond, this issue has become complicated by developments in post-Cold War western nations, as the ideal of state-subsidized public interest broadcasting is increasingly compromised by recent global economic developments. More and more, the workings of law and government are being undermined and overtaken by the power of transnational capital, while the ideals of social welfare have increasingly been undermined and eroded by the global hegemony of corporate ideology and its disdain for the values of the so-called 'welfare state' (see **ideology and hegemony**).

Mass media and the public interest

The concept of 'public interest' broadcasting has theoretically meant regulation of the granting of licences and monitoring the activities of broadcasters in both Great Britain and the United States

(see **broadcasting, the United Kingdom; broadcasting, the United States**). In brief, this principle would mandate broadcasters to adhere to certain guidelines pertaining to universal service, diversity, editorial independence, social responsibility and accountability, cultural quality and public financing or non-profit operation (McQuail 1994). In practice, however, in the UK, and especially in the United States, where since its inception television has been almost exclusively funded through **advertising** revenue and public broadcasting has only minimal support even from the public, the principle has never been fully realized. Market forces and the role of political regulation, rapidly expanding in recent years, have always encroached on this ideal. These forces, and the vast expansion and diversification of communication technologies, have threatened to do away with public interest broadcasting.

As a set of principles ensuring democratic use of the airwaves – that is, a public resource – however, it has figured centrally in discussions of the public sphere in the United Kingdom and, to a lesser extent, in the United States. As Habermas noted, if there is any arena that can properly (or potentially) be thought of as a public sphere in today's electronically mediated world, it is the mass media. With all its contradictions, it is the only potentially viable candidate for the role of universal public sphere. As much as any other aspect of today's globalized, corporatized universe, it offers fertile theoretical ground for speculation on how such a system might be made to operate. It is the only arena in which 'members understand themselves as part of a potentially wider public...a public at large' (Fraser 1991: 67) and 'the only form of expression that links the members of society who are merely "privately" aggregated...by combining their unfolded social characteristics with one another' (Kluge 1990: 66). From a critical point of view, the ideal of democratic public sphere has functioned as a 'mobilizing fiction' (Robbins 1993: 3) in discussions of the intersection of media and democracy. In particular, it has been important in pointing to the coercive role of the state in regulating media, and the profiteering, essentially cynical role of the corporate media in undermining the democratic ideals which ostensibly govern licensing and regulating procedures (Livingstone and Lunt 1994: 17).

Complicating this debate is the related issue, historically central to theories and debates surrounding mass media themselves, of distinctions among the 'masses', the 'public' and the audience. With its roots in the **Frankfurt School**, with whom Habermas and his theories are associated, the term 'mass' has referred to an essentially passive, undifferentiated, highly manipulable entity with little means of resistance to the overpowering and hegemonically normative messages of a government regulated and corporate-owned media. The concept of a public, on the other hand, implies an active, egalitarian grouping capable of forming and responding to opinions received and having access to the means of communication and the ability to influence public affairs through the power of democratically formulated public opinion.

Much debate about media and democracy concerns this dichotomy. The question of whether or not a true, even a limited, version of a mediated public sphere is possible under current conditions revolves around the question of whether audiences are indeed passive or active; massified or differentiated according to group and individual characteristics and experiences or the social contexts within which viewing takes place. Recent media reception theory, positing active viewers able to read 'against the grain' supports the idea that audiences can be characterized as active, involved 'publics' (see **reading and reception theory**). Such a formulation of active viewers, capable of judging and responding actively to what they see and hear, opens the possibility of theorizing the media as a public sphere in the sense that Habermas meant the term. Of course, theorists making such claims are aware of the necessarily impure, contradictory and limited ways in which such a sphere functions. Nor are they uncritical of the many ways in which economic and political forces make the workings of such a sphere less than ideal and often even damaging to democratic public discourse (Liebes and Katz 1986; Rapping 1992 and 1998).

Theorists who make use of theories of reception in which audiences are seen as individually and ethnographical active and even **oppositional** tend to be cultural theorists. But even social science-oriented media analysts have developed theories of '**uses and gratifications**' that allow them to analyse viewers and viewing habits in terms of individual habits and practices and to move beyond views of media which analysed the transmission of messages with little regard for the processes of reception.

Out of all this theoretical development in the areas of audiences, publics and the media as public sphere, has arisen a variety of interesting studies of the uses of the media for relatively democratic, affirmative ends. Nicholas Garnham (1993) has argued influentially for the revitalization of the public service ethos in the context of current media conditions, and James Curran (1991) has argued in a similar vein that the media today have the potential for allowing for radical-democratic initiatives.

Out of this work have also arisen studies of daytime and night-time talk shows as complex, but in some sense liberatory, arenas where public discourse on important social and political issues take place, and where elements of the population least likely to be given a voice and representation are empowered to speak and be heard. Such forums may also create a discursive space within which audiences and participants share in a public debates which approximate the kind of public sphere discourse theorized by Habermas. Livingstone and Lunt (1994: 1–70) sum up the basic issues or questions raised and analysed in these works thus: 'Is this a new form of public space or forum, part of a media public sphere? Or is this a travesty of real political debate with no real consequences? Do such programmes offer new opportunities to the public to question established power or are the programmes part of a media diversion from real political and social action?'

As Lunt and Livingstone make clear, the main issue for scholars and political analysts is the extent to which a commercial, state-regulated medium may allow for open discussion of contested issues in which the state and corporate sponsors have a clear interest. To what extent will open discourse and challenges to hegemonic norms be allowed, in the interest of allowing, or at least approximating, the kind of discourse necessary for the workings of a democratic society? This debate has been joined by many others: of particular interest are Carpignano *et al.* (1990), Munson (1994) and Priest (1995).

While not all analysts of the talk show form (see **chat/talk show**) have focused on gender issues, many specific studies have indeed focused on the specific negotiation of issues of special concern to women. Masciarotte (1991), in particular, analyses *The Oprah Winfrey Show* as a site of 'resistance within the television spectacle' for women participants and for the hostess who is a transgressive presence – Winfrey is African-American, sometimes overweight, and a self-identified 'survivor' of sexual abuse – opening a space for oppositional discourse. Many scholars, in particular Peck (1995) and White (1992), have noted the use of therapeutic discourse on television generally, especially on talk shows, as a mechanism whereby issues associated with the feminine, particularly gender, sex and family issues, can be introduced into public debate and articulated and negotiated within a mediated public sphere.

Analyses of the ways in which various subaltern groups attain representation in certain forms of media and in certain contexts of general political debate have been made by those positing the notion of 'oppositional public spheres' created by various groups, who identify as members of a particular unrepresented grouping and then contest for power by intervening, in various ways, in mainstream media discourse. Nancy Fraser (1991) and others have theorized and documented the complex dynamic by which oppositional voices have intervened in public sphere debates and representation issues within American mainstream media, where the commercial media have already achieved a culturally and politically dominant status as a public sphere arena. Such interventions are suggestive of the ways in which oppositional subaltern voices and forces intervene in public sphere politics globally through their roles as participants in the production and reception processes of media everywhere.

In Fraser's terminology, for example, feminists today comprise a 'subaltern counterpublic' with the ability to intervene in mainstream discourse and representation in a way that challenges dominant hegemonic messages with ideas and images which are 'potentially emancipatory'. Horace Newcomb (1994), borrowing from Mikail **Bakhtin**'s theories of dialogism, makes a similar point when he suggests that the media is a forum within which a variety of voices and discourses participate to produce a kind of public dialogue. Felski (1989) also theorizes a 'feminist public sphere' in which 'plural audiences' are constituted. She cites the 'enormous female participation in the consumption of mass culture forms', and the existence of the 'pluralist audiences' constituted within them, as grounds for a re-evaluation of traditional cultural biases and a recognition of the progressive political potential of mainstream media. Wicke (1998) argues that the media must now be seen as a major arena of feminist political struggle, for 'celebrity discourse' – by which she means the discourse around key feminist issues in which figures like Gloria Steinem and Oprah Winfrey participate – 'is a powerful political site...where feminism is negotiated' (1994: 756–7).

Finally, for public sphere theorists, there are two dominant models of how such a sphere would operate to serve democratic ends. In Habermas' view, the goal to be achieved would be an arena in which every voice was given equal access and all opinions would be heard and deliberated on in ways that allowed for the development of a common 'public opinion'. More recent theorists, however, following a more Gramscian view of how hegemonic norms – which are always unstable, dynamic, contradictory and contested – develop, work through a process by which various groups with varying agendas and views contest for a voice with an always negotiated, multifaceted and contradictory result.

See also: feminist theory; globalization; Gramsci, Antonio; public service broadcasting; regulation

References

Calhoun, C. (ed.) (1996) *Habermas and the Public Sphere*, Cambridge: MIT Press.

Carpigniano, P. *et al.* (1990) 'Chatter in the Age of Electronic Reproduction', *Social Text*, nos 25/26, pp. 33–55.

Curran, J. (1991) 'Rethinking the Media as Public Sphere', in P. Dahlgren and C. Sparks (eds) *Communication and Citizenship*, London: Sage.

Eley, G. (1993) 'Nations, Public and Political

Cultures', in Craig Calhoun (ed.) *Habermas and the Public Sphere*, Cambridge: MIT Press, pp. 289–339.

Felski, R. (1989) *Beyond Feminist Aesthetics*, New York: Routledge.

Fraser, N. (1991) 'Rethinking the Public Sphere', *Social Text 8*, no. 3, pp. 56–80.

Garnham, N. (1993) 'The Media and the Public Sphere', in Craig Calhoun (ed.) *Habermas and the Public Sphere*, Cambridge, MIT Press, pp. 359–76.

Habermas, J. (1984) 'The Public Sphere: An Encyclopedia Article', *New German Critique*, Autumn, pp. 49–55.

—— (1987) *Theory of Communicative Action*, Boston: Beacon Press.

—— (1989) *The Structural Transformation of the Public Sphere*, Cambridge: MIT Press.

Kluge, A. (1990) 'The Public Sphere and Experience: Selections', *October*, 46, pp. 60–83.

Liebes, T. and Katz, E. (1986) 'Patterns of Involvement in Television Fiction', *European Journal of Communication*, vol. 1, pp. 151–71.

Livingstone, S. and Lunt, P. (1994) *Talk on Television: Audience Participation and Public Debate*, New York: Routledge.

Masciarotte, G.-J. (1991) 'C'mon Girl: Oprah Winfrey and the Discourse of Feminine Talk', *Genders*, Fall, pp. 81, 111.

McQuail, D. (1994) *Mass Communication Theory*, London: Sage.

Munson, W. (1994) *All Talk: The Talk Show in Media Culture*, Philadelphia: Temple University Press.

Newcomb, H. (1994) 'Television as Cultural Form', in *Television: The Critical View*, Oxford: Oxford University Press.

Peck, J. (1995) 'TV Talk Shows as Therapeutic Discourse: The Ideological Labour of the Televised Talking Cure', *Communication Theory*, February, pp. 58–82.

Priest, P. J. (1995) *Public Intimacies: Talk Show Participants and Tell-all TV*, Cresskill, NJ: Hampton Press.

Rapping, E. (1992) *The Movie of the Week: Private Stories/Public Events*, Minneapolis: University of Minnesota Press.

—— (1998) 'Talk Shows, Feminism and the Discourse of Addiction', in Annabelle Sreberny-Mohammadi and Liesbet van Zoonen (eds) *Women's Politics and Communication*, Cresskill, NJ: Hampton Press.

Robbins, B. (1993) *The Phantom Public Sphere*, New York: Social Text Collevtive.

Ryan, M. (1993) 'Gender and Public Access', in Craig Calhoun (ed.) *Habermas and the Public Sphere*, Cambride: MIT Press, pp. 259–88.

White, M. (1992) *Tele-advising: Therapeutic Discourse in American Television*, Chapel Hill, NC: University of North Carolina Press.

Wicke, J. (1998) 'Celebrity Feminism', in Joan Landes, *Feminism: The Public and the Private*, Princeton: Princeton University Press.

ELAYNE RAPPING

Pudovkin, Vsevolod Ilarionovitch

b. 1893; d. 1953

Pudovkin was best known in his lifetime as a film director but his reputation now is more as a film theorist. Like Lev Kuleshov, Sergei **Eisenstein** and Dziga **Vertov**, he was one of the generation of filmmakers and theorists who flourished briefly during the 1920s. Supported by the Soviet government in the period immediately following the revolution, these artists made detailed explorations of the formal qualities and communicative potential of cinema.

Like Eisenstein, Pudovkin had intended to become a scientist and he shared Eisenstein's interests in theatre and music. Both men were fascinated by the distinctive meaning-making potential of film: how space and time could be transformed to recreate reality, and how the meaning of one piece of film could be altered through its juxtaposition with another. However, where Eisenstein wanted to create new meaning from the collision of the elements edited together, Pudovkin was more interested in building up these elements, one after another, to develop ideas with emotional force. His characterizations used external appearances and traits to suggest moral character – typage – but **acting** in his films also drew on Stanislavski's methods for the expression of internal feelings. Though he made films until 1946, his most highly regarded films are the earlier ones, *Mother* (1926) and *The End of St Petersburg* (1927).

See also: Kuleshov effect

Further reading

Pudovkin, V. (1960) *Film Technique and Film Acting,*

ed. and trans. Ivor Montague, New York: Grove Press.

PHILIP SIMPSON

Q

queer theory

Queer theory often prides itself on being undefinable – and, for some writers, this is a central part of what makes it queer. Nevertheless, it is possible to identify some of the histories of queer theory – the ways in which the term has been used – even if one accepts that a final and exclusive definition cannot be reached.

The term 'queer theory' was introduced by Teresa de **Lauretis** in 1990, as the title of a conference at the University of California, Santa Cruz and of the 1991 special issue of the journal *differences: A Journal of Feminist Cultural Studies* which emerged from that conference. As initially conceptualized, the term served to question the term 'lesbian and gay' as it was being used by contemporary **identity** politics of **sexuality**. It challenged the idea that 'lesbians' and 'gay men' were coherent and homogeneous groups of people, with identifiable and common characteristics and political ends. In its simplest sense, it moved away from essentialist ideas of identity – that gay men and/or lesbians are essentially linked by some (presumably natural) set of characteristics – and instead turned to the discursive constitution of sexual subjectivity (see **discourse analysis; structuralism and post-structuralism**). Queer theory does not see identity as natural and emerging from within, but rather as a surface – an intersection of cultural sites by which individuals make sense of who they are, with no internal 'authentic' self.

In this project, queer theory has found the work of Michel **Foucault**, in his writings on *The History of Sexuality*, most useful. Foucault famously asserts that before the nineteenth century, there was no such thing as a homosexual. Before medical institutions invented the name and the identity – the idea that there was a particular kind of person called 'the homosexual', whose whole being, personality, behaviour and social meaning could be thought to cohere around this one aspect of their life – there was no possibility for self-naming as 'homosexual'. There were indeed individuals who engaged in same-sex acts (much historical information is available on this point), but this was not the same thing as 'being' a homosexual. For Foucault, then, the very category of 'gay' is to be examined as a discursive construct – not appealed to as an essential link between individuals.

The strand of queer theory which emerges from de Lauretis' use of the term challenges 'heteronormativity' – the ways in which sexual identities are constructed and enforced in a **binary** couplet, homosexual/heterosexual – with heterosexuality seen as the dominant and 'natural' term. The canonical writers in this project are Eve Kosofsky **Sedgwick** and Judith **Butler**. Kosofsky Sedgwick's work emerges from the discipline of English literature, and examines the ways in which homosexual and heterosexual identities are constructed, and necessarily intertwined, in nineteenth- and twentieth-century literary texts. Judith Butler's cultural theory examines the degree to which both **gender** and sexual identities, and even sexed bodies themselves, can be understood as products of **discourse**.

However, this 'pure' version of queer theory gives little sense of the variety of, often contradictory, ways in which the term currently functions in writing about film and television. The multiplication of positions brought under the ambit of the term has been facilitated by many writers and publications removing the 'theory' from 'queer theory', so that 'queer' is now used as an adjective without necessarily requiring any connection to de Lauretis' 'queer theory' – in books which discuss 'queer readings', 'queer film' and so on.

A provisional list of some of the ways in which 'queer' now functions in cultural theory might begin with the following.

1 Any work which analyses the construction of gay and lesbian roles in culture can be named 'queer'. This seems to contradict de Lauretis' intention in coining the term, but has now become commonplace – as in, for example, the book *Queer Representations: Reading Lives, Reading Cultures* (Duberman 1997). In these texts, 'queer' is used as an inclusive synonym for 'lesbian and gay'. The advantages of 'queer' are that it does not rely on a distinction by gender; and that it appears to have a certain trendy cachet of which publishers are well aware.

2 Work which addresses transgressive cultural project, produced by 'queers'. This use of the term posits 'queer' as being the opposite of 'lesbian and gay'. In this sense, while 'lesbian and gay' is 'polite' or 'assimilationist', the former is loud, dangerous and oppositional. This use of 'queer' ties to the 'queer' politics of anti-assimilation groups such as 'Queer Nation' in the United States. In this understanding of queer, suitable objects of cultural analysis are only those which are challenging, transgressive and **avant-garde**. Examples of this form of queer include the essays in the book by Martha Gever, John Greyson and Prathiba Parmar, *Queer Looks* (1993). In a sense, this kind of 'queer' is not post-identity – rather, it posits new, transgressive 'queer' identities. The most important feature of these 'queer' identities is that they are not polite, middle class, monogamous, suburban or 'assimilationist'. Bisexuality and sadomasochism in particular have been championed in this version of 'queer'. It bears no necessary relation to the post-identity queer established by de Lauretis. Whereas de Lauretis

challenged the ways in which the categories 'gay and lesbian' were constructed, this transgressive queer rather attacks individuals who might be named 'gay and lesbian' – an identity which they see as involving assimilation. This is perhaps aided by the fact that most of the canonical writers in queer theory show little interest in popular culture – thus providing no argument against the denigration of mass culture by these writers. To them, mass culture is, by definition, not queer; indeed, it is constituted as a binary opposite, 'mass culture: queer culture'. In such writing, a model of culture as divided into a mainstream/marginal binary, where the marginal is more challenging interesting and transgressive than the homogeneous, bland mainstream (familiar from avant-garde discourses of artistic production) is accepted without challenge.

3 In the sense which most obviously refers to the work of de Lauretis, 'queer' can also refer to post-identity analyses of sexuality in culture. Alexander Doty's book *Making Things Perfectly Queer* (1993), for example, challenges interpretations of culture and the uses made by subjects of cultural texts which rely on the concept of sexual identity. In previous writing, identity politics informed cultural theory, leading to the suggestion that particular social groups were essentially related to particular kinds of culture. For example, the lesbian filmmaker Barbara Hammer asserted that lesbian stories could never be told in the 'patriarchal' form of linear **narrative** (see **patriarchy**). With this previous approach to culture, the **authorship** of films by lesbians or gay men was all important in understanding their content. Similarly, in addressing audiences, gay men and lesbians were understood to have particular '**camp**' preferences in film viewing and production. By contrast with this earlier writing, Doty takes a 'queer' approach, and offers a post-identity way of understanding cultural production and consumption. This version of cultural theory rejects the idea that individuals use cultural texts to form stable identities and positions for themselves, and suggests instead an understanding of the intersection between subjectivities (see **subject and subjectivity**) and other elements of

culture which are fluid, contingent and always partial. Neither identities nor culture can adequately be described by rigidly bounded binaries (such as centre/margin). People may make use of culture to think of themselves in different ways at different times – or even at the same time. This sense of queer need not be tied to lesbian and gay identities at all – all sexualities can be, to some degree, 'queer'.

4 As the ways in which queer theory can be employed have expanded and been explored, writers have suggested that the term need not even be tied to sexuality – it is also possible to think of 'queer' versions of race, which have nothing to do with sexuality. It is simply a way of discussing cultural theory without appealing to ideas of essentialized identities.

The first of these versions of 'queer' is often dismissed by hardline queer theorists as being 'not really queer', and perhaps represents more of publishers' attempts to mobilize a term which is recognized as having critical currency. The second and third senses are contradictory; yet are often used as though they were complementary. The ways in which they are contradictory can be illustrated with reference to a term like 'assimilation'. The second form of 'queer' is anti-assimilation – insistent that marginal and transgressive identities must not be allowed to be 'assimilated' to the cultural centre. However, the third form of queer rethinks our models of culture, so that there are no longer centres and margins, and assimilation is no longer such a threat. The second form of queer champions the most transgressive forms of sexuality; while the third form accepts all forms of sexuality which are not 'normative' – and with a definition that becomes so broad that this can include basically everyone who has any form of sex (or who has no sex at all).

Debates have taken place about whether this third version of queer – which allows everyone, whatever their position in culture, to be queer – lacks political effectivity. Lesbian and gay identity politics (which were attacked by de Lauretis' use of the term 'queer theory') relied on the fiction that there was such a thing as a generally homogeneous group of homosexual subjects, with relatively common interests, who could work together in a relatively unproblematic way in order to effect social change. Some writers fear that in dismantling identity, queer theory may disable political attempts to change culture and representation. However, other writers have proposed that other ways of thinking about political affiliations – which focus on **hybridity** and contingency without a necessary insistence on essential similarity – overcome this problem (see Cindy Patton's essay in Warner 1993).

In a similar vein, some cultural theorists worry that the version of queer theory proposed by Alexander Doty, where every subject and point in culture can be simultaneously queer and non-queer, rejects the specificity of experience of lesbians, gay men, bisexuals, transgenders and other groups who remain discriminated against in contemporary culture (Probyn 1996).

The fourth of the 'queer theories' outlined above is the one which is most congruent with the project proposed by de Lauretis, and involving Kosofsky Sedgwick and Butler. In pointing away from the rigid identity politics which had informed feminist and lesbian and gay film and television studies, queer theory has enabled different conceptions of the functions of cultural texts and the formation of identity.

References

de Lauretis, T. (ed.) (1991) *differences: A Journal of Feminist Cultural Studies*, vol. 3, no. 2.

Doty, A. (1993) *Making Things Perfectly Queer: Interpreting Mass Culture*, Minneapolis: University of Minneapolis Press.

Duberman, M. (ed.) (1997) *Queer Representations: Reading Lives, Reading Cultures*, New York and London: New York University Press.

Gever, M., Greyson, J. and Parmar, P. (eds) (1993) *Queer Looks: Perspectives on Lesbian and Gay Film and Video*, New York and London: Routledge.

Probyn, E. (1996) *Outside Belongings*, New York and London: Routledge.

Warner, M. (ed.) (1993) *Fear of a Queer Planet: Queer Politics and Social Theory*, Minneapolis and London: University of Minnesota Press.

Further reading

Jagose, A. (1996) *Queer Theory*, Melbourne: Melbourne University Press.

McKee, A. (ed.) (1999) *(Anti)Queer, Social Semiotics*, vol. 9, no. 1.

ALAN McKEE

quiz shows

A popular television **genre**, the quiz show occupies a considerable amount of peak time scheduling (see **prime time**). Often cheap and easy to produce, they tend to be formulaic and usually have a set of common characteristics: a known personality who is the host, often an ex-comedian, usually male and supported by female assistants; a live audience and 'real' people as contestants; a 'jackpot' or knock-out-rounds to create excitement and tension; glamour through exotic holidays or expensive consumer goods offered as prizes; and particular catch-phrases associated with the show or the host.

See also: live television; popular, the

PHILIP RAYNER

R

race

Race as taxonomy

'Race' is a taxonomic category by which human beings are divided into distinct groups along biological lines. The idea that such a division into races has any scientific basis has been refuted by the biological sciences since the 1950s. Genetically, it has been shown that all human beings share the vast majority of our genetic information, and there are no clear-cut boundaries that allow us to divide people into groups. The lack of ability of scientists to agree – even in the nineteenth century, when the idea of distinct races was commonplace – on how many races humans should actually be divided into – is another powerful argument against the idea.

However, the notion that we belong to separate 'races' still retains a great deal of explanatory power in contemporary, non-academic accounts of culture. Indeed, the term still holds the status of **common sense** in many discursive arenas. The idea that people of different 'races' have different personalities and behavioural attributes is also often circulated in the media as common sense – but again, this has no scientific, biological or genetic foundation. It is now recognized that the 'races' with which we are familiar, and the characteristics which are associated with them, should not be understood as 'essential', but as 'social constructions': that is to say, we have moved from ascribing these roles and characteristics to a natural, biological difference, to understanding them as constructed within **culture**.

This does not mean that the term can simply be dismissed in analyses of culture – for the idea of different races still has great explanatory power. The ways in which people are represented, treated in everyday situations, the cultures with which they are affiliated, and the histories on which they draw, all involve this fictional, but powerful notion.

In this, the idea of race has much in common with other identities (see **identity**), such as **gender** and sexuality (although there are also important differences in the way they function). It is now commonplace to suggest that in all of these cases, the identity is a 'necessary fiction': it has no simple basis in nature or biology, but it must be retained in order to explain the ways in which culture currently functions.

Stereotypes

As with the writing emerging from other areas of identity politics (see **gender; sexuality**), race initially entered cultural theory through a concern with stereotypes (see **stereotype**). Indeed, it is in relation to race – and in particular, to representations of black Americans – that the term 'stereotype' is still most commonly used. The work of writers like Donald Bogle, Jim Pines and Thomas Cripps analysed the representations of black Americans in feature films, and concluded that they were repeatedly consigned to a very limited number of character roles. Bogle specifically identified these, in the title of his 1974 book, as *Toms, Coons, Mulattoes, Mammies and Bucks*.

The terminology of the 'stereotype' and the 'positive image' also informed work on race in sociologically-informed mass communications research. The work of television researchers like Charles Hartmann and Phil Husband (1974) relied on contents analysis of television news, and newspapers, in order to discuss the ways in which people of colour were represented through 'stereotypes' rather than 'positive images'. This kind of mass media analysis invariably discovered that people of colour were represented in a very limited repertoire of ways – as criminals, or as the victims of social problems.

The black aesthetic

As well as concerns about the kinds of characters which have been represented, film theory has addressed the racial implications of particular aesthetic forms. Writing in this tradition has sought to promote a 'black aesthetic' – distinctly 'black' forms of filmmaking and cultural production. Developed from literary and visual arts culture, where it was employed in regard to movements such as Negritude and the Black Arts Movement of the 1960s and 1970s, the term has proven important in the critical writing of the African diaspora, both in the United States and in Britain. Writing on the black aesthetic uses a terminology of 'authenticity' in order to suggest that cultural products which do not partake of these particular aesthetic forms are less 'black'. The best-known proponent of the black aesthetic in film studies is Manthia Diawara.

The elements of a black aesthetic are tied to other forms of African-American culture: structures such as repetition, antiphony (call/response), the use of folkloric elements, and polyvisual structures. Manthia Diawara suggests that a black form of filmmaking involves a 'narrative contain[-ing] rhythmic and repetitious shots going back and forth between the past and the present...themes involv[ing] black folklore, religion, and the oral traditions which link black Americans to the African diaspora' (Diawara 1993: 10).

This approach draws attention to the specificity of cultural forms, and the fact that there are alternatives to the dominant modes of representation. It also usefully draws attention to questions of **authorship**. In a situation like that of black Americans, where part of the prejudice against a group has been the belief that they were savages, and lacking civilization, the very fact of visible cultural production – that black directors are publicly seen to be making films – is in itself an important part of challenging such preconceptions.

However, the idea of the black aesthetic is also an approach which refuses the possibility of **hybridity** and of creole cultural expression. In assigning races to forms, it tends to underemphasize the ability of aesthetics to evolve, adapt and take on new meanings in different contexts.

Post-colonial writing

The field of post-colonial theory, which has been most strongly developed in the field of English literature, has also contributed to film and television theory. The most familiar point is that taken up from Edward **Said**'s work on **Orientalism**. Said points out that in the representations of Empire, colonized people are often silenced. The belief is that they cannot represent themselves and they must therefore be represented by the colonial powers. Film theory has taken this up to suggest that representations of colonized people often represent them as without agency: figuratively, if not literally, silent and thus powerless (again, this might explain why it is so important for black filmmakers to be seen to be making films). 'The post-colonial gaze' is posited as equivalent to 'the male gaze' (see **gaze, the**).

However, it should be noted that most post-colonial writing is *not* about race (although it is often interpreted that way); it is usually about *nation*. The work of Gayatry **Spivak**, Edward Said and Homi K. **Bhabha**, for example, analyses the ways in which nations are formed – and how natives are represented. This is not the same as an analysis of racial representation, and it is only occasionally that post-colonial writing produces useful insights into the representation of race.

Thus, post-colonial studies of filmmaking in Brazil, or in African countries, for example, is not actually about race: it is about the filmmaking practice of particular nations. These two are often collapsed together, probably due to that exnomination which sees every production of black filmmakers as being about race; while the work of white filmmakers is not perceived in that way

('Exnomination', a word coined by Roland **Barthes**, refers to the way in which dominant groups in society do not need to give themselves a name, as they see themselves as the 'norm' against which everything else is measured.)

Post-structuralist approaches

To some degree, both writing on stereotypes – which is often concerned with the perceived inaccuracy of images (relying on the assumption that it would be possible to produce an 'accurate' representation of a black person) – and on the black aesthetic – which is concerned with 'authenticity' of cultural production – is essentialist: that is, it relies on the idea that all black people have something in common, and that some representations are more accurate than others of what black people are 'really' like. Such traditions are by no means outdated in cultural theory. For example, the writing of bell **hooks**, one of the most prominent black film critics in the United States, draws strongly on all of the approaches outlined above. hooks attacks stereotypes and decries the silencing of black voices in film, with the aim of promoting 'authentic' black voices.

By contrast, post-structuralist writing on race emphasizes the fact that there is no 'natural' category of black people – that the boundaries surrounding this racial group, like all others, are invented and circulated in language and, more widely, in culture. Critical writing in this approach seeks to trace the histories of the ways in which such a project of constructing races has taken place. Such writing is part of a general move away from 'identity politics' to an exploration of the way in which subjectivity is constructed discursively (see **subject and subjectivity; discourse**).

As Stuart **Hall**, a well-known British writer on the representation of race, puts it:

> The essentialising moment is weak because it naturalizes and dehistoricizes difference, mistaking what is historical and cultural for what is natural, biological and genetic. The moment the signifier 'black' is torn from its historical, cultural and political embedding and lodged in a biologically constituted racial category, we

> valorize, by inversion, the very ground of racism we are trying to deconstruct.
>
> (Hall 1997: 130)

It is sometimes suggested that this kind of writing is dangerously apolitical. Seeing it as a post-modern project, some writers think that if you deny that there are essential similarities between all black people, then you are making political affiliations much more difficult. Similarly, the insistence that such categories are created and sustained in language are sometimes taken as an argument that there is no 'reality' outside of discourse. Such debates resemble those between other post-structuralist and more traditionally political movements (for example, those between **queer theory** and gay and lesbian political groups).

One solution to this perceived problem is Spivak's notion of 'strategic essentialism' – a suggestion that members of oppressed groups, although acknowledging that there are many differences between them, should band together as though there were a common link between them all, in order to make political change. Hall goes even further, insisting that this perceived depoliticization of post-structuralist writing on race is not really a problem. For him, the move away from essentialism simply means paying attention to the way that discourses work over time: '[a] movement beyond . . . essentialism is not an aesthetic or critical strategy without a cultural politics. . . . What it does is move us into a new kind of cultural positionality' (Hall 1997: 130). He calls for a contingent politics: that which does not make statements about all black people, and how they should always behave, but rather pays attention to the specificity of particular cultural moments and their peculiar demands. Hall cites the work of black British cultural critic Paul Gilroy to illustrate his case:

> blacks in the British diaspora must, at this historical moment, refuse the binary black *or* British. They must refuse it because the 'or' remains the site of *constant contestation* when the aim of the struggle must be, instead, to replace the 'or' with the potentiality or the possibility of an 'and'. . . . You can be black *and* British, not only because that is a necessary position to take in 1992, but because even those two terms, joined now by the coupler 'and' instead of

opposed to one another, do not exhaust all of our identities.

(Hall 1997: 130)

The political persuasion of such post-structuralist writing is to trace the specificity of the ways in which race has been constructed at particular moments; and thus to recommend, as is suggested above, strategies which are specific to particular moments and times rather than grand projects which treat the situations of all black people as the same.

Thus, recent critical writing has also been interested in the concept of 'racism'. Rather than accepting that 'racism' is a singular, unified and coherent project, which can be identified working in all colonial societies at all times, in the same way, writers such as Greg Denning have begun to explore the different ways in which racist discourses function in particular cultures at particular times.

The expansion of 'race'

Throughout this entry, various approaches to race in film and cultural theory have been outlined in relation to black American and black British representations. This does not give a proper sense of the many new objects of study which have emerged since the 1980s – the construction of various Asian races, Chicana/o theory in the United States – and, especially, the emergence of 'whiteness' as an object of study for cultural theory. As with other forms of identity in film and television theory, writing on race has been developed in a way which has exnominated many racial groups. It is only from the 1980s onwards that the construction of 'whiteness' becomes an object of investigation in film studies. Particularly important in this context is the work of Richard **Dyer**. Dyer has examined the ways in which the 'raced' identity (or rather, lack of identity) of white people is accomplished and sustained in culture, exploring the various meanings which whiteness takes on in culture – including those of civilization, rationality and boundedness.

In this sense, the focus on 'blackness' in this entry does give some sense of the predominance of this racial category as the preferred object of study

in cultural theory, and its central place in the representational theory which has been developed around race. As well as the exnomination of whiteness, another interesting aspect of the dominance of 'blackness' as the object of study for writing on race in culture has been the peculiar effacement of national difference within that label itself. Take for example the case study of indigenous Australia. The representational theories – the stereotype, the black aesthetic – developed in relation to representation of black Americans are often transferred to study of indigenous Australians who have little in common with the situation of the African diaspora in America beyond skin colour. In this, the focus on blackness has proven to be limiting to representational theory: giving limits which are only now being challenged by the call for specificity involved in post-structuralist writing on race. It is important to note that those techniques for describing the construction of race which are developed in relation to one particular cultural moment might not be suitable for making sense of other cultures, or of other times.

See also: structuralism and post-structuralism; white

References

Bogle, D. (1974) *Toms, Coons, Mulattoes, Mammies and Bucks*, New York: Bantam.

Diawara, M. (ed.) (1993) *Black American Cinema*, New York and London: Routledge.

Hall, S. (1997) 'What Is This "Black" in Black Popular Culture?', in Valerie Smith (ed.) *Representing Blackness: Issues in Film and Video*, London: The Athlone Press.

Hartmann, P. and Husband, C. (1974), *Racism and the Mass Media: A Study of the Role of the Mass Media in the Formation of White Beliefs and Attitudes in Britain*, London: Davis-Poynter.

Further reading

Dyer, R. (1997) *White*, London and New York: Routledge.

Gilroy, P. (1993) *The Black Atlantic: Modernity and Double Consciousness*, London and New York: Verso.

hooks, b. (1996) *Reel to Real: Race, Sex and Class at the Movies*, New York and London: Routledge.
Screen (1983) 'The Last Special Issue on Race', vol. 24, no. 2.

ALAN McKEE

reading and reception theory

Mapping out a chronology of reception theory and paradigms of audience interpretations with regard to screen texts is inevitably problematic. Much of the 'academic', theoretical debate over constructions of textual meaning and the process of reading – from the Anglo-American **Formalism** of the 1940s to the German *Rezeptionaesthetik* of the 1970s – has been concerned with 'higher' culture, like poetry and the novel. Conversely, studies of **audience** response to screen texts within a similar time-frame – the 1940s to the 1970s – were grounded in the very different spheres of sociology and psychology, often informed by a commercial or political agenda.

These twin lines of inquiry never fully converged. However, by 1980 they appeared to intersect. The sociological study of film and television audiences gained a sharper focus in the 1960s and 1970s in the United Kingdom as it passed through the Birmingham Centre for Contemporary Cultural Studies, taking a left-wing slant and concerning itself with issues of hegemony, **class** and **sexuality** in British society. During the 1980s, the cultural studies approach became less sociologically-based, beginning to draw on contemporary French cultural theory and the model of increasingly dispersed social power and resistance suggested by Michel **Foucault**, Pierre **Bourdieu** and Michel de **Certeau**.

At this point – in the late 1970s and early 1980s – theories of literary interpretation began to overlap with the study of screen audiences. Certeau, for instance, extended the concept of reading as appropriative 'poaching' to include behaviour in the workplace and walking in the city (see **flâneur**). Umberto **Eco** and Roland **Barthes**, key participants in the debate over literary reception, also turned attention to popular texts such as advertisements and comics books (see **advertising**).

These investigations became the filter through which cultural studies crossed the Atlantic from the localized and specific British tradition to the emerging American, and later Australian, brands of cultural theory. John **Fiske**, for example, views television audiences within a framework of 'micropolitics' drawn from de Certeau, and employs Eco's concepts of semiotic struggle over meanings to describe the conflicts between viewers and producers. Subsequent research, like that of John Tulloch and Henry Jenkins on **science fiction** audiences, explores similar issues of fan resistance to imposed meanings and draws explicitly on European theory of power and resistance.

Literary theories of 'reading', then, began to include popular forms within their remit at the same time as *Screen* theory began to celebrate the active and participatory audience, using the term 'reader' in preference to the more passive word 'viewer'. From the 1940s to the late 1960s, however, reen research had little connection to contemporary debate on literary reception. Even in the 1970s, when parallels emerge between the two fields, similarities which now seem clear went unremarked at the time.

The 1940s and 1950s: audience readings of cinema

In contrast to this overlap between literary and screen theory, research into film audiences during the post-war era bore no relation to the formalist theories of literary reception circulating in the same period. Rather, it sought to discern the '**effects**' of films on their viewers, based on the assumption that a given media stimulus would produce a quantifiable and predictable audience response. This 'stimulus-response' approach is also known as the **hypodermic model** because of its cause–effect hypothesis: producers were assumed to be able to 'inject' a message into their viewers and follow up with research to discover whether the message had been 'correctly' absorbed. Given that the films in question were **propaganda** vehicles – some more thinly disguised than others – viewers would, it was hoped, accept the intended meaning into their own personal world-view, change their attitudes and ultimately alter their behaviour. These rather crude notions of media and the individual – with culture imposed from 'above' on a passive, malleable audience – were shared by the members of the **Frankfurt School**, although with a very different project.

For obvious reasons, inquiry into media 'effects' and influence was of interest to advertisers; but it was also employed by psychology and public opinion research to trace the passage of a film's intended 'message' to the 'receivers' in the audience. Frequently, though, the results confounded expectations and, whether the researchers accepted it or not, suggested a far more complex model of audience reaction than was implied by the study's original premise.

Exemplary of this practice is the research carried out into audience response to two feature films of 1947, *Gentlemen's Agreement* (Elia Kazan) and *Crossfire* (Edward Dmytryk), both intended to challenge anti-Semitic prejudice. The purpose of the research, based on questionnaires and interviews, is explicitly stated in both cases: to study 'changes in group attitudes towards Jews following... the viewing of the motion picture *Gentlemen's Agreement*', and to ascertain whether *Crossfire* would 'have any effect on audiences; that is, would they be the better or the worse, or the same, for having seen the picture?' The questions set to the test groups readily confirm the rather simplistic 'before and after' assumption which then dominated audience research: for example, from the *Gentlemen's Agreement* paper, a question was: 'Did the picture change your attitude towards Jews? Answer: Yes, No'.

While the researchers clearly hoped to be able to measure an appreciable change in attitudes on the part of the 'experimental groups' viewing the motion picture, the results in these and most other studies of the time prove inconclusive or unexpected. With regard to *Crossfire*'s audience, for instance, the results consistently testify that 'no significant change occurred'. In other cases, audience responses are less bland but more challenging to the 'effects' model: prejudiced viewers who were shown a series of pro-tolerance cartoons managed to evade the intended message and even distort it to support their own bigotry. Further studies even revealed a 'boomerang' effect whereby the film shown produced entirely the opposite effect to that intended.

These findings were echoed by two key works of the period, Paul Lazarsfeld's *The People's Choice* (1944), on the presidential election of 1940, and Robert Merton's *Mass Persuasion* (1946), on Kate Smith's marathon war bond drive of 1943. Both studies concluded that the relationship between media stimulus and audience response was more complex, and depended to a great deal on the social and cultural context. Lazarsfeld's findings in particular – that no direct link existed between party propaganda and voter response – had particularly radical implications for the understanding of the relationship between media and audience. Rather than viewing society as a mass of autonomous, independent members, as was assumed by the laboratory studies of that decade, Lazarsfeld's research describes interlinking and overlapping social networks. The individual was no longer seen as isolated but as subject to peer pressures, loyalties and allegiances that could affect both attitudes and behaviour far more powerfully than any media stimulus. Information reached the public, therefore, through a 'two-step flow' rather than a direct 'injection', and was mediated by the individual's social environment.

Such a model implies both an active, discriminating audience who take from the media only those messages which fit their existing frame of belief, and acknowledges the importance of what Stanley Fish (1980) would later call the 'interpretive community' in the reception of textual meaning.

The 1970s and 1980s: theories of reception

The model of a selective, active viewer and listener suggested by such studies as *The People's Choice* did not immediately change the nature of audience research. However, these findings did filter into subsequent enquiries, replacing the 'hypodermic' or 'effects' paradigm with a more fluid notion of viewer response. To give one example, Winick's 1963 study on *The Man with the Golden Arm* (Otto Preminger, 1955) readily accepts that audiences read screen texts according to their own frameworks, for their own meanings. Although the movie was intended as a moral anti-drug **narrative**, the group of addicts who viewed the film saw the casting of Frank Sinatra in the junkie role as a reinforcement of their fantasies and validation of their chosen lifestyle. Many went to see the picture several times and established a something of a cult around what was intended as a harrowing educational drama. Winick concludes: 'the movie was almost a different movie for... addicted members of the audience. Each group perceived the film in a manner consonant with its own tendency system.'

Replacing the 'hypodermic' paradigm, this revised concept of audience – which, while still concerned with the corruptive 'effects' of the media and its relation to delinquency and violence, acknowledged very different interpretations on the part of different social groups – became known as the **uses and gratifications** model. The concept that viewers are able to make their own meanings continued to inform audience research into the 1970s; indeed, it remains central to the concepts of 'appropriation' and 'reading against the grain' of today's cultural studies.

In the parallel sphere of literary theory, the mid- to late 1970s saw debate circulating around the process of reading, the production of meaning and the relationship between author, **text** and reader. While the greater part of this debate, as indicated above, never touches on film and television – the latter still widely regarded as 'low' culture, and thus unworthy of academic study – the theories of Wolfgang Iser, Stanley Fish and E. D. Hirsch remain important to any discussion of audience interpretation, and deserve to be briefly outlined.

Wolfgang Iser, author of *The Implied Reader* (1974) and *The Act of Reading* (1980), is associated with the *Rezeptionsaesthetik* – usually translated as 'reception theory' – of the University of Konstanz, Germany. Iser's theory is indebted to the work of the Polish philosopher Roman Ingarden, whose *The Literary Work of Art* was first published in 1930. Ingarden proposes that the literary text contains gaps, 'spots of indeterminacy', which the act of reading fills in, or 'concretizes'. The text itself only holds meanings 'in readiness'; the reader brings them out, and in so doing can generate meanings never intended by the author. However, like those researchers of the 1940s to whom unexpected viewer interpretations counted as a 'failed' message, Ingarden saw certain concretizations as inappropriate 'obscurations' of the intended meaning.

Building on these concepts, Wolfgang Iser saw reading as a dynamic act which brought meaning

to a previously incomplete text. This creative process could result in various different interpretations of the same work as each reader filled in the blanks according to his or her individual expectations and predispositions. Again, though, the text is considered by Iser to exist outside and prior to the reading process; the role of the reader is limited to closing gaps in a given framework.

As should be clear, these approaches to the reading process correspond roughly, albeit coincidentally, with the models of audience response emerging from psychological and social studies research into television and film viewers during the same broad period. This liberal, rather than radical, stance towards the fluidity of textual meaning – with the proviso that an 'original' meaning still exists, even if readers are able to construct their own new meanings according to context – finds a parallel in Umberto Eco's *The Role of the Reader* (1981). Eco argues that 'closed', popular texts – he uses the refreshing example of Superman comics – are open to an infinity of readings depending on the context of their reception. Such interpretations, Eco writes, do not 'betray the nature' of the text; rather, the meaning is 'co-operatively generated' by the reader. Nevertheless, he still labels those interpretations not envisaged by the writer as 'aberrant decoding', implying a hierarchy of meaning with the authorial intention given priority.

On either side of these relatively similar positions are the two opposing poles of E. D. Hirsch and Stanley Fish. Hirsch, in *The Aims of Interpretation* (1976), states firmly that our duty as readers is to seek out the stable and 'correct' meaning of a text, which is almost invariably that of the author. He sees the alternative as a 'cognitive atheism'; a chaos of meanings or, worse, no meaning at all. He distinguishes the 'meaning' of a work, which must remain stable, from the 'significance', which can vary through different interpretations. While some interpretations, Hirsch admits, may serve a useful purpose within a certain context, the author's remains the original and best.

Such a position is radically opposed to that of Stanley Fish, whose *Is There a Text in This Class?* (1980) embraces a potential infinity of meanings. To Fish, the text has no stable, external prior existence but is generated in the act of reading itself; and there can be as many different interpretations of a text as there are readers, with each specific meaning seeming perfectly valid and obvious to the person who receives it. The result is not quite the semiotic anarchy feared by Hirsch, however. Readers, in Fish's view, do not stand in isolation, each with their own esoteric and unpredictable patterns of interpretation, but are part of 'interpretive communities' which govern the way they understand a text; a notion which is not far removed from that proposed by *The People's Choice.*

Fish's model of readings is, in fact, more radical than even the current state of screen theory on audience reception, for it claims no 'original' meaning which viewers then react against; the text is formed only in the act of reading. However, there remain strong parallels between the literary-based theory of Iser and his contemporaries and the concepts of audience debated around the same period in British cultural studies, largely centred on the Birmingham Centre for Contemporary Cultural Studies.

The 1980s and 1990s: cultural studies and popular readings

Rather than seeking proof of 'effects' through questionnaires, as in the more simplistic of the 1940s audience studies, much of the work emerging from Birmingham's postgraduate research groups was based on **ethnography**, field studies and interviews, often involving lengthy transcripts whose nuances were analysed in detail. A prime example is David Morley's *The 'Nationwide' Audience* (1980), a key work in the study of television viewer response. Morley applied the concepts of Stuart **Hall**, his mentor and head of the Birmingham Centre, to groups of viewers who were asked to watch and comment on the British news programme *Nationwide*. In Hall's model, audiences may respond to a text either by accepting the 'preferred' intended meaning, by taking an '**oppositional**' stance and rejecting the message or, as is most likely, by 'negotiating' their own interpretation – agreeing with that part of the message which fits their beliefs and rejecting, or qualifying, other aspects. Morley's results are used as the basis for a discussion of the fluidity of meaning, informed by a

view of class-based 'interpretive communities' – trades union members, Conservative Party voters and schoolboys – which can be seen in retrospect as overdeterminative.

Morley stresses that while a message always contains more than one potential meaning, and can always be 'decoded', or read, differently from the way it was 'encoded', or intended, the number of potential meanings is not infinite. A message remains 'structured in dominance' around the preferred, original meaning, although it can never remain entirely fixed (see **encoding; encoding-decoding model**).

This carefully moderate stance towards interpretation, admitting the potential for reading 'against the grain' of the intended meaning yet arguing that these reader interpretations are always formed in reaction to a preferred original, informs most of the cultural studies work on audience of the 1980s and 1990s. Janice Radway's influential *Reading the Romance* (1987) brings issues of **gender** to the debate, detailing a group of female readers' complex responses to both the patriarchal and the 'resistant' elements of popular romance fiction. While it represents the successful transition of the British cultural studies approach to the United States, it might be noted that *Reading the Romance* has been criticized for its avoidance of class and its refusal to address the social distance between the researcher and her subjects.

The concern with gendered readings has continued in studies of film and television, notably by Ien Ang, Jackie Stacey and Christine Gledhill and in the British journal *Screen* (see **Screen theory**). This research has often been concerned with viewing positions within **patriarchy** and has debated the controlling power of the male gaze, a concept first proposed by Laura **Mulvey** (see **gaze, the**).

During this period John Fiske published what was effectively a trilogy on readings of popular texts: *Television Culture* (1987), *Reading the Popular* (1989) and *Understanding Popular Culture* (1989). Like Radway's study, Fiske's work embodies a shift in cultural studies – part of the journey from the UK to the US via France – towards a more dispersed model of cultural power after Foucault, de Certeau and Bourdieu. At the same time, Fiske moves towards a study of popular texts in themselves rather than audience research. The viewer emerges in Fiske's work from a close examination of the text in question, in much the same way that reception theory had projected the reader through analysis of literary prose. Here, however, the objects of study are not John Milton and William Blake but the television shows *Cagney and Lacey, Miami Vice* and *The A-Team*.

While still assuming a 'correct' original which the viewer must read against, Fiske celebrates audience readings which run contrary to the intended grain as 'resistant' on a level of 'micro-politics', which he sees as potentially more effective than organized political struggle. This approach, presupposing an original meaning on the part of the author/producer but claiming a vaguely political 'subversion' in audience readings, became particularly common in feminist and queer screen theory of the 1980s and 1990s (see **feminist theory; queer theory**).

John Tulloch and Henry Jenkins follow on from Fiske in *Science Fiction Audiences* (1995), also employing de Certeau's model of textual 'poaching', yet draw more sober conclusions about the relative powerlessness of audiences in the face of multi-media ownership and the vast institutions of capitalist production. While valuing audience creativity, Tulloch and Jenkins remain unconvinced that frameworks of power can be subverted merely through the act of viewing.

The current dominant paradigm of screen reception proposes fluid readings within a framework. It presupposes an 'original', intended meaning, contra Stanley Fish, but does not assume this will reach its audience, or audiences, who are seen in turn as communities making their own uses and meanings which may be 'better', that is more useful to them, than the 'original'.

In theory, then, there is no 'right' meaning, and producers are accepted as having no divine right to claim theirs as the correct one. In practice, however, the space between audiences and producers of screen texts is not a democratic arena. Production companies are in a position to rigorously enforce their own meanings simply through economic dominance and control over distribution. While this may seem a pessimistic conclusion, it by no means rules out the potential for struggle and debate over meaning between producers and audiences – for instance, in the form of organized fandom's low-budget magazines, conventions, protest campaigns and **Internet** sites (see **fandom**). We must remember, though, that – as Bourdieu would readily accept – the playing field between the two sides is rarely level.

References

Eco, U. (1979) *The Role of the Reader,* Bloomington: Indiana University Press.

Fish, S. (1980) *Is There a Text in This Class?,* Cambridge: Harvard University Press.

Fiske, J. (1987) *Television Culture,* London: Methuen.

Hirsch, E. D. (1976) *The Aims of Interpretation,* Chicago: Chicago University Press.

Ingarden, R. (1973) *The Literary Work of Art,* Evaston: Northwestern University Press.

Iser, W. (1974) *The Implied Reader,* London: Johns Hopkins University Press.

—— (1980) *The Act of Reading,* Baltimore: Johns Hopkins University Press.

Lazarsfeld, P. F., *et al.* (1944) *The People's Choice,* New York: Columbia University Press.

Merton, R. (1946) *Mass Persuasion: The Social Psychology of a War Bond Drive,* New York: Harper and Brothers.

Morley, D. (1980) *The 'Nationwide' Audience,* London: BFI Publishing.

Radway, J. (1987) *Reading the Romance,* London: Verso.

Raths, L. E. and Trafer, F. N. (1948) 'Public Opinion and Crossfire', *The Journal of Educational Sociology,* vol. 21.

Rosen, I. (1948) 'The Effect of the Motion Picture *Gentlemen's Agreement* on Attitudes Towards Jews', *Journal of Psychology,* vol. 26.

Tulloch, J. and Jenkins, H. (1995) *Science Fiction Audiences,* London: Routledge.

Further reading

Jenkins, H. (1992) *Textual Poachers,* New York: Routledge.

Winick, C. 'Tendency Systems and the Effects of a Movie Dealing with a Social Problem', *Journal of General Psychology,* vol. 68.

WILL BROOKER

real time

A scene of a film or television programme is said to take place in real time when its duration on the screen is equal to its **plot** duration. Conventionally, **continuity editing** techniques work to make screen duration shorter than plot duration by the temporal elision that takes place at the cut between two shots. The film *High Noon* (Fred Zinnermann, 1952) is (mistakenly) celebrated for being shot in real time since its 85 minutes of screen time is thought to represent a continuous 85 minutes of plot time. The term is normally used at the level of the sequence, scene or film rather than the individual shot.

See also: realism; reality effect

ANDREW BIRTWISTLE

realism

There is probably no critical term with a more unruly and confusing lineage than that of realism.

(Hill 1984: 57)

'Unruly' discussions about realism and the media take place as much outside as inside academic contexts. Asserting that a film or programme is realistic is often a covert way of expressing, and inviting, a favourable attitude towards it; denying that it is realistic seems to imply that the representation has been misread, or even worse, that the 'real' world has been misunderstood. At issue is a way of seeing the world and a way of judging representations of it, and both are matters about which there is a long history of disagreement – often emotive. Such disagreements pre-date film and television, but have been made more acute by the pervasiveness of these media, and by their **indexical** and iconic' qualities (see **icon**).

Outside an academic context the argument is often based on the assumption that we all see the world in more or less the same way, and can therefore agree whether or not any given representation is accurate. The passport photograph gives this view an almost universal legal status. But even the briefest reflection shows its limitations: the passport photo is a two-dimensional; its object is three-dimensional; at a certain point in history the passport photo was monochrome; its size is arbitrary; and so on. And, as someone inevitably says, 'It doesn't *really* look like you …'. Perhaps it is the *desire* to believe the world is unproblematically available to us all in the same way that makes us think that its representation could be similarly accessible. **Photography** and film are only the most recent phenomena that have seemed likely to meet that unfulfillable desire.

The 'unruly and confusing lineage' of Realism is not dealt with in its entirety in this entry; indeed, many other entries in this volume, including those on **ideology and hegemony**, subjectivity (see **subject and subjectivity**), **ontology**, **Hegel**, **Merleau-Ponty** and **Marx** contribute to this lineage. Instead, this entry outlines some of the ways in which the term has been used in theoretical and critical discussion of film and television. Every usage of the term in this context, then, carries its own history, and is usually part of a polemical argument, rather than a mode of enquiry, about how the world exists and how we are to represent and understand it in film and television. The entry begins by referring to one of the first discussions of the explicit use of Realism as a practice in the visual arts, but there is no single style or practice that can be identified once and for all as Realism.

Representation, reality and realism

Theories of the mimetic function of art go back at least to Aristotle, but Realism as a term gained circulation among writers, painters and critics in the middle of the nineteenth century (see **mimetic/mimesis**). Linda Nochlin argues that painters like Gustave Courbet and Edouard Manet painted in styles which consciously contrasted with those of their predecessors not only because they could see that rapid urbanization and industrialization were changing the appearance of the world around them but also *because they saw that world differently*. The development of the natural sciences and positivist philosophy had encouraged a commitment to the scientific attitude:

Impartiality, impassivity, scrupulous objectivity, rejection of *a priori* metaphysical or epistemological prejudice, the confining of the artist to the accurate observation and notation of empirical phenomena, and the description of how, and not why, things happen.

(Nochlin 1980: 4)

Not surprisingly, Realist painters like Courbet, Manet and Edgar Degas even made use of the emerging technology of photography to assist them in capturing surface appearances.

Nochlin's argument in *Realism* is that changes in aesthetic style relate to more general changes in the climate of ideas, but the above quotation implies some other features of Realism. Essentially, nineteenth-century Realism is concerned to reproduce surface appearances rather than indicate the causes of those appearances. The reference to 'metaphysical or epistemological prejudice' draws attention to the rejection of a previous style in painting which subscribed to the belief that the artist's task was to recognize that appearances were no more than a means of suggesting 'the reality of something other and beyond that of the mere external, tangible facts they held before them' (Nochlin 1980: 45). In this metaphysical sense, even classical painters like Caravaggio in the early seventeenth century could have claimed to be realist. Furthermore, within the period of Realism, painting was not uniform: Courbet differed from Manet, but the point is that both were committed to finding a style that matched their conception of the real.

Realism and film

The nineteenth-century's conception of Realism has much in common with the notion of naturalism, in its concern to represent appearances (see **naturalism and non-naturalism**). The nature of photography furthered this conception, and the potential of film to add movement made it almost inevitable that claims would be made for the value of film in reproducing the real. Contemporary painting and photography were also deploying and reinforcing the coding which transforms a three-dimensional world into a framed, two-dimensional one. As Roman **Jakobson** points out, in order to 'see' a picture we first learn the conventional language of painting, and this conditions the act of visual perception in a way which moving pictures could draw on. At the same time, in order for us to

characterize what we see as realism, it has to be perceived by the person judging it as 'true to life'. In the case of the Realist movement in nineteenth-century painting, both artists and public shared the same sense of truth-to-lifeness, a perception which was shaped by the current ideas of the time.

If film in its early years might be said to continue this kind of Realist tradition, it was soon challenged by different visual styles, each making claims to be more real than its predecessor. Soviet filmmakers made the most consciously theorized claims in the 1920s. Once again it could be argued that what was behind the challenge to the predominantly **narrative**, non-fiction realist cinema already associated with Hollywood was a changed perception of how reality might be seen. In some formulations this was related to the view that the dominant (bourgeois) ideology inhibited a general perception of the real conditions of existence (see **dominant ideology**). If the technical apparatus of early cinema had been developed to exploit cinema's potential to reproduce the nineteenth-century modes of perception both in art and in reality, a different deployment of that apparatus might be needed to reproduce another perception of reality. Already in film, as Jakobson has pointed out in relation to literary realism, a new version of realism was challenging that which had become the accepted norm on the grounds that the earlier form no longer represented reality accurately.

Using the proportionate representation which was typical of nineteenth-century Realism as an example, **Eisenstein** argued that the kind of perception proposed by such realism was 'simply the function of a certain form of social structure'. For Eisenstein, film could achieve what all the arts aimed for: 'to reconstruct, to reflect reality, and above all the consciousness and feelings of man' (Williams 1980: 19). This led to the experiments with **acting**, editing and subject matter that characterize Eisenstein's early films. Eisenstein explored the specific signifying practices of film by reformulating its relation to the world, and attempting to change the way these relations were to be understood (see **signifying practice**). He claimed that his modes of montage editing altered the way films would be perceived by the spectator, breaking with the perceptions of nineteenth-century Realism. Eisenstein's conception of realism owed less to surface appearances and much more to the (assumed) work of the viewer.

A more radical realist aesthetic was proposed by Dziga **Vertov**. His argument was that the characteristic narrative dramas of fiction films betrayed the potential of film for the working class by placing artifice between the spectator and the film's capacity to show the appearance of the world. Like Courbet, Vertov wanted to make working people the subject of his representations, a practice followed in realist aesthetics from Emile Zola's novels to Ken Loach's films. But Vertov also wanted to demonstrate film's capacity to see more and reveal more than the naked eye by placing his camera where the eye could not go – just as a microscope is used to reveal hidden realities. Vertov's spectator would be encouraged by his films to see 'the world as it is and to reveal its bourgeois structure to the workers' (Williams 1980: 27). But, in a move that paradoxically anticipates an **avant-garde** anti-realist position, he was also concerned to foreground the technology of reproduction in the interests of realism. *The Man with a Movie Camera* (1929) deliberately shows the techniques of editing and projection necessary to deliver 'the world as it is'.

For realism in cinema

Though differing in practice, Vertov shared the **documentary** filmmaker John **Grierson**'s view that actuality could be treated creatively; both men proposed 'realisms' that were different from the dominant form, that of Hollywood. Some versions of 'Hollywood realism', however, were celebrated by André **Bazin** whose own understanding encompassed more than one form. Indeed, Bazin proposed:

> There is not one, but several realisms. Each era looks for its own, that is to say the technique and the aesthetic which can best capture it, arrest and restore *whatever one wishes to capture of reality.*
> (Williams 1980: 41; my emphasis)

Bazin's writing on realism in cinema is sophisticated and suggestive. He starts from a conception of reality that he describes as ontologically ambiguous and immanent, implying that there are meanings in any fragment of reality which may only emerge when a context is provided, even if this is a metaphysical one. In relation to cinema this might be understood through his analogy:

> Facts are facts, our imagination makes use of them but they don't exist inherently for this purpose. In the usual shooting script . . . the fact comes under the scrutiny of the camera, is divided up, analysed, and put together again, undoubtedly without entirely losing its factual nature; but the latter is enveloped in abstraction as the clay of a brick is enveloped by a wall.
> (Bazin 1971: 37)

Conceding that 'in cinema there can only be a representation of reality', Bazin develops an argument for a realist aesthetic which is flexible enough to embrace filmmakers as diverse as the neo-realist Roberto Rossellini and the Hollywood filmmakers William Wyler and Orson Welles.

Bazin argues that reality must be 'respected' even if artifice is required to do that. In the case of neo-realist filmmakers, respect is exhibited in their desire to show the reality of post-war Italy as transparently as possible by relying on indexical re-creation and avoiding the use of objects and places merely for dramatic **mise-en-scène**. In the case of Wyler and Welles the argument is more complicated. Working within a regime where the 'authentic document' of the outside world is not available because Hollywood preferred studio production, both directors use other cinematic resources. Wyler's *mise-en-scène* is unemphatic and austere and, like Welles, his use of **depth of field** and fewer cuts than was normal in Hollywood respects the continuity of time in the real world and also the spectator's 'real world' perception. He or she *chooses* what to look at on the screen, especially in the case of Wyler's films

Bazin's version of realism suggests a more complicated relationship between text and world. For him, a realist aesthetic can be discerned from films which 'capture' what they want from the world using different techniques and technologies. Bazin also thought that we see the world in much the same way as we see a film, selecting those things to which we wish to pay attention. As with other realist aesthetics, assumptions are made about the ways in which representations are understood and become part of the rhetoric of the argument.

Hollywood emerged as the location of the dominant film industry in the teens of the twentieth century and its aesthetic practices in relation to realism have since been a source of discussion and even hostility. The technical, social and aesthetic conjunctures surrounding the rise to dominance of the Hollywood studio system are described elsewhere (see **classical Hollywood cinema and new Hollywood cinema**), as are its characteristic narrative strategies. The combination of **continuity editing**, psychologically convincing characterization, a narrative fiction with a referential relationship to lived experience, and the indexical and iconic power of film made Hollywood realism the dominant convention – a dominance supported by economic power. It was also a form of realism with many of the features of nineteenth-century painting and literature.

Against Hollywood

In the 1970s, Colin MacCabe's influential account of the '**classic realist text**' moved discussion of film realism away from film's relationship to its referent and more towards those structural features of narrative operations in Hollywood films which maintained the illusion of reference to reality for ideological purposes. MacCabe's argument draws on theoretical models derived from Jacques **Lacan** and Althusserian Marxism (see **Althusser, Louis**) and a structuralist background which questioned the referentiality of all **sign** systems (see **structuralism and post-structuralism**). Theoretically, the classic realist text held spectators in ways which made them incapable of being aware of the internal contradictions in the film, or of feeling contradictions induced in them as spectators. The false understanding of the world produced by this position could be destroyed by film practices that systematically countered Hollywood realism. Indeed, 'realism' in the Hollywood context was an ideologically-biased illusionism.

Subsequent challenges to the idea of the classic realist text questioned its general application and its disregard for actual, rather than theoretical, spectator positions. Christopher Williams' (1994) critique is particularly interesting because it

reminds us that, within twenty years of its rise to pre-eminence, Hollywood had developed popular genres whose relationship to reality was not seen as straightforwardly referring to the world. Within a musical, for example, spectators could deal with highly stylized representations which might play on nineteenth-century melodramatic or operatic conventions, along with a *mise-en-scène* which had the features of the nineteenth-century realist novel or painting (see **melodrama; musical, the**). Though the Hollywood form could be called 'classical' in relation to other cinemas, its heterogeneity thus embraced a series of complex relations with reality. Over time, as Paul Willemen (1972) suggests, a film could be understood as 'true and real because it was like other films of the same type within the genre, and therefore realistic' (see **verisimilitude**). Conversely, when the **genre** had become too familiar, a deliberate break with only *some* aspects of its conventions could be presented, and viewed, as a move to greater realism: the Western, *Unforgiven* (Clint Eastwood, 1992), is an example (see **Western, the**).

Television realism: referentiality and genre

If a dominant form of cinematic realism, the narrative fiction film, can sometimes be partially understood within realist aesthetics derived from art forms like painting and the novel, television is less easy to accommodate in this context. Indeed, one of the best articles on the topic begins with the rueful observation that the very notion of television 'realism' 'is close to being devoid of all useful analytic meaning' (Corner 1992: 97). The diverse nature of television output – drama, news, current affairs, sport, chat shows – its ubiquitous presence *as a part of* our reality, and the manner in which the medium is used and researched resist a single theoretical explanation. There is space here only to indicate some arguments about non-fiction and fiction television which have recently developed, and to suggest that increasingly subtle uses of audience research in television call into question some of the assumptions made about the modalities of realism in relation to audiences. None the less, 'unruly' discussions about television and realism, inside and outside the academy, now seem to be as common as those about film.

One approach to realism in non-fiction television is to remember that the theorization of *non-fiction film* also has a long history. Though there are no simple answers to fundamental questions here either, the 1980s saw sustained attempts to come to terms with the distinctive nature of non-fiction film as documentary. Bill Nichols (1991) moved discussion of documentary away from merely text-based accounts, but the distinctions he makes between fiction and non-fiction film in their reference to the world are helpful. Nichols argues that documentary relies on the indexical quality of the image for evidentiary purposes – it offers evidence of the world, of a historical reality that becomes part of an argument rather than a story. Where the fiction film has a metaphorical relationship to reality and can create *a* plausible world that may seem real even when fantastical, realism in documentary uses indexicality as the basis of an argument about *the* world which must match some spectators' perception of that everyday world.

Michael Renov refines this position in arguing that the relationship of documentary to the world is distinctive:

> what differs is the extent to which the reference of the documentary sign may be considered as a piece of the world, plucked from its everyday context rather than fabricated for the screen.
>
> (Renov 1993: 7)

Though Renov's remark only concerns documentary it may have implications for other 'pieces of the world' like news and sport which television plucks from their everyday context and offers to us in the 'argument' of news or sports reporting.

Fiction television's relationship with the real has been examined by John Caughie (1991) in the context of Roman Jakobson's argument. Jakobson argues that once a specific current of art, such as nineteenth-century Realism, becomes the dominant form of realist representations, some will see deviations from this form as a distortion of reality but others will claim that this is a more accurate rendition of reality – the argument we noted above as verisimilitude. Though there is not, in television, any dominant form of cinema comparable with Hollywood, some genres, or subgenres, of American television such as the crime series create a model (e.g., *Kojak*) to which later series (e.g., *Starsky*

and Hutch and *Charlie's Angels*) conform. Challenges to this form which revitalize it can come from a series like *Cagney and Lacey*, *Hill Street Blues* and, later, *NYPD Blue* and *Homicide: Life on the Street*. The conventions of representation which seem to have been acceptable to a mass audience at one time are rejected by later audiences often on the grounds that the latter conventions offer a greater realism, or, in Caughie's phrase, are more 'grounded in social reality'. In the police genre in British television, the 'realist' nature of the challenge is very apparent when the flexible conventions of long-running British series *The Bill* are contrasted with *The Cops*, a series which deliberately adds the referential and argumentative *appearance* of documentary film to the narrative structures and psychological characterization of fiction film. In this way, Jakobson and Caughie shift the theorizing of realism more towards the responses of the spectator.

Discussion of realism in film and television, then, inevitably moves towards the nature of aesthetic conventions and the spectator's perception of them, and of his or her own circumstances in the world. More ethnographic research practices, like those of Ien Ang and David Morley, increasingly used in television, may yet give us more concrete evidence about the correspondence between the viewer's perception of reality in relation to its representation (see **ethnography**). So far, much theorizing about realism in film and television has been based on *assumptions* about how people see representations of reality and understand and use them rather than the kind of research which deals with their *actual* experiences. However, framing questions about what and how people conceive reality to be brings its own complexities.

In the meantime, in his argument for the importance of retaining realism as a critical concept, Christopher Williams reminds us that what we are dealing with are conventions on both sides of the screen:

> The use of realist conventions does not, in itself, provide or imply 'knowledge of how things really are'. On the other had, it may, and quite often does, work within the framework of, or in relation to, social conventions. It would be

difficult to tell a love story without appealing, at one level or another, to some people's knowledge of what love is like.

(Williams 1994: 281)

This is not a naïve appeal to people's experience as some unproblematic access to a 'real world' against which to check out the realism of a text, but a recognition that experience itself needs to be understood, like realism, 'in conjunction with concepts like convention, language, structure and discourse'.

Conclusions

- There is not one epistemological or aesthetic realism but there are realisms;
- realisms change over time;
- changes in realisms usually relate to preceding forms and shifts in critical or public opinion;
- realisms operate through conventions; perceptions of the real also operate though conventions;
- realist texts may be heterogeneous and may include anti-realisms;
- the ideological and social consequences of realism are not uniform and relate to the spectators' perception of reality;
- realism as a critical concept has particular significance in film and television because of their indexical qualities;
- attitudes or claims to realism offer insight into the history of film and television forms and genres, and theoretical and critical writing about film and television.

See also: chat/talk show; cop shows (police drama); live television

References

Ang, I. (1991) 'Wanted Audiences. On the Politics of Empirical Audience Studies', in E. Seiter *et al. Remote Control*, London: Routledge.

—— (1991) *Desperately Seeking the Audience*, London: Routledge.

Bazin, A. (1971) *What Is Cinema? Volume 2*, trans. Hugh Gray, London: University of California Press.

Caughie, J. (1991) 'Adorno's Reproach: Repetition,

Difference and Television Genre', *Screen*, vol. 32, no. 2.

Corner, J. (1992) 'Presumption as Theory: "Realism" in Television Studies', *Screen*, vol. 33, no. 1.

Hill, J. (1984) *Sex, Class and Realism*, London: BFI Publishing.

Jakobson, R. (1978) 'On Realism in Art', in L. Matejka and K. Pomorska (eds) *Readings in Russian Poetics: Formalist and Structuralist Views*, Michigan: University of Michigan Press.

MacCabe, C. (1974) 'Realism and the Cinema: Notes on Some Brechtian Theses', *Screen*, vol. 15, no. 2.

Morley, D. (1986) *Family Television, Cultural Power and Domestic Leisure*, London: Comedia.

—— (1992) *Television, Audiences and Cultural Studies*, London: Routledge.

Nelson, R. (1997) *TV Drama in Transition*, Basingstoke: Macmillan Press.

Nichols, B. (1991) *Representing Reality*, Bloomington: Indiana University Press.

Nochlin, L. (1980) *Realism*, London: Penguin.

Renov, M. (1993) *Theorising Documentary*, London: Routledge.

Williams, C. (ed.) (1980) *Realism and Cinema*, London: Routledge/BFI Publishing.

—— (1994) 'After the Classic, the Classical and Ideology: The Difference of Realism', *Screen*, vol. 35, no. 3.

Willemen, P. (1972) 'On Realism in the Cinema', *Screen*, vol. 13, no.1.

PHILIP SIMPSON

reality effect

According to Stuart **Hall**, reality effect is produced when encountering a text organized along familiar lines – it seems not to be an organized text at all but rather a vehicle for showing 'how things really are'. Television in particular can appear 'to reproduce the actual trace of reality in the images' that it transmits (Hall 1982: 75–6).

See also: live television; real time; realism

References

Hall, S. (1982) 'The Rediscovery of "Ideology":

Return of the Repressed in Media Studies', in Michael Gurevitch, Tony Bennett, James Curran and Janet Woollacott (eds) *Culture, Society and the Media*, London: Methuen.

CLAY STEINMAN

referent

In sign analysis models like the one suggested by Charles S. **Peirce**, the referent is the 'real' object that a **sign** stands for while it denotes the concept of that object in the sign-users mind; the distinction is necessary since the concept a sign-user employs might be quite different from the 'real' object. Cognitive linguists like Jackendoff have even suggested a fourth level of differentiation, placing the 'referent' in a 'projected world' as a world perceivable within the constraints of human perception and cognitive processes, while the 'real world' – and consequently the 'real object', if there is one – cannot be objectively described or referred to.

See also: cognitive theory

EVA VIETH

reflexivity

In simple audio-visual terms, reflexivity (often referred to as 'self-reflexivity') describes the process by which a film or television programme draws attention to itself, reminding the spectator of its textuality and status as a media construct. While recognizing that reflexivity is not exclusive to the audio-visual realm, several theorists, among them Noël Burch (1973) and Robert Stam (1992), have attempted to account for reflexivity in terms of the specificity of film and television. In broader cultural terms, however, concepts of reflexivity have been theorized for several centuries, and have been employed practically within a diverse spectrum of cultural fields – from ancient poetry to quantum physics, wood carving to abstract art.

The term 'reflexivity' is derived from the Latin *reflexio/reflectere* meaning, 'to bend back on'. Applied to audio-visual practice, by extension of this etymological root, reflexivity refers to the capacity of film and television texts to draw attention to their existence as constructs. It is the process by which texts foreground their authorship and production, acknowledging their status as representation.

Within this schema of audio-visual reflexivity, we can identify a series of such devices: strategies of fracture, distanciation, interruption, discontinuity. Stylistic virtuosity, as one example, operates according to these principles, and involves an exaggerated, self-conscious use of style that draws the spectator's awareness to the fact that he or she is watching an audio-visual construction. We become alert to the role of the director and the artifice on which all filmmaking and television production is predicated.

Other reflexive strategies draw direct attention to the formal materials and processes of media construction, literally revealing to the spectator both the tools of production (camera, microphone, lights and so on) and the physical objects of audio-visual communication (for instance, a strip of film). Within this textual focus, it is the medium that becomes the critical area of interest. In popular animated series like *The Simpsons* and *The Ren and Stimpy Show*, the animation process is revealed to ironic, comic effect through **pastiche** and textual reference to production technique. While in Dziga **Vertov**'s *Man with a Movie Camera* (1929), the filmmaking apparatus is similarly revealed through a systematic focus on the film's own production. Clearly, the reflexive canon encompasses a wide range of devices, the most explicit among them being direct address to the camera, narrative discontinuity, authorial intrusion, essayistic digression, display of process and apparatus, reflexive inter-titles, and other meta-cinematic devices such as the frame-within-the-frame and the film-within-the-film.

Yet the motivation behind such self-consciousness differs from text to text. Historically, reflexivity has often been aligned with political ideology. Such an allegiance points to the assumption that both film and television are based on a desire for illusionism, a fictitious other world within which we, as spectators, can immerse ourselves. More contentiously, theorists have argued that such audio-visual illusionism directly supports the dominant political ideology (see **dominant ideology**).

When reflexivity deconstructs this type of illusionism, it is argued, the reflexive strategies take on a subversive or radical dimension, critiquing the society that generates such self-serving audio-visual fictions.

On the one hand, then, reflexive devices can be considered in political terms, part of the modernist artistic project that draws attention to the materials with which film and television programme-makers work, and the creative processes that engender their texts. On the other hand, post-modernist theory poses a problematic or mutated continuation of this reflexive tradition. As self-conscious hybridization, reference, pastiche and textuality have become the cultural norm, the status of reflexivity has evolved. Within the context of post-modernism and beyond, reflexivity has assumed a new, dominant position within the fun-house of self-conscious style.

See also: Bahktin, Mikhail; Brecht, Bertolt; intertextuality; modernism and post-modernism

Further reading

Burch, N. (1973) *Theory of Film Practice*, New York: Praeger.
Stam, R. (1992) *Reflexivity in Film and Literature: From Don Quixote to J-L. Godard* (revised edn), New York: Columbia University Press.

ANDREW UTTERSON

regression

According to Sigmund **Freud**, dream activity is a regression, or reversal in the normal processing of stimuli. While mental processes in waking life progress from perceptual stimuli to motor activity, dreaming entails regression towards heightened perceptual activity (Freud 1953: 548). The concept is useful in drawing parallels between viewing conditions and dreaming, since reduced mobility and increased perceptual stimuli characterize both. If viewing is comparable to dreaming, then perhaps viewers are inclined to process screen images as if they were dreams, or articulations of their own fantasies and desires.

See also: desire; fantasy; psychoanalysis

References

Freud, S. (1953) *The Interpretation of Dreams*, New York: Basic Books.

JEN NEUBER

regulation

This entry examines how broadcasting systems in the United Kingdom and the United States have evolved by outlining the regulatory schemes which have guided them and the values that these call on. This involves investigating the organizational frameworks within which broadcasters have had to operate in order to gauge the ways in which policy has been formulated. Regulation shapes the nature of the mass communication system and determines the means by which information comes about and how it is available. In order to comprehend how regulation has been devised, the wider political context within which broadcasting functions needs to be articulated. In addition, the technological and social pressures, and their influence on the rules of broadcasting, have to be pinpointed. This approach focuses on a number of central issues, namely the purposes of regulation, the underlying relationship of governments to broadcasters and the specific premise on which broadcasting activity is based.

Regulation can best be understood as a set of institutionalized routines directed towards the achievement of certain desirable ends (Gibbons 1998: 4). As such, it proposes a working structure within which all actors, be they governments, broadcasters or regulators, have to operate and in which their duties should be clearly defined. It is imperative, then, to investigate these objectives so as to trace the normative values that lie at the core of broadcasting regulation before observing whether the existing frameworks enact such principles. This entails identifying the ways in which broadcasting systems have developed and directions to which they are being guided.

The aims of regulation

The engine behind broadcasting regulation has been the notion of 'public interest' and the complementary notion of democracy that it encapsulates. Policy-makers have recognized broadcasting's role in providing information, and the concern has been to stimulate a steady stream of knowledge to serve the ends of democracy. As Feintuck (1998: 40) observes, 'effective communication depends upon the effective regulation of communication', and so the urgency of a strong working arrangement to elicit broadcasting's representative obligations is paramount. A healthy democracy requires its citizens to be sufficiently informed so that they are able to make rational choices from the range of views on offer. These requirements necessitate that a free flow of information is supplied, preserving freedom of speech and enabling the full participation in civic affairs, as illuminated here by Keane:

> Public regulation of the [broadcasting] market should seek the creation of a genuine variety of media which enable little people in big societies to send and receive a variety of opinions. It should aim to break down media monopolies, lift restrictions upon particular audience choices and popularise the view that the media of communication are a public good.
>
> (Keane 1991: 155)

The pursuit of citizenship has formed the nucleus of broadcasting regulation since broadcasting has been a primary source of information, and has had to be geared in such a way that the flow of ideas is not subject to state or private constraints. These social obligations, borrowed from the public utility legislation, orient public ownership of broadcasting and channel regulation towards the interests of the public. Liberal democracy requires a full representation of a diverse body of views and that impartial commentary on issues of public concern is disseminated and universally accessible to all. Thus, the need to create a literate citizenry has demanded the inclusion of political balance, accuracy and impartiality in political news as important tenets of legislation (see **bias**).

Regulation, then, must seek to secure the social and cultural mechanisms which would allow broadcasting to execute these functions. The public obligations stem from the belief that broadcasters control an important resource, one that has demanded careful attention because of its reach and because of **spectrum scarcity**. Regulators need to monitor output to ensure the criteria of public interest are met by sifting out material which violates qualities of 'taste and decency' (Feintuck 1998: 46). A recurrent pattern in the history of broadcasting has been the perceived danger that it poses to the moral fibre of the citizenry, the idea being that individuals need to be protected against any damaging material that the power, immediacy and intrusiveness of broadcasting allegedly offer. This highlights a central tension within content regulation: the necessity to protect set alongside the freedom to express, and the need for a diverse output.

Regulatory arrangements have also to make explicit the grounds for intervention on those occasions where the public interest has not been met. However, given that an element of critical distance is required for broadcasters to carry out their role as impartial information providers, a certain degree of autonomy from state pressure is essential. The understanding has been that the state should be involved in broadcasting regulation but the extent to which this intrudes on the day-to-day functioning of the institution has been contested (Gibbons 1998: 41). The requirement here is to have an adequate level of institutional separation, which establishes the broadcasters' independence and the ends of citizenry above all other aims. Thus, an arms-length model of government-broadcaster relations, as mediated through regulatory structures, is required. This demands that an element of transparency in regulation exists, so that the public can see how rules have been formulated.

Regulation in the United Kingdom

Broadcasting regulation in Britain has been implemented through a plethora of bodies, which have changed in response to new media technology and shifts in the political system. The central problem associated with this pragmatic, inconsistent and historically contingent basis of regulation has been the fuzziness of the term 'public interest' (Feintuck 1998: 77). The absence of a written constitution confers the definitional rights at the core elements of public interest on the incumbent government. This, aligned with the scope for pressure via institutional arrangements, has led to the questioning of broadcaster autonomy.

The British Broadcasting Corporation (BBC) has public interest requirements built into its **public service broadcasting** remit as a means by which it should discharge these democratic aims, summarized in its capacity to inform, educate and entertain. Broadcasting has become a major factor in British politics, and the BBC's status as a core national institution has led to acute government scrutiny in periods of political crises (see Gibbons 1998). While legal statutes such as the Official Secrets Act and the D-Notice system offer a formal means of suppression, the very organizational arrangement of the BBC's regulatory framework leave it vulnerable to governmental pressure.

The BBC operates under a Royal Charter, granted by the government and renewed every ten years, which constitutes its general policy objectives. Its structure attests to a potentially high level of political interference with the Board of Governors, headed by a Chairman, and the Director General all being government appointees. They constitutionally represent the BBC and guarantee that the Corporation meets its legal requirements so that the public interest is continually upheld. They are also responsible for appointing the Corporation's Director General and Board of Management who organize the BBC on a day-to-day basis. Such an arrangement holds the BBC directly accountable to Parliament and leaves it to work through a certain understanding of what is permissible.

This model has endowed the state with the power to direct the BBC closely, on occasion too closely for it to faithfully declare itself an autonomous institution. There have been periodic skirmishes between the BBC and governments of the day, with the latter being able to use the licence fee as a means by which to coerce broadcasters. The Thatcher administration launched a sustained assault on the BBC's independence during the 1980s and early 1990s (for a complete discussion of

this, see Negrine 1994). The government stringently questioned the BBC's commitment to the public interest in its coverage of political news. These shortcomings, as conceived by the government, led to the appointment of Conservative Party sympathizers to the Board of Governors on the grounds of public interest and culminated in the resignation of Alisdair Milne, the Director General, in 1987. Experience indicates that the BBC is subject to strict regulatory supervision, although formal measures only constitute part of the picture.

Currently, commercial television in Britain is regulated by the Independent Television Commission (ITC), who is responsible for awarding franchises to regional operators based on a quality criteria stipulated in the 1990 Broadcasting Act. The ITC has to check whether the guidelines of due impartiality and accuracy are met in relation to content and advertising. It also has to encourage fair competition across the whole sector, in addition to monitoring the commercial activities of the BBC. In its position of overall guardian of commercial broadcasting, the ITC has to ensure content fulfils a roughly public service ethos, with due care given to diversity. The ITC also takes a prohibitive stance on material of a sexual and violent nature in a manner similar to that which curtails the BBC (Feintuck 1998: 110). Another strand to the ITC's work has been to ensure that the Independent Television Network (ITV) provides a strong regional service by catering for local communities.

The ITC consists of a governing board of ten members together with a Chairman and Deputy, all of whom are political appointees. The ITC has been through different incarnations (originally the Independent Television Association, then the Independent Broadcasting Authority), and its responsibilities include monitoring content on the proliferating **cable and satellite** channels to ensure standards are upheld. The regulation of commercial television is subject to governmental pressure, particularly as control over transmission rests with the Home Secretary (Negrine 1994: 116). Government, who set its scope of influence, determines the range of powers the ITC exercises. The 1990 Broadcasting Act took away some of the regulatory power of the ITC to create a licensing body whose authority is somewhat lighter than in its previous form as the IBA (Feintuck 1998: 129).

The deployment of new technology, aligned with a political system characterized by free-market competition, has changed the broadcasting terrain with new regulators entering to oversee emerging broadcasters. This has given way to the implementation of 'light touch' economic regulation to create a system whereby market forces are the principal regulatory tool, accompanied by competition law to secure a level playing field. The Department for Culture, Media and Sport aims to improve the international competitiveness of the British audio-visual sector and as such is the core government department with responsibility for broadcasting policy. The Office of Telecommunications, a non-ministerial government department, acts as the watchdog for the telecommunications industry, an increasingly important feature of broadcasting as **convergence** grows. It regulates the digital gateway to ensure competition law is upheld so that maximum choice and value accrue to audiences. The Monopoly and Mergers Commission (MMC) keeps a watchful eye with regard to take-overs and alliances in the broadcasting sector, which involves a careful scan over other industries.

It must be emphasized that regulation was formulated in a national context and such confinement is no longer fully warranted as all British broadcasting policy takes place within an extended and now interlinked European sphere. The Television Without Frontiers Directive (1989) attempts to promote common standards across all European member states to facilitate the free flow of programming (Gibbons 1998: 16). Satellite technology allows a greater penetration of television programmes and the concern has thus been to implement an array of supranational laws to combat the content and economic discrepancies between member states. While such measures have been tentative and minimal, the growing transnational character of broadcasting justifies a rethink of the regulatory structures of a broadcasting system which has been through substantial transformation (Negrine 1994: 200).

Regulation in the United States

Broadcasting in the US is regulated by the Federal Communications Commission (FCC) which emerged from the Federal Communications Act, 1934. It declares its mission is 'to encourage competition in all communications markets and to protect the public interest' (FCC 1999). The FCC issues licences over a vast, decentralized system to a multitude of broadcasters who operate largely on a regional basis. The FCC is a state authorized agency directly responsible to Congress from whom, along with the Supreme Court, it receives guidance. Five commissioners, politically designated, assure it functions within the parameters of 'public interest, convenience and necessity' as defined by Congress (Comstock 1991: 4).

Over time, the FCC has evolved into a 'super-regulator' with responsibility over all facets of American media activity under its authority, organized through major offices, each dealing with a separate media channel. The Mass Media Bureau regulates television and radio; Cable Services monitors cable television and other cable services; Common Carrier deals with developments in telegraph and the telephone industries; Compliance and Information allocates radio spectrum and examines infringements of communications law; Wireless Telecommunications oversees cellular telephony and private radio; and International observes satellite, telecommunications and international issues. Such a concentration of regulatory power confers on the FCC the potential to adopt an integrated programme across the whole media system and promote convergence more effectively.

While the public interest clause has similarly been invoked as a general point of practice, in the US setting it has constitutional verification. The First Amendment guarantees Americans freedom of speech, a condition which has been translated into a measurable principle against which media activity can be gauged. The striking feature of the American system of regulation is its belief that competitive markets will guarantee quality as they steer broadcasters towards audience demand (Croteau and Hoynes 1997: 70). The FCC observes competition trends to ensure monopolies do not take root, with limitations on ownership, and that no reduction in standards results from the pursuit of the largest market-share. Thus, a safety net exists to guard diversity against the possibilities of market failure.

The profit-driven basis of American broadcasting has been curtailed, if only in a small way, by the existence of the Fairness Doctrine (1949). This legal requirement stipulated that broadcasters had to seek out controversial issues of public importance and present them in such a way which provided a significant platform for varying opinion (Comstock 1991: 5). Such measures dictated that there was to be balance across the whole broadcasting schedule, in order to preserve public interest, by allocating air-time to views which may not otherwise have been heard. Content regulation has formed a major concern in the US, with charges of on-screen violence causing copycat behaviour. The apparent credibility of this view impelled the FCC to implement strict watersheds for such material and levy fines. In 1996 Congress passed legislation compelling television manufacturers to install a computer chip – a 'V-chip' – in new sets which could detect and then block material of a sufficiently violent nature (Croteau and Hoynes 1997: 87). This procedure indicates the level of anxiety authorities have expressed towards the protection of minors which has subsequently justified a strong system of regulation.

The ideological thrust of the Reagan era advanced unadulterated competition as the basis of broadcasting. The relaxation of economic regulation was matched by the abolition of the Fairness Doctrine in 1987, with the understanding that a plethora of broadcasters would itself cover a diverse range of opinion. It was felt that the prohibitive nature of the doctrine did not cohere with the process of *laissez-faire* which broadcasting has adopted (Comstock 1991: 38). The belief has been that market forces foster plurality, and any intervention is undesirable since it impairs the efficiency of the market. Such a climate of open competition has continued with the Telecommunications Act 1996, further easing restrictions on ownership.

Conclusions

Social purposes, citizenry rights and economic safeguards comprise the core of broadcasting regulation. While these values have collectively formed 'the public interest' it must be stressed that the very term has been conceptualized by regulators, whose close proximity to governmental institutions throws doubt on its neutral standing. The ability to appoint designated representatives, to persuade and even to threaten, ensure that broadcasters operate within boundaries which are governmentally defined. This authority enables governments to guide broadcasting systems as they so choose, a fact which explains why broadcasting functions in parallel to a wider economic ideology, and has become a part of larger conglomerate interests.

Recent history has been characterized by the introduction of new technologies which have exacerbated commercial pressure, through the withdrawal of economic ceilings, at the expense of public interest values (Keane 1991: 155). Yet the spirit of deregulation in market structures has not permeated the whole field of activity; regulation in content and overall supervision has remained tight within centralized regulatory systems. The relaxation of economic laws has opened the floodgates for cheaply produced and often imported programming, some of which fall foul of the 'taste and decency' proviso. This has led to charges of falling standards in overall broadcasting output as commercial logic drives it towards the lowest common denominator (Croteau and Hoynes 1997: 72). With **technological change**, the justification of spectrum scarcity for public interest has been eroded as no single public exists. In its place is a fragmented **audience** whose members can tailor their programming to meet their individual needs. The danger this presents is that the public property of information becomes a privatized, commercial good to be packaged and sold. In such instances, regulation has to guard against one operator controlling the whole market through the control over technological gateways (Keane 1991: 160). It is clear, then, that regulatory schemes need to be geared to working within an international dimension to sustain citizenry values, before fulfilling the commercial opportunities technology brings, and to harnessing these to the ends of democracy. At the same time, the grounds for the state to intercede in relation to content must be clearly defined so that intervention occurs on an established basis as opposed to political expediency.

See also: broadcasting, the United Kingdom; broadcasting, the United States; deregulation, the United Kingdom; deregulation, the United States; public sphere; Reithian

References

Comstock, A. (1991) *Television In America* (2nd edn), Newbury Park, CA: Sage.

Croteau, D. and Hoynes, W. (1997) *Media/Society: Industries, Images and Audiences*, Thousand Oaks, CA: Pine Forge Press.

Federal Communications Commission (1999) *FCC Homepage*. Online. Available: http://www.fcc.org/ (15 April 1999).

Feintuck, M. (1998) *Media Regulation, Public Interest and the Law*, Edinburgh: Edinburgh University Press.

Gibbons, T. (1998) *Regulating The Media* (2nd edn), London: Sweet and Maxwell.

Keane, J. (1991) *The Media and Democracy*, Cambridge: Polity Press.

Negrine, R. (1994) *Politics and the Mass Media in Britain* (2nd edn), London: Routledge.

Further reading

Bagdikian, B. (1992) *The Media Monopoly*, Boston: Beacon Press.

Blumler, J. (ed.) (1992) *Television and the Public Interest: Vulnerable Values in West European Broadcasting*, London: Sage.

Collins, R. (ed.) (1996) *Converging Media? Converging Regulation?*, London: Institute of Public Policy Research.

Dahlgren, P. (1995) *Television and the Public Sphere: Citizenship, Democracy and the Media*, London: Sage.

Hoffmann-Riem, W. (1996) *Regulating Media: The Licensing and Supervision of Broadcasting in Six Countries*, New York: Guilford Press.

RAKESH KAUSHAL

reification

Reification is the process endemic in late capitalism whereby people come to perceive their world, and even themselves, as inert, isolated objects or things.

The concept was introduced in 1923 by the Hungarian Marxist, Gyorgy **Lukács**, in an effort to account for the unexpected failure of the European working classes to achieve class consciousness and thereby realize their revolutionary potential in the years after the First World War. The problem, he surmised, was attributable to the reification of proletarian consciousness, or in other words the stifling of the proletariat's ability to grasp society as a totality, and itself as a subject, a collective agent of historical change.

The origins of the concept can be traced back more than fifty years earlier to the first chapter of the first volume of *Capital*, in which **Marx** describes the double structure of commodity **fetishism**. With the development of a market economy, the physical work which goes into the manufacturing of a commodity and which enables its users to satisfy their needs – to extract 'use value' – is repressed. Instead, the commodity is perceived as an abstract and alienable unit of monetary or 'exchange value'. Complex social relations of production and use are thus subsumed by **commodification** into a simple exchange of things.

From Marx's specific analysis of the commodity, Lukács extrapolated a general social theory of reification, in effect by privileging the commodity as the cell-form or prototype for the rest of society. Drawing on Max **Weber**'s sociology of rationalization and employing **Hegel**'s dialectical method, Lukács argued that this congealing of real human needs and labour into a rigid mould of abstraction and objectivity is evident not only in the factory and marketplace, but also in the superstructural spheres of law, knowledge, philosophy and the state (see **base and superstructure**). Under the regime of the commodity all consciousness (even that of the philosopher or cultural critic) succumbs to a blind, compulsive desire to quantify and rationalize the external world. The culture of bourgeois capitalism is excessively rational, or rather, from Lukács' standpoint of a higher rationality, fundamentally irrational.

By the late 1930s, in the writings of Theodor **Adorno**, Max **Horkheimer** and other members of the **Frankfurt School**, the stultifying effects of reification would be discovered even further afield: in cinema, radio, **advertising** and jazz. **Culture**, in their view, had been subjected to the dictates of mass production and economic necessity, which had in turn severely eroded the ability of the audience to watch or listen in a critical fashion. The only solid ground for autonomous critique that now remained, given the shattering of working-class movements by the fascists during the same decade, was the high art of modernism (see **modernism and post-modernism**).

In recent decades, however, the logic of reification has largely fallen out of fashion. **Gramsci**'s version of Marxism was found to be less totalizing and negative in its conception of the social, and thus more fruitful for the popular cultural studies of the Birmingham School in the 1970s (see **Hall, Stuart**). Meanwhile, there were doubts as to the elitist self-positioning and self-legitimation of the Lukácsian critic. The fact that the Marxist theorist is able accurately to discern the distorting effects of reification presupposes some privileged and authentic standpoint outside and above the society he is describing. Conversely, true class consciousness is affirmed simply by appealing to its inherent 'truth'. Those Marxist critics who continue to use the term therefore tend to qualify their position: in a study of popular films, *The Godfather* (Francis Ford Coppola, 1971) and *Jaws* (Steven Spielberg, 1975) for instance, Fredric **Jameson** perceives the manipulative effects of reification as intimately bound up with utopian fantasies of emancipation.

See also: utopia and dystopia

Further reading

Adorno, T. (1978) 'On the Fetish-Character in Music and the Regression of Listening' (first published 1938), in A. Arato and E. Gebhardt (eds) *The Essential Frankfurt School Reader*, New York: Seabury Press.

Adorno T. and Horkheimer M. (1972) *Dialectic of Enlightenment* (first published 1944), trans. John Cumming, New York: Seabury.

Jameson, F. (1979) 'Reification and Utopia in Mass Culture', *Social Text*, vol. 1, no. 10, pp. 130–48.

Lukács, G. (1971) *History and Class Consciousness: Studies in Marxist Dialectics* (first published 1923), trans. Rodney Livingstone, Cambridge, MA: MIT Press.

Marx, K. (1976) *Capital, Volume I* (first published 1867), trans. Ben Fowkes, London: Pelican.

NICK YABLON

Reith, John
b. 1889; d. 1971

Appointed as General Manager of the newly established British Broadcasting Comapany (BBC) in 1922, John Reith became its first Director General (1927–1938) when it was made a Corporation in 1926, masterminding its approach towards radio and television broadcasting. He believed that radio and television could create an informed and educated public, aware of their civil duties and nurtured by the arts. Consequently, he stressed the importance of maintaining the BBC's monopoly, believing that choice might tempt the people away. Committed to the idea of **public service broadcasting**, he moulded the BBC as a national broadcaster to draw together the people of Britain.

Reith believed in strong guidance and kept the BBC separate from government. He helped steer its expansion into television, authorizing John Logie Baird's use of a BBC transmitter for his television experiments in 1929. In 1932, he established the World Service, placing public service values into an international arena.

Reith's influence continued after he left the BBC but gradually he was seen as an elitist and someone who was out of touch. He opposed the Corporation's division of radio into the Home Service, the Light Programme and the Third Programme, believing that choice diluted the BBC's mission, and maintained a fierce opposition to commercial broadcasting.

See also: broadcasting, the United Kingdom; deregulation, the United Kingdom; deregulation, the United States; national, the; regulation; Reithian;

Further reading

Stuart, C. (1975) *The Reith Diaries*, London: Collins.

MOYA LUCKETT

Reithian

It is rare for someone's surname to be turned into an adjective, but it often signifies widespread approval of an individual's achievements. In the case of John **Reith**, however, the word signifies a range of reactions – from admiration for his creation of **public service broadcasting** at the British Broadcasting Corporation (BBC) to a deep dislike of his autocratic style and narrow puritanical morality.

Born 1889, the son of a Presbyterian minister, Reith's high, moral tone is hardly surprising and his writing and volumes of autobiography are heavy with a sense of divinely guided purpose. 'I am properly grateful to God for His goodness in this matter', he wrote of his appointment as Managing Director of the BBC, in his diary in 1923. By this time he was 34, and his beliefs and philosophy had already been firmly formed. Regarded as academically backward, he had struggled to prove his family wrong through an engineering apprenticeship in Glasgow followed by evening classes. He was dedicated to his employment and later he expected no less from those who worked for him at the BBC. In his spare time he was a passionately enthusiastic member of the volunteer Territorial Army. When the First World War broke out, Reith, by now with substantial engineering management skills, combined with his devotion to God and country, was in his element. He was seriously wounded and spent the latter part of the war 'behind the lines', supervising armament production in the United States. All these qualities and experiences came together in his management of the BBC. His belief in structure and order led to his recruiting of ex-service personnel in order to create a highly bureaucratic organization, which made it easier for him to exercise his leadership and moral authority.

Although the BBC was conceived initially as a sales medium for a consortium of radio set manufacturers, it was never funded directly by advertising: a licence fee linked to the sale of radio sets was used to pay for the company's staff and output. This fitted well with Reith's belief that broadcasting should be left to the broadcasters themselves, acting in the 'public interest'. Neither advertisers nor government should be allowed to interfere. Such an institution should be a monopoly and this would permit 'unified direction', by which Reith meant direction by a single individual, himself. Nevertheless, Reith's autocratic view was to be exercised on behalf of the nation, as he saw it. Borrowing a phrase from the American broadcasting pioneer David Sarnoff, the founder of RCA, Reith believed that 'entertaining, informing and educating the nation' was a fundamental principle of broadcasting.

The early BBC programmes put this philosophy into practice. 'Our responsibility is to carry into the greatest possible number of homes everything that is best in every department of human knowledge, endeavour or achievement', wrote Reith. This meant educational talks for adults, programmes for children and schools, religious services, symphony concerts, serious drama and unbiased news bulletins. The Reithian Sunday, dedicated to serious talks, religious services and classical music, was far from popular and unwittingly built audiences for commercial radio stations. Space was found in the BBC for sports coverage, popular music and comedy, but it was the effort to 'improve' public taste that predominated. Reith recruited leading public figures to advisory committees which provided expert advice to the programme-makers, and acted as a defence against government interference.

For Reith, broadcasting was of key importance in binding the nation together and educating its population. It would provide a focus as important as the monarchy, the Christian religion and Parliament; a kind of national pulpit from which the Great and the Good could preach the virtues of a civilized society, confirming the **dominant ideology** and constructing a national identity.

As the BBC's licence fee grew during the 1930s, so expansion became possible. Reith launched the Empire Service in 1932 in order to extend worldwide the values which he believed in. In 1936 television was launched in the UK, and in 1937 the abdication by Edward VIII was broadcast on radio, personally supervised by Reith. Within a year, though, Reith had left, resigning at the peak of his power and influence, and claiming later that he no longer felt 'stretched' by his work. His years at the BBC (1922–1938) were the only truly 'Reithian' period of his life.

He left a world famous institution behind him, with a staff of thousands and an outstanding programme-making reputation. Two features of his BBC tenure survive in the foyer of Broadcasting House in London, and symbolize his achievement. One is a carved inscription in Latin that begins, 'Hoc templum artium et musarum' ('This temple of the arts and muses'), the other is Eric Gill's massive sculpture in which a sower scatters seed on the ground, 'broadcasting' it, for the benefit of others.

See also: broadcasting, the United Kingdom; deregulation, the United Kingdom; deregulation, the United States; regulation

DICKON REED

representation

Following on from Aristotle, W. J. T. Mitchell asserts that 'man for many philosophers both ancient and modern, is the "representation animal"... the creature whose distinctive character is the creation and manipulation of signs – things that "stand for" or "take the place of" something else' (Mitchell 1990: 90). Raymond Williams tells us that the verb to represent appeared in the English language in the fourteenth century, the range of meanings it almost immediately took on indicating the complexity of the concept: 'Represent quickly acquired a range of senses of making present: in the physical sense of presenting oneself or another... but also in the sense of making present in the mind...and of making present in the eye, in painting...or in plays.... But a crucial extension also occurred in [the fourteenth century], when represent was used in the sense of "symbolize" or "stand for"' (Williams 1976: 222–3). While represent can be used in the political sense (as in representative government for example), for media studies, representation usually implies the semiotic systems (see **semiotics**), such as language, writing, painting and the various media that re-present reality in textual form (see **realism**).

Representation in this sense indicates a complex circuit amongst aspects of reality, means of representation, creators of representations and perceivers of representations, in which the conventions of representation must be to some extent shared by creators and perceivers for communication to occur. If a creator puts a dab of paint on his/her canvas intending to represent a stone, the perceiver must be familiar with the means and conventions of representing three-dimensional objects in two-dimensional form in order to recognize it as such. Representation is always deeply social and deeply cultural. To give a more complicated example, Umberto **Eco** (1985) tells us that the ancient Romans used the same word for blue and green. Given that colour is in some sense a natural, scientific phenomenon based on light waves reflecting off surfaces to the human eye, we might expect that all cultures would break up the spectrum in the same way, but apparently the Romans distinguished among colours differently than we do.

The social and cultural nature of representation ties it to ideology (see **ideology and hegemony**). Much of the early work in cultural studies-inflected film and television studies argued that media representations constitute a key component in the naturalization of the dominant ideology and the positioning of subjects within it. But representations can subvert as well as support, reflecting the contradictions always inherent within the hegemonic. For example, the several series of the long-running television programme *Star Trek* might be seen as legitimizing American imperialism, but a more nuanced reading of the text might reveal that particular episodes critique rather than praise the consequences of the pax Americana.

The connection between representation and ideology has meant that much media studies work in the area has focused on **gender**, **race** and **ethnicity**. Research on stereotypes assumes that representation works directly in the service of the dominant, who reinforce the hegemonic order with false images of the **Other**, such as women and people of colour, that do not correlate with the 'real' world. Stereotypes are criticized as deliberate misrepresentations (see **stereotype**). Post-modern and post-structuralist approaches reject the idea of misrepresentation, questioning whether images can ever be 'accurate' or 'authentic' (see **modernism and post-modernism; structuralism and post-structuralism**). Rather than comparing representations with a 'real' world, such approaches compare representations with representations, without necessarily assuming one representation to be more 'authentic' than another. For example, taking a synchronic approach, one might contrast images of Native Americans in commercial film and television with Native Americans' own self-representations in the indigenous media. Or one might look at a range of contemporaneous texts in order to ascertain how their specific representations of Native Americans relate to the ideologies of particular groups of producers and consumers. One might also take a diachronic approach, looking at the representation of Native Americans in the commercial media over time to connect changing images to reconfigurations of the hegemonic order.

References

Eco, U. (1985) 'How Culture Conditions the Colours We See', in Marshall Blonsky (ed.) *On Signs*, Baltimore: The Johns Hopkins University Press.

Mitchell, W. J. T. (1990) 'Representation', in Frank Lentricchia and Thomas McLaughlin (eds) *Critical Terms for Literary Study*, Chicago: University of Chicago Press.

Williams, R. (1976) *Keywords*, New York: Oxford University Press.

ROBERTA E. PEARSON

retro/nostalgia film

The nostalgia film, or 'a mode retro' – retrospective styling – is Fredric **Jameson**'s term for a specific mode of post-modern cinema (see **modernism and post-modernism**). In many ways it embodies the aesthetic Jameson (1988) had identified in his account of post-modern **pastiche**: 'to imitate dead styles, to speak through the masks and with the voices of the styles in the imaginary museum'. In this instance, the museum is a storehouse of historical backdrops, costumes and props from which a representation of period atmosphere is reconstructed.

While Jameson's definition of the nostalgia film may be ambiguous, his use of examples is consistent. He sees *American Graffiti* (George Lucas, 1973) as the inaugural film in this aesthetic for its evocation of the United States during Eisenhower's administration, and Roman Polanski's *Chinatown* (1974) as a similar recuperation of the American 1930s. Both films recapture the atmosphere and stylistic feel of an era which, though not distant, seems somehow 'lost'. In the former movie, George Lucas looked back barely a decade from 1973 to the 1950s, but the period is bound up in his film with notions of romanticized rock and roll counter-culture and a backdrop of comparative stability. As an example from the 1990s, we might consider Richard Linklater's *Dazed and Confused* (1993), which, ironically, recalls the 1970s as a lost period of innocence and naïve rebellion. Even 1985 can now be evoked with affectionate mocking nostalgia in the 1998 comedy *The Wedding Singer* (Frank Coraci).

Jameson discusses *Star Wars* (George Lucas, 1977) as a nostalgia film not because it recreates a historical period but because of its reinvention of a half-forgotten cultural experience in the form of the Saturday matinee adventure serial. *Raiders of the Lost Ark* (Steven Spielberg, 1981), meanwhile, occupies a middle ground; set in the 1930s and 1940s, it too calls on memories of those film-serial clichés through its cliff-hangers and death-traps. We can see the continuation of this subgenre through subsequent films such as *The Rocketeer* (Joe Johnston, 1991) and *The Shadow* (Russell Mulcahy, 1994), and a further level of intertextual complexity (see **intertextuality**) in the 1990s films which attempt nostalgically to re-evoke the experience of viewing *Star Wars* itself, such as *Judge Dredd* (Danny Cannon, 1995), *Independence Day* (Roland Emmerich, 1996) and the *Star Wars* 'prequel', *Star Wars: The Phantom Menace* (George Lucas, 1999).

A further category is the ambiguous mode exemplified by *Body Heat* (Lawrence Kasdan, 1981), which, while nominally set in the 1980s, evokes through the calligraphy of its credit sequence, casting and plot 'an eternal 1930s' associated with earlier *noir* films such as *Double Indemnity* (Billy Wilder, 1944). We might now add to this group the 'neo-*noir*' aesthetic of *The Last Seduction* (John Dahl, 1994) or *Red Rock West* (Dahl, 1992), both of which transport a version of the characters and mood of 1940s *noir* to a 1990s setting (see **film noir**).

Jameson's examples beg several questions. His initial equation of the nostalgia film with the tradition of the historical novel would seem to equate the retro mode with the heritage style (see **heritage film and television**). However, he also identifies the nostalgia film with pastiche, the 'empty' copying and appropriation of earlier forms and texts. While this might ring true for *Star Wars*, the term might not be so readily accepted with regard to 'heritage' productions such as *The Remains of the Day* (James Ivory, 1993). Furthermore, the pastiche of the nostalgia mode is explicitly distinguished in Jameson's account from **parody**, which he views as an extinct practice in the postmodern era. How does this definition sit with *The Wedding Singer*, which, while steeped in nostalgia, also relies on our memory of 1980s fashions in clothing and music for most of its humour?

Jameson ultimately sees the nostalgia mode as a depressing tendency, indicative of our contemporary loss of historical sense and inability to focus on the present. In addition to avoiding any representation of our current experience, the nostalgia film can only revisit the past through clichés and stereotypical iconography, as if the 'imaginary museum' of the twentieth century were a shoddy collection of waxworks and facades. His pessimism is perhaps embodied by the dystopic cities of *Blade Runner* (Ridley Scott, 1982) and *Batman* (Tim Burton, 1989), with their chaos of *noir* **mise-en-scène**, Expressionist architecture (see **Expressionism**) and near-future technology. This finds an intriguing echo in the Alex Proyas film *Dark City* (1998), whose nostalgically 1940s-style metropolis is revealed to be a fake, a malicious experiment in control and confusion which exists outside time and space in an ahistorical void.

References

Jameson, F. (1988) 'Postmodernism and Consumer Society', in E. Ann Kaplan (ed.) *Postmodernism and its Discontents*, London: Verso.

Further reading

Brooker, P. and Brooker, W. (1997) *Post-modern After-Images*, London: Arnold.

Hutcheon, L. (1989) *The Politics of Postmodernism*, London: Routledge

WILL BROOKER

Rheingold, Howard

b. 1947

Howard Rheingold has established himself as one of the foremost contemporary commentators on computing technology, especially in relation to the **Internet**. His work cannot be pigeonholed as either popular or scholarly, for it combines the strengths of both modes of address. Rheingold's key works, *Tools for Thought* (1984), *Virtual Reality* (1991) and *The Virtual Community: Homesteading at the Electronic Frontier* (1993), provide a thoughtful and expansive description and analysis of the development of computing technologies and its application to the creation of virtual life. While aware of the dangers of overly enthusiastic adoption of technologies and the problems that virtual life may pose, Rheingold remains a persuasive advocate for the 'liberating potentials of computer-mediated communications'.

His writing in the 1980s mainly provided accessible accounts of cognitive and other sciences, but it was via membership of the influential San Francisco-based virtual community, the WELL, that Rheingold became, in his words, 'sucked into the net'. Associated briefly with *hotWired*, the online partner of *Wired* magazine, Rheingold established the Electric Minds virtual community in 1996. He also hosts the Brainstorms private community 'knowledgeable, civil, adult, fun conversation about technology, the future, life online'.

See also: cyberspace; Internet and the World Wide Web; technological change; virtual reality

Further reading

Online. Available: http://www.rheingold.com

MATTHEW ALLEN

rhetoric

Rhetoric is the art of persuasion and oratory; originally the study of the shaping of language to produce an effect on an **audience**. A contrast was made from Plato onwards between impartial reasoning in search of an impersonal truth and the manipulation of an audience by ('empty') rhetoric. But rhetoric is now increasingly validated as a way of correcting the overemphasis on a disembodied, always correct, abstract theory in film and television study; for example, on the supposed separation of observer in **documentary** practice. It engages with the ways in which movies (and film study itself; see David **Bordwell**'s *Making Meaning*) seek, precisely, to move us.

References

Bordwell, D. (1989) *Making Meaning: Inference and Rhetoric in the Interpretation of Cinema*, Cambridge, MA: Harvard University Press.

GILL BRANSTON

romance

Romanticism was an early nineteenth-century artistic movement which emphasized passion and a liberation from artistic conventions. 'Romantic' is now used in film and television studies to indicate a concentration on particular feelings and passions: those of intimate personal life, additionally often implying sexual feelings, and both a woman protagonist and a largely female audience.

Debate rages about whether the form provides important escapist (see **escapism**) and compensatory outlets for women's dissatisfactions with the intimate emotional consequences of a patriarchal order (see **patriarchy**), often via narratives involving nurturing males and yearnings dramatized by unhappy or unfulfilled outcomes. Or is it inherently masochistic and compliant with that order?

See also: feminist theory; genre

GILL BRANSTON

S

Said, Edward

b. 1935

Said's consciousness of the place and date of his birth – Palestine in 1935 – has been an exceptional determinant of his life. As a professor of Comparative Literature, a music critic and a political activist in the United States, he has consistently drawn attention to the facts of colonialism, post-colonialism and forced exile and their consequence for the cultures of those involved.

Said has written over fifteen books and over 240 journal articles. Most read in media studies are *Orientalism* (1978) and *Culture and Imperialism* (1993). *Orientalism* analyses the ways in which the **Other** has helped to define the subject: in this case, the way the Orient defines the West as its contrasting image, idea and experience. In Said's words: 'The Orient is an integral part of European material civilization and culture...beyond any correspondence, or lack thereof, with a "real" Orient'.

In *Culture and Imperialism*, Said examines nineteenth- and twentieth-century European novels from a distinctive cultural perspective. 'Culture' refers to those practices and representations, with relative autonomy from economic determinants, 'that often exist in aesthetic forms, one of whose principal aims is pleasure' (see **culture**). Matthew **Arnold**'s conception of culture is re-viewed because of its potential for severing the connection between 'such practices as slavery, colonialist and racist oppression, and imperial subjection on the one hand, and the poetry, fiction and philosophy of the society that engages in these practices on the other'.

Said's purpose in these books, as in his political activities, is not to sustain ethnic divisions or to apportion blame. Locating novels, and other representations, within the imperialist realities of their societies, he argues, does not reduce the pleasure and esteem in which they are held, 'but actually and truly *enhances* our reading and understanding of them'.

See also: Orientalism

References

Said, E. (1978) *Orientalism*, London: Routledge and Kegan Paul
—— (1993) *Culture and Imperialism*, London: Chatto and Windus.

PHILIP SIMPSON

Sarris, Andrew

b. 1928

Andrew Sarris, a professor at Columbia University since 1969 and an alliterative and punny film critic for New York's *Village Voice* from 1960 to 1989 and then the *New York Observer*, has been the most influential US advocate of the 'auteur theory', developed in the 1950s in *Cahiers du cinéma* (see **authorship; Bazin, André**). A Christian humanist and a political liberal born in New York, Sarris advocated a focus on personal sensibility and style against what he berated as sociological or literary film criticism that stressed story references or meanings. He called attention to the contract work of directors in Hollywood, elevating John Ford, Howard Hawks, Alfred Hitchcock and others to his personal pantheon precisely because they maintained individuality in the face of industry standardization. This concentration on directors' work rather than on the stories they told led to a greater appreciation for visual and aural practices, even as it supported industry promotion of brand-name directors and championed the author at a moment when Roland **Barthes** and Michel **Foucault** were insisting on an unmourned death.

Further reading

Sarris, A. (1968) *The American Cinema: Directors and Directions, 1929–1968*, New York: Dutton.
—— (1975) *The John Ford Movie Mystery*, Bloomington: Indiana University.

CLAY STEINMAN

Saussure, Ferdinand de

b. 1857; d. 1913

Ferdinand de Saussure was a Swiss linguist and the forefather of structuralism (see **structuralism and post-structuralism**). Late in his life, Saussure offered classes on general linguistic theory at the University of Geneva and, after his death, students and colleagues assembled his notes, primarily from his third course (1910–1911), as the *Course in General Linguistics* (1966). Saussure explained language as a structured, socially constructed system in which 'difference is everything'. He identified the primary unity of the **sign**, composed of a signifier (sound-image) and signified (concept), which took on meaning from conjoined yet arbitrary divisions of world and expression. Although his model focused linguistic study on a **synchronic** (one-time perspective) and social study of interpretation, the notes also reveal an interest in the production of speech and in linguistic change. His conceptual framework for mapping and interpreting underlying systems of meaning was influential in the development of **semiotics**. His reliance on systems of oppositions has shaped social sciences, humanities and film criticism of signifying and **narrative** elements.

The limitations of synchronic, interpretive studies has led to post-structuralist and **audience**-oriented approaches to communication and reading.

References

Saussure, F. de (1966) *Course in General Linguistics* (first published 1915), trans. Wade Baskin, New York: McGraw-Hill. (A critical edition in French was prepared by Tullio de Mauro [1972] *Cours de linguistique générale*, Paris: Payot.)

Further reading

Harris, Roy (1987) *Reading Saussure* Lasalle, IL: Open Court.

GARY McDONOGH

science fiction

Though used as a generic label, the status of science fiction (SF) film and television is subject to much debate. Some see it as a separate **genre**, others as a subgenre of **horror**, and yet others as a subgenre of the fantasy film, originating with the filmmaker Georges Méliès. SF movies proliferated in the 1950s and key categories now are 'alien invader', 'space flight' and 'bad futures' (or dystopias; see **utopia and dystopia**). Science fiction cinema's **mise-en-scène** is now a showcase for cutting-edge special effects (FX), for example *Star Wars: The Phantom Menace* (George Lucas, 1999) and *The Matrix* (Andy and Larry Wachowski, 1999), though its narratives combine a concern for the 'what if?' of imaginable technologized futures with elements of traditional action adventure.

Televisual science fiction was long considered primarily a children's genre, but several programmes in the 1960s altered this perception: *Dr Who*, aimed at a younger audience but embraced by adult fans, *The Twilight Zone*, which took a liberal perspective on American social problems, and *Star Trek*, the lasting popular appeal of which demonstrated the viability of the televisual genre. In the 1990s science fiction flourished on television but budgetary limitations and screen size and resolution prohibited the intensive special effects seen in the cinema. In broad terms, television science fiction focuses more on character and **narrative** than its cinematic counterpart, with some programmes, notably the various incarnations of *Star Trek*, engaging with the social and philosophical dilemmas of the turn of the millennium.

GILL BRANSTON AND ROBERTA E. PEARSON

Screen theory

'[The] opportunity must be seized by *Screen* to develop theories of film study, to analyse theories of education as these affect film study and by these operations help to define methods and techniques in both film study and film education' (Editorial, *Screen*, vol. 12, no. 1, 1971, p. 4). 'We hope that new forms of writing will develop through engagement with current events, the assessment of particular areas of intervention, and the continued development of theoretical and historical work' (Editorial, *Screen*, vol. 20, nos. 3/4, 1979, p. 13). The time of '*Screen* theory', as it has come to be known, can be located between the 1971 Spring issue and the Winter 1979 issue of the British journal *Screen* – from which these two quotations are taken.

The aim of *Screen* in 1971 was to establish the theoretical groundwork for the development of film studies, with equal emphasis on theory and education. In the same issue, the journal's new editor, Sam Rohdie, wrote a programmatic essay, 'Education and Criticism' (pp. 9–13), which began by asking a series of questions about education, theory, and their relation in film studies. The remainder of the essay attacks auteurism (see **authorship**), the dominant paradigm for studying film at that time. Rohdie sought to replace auteurism with the methods of Continental theory. But why Continental theory? To answer this question, we need to focus on another influential British journal, *New Left Review* (*NLR*), first published in 1960. *NLR* challenged the insularity of the (old) British left – including its anti-intellectualism, its moralism and its empiricism – by introducing to a British readership the work of Continental theorists. These theorists emphasized philosophy and anti-humanist values rather than the old left's anti-theoretical privileging of individual lived experience.

Screen's transformation in 1971 followed *NLR*'s lead. *Screen* established close links with European theory and attempted to synthesize the following traditions:

- a structural linguistic-based **semiotics** that located meaning, not in the director's mind, but in structures of film language which exist prior to the director's intervention;
- the Marxism of Louis **Althusser** (see **Marxist aesthetics**), which developed a theory of ideology, and a Brechtian **aesthetics** (see **Brecht, Bertolt**), leading to a critical analysis of **realism** and an endorsement of **avant-garde**, modernist film practices (see **modernism and post-modernism**);
- the **psychoanalysis** of Jacques **Lacan**, which was used to develop a theory of 'subject positioning' (see **subject and subjectivity**), and to develop a relation between psychoanalysis and feminism – epitomized in Laura **Mulvey**'s seminal essay, 'Visual Pleasure and Narrative Cinema' (1975).

However, in challenging the anti-theoretical stance of the old left, *Screen*'s theoretical advances isolated it from the pedagogic function it initially set out to achieve, then delegated it to its sister journal *Screen Education*. This is why, in volume 17, no. 2 of *Screen* (1976), four members of the editorial board resigned, citing three reasons: *Screen* is unnecessarily obscure and inaccessible; its politico-cultural analysis is intellectually unsound and unproductive; and it has no serious interest in educational matters. The eight remaining members of the editorial board replied to the charges, defending the journal's theoreticism. Yet, a few years later, one of the eight signatories, Paul Willemen, resigned and wrote a critical history of the journal, commenting that:

'[*Screen*] set itself up as a Laboratory of Pure Theory, disinterestedly producing knowledge about this, that, and the other, which knowledge was then 'available' to those who wished to avail themselves of it. A radical rhetoric was maintained while the journal in fact denied any responsibility for the politics it represented.

(Willemen 1983: 295–6)

In the 1980s and 1990s, such criticisms were also voiced outside of *Screen*. The journal was accused of placing too much emphasis on the film in positioning and determining the spectator's reading; of privileging avant-garde films as inherently progressive; of asocial analysis; and, generally, of developing a totalizing and hegemonic theory of the function and **effects** cinema creates. Cognitive film theorists such as David **Bordwell** and Noël Carroll (1995) accused *Screen* of irrationalism, mystification, an inability to construct arguments, and an attempt to unify theory in a totalizing, hegemonic framework. Their **cognitive theory** developed out of this opposition, and they argued that film theory should operate on a small-scale level. The result is a modular approach to film, developing theories of genres, **acting**, lighting, optical effects, editing, music and so on that do not flow from a small set of overarching metaphysical or political doctrines, but emerge from the data under analysis (see **genre**).

Despite these criticisms, *Screen* was none the less successful in challenging the old left, introducing Continental theory to the Anglo-American film studies community, and employing this theory to establish a theoretical foundation for film studies.

See also: feminist theory; ideology and hegemony

References

Bordwell, D. and Carroll, N. (eds) (1995) *Post-Theory: Reconstructing Film Studies*, Madison: University of Wisconsin Press.

Mulvey, L. (1975) 'Visual Pleasure and Narrative Cinema', *Screen*, vol. 16, no. 3, pp. 6–18.

Willemen, P. (1983), 'Remarks on *Screen*', *Southern Review*, 16, pp. 292–311.

WARREN BUCKLAND

Sedgwick, Eve Kosofsky

b. 1950

Eve Kosofsky Sedgwick is one of the founding writers on **queer theory**. She combines a feminist interest in the connection between **gender** or sexual relations and power relations with an interest in the mechanisms of homophobia. In *Between Men* (1985), Sedgwick uncovers male homosexuality as the forbidden driving force behind the 'homosocial' patriarchal system of male bonding (see **patriarchy**). The result of this dynamic is a system in which women are reduced to being the object of exchange (or, in the erotic triangle, the 'conduit'), legitimizing relationships between men. In *Epistemology of the Closet* (1991), she explores the function of the closet in shaping discourses of public/private, knowledge and sexuality.

Kosofsky Sedgwick's work has been incorporated into queer film theory as a means of analysing 'buddy' films of male bonding, exposing the hidden gay undercurrent in this apparently heterosexual **genre**. It provides tools for criticizing the way in which classic Hollywood cinema posits female characters as mere objects of exchange 'between men'.

See also: feminist theory

References

Sedgwick, Eve Kosofsky (1985) *Between Men. English Literature and Male Homosocial Desire*, New York: Columbia University Press.

—— (1991) *Epistemology of the Closet*, Hemel Hempstead: Harvester Wheatsheaf.

ANTJE LINDENMEYER

semantics

In the broadest sense, semantics is the study of the meaning of signs, in contrast to the study of the rules of their combination (syntax) and their use (pragmatics). Most semantic studies are concerned with the linguistic analysis of language as the most complex and most relevant **sign** system. Starting from the basic feature of human language, the ability to combine a limited number of meaningless sounds into an unlimited number of meaningful expressions, semantics analyses the meaning of single meaningful units ('semes') as well as larger meaningful units, complex words, phrases, sentences. In human communication, both aspects need to be taken into consideration. Even though sentence meaning can be said to be 'made' out of a combination of the meaning of words, the meaning of the overall sentence also influences the interpretation of the words employed; for example, the sentence 'The cat has eaten the plant', obviously uses a different concept of 'cat' than the sentence, 'The cat is one of the oldest domestic animals'.

Semantics has been further differentiated into two types: sense semantics, which is concerned with internal relationships between the meaning of different signs, and reference semantics, which concentrates on the meaning relationships between signs and their referents (see **referent**). Sense semantics is implicitly based on the structuralistic assumption that a full description of the relationships between the signs of a sign system offers a complete account of the semantic 'landscape' of a language – the relationships of relevance are synonymy, antinomy, hyponymy and hyperonymy, polysemy, etc. (see **structuralism and post-structuralism**). An extension of sense semantics is logical semantics, which analyses the logical relationship between different utterances; that is, inclusion, exclusion, contradiction and so forth.

Reference semantics, which basically tries to describe how human language 'refers' to reality and so bridges the gap between human cognition and what we perceive to be 'out there', is more problematic. First, languages differ in how they partition reality into meaningful chunks, that is, words. For example, the distinctions between basic colour terms range from three to over ten; in languages with few colour terms, 'red' is always the colour that is distinguished through an own term first, while blue and green tend to be united under one generic term. This does not mean that the speaker of such a language cannot differentiate between 'sky-blue' and 'grass-blue', but that the distinction needs to be described by a specification of the basic colour term. This seems harmless enough as long as we are talking about colour terms, but the nightmare of rendering a language like English, which differentiates gender in personal pronouns and does not have an ungendered singular pronoun for human beings, into a politically correct language may serve as an example of the difficulties.

The problem of the link between perception and expression, though recognized early in the history of language analysis, did not gain influence on 'modern' linguistic semantics – which in this case means American linguistics – until the late 1960s. Before, the paradigm of Chomskyan generative grammar assumed two completely separated instances of syntactic and semantic analysis, the semantic component basically consisting of a mental lexicon of word meanings interpreting the (syntactic) deep structure of an expression and a set of transformation rules linking those meanings to their syntactic surface forms. This 'interpretative semantics' model came under attack when, among others, G. Lakoff, J. McCawley and J. Ross developed a model of 'generative semantics' which blurred the distinction between syntax and semantics and assumed the logic-semantic form as basic structure of an expression, the string of atomic meaning-particles held together by a predicate-logic form and, through operation of both syntactic and semantic transformation rules, then transformed into the surface structure. Though this model has been attacked for the *ad hoc* character of its descriptions, as well as for its strong generative power, the loss of priority of the interpretative model opened up the field for a multitude of philosophical, logical, pragmatical and functional approaches to semantics. This led to a further reduction of the border between semantics and pragmatics, so that use-oriented approaches like the speech act theory, the Sapir–Whorf Hypothesis ('Language shapes perception', specially relevant for feminist linguistics and cultural theories based on semantics), or the rather extreme Wittgensteinian thesis, 'the meaning of a word is its usage in a language', were reconsidered and included in semantic theories.

This has led to a multitude of semantic models with different problem fields and different explanatory scope. The most promising and productive approach is 'cognitive semantics', a model that prioritizes the cognitive processes necessary to understand and use language and extends its interest to related processes that use different input sources (sight, sound, smell, touch) for pattern recognition and object identification or reference. Though already developed in the 1950s, only the possibility of combining theories of semantics with contemporary findings about neurological brain processes made it possible to use the study of language as a means to understand the bridge between perception and expression – semantics as a window on the workings of the human mind.

Further reading

Harris, R. A. (1993) *The Linguistics Wars*, New York, Oxford: Oxford University Press.

Jackendoff, R. (1983) *Semantics and Cognition*, Cambridge, MA and London: MIT Press.

Lyons, J. (1995) *Linguistic Semantics*, Cambridge: Cambridge University Press.

EVA VIETH

semic code

Semic code is a term used by Roland **Barthes** in *S/Z*, his semiotic analysis of Balzac's novella, *Sarrasine* (see **semiotics**). Barthes suggests that the units of meaning (the signifiers) in a realist **narrative** (see **realism**) are arranged according to five interrelated codes: the semic code consists of the connotations (connotative signifiers) within a **text** that provide richness and texture. A cinematic equivalent to this code is the (iconographic) system of motifs running through a film, defining its **genre** or highlighting its themes; for example, the use of costume (stetsons and dusters) and landscape (the American West) which characterizes the Western (see **Western, the**).

See also: code; connotation; icon

References

Barthes, R. (1990) *S/Z*, Oxford: Blackwell.

BRUCE BENNETT

semiotics

Semiotics is a theoretical framework for the study of meaning in films, television programmes and other cultural texts, which approaches them as a *language*. Though semiotics was founded in the early years of the twentieth century, its potential for textual analysis in film only began to be recognized in the 1950s and 1960s. It was also taken up in the study of many other areas of cultural life, such as fashion, music, literary fiction, food, with the result that by the 1970s semiotics had achieved considerable recognition in cultural and literary studies and in film theory. Though the high point of semiotics passed with the demise of structuralism, which provided its major theoretical impetus (see **structuralism and post-structuralism**), its implications for many different disciplines in the human sciences remain. It has also furnished a set of analytic terms and characteristic lines of critique which, although they have been challenged and refined by later theoretical interventions, still remain useful for the textual analysis of film and television.

Before semiotics, textual analysis of films tended to focus on characters, **plot** and internal stylistic properties, evaluating them in terms of how they represented life and how they registered the creative vision of the director. In the semiotic approach film is understood not as an expression of individual creativity, but as a **signifying practice**, in which its formal properties are likened to linguistic structures, defining the world according to particular rules and conventions. The word 'practice' captures this sense that language is an activity of defining knowledge rather than merely labelling it. Instead of seeing film as a medium that relays aspects of reality, semiotics holds that film, television and other signifying practices actively construct our sense of reality.

Semiotics proposes that the meaning of film and television texts cannot be grasped by analysing the intentions of their 'authors' (directors, editors, etc.) or the interpretations of their audiences. For semioticians, meaning is produced through a network of symbolic values and distinctions that do not originate with the film or filmmaker. Semiotics is a means of analysing these distinctions in order to identify their underlying structure. It offers textual analysis a more rigorous and methodologically self-conscious approach which, in the early days of semiotics, held out the promise of a truly scientific study of film. Christian **Metz** and other film theorists such as Peter **Wollen** were responsible for introducing semiotics into the study of film in the late 1960s. These new film 'semioticians' were influenced in turn by such figures as the structural anthropologist Claude **Lévi-Strauss** and the literary critic Roland **Barthes**.

However, it is difficult to classify semiotics as a single theoretical approach. Since it was founded, there have been different phases in its development. While semiotics was not taken up in the West until the 1950s, Eastern European linguists and literary critics had drawn on the work of Ferdinand de **Saussure**, its founding father, through several intellectual movements such as Russian **Formalism**, Prague structuralism and phonology and the Bakhtin Circle (see **Bakhtin, Mikhail**). Indeed, semiotics can be thought of as a fluid body of work which comprises all these traditions, as well as Saussurean semiology and Piercian semiotics (see below). Semiotics is also difficult to classify as an intellectual project: it can be thought of as a radical form of political critique, an academic discipline for the study of meaning, or simply as a set of methodological tools for textual analysis. There are both left-wing and centrist versions of semiotic thinking. In what follows, the objective is to present an account of semiotics' origins and broad lines of development, rather than try to do justice to all the various strands of semiotic theory.

Historical development of semiotics

That semiotics is not a monolithic body of theory is well illustrated by its beginnings: it is credited to two founding fathers – the American logician C. S. **Peirce** and the Swiss linguist Ferdinand de Saussure – who were writing at the same time as each other but who were each unaware of the other's work. These two bodies of work resulted in two different vocabularies for the terminology of signs and two different names for their study: Peirce's 'semiotic' and Saussure's 'semiology'. Now, although it is Saussure's work which has provided the most influential model for film and television theory, the Piercian term 'semiotics' has become more widely accepted.

Saussure proposed his theory of 'semiology' in a work published posthumously in 1915 by a group of his students (*Course in General Linguistics*). The *Course* defines semiology thus:

Language is a system of signs that express ideas, and is therefore comparable to a system of writing, the alphabet of deaf-mutes, symbolic rites, polite formulas, military signals, etc. But it is the most important of all these systems. A science that studies the life of signs within society is conceivable...I shall call it semiology (from Greek *semeion*, 'sign'). Semiology would show what constitutes signs, what laws govern them.

(Saussure 1959: 16)

When Saussure argues that 'language is a system of signs' he is arguing that it is a system of conventionalized distinctions through which certain physical forms (written words, sounds, images, gestures, etc.) are commonly accepted as referring to certain concepts (standing for objects and phenomena in reality). What Saussure insists on is that the relation between the forms and the concepts, between the 'physical existence of the sign' (the *signifier*) and the mental concept that it invokes (the *signified*), is an arbitrary one. The relation is based on a commonly held system of conventional distinctions and not on any intrinsic natural link between the two.

This principle, of the arbitrary relation between signifier and signified, stands at the heart of the Saussurean semiotic approach. What is at stake here is not merely the obvious and age-old view that words and their objects have no necessary correspondence. Semiotics in fact makes a radical break with the traditional notion that words refer to entities, as it does not view language as a system of naming things. Instead, it views language as an intricate grid of relative values which, by marking out boundaries and establishing distinctions, produces the conceptual map through which we make sense of the world.

Language, then, is a system of *differences*, an insight which has quite radical implications, later taken up in post-structuralism and **deconstruction**. Signifieds and signifiers, therefore, do not refer to pre-existent entities but only to each other. This point illustrates the fundamental relativity of meaning: signs only exist in relation to other signs, i.e., in relation to what they are *not*. In Saussure's terms, then, concepts 'are purely differential, not positively defined by their content but negatively defined by their relations with other terms of the system. Their most precise characteristic is that they are what the others are not' (1959: 117).

Thus, meaning depends on an abstract system of relative values. Saussure calls this system *la langue* (see **language/langue**). *Langue* is to be distinguished from actual utterances by social subjects (through sounds, physical marks on paper, etc., or thoughts and images inside people's heads). These utterances, which Saussure calls 'la **parole**', can vary widely: both my mental picture of 'river' and my way of pronouncing those sounds may be different from yours. Yet shared meanings arise because they depend on the same underlying system of distinctions which distinguish between signifieds – such as strong/weak flowing water – and between signifiers – such as *r*iver/*l*iver or river/rive*t*.

The distinction between *langue* and *parole* leads to another of Saussure's **binary** terms: **synchronic** and **diachronic** levels of analysis. For Saussure, the 'state of play' of meaning can only be grasped by studying *langue* rather than *parole*, for meaning is produced in relation to the whole system of values as it is currently constituted. This leads Saussure to propose that the synchronic level of analysis – analysis of structure at any one moment – is the most significant focus of attention for linguistics, as opposed to diachronic analysis – examining change in actual language-use (*parole*) over time.

Usage in film and television theory

Saussure was primarily concerned with linguistics, but proposed that language was merely the most characteristic instance of a general model – semiology – which described 'the life of signs' (1959: 16). We can include in semiotics any sign system (such as the traffic light or the chess game) in which there are sets of signifiers held by convention to stand for certain signifieds. Clearly, film and television texts are composed entirely of signifiers that operate in this way. However, there are certain differences between film and natural language which makes film language a special case. The following is an examination of some of the key semiotic terms in order to consider how they have been used in film and television theory.

Iconic signs and film

The principle of the arbitrary relation between signifier and signified is central to semiotic perspectives. However, several film semioticians have pointed to the fact that pictorial signs, predominant in film and television, are not purely arbitrary in the same way as linguistic signs are. Peter Wollen and Umberto **Eco** turned to Peircian semiotic terminology in order to engage with film's visual plane of meaning. Peirce distinguished between three types of sign: the iconic, the **indexical** and the symbolic sign (see **icon**). Whereas natural language is composed of symbolic signs, which are nearly always arbitrary, images comprise iconic signs, which have perceptual similarities to their referents in reality (see **referent**). Film is composed of iconic signs, which look as though they are the direct manifestations of physical reality, and which therefore appear to be motivated rather than arbitrary (see **motivation**).

However, against this, Eco argues that even iconic signs work though convention, in that understanding them requires an unconscious level of cultural training in visual perception and perspective. This is even more the case for the indexical sign, which is particularly significant in the moving image. We have to learn through our familiarity with the conventions of cultural representation that a cloudy sky means a storm is approaching. What allows signs to be meaningful for the viewer is that the text is structured by a range of different codes, which organize iconic and other signs along particular axes of meaning (see **code**). All signs gain their meaning from their position in codes. Codes approximate to the Saussurean construct of *langue*, but reflect the fact that there are many different variations of *langue* in culture (unlike the single grammars of natural languages), which operate through their own specific sign systems.

Denotation and connotation

The property of camera images just discussed, that they appear to represent reality so directly, brings us to another extension of Saussurean semiotic theory: the distinction between **denotation** and **connotation**. This distinction, introduced by

Roland Barthes, enables us to see that the visual sense-making aspect of camera images, in which we perceive what is on the screen and make sense of it, represents only one level of meaning or *order of signification*. Semioticians call this the order of denotation. The more complex cultural order of a film's *connotations* operates through both medium-specific technical codes (such as those of lighting, editing, camera angle, etc.) and the wider cultural codes of society. Connotations, then, are not fixed within the sign but derive from codes of ideology and cultural value through their usage in social settings.

Denotation should not be thought of as a value-free, 'natural' order of signification. Like connotation, it, too, can only be grasped through codes – but codes which have become profoundly naturalized (see Hall 1980). The distinction is intended to aid analysis rather than to refer to how texts are actually experienced. In practice, we rarely make sense of what is on the screen on a purely denotative level; connotative meanings simultaneously crowd in. In fact, at the same moment as *apprehending* the image, we are also *comprehending* it, and this immediately brings together the two orders of denotation and connotation.

Ideology

The distinction between denotation and connotation has been central to analysis of the role of ideology in sign systems, one of the major contributions of a radical and political semiotics such as that proposed by Roland Barthes (see **ideology and hegemony**). Barthes introduces the term **myth** to refer to the connotative level of signification, in which cultural and ideological meanings are attached to the sign through codes. Through the operation of myth, meanings which are in fact ideological come to be read as natural: as Barthes puts it, myth 'transforms history into nature' (1973: 159). What he shows is how the denotative level of meaning acts as a kind of 'alibi' for the connotative meaning, so that ideology can always hide behind the 'fact' that 'the camera never lies'. This line of enquiry has proved very fruitful for critical analysis of the ideological 'work' performed by television programmes and films (see, for example, Hall 1980).

Syntagms/paradigms

A further extension of Saussurean semiotic theory came from Roman **Jakobson**'s distinction in linguistics between the **paradigmatic** and the **syntagmatic** axes of meaning. These are two different means through which connotation operates in film and television. First, any shot gains its meaning through the kind of shot it is (high angle, low light, close-up, etc.) – the *paradigmatic* axis; and second, from its juxtaposition with preceding and succeeding shots – the *syntagmatic* axis of meaning. This pair of distinctions has aided analysis of film and television texts, in that each refers to the quintessential twin activities of filmmaking: **mise-en-scène** (how to shoot the scene) and montage (how to present what is shot).

Critiques and legacies

Some of the sharpest critiques that semiotics has attracted have been directed at the concept of *la langue*, and are also levelled at the structuralist conspectus. Critics point out that semiotics offers no means of accounting for the historical shifts in *la langue* (or, indeed, in cultural codes). In separating synchronic and diachronic analysis, Fredric **Jameson** argues that semiotics falls into an ahistoricism that cannot account for change. Bakhtin was an early critic of the structuralist concept of the fixity of *la langue* and the lack of attention to the different meanings (see **polysemic**) of signs mobilized through their deployment in specific social settings. Bakhtin's point opens up a fundamental critique of semiotics – that it fails to accord sufficient explanatory power to the specific conditions within which texts are 'read' by socially situated subjects.

The question of how far semiotics is blind to social contexts of reading is one that has led to a good deal of polemic within cultural studies. In fact, by the 1970s, semiotics was starting to address how spectatorship is constructed, to replace the earlier focus on how texts are constructed. This reflected a move into what Stam *et al.* (1992) call 'second phase' psychoanalytic semiotics, as opposed to 'first-phase' linguistic semiotics. This shift came about through the incorporation into semiotics of psychoanalytic theories of the subject and subjectivity. This body of work heralded a post-structuralist perspective, by foregrounding dimensions missing in the original semiotic endeavour – including questions of **desire**, **pleasure**, identification and **voyeurism** (see **psychoanalysis**).

However, psychoanalytic semiotics was in turn accused of limiting the question of spectatorship to the positions and identifications set up by the text, rather than examining how actual spectators react to the film they view on the screen. Critics have taken issue with the attempt to explain specific instances of reading in terms of a universalist theory of subjectivity. This debate was, and to some extent still is, reflected in an entrenched division within cultural studies between those committed to continuing the semiotic project of textual analysis, and those proclaiming a need for empirical investigations into audience readings. There have, however, been attempts, particularly within television studies, to combine the semiotic approach with audience **ethnography**.

The other major critique of the Saussurean semiotic project has come from Derridean deconstruction. Jacques **Derrida** and other critics, including the later Barthes, have subjected the notion of 'structure' to a sustained critique, arguing that, if the idea of difference is taken seriously as the principle of signification, then it makes little sense to hold onto the notion of stability and organization implied in the term 'structure'. Deconstruction points instead to the instability of the chain of signification and re-signification, and introduces the term 'differance' to capture the sense that language is a 'systematic play of traces of differences' (Derrida 1981: 27).

While the various post-structuralist critical movements have pushed the study of texts into domains that Saussure and Peirce would certainly find unrecognizable, there is no doubt that they owe their existence to the initial path-breaking work of first-phase semiotics. Semiotics has provided the philosophical foundations for many of the later post-modernist interventions, as well as giving rise to rich new areas of enquiry, such as narratology (see **narrative**). The semiotic insight that signs consist of negative differences rather than positive labels, and that, through the operation of codes, they organize our perception of the world, has proved enormously fruitful for the study of film and television. Semiotics disrupts **common sense**

assumptions that film and television simply act as windows on the world. In the process, it has developed a bank of terms and concepts which continue to provide a sophisticated and critical aid to the study of meaning.

See also: new film semiotics

References

Barthes, R. (1973) 'Myth Today', in *Mythologies*, trans. Annettte Lavers, London: Palladin.

Derrida, J. (1981) *Positions*, Chicago: University of Chicago Press.

Hall, S. (1980) 'Encoding/Decoding', in S. Hall, D. Hobson, A. Lowe and P. Willis (eds) *Culture, Media, Language*, London: Hutchinson.

Saussure, F. de (1959) *Course in General Linguistics*, trans. Wade Baskin, Glasgow: Fontana/Collins.

Stam, R., Burgoyne, R. and Flitterman-Lewis, S. (1992) *New Vocabularies in Film Semiotics*, London and New York: Routledge.

Further reading

Bignell, J. (1997) *Media Semiotics: An Introduction*, Manchester: Manchester University Press.

Culler, J. (1976) *Saussure*, London: Fontana.

Fiske, J. (1987) *Television Culture*, London: Routledge.

Hawkes, T. (1977) *Structuralism and Semiotics*, London: Routledge.

Monaco, J. (1981) *How to Read a Film*, (revised edition), Oxford: Oxford University Press.

Thwaites, T., Davis, L. and Mules, W. (1994) *Tools for Cultural Studies: An Introduction*, South Melbourne: Macmillan Education.

Tolson, A. (1996) *Text and Discourse in Media Studies*, London: Arnold.

BELLA DICKS

sender/receiver

'Sender' and 'receiver' are terms originally derived from Shannon and Weaver's (1949) process-centred model of communications, which was originally conceived as a model for the transmission of information. Sender/receiver are seen as the beginning and end of a linear process of message transfer. Although mechanistic and largely superseded by more complex notions of the active **audience** and their situated culture, the model can be useful in helping to separate out the encoding/decoding process and in identifying where problems or discrepancies in meaning may occur (see **encoding; encoding-decoding model**).

References

Shannon, C. and Weaver, W. (1949) *The Mathematical Theory of Communication*, Champaign, IL: University of Illinois Press.

PHILIP RAYNER

serial

Television serials, including soap operas, are dramatic programmes characterized by a single continuous **narrative** for the duration of their open-ended run. 'Serial' can also serve as a less pejorative way of referring to a **soap opera** – early radio soaps were called 'daytime dramatic serials', while the television production company Granada calls *Coronation Street* (1960–) a 'continuing serial' rather than a soap opera. A related narrative form is the mini-series, a multi-part, continuous narrative programme which progresses through a finite number of episodes, such as *Roots* (1977), which attracted huge audiences in international television markets.

ALISON GRIFFITHS

series

The term 'series' is most commonly used to describe the **narrative** form of much **prime-time** television drama programming, including action-adventure shows and situation comedies (see **situation comedy**). Such continuing-character episodic series retain consistent features of setting and character across individual episodes, while resolving most storylines within each episode. The episodic series represents a middle-ground between

the self-contained narrative of a television movie or drama and the continuous narrative of the **serial**. In Britain, a series attracting a small audience might get moved to a less popular time-slot, but in America a series may be cancelled mid-season due to poor ratings.

ALISON GRIFFITHS

sexuality

What is sexuality?

As it first entered film theory, the term 'sexuality' was closely tied to **gender** – or more specifically, to sex roles (male and female). When 'sexuality' became a term for consideration in the film theory of the 1970s, it was taken to mean basically the sex of one's object choice – that is, whether one was attracted to sexual partners of the same sex or of another sex. Thus, sexuality was first understood to comprise of homosexuality and heterosexuality. This is an inadequate definition (as will be discussed below), but it is important to understand this theory before challenging the definition.

Feminist film theory

It has been argued that the first wave of feminist film theory in the 1970s was too essentialist: much of the writing was about how 'women' were represented or how 'women' viewed films – as though 'women' formed a unitary and homogeneous group, with some 'essential' features in common. It quickly became obvious, however, that elements of **identity** other than gender also had to be considered. The writing of women of colour, for example, made clear that many of the feminists who wrote about 'women' were in fact writing about 'white women', where the 'white' was simply exnominated. Similarly, lesbian writers – such as Elizabeth Ellsworth, Chris Straayer, Michelle Citron and B Ruby Rich – drew attention to the exnominated 'heterosexual' in the phrase.

This introduction of sexuality to the category of 'woman' was not merely a matter of political nicety; rather, it had an important effect on theories of film spectatorship. For example, Laura **Mulvey**'s theory of the gaze suggested that men look and women are looked at (see **gaze, the**). For Mulvey, 'the gaze' was male, and it was men who took sexual pleasure from looking at women. Obviously, this theory had to be rethought with attention to those men and women who did not fit into such a totalizing schema.

Stereotypes

Another area of film theory where 'sexuality' meant homo- or heterosexuality was writing on stereotypes and positive images (see **stereotype**). The work of Vito Russo and Parker Tyler can be fitted into such a tradition. This writing was, in some ways, as essentialist as early feminist film theory. In this approach to cultural theory, it was necessary to dismiss 'negative' or 'inaccurate' representations of a sexual group, and to champion in their place 'positive' or 'accurate' representations. The problem with such an approach is that is assumes there could be an 'accurate' representation of 'a gay man' or an 'accurate' representation of 'a lesbian'. Obviously, this is not the case. It is a logical concomitant of identity politics to take such an approach – for identity politics, at least to some degree, relies on the idea of a group of people having enough characteristics or interests in common to form a coherent public group.

Authorship

Another area of film studies in which sexuality has been approached as an 'identity' is that which seeks to discuss and celebrate the homosexual '**authorship**' of various texts – either actors (such as Agnes Moorhead, Rock Hudson) or directors (Vincente Minnelli, Dorothy Arzner). This contributes to a 'history of homosexuality' writing, adding these figures to a list which includes Shakespeare, Oscar Wilde and so on. It is assumed that the fact of homosexuality is interesting to homosexual spectators, and that it contributes in some way to the qualities of the text which is produced. This work is an extension of the 'auteur' theory which was developed in the French film journal *Cahiers du cinéma* in the 1950s, and which attempted to understand films through the figure of the director.

Heterosexuality

When sexuality was introduced into film studies in these ways, it was mainly as 'homosexuality'. 'Heterosexuality' was not at first an explicit object of study. This is another example of 'exnomination'. This word was coined by Roland **Barthes** to denote the way in which dominant groups in society do not need to give themselves a name: they are simply the 'norm' against which everything else is judged. This is why the word 'homosexuality' was coined in the nineteenth century, several years before the word 'heterosexuality'. Homosexuality was perceived as an aberration which had to be named, studied and explained (and if possible, cured). Heterosexuality, by contrast, was simply 'normal'.

Psychoanalysis

The prominence of psychoanalytic approaches in film theory had particular effects on the ways in which sexuality entered the frame. The use of psychoanalysis tended to collapse sexuality and gender together as though they were the same thing. In Laura Mulvey's work on the gaze, for example, she uses **psychoanalysis** in order to explain the way in which 'the male gaze' is constructed – when in fact she is writing about the way in which 'the male heterosexual gaze' is constructed. Sexuality is an important part of this writing on the construction of gender – but, because it is heterosexuality, it is exnominated.

Indeed, if identity politics offered the object of study – leading writers to believe that sexuality meant merely 'homosexuality' and 'heterosexuality' – then it was psychoanalysis which offered the possibility for analysis – and contributed easily to the conflation of sexuality and gender. Psychoanalysis attempts to explain the production of sexual **desire** through sexual difference. In a psychoanalytic approach, it is the fact that there is difference between men and women which produces sexuality. It is worth examining this point in some detail.

The very word 'sex' contributes to the process of collapsing sexuality and sex difference. In one sense, 'sex' refers to the categories which we associate with gender difference – male and female.

But another, and equally common, meaning is quite different – for 'sex' can refer to sexual acts. These 'sex acts' need have nothing to do with gender. Masturbation, for example, or sadomasochistic sex, or fetishistic practices (see **fetishism**) need not have a gender component.

However, the link between these two meanings of sex – acts and gender – seems to be so common sense, that this double articulation often passes without comment: it seems to be too obvious to require any investigation.

In psychoanalysis, sexuality is understood to be programmed by desire. And desire, as it is understood in Freudian psychoanalysis, is directly related to the difference between the sexes. For **Freud**, desire is the search for something which every adult has lost – the original sense of plenitude which exists between the mother and child. Because we can obviously never recover that state, we search for substitutes. Desire is the name we give to that endless search. In Freud, it is presumed that the two sexes provide **binary** complements to each other – each fulfils the **lack** in the other. It should be noted, however, that in the Freudian model, there is only really masculine desire – the concept of feminine desire is a contradiction in terms.

This conception of sexuality, then, does not simply contribute to analysis of what is present on the screen – whether particular images of homosexuality are accurate or not. It rather underlies the whole theorization of the communication process. 'Desire' and 'lack' are terms which are used to explain how people watch in the cinema. More than this, these models are extended by metaphor to explain the process of communication itself. In Jacques **Lacan**'s psychoanalysis, the most important lack is the lack of the **phallus**. The phallus is a symbol, not a reality – an unattainable representation of something that does not really exist. This is taken up metaphorically to explain all representation. In a post-structuralist way of thinking about representation, symbols never represent an external reality – they always simply refer to other symbols (see **Derrida, Jacques; structuralism and post-structuralism**). In such a model, reality is like the phallus – never present, but always sought after. Metaphorically, in this model, representation is involved in desire, because it also chases after the impossible 'reality' which can fill 'lack'.

A combination of identity politics (providing the object of study) and psychoanalysis (providing the analytical tool), then, produced a film theory where sexuality was understood to be directly related to gender. This can clearly be seen in, for example, the collection *The Sexual Subject: A Screen Reader in Sexuality* (*Screen* 1992). This is a collection of articles about sex difference – male and female. The collection could be renamed '*a Screen Reader in Gender*' with no sense of violence to its contents. There is no attention to sadomasochism, necrophilia, paedophilia, masturbation or any of the other ways in which 'sexuality' might be understood.

Queer theory

Our understanding of sexuality has been radically rethought in the writing of '**queer theory**'. This writing questions what sexuality actually *is*. It does this particularly by investigating one of the key terms which is linked to it – desire. In this way, sexuality comes to be separated from identity.

As noted above, it is possible to give common sense examples of sexuality which is not defined by gender. Sadomasochistic sex, for example, does not state in its name the gender relations which it involves. A sadomasochistic woman, for example, does not, in that name, determine if her sexual partners will be male or female – and indeed, recent writing from within sadomasochistic communities (such as that of Pat Califia) suggests that gender is not the most important aspect of the sexual partners in many sadmasochistic scenes. Similarly, paedophilia does not determine gender relations in its naming; nor does necrophilia.

But although these examples provide a useful way of making clear the possibility of disarticulating sex and gender, they are still caught up in earlier ways of thinking about sexuality – for each of these names implies an *identity*. Much thinking about sexuality is now explicitly post-identity – and this allows for a radical rethinking of what sexuality is.

The History of Sexuality, Volume 1 (Foucault 1990) has gained a status in cultural theory's thinking about sexuality which can be compared with that of Laura Mulvey's essay 'Visual Pleasure and the

Narrative Cinema' in film theory's theorizing of gender. **Foucault**'s central proposition – that there was no such thing as a 'homosexual' before the nineteenth century – has now become as commonplace as Mulvey's assertion that men actively take pleasure from looking at images of passive women in the cinema. Foucault's argument – based on discourse theory – is that the term 'homosexual' was only invented in the nineteenth century. Before this, same-sex acts did, of course, occur – but the people who were engaging in these acts did not then think of them as defining their whole nature, explaining who they were, or giving them a label which they could adequately append to themselves. In short, homosexuality did not function as an *identity* before this time.

Foucault's descriptive insight has been taken up in a prescriptive way in much critical writing, as theorists have suggested that it is necessary to jettison identities – which are seen to be too constricting, limited and static a model of human nature – and find new ways of thinking about social relations. This has led to a rethinking of what sexuality is.

A particular example of this reconceptualization can be seen in the rethinking of what is meant by 'desire'. As noted above, desire is taken to be a defining part of what sexuality is in psychoanalytic theory. Some writers have accepted this articulation – and set out to rethink what is meant by desire. This is an example of discourse theory – the idea that the way we use words changes the experience that we have of reality. This thing called desire is not a simple object, upon which everyone can agree. It is, rather, an abstract concept, and the ways in which we think about what it is contribute to the ways in which we think about who we are.

In much film theory from the 1970s onward, the concept of desire is a psychoanalytic one where desire is based on *lack*. Elizabeth Grosz (1995) points out that these ways of thinking about desire form part of a recognizable western philosophical discourse which can be traced back to Plato, taking in **Hegel**, on the way to Lacan and Freud. But Grosz points out that there is another philosophical tradition, which thinks of desire quite differently – one which she traces back to Spinoza, and on to the writings of Deleuze and Guattari (see **Deleuze, Gilles and Guattari, Félix**) – which

suggests that this thing we call desire is *production*, rather than lack. She suggests that we can think of desire as being positive and productive.

This is the first part of the reconceptualization – that this thing we call desire is *not* about searching for a lost essence which will make us whole, but, rather, is a positive practice. The second shift is to reject the very idea that human beings are ever, or can ever be, a 'whole'. The rejection of identity – that we can find a label which will adequately explain who we are, and everything about us, in one coherent and stable figure – means that desire is not about completing a single, whole self. Instead, it is about surfaces and disconnected moments.

These two conceptual shifts lead to a completely different notion of what desire – and what sexuality – are:

> Sexuality and desire . . . are not fantasies, wishes, hopes, aspirations . . . but are energies, impulses, actions, movements, practices, moments, pulses of feeling. The sites most intensely invested in desire always occur at a conjunction, an interruption, a point of machinic connection, always surface effects, between one thing and another – between a hand and a breast, a tongue and a cunt, a mouth and food, a nose and a rose. In order to understand this notion, we have to abandon our habitual understanding of entities as the integrated totality, and instead focus on the elements, the parts, outside of their integration or organisation, to look beyond the organism to the organs that compose it.
>
> (Grosz 1995: 182)

This understanding of sexuality can be post-gender. For example, not all body parts belong to one particular gender. In Grosz's formulation, the sexual interaction of a tongue and a nipple need not involve the distinction male or female – for both males and females have tongues and nipples.

It can, of course, be argued that this post-identity conceptualization of sexuality and of desire is an idealist fantasy – most people are aware of, and make decisions based on, the sex of their partners. In part this is true – although it does not devalue the importance of these writings as offering an alternative way of thinking about sexuality. But it should be noted, as suggested above, that there are particular cultural sites which do seem to exhibit a post-sex sexuality. Sadomasochistic communities are one such site. Indeed, when he is writing about sadomasochistic practices, Foucault goes even further than Grosz and rejects the category of desire. Instead, he suggests thinking of sexuality as *pleasure* – a term which, he argues, is less regulated, and less tied to identities than desire has been.

Bisexual writers have also begun to challenge the simple notion that sexuality can be tied to sex differences. The term itself is an unsatisfactory one – 'bi' means two, the term implies two kinds of desire (one for male, one for female, brought together). Terms like polysexuality, ambisexuality or multisexuality might better be used for post-sex sexuality. And again, this is not simply a philosophical fantasy – this is the experience of sexuality for many ('bisexual') people.

These conceptual challenges change 'sexuality' from being about the relationship of sexed identities (homosexual, heterosexual), to being a series of desirable, or pleasurable, interactions between surfaces, objects, moments. This rethinking of sexuality has led to quite different approaches to cultural texts. Rather than seeking to check representations of gay men, or lesbians, for their accuracy, it has tended to lead to discussions of the relationship between spectators and texts which are less tied to sex differences than has previously been the case.

Texts and metaphors of sexuality

The work of Elspeth Probyn (1996) takes up the non-psychoanalytic version of desire theorized by Deleuze and Guattari in order to discuss the circulation of cultural texts. First, this moves away from the conception of representation which sees the process as based on desire, based on lack (the search for reality). It also suggests quite different ways of approaching cultural texts. Probyn, for example, discusses 'lesbian images':

> The image becomes that with which we think and feel our way from body to body...hopeful lesbian images (images that we wish were lesbian) work not in relation to any supposed point of authenticity, but in their transversal

movement, in the ways in which they set up lines of desire...the image is queer not in and of itself, but in relation to other images and bodies.... Beyond the interpretation of images that seeks the origin of meaning, that seeks to fix impossible equivalences, that wishes to interpret images for their authentic queerness.

> (Probyn 1996: 60, 61)

In this writing, sexuality is no longer seen to be something in people that controls their interpretation of texts. Rather, the very relations of spectators with texts, the moments of consumption, are sexual, desiring acts. The spectator no longer has an identity, separate from culture and bounded by the body: the sense of self is formed in multiple moments of interaction and folding with the elements of culture itself.

See also: camp; feminist theory

References

Foucault, M. (1990) *The History of Sexuality, Volume 1*, trans. Robert Hurley, London: Penguin.

Grosz, E. (1995) *Space, Time and Perversion*, Sydney: Allen and Unwin.

Probyn, E. (1996) *Outside Belongings*, New York and London: Routledge.

Screen (ed.) (1992) *The Sexual Subject: A Screen Reader in Sexuality*, New York and London: Routledge.

ALAN McKEE

Shklovsky, Viktor

b. 1893; d. 1984

A Russian literary critic born in St Petersburg, Viktor Shklovsky, along with Boris Eichenbaum, Roman **Jakobson** and Yury Tynianov, developed a theory of poetics and language known as Russian **Formalism**. A prominent figure in the Petrograd group OPAYAZ (Society for the Study of Poetic Language), Shklovsky laid out the fundamental tenets of formalist criticism in 'Art as Technique'. Although he continued to write in Moscow until his death in 1984, Shklovsky is best known for his work during the height of Russian Formalism, between 1917 and 1929.

Like other Russian formalists, Shklovsky focused on narrative design and the manipulation of literary techniques, as opposed to cultural, historical and symbolic meanings. The development of **narrative** theory in film and television studies is indebted to Russian Formalist ideas about the relationship between **story**, **plot** and **style**. David **Bordwell** and Kristin Thompson have employed Shklovsky's method of defining the conventions of narrative construction in order to advance the systematic study of cinematic narration.

See also: fabula; syuzhet

Further reading

Shklovsky, V. (1990) *Theory of Prose* (first published 1929), trans. B. Sher, Elmwood Park: Dalkey Archive Press.

Thompson, K. (1988) *Breaking the Glass Armor*, Princeton: Princeton University Press.

JEN NEUBER

shot/reverse shot

Shot/reverse shot is a Hollywood editing technique, which is typically employed to show the immediate reaction of one character to another. The technique is central to the argument that film spectators are positioned into ideology and psychoanalytic structures via the **rhetoric** of **style**.

The notion that the shot/reverse shot technique participates in the positioning of spectators in ideology was introduced to film theory by Jean-Pierre Oudart and extended by Daniel Dayan. Both writers focus on the way in which the technique assumes an 'absent one' in the 'space' between the two shots – an absent one that is unconsciously assumed by the viewer. The technique sutures viewers into the symbolic order of the film (see **suture; symbolic code**). Oudart and Dayan thus reveal one way in which film style supports structuralist notions about ideology and the **unconscious** (see **structuralism and post-structuralism**).

See also: ideology and hegemony; psychoanalysis

Further reading

Rosen, P. (ed.) (1986) *Narrative, Apparatus, Ideology: A Film Theory Reader*, New York: Columbia University Press.

DANIEL BERNARDI

sign

'Sign' is a term from **semiotics** that refers to any meaningful unit – for example, a word, an image, a sound, etc. – which stands for something else. The two founders of semiotics, Ferdinand de **Saussure** and Charles **Peirce**, theorized the sign in different ways. For Saussure, it has a **binary** composition: a signifier (its physical form) and a signified (the mental concept it represents). Peirce envisaged a triangular model, comprising a representamen (its physical form), an interpretant (the sense made of it) and an object (what it refers to in reality). Saussure emphasizes the **arbitrary** relation between the signified and the signifier – a key area of discussion for film and television theory.

BELLA DICKS

signifying practice

This term, associated with **semiotics**, was introduced by Julia **Kristeva** to describe film and other artistic discourses. The word 'practice' proposes that film is an active process of meaning-production, rather than being a passive transmitter of pre-existent meanings in reality. Furthermore, individual film texts are not discrete units, but are permeated by wider meanings (see **intertextuality**). The term draws attention to the specific forms of different practices, emphasizing, for example, the particular qualities of film as opposed to television. It also focuses attention on *how* films signify, as opposed to *what* they signify, particularly through examining how the film constructs an author and a spectator.

BELLA DICKS

simulacrum

Introduced into cultural theory by Jean **Baudrillard**, the simulacrum refers to a product in a world where truth has become redundant. In the postmodern world of the simulacrum, a copy can no longer be distinguished from an original, since the status of the original itself is questioned: no 'real' exists against which to judge (see **modernism and post-modernism**). The concept has repercussions on discussions of subjectivity and social theory: the coherence of the self is under question, together with the possibility of reasoned and effective action. The proliferation of media is both the origin and a symptom of the world of simulacra: everything becomes 'mediatized', fictional and unoriginal.

PETRA KUPPERS

single play

The single play was a form of television drama with its own specific history in British television. As the name implies, it offered television drama which was not in **serial** or **series** form. In Britain, its high point is seen as the period between 1958 and 1972, and the format was developed initially under the Canadian, Sidney Newman. Newman imported the idea from North American television when he became (in 1958) Head of Drama at ABC, an independent (commercial) company, and then in 1963, Head of Drama at the British Broadcasting Corporation (BBC). Under different programming slots, *Armchair Theatre*, *The Wednesday Play*, *Play for Today*, Newman encouraged such writers and producers as John Mortimer, Harold Pinter, Dennis Potter, Simon Raven, Jim Allen, Alan Plater, Ken Loach, Tony Garnett, Philip Saville, James MacTaggart and Kenith Trodd.

In 1958, 48 plays were produced by ABC and in 1960, 265 'dramatic works' by the BBC, so it would be false to assume that the single play had a readily definable identity. But over the period the single play came to be associated with drama that spoke to nation-wide audiences, sometimes between six and twelve million, about current issues like **race**, **class** struggle, homosexuality, urban poverty and crime and punishment in a changing

society. Often scheduled at peak time (see **prime time**) after the news, the plays frequently challenged the hegemony or consensus which the news implied, and provoked controversies which led to direct and open confrontation between the writers and the BBC, and between the BBC, the government and right-wing populist press and lobby groups (see **ideology and hegemony**).

Though the innovation of shooting on film rather than tape enabled the growth of **documentary**-style naturalism, the single play also offered the space for experiments with nonnaturalism which Dennis Potter, David Mercer and others exploited (see **naturalism and non-naturalism**). Both modes attracted controversy, but in *Up the Junction* (first broadcast 3 November 1965) and *Cathy Come Home* (first broadcast 16 November 1966), Loach directed and Garnett produced dramas which deliberately adopted the visual style of **current affairs** programmes and become known as 'drama-documentary'. The plays raised issues about working-class life, homelessness and dispossession in a manner calculated to cause public debate both about their subject matter and the provocative mixture of 'fictional' content and 'factual' style. The government of the day and the press duly responded, and some minor changes in housing policy resulted. The longer-term political consequences, however, were more apparent in the subsequent careers of Loach and Garnett.

The single play was expensive to produce, and it allowed writers and directors a space to try innovations which, at first, might fail. Audiences as low as three or four million were tolerated, but the **public service broadcasting** ethos which informed both the BBC and ITV sometimes placed dramatic innovation and social relevance over ratings. In resisting the drive always to maximize revenue or audiences, they were also prepared to risk scheduling the plays at peak times. Economic pressures in the late 1970s and 1980s, however, made even the BBC more aware that series and serials, which used and re-used the same casts and sets, were cheaper to produce. Costume dramas that dealt with the past, or versions of 'Englishness' for export rather than controversial domestic issues, could also be sold overseas (see **heritage film and television**). It was easier and safer to schedule a six- or thirteen-part series which might build an audience and which could be relied on not to offer disturbing shifts in form or content from week to week. By the end of the 1980s, moreover, the British audience was also beginning the process of fragmentation which the advent of **cable and satellite** inevitably brings. From the mid-1980s, Channel 4 and the BBC were committed to co-productions that might also have a cinematic appeal abroad as well as at home.

Though the single play in British television has its particular history, as a conjunction of issues about the relationship between institutional control, formal innovation and the social role of television, that history may have a wider relevance.

See also: broadcasting, the United Kingdom

Further reading

Brandt, G. (1981) *British Television Drama in the 1980s*, Cambridge Cambridge University Press.

Caughie, J. (2000) *Television Drama: Realism, Modernism and British Culture*, Oxford: Oxford University Press.

Gardner, C. and Wyver, J. (1983) 'The Single Play: From Reithian Reverence to Cost-accounting and Censorship', *Screen*, vol. 24, nos 4–5.

MacMurraugh-Kavanagh, M. (1997) ' "Drama" into "News": Strategies of Intervention in *The Wednesday Play*' *Screen*, vol. 38, no. 3.

—— (1997/98) 'Wednesday Play', *Media Education Journal* (Winter), pp. 10–14.

PHILIP SIMPSON

situation comedy

Situation comedy (sit-com) is a humorous depiction of a 'situation' often found in everyday life, usually resolved within the half-hour format of a television programme. A common story element in situation comedy is the experiences of the middle-classes, giving many viewers the ability to identify with the characters and events depicted. Situation comedy centres on a group of main characters who propel the action of the story. Other types of roles include supporting and transient characters. Supporting characters are regular cast members who interact with main characters on various social and professional levels. Transients appear as guest stars, occasional characters or one-time characters. British sit-com tends to be 'writer' led, while US sitcom is more reliant upon stars.

BERTO TRINIDAD

soap opera

The pejorative term 'soap opera' was coined in the American press in the 1930s for radio's daytime **serial** programmes. The term referred to the product of the sponsor-producers and to the supposed melodramatic excesses of the **genre** (see **melodrama**). Soap operas are characterized by open-ended narratives, a community of densely interrelated characters and storylines concerned with moral and social issues. There are distinct national differences in the style and content of soap operas, including those between American **prime-time** soaps such as *Dallas* and *Dynasty* and the more realist British prime-time soaps such as *Coronation Street* and *EastEnders*.

ALISON GRIFFITHS

Socialist Realism

Socialist Realism was the official art policy of revolutionary communist governments, especially of Soviet Russia and China. As an artistic creed, it expressed a similar desire to 1920s works of agitation-propaganda (see **agit-prop**) to teach official views of politics and history. However, the works of Socialist Realism adhered to much stricter artistic expressions. The Socialist Realist reform of art extended one strain of revolutionary practice to reinforce the absolute power of the state.

Lenin had initiated Bolshevik control of art in the Soviet Republic. In 1932 the Central Committee of the Communist Party, under Josef Stalin, established cultural supremacy in the name of the proletariat, or working class, by liquidating all literary institutions in the creation of the All-Soviet Union of Writers. When Mao later came to power in China, he held similar autocratic authority. Both leaders enforced Socialist Realism throughout their political parties, class-based unions and Communist nations.

Socialist Realism appeared not merely as a set of artistic rules, but as an ideology (see **ideology and hegemony**). Whoever aligned themselves with its artistic tenets also adhered to explicit ideas of social and political life. The correct, official understanding of both reality and art arose through Socialist Realism's three tenets of *partiinost* ('party-ness'), *narodnost* ('nation-ness') and *klassovost* ('class-ness').

In *partiinost*, all experience must be filtered through and express conformity with Communist Party thought. No art exists outside of the Party, and thus art became inextricable from publicizing Party doctrine. The orthodoxies of *narodnost* and *klassovost* blend indistinguishably with *partiinost*. The Party embodies the people, who are steeled by the proletariat; the proletariat leads the people forward through the Party. In its trinity of party, nation and class, Socialist Realism represents the quintessence of a fabricated national unity. Socialist Realist leaders urged the fusion of artworks with the feelings of workers, peasants and Party soldiers. As the Party supposedly embodied the essence of the nation and its working people, Socialist Realist art represented their union by depicting class, national and Party subjects in a clear and monumental style.

An exemplary Socialist Realist film, such as *Chapayev* (1934), forges the links between nation, class and Party into a heroic whole. Early in the film, a Red commander in the Russian civil war, Chapayev, compels his peasant soldiers to retrieve their rifles from a river after an attack. Workers from the city then join his newly disciplined peasant troops. The two groups become a single, devoted force under Chapayev, with the help of a commissar from the Communist Party. The commissar convinces Chapayev not to allow looting as the army passes through peasant land. As Chapayev and his proletarian squadron defend the Party, the Party – in the person of the commissar – teaches respect and devotion to the people. In terms of visual style, Socialist Realist film fused folk imagery with models of the Party's industrial and military progress (celebrating rifles and potatoes).

As Socialist Realism set forth three principles for guiding artistic understanding, it also judged art by three interwoven relationships to time. First, the artist had to draw on national traditions, but only the strain of custom appropriate to the modern Communist state. The Russian writer Maxim Gorky urged his fellow artists to learn from the classics – to purify the best in them as the new Communist regimes bettered all previous systems. Paradoxically, the artist had to grasp society's present achievement, and express it to assure Communism's inevitable triumph. Socialist Realism inextricably bound art to the government. Artistic truth illuminated current politics; politics determined realistic representations in art.

The third principle of time in Socialist Realism confirmed the reciprocity of art and political power, in merging past, present and future societies. Socialist Realism created a circular present time, to assure the future realization of its teachings. In Socialist Realism, the state claimed culture. Even more: in absorbing the subjects of culture, dictating its style, and integrating it completely into absolute authority, the state became art.

See also: Marxist aesthetics; realism

Further reading

Luker, Nicholas (ed.) (1988) *From Furmanov to Sholokhov: An Anthology of the Classics of Socialist Realism*, Ann Arbor: Ardis Press.
Vaughan, James C. (1973) *Soviet Socialist Realism: Origins and Theory*, New York: St. Martin's Press.

GABRIEL M. PALETZ

sound

In spite of the significance of the addition of integrated sound to feature films in the late 1920s, there really was never a silent cinema: filmgoers had always heard at least a musical accompaniment. Still – and, more significantly, in spite of many decades of full soundtracks – sound has often figured as a kind of afterthought in the world of film theory. The image, on the other hand, has received the most attention, and has been at the hub of most major film theoretical movements, including psychoanalytical theory, various strains of **Formalism** and textual analysis. Most theorists do not ignore sound entirely, but many implicitly assign it a lower status than the visible image.

However, beginning in the 1980s, considerable attention was paid to film sound by theorists concerned to redress its previous neglect, and to do so in ways which went beyond rehashing the technical history of sound and beyond understanding sound as a kind of adornment on film. A key and influential early publication in this period was a 1980 special issue of *Yale French Studies* (*YFS*) devoted to 'Cinema/Sound'. The ten essays in this volume fall into three categories: theory, history and music. In the introduction to the volume, editor Rick Altman suggests that:

> The source of the image's current dominance [in film theory] is closely linked to the vocabulary developed by three-quarters of a century of film critics. With few exceptions film terminology is camera-oriented.... The type and placement of microphones, methods of recording sound, mixing practices, loudspeaker varieties, and many other fundamental considerations are the province of a few specialists.
>
> (*Yale French Studies* 1980: 3)

He reviews the history of the neglect of sound by theorists (some of whom quite explicitly proclaimed the visual aspect of film to be the principal one), and describes the *YFS* volume's goal as 'remedial' (*ibid.*). In fact, the *YFS* collection did have a strong influence, though it would be difficult to argue that film theorists have grown to accept sound fully on an equal footing with visual imagery in film.

Selected theoretical issues in film sound

Much writing has been devoted to the topic of sound. What follows are some brief comments on a selection of theoretical issues of recurrent interest to theorists of film sound.

1 *Sound and the ontology of film.* Theorists have long debated the question of how sound fits into the fundamental question of what film is – that is, the question of whether film is an 'essentially' visual medium but not an essentially aural medium. As Altman (1987) points out, this debate intensified in the 1920s as sound on film was becoming a reality; a number of filmmakers

and film theorists (**Eisenstein**, **Arnheim**, **Pudovkin** and others) expressed either opposition to sound or serious reservations about the effects it was likely to have on film. This notion of sound as an add-on feature of film, rather than an essential part of it, is still debated. On the one hand, it is clear that a film without sound is still 'film', whereas recorded sound without a visual track is not 'film'. The image portion of film thus seems to have a claim to primacy. On the other hand, if – as is indeed the case – almost every film produced and seen throughout many decades, in many film cultures, does in fact have sound, it can also be argued on historical grounds that sound is an integral part of film, in any historically meaningful sense of the term 'film'.

2 *Synchronous/asynchronous sound.* One of the key characteristics of film sound is that while it can be tightly bound to the image – in such a way that the audience sees a character speak and hears the words spoken at the same time – this need not be the case. In other words, sound may be synchronous or asynchronous. Synchronous sound, with all its implications of **realism**, is only one of the options available to filmmakers, and this variability on the part of sound has figured in debates over the role of sound in film.

Certain uses of asynchronous sound do convey an anti-realist impression. However, even the standard creative palette of conventional realist commercial film includes certain asynchronous sound techniques. Voice-over narration, in particular, involves a partial or full dissociation of the human voice from any visual representation of the speaker. A voice-over may be anonymous, or the voice may be that of a known character in the film but speaking from an unspecified time and place. The matter of sound synchrony has received attention from numerous theorists (see the essays by Doane and Altman in *YFS*, and Sarah Kozloff's *Invisible Storytellers* [1988] on the subject of voice-over narration).

3 *Music.* Film music, while part of the overall topic of sound, is in some respects a subject of its own (see **music and film**). The history of film music reaches back beyond the late 1920s 'sound barrier', inasmuch as live musical

accompaniment of silent films was a virtually universal practice. The study of film music also includes biographical and stylistic analyses of particular composers, as well as **genre** studies; see in particular Rick Altman's *The American Film Musical* (1987).

4 *Sound and technological enhancement*. Even outside the cinema, recorded sound has undergone numerous changes aimed at enhancing its realism – or, more precisely, its potential to be advertised and marketed as realistic. Film sound has shadowed some of these developments, in particular the use of stereo and enhanced directional sound (so that, for instance, the sound from an off-screen car comes from the side or back of the theatre). In some cases little more than a gimmick, directional sound has at least as much claim to be taken seriously as does any other commercially-motivated, reality-imitating aspect of film (colour, sound itself, widescreen images, etc.).

Sound and television

Some of the historical and theoretical issues which have arisen in connection with sound in film pertain to sound in television; but some do not, and television sound also raises questions of its own. Television's roots are in radio. This is not to say that television is nothing more than 'radio with pictures', but rather to point to the historical continuities between the radio industry and the television industry. In Britain, both were the domain of the BBC. In America, the three dominant national radio networks (ABC, CBS, NBC) spearheaded the funding of television research and dominated the television industry even more than they had the radio industry. Programming forms from news to **soap opera** to comedy/variety were adapted from radio. In many cases, specific programmes made the transition, sometimes even being broadcast on both media at the same time.

In short, while television is more than 'radio with pictures', the television industry has often behaved as if that were indeed the essence of television, clinging closely to formats and practices established in radio. This has implications for the role of sound in television. While television offers at least as many types of asynchronous sound as film, in many cases television sound does little more than repeat information already available visually. (This phenomenon of 'redundancy'' between the visual and aural tracks has been examined in depth, in the case of film, by Rick Altman in 'Moving Lips: Cinema as Ventriloquism' [*YSL* 1980].)

Sports broadcasting provides an instructive example of redundant sound in television. For an even moderately knowledgeable viewer, baseball is an easy sport to follow on television by watching. None the less, baseball commentary – the sound portion – often takes the form of redundant narration of events and actions clearly visible on the screen ('The runner goes . . . swings and misses . . . here's the pitch', etc.). It is reasonable at least to speculate that the tradition of a redundant soundtrack has its roots, not in any thoroughgoing assessment of human cognitive processes, but in the history of the medium. As the forerunner of television in the matter of sportscasting, radio *required* verbal description of every play, and the practice of providing at least a large measure of such description has persisted, although to a greater extent in American than in British sportscasts, with American commentators far more concerned to provide running descriptions than British commentators.

The redundancy between television sound and image – or even, in some cases, the primacy of sound over image – also meshes with the fact that television viewing sometimes takes place in circumstances of distraction or partial attention. In the case of a sporting event, verbal commentary allows a viewer to wander away from the television and yet not miss any plays. An interesting example of television designed for intermittent attention has been identified and studied by Tania Modleski in her work on the soap opera. In 'The Rhythms of Reception', Modleski (1983) suggests that certain aspects of soap opera **narrative** are designed specifically to accommodate women at home in the afternoon who want to follow the story but must also attend to child care and housework which takes them away from the television. The slow pace and repetitive narrative structures of soap operas, Modleski suggests, assist in this regard; missing any given few minutes is unlikely to result in losing track of the plot lines. Sound, too, seems to play this role; much of the 'action' of a soap opera resides in the dialogue, often to the extent that visual inattention hardly has an impact on a viewer's ability to follow the narrative.

References

Altman, R. (1987) *The American Film Musical*, London: BFI Publishing.

Kozloff, S. (1988) *Invisible Storytellers: Voice-over Narration in American Fiction Film*, Berkeley: University of California Press.

Modleski, Tania (1983) 'The Rhythms of Reception', in E. Anne Kaplan (ed.) *Regarding Television*, The American Film Institute Monograph Series, Volume II, Los Angeles: The American Film Institute.

Yale French Studies (1980) special issue, 'Cinema/Sound', vol. 60, no. 1. (This issue includes the essays referred to in the entry: Mary Ann Doane, 'The Voice in the Cinema: The Articulation of Body and Space', pp. 33–50; Rick Altman, 'Moving Lips: Cinema as Ventriloquism', pp. 67–79; Rick Altman, 'Introduction', pp. 3–15.)

DAVID A. BLACK

space/place

A clock ticks on a wall above an exit sign. It is 9.05 p.m. My eyes are distracted from the screen and fixed on the clock. This momentary break in concentration makes me aware that I am in a cinema watching a film, engaged as a spectator by the architecture of the building and the light from the projector on the screen in front of my eyes. I have been made aware of the space between the screen and me while, before this interruption, I was mainly conscious of the space I occupied in relation to what was happening on screen. I tried for many years without success to have the clock moved in the cinema which I attended regularly as a child and adolescent. The space of the building, the space-time of the film and the 'real' time of the film's duration was marked out by the clock. Sometimes it was used as a measure of the film's attraction, its suspense and its visual and narrative

hold. A film without sufficient narrative or visual interest was measured by repeated looks at the clock, particularly in the closing section. A case of spatiality being controlled by temporality, as it has been in the history of narrative cinema and television where the study of **narrative**, time-based stories has tended to dominate.

Study of screen space has generally been linked with the formal properties of film, the editing, camera movement, **mise-en-scène**; this has helped to establish the significance of screen space but has routinely relegated it to being of secondary importance, as subordinate to narrative causality. This entry is an attempt to redress the balance, to accord space/place equal importance to narrative. As Peter **Wollen** (1980: 25) has argued, although 'Places are functions of the narrative (actions must take place somehow) yet the fascination of film is often with the places themselves'. The symbiotic relationship of screen storytelling and screen space is best established by renaming space as space-time, with the re-assertion of the importance of screen space and place and their contribution to the range of meanings in film alongside, rather than subordinate to, the determinants of narrative causality.

According to Yi Fu Tuan, space and place require each other for definition:

> Space is a common symbol of freedom in the Western world. Space lies open; it suggests the future and invites action. Enclosed and humanised space is place.... Human beings require both space and place. Human lives are a dialectical movement between shelter and venture, attachment and freedom.
>
> (Tuan 1974: 54)

If we think about this definition in relation to screen space-time, we move towards a possible description of how screen space-time and place overlap. Although much theoretical writing has been given over to the construction of meanings of screen space-time (see Burch 1973; Bordwell and Thompson 1976; Heath 1981; Branigan 1989), the ways in which screen *space-time* is connected with *places* represented on the screen, and their existence in the real world, has been discussed in Higson (1984), Aitken and Zonn (1994), Donald (1995), Collins (1995) and Morley and Robins (1995). The purpose of linking the words is to identify their interdependence and to offer a more holistic view of what is seen on the screen, or suggested in off-screen space; how what is seen is perceived by the spectator, and how the spectator transforms two-dimensional screen space-time into three-dimensional place in the process of looking and seeing.

The joining of space-time and place also points to the importance of the role played by the media, particularly film and television, in the mediation of place image. A place is often known first by its representation on the screen. What Collins (1995: 35) calls the 'intervention of institutionalized image-making' has become an essential part of how people see themselves, and the space/place of their lived experiences. Layers of popular narratives about Los Angeles have contributed to the ways in which that city is imagined, inhabited and envisioned by Los Angelenos and the tourist/viewer. While acknowledging the symbiotic relationship of space/place, I suggest that the terms be regarded as having some of the same properties rather than as synonyms. Their intermingling sets up their distinctive nature but holds these in tension. Although most examples are drawn from classical Hollywood and post-1960s Hollywood cinema (see **classical Hollywood cinema and new Hollywood cinema**), it might be suggested that what distinguishes **avant-garde** or **art cinema** from mainstream cinema is the way that the former works to expose audiences to the screen space-time – that is, makes them aware of its construction – while the mainstream cinema tries to hide or efface the space where the narrative is unfolding. One seeks to hide its operation, the other to make it visible. As Maltby (1995: 217) suggests, 'spatial presentation is rarely stressed in Hollywood, making it difficult to appreciate its significance...a richer understanding of a Hollywood movie can be offered by examining its visual discourse than by presuming that its meaning is located solely in plot and dialogue'.

So what is it that links cinematic space-time and place? A tentative definition might be that cinematic space-time is turned into place by *mise-en-scène* and the presence of screen characters. When the idea of space is talked about in everyday life it is often described as a static notion. Cinematic space, however, must be dynamic, hence the use of the term space-time. We measure space by using numbers, it exists in the abstract and is there objectively. Place is subjective, it exists at a number of different scales. It is our favourite house or beach or landscape or country and we invest it with **memory** and **desire**. Combining the words to help identify their shared properties enables a close examination of the dynamics of space-time and the subjectivity of audience identification with character(s) in place.

Screen space-time engenders a sense of place when we engage with it through our emotional identification with the character: when the screen space is humanized. On the roof in *On the Waterfront* (Elia Kazan, 1954) shifts from a space where the action unfolds, the murder of Joey Doyle at the beginning of the film, to a place where the emotional investment of Terry Malloy (Marlon Brando) in his pigeons portrays his more decent, humane and expressive side. It could also be said that place is used here as a metaphor for Terry's feelings about Edie Doyle (Eva Marie Saint). Screen space-time as place is not subordinate to the narrative but contributes to the performance and deepens the audience identification. The locations in *On the Waterfront* play an important part in the narrative, not just as *mise-en-scène*, or backdrop to the action, but also by working with other elements such as **sound** and dialogue – for example, when, in the scene in which Terry confesses to Edie about his unwitting part in her brother's death, part of their conversation is drowned out by the sound of the docks. Sound plays a crucial part in defining and setting the limits of screen space-time and helps to turn it into recognizable place. Thus, the audience's mapping of the narrative space-time is guided by the dialogue, music and sound effects as well as the visual discourse.

When we watch the screen as spectators our perception of screen space-time is governed by a set of rules first elaborated in the fourteenth century and regarded as 'normal' or **common sense**. Heath (1981: 30) suggests that 'the conception of the Quattrocento system is that of scenographic space, space set out as spectacle for the eye of a spectator'. Spectators are able and willing to give themselves over to this perspectival position as it allows them to apprehend three-dimensional objects on a flat screen (see **perspective**). Branigan (1995) argues that cinema has closer associations with the optical toys of the nineteenth century than with **photography**. It is the movement of each frame at twenty-four frames per second that helps to create the illusion of **persistence of vision**. Screen space-time may be visible on the screen but it is brought into being by the highly conventionalized ways of seeing and highly conventionalized expectations of viewers, depending on their knowledge of the cinema-going experience, their expectations of the **genre**, and their **gender**, ethnic and socio-economic backgrounds. Screen space-time has evolved through a series of rules or codes of production (see **code**) that begin with perspective and develop because of the specificity of the medium to include **continuity editing**, *mise-en-scène*, framing, sound, composition, eye-line matching and narrative causality.

When we view the opening scene of *Chinatown* (Roman Polanski, 1974), for instance, the illusion of three-dimensionality arises immediately as we become aware that we are watching still images of a couple engaged in intercourse. They are in black and white, and as the camera draws back to present the *mise-en-scène* we see, in colour, the office of J. J. Gittes (Jack Nicholson), private investigator. The titles of the film and the accompanying music guide us to the genre of the film and help set up expectations that will be fulfilled as the occupation of the central character is revealed. In these opening scenes through the use of period detail, the production design, the costumes, the hats, all signal the codes of a particular time and location. The space of Jake Gitte's office functions in the narrative to provide the place where the enigma is set up. It is the locus for the initial storytelling. With the departure of Curly, the husband in the opening scene who has been cuckolded as the photographic evidence proves, we see the arrival of Mrs Hollis Mulwray, whom we later find out is an impostor, her costume adding detail to the already growing period feel of the film. She sets up the surveillance of her husband whom she believes is having an affair with a much younger woman. Jake takes on the job reluctantly and so begins the watching of Hollis Mulwray. It is at this point that the space-time where the narrative of surveillance is unfolding is turned into place, not by direct naming but by architectural, newspaper, character and dialogue clues. We are in Los Angeles of the 1930s, a time recreated for the film – shot in the early 1970s – by the accurate production design and the choice of locations. It is the interactions of the central characters with their environment that turns screen space-time into cinematic place.

The functions of place

Outlining some of the functions of cinematic place should help to make its inter-connectedness with screen space-time clearer and more visible. These functions are not mutually exclusive. Nor do they suggest a subordination to narrative causality; rather they deepen and enrich the narrative. Drawing on the work of filmmaker Mark Rappaport (1980: 26), I would suggest that place can be considered in six main ways.

Place as a backdrop: this is the least sophisticated function but it can serve to invest a scene or an action with aesthetic or emotional significance. The places Thelma and Louise (*Thelma and Louise*, Ridley Scott, 1992) travel through in their picaresque journey help them to make a decision about their lives. This film draws attention to these places as sites of mythical imaginings, where other screen stories have been played out. The places, as well as a backdrop for the action, have a certain elemental quality.

Place as character: here the location becomes vital in the way the film's narrative develops. Monument Valley in John Ford's depiction of the West, particularly in his cavalry trilogy, becomes a character in his films. The narrative might be said to arise out of the locations. New York as the location for the musical journeys of the three sailors in *On the Town* (Gene Kelly and Stanley Donen, 1948) is more than just backdrop; it defines the attitudes and actions of the characters. The desert as place and character is evident in *Lawrence of Arabia* (David Lean, 1963) and *The English Patient* (Anthony Mingella, 1995) where the landscape and the characters' interactions with it helps to construct the tempo of the narrative. The spaceship Nostromo in Ridley Scott's *Alien* (1979) and the Bates Motel in *Psycho* (Alfred Hitchcock, 1960) also serve the function of place as character. These cinematic creations, rather than existing within the 'real' world, are constructed by the camera, the *mise-en-scène*, the continuity editing, the soundtrack and the music, but they help to define and develop generic expectations and narrative causality.

Place as metaphor: in *Chinatown* the strength of that place as metaphor is suggested in the early scenes between Jake and his former police colleagues when he is reminded of his past actions in Chinatown and his inability to control what happened. He ended up hurting someone whom he was trying to protect, which becomes a prophetic warning for the events at the end of the film, the only scenes to be actually located in Chinatown. The name of the film does not, in this instance, function as a location-finder for the external events of the film, but as a psychological map of the terrain of Jake's mind. He is unable to control events, or locations, even though he is the central detective, the finder-out of truths. *Paris, Texas* (Wim Wenders, 1984) is another place that functions as metaphor. It exists as a place, but the name also describes the longing to belong that the central character, Travis (Harry Dean Stanton), evokes in his seemingly aimless wandering through the desert: a landscape mythologized in countless Westerns. Travis' inability to find and humanize this place, the turning of space-time into somewhere he is free to wander without ever arriving at a destination, metaphorically describes the quest undertaken by countless immigrants on their journey westwards. It also helps to portray the alienation of the central character and his inability to make space and place legible, raising questions about how to survive the dialectic of attachment and freedom, shelter and confinement.

Place as authenticator of the narrative: this focuses on the importance of creating the illusion of geographical **verisimilitude**. The town and the beach in *Local Hero* (Bill Forsyth, 1983) do not exist in close geographical proximity but we are encouraged to believe that they do by the editing and the characters' ability to walk between locations. Despite the use of two locations the landscape is strongly coded as Scottish through music, dialogue and production design, and this helps to authenticate the actions and attitudes of the characters.

Place that cuts against the descriptive meaning and narrative flow: this can be seen in the use of locations in the opening section of *Chinatown*. Mulwray's

visits to the city's drainage sources stalls the surveillance and the uncovering of his supposed mistress, but in so doing it sets up the main storyline which centres on the ownership and control of water and power. The places of surveillance themselves become the spectacle: on one level a distraction from the progress of the narrative, while on another level, registering their importance in shaping the actions of the characters.

Place may serve a metonymic function: this is because it is space that has been humanized, where networks of social relations are apparent (see **metonymy**). A building, for example the Eiffel Tower, may code the action as taking place in France. The coded use of certain architecture, skyscrapers, tenement blocks, metonymically and ideologically locates central characters, their beliefs, values and attitudes. The opening scenes of *Boyz N the Hood* (John Singleton, 1991) locate the film not just in Los Angeles, but in a specific black neighbourhood, and they suggest a certain mismatch between character and place. The paradox of longing for belonging is indicated in the film's title, the importance of the hood identity, but this is played out as a place from which escape is necessary in order to survive. The opening of *L.A. Story* (Mick Jackson, 1991) uses the space-time and place of Los Angeles for very different purposes. The audience is encouraged, though they may choose to resist, to read the film's locations as natural – a spectacle laid out for the eye, where absences, difference and geographical unruliness which do not serve the purpose of the filmmakers or the picture of the place being represented are effaced or used as geographical irony.

The above examples of how cinematic space-time co-exists as place points to the importance of these elements in the construction of narrative and highlights the intervention of the audience in place-image identification.

Space-time becomes place through identification with character. Both words should be seen as working together but also in tension with each other, helping to signal more clearly the meanings that are suggested by the text and those which we bring with us as audiences. Space-time and place co-exist in film narrative, at times complementing, at other times counteracting the flow of the narrative. It is not a question of whether spectacle dominates over narrative but the ways in which spatio-temporal elements within the film help to achieve audience response through emotional identification. The cinematic image is at its most potent when space-time is transformed into place and the audience find themselves located in the action. The audience recognizing and existing, as I did with the clock in my home-town cinema, within and outside the diegetic and non-diegetic world of the cinematic space/place (see **diegesis**). Such is the power of cinematic representations of space/place coupled with the audience's willingness to give themselves up to this double existence: feeling *part of* but also *standing outside* the experience of cinematic space-time and place.

References

Aitken, S. and Zonn, L. (eds) (1994) *Place, Power, Situation and Spectacle*, Maryland: Rowman and Littlefield.

Bordwell, D. and Thompson, K. (1976) 'Space and Narrative in the Films of Ozu', *Screen*, vol. 17, no. 2.

Branigan, E. (1989) 'The Spectacle and Film Space', *Screen*, vol. 22, no. 1.

—— (1995) *Narrative Comprehension and Film*, London: Routledge.

Burch, N. (1973) *The Theory of Film Practice*, London: Secker and Warburg.

Collins, J. (1995) *Architectures of Excess*, London: Routledge.

Donald, J. (1995) 'The City, the Cinema: Modern Spaces', in C. Jenks (ed.) *Visual Culture*, London: Routledge.

Heath, S. (1981) *Questions of Cinema*, London: Macmillan.

Higson, A. (1984) 'Space, Place, Spectacle', *Screen*, vol. 25, no. 4.

Maltby, R., with Craven, I. (1995) *Hollywood Cinema: An Introduction*, Oxford: Blackwell.

Morley, D. and Robins, K. (1995) *Spaces of Identity: Global Media, Electronic Landscapes and Cultural Boundaries*, London: Routledge.

Rappaport, M. (1980) 'Place in the Cinema', *Framework*, vol. 13, p. 26.

Tuan, Y. F. (1974) *Space and Place: The Perspective of Experience*, Minneapolis: University of Minnesota Press.

Wollen, P. (1980) 'Place in the Cinema', *Framework*, vol. 13, p. 26.

Further reading

Bukatman, S. (1997) *Blade Runner*, London: BFI Publishing.

Clarke, D. B. (ed.) (1997) *The Cinematic City*, London: Routledge.

Davis, M. (1991) *City of Quartz*, London: Vintage.

Massey, D. (1993) *Space, Place and Gender*, Cambridge: Polity Press.

KEN FOX

spectacle

The term 'spectacle' has been established in film and television theory mainly through three traditions of thinking. These are: a sociological approach exemplified by Guy Debors; a feminist/psychoanalytical usage coined most influentially by Laura **Mulvey**; and the historical approach of Tom Gunning in his rereading of Sergei **Eisenstein**'s '**cinema of attractions**'.

Debors' 1967 pamphlet, *Society of the Spectacle*, analyses the role of capitalist development. All forms of human communication are replaced by the consumption of images: 'the principle of commodity fetishism...reaches its absolute fulfilment in the spectacle, where the tangible world is replaced by a selection of images' (Debors 1970: 16). These images of passivity and the death of democracy were resonant in the political agitation of 1968, and similar concerns have resurfaced in Jean **Baudrillard**'s **hyperreal**. Baudrillard's writing has renewed interest in the relationship between media and reality. His statement that 'the Gulf war will not take place' pointed to the mediated and spectacularized knowledge of the event. Our world is brought to us second-hand and simulated, and no 'disruptive event' such as war, emotions and affects can penetrate the conformity of endless images. All events are levelled into media fodder and spectacle. Media studies' concerns centre on the possibilities for social or political engagement in a mediated, post-modern world (see **modernism and post-modernism**).

In psychoanalytic film theory, the term 'spectacle' has become a description for inequalities in the representation of **gender** (see **psychoanalysis**). Women in film are looked at, men do the looking: this is one of the central statements of Laura Mulvey's influential essay, 'Visual Pleasure and Narrative Cinema' (1975). Modern culture's debasing use of bodies as spectacles was already noted by writers like Siegfried **Kracauer** who wrote about the 'ornament of the masses' in relation to shows such as Busby Berkeley's panoramas of female legs. Kracauer linked this use of bodies to the dehumanizing effects of modernity. Mulvey investigates the specific gendered nature of spectacularization.

In classic Hollywood cinema, the woman as passive erotic spectacle, object of the look, threatens to halt the flow of the narrative. Flow is restored by narratively punishing the woman, or by fetishizing and fragmenting her body (see **fetishism**). 'Woman' is thus always either deployed as a narrative threat or becomes a fetish without any subjectivity. Women as active individuals have no place in this ultimately narcissistic male spectatorial system. In Mulvey's essay, cinema is structured around this gendered economy of the gaze and the spectacular object (see **gaze, the**). There is no space provided for women's pleasure in film, other forms of **desire**, or forms of active display that do not objectify and disempower. Important debates in feminist film theory are structured around the re-writing of this paradigm (see **feminist theory**).

A further influential use of the term 'spectacle' emerged from film studies. During the 1980s the orthodoxy which saw film history as a teleological development towards a more developed form of communication was replaced by different approaches to early film. Early film was analysed as cinema in its own right, and not just as a simplistic precursor to classical forms. Tom Gunning's influential essay 'The Cinema of Attractions' was published in *Wide Angle* in 1986 and dovetailed with an interest in spectatorship approaches in film studies generally. Instead of seeing unsuccessful or clumsy narratives in films before 1906, Gunning points to alternative modes of address employed in these early film forms. He describes an exhibitionist cinema: 'The cinema of attractions directly solicits spectator attention, inciting visual curiosity, and supplying pleasure through an exciting spectacle' (Gunning 1990: 58). The technical possibilities of cinema such as the close-up, stop-motion or multiple exposure are wonders which have the ability to excite audiences, without the need for elaborate narratives. Gunning's concept of the spectacle pleasure of early cinema was directed at the specific situation of a defined historical period, but the concept has been taken up in discussions of late-Hollywood blockbusters such as *Jurassic Park* (Steven Spielberg, 1993) and the pleasures they afford.

See also: audience; classical Hollywood cinema and new Hollywood cinema; pre-Hollywood cinema

References

Debors, G. (1967) *Society of the Spectacle* (trans. 1970), Detroit: Red and Black.

Gunning, T. (1990) 'The Cinema of Attractions. Early Film, its Spectator and the Avant-Garde' (first published 1986), in Thomas Elsaesser (ed.) *Early Film: Space, Frame, Narrative*, London: BFI Publishing.

Mulvey, L. (1975) 'Visual Pleasure and Narrative Cinema', *Screen*, vol. 16, no. 3.

PETRA KUPPERS

spectrum scarcity

Broadcast signals were initially transmitted through a spectrum that was limited, and consequently considered part of the collective domain. In Britain it was felt that this valuable form of public property should be regulated rather than left to market forces (see **regulation**). This principle has gradually lost validity as new delivery platforms and techniques of compression have opened up the ether. With parts of the spectrum freed, ownership has passed to the private domain where commercial, satellite and digital broadcasters have emerged so that scarcity has been replaced with a virtually unlimited supply.

See also: cable and satellite

RAKESH KAUSHAL

Spivak, Gayatri

b. 1941

Gayatri Spivak is one of the pre-eminent post-colonial theorists working in the American academy. A self-defined post-structuralist, Marxist-feminist, Spivak's work spans the important early translation of Jacques **Derrida**'s *De la Grammatologie* (1976), to her influential article, 'Can the Subaltern Speak?', and her championing of Bengali Indian women writers. Her writing explores the contradictory position of the marginal subject, whether in history, literary texts or the American academy. The dilemma of explaining the position of being inside and outside the dominant power structure is also taken up in the style of her writing which is at once an example and critique of Derridean deconstructive philosophy (see **deconstruction**). In this sense, Spivak is as much a practitioner as a theorist. Her most recent work (1993) contains discussions of Indian cinema culture in a neo-imperialist global context and a critique of cultural studies.

Further reading

Spivak, G. (1987) *In Other Worlds: Essays in Cultural Politics*, London: Methuen.
—— (1988) 'Can the Subaltern Speak?', in C. Nelson and L. Grossberg (eds) *Marxism and the Interpretation of Culture*, Chicago: University of Illinois Press.
—— (1993) *Outside in the Teaching Machine*, London: Routledge.

PAULA TATLA AMAD

sponsorship

Sponsorship is a commercial method of funding for media production and exhibition. Unlike **advertising**, where companies via advertising agencies place messages in the breaks around programmes, sponsorship directly links a particular product with a specific television programme or televised event.

An organization will pay money to the broadcaster or network to associate themselves and/or their product with a particular media production – usually a television programme. A high profile example in the United Kingdom is the association of Cadbury's chocolate with the soap opera *Coronation Street*. In the United States, where broadcasting has always operated on a purely commercial basis, sponsorship has a long and established history which has its roots in radio. Indeed, the term '**soap opera**' originates from the sponsorship of serial radio drama by soap companies wanting to sell their product to housewives at home listening to the radio.

However, in the UK direct programme sponsorship was only introduced in 1991 after the liberalization of broadcasting brought in by the 1990 Broadcasting Act, and even then with close monitoring by the Independent Television Commission (ITC, the body responsible for licensing and regulating all commercial television). The regulations currently governing programme sponsorship in the UK prohibit companies or products sponsoring a programme from advertising during the same programme. There are also regulations governing the sponsorship of certain types of programmes, for example it is forbidden for alcohol or cigarette companies to sponsor children's programmes.

In the United States, where **regulation** is less strict, programme sponsors are required by the FCC to make their association transparent: Section 317 of the Communications Act requires that any material broadcast in exchange for money, service, or other valuable consideration paid to a broadcast station, directly or indirectly, be accompanied by a sponsorship identification or disclosure. Unlike the ITC in the UK, the FCC has no real powers to censor companies that violate these rules except in so far as they have the power to either renew or revoke their licence to broadcast. This difference in regulatory practice is indicative, on a more general level, of the differing discourses of the public good underpinning American and western European broadcasting (see **public service broadcasting**).

Sponsorship relies heavily on ideas of branding and association. For example, in the case of *Coronation Street* and Cadbury's, the chocolate manufacturer wants to project an image of its brand as familiar, comfortable and reliable – 'the nation's favourite' – through its connection with the UK's most consistently high-rated television programme. Advertising agencies, public relations departments and broadcasters have specialized sponsorship departments that work to find the right match between brands, for example matching the **situation comedy** *Friends*, where a group of attractive young Americans sit around drinking coffee and talking about themselves, with a coffee manufacturer.

Unlike advertising, which tends to be a more direct form of selling a particular product, sponsorship is, in effect, more subtle, relying on ideas around brand image and profile. By sponsoring a programme like *Friends*, a coffee manufacturer would not expect to tell people to drink their coffee because it tastes nice, but rather to get people to think that their brand is popular with attractive and funny people like the characters in the show. Thus, the value of the product becomes increasingly divorced from its actual use and function.

The rise of programme sponsorship as a means of revenue for broadcasters reflects the growing privatization of broadcasting in the UK after the 1990 Broadcasting Act. The notion that a programme is 'brought to you by ...' implicitly connects the production of television with commercial interests and undermines the idea that television programmes are brought to you by a team of dedicated professionals, or an independent television company acting in the public interest. Sponsorship of television events, like multi-channel broadcasting, works through making certain assumptions about the audience and the types of people who watch particular programmes; for example, Premier League football results sponsored by a razor manufacturer. There is a self-evidential market logic about these practices, but the breaking down of the **audience** into niche markets or lifestyle groups further reinforces the fragmentation of the **public sphere**.

As well as direct sponsorship of television programmes, companies can also sponsor events that get televised, most notably sport fixtures and competitions. In the UK, sporting events are more likely to be sponsored by companies selling products that are restricted in how they advertise on television, for example, tobacco manufacturers. However, in the UK the New Labour government in the late 1990s banned any kind of advertising of tobacco products.

See also: broadcasting, the United Kingdom; broadcasting, the United States; deregulation, the United Kingdom; deregulation, the United States; sport and television

HANNAH DAVIES

sport and television

The significance of sport within the history of television should not be underestimated. After the Second World War, sport was used to attract viewers to the new medium by the BBC in the United Kingdom and the major networks in the United States. In the 1980s and 1990s, sport has been used by global media companies like News Corporation to introduce **cable and satellite** technologies and pay-TV. Major sports events can provide the most intense television drama, inviting deep emotional involvement from spectators who are often viewing within a collective, festive context. Sports stars are among the most visible of entertainment celebrities, particularly those involved in the global media spectacles surrounding numerous scandals. Sport has the potential to generate massive revenue for media companies. Important sports events can earn significant pay-TV revenue, deliver large, predictable and demographically desirable audiences to advertisers, and provide invaluable indirect **advertising** for sponsors. The relationship is symbiotic – many sports have been transformed by television and **sponsorship** revenue. Contemporary media culture is unimaginable without television sport, yet television sport has remained marginal to cultural studies (see Whannel 1992). Although the substantial literature on television sport from within sports sociology needs to be recognized (see Kinkema and Harris 1998), research in the field remains underdeveloped. This entry attempts to map the main conceptual approaches that can be used to evaluate global television sport – at the same time the difficulties of generalization need to be acknowledged: instances of the production and consumption of television sport need to be understood in their specific historical and local context.

The role of television in the commodification and globalization of sport

Television plays a major role in the process of the **commodification** of sport. Whereas there has been a degree of commercialization ever since spectators were charged an entrance fee at sports events, the impact of commercial television has marked a qualitative shift in the transformation of sport into a commodity. First, where there is increasing competition in television markets sports organizations are able to charge escalating fees for exclusive rights to broadcast events and competitions. Commercial broadcasters are able to recoup their costs through selling audiences to these events to advertisers, and through pay-TV. Second, television provides the opportunity for indirect advertising through sponsorship of stadia, clothing, teams and competitions, often enabling sponsors to side-step national restrictions on the advertising of particular products. The commodification of sport has a number of implications, as many sports have become dependent on revenue from television rights and sponsorship. Sports leagues and teams are increasingly profit driven, often leading to conflict of interests over revenue generated by television. The rules and presentation of several sports have been changed to accommodate television sport, and many new competitions have been invented specifically for the medium. Finally, commodification has transformed **fandom** in many sports. If previously supporting a team was an active participatory expression of local community, commodification has tended to transform sports spectatorship into an economic relationship between business and consumer. Overall, there has been a shift in the relative importance from the spectator attending an event to the television viewer (either at home or in communal spaces such as clubs and bars). Hence television's major contribution to the commodification of sport is that

the markets for sports are no longer restrained by the limits of geography.

Television's role in the commodification of sport is inextricably related with processes of **globalization**. Marshall **McLuhan** predicted that the development of electronic media would lead to the metaphorical abolition of time and space, that television would transform the world into a 'global village'. To the extent that this vision has been realized, the Olympic Games and the soccer World Cup are its main festive events, attracting massive global audiences.

Aspects of globalization can be identified throughout the history of organized sport. The International Olympic Committee (founded to administrate the modern games from 1896 onward) and FIFA (Fédération Internationale de Football Association, organizers of the soccer World Cup founded in 1904) are by definition international organizations, providing evidence for the argument that globalization is far from a recent phenomenon. However, television has brought about a qualitative shift in the globalization of sport, as it offers corporations the potential to develop markets geographically distant from the actual sports event. A process of global conglomeration is occurring, as corporations such as News Corporation and Disney launch and acquire sports channels, and even sports franchises or clubs, on a global basis. The increasing influence of mainly US-based media companies on national sport raises concerns about the dangers of cultural imperialism. However, if global sport is becoming 'Americanized', evidence can be found in changes in marketing, advertising, sponsorship, television presentation and business methods – attempts to export the big three American sports (gridiron, baseball, basketball) have met with an uneven degree of success.

Developments in television sport demonstrate that globalization should be understood as a complex phenomenon. Whereas simplistic accounts of globalization assert that contemporary economic, political and cultural processes spell the end for the nation, television sport demonstrates the resilience and adaptability of nation-states, nationalism and national identities (see Rowe 1996). National television presentation of the most global events such as the soccer World Cup and the

Olympics encourages identification with individuals and teams as representatives of the national community. Further, national governments can and do block moves towards global conglomeration and convergence of ownership in the public interest. If tendencies towards commodification and globalization have accelerated since the development of mass television, then it also needs to be recognized that there is often local resistance to these processes from administrators, participants and fans.

The characteristics of sports television

Major sports events such as the Olympics, the World Cup and the Superbowl are archetypal media events, representing an extraordinary interruption into the routine of everyday life (see **media event**). They share characteristics with live news coverage of major ceremonial events (funerals, treaty signings) and global events (such as Live Aid; see **live television**). Viewing is mainly a collective experience, which invites a high degree of emotional engagement. These major events attract huge audiences, which in turn generate massive revenue in the form of the sale of television rights. Live coverage of prestige national leagues and competitions also attracts significant audiences and for fans of these sports are equally as significant. By contrast, recorded sport also provides extensive cheap footage that can be packaged for the proliferating number of specialist sports services.

Live sports event coverage represents a distinctive television form, sharing characteristics with both factual and fictional television genres. Live sport is similar to live news in that it is ostensibly a journalistic record of an event. The reality of sports coverage is constructed through conventions that had to be invented at the beginning of broadcasting, but have evolved and are now generally accepted (see Whannel 1992). Obviously differences can be identified between these conventions according to which sport is covered, and which national broadcaster is responsible. However, it is possible to identify some common conventions across sports coverage as a whole, although these will need to be adapted in considering different sports. For stadium-based events, the coverage of the action is anchored by a main camera position

that situates television viewers in the ideal spectator position. This camera position is fixed and pans following the action, cutting to medium-range shots at moments when the action is condensed into a small area. The cameras appear to give a transparent view of the action that corresponds closely to what a spectator would ideally be able to see at the venue. During breaks in the action close-ups are cut with slow-motion action replays and/or close-ups of the reactions of players or athletes, coaches and fans, inviting identification by the viewer. New presentational techniques have been introduced: computer-generated graphics, animation, shots from miniature cameras on the field of play, **virtual reality** reconstructions, aerial shots, etc.

Whannel (1992) proposes that the historical development of the conventions of television sport is characterized by a tension between the 'journalistic' values of realism (the desire to give as transparent a view of the sports event as possible) and entertainment values (the desire to entertain through encouraging identification through close-ups of participants' expressions, etc.). Realist values have tended to predominate in the sports presentation of a public service broadcaster like the BBC (see **public service broadcasting**), entertainment values in that of commercial broadcasters such as the US and Australian networks. However, as the political climate since the 1980s has ensured that even European public service broadcasters need to compete for ratings, entertainment values increasingly predominate.

A crucial component of television sports presentation is commentary. Television commentators adapted the conventions of radio broadcasting, and the typical combination of commentator and expert was developed early on. Although there is scope for some preparation, sport commentary represents a space for unscripted talk that has few parallels in the rest of television. In the case of live transmission of the World Cup for example, the host nation's broadcaster will be responsible for visuals and natural sound while domestic broadcasters will supply their own commentary. In offering an interpretation of events for viewers, television commentary provides important material for the analysis of the political implications of television sport. To take two different examples, the improvised nature of commentary can lead to both unthinking and conscious national and racist stereotyping, whereas the accepted conventions of sports commentary (pitch and tone of voice, use of ex-players as experts) reinforces male dominance in these occupations. Paralleling television presentation, entertainment values are becoming increasingly predominant in commentary, with some commentators and experts becoming stars in their own right.

Television sport is ostensibly a transparent record of an event constructed through commonly-held visual and aural conventions, although increasingly characterized by entertainment values. Television sport shares characteristics with television drama, particularly **soap opera**, in encouraging viewers to identify with individuals and teams through the development of narratives (although neither broadcasters, participants nor viewers can predict how the narrative will be resolved, only that it will be resolved – at least temporarily). To understand the function of identification and **narrative** in a particular sport event it is necessary to look at how characters and stories are constructed intertextually across the proliferation of related media representations – not just specialist sports television (magazine programmes, promos, advertisements, phone-ins, panel discussions), but also material on non-sports television in the form of serious and 'tabloid' documentaries on sports issues, comedy sports quizzes, sports reports on regular news, sports television dramas, movies, etc. Broadcasters seek to build audiences for sports events by promoting them as a resolution of conflict between individuals and teams.

However, just because the realist and entertainment conventions of television sport encourage viewers to identify with individual stars or teams, or the opinions of commentators and experts, does not mean that they do. Indeed, resistance to some aspects of television presentation is often seen as an essential part of sports fandom (for example, in the case of British soccer). As with any type of television, analysis needs to consider the ways in which viewers use sports television and the significance they derive from it. Research on this area is thin, and tends to focus on social issues such as the effects of television sport on encouraging violence within family relations, reflecting social science concerns. By contrast, whereas fandom has been a central part of cultural studies approaches to television in the 1980s and 1990s, sports fans have largely been absent from this work. It is possible to speculate that the absence of sports fandom within cultural studies is related to generally-held perceptions of the sport audience as predominantly white, heterosexual, male and conservative in social outlook, whereas cultural studies has tended to celebrate aspects of fandom which demonstrate resistance by dominated groups to official culture (see **Fiske, John**), or are central to the construction of minority social identities. However, whereas there is still plenty of evidence to support the stereotypical view of sports spectators, broadcasters are realizing that the potential audiences for television sport are more heterogeneous. Cultural studies needs to address the increasing complexity of television sports fandom.

The politics of television sport: gender, race and nation

Televised coverage of sport plays a major role in the construction of identities, particularly around **gender**, **race** and nation. Research in sports sociology has demonstrated that televised sport reproduces patriarchal and racist ideologies through underrepresentation and stereotyping (see Kinkema and Harris 1998). However, cultural studies approaches to the analysis of the many sports media scandals in the 1990s have argued that although the dominant messages reproduced through television sport remain resolutely conservative, the significance and complexities of such spectacles should not be reduced to the extent to which they reproduce stereotypes (see **stereotype**). Drawing on theories of identity construction which see cultural identities as complex, contingent and potentially contradictory (see **Hall, Stuart; identity**), a number of studies have argued that media sport represents a site for the contestation of identities (Baughman 1995; Boyd 1997).

Television sport marginalizes women athletes and women's sports in a way that reinforces the institutional marginalization of women in sport. First, the quantity of media coverage of men's sport substantially exceeds that of women's sport. Second, the limited number of representations that there are tend to stereotype sportswomen through sexualization and trivialization. Female athletes whose physical appearance corresponds to stereotypical definitions of femininity, such as Katarina Witt and Florence Griffith Joyner in the late 1980s, attract more coverage. Sportswomen's personal and familial relationships are covered to a greater extent than that of sportsmen. Further, representations of gender in television sport are asymmetric. The positive values and meanings that have come to be attached to sport, those of power, stamina, competitiveness and aggression, coincide with stereotypical meanings around masculinity. Those women's sports that receive more coverage are the ones that are seen as more appropriate to conventional definitions of femininity (tennis, figure skating). This asymmetry, which centralizes men's sport as the norm, reinforces the inequalities between men's and women's sport, and leads to a vicious circle in which less visibility for women's sport is related to lower participation and less resources due to lower revenue from television rights and sponsorship (see Kane and Greendorfer 1994; Duncan and Messner 1998).

However, there is more to the representation of gender in sports television than just the extent of under-representation and stereotyping. The contributors to Baughman (1995) analyse the proliferation of media representations around figure skater Tonya Harding's suspected involvement in a physical attack on her rival Nancy Kerrigan leading up to the 1994 Winter Olympics. They argue that this media spectacle foregrounded a range of inter-related social issues around class definitions of femininity, female sexuality, parental emotional and spousal abuse, within the context of the gendered significance of women's ice skating.

A number of studies within sports sociology have shown that the same themes of under-representation and stereotyping also characterize television coverage of black athletes (see Davis and Harris 1998). While the achievements of black stars can be represented in very positive ways, at the same time conventional stereotypes are reinforced. A common stereotype across many sports is that black athletes' success can be attributed to natural ability rather than training, tactics or hard work. This stereotype reinforces a situation in which black athletes may be well represented in certain sports,

but marginal in the fields of sports ownership, management and coaching.

An approach to the analysis of representations of race which focuses only on the amount of coverage and the extent of stereotyping runs the risk of missing the complex and often contradictory meanings in television sport. For example, Boyd (1997) argues that television sport provides space for images of black empowerment and resistance. The media personas of sportsmen such as the basketball player Charles Barkley represent an explicit rejection of white definitions of black identities. At the same time it is based on a specific male, working-class definition of black identity which can also be misogynistic. Further, the economic basis of discrimination within sport is left unchallenged, and indeed this type of 'bad-boy' image is highly marketable within commodity culture.

The media play a major role in the construction of national self-identities and the stereotyping of other nations. Through festive media events such as the soccer World Cup, the Olympics or the Superbowl, sport provides perhaps the best example of how television can construct a sense of national identity through linking household collective viewing rituals with that of the larger 'imagined community' of the nation. Television sport also contributes to the definition of other national identities through stereotyping in commentary, advertising, expert panel discussions, etc. This stereotyping occurs not so much through explicit references to national dress, food and culture, but more implicitly through the attribution of typical national styles of play and temperamental characteristics to individuals and teams.

The meanings of national identities in media sport should not be seen as fixed and unproblematic, but as continually contested, particularly in the current phase of globalization. As broadcasters and governments alike aggressively promote the importance of national sporting success, television sport tends to reinforce differences through representing a sense of national self-identity. However, these representations are often highly gendered and ethnocentric, reflecting tensions between traditional and modern, exclusive and inclusive visions of the nation.

References

Baughman, C. (ed.) (1995) *Women on Ice: Feminist Essays on the Tonya Harding/Nancy Kerrigan Spectacle*, New York: Routledge.

Boyd. T. (1997) 'The Day the Niggaz Took Over: Basketball, Commodity Culture and Black Masculinity', in A. Baker and T. Boyd (eds) *Out of Bounds: Sports, Media and the Politics of Identity*, Bloomington: Indiana University Press.

Davis, L. R. and Harris, O. (1998) 'Race and Ethnicity in US Sports Media', in L. Wenner (ed.) *MediaSport*, New York: Routledge.

Duncan, M. C. and Messner, M. A. (1998) 'The Media Image of Sport and Gender', in L. Wenner (ed.) *MediaSport*, New York: Routledge.

Kane, M. J. and Greendorfer, S. L. (1994) 'The Media's Role in Accommodating and Resisting Stereotyped Images of Women in Sport', in P. Creedon (ed.) *Women, Media and Sport*, Thousand Oaks: Sage.

Kinkema, K. and Harris, J. (1998) 'MediaSport Studies: Key Research and Emerging Issues', in L. Wenner (ed.) *MediaSport*, New York: Routledge.

Rowe, D. (1996) 'The Global Love-match: Sport and Television', *Media, Culture and Society*, vol. 18: 565–82.

Whannel, G. (1992) *Fields in Vision*, London: Routledge.

Further reading

Brookes, R. (2001) *Representing Sport*, London: Arnold.

Rowe, D. (1999) *Sport, Culture and the Media*, London: Open University Press.

Wenner, L. (ed.) (1998) *MediaSport*, New York: Routledge. (This book includes chapters on most of the issues introduced here by the key authors in the field.)

ROD BROOKES

star system

'Star system' is the term for the marketing strategy that uses the creation, **commodification**, promotion and publication of performers, or more properly their representations and images, to sell films (see **image; representation**). In classical Hollywood, a star was a performer with a high 'marquee value', who was able to attract audiences to a film. David **Bordwell** has defined a star as 'a monopoly on a personality', while Richard **Dyer** posits that the star is a 'structured polysemy' (see **polysemic**), or a bearer of many different intertextual meanings (see **intertextuality**), that makes him or her able to signify many things to many audience members (and thereby achieve a marketable marquee value). Though the star system of the American film industry had obviously been 'borrowed' from other performance industries, only film stardom allowed for the simultaneous mass distribution of star images around the world.

Among the most important studies of the American star system is Richard deCordova's (1985) 'The Emergence of the Star System in America', in which he challenges conventional accounts of its formation. Until deCordova's work, many scholars had assumed that stars were forced on the nascent film industry during the first decade of the twentieth century by audiences who demanded to know the names of the personalities whose performances enthralled them. According to the legendary accounts, producers – especially those associated with the 'Trust', the monopolistic trade association formed by Thomas Edison – wanted to limit the power of performers both to control their images and to bargain for the higher wages associated with demonstrable popularity. Producers refused to release their performers' names to the public until compelled to do so around 1910 by a few renegade producers, the 'Independents', who were seeking to gain their own market advantage through the use of stars as commodities.

DeCordova demonstrates, as does Janet Staiger (1983), that producers released the names of stars well before 1910, and that 'Trust' producers did so as frequently as the 'Independents'. Well-known theatrical stars were used to help legitimize film acting and to lure middle-class audiences to longer narrative films. Because stars were reliable commodities who could be used not only to draw audiences but to distinguish film products from one another – through film performances and through the circulation of publicity and other forms of discourse about their off-screen lives – they functioned to anchor and standardize the industry during the teens. As narrative film language 'evolved' to include close-ups and character-driven narratives, the star became a significant locus for audience fascination with Hollywood and other national cinemas.

Not every national cinema uses a star system. The cinema of the Soviet Union relied more on *typage*, or the casting of representative 'types' from different social classes, different regions, etc., rather than professional actors with individual character-istics. Nevertheless, audiences often identify, and patronize, films according to who is in them. There are many well-known films 'by Alfred Hitchcock', yet the most popular Hitchcock films remain those starring Cary Grant, James Stewart, Grace Kelly and other well-known stars.

The mechanisms by which stars appeal to audiences are only now receiving serious scholarly attention. Much of our identification with stars draws on the complex interplay of **unconscious** psychic mechanisms linking **desire**, **sexuality**, identification and consumption. Among the ques-tions that continue to interest scholars are what stars have meant to specific audiences in different times and places, particularly in relation to identity politics like **class** and **gender**; how stars from one field (e.g., theatre, the music industry) function when their 'intertext' changes to film; and the intersections of stars, genres, **performance the-ory**, **acting** and celebrity.

See also: audience; classical Hollywood cinema and new Hollywood cinema; fandom; feminist theory

References

Bordwell, D., Staiger, J. and Thompson, K.(1985) *The Classical Hollywood Cinema: Film Style and Mode of Production to 1960*, New York: Columbia University Press.

deCordova, R. (1991) 'The Emergence of the Star System in America' (first published 1985), in C. Gledhill (ed.) *Stardom: Industry of Desire*, New York: Routledge.

Dyer, R. (1998) *Stars* (first published 1979), London: BFI Publishing.

Staiger, J. (1991) 'Seeing Stars' (first published 1983), in C. Gledhill (ed.) *Stardom: Industry of Desire*, New York: Routledge.

Further reading

DeCordova, R. (1990) *Picture Personalities: The Emergence of the Star System in America*, Urbana: University of Illinois Press.

Dyer, R. (1986) *Heavenly Bodies: Film Stars and Society*, New York: St. Martins.

Stacey, J. (1994) *Star Gazing: Hollywood Cinema and Female Spectatorship*, New York: Routledge.

ADRIENNE L. McLEAN

stereotype

The term 'stereotype' is widely used in popular culture. It represents one of the most common ways in which to discuss and make sense of films and television programmes. It is a word which is now commonly employed in journalism and everyday **discourse**, where it is used as a means of discussing representation of particular groups. In popular discourse, it is often used in imprecise ways. This means that its use must be carefully considered in academic writing: it is too easy to use the word in its everyday senses (which, as will be suggested below, are varied and are often contra-dicted by academic thinking). As a result of this function in different discursive terrains, the term 'stereotype', as it is currently employed, is a maddeningly imprecise one.

In everyday discourse, a 'stereotype' is an undesirable representation of a particular group of people. It is worth noting first that there are at least two quite distinct implications in the use of the term 'stereotype' as it is used both in everyday discourse and in cultural theory.

1 It implies a tradition of representation. If a number of films or television programmes represent a group of people in a similar way over a period time, this might be called a 'stereotype'.

2 At the same time, there is a sense that

'stereotype' is a 'negative image' – that is, anything which shows unattractive characteristics might be called a 'stereotype'.

To these two, quite definite, senses, might be added a third, aesthetic judgement – the idea that if a representation is a stereotype then it is 'unrealistic', and vice versa. This sense might be seen in the everyday opposition of 'stereotype' with 'rounded character', or 'three-dimensional character'.

It is the confusion of these various meanings in the everyday use of the term which so often complicates things. The relative merits and problems of these various meanings are explored below.

Looking at the way in which the term is used in film theory, it is instructive to note that concerns about stereotyping emerge with various forms of **identity** politics: in particular, feminism, gay and lesbian politics, and black politics in the United States. This is unsurprising. One of the characteristics of a 'stereotype' is that it represents not a particular individual but a group. It makes a claim to be an adequate representation not of a particular person but of certain aspects that all members of a group have in common. Sociological theory suggests that people tend to employ visual and aural information in order to make sense of individuals – to place them within groups, according to the connections which are established in culture between particular groups and particular characteristics. We place people into types – groups – before we gather enough information about them to understand them as individuals. It is thus only when groups begin to gain a self-identity, usually political – as gay and lesbian, women, black – that concerns about how that group is represented can be addressed, rather than simply representations of particular individuals challenged.

Each of these movements – lesbian, gay, black, feminist – produced in the 1970s writing which examined the representation of those particular groups in films, and which began to catalogue the 'stereotypes' of those groups. In 1973, Donald Bogle published the first edition of *Toms, Coons, Mulattoes, Mammies and Bucks*. In his influential book, Bogle provided a history of the black characters in American film, pointing out that a very small number of roles were continually replayed. As the

book describes these categories: 'Toms: they served their masters well. Coons: The funny men who assured Whitey all Blacks were harmless and stupid....Mammies: Sexless Earth mothers who devoted their lives to their White charges ...', and so on.

Similarly, Parker Tyler's *Screening the Sexes: Homosexuality in the Movies* ([1972] 1993) lists the recurring roles which have been accorded to homosexuals, including 'drag queens...Hustlers, sadist killers, gay-lifers...blackmail artists...vampires, Male Dorian Grays, female Dorian Grays, courtly cupids', and so on (Tyler 1993: xv–xvi).

The work of such authors as Bogle and Tyler was very important, as it drew attention to the fact that certain groups of people were being represented in particular, limited ways. However, this approach to representational theory is also extremely limited – precisely because it confuses various different meanings together in the word 'stereotype'. When the term 'stereotype' is applied to a particular representation, it does not simply call attention to the way that representation fits into a dominant trends of characters: it also suggests that the representation is both *negative* and *unrealistic*. These are quite different things from simply pointing to a dominant tradition of representation.

In feminist film theory, for example, in the 1970s, there was a suggestion that stereotypes of women should be represented by 'positive images'. This term suggested that traditional representations of women as intuitive, emotional, physically weaker than men, homemakers and so on, were not only predominant but also *bad*: positive images, by contrast, would 'presen[t] girls and women, boys and men with non-stereotyped behaviour and attitudes: independent, intelligent women; adventurous, resourceful girls....Women flying planes, etc.' (Artel and Wengraf [1978] 1990: 9).

Similarly, gay and lesbian politics took up the cry that 'stereotypes' of effeminate men and masculine women should be replaced by 'positive images' of masculine, materially successful men, and attractive, feminine women – and the term is still heard in much of the commentary of organizations such as the American organization Gay and Lesbian Alliance Against Defamation (GLAAD) which, for example, issued a press release condemning the 1997 film *The Birdcage* (Mike Nichols) for still showing too 'stereotyped' a representation of gay men – because its characters were portrayed as effeminate.

The problem with these meanings of 'stereotype' – as 'negative image' and 'unrealistic' – is that it is not possible to agree on what might be 'negative' about an image. So, for example, in the instance of feminist film theory, it is the case that many women may want to continue as homemakers – the representation of a woman in this role is not, *in itself*, bad; it is more the case that such representations have tended to predominate to the exclusion of other possible images. Similarly, many gay men are, in fact, effeminate – but this is, for GLAAD, a 'stereotype'.

This problem arises because some critics – and again, the confusion between academic and every-day uses of the word can be seen – seem to strive for the idea that it would be possible to produce a single representation which would adequately represent the whole of a community – an 'accurate' representation of a woman, an 'accurate' representation of a gay man, an 'accurate' representation of a black woman. The very fact that these categories could overlap (is the 'accurate' representation of a woman black or white?) makes clear that this desire is an impossible one.

The use of 'stereotype' to mean 'negative' or 'inaccurate' then, is not one which can be supported in film theory – for who decides what is 'positive' and what is 'negative' for a particular group? However, the use of the term which draws attention to histories of representation – in order to argue for a greater *variety* of representation – is much more easily sustained. But, even here, care must be exercised in its use. In Bogle's work, there is a sense that the roles that were played by black actors were limited to an incredible degree – it was only as comic relief, maidservants or tragic cross-overs that these actors were allowed to perform in films. We must be aware that this approach to taxonomy might not so well serve contemporary representations. Which is to say that it is possible to continue to invoke the term 'stereotype' as a general insult, where the link between the particular representation, and the tradition to which we link it, may be one which *we ourselves* (as critics) manufacture. For example, bell **hooks** has criti-

cized the character of Aunty Entity, played by Tina Turner, in *Mad Max Beyond Thunderdome* (George Miller and George Oglivie, 1985), by asserting that the character 'evokes two racist/sexist stereotypes, that of the black "mammy" turned power hungry and the sexual savage' (hooks 1992: 68). Yet, for Bogle, the category of the mammy was defined as both 'sexless' and as 'devoted to their White charges' – in short, with hooks redefinition, there is nothing left of Bogle's original definition of the category. This is an example of the way in which an overenthusiastic search for 'stereotypes' can find them in any representation. There is always some way in which it is possible to link a representation to some perceived 'stereotype'. This tendency is exacerbated by the tendency of some critics (again, hooks is a good example) to invent new categories of stereotypes as they write, thus losing the idea that the term refers to a tradition of representation.

In attempting to describe characters in films and television programmes, we must be as attentive to *difference* as we are to sameness. It is too easy to insist that all representations of black characters, or of gay characters, are the same; but in so doing, we can lose sight of the differences between them. For example, both John Inman in the British television sit-com *Are You Being Served* and Harvey Fierstein in the film *Torch Song Trilogy* (Paul Bogart, 1988) play effeminate gay men; but whereas Inman's character is asexual, apolitical and a member of a group, Fierstein's is intensely sexual, politicized and the hero of the narrative.

The concept of the 'stereotype' is useful for drawing attention to traditions of representation of particular identity groups. However, we must also attend to the specificity of representations. If there are differences to what has gone before, we must not be too hasty to insist that nothing has changed, and that the 'stereotype' continues unaltered.

References

Artel, L. and Wengraf, S. (1990) 'Positive Images: Screening Women's Films' (first published 1978), in P. Erens (ed.) *Issues in Feminist Film Criticism*, Bloomington and Indianapolis: Indiana University Press, pp. 9–12.

Bogle, D. (1974) *Toms, Coons, Mulattoes, Mammies and Bucks: An Interpretive History of Blacks in American*

Films (first published 1973), New York: Bantam Books.

hooks, b. (1992) *Black Looks: Race and Representation*, Boston, MA: South End Press.

Tyler, P. (1993) *Screening the Sexes: Homosexuality in the Movies* (first published 1972), New York: Da Capo Press.

ALAN McKEE

story

'Story' is a term adapted by Christian **Metz** and others from **enunciation** theory. It is used in various contexts – some drawn from **psycho-analysis**, others from narratology – to character-ize the means by which classical film narratives signify themselves as being 'told from nowhere, told by nobody, but received by someone'. According to Metz, the classical film story (*histoire*; see **history/ histoire**) is actually a form of **discourse** (*discours*) that is produced by concealing or effacing the marks of enunciation through the use of the continuity system of 'invisible' editing and an impersonal narrative voice. This seems to make the spectator, through the psychic processes of **voyeurism**, the 'producer of the fiction'. A radical cinema might foreground the marks of its enun-ciation and reveal the processes by which dominant cinema seeks to deny its ideological and rhetorical purposes. Others have pointed out that dominant cinema frequently presents itself as discourse as well, implying that the ideological distinction is questionable.

See also: cinematic apparatus; gaze, the; mode of address

ADRIENNE L. McLEAN

structuralism and post-structuralism

Structuralism is a method of grasping culture as a set of rules akin to language. It points to the relational aspects of culture: all cultural representa-tions gain meaning and value in relation to each other, not by themselves. Rules (structures) govern the allocation of value within this system. With this, structuralist thought breaks with earlier, essentialist views which see cultural representation as reflec-tions of reality. 'Reality' is no longer an issue for structuralism: all our knowledge of the world is already embedded in the structures that enable us to understand our lives. But whereas structuralist thinkers conceive of basic structure as static and fixed, post-structuralism goes one step further. For thinkers such as Jacques **Derrida**, not only is the world outside culture unknowable, but also the rules and systems of knowledge exceed the analyst's grasp. Culture is seen as something that is constantly rewriting itself, in flux, malleable and unstable. Film and television studies have been widely influenced by these thought systems.

This entry will delineate the structuralist heri-tage of Claude **Lévi-Strauss** and Vladimir **Propp**, and show the application of their models to film and television. Post-structuralist thinkers such as Roland **Barthes**, Derrida and Michel **Foucault** and their impact on the field will be assessed in the second part of the entry.

The development of structuralism can be traced back to the French linguist Ferdinand de **Saus-sure**. His attempt to find a structure in language has been credited with the inception of **semiotics** – the study of the sign. Three issues emerge from his system. The relationship between a word and its referent (signifier/signified) is arbitrary. Each utterance (**parole**) becomes meaningful against the backdrop of the language system (*langue*; see **language/langue**). A language system can only be understood in its present configuration. Any element of this language is meaningless outside its own, historic structure: it gains meaning in its difference to other elements. Within film theory, Saussure's semiotics has directly influenced a semiotics of the cinema via Christian **Metz**. (This important aspect of structuralist film studies is discussed in the semiotics entry.)

Saussure's work influenced many other theorists to put forward systematic theories about the structural foundations of other aspects of culture. An emphasis on constellations of meaning meant that social scientists had to start to think about any aspect of culture as gaining meaning only through its construction and maintenance in language. Historic facts were no longer 'facts', but points of reference within the construction of culture.

One important theorist who acknowledges the Saussurean influence is the anthropologist Claude Lévi-Strauss. He developed his study *Mythologiques* after research into the myths of North and South American tribal cultures. He tried to find a common meaningful structure underlying these 'inexplicable' myths, and to relate this structure to the seemingly different narratives of western Europe. Like Saussure with language, Lévi-Strauss was interested in the binding structure of all these myths as an expression of the state of that culture, rather than in each single myth and its intrinsic value. In opposition to the many developmental theories of anthropology which chart the course of evolution from 'primitive' to capitalist 'man', Lévi-Strauss was interested in a universalist approach based on a 'mind structure' which is shared by all societies.

What he found in these cultural narratives was a language structure, with each separate myth a specific utterance (*parole*) of the underlying 'deep structure' (*langue*). This deep structure of myth is dynamic, and not expressible as one single, stable content. These underlying myths relate to contradictions in human experience, such as the tension between individual and society, or benevolent God and cruel Nature. New forms of the myths are constantly generated, for:

> The purpose of the myth is to provide a logical model capable of overcoming a contradiction (an impossible achievement if, as it happens, the contradiction is real), a theoretically infinite number of (versions) will be generated, each slightly different from the others.
>
> (Lévi-Strauss 1963: 229)

Myth is thus dynamic, driven to creativity because of the unsolvable tension that it attempts to rewrite. The contradictions of the cultural experience are repressed from the surface of society, but come back in their stories. The anthropologist (or textual critic) has to find the contradictory pairings, the binaries, which motivate the specific narrative, and which are expressive of, and specific to, the originating culture of the text.

Lévi-Strauss' system was criticized in anthropology circles. Apart from finding empirical faults with his database, scholars questioned whether this **binary** structure of structuralism is not an ethnocentric, western concept which might not be appropriate for the 'mind schemes' of other peoples.

Lévi-Strauss' thesis about the relationship between texts and culture has had far-reaching influences on cultural scholars. His complex notion of myth points to the inconsistencies and fractures of culture, which generate constant textual production. But the method also uncovered many problems: how far can the production of mass media texts within an industrial framework be likened to the production of oral myth? What is the relationship between individual expression in art texts and more general cultural concerns?

Film studies reflected Lévi-Straussian methods of analysis from the early 1970s onwards. Scholars like Peter **Wollen** initially elided the questions posed above when he used Lévi-Strauss' concerns with cultural binaries to investigate the meanings generated unconsciously in the œuvre of individual filmmakers. This auteur structuralism initiated debates about the appropriate conceptualization of the artist in film (see **authorship**).

Soon, though, the tenets of structuralism were adopted in **genre** studies. Writers saw genres with their endless recreation of the similar as close to myths, and Will Wright makes the single most extended use of Lévi-Strauss in film theory in a book-length study of the Western (see **Western, the**), *Sixguns and Society* (1975). Wright uses the transformations of binaries to explain the changes that occurred in the Western over its history. But instead of seeking deep structures lodged within the universal human mind, Wright attempts to account for the way that Westerns as myths communicated a 'conceptual order' to American society and allowed it to make sense of its social origins. The history of the Western film becomes a symbolical mapping of changing American social beliefs.

Just as auteur structuralism was haunted by calls for a satisfactory theorization of the role of individual artistic choice, genre structuralism was criticized for its inability to account for capitalist marketing practices in the creation of a film's success. How far does a film's success depend on its stars or publicity machine, and how far on its mythic power derived from its internal structures?

The main legacy of Lévi-Straussian analysis in film and television studies thus moved away from 'grand explanation' of the entire film and television industry as a mythical system, but important elements of his original formulations were retained in the study of narrative and representation. Of particular interest for film and television was the articulation of contradictory binaries in the figure of the mythical hero. Lévi-Strauss has shown how the hero functions as a repository of excess meaning: he or she carries meanings of both binaries. The hero functions as the arbiter, showing how life can go on even if the contradiction of the binary is unsolvable. In Westerns, the hero articulates the problematic coming together of nature and culture, wilderness and civilization or male and female. John **Fiske** (1987) uses mediated binaries as a starting point for an analysis of the television series *Miami Vice*. The heroes, Crockett and Tubbs, move between the worlds of the vice squad and drug dealers. They embody values of both sides – which often is a source of narrative conflict, when the two are overstepping the boundaries of straight police procedure. They enact temporal solutions to the problems posed by the clashing of the two social worlds, but these solutions never hold for longer than the time-span between one episode and the next. Fiske's analysis of a constant rewriting of conflict also acts as an explanation for the pleasures of the **serial** format in television or the genre function in film.

Other structuralists such as Tzvetan **Todorov** and Vladimir Propp have found entry into the methodological **canon** of film narrative analysis. Propp wrote his influential book *Morphology of the Folktale* forty years before Lévi-Strauss' work. After a detailed study of Russian folktales, he puts forward a tentative structure of narrative, based not on binaries but on narrative functions. He identifies positions such as the hero, villain and princess, but sees these as spheres of action rather than fixed identities. These character roles go through thirty-two narrative functions, grouped under the headings: preparation, complication, transference, struggle, return and recognition. Together, this scheme provides a narrative structure. Propp's work, like Lévi-Strauss', has been read as providing an understanding of narrative as a transformation of the conflict between order and disorder. Since all societies experience problems at the boundaries of order and disorder, individual

and group, so all narratives continue to work through a universal scheme to cover these problems.

Will Wright and Peter Wollen have applied Propp's scheme to film. Wollen analysed *North by North-West* (Alfred Hitchcock, 1959) and found that he could read its complexities satisfactorily by seeing the protagonist shifting between the positions of seeker and victim. The question is, though, whether this kind of approach to cinema can come to terms with audience identification and participation with filmic narratives. Jonathan Culler (1975) argued that although Propp's scheme appears so simple and obvious, each specific instance of narrative (as *parole*) could still engage audience suspense. It is only at the very end of a film experience that the deep structure of character and narrative functions can be identified.

These questions about audiences and pleasure move away from a universal structuring binary or conflict towards questions about the multiplicity of possible interactions of texts with other texts. This propelled thinkers such as Roland Barthes to move from a structuralist position to a post-structuralist one. This shift can be seen in his conception of the work of **myth**.

In *Mythologies* (first published in 1957) Barthes sees binaries not as universal and independent of history, but as ideologically located articulations. Myths are messages, they are used to structure social relations. Their power rests on the fact that they need not be deciphered or interpreted: their meaning is 'natural'. Two quotes from 'Change the Object Itself' show the shift occurring in Barthes' work, from an earlier (1950s) belief in the political power of myth analysis to a position which is deeply suspicious of any centre of meaning. The analysis of myth still yields results, but has not developed into an emancipatory methodology.

> Myth consists in turning culture into nature, or, at least, the social, the cultural, the ideological, and the historical into the 'natural'. What is nothing but a product of class division and its moral, cultural and aesthetic consequence is presented (stated) as being a 'matter of course'.
>
> (Barthes 1977: 164)

Denunciation, demystification has itself become discourse, stock of phrases, catechistic declaration; in the face of which, the science of the signifier can only shift its place and stop (provisionally) further on – no longer at the (analytic) dissociation of the sign but at its very hesitation: it is no longer the myths which need to be unmasked . . . it is the sign itself which must be shaken; the problem is not to reveal the (latent) meaning of an utterance, of a trait, of a narrative, but to fissure the very representation of meaning, is not to change or purify the symbol, but to challenge the symbolic itself.

(*Ibid*.: 166–7)

Myth analysis has become the new orthodoxy. With his desire to keep moving, to deny any fixity, Barthes aims at an understanding of meaning as constantly in flow. This view of meaning also relates for Barthes to the circulation of popular cultural texts: their meanings are never fixed, but constantly rewritten, added, changed, appropriated by their relation to other texts and reading practices. Intertextuality and the changing politics of media icons have propelled a wide range of studies, subsumed under the heading 'social text approach'. Work on the changing intertextual fields of *Star Trek*, Batman, James Bond or Dr Who has charted the modifications of meanings of textual fields (see **intertextuality**).

The central concern with the fluidity of meaning characterizes other important thinkers of post-structuralism: Derrida, Lacan and Foucault. Just as the subject is constantly denied access to meaning through the initial loss of self-identity in Lacanian **psychoanalysis**, the signifier always just refers to another signifier, the binary always to another binary. Structuralism dissolved the human subject by showing how subjectivity is created through discourse and structure. Post-structuralism shows how the death of the subject (see 'Death of the author' in **authorship**) as autonomous individuality is further undermined: even the structures that make up subject positions are sliding, and identity is always questionable.

Jacques Derrida is usually described as the central figure of post-structuralism. He adds a new, crucial term to Saussure's semiotics: *différance*, which means both to defer and to differ. For Saussure, meaning was always created in relational difference. Derrida shows that meaning is never

fully present – it is always deferred and different. Everything always refers to something else; this intertextual flow of meaning never stops. Traces of other meanings, referrals and intertextuality adhere to any utterance. The one-to-one structure of the Saussurian sign, where one signifier reliably (in convention) referred to one signified, is no longer given. Social interaction bears the traces of excess meanings, slippages and gaps.

Post-structuralist thought has gained entry into various fields of film and television studies. Continual displacement and lack of stable identification is the main theme governing Lacanian psychoanalytic film analysis. The search for the excesses, absences and gaps addressed by Derrida has had a less direct influence on film and television theory. Theorists such as Marie-Claire Ropars-Wuilleumier, Tom Conley and Gregory Ulmer focus in different ways on the complexity of meaning, and show the impossibility and undecidability of meaning in film. But the destabilization of meaning and identity has had far wider impact on media theory: historical film studies have rewritten orthodoxies by allowing a view of film texts as open, contradictory and shifting, exceeding any attempts to fix connotations and install ideology. New studies of Nazi German films have focused attention on the excess of meaning which swamp functional binaries associated with Nazi ideology. Linda Schulte-Sasse draws on Lacan and Slavoj Zizek to address popular Nazi cinema: its success lies in its organization of desire, instead of its creation of fixed images of identification. The desire for meaning is channelled into a looping chain of associations of community and pleasure, rather than towards the resolution of a specific binary (Aryan/Jew).

Other politics of cultural identity have equally been moved away from a stable, fixed identity which could serve as reference point for members of a group. All identity is negotiated and shifting. Alliances need constant re-inscription, but the inscription is never fully enough. This connects to Lévi-Strauss' notion of the dynamic myth, but goes beyond that concept: there is no one binary which needs to be written over by all members of a culture. Now, the concept of a shared culture (and shared binaries) is queried. Cultural products and events, such as the London Gay and Lesbian Film

Festival are now not just guarantors of connection, but also constructors of the very notion of shared identity. Theorists such as Judith **Butler** have pointed to the necessity to re-inscribe identity and gender in her concept of performativity (see **performative**). Any identity politics in a post-structuralist environment has to work as an uncertain, reiterated positioning, a politics of position.

The uncertainty of stability, fixed causes or explanations in post-structuralist projects of knowledge characterizes the work of Michel Foucault. He is a historian who stresses discontinuities, local knowledges and writes against 'total' history and its hierarchical, ordering effects. He charts a genealogy of power: power is seen as productive, creating subjectivities which are thoroughly written through by the operations of power. Thus, culture is not a system of signs, but a shifting and open constellation of sites of power, replete with resistances. In her thorough feminist investigation of structuralist approaches to cinema, *Alice Doesn't*, Teresa de **Lauretis** reads Nicholas Roeg's films for marks of these localized resistances, and shows the price that has to be paid by 'strangers' in order to posit an 'absolute negativity' to the dominant system.

Foucault's theories have been influential in writings about the **body** and visibility. He identified a 'panoptic regime', which is the controlling gaze that polices aberration, and which can be internalized to supervise correct behaviour without outer coercion. This can be applied to issues of media influence by analysing how images of 'ideal bodies' on television articulate with the shifting self-image of the watching subject.

Structuralism and post-structuralism have been major influences on the cultural landscape and on the conceptualizations of a wide range of disciplines. They have undermined belief in self-directed, autonomous subjects, and propose to replace any certainty of meaning with bewildering insights. The main challenge that faces post-structuralist thought is the necessity to provide avenues of transformation, to provide a politics of instability.

See also: modernism and post-modernism

References

Barthes, R. (1977) 'Change the Object Itself. Mythology Today' in R. Barthes, *Image Music Text*, London: Fontana Press.

Barthes, R. (1993) *Mythologies* (first published 1957), selected by and trans. Annette Lavers, London: Vintage.

Culler, J. (1975) *Structuralist Poetics*, London: Routledge.

de Lauretis, T. (1984) *Alice Doesn't. Feminism, Semiotics, Cinema*, Houndsmill: Macmillan.

Fiske, J. (1987) *Television Culture*, London: Routledge.

Lévi-Strauss, C. (1963) *Structural Anthropology* (first published 1958), New York: Basic Books.

Schulte-Sasse, L. (1996) *Entertaining the Third Reich. Illusions of Wholeness in Nazi Cinema*, Durham and London: Duke University Press.

Wright, W. (1975) *Sixguns and Society. A Structural Study of the Western*, Berkeley: University of California Press.

Further reading

Sarup, M. (1993) *Post-Structuralism and Postmodernism* (2nd edn), New York, London: Harvester Wheatsheaf. (This volume is a good introduction to the variety of post-structuralist thought.)

Stam, R., Burgoyne, R. and Flitterman-Lewis, S. (1992) *New Vocabularies in Film Semiotics. Structuralism, Post-Structuralism and Beyond*, London and New York: Routledge.

PETRA KUPPERS

studio systems

By 1908, some 10,000 nickelodeons and more than 100 film exchanges were operating in the United States, all supplied with films by manufacturers or studios. The tremendous public demand for film was met by emphasizing speed and quantity of production over 'quality' and stylistic innovation, and thus studios developed as film factories modelled on the assembly lines and management techniques of industry and mass-market manufacturing (see **Fordism**). The ease, lower cost and efficiency of the hierarchical 'studio **mode of**

production', as David **Bordwell**, Janet Staiger and Kristin Thompson (1985) call it, made it attractive to entrepreneurs responsible for the international expansion of multi-reel or large-scale narrative filmmaking in the teens. It became the dominant structure around which national film-making industries were organized on the European Continent, in Britain and in the United States from the 1920s through the 1950s.

Though the specifics of organization and structure vary among different countries, studio systems can be identified by their top-down financial control and heavy capitalization; their high degree of organization, with 'units' of production, comprised of directors, writers, de-signers, actors and actresses and other production personnel who are contracted to perform specia-lized tasks, supervised by producers, executives or some other type of manager; and their strongly marked standardization of product (e.g., 'classical Hollywood cinema' or 'Soviet cinema').

The oldest existing film studio may be Den-mark's Nordisk Films Kompagni, founded in 1906. But the most famous studio system is undoubtedly classical Hollywood itself, consolidated by the end of the 1920s (helped by the success of the transition to sound) into the 'big five' major studios (Para-mount, Metro-Goldwyn-Mayer, Warner Bros, Twentieth Century-Fox, RKO-Radio) and the 'little three' minors (United Artists, Universal, Columbia). These studios' collective designation as 'the majors' indicates their capital strength, their factory structure and routinization of the work of filmmaking, and their dependence on the contract-based **star system**. It also distinguishes them from their 'poverty row' or 'B-film' cohorts (e.g., Monogram Productions, Republic Pictures, and Grand National Films), as well as from the 'invisible' producers of race films and other forms of 'outsider' cinema in America.

The Hollywood majors controlled more than American film production through the 1930s and 1940s; their connections overseas, through 'branch offices' and theatre ownership, made them the most potent film business enterprises in the world. But US government anti-trust legislation after the Second World War officially decentralized Amer-ican film production, by forcing the studios to give up some of their monopoly control of the means of film production, distribution and exhibition. Com-bined with other factors such as post-war inflation, labour disputes, restrictions on the import of American films abroad and competition from television, the studios' divestiture of their theatre chains proved ruinous to the economic structure of the studio system. However, suburbanization and the concomitant decline of the audience base in the studios' most lucrative 'first-run' urban markets were already cutting into profits by 1952, when the divestiture was complete.

With the audience previously 'guaranteed' them by restrictive practices like block-booking gone (block-booking forced theatres to accept blocks of films in order to secure more desirable titles or star vehicles, and was made possible by the studios' control over their theatre chains), the factory-style production, which kept employees under long-term contract to make films on a continuous basis, no longer made financial sense. The studios them-selves remain powerful through their control of distribution and, increasingly, exhibition, with independent productions being used to fill the theatres now owned, along with the studios themselves, by **multinational** conglomerates and consortia.

Hollywood's dominance of international film production was never inevitable. World events helped its emergence: the two world wars deva-stated the infrastructures of European film produc-tion. But, for reasons primarily to do with efficiency and control, the studio systems of non-capitalist and non-western countries often closely resemble those of their capitalist counterparts.

The rest of this entry gives brief comparative accounts of studio systems other than Hollywood's. Because of space limitations, representative exam-ples only are discussed in order to suggest similarities and differences among the studio systems of countries of several different political ideologies.

France, Italy, Germany

Many of the major European studios were, from the beginning, multinational in their management and financing. The first major French studios were Gaumont Pictures, founded in 1895, and Pathé Frères, established in 1896. But, through their control of film stock and equipment patents (as well as their ruthless acquisitive urges), Pathé and Gaumont soon controlled production companies in Spain, Russia, Italy, Britain and America. By 1908 Pathé dominated exhibition and distribution across the European Continent, and was, as David Cook (1996) writes, marketing 'twice as many films in the United States as all the American production companies put together, and by 1909 the same situation existed in Great Britain'. Pathé Frères pioneered the film industries of Australia, Japan, India and Brazil, and Gaumont's British production studio and exhibition circuit, Gaumont-British, remained under French control until 1922, having a major impact on the development of the British film industry.

With the outbreak of the First World War, production by both companies fell, never to achieve pre-war levels and forcing the heavy reliance on American product, and the ultimate loss of control of their own market. The introduction of sound worked to cripple the industry further, as France owned no patents to sound equipment. Thus, French commercial production became somewhat 'artisanal', innovative and even experimental, as studios leased their facilities to independent filmmakers. These smaller-scale production methods would result in films and movements that made the cinema of France among the most critically acclaimed in the world during the 1930s. As was true of many European countries during the Second World War, occupying forces nationalized the film industry, but also established a French government-subsidized national film school (which remains in existence). As in the United States, from the 1950s through to the present day, independent production practices coexisted with, drew on the resources of, and were sometimes supported by, larger-scale studio systems.

Italy's film industry closely resembled that of France and America, being founded with the construction of the Cines studio in Rome in 1906, which produced mostly costume dramas and melodramas 'in the French vein'. The introduction of other Italian studios into the marketplace led to the proliferation in the mid-teens of historical epics, the multi-reeled 'super spectacles', in which producers vied with one another for supremacy and market share using enormous sets, huge numbers of extras, extravagant costumes and the latest special effects. Italy's apparent aesthetic dominance of world cinema was brought to an end by the economic and material devastation of the First World War. Ironically, Benito Mussolini was instrumental in reviving the Italian film industry in the 1920s through the formation of a state-run film studio (Cinecittà) and school in Rome. The state-subsidized industry, closely modelled on Hollywood, produced mainly melodramas, comedies and adaptations of literary works, all of which were well-crafted and popular with Italian audiences. Though movements such as Italian neo-realism, which had an enormous influence on filmmaking style around the world, arose from an impulse that was anti-studio and anti-conventional (neo-realist films used on-location shooting and non- or semi-professional actors, and tended to have a loose narrative structure), larger-scale studio production maintained its dominance through the 1960s. Today, studios like Cinecittà function much as they do in America, as resources and locations for the shooting, assembly and post-production work of 'packaged' films, television shows and international co-productions.

Germany, too, founded its own state-run studio, UFA (Universum Film Aktiengesellschaft), by government decree in 1917, which was run much like any Hollywood studio but with a higher degree of autocratic control. After the First World War, UFA became a private company – and, through financing by Paramount and Metro-Goldwyn-Mayer in 1925, a multinational corporation as well – but its internal structure remained much the same. German cinema was so completely studio-bound between the wars, in fact, that its style acquired the name 'studio constructivism'. Hitler co-opted the German studio system, with UFA at the top, to produce escapist as well as propaganda films during the war. He removed from power or exiled many of the Jewish stars, directors and technical personnel who had made German cinema so admired around the world – but the structure of the system remained largely the same. After the war, all German production facilities in the Soviet-controlled East Germany (including UFA) were nationalized, which provided capital, albeit on an extremely competitive basis, for new productions through state subsidies. In West Germany, recovery was controlled by US interests, which supported the reconstruction of distribution and exhibition venues over studios, thus preventing both the emergence of a centralized West German industry and competition with American films. Hollywood's dominance in German cinemas remains strong; even after German reunification the German film industry has come to depend more and more on state subsidies for filmmakers, international co-production financing and support from German television companies.

Though one can only cautiously attempt to generalize about similarities between the film industries of all of the countries of Europe from their beginnings to the present day, some similarities might be noted. The studio systems of Europe, whether privately owned or state-run, were organized on a model that closely resembled Hollywood, and, with the exception of state-run systems in Communist countries, most studios have now become locations for factory-style work rather than factories themselves, with independent productions or international co-productions forming the bulk of the work performed at the studio. Many functioning studios are now devoted to producing television and video rather than film. And, finally, the costs of maintaining a Hollywood-style studio are high, and few succeed without the benefits of monopolistic, coercive, or protectionist practices, and/or government subsidy.

Soviet Union

Before the Bolshevik Revolution in 1917, the cinema of Russia was also multinational, mainly European. The first Russian studios were founded in 1908 with imported equipment and film stock, and competition from American product was fierce. When Russia entered the First World War in 1914, the supply of foreign films was cut off and domestic production increased, split among escapist entertainment and propaganda documentaries meant to counter criticism of the tsarist regime. But whether the studios were large production houses or smaller firms, they resembled Hollywood studios in their organization of the means of production, distribution and exhibition. After the Revolution and Lenin's declaration that 'the cinema is for us

the most important of the arts', several central and regional film schools were founded to train filmmakers in the production of **agit-prop** and **documentary** films. Similar to Warner Bros or Paramount, the schools were organized into departments of directing, cinematography, acting, scriptwriting, film criticism and history (publicity as well), set design, and economics and organization (producing).

By 1924, the centralized Soviet film industry was again making large-scale narrative films (many financed, ironically, by the box-office receipts from American films imported by the Soviet government). Though **Eisenstein**, **Pudovkin** or Dovzhenko might have exercised a greater degree of control (at least until Stalin) over more aspects of their films through being involved in writing, directing and editing, the process by which these films were made resembled the model of the Hollywood system, following the training structure of the state film academies. Thus, Eisenstein used a shooting script and schedule, had costumes made in a costume department, and distributed other specialized tasks to personnel trained and employed to perform them. Once Stalin placed the Soviet film industry under more restrictive government control in 1930, and individual creativity was subsumed to the demands of the 'official style' of **Socialist Realism**, the Soviet system came even more closely to resemble a paranoid, impoverished and unproductive version of Hollywood. Despite various 'thaws' after Stalin's death in 1953, Socialist Realism remained officially in place until 1990. Smaller and more ethnically diverse regional companies have formed since the break-up of the Soviet Union, but their survival, despite the output of many award-winning and important films, has predictably been restrained by competition from American films, the small size of the domestic market and, in some cases, political unrest.

Asia

In *The Asian Film Industry* (1990), John Lent notes that, while it is 'utter nonsense' to refer to Asian cinema as a whole, there are also strong similarities among the industrial practices of Malaysia, Indonesia, India, Sri Lanka, Japan, China, Korea, Pakistan and other countries referred to by the

West as 'Asian'. Among the generalizations he makes about Asian cinema (besides the always-present threat of cultural co-optation by American films) are that Asia is and has been a prolific producer of movies, with India leading the world in the number of films produced per year. Another is that there tends to be a split between formulaic, commercial films manufactured for local audiences and the more pretentious or '**art cinema**' generated for international film festivals and distribution. In all cases, concentration of owner-ship of the means of film production has plagued Asian cinema. In Japan and the Philippines, for example, four or five large studios control not only the bulk of indigenous film production but also distribution and exhibition as well – and often have multinational owners and interests in 'non-film' industries, which are interlocked, Lent writes, with 'large business and political concerns'.

As this brief outline has suggested, one of the reasons for the international dominance of the studio system as a filmmaking practice is that, even in its America incarnations, it *is* an autocratic form. It has thus tended to flourish not only in capitalist economies, driven by the marketplace, but in fascist, socialist or Communist states as well. Taken together, the popular cinemas of the United States, Europe, the former Soviet Union, Asia and else-where all have evolved on the assembly-line and hierarchical model of Hollywood. If few studio systems today function generically as film factories, in which workers labour at their specialized tasks to make films continuously for a guaranteed market, narrative filmmaking as a practice continues to use the divisions of labour that marked studio systems around the world for more than thirty years.

See also: classical Hollywood cinema and new Hollywood cinema

References

Bordwell, D., Staiger J. and Thompson, K. (1985) *The Classical Hollywood Cinema: Film Style and Mode of Production to 1960*, New York: Columbia University Press.

Cook, D. (1996) *A History of Narrative Cinema* (3rd edn), New York: Norton. (This book provides a history of almost all national cinemas and their major production facilities, and contains a comprehensive bibliography.)

Lent, J. (ed.) (1990) *The Asian Film Industry*, Austin: University of Texas.

Further Reading

Guback, T. H. (1969) *The International Film Industry*, Bloomington: Indiana University Press.

ADRIENNE L. McLEAN

style

Any film or television **text** (or indeed any text, from anywhere) can be said to have some sort of style by virtue of its being the product of human labour. Since all films or television shows make use of techniques, devices and assumptions that govern the production of a wide range of similar texts, they all can be analysed and discussed in terms of the choice and organization of those elements. Film style, therefore, can be defined, in the words of David **Bordwell** and Kristin Thompson (1997), as the 'repeated and salient uses of film techniques characteristic of a single film or a group of films (for example, a filmmaker's work or a national move-ment)'. An individual filmmaker thus exhibits his or her own style (e.g., Jean Renoir, Maya Deren, Sergei **Eisenstein**), a group of similar filmmakers their own (e.g., French poetic realism, the Amer-ican **avant-garde**, Soviet-style montage), an industry yet another (e.g., classical Hollywood cinema, the European **art cinema**). Historically, however, style has been associated with **aes-thetics**, as a component of the *art* of film (which will be the focus of this entry) rather than its status as an industry or system of technology.

The fact that film is always a system of technology, and for much of its history has also been an industry, complicates this assumption. Nevertheless, the history of film style tends to read as a history of film artistry as it has been defined at various times and places. As such, as Bordwell's definitive work (1997) on film style shows, the 'grand narrative' of film style begins when cinema turned away from the recording of events towards the manipulation of their representation. When art historian Irwin Panofsky wrote 'Style and Medium in the Moving Pictures' (1934), he helped to grant film the status of 'the seventh art' by tracing how film had developed its specific aesthetic identity: 'It is the movies, and only the movies, that . . . organize material things and persons, not a neutral medium [like paint and canvas], into a composition that receives its style, and may even become fantastic or pretervoluntarily symbolic, not so much by an interpretation in the artist's mind as by the actual manipulation of physical objects and recording machinery. The medium of movies is physical reality as such.' While other theorists, such as Rudolf **Arnheim** and Hugo Münsterberg, had posited that film's special power lay in the recognition of how profoundly the film image differs from physical reality, the emphasis in virtually all writing about film as art lay in defining film's 'essential nature'. Until we agreed on what made film *film*, this aesthetic tradition went, we could not agree what made film art.

Linking film to other art forms, if only to define its distinguishing characteristics, set the terms for one sort of stylistic evaluation of film. As Hollywood cinema and its narrative form came to dominate world cinema, the aesthetics of the sound film and how film worked as a narrative language also became a nexus of evaluation. Arguments about the value of montage over **mise-en-scène** aesthetics (and vice versa) have consistently marked the grand narrative of the history of film style. But, as Bordwell shows, style can never be more, nor ever less, than a film's 'systematic and significant use of techniques of the medium. . . . Style is, minimally, the texture of the film's images and sounds, the result of choices made by the filmmaker(s) in particular historical circumstances.'

See also: authorship; classic realist text; classical Hollywood cinema and new Hollywood cinema

References

Bordwell, D. (1997) *On the History of Film Style*, Cambridge: Harvard University Press.
Bordwell, D. and Thompson, K. (1997) *Film Art: An Introduction* (5th edn), New York: McGraw-Hill.
Panofsky, E. (1934) 'Style and Medium in the Moving Pictures,' in L. Braudy and M. Cohen (eds) (1998) *Film Theory and Criticism* (5th edn), New York: Oxford University Press.

ADRIENNE L. McLEAN

subconscious

Sigmund **Freud** assumes three different states of awareness of mental processes: **unconscious** processes, which cannot be made conscious (e.g., first language acquisition), conscious processes, and preconscious processes which function as a 'screen' between the conscious and the unconscious and can be made conscious through **psychoanalysis** or introspection. Though Freud himself refutes the term, it is the latter processes which have in normal language usage been named 'subconscious'. The exploration of such 'screened signals' like dreams, phobias or traumata forms not only an important part of psychoanalysis, but is used as a marked system of signification in all art forms. The popularization of Freudian psychology in the 1940s resulted in Hollywood producing a cycle of films predicated on finding the key to a character's subconscious; for example, *Spellbound* (Alfred Hitchcock, 1945) and *The Snake Pit* (Anatole Litvak, 1948).

See also: Lacan, Jacques

EVA VIETH

subculture

Subculture, as defined in Dick Hebdige's (1979) influential study of that title, denotes a social group whose members are both marginalized from 'mainstream' society and share a commonality which binds them together. This shared identity may stem from a style of music, from fashions in dress and hair, from a sense of disempowerment within established social structures or, frequently, from a combination of these elements. This was the case, for instance, with the 'grunge' movement which originated in Seattle in the early 1990s. Based around bands like the late Kurt Cobain's Nirvana, grunge followers, most of them teenagers, adopted a thrift-store style and a disenchanted, 'slacker' mentality towards work and education.

The relationship between subcultures and mainstream society – including television and film representation of subcultural groups – has often proved ambivalent, progressing from outrage on the part of the establishment to a gradual acceptance, leading to the point where subcultures become incorporated, often in a tamer form, into mainstream representation.

While the process of imposing a framework on social groups and labelling certain types as 'deviant' or 'delinquent' is, as Michel **Foucault** has shown, not a twentieth-century phenomenon, the idea that these categorizations could come defiantly from 'below' – that is, from the subcultures themselves – is a more recent concept and can be traced back to the 'teen-age' culture of the 1950s. Changes in youth behaviour in the postwar years appalled and often baffled the adult worlds of psychology, education and policing. Parents were confronted with the fact that their children had developed an independent culture of their own, with an alien style of music, fashion and even vocabulary. Yet as James Gilbert (1986) reports in *A Cycle of Outrage*, mainstream culture gradually began to take its cue from these new styles. Clothing stores employed teenage researchers, while magazine articles provided lists of teen argot and rock and roll movies offered the new market a flattering reflection of its own rebellion. By the early 1960s, adolescents were seen not just as a powerful consumer group but as a key electoral target and potent social force.

The research of Dick Hebdige and his colleagues at the Birmingham Centre for Contemporary Cultural Studies (see **Hall, Stuart**) traced the evolution of subcultural groups in 1970s and 1980s Britain. Paul Willis investigated the lifestyles of schoolboys, bikers and hippies, while Hebdige offered an overview of mods, teds and Rastafarians, with a particular emphasis on punk rock. Angela McRobbie drew attention to the less visible and often overlooked subculture of teenage girls. Hebdige's case study of punk vividly illustrates that the process of incorporation and absorption described by Gilbert with relation to the teenager of the 1950s was still active in the late 1970s. He details the shift from news articles denouncing the freakish hairstyles and fashions of punk rockers to magazine features showcasing house-trained punks

with their proud mothers. This initially shocking subculture was effectively subdued, tamed and contained until it became a suitable subject for tourist postcards.

The ambivalent relationship between subculture and establishment can be traced through a variety of marginalized groups and movements to the present day. Comic-book, film and television **fandom**, which evolved during the late 1960s and 1970s, is in a constant process of debate and negotiation with the industry as fans argue for their own meanings through letters pages, conventions and electronic bulletin boards. As discussed by John **Fiske** in his work on resistant 'readings' of 1980s texts, and by Henry Jenkins with reference to **science fiction** audiences, producers have the institutional power to impose their own meanings but also rely on dedicated fan support for continued sales and viewing figures.

Most recently, the **Internet** subculture has been the subject of sensational news articles about cybersex and on-line porn and of films – *Hackers* (Ian Softley, 1995), *Killer Net* (Geoffrey Sax, 1998) – which depict users either as streetwise rebels or as victims of a dangerous addiction. Once again, the mainstream wavers uneasily between romanticization and moral panic, spinning out a love-hate relationship with subculture which has barely altered since the 1950s.

References

Gilbert, J. (1986) *A Cycle of Outrage*, New York: Oxford University Press.

Hebdige, D. (1979) *Subculture: The Meaning of Style*, London: Methuen.

Hutcheon, L. (1989) *The Politics of Postmodernism*, London: Routledge.

WILL BROOKER

subject and subjectivity

'Subject' and 'subjectivity' are fiercely contested terms in social and cultural theory. Competing theories of subjectivity, variously derived from humanism, Marxism, **psychoanalysis**, post-structuralism and feminism, have become important in media and cultural studies (see **feminist theory; structuralism and post-structuralism**). At the centre of these debates is the *humanist subject* with which other models take issue. The humanist tradition of social and political thought has been of major importance in the West since the Renaissance. Humanist ideas about subjectivity first developed in opposition to the medieval cosmology in which the human subject was defined by the Divine Order. Humanist models of the subject privilege the individual, **consciousness** and lived experience over theories which ground the human either in biology and natural science or in social structures. In humanist thought the subject and subjectivity are assumed to be unified and rational. The subject is governed by reason and free will, which give it agency. Key humanist theories within twentieth-century social thought include **phenomenology** and existentialism.

The subject of ideology

One of the most important challenges to humanist ideas of subjectivity has been Marxism. In **Marx**'s writings and the varied traditions of Marxist thought derived from them, the sovereignty of the humanist subject is challenged by theories of **class** and ideology (see **ideology and hegemony**). For Marxism, subjectivity is always class subjectivity. Marxism theorizes **history** as a series of modes of production (slave-owning, feudal, capitalist) governed by specific forms of class relations. The capitalist **mode of production** is founded on a fundamental class antagonism between capital and labour. The capitalist class owns the means of production: the capital to set up and run factories and to employ labour to produce both goods and surplus value. The proletariat has only its labour power; that is, its ability to work. Class is first and foremost an economic category, determined by whether or not an individual has access to control of the means of production. Yet class position is also a crucial determinant in the formation of subjectivity. In modern capitalist states, which do not rely on indentured or slave labour, the relations between capital and labour appears in the form of contracts between apparently free individual subjects – worker and employer. These relations of

production are secured by ideology which is embedded in social and cultural practices.

In Marxist theory, ideology shapes subjectivity. As Marx and Engels put it in their early formulation in the *German Ideology*: 'Life is not determined by consciousness, but consciousness by life' (1970: 47). The forms which ideology takes vary in different Marxist texts, ranging from ideology as false consciousness to the Althusserian notion of ideology as 'the imaginary relationship of individuals to their real conditions of existence' (Althusser 1971: 153). It is this latter formulation that has been most influential in media and cultural studies. The Althusserian theory of ideology and subjectivity is sketched in an essay entitled 'Ideology and Ideological State Apparatuses. Notes Towards an Investigation' (Althusser 1971). This essay, which falls into two main parts, is concerned with what Louis **Althusser** calls ideological state apparatuses and the role they play in the reproduction of capitalist relations of production via the constitution of subjectivity (see **ideological state apparatuses**). These apparatuses, which include, for example, education, religion, the political apparatus, trade unionism, **culture** and the media, play a central role in the reproduction of a willing work force and the other social strata that make up society. Each apparatus contributes to the reproduction of capitalist relations in its own specific way: 'The political apparatus by subjecting individuals to the political State ideology, the "indirect" (parliamentary) or "direct" (plebiscitary or fascist) "democratic" ideology. The communications apparatus by cramming every "citizen" with daily doses of nationalism, chauvinism, liberalism, moralism etc.' (Althusser 1971: 146). Unlike the police, the army and the courts – i.e., the repressive state apparatus – the ideological state apparatuses 'function massively and predominantly *by ideology*' (Althusser 1971: 138). Ideological state apparatuses operate by interpellating individuals as subjects within specific ideologies. These subjects internalize particular meanings and values according to which they then live.

In the second part of his essay, Althusser turns his attention to what he terms 'ideology in general', which is the precondition of both subjectivity and human sociality. At the centre of this theory is the category of the 'Subject' which 'is constitutive of all ideology in so far as all ideology has the function (which defines it) of "constituting" concrete individuals as subjects' (Althusser 1971: 160). Here Althusser draws on Jacques **Lacan**'s theory of the **mirror stage**, a process based on misrecognition (see below). 'Good' subjects, interpellated within specific ideologies, will work independently to reproduce capitalist social relations without recourse to the repressive state apparatuses.

The subject of language

A second site for the contestation of humanist models of language and subjectivity is linguistics. Here two theorists in particular have been central in the formation of alternative post-structuralist ideas of subjectivity: the Swiss linguist Ferdinand de **Saussure** who is seen as the founder of semiology (the study of signs) and the French linguist and **discourse** theorist Emile Benveniste. The work of Saussure does not directly address the question of subjectivity but has none the less had profound implications for post-structuralist theories of language and subjectivity. In a series of lectures, collected posthumously by his colleagues and students and published in 1916 as *Cours de linguistique générale* (*A Course in General Linguistics*, 1974), Saussure broke with reflective theories of language according to which words labelled meanings that already existed in the external world. Saussure suggested that language, far from being a set of labels for already given meanings, was a system of differences (see **difference**). Individual signs in the language system were composed of signs (see **sign**): signifiers (sound or written images) and signifieds (meanings). The link between signifiers and signifieds was an arbitrary conventional effect of language which had no external guarantee in the world of referents beyond language. In post-structuralist appropriations of this theory, it is read as having profound implications for how subjectivity is conceived. Since there is no longer fixed meaning in the world which the knowing subject perceives, the subject no longer controls meaning but is an effect of it.

Benveniste takes up the idea that language produces the subject. He starts from Descartes' famous premise '*cogito, ergo sum*' ('I think, therefore I am'), according to which the act of thinking points

to the existence of the subject as the source and guarantee of meaning. Benveniste challenges and complicates this model by insisting on the distinction between the subject of the **enunciation** and the subject of the enounced (a distinction that is also important in Lacanian psychoanalysis). According to Benveniste, the subject who says 'I think' should be held distinct from the subject whose existence is assumed in the act of thought. Thus the subject can no longer be seen as unified and the self-present source of knowledge and truth. It is the very structure of language that points to the implausibility of such models of subjectivity.

The subject of psychoanalysis

In the work of Sigmund **Freud**, the humanist subject is radically decentred and becomes but one dimension of subjectivity, equivalent to the ego, governed by a rational consciousness which is no longer assumed to be sovereign master in its own house. The ego, far from being unified and in control, is, for Freud, a product of repression and is constantly subject to the laws of the **unconscious**. It is, however, the rereading of Freud by the French psychoanalyst Jacques Lacan that has been most important in recent psychoanalytic theories of subjectivity which have profoundly influenced film and media studies. Like Benveniste, Lacan takes as his starting point Descartes' *cogito, ergo sum*. However, he rewrites Descartes' proposition as, 'I think where I am not, therefore I am where I do not think' (Lacan 1977: 166). Privileging one particular emphasis in Freud's work which can be found in such texts as *The Interpretation of Dreams* (1976) and *The Psychopathology of Everyday Life* (1975), Lacan develops Freud's theory of the acquisition of gendered subjectivity into a general theory of society and culture. Lacan argues that the symbolic order of language, law and meaning is founded on the unconscious which is itself structured like a language. Subjectivity is an effect of language, governed by repression and the realm of the unconscious. The intentional subject (which is equivalent to the ego) is a subject based on a structure of misrecognition, laid down in the mirror stage.

According to Lacan both meaning and subjectivity are structured in relation to a primary signifier, the **phallus**, which governs the symbolic order of society and culture. Control of the phallus is control of the laws and meanings of society. This position of control is the position of the **Other**. It is not a position open to either men or women. (It could only ever be occupied by figures such as the all-knowing, self-present God of the Judaeo-Christian tradition.) Subjectivity is founded on the misrecognition by the individual of himself as Other.

In the mirror stage the infant misrecognizes itself as a whole, unified and autonomous being. The pre-Oedipal experience of the body in fragments, that is the lack of a definite sense of unified, embodied self, separate from the world around it, defines the state of the pre-mirror stage infant. This is compounded by the lack of control over the satisfaction of needs and **desire** which will become the motivating force behind language. Governed by a fragmented sense of self and unable to distinguish itself as a separate entity, the infant overcomes its fragmentation by identifying with an 'other', an external mirror image.

> We have only to understand the mirror stage *as an identification*, in the full sense that analysis give to the term: namely the transformation that takes place in the subject when he assumes an image – whose predestination to this phase-effect is sufficiently indicated by the use, in analytic theory, of the ancient term *imago*.
>
> This jubilant assumption of his specular image by the child at the *infans* stage, still sunk in his motor incapacity and nursling dependence would seem to exhibit in an exemplary situation the symbolic matrix in which the *I* is precipitated in a primordial form, before it is objectified in the dialectic of identification with the other, and before language restores to it, in the universal, its function as subject.
>
> (Lacan 1977: 2)

This process of misrecognition becomes the basis for all future identifications by the subject of itself as autonomous and sovereign once it has entered the symbolic order of language. In reality, subjectivity is divided, based on misrecognition. It is the subject's lack of fullness, lack of self-presence and inability to control meaning that motivates language. The process of assuming subjectivity invests the individual with a temporary sense of

control and of sovereignty which evokes a 'metaphysics of presence' (Derrida 1973) in which he/she becomes the source of the meaning he/she speaks and language appears to be the expression of meaning fixed by the speaking subject. Yet, in Lacanian-based theories, the speaker is never the author of the language within which he/she takes up a position. Language pre-exists and produces subjectivity and meaning. The subject 'I' is an effect of language and marks the points at which the individual is inserted into the symbolic order of language, law and meaning.

It was in the British journal *Screen*, first published by the Society for Education in Film and Television in 1969 (SEFT was founded by the British Film Institute in 1950), that psychoanalytic theories of subjectivity began to make an impact on film and media studies (see **Screen theory**). The main focus of *Screen* in the 1970s was the relationship between semiology, Marxism and **psychoanalysis**. Also important in these debates was feminism. Among the most influential interventions in *Screen* was Laura **Mulvey**'s essay 'Visual Pleasure and Narrative Cinema' (1975), which used psychoanalysis and feminism to problematize the question of the female spectator. Mulvey argues that traditional film forms portray female characters as objects of the male gaze which depends on narcissistic and fetishistic scopophilia (see **gaze, the; fetishism**) involving male **voyeurism** and female exhibitionism. The filmic realization of a non-patriarchal female subjectivity requires, Mulvey suggests, new filmic forms (see **patriarchy**).

The post-structuralist subject

Semiology and psychoanalysis both played direct roles in the development of post-structuralist theories of subjectivity. Marxism was also important as a key discourse against which forms of post-structuralism defined themselves. The terms subject and subjectivity are central to post-structuralist theories which see them as effects of language and discourse. Post-structuralist theories as developed in the work of Jacques **Derrida**, Jacques Lacan and Michel **Foucault** are concerned with four key areas: meaning, subjectivity, discourse and power. Derrida has been important both for his critique of the self-present, humanist subject and his deconstructive (**deconstruction**) approach to language (Derrida 1973 and 1976). Lacan has been important for his theory of the split subject laid down in the mirror stage, for his conception of the symbolic order and for feminist appropriations of his work in Julia **Kristeva** (1986) and Luce **Irigaray** (1985 and 1991). Foucault is best known for his theory of subjectivity, discourse and power (1979 and 1981).

In post-structuralist models, meaning is constituted in language. It does not already exist in a world outside language. Thus language *constitutes* rather than reflects or expresses the meaning of the world, society, our experience and our sense of ourselves. Post-structuralism takes issue with the self-present Cartesian subject, theorizing subjectivity as an effect of language. Subjectivity (defined as our conscious and unconscious sense of self, our emotions and desires) is constituted in language. Rational consciousness is only one dimension of subjectivity. It is in the process of using language – whether as thought or speech – that we take up positions as speaking and thinking subjects. Language exists in the form of many competing and often contradictory discourses (see Foucault 1981). For Foucault, discourses constitute our subjectivity for us through material practices that shape bodies as much as minds. Discourses involve relations of power. Some discourses, and the subject positions and modes of subjectivity that they constitute, have more power than others. Power is a relationship which involves resistance. It is not something held by a particular group, though as a relationship which inheres in all discourses (economic, media, familial and so on), it serves particular interests. Power comes from below and is not centred in any one institution. It is dispersed. Power functions through the discursive constitution of embodied subjects within discourses.

In Foucault's work discourses produce subjects within relations of power which potentially or actually involve resistance. The subject positions and modes of embodied subjectivity constituted for the individual within particular discourses allow for different degrees and types of agency both compliant and resistant. The discursive field, which produces meanings and subjectivities, is not homogeneous. It includes discourses and discursive

practices which may be contradictory and conflicting and which create the space for new forms of knowledge and practice. While there is no place beyond discourses and the power relations that govern them, resistance and change are possible from within. In the *History of Sexuality. Volume One*, for example, Foucault (1981: 43) gives the example of the homosexual who is the creation of a set of discourses that endow him with a subjectivity which facilitates the production of a resistant reverse discourse.

The embodied subject and performance

In the work of Foucault and in subsequent appropriations of it, subjectivity is always embodied. Judith **Butler** (1990 and 1993), for example, has drawn directly on Foucault in an attempt to theorize the materiality of the **body** and the ways in which 'bodies are materialised as sexed' in the light of a critique of heterosexism. Starting from the premise 'that bodies only appear, only endure, only live within the productive constraints of certain highly gendered regulatory schemas' (1993: xi), Butler suggests a way of theorizing these schemas via the concept of performativity (see **performative**). Here she draws on speech act theory. Gendered subjectivity is acquired through the repeated performance by the individual of discourses of **gender**. Moreover, Butler argues that 'there is no gender identity behind the expressions of gender...Identity is performatively constituted by the very "expressions" that are said to be its results' (Butler 1990: 24–5). This 'performativity must be understood not as a singular or deliberate "act", but, rather, as the reiterative and citational practice by which discourse produces the effects that it names' (Butler 1993: 2).

Butler's appropriation of Foucauldian theory involves a decentred notion of subjectivity and agency:

> the agency denoted by the performativity of 'sex' will be directly counter to any notion of a voluntarist subject who exists quite apart from the regulatory norms which she/he opposes. The paradox of subjectivation (*assujetissement*) is precisely that the subject who would resist such norms is itself enabled, if not produced, by such

norms. Although this constitutive constraint does not foreclose the possibility of agency, it does locate agency as a reiterative or re-articulatory practice, immanent to power, and not a relation of external opposition to power.

(Butler 1993: 15)

Here Butler, following Foucault, locates resistance and the possibilities of transforming the *status quo* within the discursive field which produces both existing power relations and forms of subjectivity. There is no possibility within this model of either fully autonomous subjectivity or a space beyond power from which to act. Agency can, however, transform aspects of material discursive practices and the power relations inherent in them. In bringing Foucault to bear on feminist and **queer theory**, Butler challenges those distinctions between sex and gender which see sex as the biological basis on which gendered subjectivity is inscribed. For Butler, sex is as much a matter of culture as is gender and the very distinction between the two is 'the effect of the apparatus of cultural construction designated by gender' (Butler 1990: 7).

Foucauldian models of discourse, subjectivity and power require analyses that start from the detailed examination of the many localized forms which subjectivity and power relations take in particular areas of discursive practice. Yet Foucault's view of power and subjectivity is controversial because it denies the possibility of a place exterior to power from which the subject could ground transformative political action. Feminists hostile to post-structuralism, for example, argue that feminism needs grounded ideas of subjectivity and positions outside of power from which woman can speak and act in order to effect change. Post-structuralists argue against this, that the theory that all discursive practices and all forms of subjectivity constitute and are constituted by relations of power is only disabling if power is seen as always necessarily repressive. It is precisely such singular notions of subjectivity and power as repression that Foucault attempted to question in his historical studies.

References

Althusser, L. (1971) 'Ideology and Ideological State Apparatuses (Notes Towards an Investigation)' (first published 1969), in *Lenin and Philosophy and Other Essays*, trans. Ben Brewster, London: New Left Books, pp. 121–73.

Benveniste, E. (1971) *Problems in General Linguistics* (first published 1966), Miami: University of Miami Press.

Butler, J. (1990) *Gender Trouble*, New York and London: Routledge.

—— (1993) *Bodies That Matter*, New York and London: Routledge.

Derrida, J. (1973) *Speech and Phenomena* (first published 1967), trans. D. Allison, Evanston, IL: Northwestern University Press.

—— (1976) *Of Grammatology* (first published 1967), trans. G. Spivak, Baltimore, MD: Johns Hopkins University Press.

Foucault, M. (1979) *Discipline and Punish*, Harmondsworth: Penguin.

—— (1981) *The History of Sexuality. Volume 1. An Introduction* (first published 1976), trans. R. Hurley, Harmondsworth: Penguin.

Freud, S. (1975) *The Psychopathology of Everyday Life* (first published 1901), trans. A. Tyson, Harmondsworth: Penguin.

—— (1976) *The Interpretation of Dreams* (first published 1900), trans. J. Strachey, Harmondsworth: Penguin.

Irigaray, L. (1985) *This Sex Which Is Not One* (first published 1977), trans. C. Porter and C. Burke, New York: Cornell University Press.

—— (1991) *The Irigaray Reader*, ed. Margaret Whitford, Oxford: Blackwell.

Kristeva, J. (1986) *The Kristeva Reader*, ed. Toril Moi, Oxford: Blackwell.

Lacan, J. (1977) 'The Mirror Stage as Formative of the Function of the I', in *Ecrits. A Selection* (first published 1949), trans. A. Sheridan, London: Tavistock, pp. 1–7.

Marx, K. and Engels, F. (1970) *The German Ideology* (first published 1845), trans. C. J. Arthur, London: Lawrence and Wishart.

Mulvey, Laura (1975) 'Visual Pleasure and Narrative Cinema', *Screen*, vol. 16, no. 3, pp. 6–18.

Saussure, F. de (1974) *A Course in General Linguistics* (first published 1916), trans. W. Baskin, London: Fontana.

CHRIS WEEDON

subliminal

A subliminal image or sound in film or television is one that is seen or heard under the threshold of **consciousness** but is understood to make an impression. If one frame of a different image is inserted into a uniform series of images, the image may be received but not acknowledged. Most **advertising** authorities will not allow the inclusion of subliminal images, as the subconscious suggestion of products would seem overtly manipulative.

Subliminal **sound** may be more common in film, for example: animal noises in *Raging Bull* (Martin Scorsese, 1980) add to the dramatic effect, but are not recognizable.

NICK BURTON

subversion

Classical Hollywood cinema offers a relatively dominant mode of representation which is often considered to be the norm; consequently, audiences often have a particular set of expectations when experiencing film or television. Some texts play on these expectations by subverting them as they deconstruct the classical form (see **deconstruction**). In some cases this subversion may be within the **narrative** or within the construction of screen space. *Last Year in Marienbad* (Alain Resnais, 1961), for example, subverts both narrative and spatial expectations. The narrative in the film is inconsistent and ambiguous, and the conventional logic of the space is broken by, among other things, the unusual juxtapositions of shots.

See also: avant-garde; classical Hollywood cinema and new Hollywood cinema

NICK BURTON

suspense

Defined literally as a deferral or as a state of nervous or excited uncertainty, suspense is associated principally with unrestricted or omniscient narration whereby viewers have more knowledge than the characters. The viewer's superior range of knowledge creates suspense because he or she can anticipate effects which the character can not – for example, that a bomb in a room is about to explode. The deferral of this event increases suspense, frequently emphasized by more rapid rhythms of music and editing. The structure of suspense thus serves to draw viewers into anticipating forthcoming events and is characteristic of the **narrative** structure of classical Hollywood cinema (see **classical Hollywood cinema and new Hollywood cinema**).

LEE GRIEVESON

suture

From psychoanalytic theory, suture refers to the 'sealing' or 'completing' of an identity through **discourse** (see **psychoanalysis**). The psychic process that forms subjectivity is reproduced between the subject-spectator and the chain of filmic discourse. The **shot/reverse shot** structure is the technical process by which the spectator is positioned to make a film coherent *and* produced as a subject (see **subject and subjectivity**). In cultural studies, the concept of suture has been used as a correlative to Marxist theories of **class** consciousness in order to understand how competing political identities (**race**, **gender**, **sexuality**, nationalism) are always precarious and open to new articulations. Identities are temporarily sutured forming new political subjects. Current reinterpreters of the concept include Judith **Butler** and Chantal Mouffe.

Further reading

Laclau, E. and Mouffe, C. (1989) *Hegemony and Socialist Strategy: Towards a Radical Democratic Politics*, London: Verso.

Miller, J.-A., Oudart, J.-P. and Heath, S. (1977/1978) 'Suture', *Screen*, vol. 18, no. 4, pp. 24–34.

PAULA CHAKRAVARTTY

symbolic code

One of five codes deployed by Roland **Barthes** in deconstructing a text (see **deconstruction**). The **text** is seen as a network of threads which we work back along to ascertain the code. The symbolic code allows access for structural or psychoanalytic criticism by indicating the symbolic structure. One familiar symbolic form is antitheses: the Western is sometimes structured around antinomies such as the wilderness and the garden, savagery and civilization (see **Western, the**); **film noir** around light and dark, past and present, masculinity and femininity. In other genres the symbolic code is less obvious, but in all cases the code works to position the reader within a framework of assumed oppositions or differences.

PHILIP SIMPSON

synchronic

Synchronic language analysis is based on the assumption that speakers of a language, while their language competence and performance (see **language/langue; parole**) is complete, usually have little or no knowledge about the historic or **diachronic** development of that language. This leads to the conclusion that the elements of a language system must be describable without reference to the development of the language from earlier forms. While language analysis from **Saussure** to the Chomskyan decades has placed the greatest relevance on purely synchronic language descriptions, recent developments in the field of linguistics have revived the interest in historic language development. The term has been taken up by film scholars to refer to contemporary analysis as opposed to a diachronic, or historical, analysis.

EVA VIETH

synergy

Synergy is the process by which media companies acquire and harness relations between two or more elements of a media production and distribution process. The aim is to increase business efficiency and to avoid duplication of resources or to market two or more complementary products simultaneously where it is hoped that the success of one will promote the success of the other.

A successful example of synergy occurred in Britain in the late 1980s when Levi jeans used a series of classic pop songs in its advertisements. The adverts raised awareness of the revived songs which then entered the top ten chart and helped increase awareness of the jeans adverts. Films such as *Titanic* (James Cameron, 1997), *The Bodyguard* (Mick Jackson, 1992) and *Forrest Gump* (Robert Zemeckis, 1994) have all had singles or soundtrack albums which have dominated the music charts and have benefited from the success of the films.

The release of such blockbuster movies as *Jurassic Park* (Steven Spielberg, 1993) or *Dinosaurs* (1998) can often involve multi-million dollar tie-ins with fast food companies like MacDonalds or KFC, as well as promoting a range of toys, foods and clothing. These tie-ins are an increasingly crucial part of a movie's financial success and, as Wasko (1994) notes, companies like Coca-Cola can have a significant influence on how a film is produced.

A common form of synergy is where media conglomerates are able to take advantage of their cross-media ownership to promote products within the company. In Britain, Rupert Murdoch's News International-owned newspapers, for example the *Sun* and the *Sunday Times*, have consistently promoted the News International-owned satellite company BSkyB. BSkyB has also linked up with the German media group Kirch to set up a European-wide pay-TV company. Kirch has programme agreement with Viacom, the US company which owns Paramount film studios and MTV.

Increasingly in Britain media companies are being absorbed into larger, more economic groups, as a result of the relaxation of ownership rules in the 1996 Broadcasting Act. Regional commercial television companies are looking to merge their regional infrastructures with local newspaper groups to share news gathering and advertising resources and to cut overheads. The local commercial radio sector in Britain is dominated by a small number of large companies such as EMAP and GWR. Stations within the GWR group offer a similar format and conform to a group-wide music policy irrespective of where their broadcasts originate. Using ISDN and satellite links it is possible to feed a 'local' radio service to a community many hundreds of miles away. EMAP Radio, apart from owning several local radio stations, is now offering a television version of its popular dance-music based stations, KISS-FM. One of the world's largest multimedia conglomerates is the American company Time-Warner who have interests in film production, television (through its production company Lorimar), satellite services (CNN) and music (Warner Music Group who 'own' acts such as Simply Red, The Cure and Genesis), as well as book and magazine publishing.

The digital 'revolution' means that this concentration and integration of media, entertainment and communications companies will continue. It is predicted that eventually some households will have one digitally-based communications centre which will offer both television and radio via terrestrial, satellite and cable channels, a personal computer with **Internet** access and telephony and interactive services such as shopping and banking.

Although there have been examples of unsuccessful attempts at creating synergy, most notably Sony and Matsushita's attempts to take over the Hollywood studios Columbia/TriStar and MCA/Universal, the trend is increasingly towards large media conglomerates like News International who are now looking to combine computer and telecommunications activities with their media and entertainment resources. The drive to greater synergy can be seen as likely to increase the domination of a few, largely western-owned, multinational conglomerates, and to offer audiences less choice and fewer opportunities for independent and alternative productions.

See also: globalization; multinational

References

Wasko, J. (1994) *Hollywood in the Information Age beyond the Silver Screen*, London: Polity Press.

PHILIP RAYNER

syntagmatic

Whereas **paradigmatic** rules govern the selection of elements from a group that bear a basic similarity relation, syntagmatic relations are relations of contingency and syntagmatic rules govern the sequence or composition of different elements – for example, the composition of a sentence in the sequence subject–verb–object. The cognitive process of understanding syntagmatic relationships is essential not only for sentence construction but it also influences the ability to understand and employ metonymies, which is essential for Jacques **Lacan**'s theories on **metaphor** and **metonymy**. Christian **Metz** examined the syntagmatic conventions of the cinema, that is the linear organization of film narratives, and evolved the theory of the 'large syntagmatic categories'.

EVA VIETH

syuzhet

Syuzhet: from Russian **Formalism** and the oppositional term to **fabula**. Within the *syuzhet*, events are transformed from their ordinary chronological unfolding and subjected to artistic intervention, rearrangement and organizational shifts. The effect enables the reader/viewer to see the action freshly, as distinct from everyday occurrences. *Last Year at Marienbad* (Alain Resnais, 1961) provides a cinematic example of the rich possibilities of foregrounding *syuzhet*: the narrative chronology remains hazy and mysterious due to continual repetitions (always with differences), gaps that elide cause-and-effect sequence, unexplained and unpsychologized character motivation, and even spatial uncertainty produced by the flowing camera movement.

KAREN BACKSTEIN

T

tabloid television

Tabloid television refers to a type of news and current affairs programming which effaces distinctions between public and private, serious and sensationalist, critical and sceptical. It tends to be moralistic in style and tone, blurring the lines between fact and fiction, news and entertainment (see Fiske 1992).

Bob Franklin (1997) employs the term 'newszak' to characterize what he sees as a contemporary trend in British journalism to retreat from investigative, 'hard' news reporting in favour of ever 'softer', 'lighter' stories:

> 'Newszak' understands news as a product designed and 'processed' for a particular market and delivered in increasingly homogenous 'snippets' which make only modest demands on the audience. Newszak is news converted into entertainment.
>
> (Franklin 1997: 4–5)

Entertainment-led journalism is being subjected to ever-closer scrutiny, a development connected with recent revelations in Britain about 'fakery' in televisual documentaries and that several talk shows allegedly hired actors from talent agencies to pose as guests (see **chat/talk show**). These incidents have prompted strong reactions from critics questioning the ethical standards of programmes that purport to offer audiences factual and reliable information on a range of important public issues.

In light of such developments, both journalists and audiences are struggling to come to terms with important ethical questions. It appears that in the current news environment, what counts as 'truth' is in danger of becoming blurred amid the drama and superficiality of news formats obsessed with sex, crime and scandal (see Allan 1999; Lull and Hinerman 1997). Some commentators in both the United States and the United Kingdom vigorously contend that this apparent 'dumbing down' of the news will have profound consequences for the future of parliamentary democracy, not least because the number of reliable sources of information is shrinking.

An editorial leader in the British broadsheet newspaper *The Independent* (6 March 1999: 3) maintains that, taken overall, the so-called 'dumbing down' of British culture is in fact a 'broadening out'. That is, an increased emphasis on popular culture, the editorial voice maintains, is actually making British cultural life more open and democratic. Nevertheless, news is identified as a crucial exception to this argument:

> But there is one area where the drive towards the lowest common denominator should genuinely be worrying, and that is in journalism. . . . the convergence of tabloid and broadsheet newspapers on the middle ground of celebrity soap opera is a real threat, not to our cultural life but to our democratic citizenship.
>
> (*The Independent*, 6 March 1999: 3)

In Britain, commercial television newscasts currently exhibit many of the features typically associated with their counterparts in the tabloid press. With regard to changes in news selection and treatment, the commercial news provider Independent Television News (ITN), for example, has become more 'tabloid' in its orientation, placing greater emphasis on crime and human interest stories and offering fewer foreign and political news stories than the publicly owned British Broadcasting Corporation (BBC) news. Commercial pressures have also prompted ITN to place a higher emphasis on reporting sports activities. Increasingly, then, it appears that discourses of 'the market' and 'the bottom-line' are systematically shaping what is reported in the news, and how. Such changes in emphasis have not necessarily resulted in the reporting of falsehoods, but rather in a further simplification of the news and sometimes in a failure to explain adequately the significance of certain events.

Commentators on both sides of the Atlantic seem to agree that journalists are becoming increasingly uncomfortable about challenging those in positions of power in society because of a possible negative impact on ratings and thus revenue. What is lost, some suggest, is the journalistic objective to operate in the public interest. This is a corruption of the profession in the name of commercialism.

See also: broadcasting, the United Kingdom; broadcasting, the United States; live television

References

Allan, S. (1999) *News Culture*, Buckingham and Philadelphia: Open University Press.

Fiske, J. (1992) 'Popularity and the Politics of Information', in P. Dahlgren and C. Sparks (eds) *Journalism and Popular Culture*, London: Sage.

Franklin, B. (1997) *Newszak and News Media*, London: Arnold.

Langer, J. (1998) *Tabloid Television: Popular Journalism and the 'Other News'*, London: Routledge.

Lull, J. and Hinerman, S. (eds) (1997) *Media Scandals*, Cambridge: Polity.

CYNTHIA CARTER

technological change

Film and television are technologically intensive media: they cannot exist without elaborate electrical machinery at all phases of production and exhibition. Consequently, theorists and historians of film and television have a stake in many aspects of the study of technology in general, including histories of technology and theories of technological change.

Technological determinism

Informally, it is easy to get the impression that technological developments – inventions, subsequently exploited on a commercial basis by manufacturers – play a decisive or determining role in much of our culture. Television is said to produce 'effects'; the film industry influences behaviour and fashion; more significantly, wars are fought over the oil which fuels the energy-hungry lifestyle of many countries.

Furthermore, technologies often appear to grow or develop in a progressive, linear way. Televisions receive *more* channels and have *larger* screens. Films, thanks largely to computers, increasingly succeed in representing scenes and spaces which are unfilmable (and do not exist) in traditional terms. Technologies are often spoken of almost as living things: they 'grow', 'develop' or become 'mature'. Earlier versions of the same technology become, in retrospect, 'first steps'.

Technology, in other words, not only looms large in modern culture, but also gives the impression that it achieved this position through a *natural* process, a process of growth and maturation. This way of looking at technology and technological change – namely, that technology has a life of its own, and that one technology gives birth to another in a forward-moving, upwardly progressive sequence – is known as *technological determinism*. Technological determinists often use natural or biological metaphors to describe technological change: radio is an ancestor of television, computers descended from the typewriter (or the abacus) and so forth.

The important point about technological determinism is that it paints a picture of society (including government and industry) as a kind of passive witness to the growth of technology. One machine spawns another; 'simple' inventions 'lead' to more complex ones; and human beings make the best of it. What this view tends to obscure is the role that human beings play in the history of technology in the first place. Technological determinism has encountered some powerful objections, many of which focus on the ways in which social and economic forces have *determined* – not always been determined *by* – the history of technology. An anti-determinist position on technology would suggest that new machines do not appear in the world because their moment has arrived in the independent history of technology, but because decisions have been made, and actions taken, by governments, corporations, banks and investors.

Still, even anti-determinists have to come to terms with some compelling truths about the history of technology. Inventions do not occur entirely at random; computers were not invented in ancient Rome, nor could motion pictures exist before photography. To a large extent, technologies often do depend on what comes immediately before them. However – and this point is central to the anti-determinist position – technology does not follow one, preordained, inevitable path, but rather develops and changes in ways which depend on available resources and historical conditions.

A good reminder of the non-technological factors which influence the history of technology is the American space programme, which got underway after the Second World War due in part to war-time technologies, but thanks even more to the political climate which generated competition with the Soviet Union. Another example is the recent history of microcomputers. The 'microcomputer revolution' depends on certain technological achievements; but the popularity of computers is not a *direct* result of scientific breakthroughs, nor are those breakthroughs the result of natural 'growth' in the technology. Rather, the manufacturers of the technology saw potential in it which they decided to exploit – or, more accurately, to exploit those limited aspects of it which seemed to promise the greatest profits.

Another set of objections to the technological determinist position can be made on ideological or moral grounds. Consistently through history, developments labelled as technological 'progress' have brought about increased automatization in the workplace and consequent loss of jobs. In this light, technology has a destructive effect on society, in very tangible ways in the lives of real, identifiable

people. A strict technological determinist view would maintain that technological developments, including automation and factory streamlining, come about naturally and inevitably (because the time is right for them to do so, in the 'life history' of technology), and cannot be fended off. A dissenting view would maintain that every job lost to a machine is lost because an employer *decided* to use a machine. Such a view, in other words, would see human action and behaviour as the determining force in history.

Technological determinism and film and television

Film and television provide important examples of almost every issue in the areas of technological change and the debate over technological determinism. Not least of these, for film and television theory, is the matter of how history is told. Clearly, technology looms large in the history of these media. But historians still have to make choices. Should the history of film and television be told as the history of technology? Should the historian take a technological determinist position, describing early machinery as 'primitive' or 'immature', and later developments as 'growth' and 'progress'? Or, do the histories of film and television lend themselves to wider, less techno-centric interpretations?

In *Film History: Theory and Practice*, authors Robert C. Allen and Douglas Gomery (1985) address the question of the role of technology, and technological change, in the project of telling film history. Allen and Gomery recognize the centrality of technology and its history to the history of film, but advocate an approach to history which puts technology in a wider context:

The basic task of the historian of cinema technology is the examination of circumstances surrounding the initial development of the cinematic apparatus (camera, printer, projector) and those attending the subsequent alterations, modifications, and extensions. This does not mean merely cataloging inventions in historical sequence; machines do not invent themselves. The technological history of the cinema necessarily must also entail how particular pieces of technology came to be developed at a particular time, their relationship to the existing state of technology, the extent and nature of their use, and the consequence of that use – whether foreseen or unforeseen.

(Allen and Gomery 1985: 110)

Having taken this position, Allen and Gomery go on to deal directly with technological determinism. In arguing for a more inclusive approach to film history, they point out that technology does not always lead the way; sometimes an available technology will be neglected, if there are economic and industrial reasons for not using it: 'the simple availability of technology does not in itself determine filmmaking practice, nor does it necessarily specify a general direction for artistic innovation. For example, lightweight, portable 16mm filmmaking equipment was "available" to Hollywood in the 1950s and 1960s, but did not find its way into use in Hollywood' (*ibid.*: 113).

A particularly pointed example of the ways in which technological change does or does not play a determining role in history is the case of American commercial television. The technical preconditions for a fully-fledged commercial television industry existed twenty years before the industry got underway; reasons for this delay cannot be found in anything in the 'natural' life-cycle of the technology, but must be sought in the historical, institutional and economic forces which were at work in the world before, during and after television's introduction.

In *Media Technology and Society: A History: From the Telegraph to the Internet*, Brian Winston (1998) discusses this period in detail, offering it as a prime example of what he calls 'the "law" of the suppression of radical potential'. This 'law' is the cumulative effect of the existing interests – financial and political – of the corporate and government forces to whom the task of introducing new technologies into society has fallen (or who have seized and monopolized that task). Winston argues that, in spite of the frequent pronouncements we hear to the effect that technological innovations drastically alter society and even human consciousness, the underlying structures of economic and social power in industrialized societies has not

changed very much for decades, or even in some respects for centuries.

Film and television: the special case of realism

In general, technological change (including minor change marketed and promoted as significant change, as in the case of new car models or clearer phone lines) finds itself greeted with enthusiasm, praise and money. It hardly matters what the change consists of, as long as it can be quantified in some manner and as long as the advertising agents depicting it publicly are good at what they do.

In the cases of film and television, much technological change over the decades has followed something like a pre-written script: namely, incremental movement along a path defined in terms of realism. Indeed, this path may be understood as having started long before film, culminating along one route in the development of **photography**. Film – motion or moving pictures – may be understood crudely as photography-plus-motion, motion being an empirical characteristic of reality not found in still photographs. The 'addition' of **sound** to movies in the 1920s represented another step along the realist path, another juncture at which an empirically verifiable characteristic of reality became a characteristic of film.

The path continues: black-and-white film gives way, at least in many contexts, to colour, computer-generated film sequences allow for the illusionistic representation of imaginative and physically impossible realms of action and so forth. Along the way, even some of the film industry's failures have taken the form of attempted enhancements of realism, such as 3-D movies. More recently, directional sound has become commonplace in cinemas.

Television, too, has developed according to a crude realist agenda. In the United States, colour television broadcasting largely took over from black and white in the 1960s. The 1980s saw the beginnings of what became a wave of pseudo-**documentary** camera techniques – jerky, hand-held camera movement, off-centre framings – designed to confer on the televised material the veneer of realism and plausibility. (Thus many viewers who had never set foot in a police precinct found themselves declaring *Hill Street Blues*, NBC's pioneering unsteady-camera effort, to be 'realistic'.)

At one level, the incremental addition of characteristics of reality to film and television – sound, colour, motion, directionality – cannot be gainsaid: empirical reality does indeed display those characteristics, and their selection as the agenda items for commercial media is not entirely random. At the same time, however, there is more to this ostensible march toward perfect **verisimilitude** than there might at first appear to be.

In spite of the apparent linear movement – progress – involved in going from silence to sound, grey to colour, still to moving, an equally important factor in the history of these photo-reproductive technologies is that *at almost any given time in their histories*, however early, they are praised for their **realism** and illusionism. In other words, while early twenty-first century consumers of film and television may find the media products of fifty or a hundred years ago laughably unrealistic, the consumers of those earlier times did not – or, at the very least, some of them did not and, importantly, promotion and advertising for those products *already* emphasized realism (see **pre-Hollywood cinema**).

The complexity of studying the realist agenda for technology, then, is that realism to a great degree is in the eye of the beholder, or the mind of the viewer. Fifty years from now, consumers of film and video (or whatever mixed or hybrid media then exist) will react to early twenty-first century media as we do to turn-of-the-twentieth-century films. It is important for media industries to promote this endless 'progress' (since, if we *really* believed that today's television sets offered stunningly realistic pictures, we would never replace them), but also to make the 'perfection' of the moment seem real. Consumers must be persuaded to buy a new device because it supersedes an older one, in exactly these terms (greater realism); but the same consumers must also, and without loss of faith, be persuaded a few months or years later that the product they purchased in fact falls laughably short of perfect realism.

The realist agenda is thus part of the agenda of 'planned obsolescence', the deliberate circularity of the processes of invention, promotion, and dissemination of technologies and other products and services.

See also: digital communication; Internet and World Wide Web

References

Allen, R. C. and Gomery, D. (1985) *Film History: Theory and Practice*, New York: Alfred A. Knopf.
Winston, B. (1998) *Media Technology and Society: A History: From the Telegraph to the Internet*, London: Routledge.

Further reading

Smith, M. R. and Marx, L. (eds) (1994) *Does Technology Drive History? The Dilemma of Technological Determinism*, Cambridge, MA: MIT Press.

DAVID A. BLACK

teleological

Combining *telos* (end, purpose or goal) and *logos* (principle), teleology refers to one of the principles commonly used by theorists to explain change and movement. As a metatheoretical principle, it says that all phenomenal changes in nature, such as the elliptical movement of stars in heaven, the growth and decay of a tree, or the actions of intentional agents like human beings, are phases within a process that moves towards a goal state. An explanation can therefore be described as teleological when it posits either a predetermined end or a final cause as the driving force behind the phenomenon. In his metaphysics, Aristotle invests natural beings with goals – what he calls the internal teleology. In modern times, **Hegel** shifts the teleological thinking to a new idealist height, constructing a system by which world history is supposedly rendered intelligible as an Odyssean journey where the human spirit returns to its own truth in the final stage of perfect knowledge.

BRIANKLE G. CHANG

text

A text is a signifying structure organized by codes and conventions, capable of creating meaning, capable of being read. Traditionally, the word has been used to refer almost exclusively to the written word, but since the 1960s it has been used within film and television studies to refer to television programmes, films, photographs or indeed any visual or aural signifying structure which has a material existence independent of sender or receiver (see **sender/receiver**). The term is sometimes used interchangeably with 'message', despite significant differences in meaning: an offensive hand gesture, for example, sends a message, but is not in itself a text. Texts are 'read' by their audiences or consumers, the process by which meaning is constructed from the signs contained within it.

Use of the word 'message' within film and television studies stems from the growth of the social sciences in the United States in the 1940s and 1950s, when critical attention was first focused on mass communication. Studies during this period were concerned almost exclusively with the process of communication, the way in which messages are transmitted and received. The 'message' itself was taken as an unproblematic given, and content analysis limited to studies of the frequency of words in newspaper articles, or comparisons of the amount of newsprint devoted to different topics. The term is now mainly used within sociology, psychology and engineering to refer simply to that which is transmitted.

Structuralism introduced the notion of 'text' to film and television studies in the 1960s and 1970s, marking a conceptual shift away from use of the more inert term 'message' (see **structuralism and post-structuralism**). Structuralist theory proposes that any signifier derives its meaning from its location within a sign system, and that these systems are governed by their own internal logic. Structuralist studies of film, like those by Wright (1975) and **Wollen** (1982), proposed that a filmic text could be seen as an autonomous object, obeying its own inner logic, rather than simply the intentions of the author. For writers on television, such as John **Fiske**, Richard **Hoggart** and Raymond **Williams**, the codes and conventions that govern a text have socio-cultural underpinning, and thus an ideological function and significance.

Roland **Barthes**' work on the notion of text broke the link between text and author that had dominated critical thinking about the arts for so long. Asserting that a text 'reads without the inscription of the father' (1977: 161), Barthes displaced the author as the primary source of meaning, drawing attention to the internal rules which govern the way signs are organized within a signifying system (see **symbolic code**). Such an approach frees up those texts to which it might be difficult or unhelpful to attribute **authorship**, including many products of popular culture. In the 1960s, this position provided a methodology for the growing interest in **genre**, radically challenging the dominance of the concept of authorship in film criticism. Barthes conceived the text as a space in which multiple and sometimes incompatible voices could blend and clash, replacing the notion of the text as an organic whole with the model of a network in which, and through which, the codes that organize it interweave. The act of reading a text is, for Barthes, one of production rather than consumption, the task being to actively produce meaning from what is offered by the text, rather than simply decoding a trail of signs left by the author. Barthes' work on the codes that structure literary texts, like that of **Metz** on the filmic text, has been criticized by post-structuralist critics, who see the project of identifying a totalizing and all-embracing set of codes as essentially flawed. Stephen Heath (1981) has suggested such codes should be seen as loose systems of constraints or possibilities, and that 'text' should be viewed as a process or operation rather than an object, reinforcing the importance of the relationship between text and **audience**.

References

Barthes, R. (1977) *Image-Music-Text*, trans. S. Heath, London: Fontana.

Heath, S. (1981) *Questions of Cinema*, London: Macmillan.

Wollen, P. (1982) 'North by Northwest: A Morphological Analysis', in *Readings and Writings*, London: Verso.

Wright, W. (1975) *Sixguns and Society*, Berkeley: University of California Press.

Further reading

Metz, C. (1974) *Language and Cinema*, trans. M. Taylor, New York: Oxford University Press.

ANDREW BIRTWISTLE

theory

In everyday usage, 'theory' tends to mean a set of ideas with relation to practice: a book about the theory and practice of car maintenance would probably tell us the how and why of keeping a car running. There are, of course, books about the practicalities of making of films and television programmes but in this Dictionary 'theory' refers to the attempt to understand and explain aspects of film and television.

In general terms, theory might be seen as the attempt to explain systematically the existence of a phenomenon or practice. Conventionally, in the natural and physical sciences, the set of propositions which make up a theoretical explanation of phenomena can be so precise and powerful that predictions can be made about them. Film and television theories have never attained this degree of scientific rigour. Though accounts of perception of the moving image or the speed of electronic bombardment clearly draw on the physical sciences to explain some of the visual phenomena of these media, media theory has more often drawn on the social sciences and **history**.

This is because the dominant theoretical questions for media theorists concern less a relatively simply described *phenomenon* like the images on the screen, and more the *relationships* between images and the groups and individuals producing and receiving them. At a more complex level, the questions are also about which fields of knowledge are most appropriate for understanding that relationship. Thus, both objects and modes of theorization are problematized in film and television theory. Some early film theory concerned itself with establishing the specific nature of film in relation to the other arts, an approach which assumed that modes of explanation drawn from aesthetics were appropriate. Sergei **Eisenstein**, Dziga **Vertov** and André **Bazin** theorized the ways in which different editing strategies offered different meanings to audiences, simply making assumptions about perception and behaviour. Theories of **realism** in cinema fit into this context. Christian **Metz**'s theorization of film as a language draws on **semiotics**, purportedly a 'science of signs' but lacking the rigour and predictability of the model offered by the physical sciences.

The so-called '**Screen theory,**' of the 1970s drew on a different, more explicit, set of theories to explain the operations of mainstream cinema. As well as emergent feminist theories (see **feminist theory**), *Screen* theory drew on Freudian, Lacanian and Althusserian explanations (see **Althusser, Louis; Freud, Sigmund; Lacan, Jacques**). In some senses, *Screen* theory was an advance because it embraced systematic modes of explanation or 'critical theory' which challenged conventional scientific explanation by recognizing the social construction of knowledge and its objects. In other senses, *Screen* theory did not mark a decisive break from earlier theorizing. Categories of explanation from other fields were still being used, perhaps with more explicitness, to constitute and explain the operation of the object of study and its relation to the viewer, without widely accepted models for conceptualizing and verifying viewer engagement.

When television became more widespread as the object of study in the 1970s and 1980s, the limitations of screen theories were more exposed. Debates about the relationship of audiences to the screen (see **audience**), sometimes couched in terms of '**effects**', 'measurement' and '**uses and gratifications**', and the sheer pervasive 'everydayness' of the medium, made it more difficult to construct television as an object separable for the purpose of analysis from people's experience of it. More recently, the work of, for example, Ang (1982) and Morley (1986), reveals an awareness of the subtlety of 'meaning making' by groups and individuals in relation to television. Attention turned more emphatically to those social sciences – **ethnography** and other participatory observational studies – which might deliver an understanding about how television existed within a social framework. Some theoretical ideas which had developed in film theory such as **genre**, **narrative** and **intertextuality** helped the understanding of the screen 'text', but the shift of emphasis to audience interaction beyond simple quantification called into question the value of much film theory to television studies. Parallel with this development in the theories relevant to the study of audiences has been the development of how television and film were and are produced institutionally (see **institution**) – explanations which concern history as much as social science.

The everyday sense of 'theory' in film and television study is still useful as a way of signalling an activity different from 'practice' or 'criticism', though these activities are often shaped, consciously or not, by the kind of theoretical perspectives mentioned here. Rather than speak of film or television 'theory', though, it may be better to be aware of the *range of theoretical approaches* which are deployed in understanding and explaining these forms.

References

Ang, I. (1982) *Watching Dallas: Soap Opera and the Melodramatic Imagination*, New York: Methuen.
Morley, D. (1986) *Family Television: Cultural Power and Domestic Leisure*, London: Comedia.

Further reading

Horkheimer, M. (1976) 'Traditional and Critical Theory' (first published 1937), in *Critical Sociology*, ed. Paul Connerton, London: Penguin.
Williams, R. (1976) *Keywords*, London: Fontana.

PHILIP SIMPSON

Third Cinema

The term 'Third Cinema' refers to the revolutionary form of filmmaking proposed by Third World directors, primarily during the 1960s, and the theoretical arguments from which it developed. Influenced to a large extent by the success and ideology of the Cuban revolution, Third Cinema strove to challenge the spectator, examine political

and economic realities, particularly the effects of capitalism, and redefine traditional aesthetics. As such, it served as an alternative both to the dominant commercial movies of Hollywood – seen as being imperialist – and to the often apolitical 'author cinema' (see **authorship**).

Using techniques derived from such diverse styles as neo-realism and **Eisenstein**'s dialectics of montage, directors in Latin America, Africa and Asia – as well as disenfranchised filmmakers in the 'first world' interested in effecting political change – developed ways of making films suited to their own particular environments and needs.

The term 'Third Cinema' was originally posited by Argentinean directors and theorists Fernando Solanas and Octavio Getino, who made the seminal film *La hora de los hornos (Hour of the Furnaces)* between 1966 and 1968. In their article 'Towards a Third Cinema', published in 1969, Solanas and Getino called for 'films of decolonization' that 'succeeded in bearing witness to the decay of bourgeois values and testifying to social injustice'. Rejecting the separation of politics and art, and insisting that the intellectual should play an important role in convincing the masses of the need for change, they saw the filmmaker as 'one more worker, functioning on the cultural front'. The three-part *La hora de los hornos* put these concepts into practice: it analyses Argentina's history from colonization to modernity using montages that sharply contrast the 'haves' with the 'have nots' and incorporates intermissions in the **text**, during which workers could engage in discussion of their own situation and strategic revolutionary planning.

Cuban writer and filmmaker Julio García Espinosa and the Brazilian director Glauber Rocha waged the battle on the aesthetic front, suggesting that Third World films should not even attempt to reproduce the glossy technique and expensive look of their Hollywood counterparts: instead they should reveal poverty and lack in their very texture. García Espinosa's 'For an Imperfect Cinema' (1969) addressed the burgeoning Cuban film industry, and urged directors to avoid the temptation of producing a technically masterful but reactionary cinema. He argued for overcoming the bourgeois elitism associated with artistic practice and making the tools of filmmaking available to all.

Carrying the modernist idea of the active spectator to its logical conclusion, García Espinosa suggested, would eventually eliminate the difference between producer and viewer. Those already privileged enough to have a camera in the hand must practice filmmaking as a committed art – which most Cuban filmmakers did. Santiago Alvarez's fiercely partisan documentaries handled such diverse topics as Fidel Castro visiting the countryside and the war in Vietnam. Sara Gómez's *De cierta manera* (*One Way or Another*, 1974) mixed documentary and fictional footage to present the changing landscape of Havana.

Glauber Rocha coined the phrase 'an aesthetic of hunger' to describe a cinema that made the misery of Third World nations palpable. Referring to the Cinéma Novo's (new Latin American cinema) output as 'screaming, desperate films', he asserted that 'the cloak of Technicolor cannot hide, but only aggravates' this cancer of poverty, this starvation that is 'Brazil's national shame' (Stam and Johnson 1982: 70). Rocha believed that Third World cinema must have a commitment to truth, and required political freedom in order to flourish. From documentary-style filmmaking to a didactic contrast of high and popular culture to bravura camerawork, four of his major films – *Barravento* (1962), *Deus e o diabo na terra do sol* (*Black God, White Devil*, 1964), *Terra em transe* (*Land in Anguish*, 1967) and *Antonio das Mortes* (1969) – manifested the anger and violence that Rocha considered a requirement of committed cinema.

Although many Latin American nationals still possessed the social conditions to forge a new cinema at the beginning of the 1960s, by the decade's end military dictatorships had stamped out revolutionary filmmaking. However, Third Cinema continued to develop and grow – sometimes aided by revolutionary European directors such as Jean-Luc **Godard** and Chris Marker – in Africa (Ousmane Sembene in Senegal, Haile Gerima in Ethiopia, and the Italian Gillo Pontecorvo in Algeria), in India and in the Middle East.

References

Solanas, F. and Getino, O. (1983) 'Towards a Third Cinema' (first published 1969), in M. Chanan (ed.) *Twenty Five Years of the New Latin American Cinema*, London: BFI Publishing/Channel 4.

Stam, R. and Johnson, R. (1995) *Brazilian Cinema* (expanded edn), New York: Columbia University Press.

Further reading

Armes, R. (1987) *Third World Filmmaking in the West*, Berkeley: University of California Press.

Burton, J. (ed.) (1990) *Cinema and Social Change in Latin America*, Texas: University of Texas Press.

Chanan, M. (1985) *The Cuban Image: Cinema and Politics in Cuba*, London: BFI Publishing.

Diawara, M. (1993) *African Cinema*, London: Routledge.

Pines, J. and Willemen, P. (eds) (1990) *Questions of Third Cinema*, London: BFI Publishing.

KAREN BACKSTEIN

Todorov, Tzvetan

b. 1939

A theorist of linguistics, narrative discourse and culture, Tzvetan Todorov serves as a crucial link between the Russian formalists (see **Formalism**) and the French structuralists (see **structuralism and post-structuralism**), and has influenced major writers like Gérard **Genette**. Among his more linguistically focused works are groundbreaking studies of literary theorist Mikhail **Bakhtin** and a collection of articles on Russian formalists.

Todorov examines questions of narrative temporality and what he refers to as *aspect*, or the narrator's perception or events versus the character's. His analyses range from the nature of the literary and the state of literary theory to the rules and conventions of **narrative** and the elements of **genre**. In *The Fantastic: A Structural Approach to a Literary Genre* (1975), he rigorously outlines that genre's use of language, its themes and its place in the **canon**, while *The Poetics of Prose* (1977) includes discussion of the transformation of language into literature, the emergence of literary forms, the formation of character and the difference between **verisimilitude** and reality. Since *histoire* in French means not only story, but also history, he has taken on the larger concerns of nationalism, **race** and nationhood, always linking them to the 'master narratives' that affect real life (see **history/ histoire**). Two outstanding examples are *The Conquest of America: The Question of the Other* (1999) and *Facing the Extreme: Moral Life in the Concentration Camps* (1997), an examination of the heroic spirit, free will and a devotion to the 'ideal' in extraordinary circumstances.

References

Todorov, T. (1975) *The Fantastic: A Structural Approach to a Literary Genre*, Ithaca, NY: Cornell University Press.

—— (1977) *The Poetics of Prose*, trans. Richard Howard, Ithaca, NY: Cornell University Press.

—— (1997) *Facing the Extreme: Moral Life in the Concentration Camps*, New York: Henry Holt and Company

—— (1999) *The Conquest of America: The Question of the Other* (first published 1992), Norman: University of Oklahoma Press.

KAREN BACKSTEIN

transparent

One function of the **classic realist text** is to efface traces of its own making, so that its story seems present while camera, editing, lighting, etc., seem absent. In that moment, the film can seem transparent, a window on the world rather than a two-dimensional screen. Transparency is not, however, solely a product of cinematic manipulation. It also requires a decoder in each viewer's mind to make film technique invisible. In that sense, the classical Hollywood cinema as an institution includes a mode of consumption as well as a **mode of production**.

See also: classical Hollywood cinema and new Hollywood cinema; realism; reality effect

CLAY STEINMAN

U

uncanny

The uncanny refers to a feeling of non-familiarity which has a threatening and undermining aspect. Its use in this sense can be traced to Sigmund **Freud**, who introduces the term in a psychological study of terror. Freud describes as uncanny that which is on the limit of the familiar, and which thereby destabilizes clear boundaries. In uncanny situations, the strange infiltrates the familiar, questioning sanity, reason and self-assurance. The uncanny can be seen as one sensation invoked by **horror** films or *déjà vu* effects – a creeping feeling of something being not quite right.

PETRA KUPPERS

unconscious

A fundamental concept of **psychoanalysis**, the unconscious is a psychical system whose contents are the repressed ideas originally attached to the instincts. The unconscious must be seen as a dynamic system in continual interaction with all the psychical agencies. Thus the content of the unconscious continually strives to become conscious, but because the unconscious is governed by the primary processes of **condensation** and **displacement**, this content only reaches consciousness in the disguised forms of symptom, dream or parapraxis. Psychoanalytic textual analysis holds that all complex signifying systems overlap unconscious processes and so can be analysed symptomatically.

ANGELO RESTIVO

uses and gratifications

Uses and gratifications theory is a socio-psychological theory of media use, arising in the 1940s, as a response to the **Frankfurt School** concept of the mass **audience** as inert, passive recipients of media **effects**. In simple terms, uses and gratifications theory is concerned with what people do with media, not what media do to people. Media use is nearly always defined as 'watching television' – a limiting aspect of the theory, which does not usually consider the gratifications people derive from other cultural experiences, or from leisure activities in the past, before the invention of television.

The theory and its application have derived primarily from survey studies asking viewers to give reasons why they watch television. Katz, Blumler Gurevitch and Hass (1973) grouped thirty-five of these reasons into five categories: cognitive (learning); affective (emotional satisfaction); personal integrative (help with issues of personal identity); social integrative (help with issues of social identity); tension release (relaxation). Greenberg (1974) analysed 180 essays of London schoolchildren aged between 9 and 15 and found eight main reasons for using television: to pass time; to forget; to learn about things; to learn about myself; for arousal; for relaxation; for companionship; and as a habit. Rubin (1984) further reduced these categories to two: 'instrumental' uses (learning) and 'ritual' uses (habit and relaxation). Rubin also found that there were strong life-cycle influences on television use, with elderly people, for instance, relying on 'instrumental' uses to stay in touch with society.

More recently, Kubey and Csikzmentmilhayi (1990), in a study on television and 'the quality of life', attempted to set television viewing in a broader context of everyday life, characterizing it as part of a pattern of activities which helped 'reality maintenance'. Their method required individuals to make a note of their emotional state at different moments as they went about their daily business. The study, unusually, was thus able to compare the uses and gratifications of television watching with the satisfactions derived from other activities: working; public leisure; cultural and entertainment events; 'idling'; and meals. Kubey and Csikzcentmilhayi found that television was the most relaxing of all activities, and that it was one of the most enjoyed. But it was also the one that required least 'concentration, challenge and skill'. A simpler view of the uses of television is that viewing is primarily determined by 'availability to view' (Barwise and Ehrenberg 1996). In other words, if people have other things to do, they do not watch, and they are most likely to watch at '**prime time**' in the evening, because the day's work is over. This raises the question of whether content most determines people's choices about watching television, or whether they simply enjoy the act of viewing.

Critics of the theory have pointed out that, although it usefully describes what people do 'with television', it does not explain why they do it. Critics have also pointed out that uses and gratification theory does not take sufficient account of socio-cultural factors. Thus, for instance, the institutional fact that television is a major marketing tool, designed to influence patterns of **consumption** both of products and of ideologies, may not be seen as a major determining factor in how people 'use' or 'enjoy' it (see **ideology and hegemony; institution**).

A further drawback of the theory, ironically, is that it does not take account of effects. Although it rejects a simplistic effects model of television viewing, the question of social and cultural outcomes is still raised by findings that people rely heavily on television for information and for leisure. What are the consequences of this? From an institutional perspective, what are the implications for journalism, for instance, of people's desire to find television 'relaxing' (see **tabloid television**)? Uses and gratifications theory does not provide full answers to these questions.

References

Barwise, P. and Ehrenberg, A. (1996) *Television and its Audience*, London: Sage.

Greenberg, B. S. (1974) 'Gratifications of Television Viewing and their Correlates for British Children', in J. Blumler and E. Katz (eds) *The Uses of Mass Communications: Current Perspectives on Gratifications Research*, Beverly Hills, CA: Sage.

Katz, E., Blumler, J. and Gurevitch, M. and Haas, H. (1973) 'On the Use of Mass Media for Important Things', *American Sociological Review*, vol. 38, pp.164–81.

Kubey, R. and Csikzmentmihalyi, M. (1990) *Television and the Quality of Life*, Hillsdale, NJ: Lawrence Erlbaum Associates.

Rubin, A. (1984) 'Ritualized and Instrumental Television Viewing', *Journal of Communication*, vol. 34, pp. 67–77.

MAIRE MESSENGER DAVIES

utopia and dystopia

Sir Thomas More first coined 'utopia' in the sixteenth century, combining *eutopia* ('good place') and *outopia* ('no place') to suggest there is no place beyond contemporary life in which all things will be good (*Utopia*, 1516). Since More's invention, utopia has been used both as an inspiration for thinking about and planning for the future, and as a tool for analysing the failings of the present. More implied an ironic pessimism that now seems largely to have been forgotten. The irony was that people who seek utopia are blinded to its impossibility by their *desire* for perfection. Moreover, as Marxian critiques of utopian socialism show, utopian thought often fails to offer substantive changes in the present because of its fascination with the envisioned outcome (see **Marxist aesthetics**).

Nevertheless, utopian writing has enabled important political analysis, perhaps because the utopian genre serves as a legitimate arena for propositions of radical change. Charlotte Perkins Gilman's *Herland* (1915), for example, proffered a vision of **gender** equality in the context of socialism that was remarkable and radical for its time. Perhaps, then, utopia is its *own place*: an ideal genre in which surly pragmatism can be dismissed in pursuit of a vision that, by its very fictionality, comes to play an important role in the factual world.

Yet More's joke has turned sour in a society whose ultimate legitimacy rests squarely on myths of scientific-technological progress. Utopia now serves less as a critical insight and more as a description of the kinds of marketing strategies found, most recently, in relation to information technology and biomedical engineering.

Fundamentally, the quest for utopia is not merely part of western culture but its foundation. The kinds of scientific elites once seen as the revolutionaries to bring utopia into being (Bacon, *The New Atlantis*, 1627) have become the ghosts in the contemporary world machine. They do not exist as a governing force (as proposed in H. G. Wells' utopian *The Shape of Things to Come* [1933], filmed in 1936 by William Cameron Menzies as *Things to Come*), but as the inner logic to all that we propose as 'technological progress'. The impact and meaning of utopia no longer has the same critical force in societies which, ideologically, accept the quest for utopia as the justification for increasingly arbitrary and illiberal present policies.

Dystopian thought is a much more recent phenomenon than its utopian corollary, emerging with the generalized dominance of scientific thinking. It consists mainly in cultural and political criticism that implies the need for change in the present, not as a search for a better tomorrow, but in pursuit of a world that is, at least, not as bad as predicted. If Wells and Gilman stand as classic texts of utopia, then they find their dystopian counterparts in George Orwell's *1984* (1948) and Margaret Attwood's *A Handmaid's Tale* (1985).

Dystopian thought can be found principally in **science fiction**, both in print and in film and television. While science fiction has often served as the cultural force that gives meaning and substance to the logic that humanity commit itself to the path of scientific achievement, it has also been the pre-eminent critic of science, undermining its hubris and pervasiveness. *Blade Runner* (Ridley Scott, 1982), with its technologically charged vision of the future, merges with the *œuvre* of numerous **cyberspace** writers in successfully creating dismally dystopian worlds that are wrong precisely because of an overweening reliance on science and technology.

Utopianism may live on in eager **propaganda** about the way the **Internet** is reshaping human life. The Internet not only provides a means for many groups to disseminate utopian beliefs but also serves as the technological touchstone by which utopia may be achieved. The extent to which fictional accounts of cyberspatial futures are dystopian exemplifies the extent to which critical commentary on the supposed paths between the present, and the present-to-come, is now grounded in undercutting the utopian ideologies of late techno-capitalism.

Further reading

Kumar, K. (1987) *Utopia and Anti-Utopia in Modern Times*, Oxford: Blackwell.

Segal, H. P. (1987) *Technological Utopianism in American Culture*, Chicago: University of Chicago Press.

The Society for Utopian Studies, University of Toronto. Online. Available: http://www.utoronto.ca/utopia/

MATTHEW ALLEN

V

verisimilitude

Verisimilitude is sometimes used to propose that a plausible or believable relationship exists between a **text** and its referent in the world of experience, or, in more sophisticated terms, those discourses that are used to represent it (see **discourse**). In this usage, events and characters are believable or plausible, possess verisimilitude, if the reader or viewer can accept that such things are possible. Given the range and diversity of texts that might meet this condition, a more precise account of this concept would be needed for it to be analytically useful.

To some extent, Tzvetan **Todorov** (1997) offers this in theorizing literary genres (see **genre**). Genres, he argues, systematically exploit certain expectations on the part of the reader by creating their own regimes of verisimilitude, but not simply with regard to the world of experience. Todorov proposes that we can identify *two* ways in which verisimilitude is used in the analysis of fiction. There is a verisimilitude where a specific text relates to 'another generalized text which is called "common opinion" ' – that is, what people believe to be true, a discourse independent of the text. But in a generic text there is a verisimilitude where a specific text conforms to the rules of the genre, that is, to other discourses related to that text. The former is true to the norm of 'public opinion'; the latter to the norm of the genre, and there are as many verisimilitudes, in this sense, as there are genres.

Steve Neale (1990) has thoughtfully explored the implications of the ambivalence of verisimilitude in relation to fiction film. He makes the point that where some film genres draw on discourses independent of the text for what he calls the authenticity of 'cultural verisimilitude', instancing war films or police procedural thrillers which might use maps or newspaper headlines, other genres such as gothic **horror** and **science fiction** make more appeal to generic verisimilitude. Neale notes that some genres, he cites **melodrama** and war films, often seek to blur the distinctions between the two forms of verisimilitude and are marked by this tension. In consequence, the discussion of such films can also move confusingly between the forms when, for example, the lack of cultural verisimilitude is used to dismiss the generic heroics of a film like *The Deer Hunter* (Michael Cimino, 1978). But, as Todorov and Neale point out, the two notions of verisimilitude can melt into each other. The chief pleasure of a musical may be the singing and the dancing, its most generic elements and the points where cultural verisimilitude is least apparent (see **musical, the**). On the other hand, these generic features are now so widely known as to be part of the public's cultural knowledge.

Realism, in either a fictional or non-fictional mode, can be seen as a type of generic verisimilitude open to the same critical approach. Some texts, according to Todorov, appear to be shaped by the need to correspond to their referent when they actually correspond more to the 'laws' of their genre. A **documentary** film, whether expositional like those following the structure of the British Documentary Movement or observational like those of Frederick Wiseman, offers a referent drawn from historical reality, but the film will be consistent with the norms of the form. Both Roman **Jakobson** (1978) and Todorov (1977) associate what Neale later calls generic verisimilitude with 'classical form' so that challenges to this form are often rejected by conservative tendencies or embraced as radical departures in the name of greater realism. Wiseman's documentaries evoked this response.

In recognizing verisimilitude as an ambivalent concept, Jakobson, Todorov and Neale remind us of the obvious fact that the concept is as much about the relationship between the text and the viewer as the text and it referent.

References

Jakobson, R. (1978) 'On Realism in Art', in Ladislav Matejka and Krystyna Pomorska (eds) *Readings in Russian Poetics: Formalist and Structuralist Views*, Ann Arbor, MI: University of Michigan Press.

Neale, S. (1990) 'Questions of Genre', *Screen*, vol. 31, no.1, pp. 35–57.

Todorov, T. (1977) 'An Introduction to Verisimilitude', in *The Poetics of Prose*, trans. Richard Howard, Ithaca: Cornell University Press.

—— (1977) 'The Typology of Detective Fiction', in *The Poetics of Prose*, trans. Richard Howard, Ithaca: Cornell University Press.

Further reading

Caughie, J. (1991) 'Adorno's Reproach: Repetition, Difference and Television Genres', *Screen*, vol. 32, no. 2.

PHILIP SIMPSON

vertical integration

A company is vertically integrated when it owns and controls every area of its enterprise: manufacturing, wholesaling and retailing. In the film and television industries, vertical integration requires ownership of production, distribution and exhibition facilities. This strategy emerged very early in the American film industry, and the Hollywood studio system became a model for integrated media ownership (see **studio systems**). Contemporary audio-visual industries are integrated via cross-media ownership, with **multinational** media corporations controlling multiple distribution outlets including film, television and home **video**. At the same time, horizontal integration – the ownership of different entertainment media by a single corporation – allows companies to market film and television through ancillary products such as soundtrack recordings, radio networks and print publishing. Historically, the result of vertical integration has been a high degree of market control by a small number of companies – an oligopoly.

In the first decade of the American film industry, Thomas Edison's Motion Picture Patents Corporation attempted to form a monopoly through technology patent pooling and licensing. The failure of this strategy in 1912–1915 was followed by the formation of vertically integrated studios during the rapid expansion of the American industry. Famous Players-Lasky initiated this shift by purchasing the Paramount distribution company in 1916 and a large chain of first-run theatres by 1925 (Gomery 1986: 27–8). Other studios followed suit, forming a structure of market hegemony (see **ideology and hegemony**) that effectively forced all other producers to distribute through the 'big five' and 'little three' studios (the 'big five' major studios were Paramount, Metro-Goldwyn-Mayer, Warner Bros, Twentieth Century-Fox, RKO-Radio; the 'little three' were United Artists, Universal, Columbia). Ownership of first-run theatre chains was the studios' primary advantage, because no other distribution company could gain an equal share of the market in major cities. Theatres represented 90 per cent of the assets of the 'big five' studios, and their box-office figures were used to determine each year's production budgets and schedules. With the country divided geographically to allow each studio control over exhibition in a particular region, the system allowed the studios to operate as a 'collusive unit', maximizing profit and minimizing risk for all (Gomery 1986: 14).

By 1925, international export amounted to roughly one-half of the American film industry's revenue (Gomery 1986: 18), and the 1945 formation of the Motion Picture Export Association allowed Hollywood studios to consolidate foreign distribution and exhibition even as they were being prosecuted under anti-trust laws in the United States. In 1948 Paramount was ruled to be an illegal monopoly, and a 'divorcement decree' forced the studio and others to sell off their domestic theatre chains. Foreign ownership was not affected by the decree, however, and US studios continued to operate a distribution cartel overseas (Guback 1985). The post-divorcement trend towards cross-media integration was initiated by the Disney studio, which added television production and theme parks to its feature film business, using each new entertainment outlet to promote the others. The rest of the Hollywood studios quickly moved into television production, though they were prevented from owning broadcast licences by cross-media ownership regulations. The take-over and recapitalization of film studios in the 1980s and 1990s resulted in the incorporation of film studios into larger frameworks of media production and marketing, with integration between all aspects of film, video, television, music and merchandise production and dissemination.

The **regulation** of broadcasting in many countries has been based on the notion of a 'natural monopoly' governed by the state because it was a singular medium of communication requiring monitoring for political content and technical quality. In most countries, therefore, broadcasting networks were either non-commercial or regulated to remain economically independent from other large media corporations. The 1980s and 1990s, however, saw the widespread deregulation of television ownership, spurred by new delivery systems which challenged the 'natural monopoly' argument and fuelled a transnational media economy (Barker 1997: 29). In countries like Mexico and Brazil, the lack of cross-media ownership regulation has resulted in broadcast companies that produce the majority of their own programming as well as owning distribution outlets like cable and home video (Sinclair *et al.* 1996: 49).

See also: classical Hollywood cinema and new Hollywood cinema; deregulation, the United Kingdom; deregulation, the United States

References

Barker, C. (1997) *Global Television: An Introduction*, Oxford: Blackwell.

Gomery, D. (1986) *The Hollywood Studio System*, New York: St. Martin's Press.

Guback, T. (1985) 'Hollywood's International Market', in T. Balio (ed.) *The American Film Industry*, Madison: University of Wisconsin Press.

Sinclair, J., Jacka, E. and Cunningham, S. (eds) (1996) *New Patterns in Global Television: Peripheral Vision*, Oxford: Oxford University Press.

SARAH BERRY

Vertov, Dziga (Denis Kaufman)

b. 1896; d. 1954

Renewed interest in politics and film form in the late 1960s revived engagement with the work of Denis Kaufman, born in Bialystok (now in Poland). Under the name 'Dziga Vertov', usually translated as 'spinning top', Kaufman was committed to making films which demonstrated their potential as mass medium and art form. He wanted to bring the ideals and images of the emergent Union of Soviet Socialist Republics to its disparate populations, many of whom were illiterate. To this end, he edited and filmed newsreels, including the monthly *Kino-pravda* ('Film-truth', or 'Cine-truth') from 1922 to 1925, and went on to make documentaries of which *One Sixth of the World* (1926) and *The Man with the Movie Camera* (1929) are the most famous. Concurrently, he wrote polemical manifestos attacking existing cinematic forms.

Vertov vigorously opposed studio-based fictions and wanted to disseminate awareness of the new realities of Soviet Russia by making and screening documentaries, using the Agit-train for screenings, as he travelled round Russia. He undercut the illusionism of even **documentary** film by using techniques – dissolves, repetitions, split images, ellipses, unusual montages and rhythms – whereby spectators were constantly re-oriented in relation to the realities on- and off-screen.

Audiences found his films difficult then, as audiences do now, and he lost government support in the 1930s. But the compulsion to both theorize and demonstrate the potential of film in a cause beyond the personal has proved inspirational to subsequent filmmakers.

PHILIP SIMPSON

video

The smallest and least expensive video production tools are the camcorder and the video cassette recorder (VCR). These instruments have found their way into many homes, with interesting results for the status of the video medium. As in the cases of commercial and artistic uses of video technology, video in the home reflects a mixture of purposes: in part, it represents a new way of achieving familiar goals; in part, it provides new or significantly enhanced functionalities. As with video art (see **video and art**), the expansion of video technology into the home – into the hands of members of the general public, as opposed to specialists and production companies – raises questions about the traditional divisions, in television and video, between those in control of the means of production and those in the role of consumer. It would be very misleading to suggest that any real revolution has taken place in these areas, but at the very least some important and intriguing shifts have begun to take place.

The VCR has been hailed as a tool of liberation for the traditional television viewer. It offers a means of rearranging the broadcast schedule through taping programmes and watching them at unscheduled times (thus interfering with the careful competitive planning of the various stations and networks) and the means to remove (or speed up through) commercials, a viewing strategy which, if pursued consistently, entirely strips the medium of commercial television of its single reason for existence. Viewers are also able to bypass regularly scheduled television programming entirely by renting or purchasing film and video material for VCR playback. It has never appeared, however, that these freedoms have led to any radical public reassessment of the nature of the medium, or of the power structures imposed on and expressed through it.

Compact video cameras – so-called camcorders – offer yet another level of freedom, this time in the matter of production. While not sophisticated in comparison with professional-grade production equipment, camcorders do allow non-professionals access to video technology for a variety of purposes, which was rarely the case prior to the miniaturization and popularization of video cameras. Many uses of camcorders duplicate, or nearly duplicate, the functionalities of other media and materials; the camcorder has almost entirely replaced the home-movie camera (and is probably in more widespread use than the home-movie camera had been), and in some cases fulfils the role of the photograph album. Most camcorder usage among the general public has been along these lines; thus the dissemination of video technology in this fashion has not, in the event, generated any serious shifting of the balances of power and control in the media and image-making industries.

Indeed, the popularization of camcorders coincided with the development, on commercial television, of programmes consisting largely of home-video footage donated to the networks (such as *America's Funniest Home Videos*). Such footage only amounts to a few hours a week – a tiny percentage of existing home-video footage overall – but the prominent use of this material as an object of ridicule suggests one strategy in use by the existing broadcast industry for containing any disruptive potential that the public's access to video production technology might have created.

But camcorders and amateur videography have also played a more serious role with respect to modern culture, including mainstream television. Sometimes by chance and sometimes with planning, amateur videographers have documented on tape a number of important social and political events; the most famous of these is the 1992 tape showing the police beating of Los Angeles resident Rodney King. Politically-active citizens have used camcorders to document events of many kinds: riots, meetings, demonstrations, strikes, etc. – and in some cases have made their tapes available on a wider basis, through public access presentations or distribution by television production collectives such as Paper Tiger Television.

DAVID A. BLACK

video and art

In the same way that the media of film and television share many characteristics but are not identical, so too the medium of video is closely related, but not identical to, television. Technically, video refers to the videotape medium, which in many cases figures in television production but need not do so (for example, when television is broadcast live or produced on film). In some respects, video is a less expensive medium than film. Supplies are cheaper, and there is no need for chemical development. Over a period of years, video technology has become available in a number of cheaper, smaller, more portable forms. This has made video technology more widely available for use outside of the mainstream of professional, commercial television. Video is certainly the medium of choice for use in the home, for both production and exhibition.

Videotape was introduced in the mid-1950s. The new technology played two principal roles in commercial television (to which its use was almost entirely restricted until trends towards miniaturization made equipment more widely accessible in the 1960s and beyond). First, video served as a new production medium in place of film; tape could be edited, it could be brought to air faster and without chemical development. Video never replaced film as a television production medium, but it did offer an alternative in cases where it made sense for economic and/or scheduling reasons. Second, videotape offered a new means of capturing and preserving live broadcasts, which had previously either vanished forever or been saved only in cases where a kinescope – essentially a film camera recording a broadcast off a television screen – was available. The easy recording of live broadcasts also made for easier re-transmission, or even the use of real-time, live-looking production techniques in instances where broadcasting did not take place at the same time (see **live television**).

In commercial broadcasting, video technology thus provided an alternative means for achieving some of the existing functionality of film, while also introducing new or significantly transformed functionalities. The same pattern – partly a new means to a familiar end, partly a new functionality – emerges, too, in the areas outside of commercial television where video technology has played a major role.

Video art

Since the 1960s, video has emerged as the medium of choice in the work of a great number of artists. The very idea of video as an art medium required a certain amount of acclimatization on the part of the art world; both the technological basis of the medium and its associations with commercialism and triviality created a certain amount of resistance. However, the achievements of artists in the field brought about recognition of the medium by critics, archives and museums, non-commercial broadcast organizations such as the American PBS, and governmental arts funding agencies.

Not surprisingly, considering the sensory richness of their medium, video artists often come to video with backgrounds in other arts, with the result that video art is wide-ranging and eclectic. In their book *Illuminating Video*, Doug Hall and Sally Jo Fifer make the observation that: 'Video's pedigree is anything but pure...its stock of early practitioners includes a jumble of musicians, poets, documentarians, sculptors, painters, dancers, and technology freaks. Its lineage can be traced to the discourses of art, science, linguistics, technology, mass media, and politics' (Hall and Fifer 1990: 14). Video artists differ from one another as much as artists in any medium do; there is no single style or artistic philosophy characteristic of video art. Still, video artists do confront certain issues in common, and share a number of constraints and challenges – some specific to their medium, some more widely shared by artists in other media as well.

Video is an expensive medium for an artist. Unlike writing, for instance, which calls for minimal materials, even the simplest work of video art requires complex electronic equipment. Technological issues have always rested at the heart of video art. The beginnings of the flourishing of video as an art form are often traced to the appearance in the mid-1960s of the Sony PortaPak, a relatively affordable and light-weight video camera which brought about an explosion in video production of various kinds, including **documentary**, on the part of independent videographers and artists. With regard to the availability of technology as well as its use for innovative purposes, video artists exist in a somewhat uneasy symbiosis with the world of commercial television. Sometimes the artists take the initiative, as in the case of the Paik-Abe synthesizer, an image synthesizer co-invented by influential artist Nam June Paik and, in its time, on the cutting edge of image manipulation. Sometimes commercial television provides technologies or even 'found' video materials for artists; a well-known example is the video *Wonder Woman* by Dara Birnbaum, which consists of ironic, even comic repetitions and manipulations of images of Lynda Carter in the role of Wonder Woman from the television programme of that name.

In one sense, much of the work of video artists is **oppositional** to commercial television, often explicitly inviting the viewer to think critically about commercial image-making (as in the Birnbaum tape) or implicitly leading the viewer to understand that video technology can serve other purposes than that of providing frenetically paced, commercially motivated entertainment (as in the slow, meditative, oversized video installations of Bill Viola). But at the same time, experimentation by video artists can find its way into the commercial mainstream. Much of the now-hackneyed image manipulation of MTV, for example, looks a lot like earlier video art; this is true even of television commercials. As Martha Rosler writes in her essay 'Video: Shedding The Utopian Moment': 'Nothing could better suit the consciousness industry than to have artists playing about its edges embroidering its forms and quite literally developing new strategies for ads and graphics' (in Hall and Fifer 1990: 49).

Lacking the history and traditional credibility of arts like painting and poetry – which, themselves, have suffered tremendous neglect by modern societies and governments – video art has had to fight for recognition as a legitimate art form. The very idea of visiting a museum to see video tapes or installations still strikes many people as absurd. None the less, certain key museums have taken the lead in presenting video art to the public and thereby conferring on it a certain institutional legitimacy; these include the Museum of Modern Art (MOMA) and the Whitney Museum of American Art, both in New York City. Archives devoted to the preservation and study of video art have also been established, notably Electronic Arts Intermix in New York. In 1970, the New York State Council on the Arts became the first governmental arts funding agency to award grants to independent video-makers (Hall and Fifer 1990: 56).

Still, even legitimacy of this kind is controversial among video artists. Museum exhibition signals a kind of acceptance into mainstream culture which, for some artists, carries dangerous baggage. 'Perhaps the hardest consequence of museumization,' writes Martha Rosler, 'is the "professionalization" of the field, with its inevitable worship of what are called "production values." These are nothing more than a set of stylistic changes rung on the givens of commercial broadcast television' (in Hall and Fifer 1990: 49). To the extent that museums and other mainstream institutions, in spite of their non-commercial status, tend to internalize the aesthetic values of commercial television, only those video works which reflect those values will be acceptable to those institutions. This puts artificial and troubling limits on the extent to which video artists eschewing those values – for aesthetic, political or even financial reasons (as the achievement of what Rosler calls 'production values' can be very expensive) – can be accepted by the art establishment.

References

Hall, D. and Fifer, S. J. (1990) *Illuminating Video: An Essential Guide to Video Art*, New York: Aperture Foundation, Inc. (This collection includes essays by artists, critics and curators, covering a wide range of historical, aesthetic and political topics related to video art and documentary practices.)

Further reading

Zippay, L. (ed.) (1991) *Electronic Arts Intermix: Video*, New York: Electronic Arts Intermix.

DAVID A. BLACK

viewer

The simplest meaning of the term 'viewer' is a person who watches (and listens to) a film or television show. Film theorists have expanded on this **common sense** definition, however, by drawing on Wayne Booth's literary notion of the implied reader. This structuralist account suggests that the actual reader of a novel, poem or play must be distinguished from the implied reader, which is a subject *position* within the text, part of the **narrative** contract (see **subject and subjectivity**). By analogy, then, the film and/or television viewer is not just a flesh-and-blood individual but also a cultural construct of the **text**, a complex, overdetermined *function* whose perceptions (and conceptions) are positioned and determined by the **style** and ideology of any given film or television show (see **determination; ideology and hegemony**).

Whether derived from Lacanian **psychoanalysis**, Althusserian Marxism, **sender/receiver** or apparatus-based model, or the system of the **suture**, this notion implies that the viewer automatically identifies with the camera and/or a **character** within the **diegesis** (see also **Althusser, Louis; Lacan, Jacques; Marxist aesthetics**). Most assume that it is *the text* that is doing the meaning and, therefore, that the viewer is positioned as a mere manipulandum of textual interpellation.

Alternatively, the viewer can be seen as a part of one or more demographic groups – based on **race**, **class**, **gender**, age, sexual orientation, etc. – that determines his/her understanding of media texts. Other theories, such as **phenomenology** and reception theory (see **reading and reception theory**), give the viewer more credit (and freedom) to interpret a text according to his/her own interpretative schema.

See also: encoding-decoding model; feminist theory

Further reading

Baudry, J.-L. (1974–75) 'Ideological Effects of the Basic Cinematographic Apparatus', *Film Quarterly*, vol. 28, no. 2, pp. 39–47.

Browne, N. (1976) 'The Spectator-in-the-Text: The Rhetoric of *Stagecoach*', *Film Quarterly*, vol. 29, no. 2, pp. 26–38.

Mayne, J. (1993) *Cinema and Spectatorship*, London: Routledge.

FRANK P. TOMASULO

violence

The concept of violence has much currency in film and television studies. In this entry, the relationship between the concept and various areas are investigated, grounded in media effects debates and representation debates. Television and film and the ways in which they are consumed are not thought to directly or physically harm people, but many groups within society claim that they perpetrate other forms of harm. The nature of this harm relates to the definition of violence that is used. The entry discusses two main questions: what is conceptualized as being violated by film and television forms and representations, and how does the violation occur?

The violence done by media forms to sections of the public is a long-standing theme in the discussion of cultural products. At all points in the history of mass media, panics have surrounded the accessibility of certain products to certain populations, and claims for **censorship** surround most media practices. In these debates, a group of 'experts' argue for restrictions to be put on certain media in order to protect members of society who are conceptualized as 'weak'. Media studies conceptualizes the violence envisaged by these experts as the violence of disruption of the *status quo*, and their worries are analysed as expressions of fear of a shifting of social relations.

Women's literary output and access to reading material was under constant discussion from the 1600s onwards. They were considered weak and easily influenced. Women's minds were constructed as 'inferior', and not only were universities closed to them, but their minds were feared to be easily 'infected' by highly emotional material.

In the nineteenth century, penny-dreadfuls (in the United Kingdom) or dime novels (in the United States), cheap, individually-bound thrillers with action plots, available to buy from travelling salesmen, were attacked for perverting minds with the seeds of violence and moral corruption. These pamphlets were accessible to many who were not usually considered traditional 'readers', and issues of **class** entered the debate. At the turn of the century, music halls provided a similar focus for upper-class fears of lower-class 'revelry', debauchery and overexcited stimulation. The violence at stake here was unrest and revolt. Matthew **Arnold** characterized popular culture as 'anarchy': as a culture that questions social stability. Schools in working-class areas were seen as beacons of civilization and outposts in a barbaric environment: 'good culture' was something brought to the lower classes by the upper classes.

These two examples of **gender** and class issues show how social roles, moralities and beliefs are associated with assumptions about the violent influence of media. The fact that commercial mass media, from the cheap reproduction of sensationalist writings to the transnational availability of the satellite network BSkyB, are hard to control and police by a self-appointed elite make these debates more urgent for those who see their values threatened by popular culture.

In the mass media violence debates of the twentieth century, a new group is conceived as under threat: children. A range of scholars have argued that similar to women and the lower classes, children act as signifiers for a specific cultural self-image. The values invested in them underlie the ideological foundations of society. The values of innocence and purity can be seen in this light: in a social world influenced by latent religious systems, the purity of the child can function as a repository for all that is lost to adults, as a utopian vision. Conceptualizing children not as inherently different from adults but as equally guided by 'base instincts' can destroy a core focus of social endeavour and activate feelings of uncertainty. The mass media have generated many sources of information, world-views and belief systems, and their multiple voices undermine coherence. The anxieties associated with modernism have focused on the detrimental effects of the mass media, most influentially in the **Frankfurt School** (see **modernism and post-modernism**). Bringing children and the mass media together therefore acts as a powerful source of social unease (see **children and media**).

Various effect models have consequences for the conceptualization of violence in the mass media. The main thrust of research into television effects did not initially focus on issues such as potentially raised fear through continued exposure to images which show violence in society, but on the copying of watched behaviour by children. How can aggressive behaviour be linked to television, film or video watching? The positions can be polarized into two main arguments: the '**hypodermic model**' and the '**uses and gratifications** model'. The first model sees the consumer of media products as passive, and likens the effect of media representation to an injection or infection. Following the view of the mass media as a levelling, damaging, capitalist venture, put forward by the Frankfurt School, mainly American researchers in the 1950s and 1960s attributed rising social violence to the influence of the new television medium. Experiments were conducted, influenced by behaviourist models such as B. F. Skinner's. One of the most famous experiments shows the methodological problems encountered by the hypodermic model. The 'Bobo doll experiment' was documented by Bandura and Walters in 1963, and focused explicitly on copied aggression in children. Simply, the experiment exposed children to films of adults damaging a doll. Later, the children were left alone with similar dolls, and showed behaviour patterns similar to those seen in the adults: they hit their dolls. The conclusion drawn at the time was that violent images on television are equally enacted directly by the children.

This experiment saw the children as mindless and empty, without any thought patterns of their own. The researchers were not interested in finding the meanings that the children attributed to the experiment situation. This included the possibility that the children construed the necessity to please the researchers by manipulating the doll – why else were they put into a room with it? Furthermore, the experiment did not take into account the complex situations in which media consumption takes place. This includes patterns specific to the media products, such as genre and narrative, as well as social patterns such as peer pressure or framing of the media experience by the (dis)comfort of home.

In opposition to the hypodermic model, the 'uses and gratifications' model of media effects sees the consumer of representations as an active, informed maker of choices. The media are used for psychological and social purposes such as to define oneself as part of a group. This relates to research in constructivist psychology, which sees media consumers engaged in writing and rewriting scripts of their interaction with the social and cultural world. Viewers process and evaluate information, building up 'media competences'.

These two opposing views of viewers as active or passive, subordinated to representation or shaping it in their reading, are supplemented by research in the field of cultural studies, which sees viewer choice and negotiation within the boundaries and constraints of the media industry. A child watching 'H-Man' comics on satellite television would thus be able to categorize the experience according to his/her media literacy, drawing on his/her understanding of genre codes. Interaction with parents or schoolmates would anchor this form of knowledge. The violence seen would be processed as appropriate to the generic conventions of the cartoon, but not the 'real world'. This message is reinforced in the narrative: good wins over evil, and the excessive force used in this struggle socializes the child not into 'disruptive' violence, but to the codes of a social world which relies on 'justified' exertion of brutality (such as police control or the death penalty).

This approach which views media violence as embedded in a social system tends not to polarize 'good' and 'bad' violence, but to investigate the social structures that underlie these value judgements. From this point of view, the violence inherent in the Bible, accepted forms of 'high art' including images of the bleeding and broken body of Saint Sebastian, or news reports of Rwanda, is of as much interest as the reported reactions to *Natural Born Killers* (Oliver Stone, 1994). Violent representations are seen as concordant with 'accepted' values in a social system: H-Man's use of physical strength to 'positive' purposes dovetails with images of masculinity in western society. The content of 'violence' is set by dominant views in a hegemonic system, and is layered with meanings emerging from other aspects of a culture, such as gender roles.

This discussion links to another area concerned with the analysis of violent images. Many political interest groups have used textual analysis of media texts to point to inequalities and violence perpetrated and perpetuated by images. The most visible of these debates emerged from **pornography**. From an analysis of the violence enacted on women in hard-core pornography developed a critique of all objectifying representations of women – gender violence is seen as the core of visual representation. This critique echoes Laura **Mulvey**'s analysis of **patriarchy** structured into the narrative and visuals of Hollywood cinema (see **feminist theory**). A similar argument was launched by minority groups: the exclusion of images of gay, lesbian, people of colour or disabled people from the mainstream is an enactment of social violence. A call for 'positive images' tried to redress the imbalances of representation. As a result, television series such as *Star Trek* spin-offs or *Roseanne* include the occasional lesbian or disabled character. But since these characters are still marked as 'special', they cannot carry the utopian values of a society without divisions (see **stereotype**).

The view that all representation is violent since it necessarily silences many voices has shaped the political concerns of cultural studies and has found entry in a range of textual-based disciplines. The awareness of the consequences of representation in all media has led the way to new ways of engaging with representation, from interdisciplinary conceptual art practices in the fine arts to consumer consultancy groups and minority programming on **public service broadcasting**.

Taking this point further, the relationship between language and violence is investigated by theorists such as **Foucault** and **Derrida**, and Teresa de **Lauretis** shows how these theories of representation themselves are implicated in the violence of naming, of dividing and allocating positions. She shows the consequences of the positions taken by some philosophers, who want to dislodge power structures by 'becoming Woman'. With this, they mean that philosophy should enter the undifferentiated, other space to the male centre. But by gendering this other space, the binary of man/woman and the power structure implied is naturalized. Women are doubly put into their places.

The multiple uses of the term 'violence' in relation to media show that the concept is highly evocative, if vague. Acting violently, physically or symbolically is of vital importance to a culture which exists through power differentials, and where one group is elevated based on the subjection of another. The media have been seen as the language by which a culture tells its origin and workings, and maintains and contests its power distributions. For this reason, questions of media violence can never be limited to media psychology, but will always point to the larger value systems of culture.

Further reading

Barker, M. and Petley, J. (1997) *Ill Effects: The Media/Violence Debate*, London and New York: Routledge.

de Lauretis, T. (1989) 'The Violence of Rhetoric. Considerations on Representations and Gender', in N. Armstrong and L. Tennenhouse (eds) *The Violence of Representation*, London and New York: Routledge.

PETRA KUPPERS

Virilio, Paul

b. 1932

Architect, aesthetic philosopher and critic, Paul Virilio's trajectory has been shaped by wars (the Second World War, Algeria and the Gulf War), engagement with built forms and a quest for social justice. Co-founder of *Architecture principe* (1963) and professor and president of the Ecole spécial d'architecture in Paris, he has also produced provocative works of social theory. His work reverberates with the implications of modernities – speed, technology, elimination of space and time. With cinema and television, he focuses not on **text** or **audience**, but on the implications of media as social and cultural phenomena: the creation of virtual experience, the manipulation of movement, time and space in simultaneity and imagery, and the relation of these to new forms of society, the city and the state. His analyses, political and formal,

underscore the crisis of late capitalism taking shape through **globalization** and a loss of local meanings.

Further reading

Derian, J. (1998) *The Virilio Reader*, Oxford: Basil Blackwell.

Virilio, P. (1989) *War and Cinema: The Logistics of Perception*, London: Verso.

GARY McDONOGH

virtual reality

Virtual reality (VR) usually suggests computer-generated simulations of sight, sound and touch that overwhelm users' disbelief, render imagination irrelevant and make the computer mediation completely invisible. Yet any attempt to understand VR simply in this fashion will fail. Indeed, because virtual reality technology – as it is ideally understood, commercially promoted and so regularly represented in popular culture – remains as fictional as the simulated worlds it might one day create, the meaning of 'virtual reality' must necessarily be a matter of the subtleties of **discourse**, rather than the operation of machines. Sherman and Judkins (1992: 33) implied as much when they described the phrase 'virtual reality' as 'poetic, mysterious, elusive'. They suggest that Jaron Lanier, who originated the term, made his most significant contribution to the technology of computer-generated simulations by giving it a label whose power far exceeds its capacity to deliver what it claims.

Contrary to the technological hopes of pioneers such as Lanier, virtual reality's most significant status comes from its use in popular cultural discussions of the future of computing. Moreover, even by the accelerated standards of cultural production, virtual reality has enjoyed a short public importance. Virtual reality hardly registered on the collective screen of media consciousness until the late 1980s. By the mid-1990s, however, public attention was focused increasingly on the **Internet**: 'cyberspace' had become the new motif of high technology dreaming. With this change, too, came public awareness of the extant realities of networked computer-based communication between humans which, even in plain text, were more fulfilling than promises about human–computer interaction.

In the few short years between those dates, virtual reality occupied a prominence out of proportion to what was technologically possible. Sustained by mythic western uncertainty about the status of the fleshy body – the '**body**' that was simultaneously vulnerable to viral infection and so amenable to cyborg augmentation – VR captured the public imagination. The science fiction writer J. G. Ballard's claim that 'sex + technology = the future' made perfect sense as 'teledildonics' (proposed computer-mediated sex as good as the 'real' thing, without the risks inherent in actual bodily contact) provided another media headline (see Springer 1996: 52 ff.). What VR meant, then, was the utopian or dystopian *idea* of experiencing sensations and events without them actually occurring (see **utopia and dystopia**). It was an easy leap from there to using VR to signify almost anything that people thought computers might do one day.

Perhaps the real desires being satiated by VR were more prosaic. Seeking to continue the *personal* computer revolution, the information technology industry benefited from the popularization of human–computer interaction promised by VR even while, in most cases, it was selling forms of entertainment that were as two-dimensional and screen-based as the media with which it was competing. At the same time, the military connections of VR came more clearly into focus through the televised images of the Gulf War in 1990. The research and development of VR technology (notably helmet-mounted displays) was in large measure funded by the US Air Force. Furthermore, many of the consumer-oriented battle simulations that are currently the main form of mass VR technology were the re-application of combat training technologies to the commercial market.

Yet virtual reality has a contested meaning. The term is also used more loosely to describe the *highly* imaginative acts of creation, maintenance and activity in online, computer-mediated communities of discussion (Turkle 1996). Some people continue to use VR to describe the forms of social space found in 'virtual communities' and 'virtual universities', perhaps as a more direct alternative to the overused 'cyberspace'.

Virtual reality research and development continue; the combat and flight simulations available to both military or aviation personnel and consumers are inspiring in their ability to mimic reality and immerse users in an environment which they believe to be real. Yet, in popular consciousness and commercial publicity, VR no longer has the same relevance it once did, principally because the Internet has produced a new form of understanding about the relationship between societies, human individuals and information technologies.

See also: Internet and the World Wide Web; technological change

References

Sherman, B. and Judkins, P. (1992) *Glimpses of Heaven, Visions of Hell: Virtual Reality and its Implications*, London: Hodder and Stoughton.

Springer, C. (1996) *Electronic Eros*, Austin: University of Texas Press.

Turkle, S. (1996) 'Constructions and Reconstructions of Self in Virtual Reality', in Timothy Druckery (ed.) *Electronic Culture: Technology and Visual Representation*, New York: Aperture.

MATTHEW ALLEN

vox pop/man in the street

Vox populi, Latin for 'voice of the people', is a convention widely used in much media output. Producers like vox pops because they are easy and cheap to produce and are generally popular with audiences who often find them humorous, as well as appearing to let the general public give their point of view. In television, the public's answers are often strung together to give a variety of voices and opinions or perhaps a common point of view, depending on the editing.

PHILIP RAYNER

voyeurism

The term voyeurism refers to a form of behaviour linked to a psychological condition: a sexualized desire to see, in particular to witness, sexual acts indirectly. The voyeur has a distanced relationship to the world, and cannot engage directly with his or her object of desire. Instead, sexual gratification is achieved via the prying, violating gaze (see **gaze, the**). The mechanism of cinema, where anonymous spectators sit in the dark and watch a spectacle unfold, has been called voyeuristic, thereby sexualizing the cinematic engagement. The term has strongly resonated within film studies, in particular in feminist film theory and the writings of Laura **Mulvey**.

See also: feminist theory

PETRA KUPPERS

W

watershed

The notion of a 'watershed' was introduced in Britain by the British Broadcasting Corporation (BBC) to create a division between 'family viewing' and television programmes that may contain more 'adult' language and/or sex and violence, and to signal parental responsibility for post-watershed viewing. It is a voluntary practice that now generally informs terrestrial broadcasting in Britain, but is often a cause for debate and criticism by those who complain when broadcasters show material before the 9 p.m. watershed which they consider unsuitable for younger audiences. Its effectiveness is becoming difficult to gauge with the increased range of **cable and satellite** services and increasing 'time-shifting' as a result of rising **video** cassette recorder ownership, often by younger viewers.

See also: censorship; children and media

PHILIP RAYNER

Weber, Max

b. 1864; d. 1920

A founder of the discipline of sociology, Max Weber was heavily engaged in the project of nation-building in Germany in the 1890s. Weber was primarily interested in the relationship between shared world-views and social structure evident in his most famous book, *The Protestant Work Ethic and the Spirit of Capitalism*. Weber studied the genesis of western civilization, and developed many of the historical and sociological methods of research used and critiqued in cultural studies today. Weber was a profoundly influential scholar of religion, language and law, though today he is remembered most for his contributions to theories of modernity.

Weber, like Karl **Marx**, was primarily interested in understanding human society under western capitalism. However, whereas Marx focused on alienation, Weber was mainly interested in rationalization. Synthesizing theories of Marx and **Nietzsche**, Weber argued that modern economy and science subjects human beings to the universal rationalization of life. The 'iron cage' of subordination to rationality depends on forces that are themselves irrational. Weber was neutral about rationalization because he saw its achievement in creating the institutions of modern western society as ambiguous. Weber's influence in cultural studies as a proto-theorist of **discipline** and power, taken up by Michel **Foucault**, is often unacknowledged.

See also: Orientalism

Further reading

Lowith, K. (1993) *Max Weber and Karl Marx*, London: Routledge.
Giddens, A. (1972) *Politics and Sociology in the Thought of Max Weber*, Hong Kong: Macmillan.

PAULA CHAKRAVARTTY

Western, the

One of the most enduring of American film genres (see **genre**), the Western draws its subject matter and iconography from the cowboys, 'Indians', outlaws, settlers, horses, towns, covered wagons and other figures and tropes of American popular culture and history (see **icon; popular, the**). The Western's semantic components and meanings (see **semantics**) have undergone shifts in response to changing attitudes about the frontier and western expansion and the concomitant genocide of Native American cultures, or about the (im)possibility of heroism in the modern world. Structurally, the Western in any of its guises still remains focused on the opposition between rugged individualism and community concerns, law and order, savagery and civilization, domesticity and independence, white and non-white.

ADRIENNE L. McLEAN

white

In his book *White*, Richard **Dyer** explores representations of **race**, and concludes that: 'Non-whiteness...is always...particular and has no ordinariness. Whites are the one particular group that can claim to take up the non-particular position of ordinariness' (Dyer 1997: 222–3). The status of 'whiteness' as a social construction has often been passed by in work on race, leaving whiteness – as a dominant position – relatively unexamined (Pfeil 1995).

Filmic representations of white masculinity in the 1990s, especially in the film *Falling Down* (Joel Schumacher, 1993), have provoked work examining how the dominant subject position of straight white masculinity has become less able to claim a universal or non-particular status (Davies 1995; Gabriel 1996).

See also: queer theory; subject and subjectivity

References

Davies, J. (1995) ' "I'm the Bad Guy?": *Falling Down* and White Masculinity in 1990s Hollywood', *Journal of Gender Studies*, vol. 4, no. 2, pp. 145–52.

Dyer, R. (1997) *White*, London: Routledge.
Gabriel, J. (1996) 'What Do You Do When Minority Means You? *Falling Down* and the Construction of "Whiteness" ', *Screen*, vol. 37, no. 2.
Pfeil, F. (1995) *White Guys: Studies in Postmodern Domination and Difference*, London: Verso.

MATTHEW HILLS

White, Hayden

b. 1928

Since the 1970s, Hayden White's work on the nature of historical writing has been widely influential in the critical terrain of **structuralism and post-structuralism**. The central argument of his work can be (too) simply summarized: history is a narrative discourse and its content is as much imagined and invented as found. For White, the imposition of certain **narrative** structures on historical events necessarily distorts those events; past events simply do not have the shape of stories and **historiography** imposes meaningful forms onto a meaningless past. This imposition will be closely linked to **ideology and hegemony**; furthermore, it will link history writing to fiction writing.

For film and television studies, White's work has been influential in three main ways. First, and implicitly, in the conception of cinema history emerging in recent revisionist historical work, especially on early cinema. This work challenges previous historical narratives of 'progress', arguing against the dictates of teleology and challenging assumptions that historical changes were linked solely to the actions of 'great men'. Second, White's work has been influential on debates within **documentary** theory, in particular his suggestion that all **discourse** bears the traces of tropes which link it to fiction. Third, and more recently, scholars have pursued the ways in which film and television respond to, interrogate and create contemporary history in the light of what White sees as a dissolution of the significance of the historical 'event' correlative with modernity and 'modernism' and the traumatic events of the twentieth century.

See also: history; modernism and post-modernism

Further reading

Sobchack, V. (1996) *The Persistence of History: Cinema, Television, and the Modern Event*, London: Routledge.

White, H. (1987) *The Content of the Form: Narrative Discourse and Historical Representation*, Baltimore: Johns Hopkins University Press.

LEE GRIEVESON

Williams, Raymond

b. 1921; d. 1988

Born in the rural Welsh village of Pandy, Abergavenny, Williams won a scholarship to Trinity College, Cambridge, where his background marked him as an outsider. His experience with the journal *Politics and Letters* and his work in adult education fed directly into his first major book, *Culture and Society, 1780–1950*. *The Long Revolution* followed in 1961, by which time Williams was lecturing at Cambridge. Until his death Williams continued to write critical fiction and non-fiction, making a major contribution to the debates that constitute cultural studies.

Raymond Williams' project in the two major works cited above is, like that of Richard **Hoggart**, very much concerned with the past. Williams sees **history** as a process whereby cultural forms shape and are shaped by the wider context of their period, finding expression in a representative 'structure of feeling'. Through a debunking of received ideas about historical progress he was able by extension to challenge the myths about modern 'mass' culture at this crucial point in society's 'long revolution', and so to look dynamically to the future with a convincing agenda for progressive social change.

Further reading

Eagleton, T. (ed.) (1989) *Raymond Williams: Critical Perspectives*, Cambridge: Polity Press.

WILL BROOKER

Wollen, Peter

b. 1938

Peter Wollen began his professional career as a journalist and screenwriter. Although successful as a screenwriter, Wollen found greater acclaim through the publication of his first book, *Signs and Meaning in the Cinema* (1969). Although *Signs and Meaning* may be one of the most famous of cinema books, it by no means defines its author. Writing and directing six feature films between 1974 and 1987, Wollen also served as an associate editor of *Screen*; a contributor to the British film journal *Sight and Sound*, and to *The London Review of Books*; and as a teacher at universities in the United Kingdom and in the United States.

Wollen remained active during the 1990s, publishing a number of books including *Singin' in the Rain* (1993) and *Howard Hawks, American Artist* (edited with Jim Hillier, 1996), writing more than thirty articles, and curating art exhibitions around the world. Wollen's last feature film was *Friendship's Death* (1987). Wollen has been a professor of Film Studies in UCLA's Department of Film and Television since 1988, and was appointed Chair of that department in 1998.

Further reading

Wollen, P. (1969) *Signs and Meaning in the Cinema* (reprinted 1972, 1974, 1998), London: BFI Publishing.

—— (1993) *Singin' in the Rain*, London: BFI Publishing.

—— (1993) *Raiding the Icebox, Reflections on Twentieth Century Culture*, London: Verso.

JAMES FRIEDMAN

Index

Page numbers in **bold** indicate references to the main entry.